Democratic Faith

NEW FORUM BOOKS

Robert P. George, Series Editor

A list of titles in the series appears at
the back of the book

LIBRARY OF CONGRESS CATALOGING-IN-PUBLICATION DATA

Deneen, Patrick J., 1964–
   Democratic faith / Patrick J. Deneen.
    p. cm.
   Includes bibliographical references and index.
   ISBN 0-691-11871-X (acid-free paper : cl.)
   1. Democracy—Philsophy. 2. Democracy—History. 3. Democracy—
   Moral and ethical aspects. I. Title.
   JC423.D382 2005
   321.8'01—dc22   2004058964

British Library Cataloging-in-Publication Data is available

This book has been composed in Sabon

Printed on acid-free paper. ∞

pup.princeton.edu

Printed in the United States of America

10 9 8 7 6 5 4 3 2 1

Democratic Faith

PATRICK J. DENEEN

PRINCETON UNIVERSITY PRESS

PRINCETON AND OXFORD

TO WILSON CAREY MCWILLIAMS

teacher, mentor, and friend

There are opposite ages, really democratic, where people give up this faith, and a certain cocky faith and opposite point of view advance more and more into the foreground—the Athenian faith that first becomes noticeable in the Periclean age, the faith of the Americans today that is more and more becoming the European faith as well: The individual becomes convinced that he can do just about everything and *can manage almost any role*, and everybody experiments with himself, improvises, makes new experiments, enjoys his experiments; and all nature ceases and becomes art.

—FRIEDRICH NIETZSCHE,
The Gay Science, aphorism 356

This book has been written against a background of reckless optimism and reckless despair. It holds that Progress and Doom are two sides of the same medal; that both are articles of superstition, not of faith.

—HANNAH ARENDT,
The Origins of Totalitarianism

CONTENTS

ACKNOWLEDGMENTS

THIS BOOK BEGAN as a passing idea, matured as an article, and finally grew up to be an ungainly tome. During the expanding length of time that it has taken to complete, I have gained invaluably from many conversations. When my interlocutors see some of the results of our discussions, they will almost certainly conclude that I learned too little; I can only assure them that this book would have been much worse but for their generous and challenging words. By naming them, I acknowledge at once my gratitude and my own shortcomings. Special thanks go especially to Ruth Abbey, Lawrie Balfour, Benjamin R. Barber, Larry Bartels, Aurelian Craiutu, Denise Dutton, Peter Euben, Eugene Garver, Eddie Glaude, Russell Hanson, Clarissa Hayward, Matthew Holland, Jeffrey Isaac, Gary Jacobsohn, Peter Lawler, Daniel Mahoney, Bill McClay, Jim McCullough, Sara Monoson, Lynn Robinson, Melvin Rogers, Nancy Rosenblum, Mark Schwehn, James T. Schleifer, Paul Seaton, Heda Segvic, Tracy Strong, Norma Thompson, Dana Villa, Cornel West, and James Boyd White. Several colleagues at Princeton University were frequent interlocutors, and I'd like warmly to thank Robert George, Eric Gregory, George Kateb, Jeffrey Stout, and Maurizio Viroli. Paul Carrese, Robert Faulkner, Charles Mathewes, Joseph Reisert, Joseph Romance, and John Seery read much or all of the manuscript, and I am grateful for their numerous helpful comments. For extraordinary help in preparation of the manuscript I am grateful to Ethan Schoolman and John Lombardini. My thanks also to Rita Bernhard for superb copyediting assistance.

I received many invitations from wonderful institutions to present portions of this book, and I am grateful for the challenging but always helpful colloquy with people at the following places: the Walt Whitman Center at Rutgers University; the Political Philosophy Colloquium, the Program in Law and Public Affairs, and the Center for the Study of Democratic Politics at Princeton University; Christ College at Valparaiso University; Harvard University; The Ohio State University (with special thanks to the Mershon Center); Indiana University; the Institute for Advanced Studies in Culture and the Center on Religion and Democracy at the University of Virginia; Cornell University Law School; University of Oregon (with sponsorship by the Christian Scholars Lecture Series Program and with special thanks to Father Mike Fones); Berry College; Villanova University; and Yale University.

For invaluable material support I would like to thank the Pew Evangelical Scholars Program; the Erasmus Institute at Notre Dame; Princeton University for several research grants as well as support from Princeton's University Center for Human Values, Center for the Study of Religion, and the James Madison Program; the Higher Education Initiatives Foundation; and, especially, the Earhart Foundation for an extraordinarily timely and generous grant that allowed me a sabbatical year.

My thanks to Ian Malcolm of Princeton University Press for his willingness to consider the project, for his patience in awaiting its completion, and for his insistence that I finally finish it.

My greatest intellectual debt—one that should be evident on every page—is owed to my teacher, mentor, and friend, Wilson Carey McWilliams. I am grateful for every encounter with Carey, and simply marvel that such incomparable gifts can be bestowed from such depths of friendship and, because of his generosity, that such debts can be borne with joy. I dedicate this book to Carey.

Finally, unending thanks go to my family, who help sustain my faith in so many ways. To my parents, Richard and Irene Deneen, I owe far more than filial gratitude for fostering a spirit of generosity and the love of learning that is evident in every member of our family. To my wife Inge and our children, Francis, Adrian, and Alexandra, nothing I could write here would capture the gratitude and sustaining hope that can only be lived with those whom one loves.

WORSHIPING DEMOCRACY: THE PANTHÉON

AND THE GODDESS OF DEMOCRACY

> The aspects of things that are most important for us
> are hidden because of their simplicity and familiarity
> (One is unable to notice something—because
> it is always before one's eyes).
>
> —Ludwig Wittgenstein, *Philosophical Investigations*

BETWEEN OCTOBER 9 AND 11, 1794, the remains of Jean-Jacques Rousseau were transported from Ermenonville on the Isle des Peupliers to his current and final resting place in the Panthéon of Paris. The procession, which at various points along the journey sang songs written by Rousseau, was met at Tuileries by a large crowd who shouted "*Vive la Republique! Vive la mémoire de Jean-Jacques Rousseau!*" At the end of the procession in Paris were members of the national legislature who held aloft a copy of *The Social Contract*, as a priest would hold aloft a Bible at a funeral. Deep in the bowels of the Panthéon Rousseau's coffin was placed in a crypt directly across from that of his great adversary and bête noire, Voltaire, and today one can still visit the site, standing literally between the two heroes of the French Republic, enemies in life, neighbors in death.[1]

It is both wildly inappropriate that Rousseau's remains were disinterred from the bucolic "Island of Poplars" for burial in Paris, the cosmopolitan city where he had been scorned and persecuted especially in the later years of his life, and yet strangely fitting that he should be buried in the Panthéon in that same city. Writing against D'Alembert in 1758, and by proxy the real target of his enmity, Voltaire,[2] Rousseau condemned the introduction of a theater in Geneva and more broadly attacked the cosmopolitan culture of city life that offered only corruption and moral laxity to its residents, suggesting that where a theater could only ruin the virtue of Genevans, it might otherwise valuably distract the otherwise corrupt citizens of such a city as Paris:

> In a big city, full of scheming, idle people without religion or principle, whose imagination, depraved by sloth, inactivity, the love of pleasures, and great needs, engenders only monsters and inspires only crimes; in a big city, where morals [manners] and honor are nothing because each, easily hiding his conduct from the public eye, shows himself only by his reputation and is esteemed only for his riches; in a big city, I say, the police can never increase the number of pleasures permitted

too much or apply itself too much to making them agreeable in order to deprive individuals of the temptation of seeking more dangerous ones.[3]

If Rousseau's contempt for big city life underscores the irony of his eventual apotheosis in that city, another aspect of his writing suggests a certain fittingness to his entombment in the Panthéon. Following the successes of the French Revolution, in 1791 the national assembly voted to desacralize the Cathedral of Saint Geneviève and rededicate the basilica as a resting place for France's revolutionary heroes. Above its doors were carved the words, "Aux grands hommes la Patrie reconaissante" (The nation honors its great men).[4] Battles over the status of the building continued through the nineteenth century, with the building's resacralization in 1821 after the Bourbon restoration and its subsequent rededication as the "Temple of the Nation" in the Second Republic. Rousseau had written in praise of purely civil forms of religion for its ability to inspire social concord and manly courage in civil life, even as he had criticized Christianity for its enervating effects on wholly civic virtues.[5] That a Christian church was converted to a secular pantheon in order to display his remains is both at once appalling—regarding Rousseau's disdain for Paris—yet also curiously fitting, given his praise of the role of civil religion in the service of civic virtue.

The National Assembly's choice of the Cathedral of St. Geneviève for its civic "necropolis" was an inspired one for reasons beyond the church's central and prominent location, ones that accorded with this endorsement of Rousseau's recommendation of a human-created and human-centered civil religion. St. Geneviève became known as the patron saint of Paris for her role in saving the city as it faced imminent invasion by Atilla and the Huns in 451. She represented the sacred opposite of the secular *grandes hommes* who replaced her remains: faced with imminent invasion, she admonished the inhabitants of Paris to remain in the city and pray for divine protection and blessing. Wholly exposed to the invading forces renowned for their merciless butchery of civilian inhabitants, the people of Paris left their fate in the hands of God and believed their prayers answered when Atilla and his invading forces turned southward and instead attacked the city of Orleans. In contrast to the fighting female saint that would later come to defend that benighted city, Jean d'Arc, Geneviève was canonized as the patron saint of Paris for her faith and her ability to stoke the faith of others—a faith in divine intervention that required no action or intervention on the part of humanity, with the exception of prayer that importuned but did not demand or set terms. She was a protectress of the city who did not protect, a defender who did not fight, one who surrendered but who did not lose faith. To desacralize the church raised in her honor, declaring the city's preeminence over God's, and celebrating the role of men of action and men of thought whose ideas sparked action, represented in the most direct terms a repudiation of the frail and uncertain faith of the ancients, and an affirmation of modern secular belief in human ability, power, and autonomy.

In May 1989, almost two hundred years after the onset of the French Revolution, Chinese students protesting authoritarian rule in Tiananmen Square assembled a Styrofoam and papier-mâché sculpture that they called the *Goddess of Democracy*. Based on a classic statue of a Chinese peasant (and sometimes mistaken for the American Statue of Liberty),[6] the statue stood for five days at the Gate of Heavenly Peace, in the shadow of the Forbidden City—ancient home of the emperor, barred to common people—and near the Monument to the People's Heroes, a secular temple to Communist China's leading figures (a building that resembles in function if not in form the French Panthéon).

In this public space fraught with political, religious, and secular meaning, they unveiled the statue with a speech:

> Democracy, how long has it been since we last saw you . . . ? You are the Chinese nation's hope for salvation! Today, here in the People's Square, the people's Goddess stands tall and announces to the whole world: A consciousness of democracy has awakened among the Chinese people! The new era has begun! From this piece of ancient earth grows the tree of democracy and freedom, putting forth gorgeous flowers and a bountiful harvest of fruit.
>
> The statue of the Goddess of Democracy is made of plaster, and of course cannot stand here forever. But as symbol of the people's hearts, she is divine and inviolate. . . . We have strong faith that that day will come at last. We have still another hope: Chinese people arise! Erect the statue of the Goddess of Democracy in your millions of hearts![7]

At the conclusion of the speech, the protesters chanted "Long Live Democracy!" and several times sang *The Internationale*.[8] Themes both religious and secular covered and disclosed each other, almost indistinguishably intermingling in this call to worship a deified form of secular political rule.

The symbol of the Goddess of Democracy has continued to resonate since its brief appearance in 1989. Indeed, rather than looking on this iconic deification of democracy with suspicion or bemusement, Western democrats have often adopted the symbol as a sign of solidarity with the Chinese dissidents and, more, an expression of common discontent with shortcomings in existing democracies and an acknowledgment of a shared faith in democracy. Permanent replicas of the statue can be found, among other places, in Washington, D.C., San Francisco, and Vancouver. Frequently the gathering site for groups that are otherwise hostile toward the unreasoned faith of religion (sharing, in principle, Marx's critique of religion as the "opium of the masses"), this approximate adulation of the Goddess of Democracy is neither so uncanny nor incongruous as first glance might suggest.

If the transformation of the Cathedral of Saint Geneviève represents the movement of *desacralization* and the rise of eighteenth-century forms of civil religion, the *sacralization* of a papier-mâché statue into a deified image of democracy itself represents a curious and seemingly contradictory movement. Yet, the very images of Paris's saint-protectress in the main chambers of the basilica that remain in spite of its contemporary usage suggest that "desacralization" was never complete: like a medieval palimpsest, the older sacred writings were never wholly erased or covered over by modern secular signs but remained subtly beneath the surface, radiating divine legitimacy to secular efforts even as those endeavors were undertaken in direct antipathy toward those older sacred practices and beliefs. That democracy came to be enthusiastically accepted, if only symbolically, by radically secular thinkers as itself an object of worship and deification is suggestive less of thoughtlessness or hypocrisy than subtle acknowledgment of the sacred amid the profane, of faith amid unbelief, even the possibility of true belief amid mistrust of fanaticism. If faith is a belief in that which is unseen, then it may be that democracy is as justifiably an object of faith as a distant and silent God. This is particularly the case for those who perceive a radical gulf between that system of government that we now call democracy—rife with apathy, cynicism, corruption, inattention, and dominated by massive yet nearly unperceivable powers that belie claims of popular control—and the vision of democracy as apotheosis of human freedom, self-creation, and even paradisiacal universal political and social equality that coexists seamlessly with individual self-realization and uniqueness. In the absence of such a faith, ambitions might wither amid cruel facts and hopes dissipate in the face of relentless reality.

Democracy—that ancient combination of ancient words meaning "power of the people"—is almost universally acknowledged to be the sole legitimate form of governance remaining in the world today. After centuries of rejection by thinkers in antiquity, vilification by the medieval schoolman, suspicion during the humanistic period of the Renaissance, scorn by the Enlightenment "founders" of that oldest continuous regime that we call democratic— America—democracy is, almost against all odds, the only regime most living humans now deem worthy of serious consideration, exploration, clarification, articulation, exportation, importation, and, finally, faith. In the wake of the horrific encounter with twentieth-century forms of secular utopian totalitarianism that resulted in the murder of millions of people in the name of perfection in politics, democracy has risen supreme as that one form of government that eschews any claims to perfection on earth, that avoids any claims to fundamental knowledge of truth in politics, that permits most widely the proliferation of distinctive lifestyles and life paths while still governing in the name of the common weal.

How is it, then, that this form of rule based on epistemic modesty and an embrace of imperfection and human fallibility, undergirded not by any claims to truth but instead by pragmatic adjustment and prudential calculation of interest and accretion of popular assent, at the same time can be frankly acknowledged to be, and further be embraced as, an *object of faith*? Is there an unperceived utopianism lining the anti-utopian mantle of democracy, even a degree of overconfidence amid otherwise humble claims of democracy's rejection of overconfidence? Does the palimpsest of the sacred underlying the profane in fact only convey an incomplete text, raising up the prospects of human perfectibility by humble democratic means, retaining faith as willed belief even as it rejects the ancient and religious admonition to avoid hubris? If contemporary theoretical endorsements of democracy recommend the rejection of claims to truth in the daily operation of democratic politics, how can that be reconciled with inquisitorial denunciations of any such perceived "truth claims"? Is it possible to be fanatically anti-fanatical? Is this not fanaticism of a sort? Is the faith in democracy finally as susceptible, or possibly even more susceptible, to the very kinds of dangerous extremes of belief that the democratic faith otherwise claims to avoid and forestall?

This is a study of paradox, an inquiry into how a political system designed to minimize claims of faith itself rests on faith, how a regime embraced for its modesty may be immodest in that embrace, how the rejection of truth in politics has led to the creation of a guiding truth in politics, and how that most anti-utopian regime may become most dangerously utopian at the moment it congratulates itself loudest for its defeat of utopianism in politics. It is further a call for the recognition of this paradox and a reminder that such recognition itself functions as a form of modesty that should be embraced by democrats even as it calls upon ardent believers in the democratic faith to allow for the possibility of doubt amid that faith, and a faith that can support that doubt. This study seeks to remind that faith can be a healthy accompaniment to corrosive skepticism, and skepticism a necessary corrective to overweening faith—a belief that faithful democrats curiously evince in nearly all regards except in respect to democracy itself. We do not betray democracy by questioning the faith: by making ourselves uneasy, we hold at bay the dangerous extremes of any faith toward unwarranted optimism, utopianism, and fanaticism, even as we do not lose our democratic hopes.

Democratic Faith

Dynamics of Democratic Faith

> For better or worse, democracy cannot be disentangled from
> an aspiration toward human perfectibility.
>
> —Herbert Croly, *The Promise of American Life*

DEMOCRACY IS REGNANT in practice and triumphant in theory. While many thinkers object to suppositions that we have reached philosophically the "end of history," nevertheless in Western political thought there is no formidable or even noticeably significant challenge to the near-universal embrace of democracy as the sole legitimate form of government.[1] Particulars differ radically—sometimes it appears that various camps fight to assume the label "democratic" in order to assert their unimpeachable legitimacy and dismiss the claims of philosophical opponents, just as the term "antidemocratic" constitutes opprobrium of the highest order—yet, at base, an underlying embrace of certain democratic tenets centered around a belief in universal human suffrage, political equality, economic and personal liberty, and inherent human dignity constitute shared features of various schools of democratic thought. In political theory—a "field" invented some twenty-five hundred years ago in order to discern the relative virtues and deficiencies of different regime types, and often identifying democracy as inferior to monarchy and aristocracy—it is no longer necessary, by and large, for its contemporary practitioners to demonstrate the grounds for democracy's superiority.

Yet, at the risk of contrariness, if not outright overstatement, democratic theory is in a state of quiet crisis, reflecting (if inadequately) the more serious crisis of democracy itself. The quiescent assumption that democracy's superiority can and ought to be taken as a matter of unchallenged belief rests on a set of largely unexamined presuppositions that point to a quiet desperation underlying much of contemporary democratic theory—a desperation, indeed, that has always been present in democratic theory from its earliest articulations in antiquity. That desperation has been more evident in ages with high degrees of democratic suspicion, and has taken the form of forcefully articulated statements of democratic faith. In the absence of such widespread opposition in the contemporary era, such strong statements of democratic faith have become less evident within mainstream analyses of democracy, but even their pale counterparts evince no less anxiety—albeit less self-awareness of that anxiety—than their more explicit earlier counterparts. This desperation takes the form of an inherent fear that "faith" is not sufficient—that belief in democracy will not be repaid in reality—and thus that either democracy must give way to the reality of human shortcomings or human shortcomings must be overcome to realize democracy. While claiming to take "men as they are," democratic theory from its inception, even to its dominant contemporary expressions, exhibits anything but satisfaction for the civic capacities of ordinary humans, and seeks, sometimes to a major extent, to alter that condition for democratic ends.

In the first line of Rousseau's *Social Contract*, Rousseau declares his intention to "take men as they are and the laws as they might be."[2] A less utopian yet more idealistic formulation perhaps cannot be found in the history of political thought. Men, Rousseau suggests, are sufficiently capable as they are to create good laws—laws that could serve as the basis of an excellent regime, but which yet elude them. Such law might be realized if the inherent decency of humans could itself be either recovered or actualized for the first time. "Man is born free, but is everywhere in chains": our freedom is inherent in our deepest origins but has been shackled by institutions and practices that deceive or divert men from their true condition. Rousseau formulates the modest yet radical premise of democracy: democracy is based upon a belief in human decency, even potential for individual and collective goodness, and needs only to achieve the realization of this inherent decency to bring about democracy in its most fully manifested, even ideal form.[3]

Democracy, in this succinct formulation, seems the most appropriate, even most natural regime for human beings. While reviled in past ages as according too great faith in human goodness—trusting otherwise selfish and self-involved humans to extend as much respect and consideration to the views, interests, and property of others as those that underlie one's own motivations—previous philosophers ranging from antiquity to the middle ages and even into modernity have held democracy to be an idealistic but finally unworkable form of utopian fantasy.[4] Contemporary devotion to democratic forms reflects a worldwide embrace of the belief that ordinary humans are capable of, at the very least, minimal decencies and, at best, deep devotion both to those dreams and interests they hold dearest and to those same dreams and interests held by their fellow citizens. Democracy assumes that extraordinary virtue becomes ordinary, that ordinary humans are capable of extraordinary virtue. As stated by George Santayana,

> If a noble and civilized democracy is to subsist, the common citizen must be something of a saint and something of a hero. We see, therefore, how justly flattering and profound, and at the same time how ominous, was Montequieu's saying that the principle of democracy is virtue.[5]

It is easy, given modern assumptions, to view those ancient, medieval, and even modern thinkers who regarded democracy with suspicion, misgivings, and even outright hostility as overly dour and even pessimistic. We resist any rejection of democracy as informed by an ideology or even faith that has since been superseded. We can perhaps fruitfully mine other parts of such philosophies for interesting and provocative observations, but at the point in which all regimes—including democracy—are considered, weighed, and almost inevitably found wanting, we balk and point to anachronistic, recidivist, and even reactionary assumptions.

Yet, do we overly flatter ourselves, as Santayana suggests, in quickly brushing off those misgivings and even outright expressions of "antidemocracy"? Perhaps we think not, because, more often than not in contemporary philosophy and theory, we believe that we theorize implicitly and oftentimes explicitly under Rousseau's dictum, "taking men as they are." We are not utopian—indeed, we do not even wish to dwell on considerations of "virtue"—because we do not seek to alter human beings to "become" democratic creatures, to "make" men worthy of democracy. Our ambitions are altogether modest: we seek to advance democracy at home and in the world to provide all humans with the requisite freedom from oppression and arbitrary rule, and freedom to become what their capacities allow, and not to make humans other than they already are. We seek, as Rousseau suggests, to align "men as they are" with "laws as they might be."

Yet, if this simple dictum of Rousseau, if only implicitly, underlies apparently modest democratic endorsement that most largely share—if, further, it renders us unwilling, perhaps even incapable of considering, much less accepting, the "antidemocratic" proclivities of most of the philosophers in the history of political thought—then how are we to understand Rousseau's argument, several brief chapters after his opening sentence, that citizens in a just society with democratic underpinnings need to undergo a fundamental transformation? Because of the limitations of human beings to see past their own interests, to take into account the good of the whole, which they cannot easily perceive much less achieve a willingness to embrace even were it perceptible—indeed, arguably because human beings are so riven by difference as to be incapable of becoming a "whole"—Rousseau invokes a *lex ex machina*, the "Legislator," who takes human beings as they are and undertakes to "change their nature, so to speak." A regime in which the good of the whole is considered and embraced, in which laws are conceived and promulgated in light of that whole—in which individual preferences cease, in some way, to become foremost in people's minds, thereby rendering automatic a "view of the whole"—one can expect that all subsequent public considerations will be undertaken in a similar spirit and vein. Such an idealized regime would be capable of molding generations of such citizens, able to rely on its own "social spirit" to continuously cultivate this devotion to the whole. But Rousseau realizes that in order for such a regime to come into existence the "effect must become the cause," that such civic excellence must first come into existence without the benefit of an existing regime to form those excellences. Hence the recourse to the Legislator: "For a nascent people to be capable of appreciating sound maxims of politics and of following the fundamental rules of reason of State, the effect would have to become the cause, the social spirit which is to be the work of the institution would have to preside over the institution itself, and men would have to be prior to laws what they ought to become by means of them."[6]

If there is a distance between the "reality" of men as they are and the laws as they might be—between those manifest limitations of human beings and the ideal of a democracy in which universal justice might be achieved—then we must either attribute this fact to one of two main causes: either men "as they are" do not currently exhibit the kinds of imagination, sympathy, or rationality that needs to inform the willingness to cede some individual desires and satisfactions for the good of the whole; or, democracy is too good for the people, and people cannot be changed to become worthy of the ideal. In a democratic age the latter option—once the prevailing view of most political philosophers for most of human history—is unthinkable. Thus, with the recognition that there is some distance between "men as they are" and democracy as it might be, an attempt to bring the two together leads to an implicit dissatisfaction with "men as they are," and perhaps even an inclination to seek their transformation to "democratic men as they might be."[7] If "men as they are" *do* in fact possess the requisite features that could lead to a realization of democracy, then something *external* to them is preventing its manifestation. This assumption underlay the revolutionary ideologies of the nineteenth and twentieth centuries, in which the assumption that a combination of institutions and various ideologies that gave rise to "false consciousness" prevented human beings from realizing the utopian universal regime in which all alienation was overcome. However, if in our more modest age we are less inclined to such revolutionary inclinations—more inclined to claim to be content with "men as they are"—even modern democrats remain uncomfortably aware that men are not quite what we might wish them to be, and that they are not yet wholly commensurate with "democracy as it might be." If humans are capable of becoming ideal democratic citizens—ones that are simultaneously fully realized autonomous individuals yet also willingly seek to understand and embrace more general human concerns—then we must attribute this gap to insufficient realization of what humans *are* or *could be*. Embedded in this seemingly modest claim to contentment with basic human motivations is a subtle but undeniable transformational impetus. If less obvious and even objectionable than the tack adopted by Rousseau, this tendency to make humans into what they *really* are—or what they really might be—may indeed require some kind of intervention by those who have adequately realized such grounds, if only in theory and not yet in fact.

In order not to abandon a belief in democracy, nor to embolden those who would find democratic discontent as a sign of democracy's peril, assertions of "democratic faith" insist upon the possibility of *democratic transformation*. In particular, by advancing a conception of human beings as both infinitely malleable and ameliorable, along with an accompanying belief in the compatibility or malleability of nature and the universe to such perfectionist inclinations, the impulse to "perfectibility" becomes an integral component of democratic faith. Alexis de Tocqueville observed this belief in widespread human "perfectibility" as an evident and overwhelming feature of modern democracy during his visit to America in the nineteenth century.[8] Even if a final vision of fully "realized" democratic humanity cannot be advanced—indeed, such accounts typically resist a full statement of democratic apotheosis in favor of depictions of infinite change (change that invariably takes the form of "improvement" and progress) but, according to Richard Rorty, "carries us beyond argument, because [it is] beyond presently used language"—"democratic perfectionism" serves as the implicit, and often explicit, object of democratic faith.[9] Because of this belief in amelioration without limit, of mutability without *telos*, of progress without boundary, and of faith without grounding, one finds especially strong expressions of "democratic faith" in "antifoundational" and pragmatic theories. Democratic theory is particularly inclined toward conceptions of human growth and improvement that reject "foundations," appeals to "nature," or invocations of necessary limits and cautions. Democratic faith tends to reject tragedy.

For this reason, antifoundational believers in democracy are concomitantly hostile to forms of philosophy and "faith"—particularly ancient philosophy and traditional religious faith—that seek to chasten such human visions of perfectibility with warnings against hubris, invocations of human nature and human teleology, and reminders of inescapable human shortcomings. "Traditional" teachings—especially religious and in particular the Judeo-Christian belief of fundamental human depravity—do not appear to accord with "democratic faith." Indeed, according to the "democratic faithful"—whose faith is premised to a lesser or greater extent upon the prospects of transforming individuals into citizens fitting for democracy—then "traditional" views of ineradicable human imperfection are, on their face, *antidemocratic*. Ironically such opposing positions are rejected as being motivated by so much faith—now *bad* faith—even while its critics invoke "democratic faith" as a superior form of belief. In this choice between two faiths, it is simply a matter of having the "will to believe" in democratic faith.

If the distance between "men as they are" and "democracy as it might be" suggests the necessity of changing humans or viewing them as malleable and subject to alterations of the social conditions in which they are embedded, then any assumptions of human depravity or even strong statements of human limitation must be rejected a priori. If this is the case, one would expect to see among such "democratic faithful" thinkers an aggressive rejection of religious belief that asserts the existence of certain unalterable human conditions, including those of sinfulness, pride, self-aggrandizement, a propensity to irrationality, and a fundamental condition of alienation. At the same time, however, the "faith claims" of transformative democratic theory can often go unnoticed—submerged beneath aggressive and dismissive attacks upon traditional religious faith, and thus taking on the semblance of a school of "skeptical" theory—thereby leaving democratic "faith" assumptions unacknowledged and unexamined. Arguably, accompanying the as-

cendancy of democracy in the present age is an increasing inability to recognize, much less examine, presuppositions that undergird democratic faith
precisely *because* it is rarely recognized as a form of faith, even one with theological underpinnings that draw from Gnostic, Pelagian, Montanist, and
antinomian traditions, all forms of millenarian belief that humans can bring
about their own salvation in some form. Satisfied with its apparent skeptical secularism, "democratic faith" neglects its theological assumptions about
human anthropology, even as it excoriates the faith claims of "religious"
believers.

Yet, the most robust theories justifying democracy almost inevitably contain a shadow theology. Perhaps more than any other regime, democracy requires a reconciliation of the apparently irreconcilable—in its most ancient
formulation, "the one" and the "many"; in contemporary parlance, the individual and the community; and even in some recent articulations, the individual and the global. Arguably much contemporary (if not simply *all*) political theory is devoted to an exploration of how to preserve a robust form
of individual flourishing while inculcating the necessary disposition of toleration, respect, even care for the whole. Alienation remains a primary source
of dissatisfaction, as it has since the dawn of human consciousness. The attempt to overcome this seeming dichotomy built into the human psyche—
the praiseworthy and equally damnable love for one's own and sometimes
evident but often insufficient care for the good of the whole—can be understood to undergird many theological accounts and equally underlies many
secular variants that stress the possibility of a kind of "democratic transcendence" and an overcoming of human alienation.[10] Again, Tocqueville's
observations at the dawn of modern mass democracy are instructive, inasmuch as he saw that democracy had a tendency to lead simultaneously to a
belief in individualism, on the one hand, and "pantheism," on the other.
Democracy bridles against differentiation and borders, and hence tends to
break down any hierarchies and rejects attempts to preserve or create boundaries or exclusion: one is left with one *and* many but not with "some." Democracy, so conceived, sees its main challenge as the reconciliation of the individual with a greater diversity but ultimately, almost unavoidably, appeals to
the possibility of cosmopolitan transcendence of all arbitrary limitations. Individualism and pantheism are two sides of the same modern democratic coin.

If traditional theological accounts of this transcendence of the divide between the "one" and the "many" invoke divine assistance or even suggest its
possibility only in an eventual "City of God," secular variants on this theology require some means or method of "transformation"—and, indeed, the
language of "transformation" is almost unavoidable in much of contemporary democratic theory. Because the ideal of "transformation" contains at
least faint echoes of enforced or hierarchic attempts to alter human nature,
much of contemporary democratic theory rests content with calls for "self-
transformation," impersonal mechanisms such as "constitutional transfor-

mation," or by means of an education that will make us adequately and simultaneously individualistic and liberal.[11] Many approaches have been
urged and pursued in closing this gap between the perceived disappointing
reality of democracy as it is and democratic citizens as they might be. While
this book does not claim to offer an exhaustive analysis of the various endeavors to fashion a democratic citizenry, two "methods" in particular will
be analyzed in further depth: first, the call for various kinds of "civil religion" as a means of reconciling democratic individualism and social solidarity (which include various articulations of specifically democratic education aimed toward the realization of the "kingdom of God on earth," such
as that advanced by John Dewey); and, second, the embrace of science as a
form of inquiry, and as a project with a promising set of outcomes, that aim
to overcome limiting features of humankind that have thus far thwarted the
realization of an idealized democracy. Both these undertakings are born of a
set of theological presuppositions about the relationship of God and man, of
human potential and the possibility of earthly redemption, and thus more
deeply align "democratic faith" with theological faith in ways that its adherents rarely acknowledge or even realize. It remains a suggestive question
whether the decline of contemporary "faith" in the *means* of transformation,
without a concomitant decline in "democratic faith" itself, represents a lessening or an exaggeration of faith in democracy. I discuss such efforts at
"democratic transformation" in chapter 2.

Does democracy necessarily, whether implicitly or explicitly, give rise to a
"perfectionist" impulse? Is democracy tenable without such a belief, or does
powerful empirical evidence of citizen shortcomings in the form of political
apathy, poor political knowledge, prejudice, parochialism, and the absence
of real progress made toward human "transformation" suggest that "democratic faith" is misplaced and misconceived? If democracy rests upon the
"evidence of things unseen," are these material factors likely to be the eventual source of disillusionment, disappointment, and despair? If a dynamic
within democratic theory tends toward dissatisfaction with the gap between
"men as they are" and democracy as it might be, and means of closing the
gap tend toward a belief in infinite human amelioration, then democratic theory, which appears to contemporary eyes to be the only political theory intended for human beings as they are, may be ironically a political theory
most inclined to arrive at dissatisfaction with ordinary humans. The "quiet"
crisis of contemporary democratic theory is reflected in the very vocal dissatisfaction with democratic politics generally in the populace, and is imperfectly articulated among most democratic theorists as dissatisfaction with
unrealized democratic capacities of those self-same people. Civic discontent
is manifested as antipolitical democratic populism; academic dissatisfaction,
by contrast, is frequently expressed as thinly veiled contempt for such populist dissatisfactions. Academia believes itself to be responding to civic discontent, when, in fact, taking the genealogy of its own "democratic faith"

into consideration, it could be argued that intellectual elites actually *contribute* to democratic dissatisfaction. There is a blithe assumption that elite recommendations for democratic "transformation" represent a solution to present discontents rather than further contributing to civic disillusionment as a result of setting the bar for legitimate democratic politics beyond what any politics will bear. Very few contemporary democratic theorists actually can be said to believe in humans "as they are" but, rather, prefer to envisage democracy as it might be—if people can only be transformed into beings good enough for democracy.

"Democratic faith" may thus in fact contribute to democratic disillusionment and cynicism.[12] "Democratic faith" and "democratic cynicism" arguably coexist in a mutually reinforcing cycle: democratic faith's exaggerated and unrealizable vision of democracy leads to disillusionment; a response that dismisses "faith" is the result, leading to a cynical democratic theory premised upon the inescapability of interest and manipulation; in turn, idealists resort to more fervent calls for democratic faith and ever greater resulting expressions of disillusionment, even despair.[13] In the end, calls for a moderate and decent democracy are abandoned in this struggle between soft-hearted (headed?) true belief and hard-headed (hearted?) cynicism. Indeed, the increasing inability of "normative" democratic theorists and "realist" empirical analysts of democracy to speak with each other suggests a worrisome divide: democratic theorists today prefer the company of members of philosophy departments, whereas political scientists find more in common with faculty in economics departments. Connections to the world of politics, politicians, and citizens are in jeopardy, thus suggesting a problem that is more than merely "academic" in nature.

Against the growing (and related) tendencies toward democratic "faith" and democratic "cynicism," I would like to recommend instead a form of "democratic realism." The challenge for democratic theory and, more important, for democracy is to escape the dynamic that reinforces, on the one hand, the cynical complacency of pluralist and interest-group (and, increasingly, rational-choice-based) conceptions of political conflict and, on the other, unrealistic conceptions of democracy premised upon a fundamental transformation of political conditions, citizens, or both.[14] One means of stepping outside this reinforcing vicious circle, it has been suggested, is by finding a "mean" between these two extremes. Resorting to a distinction articulated recently by the ethicist William F. May, such a mean might be achieved by identifying democracy in the dynamic tension between two impulses, one that is "accepting" of people in all their imperfection, and the other "transforming" in an effort to challenge people to improve and go beyond what is strictly given.[15] Indeed, much contemporary democratic theory falls into one camp or the other, leading in the former case to complacency and a politics of low expectations and, in the other, to heightened expectations, disappointment, eventually even despair and democratic disgust. In terms that have been suggested by Margaret Canovan, "pragmatic" democracy needs a "redemptive" face, and utopian "redemptive" democracy needs a strong dose of "pragmatism."[16]

Yet, I would like to suggest that this idea of a democratic "mean," while attractive, does not do sufficient justice to the Aristotelian conception of "mean" from which it is implicitly drawn and, in particular, does not recognize that a "mean" must always be achieved prudentially with full recognition of the likely temptations that will draw such a conception of democracy inevitably back toward one dominant extreme.[17] I would rather recommend an alternative "dynamic," one that begins with a stronger initial assertion of what May describes as an "accepting" attitude, since, in particular, "acceptance" (here, in his discussion, of a parent for a child) is antecedent to, and necessarily informs and moderates, the efforts at "transformation." Consider the opposite assertion of priority, which places "transformation" before "acceptance." This priority reflects "democratic faith's" vision of the future transformation of inadequate people into fully fledged democratic participants, people who are worthy of democracy. "Acceptance" comes after "transformation." Unsurprisingly proponents of "democratic faith" frequently evince dissatisfaction and at times even contempt toward the yet untransformed masses. A strong dose of "elitism" courses through the thought of such democratic faithful as Emerson, Mill, and even at times Whitman. It is too short a distance from the "democratic" superiority of these thinkers to the antidemocratic "transformative" philosophy of Nietzsche (a fact Nietzsche implicitly acknowledged through his deep admiration of Emerson). Alternatively "democratic realism" begins from a disposition of "acceptance," one that begins with a firm sense of human limitations and imperfection, even imperfectability, and, by means of "acceptance," results in a chastened "transformative" impulse that stops well short of endorsing the perfectionist "transformative" enterprise of "democratic faith." Rather, beginning from an attitude of acceptance, the possibility of democratic *caritas* arises, one that is resistant to a smug superiority or condescension, one that is *accepting*, and, through being accepting, seeks a more gentle "transformation" through humility and forgiveness. Our acceptance in the first instance "transforms" our expectations and prompts our admiration of (rather than disgust for) imperfect striving; encourages efforts to assist inevitably broken communication; and promotes compassion for suffering that we share alike to different degrees and in different forms, albeit all with a final view toward human mortality and finitude.

"Democratic realism" begins with—and does not abandon—a strong premise of human imperfection (a belief akin to, perhaps indistinguishable from, original sin, in theological terms), thereby rejecting the temptation for any form of democratic perfectionism or political utopianism more generally.[18] At the same time democracy can resist complacency through the very resources offered by that strong initial recognition of human imperfection: rather than recommending resignation to complacent or cynical versions of what John Rawls called "modus vivendi" democratic politics, the recognition of individual imperfection, fallibility, and insufficiency affords powerful grounds for an endorsement of democracy that calls upon chastened qualities of "heroism" and "saintliness" of ordinary citizens, even an imperative for democratic *caritas* based upon a starting acknowledgment of human need. As none of us is capable of self-sufficiency, all politics are premised upon a mutual endeavor to secure for the common what each would be incapable of achieving alone; democracy, by extension, represents the common effort to transcend "mere life" and, rather, to provide the possibility of "the good life"—one impossible for each alone—for all citizens.[19] "Democratic realism" results in a strong articulation of political and more profound human equality *not* premised upon our eventual or ultimate perfectibility, on the one hand, nor upon the theoretical realization of our individual capacities within a meritocratic order, on the other (so-called equality of opportunity) but rather an equality born of our shared *dependency* and mutual *insufficiency*, and therefore a concomitant recognition of our shared obligations to, and concern for, one another.[20] Democracy is ultimately justified because of our shared weakness and imperfection in view of our shared equal condition of need and insufficiency and not because of the promise of ultimate autonomy or perfectibility. Indeed, contemporary endorsements of democracy premised upon belief in progress, human agency, control of nature, thorough autonomy, and self-transcendence actually *imperil* democracy to the extent that these visions delude individuals into believing in fantasies of total freedom from necessity, nature, and one another, rather than keeping in view our shared equal condition of need and insufficiency. Libertarianism or tyranny, not democracy, lies at the end of that road.

Undoubtedly some will simply see my own alternative of "democratic realism" as a form of "democratic faith" by another name. Defined appropriately—that is, not premised upon a belief in human or societal transformation but, in the first instance, firmly insistent that democracy is best justified by means of an embrace of a belief in human imperfection and insufficiency—it is a duly modified label I am willing to accept. It places me in the very good company of G. K. Chesterton, who wrote in *Orthodoxy*:

> This is the first principle of democracy: that the essential things in men are the things they hold in common, not the things they hold separately. And the second principle is merely this: that the political instinct or desire is one of these things which they hold in common. . . . [It is] a thing analogous to writing one's own love-letters or blowing one's own nose. These things we want a man to do for himself, even if he does them badly. . . . In short, the democratic faith is this: that the most terribly important things must be left to ordinary men themselves—the mating of the sexes, the rearing of the young, the laws of the state. This is democracy; and in this I have always believed.[21]

Democracy premised not on "perfectibility" but rather on inescapable *imperfection* is one that retains a commitment to amelioration premised first on an "accepting" disposition that motivates out of democratic *caritas*. "Acceptance" is not despairing; *hope without optimism* distinguishes its view toward the future. While much of contemporary democratic theory rightly rejects the complacency born of a pessimistic impulse, it can be argued that democracy premised upon "transformation" and perfectibility betrays the fundamental justification for democracy, which is better understood not as the realization of ultimate human *potential* for a kind of earthly divinity but rather as that which begins from, and never has far from sight, an acknowledgment of human *shortcomings*. An initial recognition, even embrace, of human imperfection, and concomitant rejection of the vision of thoroughgoing transformation, opens up the possibility of an amelioration of democratic politics and democratic culture—a prospect that would fall so short of "transformation" that any improvement might be, if not disillusioning and unsatisfying, outright indiscernible to the democratic utopian but would serve as a source of ongoing hope to the "democratic realist."

One source of that realism often derives from religious faith, a self-critical form of belief which can exercise a chastening force on democratic ambitions. In contrast to the "democratic faithful," whose belief in human malleability frequently leads them to reject traditional religious belief as undemocratic, "democratic realism" finds, in the religious stress upon human fallibility, insufficiency, and humility, an extraordinary chastening and democratic resource. While many contemporary academics and leading intellectuals view religious believers as a threat to democratic politics, it can be argued that religious belief—properly understood—can contribute to the strengthening of our commitments to "ordinary" democracy. Without calling for religious belief by those who do not share such faith, secularists might be persuaded to see the invaluable democratic resources afforded by religious believers. Far from posing a threat to democracy, religious belief so conceived can be seen as the first line of defense against the threat to democracy that "democratic faith" can engender. Those of religious faith can serve as a witness by reinforcing our sense of imperfection and chastening utopian forms of "democratic faith," by fostering a shared belief in common neediness that rejects the sense of self-satisfied desert or self-loathing failure in increasingly meritocratic societies, and commending to the populace as a whole an exemplary kind of "democratic *caritas*."[22] Contemporary critics of religious belief in many cases rightly perceive an absence of these democratic resources among many of the most strident, and hence most visible, of today's religious adherents. Mutual hostility between the "faithful" and "nonbelievers" has hardened each camp and undermined the charitable impulses that might be called upon to bridge the divide, and even encourage each side to overlook the many that both sides share in common concerns for social justice.[23] Above all, each camp is becoming increasingly incapable of articulating the danger to democracy posed by the loss of corrective religious resources, that faith which might serve to chasten forms of "democratic faith" lacking any such restraining internal resources. This danger I take to be the fault of all concerned, secular and religious-minded alike, who, locked in a series of discrete battles often in the realm of symbolic politics, fiddle while Rome burns and increasingly imperil democracy. In the third part of the book I call for a reconsideration of some powerful articulations of democracy's "friendly critics" (Plato, Tocqueville, and the Americans Reinhold Niebuhr, Christopher Lasch, and Abraham Lincoln) who caution against the democratic impulse toward self-flattery.

Among a number of these critics "democratic faith" is countered by "religious faith," and suggests finally that democratic theory may be best understood in light of theological assumptions rather than as a debate among wholly secular philosophers or between "believers" and "secularists." One of the aims of pointing to the existence of "democratic faith" is to highlight how democratic theory is often, perhaps always, a battle between different systems of belief. In the pages that follow I attempt to trace some of the "dynamics" of this faith in democracy, its concomitant temptations toward Promethean perfectionism, its attendant tendency toward fostering democratic despair, and, finally, a possible source of reconceiving a "democratic realism" that takes men as they are without inclining toward a belief in democratic perfectionism, on the one hand, or succumbing to self-satisfied complacency toward imperfection, on the other.

This is not a book that calls for "democratic quiescence"; rather, my aim is to offer a sobering assessment of how difficult "belief" in democracy in fact becomes when shorn of easy recourse to "democratic faith." Democracy is not an undertaking for the faint of heart: it calls for limitless reservoirs of hope against the retreat into easy optimism or the temptation to a kind of democratic cynicism or despair. "Critics" of democracy—ranging from Plato to Tocqueville to Niebuhr and Lasch—are often mistaken as being hostile toward democracy proper, because they seek to warn against democracy's most dangerous internal tendencies, especially expressions of versions of "democratic faith" that ironically yet ultimately threaten to imperil the prospect of democracy itself. Such voices are better understood as "friendly critics" of democracy, offering a set of diagnoses that represent a form of "democratic realism." It may be that the best protection against eventual democratic disillusionment is not to stoke the flames of "democratic faith" but instead to temper their white hot flames—flames that burn too quickly, leaving only fading embers—with cold water. The cure for ailments of democracy may not be more democracy but rather chastened self-reflection over the nature of the faith in that very "cure" that likely only worsens the ailment.

PART ONE

Democratic Faith and Its Discontents

CHAPTER ONE

Faith in Man

> Our doubts are traitors,
> And make us lose the good we oft might win,
> By fearing the attempt.
>
> —William Shakespeare, *Measure for Measure*

FAITH IN DEMOCRACY

To THE EARS OF MANY, linking the words "faith" and "democracy" is strange, uncanny, bizarre, objectionable, and, for some, even sacrilegious. Faith is belief in the unknown or the unknowable: as expressed by Nathan Rotenstreich, "faith and belief connote assent to something beyond observation."[1] By contrast, democracy is a manifest and observable form of government, one that has been in existence during various periods throughout human history and is currently the form of governance most frequently found in nations throughout the world, and especially in the West. The longest continuous constitutional form of government, that of the United States of America, in existence since 1789, is considered a preeminent form of democracy in the modern era. For many observers, an object so obviously perceptible cannot and should not be considered as either (in the eyes of some) worthy as an object of faith or (in the eyes of others) as requiring or necessitating any invocation of faith.

Yet, that most preeminent modern democratic nation was fashioned to considerable extent out of *distrust* or lack of faith in the general populace. This is perhaps most visible in the epistemological assumptions that once resulted in the *mistrust* of the electorate, and which now quite ironically can be seen to undergird the two leading schools of democratic theory. We might characterize contemporary forms of faith in the people to take one of two forms—a "weaker" version that is reflected in contemporary liberal theory and a "stronger" form we might characterize as "agonistic." Each evinces considerable "faith" in the capacities of ordinary people for self-governance, although liberalism is more inclined to seek procedural and institutional constraints upon democratic decision making—albeit while increasingly placing greater faith in the rational "deliberative" faculties of ordinary citizens—whereas "agonistic" democratic theory places more reliance upon the transformative nature of democratic politics toward the end of securing democratically desirable outcomes by democratically driven means. Strikingly, each approach rests upon a set of epistemological assumptions whose origins were explicitly antidemocratic—that is, they rejected faith in democratic capacities of ordinary people—and that have since been considerably "democratized" in recent years on behalf of democracy. Further, each theory demonstrates considerable potential for and some real evidence of "despair" toward democracy, inclining each toward a tendency to retreat from the actual practices of democracy and into a form of democratic despair manifested as cynicism or even contempt toward ordinary citizens.

Versions of democratic theory rest substantively on articulated theories or implicit assumptions about human knowledge and the possibility of realizing democratic capacity based on, or in the absence of, certain kinds of knowledge. Epistemological assumptions that stress the role and promise of *reason* in judgment inform theories of liberal democracy with a concomitant stress on rights, procedures, constitutionalism, rule of law, and a greater role for deliberation, whether juridical or more popular. Alternatively theories that center on epistemological assumptions of deep pluralism, irreconcilable value commitments, and an antifoundational rejection of the possibility of fundamental preliminary agreement *antecedent to* democratic decision making instead stress versions of radical or participatory democratic politics. Both epistemologies, while deeply opposed, are largely employed by contemporary political thinkers in the service of arguments for and justifications of democracy.

Although both epistemological assumptions are employed in justifications of democracy in modern political theory, neither epistemology can or should be regarded in the end as essentially democratic; each can lead with equal and possibly greater facility to *rejections* of either democratic equality *tout court* or democracy in its more robust popular conceptions. Indeed, one might argue that each epistemology arose or gained prominence during various historical periods, if not even initially, as a response to fears provoked by democratic equality, whether ancient or modern, and was philosophically developed as a means of combating what were regarded as worrisome democratic assumptions or conditions. This is one understanding at least of Plato's rationalist response to the perceived unjustness of democratic Athens, just as conversely it is seen as animating in part Nietzsche's or Schmitt's antifoundationalist aversion to liberal forms of modern democracy.

While one might look at these and many other places in the history of political thought for examples of the ways that "rationalist" and "fallibilist" epistemologies did not lead necessarily to strong democratic endorsements, a more "familiar" source—the *Federalist Papers*—suggests how these two epistemologies have lent themselves at the very least to extensive suspicions of democracy even within the more democratically sympathetic American setting. While the *Federalist Papers* are often regarded as guided by a single voice and single vision despite multiple authorship, tensions between the two primary authors—Hamilton and Madison—occasionally erupt and even foreshadow the political divisions between the two figures in later years.[2] While both endorsed popular sovereignty throughout the *Federalist Papers*, each evinced a deep suspicion toward deliberative or participatory democratic models that called upon an extensive belief in democratic capacities. Hamilton and Madison held such suspicions arguably not *despite* but *because of* beliefs in "rationalist" and "fallibilistic" epistemologies, respectively.

Hamilton reveals the full extent of his belief in a form of "rationalist" epistemology in *Federalist* 31:

> In disquisitions of every kind there are certain primary truths, or first principles, upon which all subsequent reasons must depend. These contain an internal evidence which, antecedent to all reflection or combination, commands the assent of the mind. . . . Of this nature are the maxims in geometry. . . . Of the same nature are these other maxims in ethics and politics . . . [which], if they cannot pretend to rank in the class of axioms, are yet such direct inferences from them, and so obvious in themselves, and so agreeable to the natural and unsophisticated dictates of common sense that they challenge the assent of a sound and unbiased mind with a degree of force and conviction almost equally irresistible.[3]

Hamilton expresses dismay at the resistance by opponents to the Constitution to what he regards as "axiomatic" political foundations as those endorsed throughout the *Federalist Papers*. He admits that while such "axioms" should be evident to every person's common sense, even "men of discernment" can be all too easily swayed by irrational impulses. "The obscurity is much oftener in the passions and prejudices of the reasoner than in the subject. Men, upon too many occasions, do not give their own understanding fair play; but, yielding to some untoward bias, they entangle themselves in words and confound themselves in subtleties."[4]

If Hamilton suggests that reason *can* settle divisive political issues, even if biased or impassioned people may be resistant to its conclusions, in *Federalist* 37 Madison is far less sanguine about the ability of reason to act as an infallible guide for human political judgment. While Madison shares Hamilton's view that some "delineations [of nature] are perfectly accurate," he holds that the medium of human perception is permeated with imperfection and uncertainty.[5] Moreover, once one moves from an examination of natural or mathematical phenomena to a consideration of human affairs, "the obscurity arises as well from the object itself as from the organ by which it is contemplated."[6] Beyond the uncertainties produced by both the object and "organ" of perception themselves, further uncertainty is introduced through the medium of language, by which such perceptions are communicated (and miscommunicated) to other humans:

> But no language is so copious as to supply words and phrases for every complex idea, or so correct as not to include many equivocally denoting different ideas. Hence it must happen that however accurately the discrimination may be consid-

ered, the definition of them may be rendered inaccurate by the inaccuracy of the terms in which it is delivered. And this unavoidable inaccuracy must be greater or less, according to the complexity and novelty of the objects defined. When the Almighty himself condescends to address mankind in their own language, his meaning, luminous as it must be, is rendered dim and doubtful by the cloudy medium through which it is communicated.[7]

Divine revelation itself—the very definition of Truth by some estimations— is itself rendered dubious by its mediation through language. Human understanding is always subject to uncertainty—uncertainty that is tainted by our sinful and fallen natures—and hence division and disagreement, even when the object of perception—whether natural or divine—are otherwise "perfectly accurate."

For Hamilton and Madison, the political implications of these divergent epistemological assumptions are the same for the purposes of the *Federalist*: widespread popular self-government is both implausible in theory and dangerous in reality. In the first instance, the Federalists doubt whether reason can be expected to be sufficiently present in enough of the population. Dismissing calls such as those by the more democratically optimistic Jefferson to subject the Constitution itself to frequent democratic reconsideration, Madison insists on the importance of "veneration" that he hopes will be accorded to the Constitution over time. Such "veneration" has to be inculcated precisely because of the unreliability of *reasoned* devotion: "In a nation of philosophers, this consideration ought to be disregarded. A reverence for the laws would be sufficiently inculcated by the voice of an enlightened reason. But a nation of philosophers is as little to be expected as the philosophical race of kings wished for by Plato."[8] Here Madison does not mean for us to assume for an instant the feasibility of achieving such a "nation of philosophers," since he has little confidence that the faculty of "enlightened reason" is ever likely to be widespread.

To confirm that this remark is more a dismissal than a fondly desired hope, Madison reveals the full extent of his misgivings over reason's domain in his denunciation of antifederalist arguments for increasing the size of the House of Representatives. While human beings may be capable of following the dictates of reason in contemplative isolation, the Federalists view the faculty of reason to be insufficiently resilient in resisting those passions and biases that can be expected to be stoked and aggravated in more crowded democratic settings. Madison stresses the need to maintain a comparatively small legislature "in order to avoid the confusion and intemperance of a multitude. In all very numerous assemblies, of whatever character composed, passion never fails to wrest the scepter from reason. Had every Athenian citizen been a Socrates, every Athenian assembly would still have been a mob."[9] He concludes that there is no possibility of a "nation of philosophers," since the multitude of a "nation" would undermine philosophy qua reason in every event. Even the philosopher who envisions the possibility of a rationally governing philosopher-king—Socrates, via Plato—would be just as susceptible to mob-provoked irrationality. His rational wisdom comes not only from within but from his practice of remaining aloof from the greater populace and speaking only with one or very few interlocutors at any time.

These two epistemological approaches—one a "Hamiltonian" trust in an ordered structure in nature and potentially also in human affairs, a belief in the discernibility of such order through the faculty of reason, and even the potential for near-universal agreement upon that basis; the other a "Madisonian" suspicion of human faculties of perception and the rationality of human affairs themselves, combined with an acknowledgment of the elusiveness of common perception once mediated through the course and imprecise medium of speech—these two approaches represent a version of what John Gray has termed the "Two Faces of Liberalism."[10] The former, a liberalism based upon "universal principles," seeks to construct institutions that maximize the possibility of reasoned analysis and deliberation with an aim toward achieving not mere consensus but correct answers based upon reasoned inquiry, and, in particular, favors juridical approaches to conflict resolution, thereby suggesting that conflict itself can be settled by "reasonable" deliberation.[11] The latter, a liberalism based upon a recognition of eternal conflict and irresolution, seeks tolerantly at once to allow the flourishing of political disagreement even while considering ways of minimizing potential social disarray that could result from the most virulent and enduring forms of political conflict.

Hamilton, interested in establishing government not by "accident and force" but by "reflection and choice" was particularly attracted to the roles of courts, and especially the Supreme Court.[12] In *Federalist* 78 he recommends the lifetime appointment of judges as a means of protecting judges from the temporary and heated passions of the populace, and thus form a "bulwark" against "those ill humors which the arts of designing men, or the influence of particular conjunctures, sometimes disseminate among the people themselves."[13] By contrast, Madison argued that "the latent causes of faction are sown in the nature of man," and ingeniously argued for the preservation of the "diversity in the faculties of men" by allowing the free exercise of that diversity in the political realm, both by means of representation, and especially by "extending the sphere," that is, by expanding the very physical dimension of the polity, thereby making it difficult for people to concert together or at length.[14] Through both these means, juridical and social, Hamilton and Madison sought to establish institutions or structures that would alternately maximize rationality in politics while both permitting diversity yet minimizing the consequences of inevitable conflict in politics. The solution favored by each reflected their respective assumptions about human perception and the potential for a rationally ordered polity, but both solutions continue to be regarded as having been spurred by fundamental mistrust of government by the people—democracy.

Ironically, with the rise of democratic devotions in the intervening centuries, the respective epistemological assumptions of Hamilton and Madison have been put *in the service* of justifications of democracy rather than used as means of attempting to rein in the rule of the people. Indeed, contemporary versions of these two epistemologies, instead of Gray's "Two Faces of Liberalism," might today be dubbed even more appropriately the "Two Faces of Democracy." Whereas, for Hamilton, reasoned deliberation was thought to be achievable only by relatively few well-educated and insulated people, contemporary liberal thinkers are far more sanguine about the capacity of deliberation by every citizen. Whereas, for Madison, the brute natural fact of "diversity of faculties of mankind" led inexorably to "the mischief of faction," which in its thoroughgoing democratic form resembled the *stasis* of democratic Athens, for contemporary radical democrats the fact of inexpugnable difference affords the promise of "agonistic" democratic politics shorn of foundational limits and institutional constraints. Epistemologies once believed to require the constraint or even outright rejection of democratic forms are now assumed to be fully supportive of democratic means and ends. The "democratic turn" of each epistemology has resulted in two contested and contestable contemporary theories of democracy, the "deliberative" and "agonistic" models of democracy. Whereas each rests explicitly on a rejection of the place of faith in democracy, each evinces a substantial and implicit form of faith in individual capacity that transforms a formerly antidemocratic epistemology into a support for democracy.

Adherents of these two preeminent schools of democratic theory today—the liberal "deliberative democratic" school and the antiliberal, radical "agonistic democratic" school—have been so long arrayed against each other, like armed hostile camps whose attention is diverted for the most part toward an opposing army, that it is easy to overlook the profoundly antidemocratic origins of the two positions. Each side has taken on a democratic "face" largely by refusing to "take men as they are" and, instead, painting an idealized portrait of humanity as it might be. Their respective articulations of democracy are premised upon an idealized portrait of humanity that subjects each position to the danger that, short of their realization, each becomes susceptible to democratic disillusionment. In the following sections I consider the apparent democratic claims of each in order to suggest that they are not, in fact, the best friends of democracy, resting upon a "faith" that inclines its adherents toward an underlying democratic "cynicism" as the conditions of democracy fail to live up to that faith.

Liberal Faith: Deliberative Democracy, Rational Capacity, and Overcoming Politics

While Madison and Hamilton coauthored the *Federalist Papers* in 1787–88 in order to secure ratification of the Constitution, the differences of their epistemological assumptions reflected, in fact, deep philosophical divisions that were eventually manifested in the political sphere, with Hamilton remaining a lifelong Federalist, while Madison joined forces with Jefferson in the Democrat-Republican Party. While Hamilton retained his aversion for populism, writing in several late letters of his distaste for "democracy,"[15] Madison came to share Jefferson's greater confidence in the democratic capacities of the populace, reflected in part by his confidence in the role of the Bill of Rights, which he viewed otherwise as "parchment barriers," toward forming a democratic spirit among the people.[16] By declaring the rights "in that solemn manner," they would "acquire by degrees the character of fundamental maxims of free Government, and as they become incorporated with the national sentiment, counteract the impulses of interest and passion."[17] Without abandoning his belief that division and disagreement would always mark political activity owing especially to the deficiencies of perception that he described in *Federalist 37*—deficiencies that were only exacerbated by the perceptual limitations imposed by self-interest—Madison nevertheless believed that an underlying commitment to democratic freedoms could be secured by means of subtle education in mutual recognition embodied, for example, in the First Amendment's protections of freedom of speech. Rather than seeking to minimize the "virulent subdivisions" that Hamilton feared, Madison believed that widespread conflict within a broader democratic consensus would be the best defense of the collective basis of democracy and "the diverse faculties" of individuals.

The eventual divisions between Hamilton and Madison are, if anything, more intensely reflected in their various direct or indirect intellectual heirs, expressed by what I have termed "the two faces of democracy"—liberal "deliberative democrats" and antifoundational, agonistic democrats. If the "antifoundational" camp can be viewed as resting their democratic confidence on unexplored "faith" commitments, does the Hamiltonian liberal camp offer a more skeptical approach to democratic theory? Has the move to embrace the democratic potential of Hamiltonian (or Lockean or Kantian) "rationality" resulted in a democratic theory at once sufficiently constraining and open to democratic outcomes? Have "deliberative democrats" avoided "democratic faith" while remaining faithful to democracy? Is their greater cautiousness also an effective barrier to possible democratic disillusionment?

While theorists like Ronald Dworkin maintain a deep suspicion of majoritarianism and an equal confidence in the capacity of reason to settle conflict through the deliberative functions of the judiciary, increasingly the term "deliberation" has come to be combined with "democracy" in an effort to broaden the numbers of deliberators, no longer to be confined to a small circle of specially trained judges but rather to include the citizenry at large.[18] Liberal "deliberative democrats" import many of Hamilton's assumptions, yet now in support of democracy, in particular with an aim toward advancing a conception of democracy that contains disagreement within deliberative limits that have been previously established themselves by recourse to rational deliberation.[19] Many, if not most, "deliberative democrats" explicitly adopt the philosophical underpinnings afforded by John Rawls in *A Theory of Justice* and *Political Liberalism*—especially the starting assumptions of the necessary conditions of political justice that derive from Rawls's rational-choice–inspired thought experiment of the "original position" and the consequent commitments to political liberalism and "the difference principle"—but such theorists seek to make far more explicit than Rawls the expectation that *every* citizen is both capable of, and to be expected to, personally undergo such a thought experiment and thereby arrive independently at the conclusions Rawls himself endorses.[20] Whereas for Rawls "the original condition" functions largely on justificatory grounds, for "deliberative democrats" the greater confidence in the rational capacities of the public leads to the recommendation and belief that each individual can and will personally arrive rationally at similar conclusions—conclusions that justify a liberally grounded conception of deliberative democracy—and, moreover, that such conclusions will be reached publicly and discursively rather than in solitary reflection. By democratizing rationality itself, they democratize both Hamilton and Rawls.

The democratic turn in liberalism requires far greater trust and even faith than that exhibited by Hamilton in both the faculty of reason in each individual, as well as in the "reasonableness" of each individual to willingly engage politically in a "rational" manner. The outcome is an endorsement of "public reason," a form of open and public justification that requires political actors to offer reasons and justifications that can be accepted by "reasonable" people and resist "rational" scrutiny. "Comprehensive doctrines" that foreclose acceptance by those who do not share its base assumptions must be held in abeyance because of the strictures of "rational" and "reasonable" deliberation. This has the pointed effect of disallowing religious justifications, in particular.

For many deliberative democrats, John Locke is regarded as the founder of democratic liberal theory for his "democratizing" of both justificatory reasoning and resulting regime preferences.[21] Locke lodges sovereignty always finally with the People who originally contract with one another to form a government, and can, if that government itself proves more onerous than the State of Nature (one conceived in terms far less hostile than Hobbes's version), organize to overthrow the repressive regime and contract to establish another in its place. Because of Locke's acknowledgment of ultimate popular sovereignty, he has been viewed by some as "the first liberal democrat."[22]

Yet, Locke is not as friendly to the democratic inclinations of "deliberative democrats" as is often assumed, and indeed suggests the vast theoretical distance that separates them. Locke's deep mistrust in both reason and "reasonableness" points to an implicit "democratic faith" in the assumptions of "deliberative democrats," which Locke does not remotely share, and raises questions about the "faith-based" assumptions of deliberative democrats that are often regarded as long-settled (often by means of incomplete reliance upon Locke, supplemented by a healthy dose of Kantian ethics).

While Locke could speak of abstract humanity as capable of both knowing and protecting its own basic self-interest and ultimate sovereignty when
discussing the State of Nature and the foundations of government particularly in the *Second Treatise*, it would be a mistake to assume that Locke was
sanguine about the prospects of democratic rule based extensively on assumptions of the "reasonableness" of the populace. For Locke, reason alone
was not, nor could be, a sufficient basis for morality and good judgment in
politics. As he writes in his late, important, if less-often read treatise, *The
Reasonableness of Christianity*, "'tis our mistake to think, that . . . we had
the first certain knowledge of [truths] from [reason], and in that clear Evidence we now possess them. The contrary is manifest, in the *defective Morality of the Gentiles* before our Saviour's time. . . . Philosophy seemed to have
spent its strength, and done its utmost."[23]

Locke admires the thoroughgoing reasonableness of the ancients but still
finds them lacking in morality that only became possible after revelations
from "our Saviour." Locke writes that one might attempt to collect the wisdom of the ancients, but "the world nevertheless stood as much in need of
our Saviour, and the Morality delivered by him." While Locke states that the
laws of the New Testament conform to principles that are discoverable by
reason, nevertheless he acknowledges that "the truth and *obligation* of its
Precepts have their force, and are put past doubt to us, by the evidence of
[Jesus Christ's] mission. He was sent by God: His miracles shew it; And the
Authority of God in his Precepts cannot be questioned." Thus Locke con-
cludes that the unaided reason of the sort demonstrated by ancient philoso-
phy was insufficient to discover the grounds of morality and, further, the vol-
untary observation of such morality, independent of religious revelation:
"And we see, [reason] resolved not the doubts that had arisen amongst the
Studious and Thinking Philosophers; Nor had yet been able to convince the
Civilized parts of the World, that they had not given, nor could without a
Crime, take away the Lives of Children, by Exposing them."[24]

Further, Locke was not sanguine about the prospects for democracy. Locke
continues his analysis by supposing for a moment that reason is a sufficient
guide for human morality and judgment (a point on which, it must be
stressed, he was insufficiently confident to begin with). Thus he writes
(wholly in the conditional):

> Or if it [i.e., rationalistic philosophy] should have gone farther, as we see it did not,
> and from undeniable Principles given us *Ethicks* in a Science like *Mathematicks* in
> every part demonstrable, this yet would not have been so effectual to man in this
> imperfect state, nor proper for the Cure. The greatest part of mankind want *leisure
> or capacity* for Demonstration; nor can they carry a train of Proofs; which in that
> way they must always depend upon for Conviction, and cannot be required to as-
> sent to till they see the Demonstration. Wherever they stick, the Teachers are al-
> ways put upon Proof, and must clear the Doubt by a Thread of coherent deduc-
> tions from the first Principle, how long, or how intricate soever that be. And you

> may as soon hope to have all the Day-Labourers and Tradesmen, the Spinsters and
> Dairy Maids perfect Mathematicians, as to have them perfect in *Ethicks* this way.
> Hearing plain Commands, is the sure and only course to bring them to Obedience
> and Practice. The greatest part cannot know, and therefore they must believe.[25]

He concludes, even were reason to be assumed to be the best guide for moral
judgment, that nevertheless "the Instruction of the People were best still to
be left to the Precepts and Principles of the Gospel."[26]

Owing to Locke's *lack* of faith in both reason's sufficiency and in reason's
accessibility and *comprehensibility* to the "greatest part" of humanity, he instead recommends a thoroughgoing reliance upon the precepts of revealed
religion. While unclear whether it is merely because of the absence of
"leisure" or also (or exclusively) to the deficiency in "capacity," the general
conclusion of Locke's analysis is that reason, by itself, will always be insufficient as a basis of political decision making. As such, Locke's conclusion severely constrains the possibility of democratic self-governance, both to the
degree that it questions the extent to which those wanting "leisure or capacity" can be expected to govern at all—since in the absence of the time
and even ability to deliberate, they must simply "believe"—as well as raising significant questions about the possibility of reason's sufficiency in arriving at ethical decisions were such "leisure and capacity" assumed to exist.

Locke's lack of confidence in reason or the capacities of ordinary citizens
sheds a good deal of light on a controversial argument in which Locke further commends religious belief as a basis to his Social Contract theory. In the
Letter concerning Toleration—otherwise a core text in liberal political philosophy—Locke insists that toleration is not to be extended to atheists, since
they cannot be trusted to keep to the agreements of the Social Contract on
the basis of reason alone:

> Lastly, those are not to be tolerated who deny the Being of a God. Promises,
> Covenants, and Oaths, which are the bonds of Humane Society, can have no hold
> upon an Atheist. The taking away of God, tho but even in thought, dissolves all.
> Besides also, those that by their Atheism undermine and destroy a Religion, can
> have no pretence of Religion whereupon to challenge the Privilege of a
> Toleration.[27]

Atheists will not honor their contracts—including that most fundamental
contract undergirding society itself, the Social Contract—and thereby cannot be trusted to keep their oaths and promises. In the absence of a
"Leviathan"-like state that can detect all infractions of law and morality,
Locke relies extensively upon the assumption that human morality requires
a basis beyond mere rationality (or perhaps, better put, that morality cannot
survive calculating and instrumental rationality), lest fragile human society
devolve into a State of Nature scenario of unadulterated self-interest. An
atheist threatens to "dissolve all," since the prospect of even one contract-
ing member who will circumvent the stipulations of the contract thereby
threatens to unravel the contract as a whole (e.g., why should *I* pay all my

taxes when I know that everyone else isn't?). For Locke—less sanguine about the ability of reason to settle ethical matters, about people's ability to discern the dictates of reason even if this were due to the absence of leisure and ethical training, and finally about the widespread existence of what Rawls would call "reasonableness" itself—*religious* faith, or "saving faith" as Locke puts it, is a base requirement for felt confidence in the moral, even democratic, capacities of "the greatest part" or "bulk," as he describes it elsewhere.[28] If Locke is the first "liberal democrat," he is significantly less democratic than sometimes supposed, and certainly less liberal than almost always assumed.[29]

Contemporary democratic liberals (self-styled, inaccurately in my view, as "liberal democrats"), particularly those that claim the label "deliberative democrats," appear to reject Locke on both counts: deliberative democrats express profound faith in the promise of "reasonableness" as a basis on which to resolve persistent political controversies, and furthermore express extensive confidence in the widespread capability of a democratic public to engage in efforts to forge consensus on the basis of reasoned agreement and principled reflection that transcend partial, sectarian, or factional interest. If the roots of liberalism reflect deep suspicion toward the ordinary capacities of people generally, and toward the plausibility of a functioning democracy specifically, contemporary theorists appear to have jettisoned any lingering doubts and embraced wholesale and without reservation a form of liberal democratic faith.

Reservations about the rational capacities of ordinary citizens such as those Locke expressed have largely been overcome as unduly pessimistic toward the prospects of human amelioration and progress. John Stuart Mill's and John Dewey's confidence in moral progress through education, open deliberation, and the scientific control of nature form background assumptions in contemporary liberalism's willingness to embrace the democratic potential of the populace, and particularly the turn in recent years toward models of "deliberative democracy."[30] Education opens human vistas to new knowledge and engagement with other forms of thinking and believing; the open flow of discourse and information enables all humans to more closely approach the truth of fundamental matters, while leaving open the possibility that working hypotheses can be overturned in the process of further discussion and investigation; and, further, technological progress allows greater flow of information and physical mobility, breaking down barriers and overcoming local parochialism, thereby leading to the promotion of greater mutual understanding and the homogenization of modernist culture. "Deliberative democracy" claims to address the problem of "people having interest solely [in themselves], or at least failing to demonstrate sufficient regard for the interests of others."[31] Liberalism ultimately views itself as "transformative": it forges people in its own image—open, tolerant, even capable finally of transcending individual interests in the embrace of rational reflection of the common good.[32]

Indeed, at its furthest extreme, liberalism begins to sound little different from the religious sensibility it claims to displace. Gutmann and Thompson reveal that "deliberative democracy" presupposes the democratic virtue of "mutual respect." Mutual respect "requires a favorable attitude toward, and constructive interaction with, the persons with whom one disagrees. It consists in an excellence of character that permits a democracy to flourish in the face of fundamental moral disagreements."[33] Deliberative democracy thus presupposes a kind of democratic charity, a preliminary "agreement to disagree," a more fundamental commitment to democracy than any other value or belief. Democracy is to supercede all our other "comprehensive doctrines." A deliberative character is assumed to undergird deliberative democracy; that is, deliberation can only occur when people have developed the dispositions of character and deliberative abilities that incline them to the deliberation that, presumably, is necessary to develop those dispositions. As Rousseau described the creation of the "General Will," the effect must become the cause. This occurs when democracy can assume the mantle of "religion" from the "religious." Stephen Macedo, for example, gives liberalism credit for evidence of widespread American endorsement of the claim that people ought to "love their neighbors": "the three great religions of America have [followed] . . . the basic imperatives of political liberalism in America."[34] The "golden rule" is embraced by Americans of varying religious backgrounds because of the "transformative" power of liberalism; it took liberalism to actualize latent religious beneficence by overcoming pervasive sectarianism.

Modern deliberative liberalism lays claim to the most idealistic, even "religious" transformative impulse, but in so doing jettisons the accompanying traditional religious belief in ineradicable human sinfulness, self-interest, and self-deception. It regards the propect of universal reason and democratic deliberation as eminently realizable; it is not viewed as "utopian" but as a practicable goal. The failure to realize a fully deliberative polity lies not in the nature and limitations of human character but rather is attributable to an insufficiently realized democratic populace. As such, the very "idealism" of deliberative democracy contributes to its deeper antidemocratic trajectory. To the extent that people fail to demonstrate their receptiveness to liberalism's "transformative" character, liberalism exhibits its foundational hostility toward nontransformed, average people. In this regard, "deliberative democracy" is formulated as a mirror (i.e., an identical but reversed) image of Locke's liberalism endorsed especially in order to exclude religious justifications in the public sphere. Ironically Locke sought to exclude *nonbelievers* from public life for many of the same reasons that contemporary deliberative democrats seek to exclude arguments of religious *believers* from the public sphere: each, respectively, is perceived to pose a threat to liberal public order.[35] To the extent that some groups do not evince liberal forms of "transformation," and rather evince "unreasonableness" in the actual practices of contemporary politics, "deliberative democrats" are forced to admit that their devotion is finally less toward democracy and rather in favor of a liberalism that rules in the name of the people. Democracy is endorsed to the extent that people exhibit transformed dispositions of "perfectionist liberalism." To this extent, liberals begin more fully to resemble that aspect of Locke they have largely denied, ignored, or never encountered, namely, Locke who argues in *The Reasonableness of Christianity* that "Day-Labourers and Tradesmen, the Spinsters and Dairy Maids" are likely not leisured or capable enough to exercise reasoned self-rule, and will instead be led by wiser authorities.

Thus, in instances in which a local majority may legitimately vote for the introduction of religious-based practice in a public forum (e.g., a school), "deliberative democrats" will seek to exclude such majoritarian democratic outcomes by means of the familiar Hamiltonian juridical regime.[36] When the situation comes to a head, liberal "public reason" will always trump the democratic "public," and courts and enforcement of the state will ensure that "unreasonable" voices are barred from the public sphere.[37] Yet, because of apparent democratic commitments, the rejection of such "unreasonable" majoritarian decisions will be done in the name of the people and democracy more generally, particularly with the proviso that liberal decisions are the only ones that could be reached by "reasonable" people.[38] Legitimate democratic citizens are defined exclusively as "reasonable": a people must either conform to that rational ideal or forfeit the right to be considered full-blown members of the democracy. What constitutes legitimate "deliberative democracy" ultimately is dictated by the demands of "reasonableness," whether that outcome is reflected by the populace or not. Reasonableness becomes a proxy for the voice of the people, and where the people fail to be reasonable, an opposite outcome can be derived in the name of "deliberative democracy." This is the conclusion reached by Rawls in his later work, *Political Liberalism*:

> Our exercise of political power is proper and hence justifiable only when it is exercised in accordance with a constitution the essentials of which *all citizens* may reasonably be expected to endorse in the light of principles and ideals acceptable to them as reasonable and rational.[39]

"All citizens" include everyone except those who do not conform to what is "reasonable and rational"; thus the "reasonable and rational" becomes tantamount to the people itself—a stand-in, or re-presentation, of legitimate democratic citizens that are conjured in the minds of Rawlsian liberals if not existing in fact. The "reasonable" come to represent "the people," and thus "deliberative democrats" cleave closely to the original Federalist mistrust of democratic citizens, whose views must be "filtered" by the enlightened representatives.[40] Democracy is carried out by a reasonable elite in the name of the people.

Democracy is preserved, but at the potential expense of vast numbers of people, if Locke's assessment of the unlikelihood of widespread "rational-

ity," so-defined, is to be credited. Because such an outcome is untenable, a belief in widespread education in rationality and human amelioration along liberal rationalist lines is recommended and pursued. Of concern, however, is
the possibility that such undertakings will not arrive at the desired outcomes,
spelling either the demise of liberal democratic commitments (however unlikely) or the rhetorical adherence to the language of democracy even as governance is undertaken by a small elite of liberal activists (likely, if not in fact
increasingly, the reality).[41] Democracy appears to be too good for the people,
and must be salvaged in their name. In short, in the thoroughgoing retreat
from Lockean pessimism and the embrace of Millian liberal perfectionism,
liberalism goes from outright rejection of democracy to the practical replacement of democracy by the rule of educated liberal elites who "stand in" for
a reasonable public.[42] Liberal "democratic faith" tends to lead to the rhetorical embrace of democracy, but the effectual rejection of all but an ideal form
of liberal, that is, "rational and reasonable," democracy—precisely because
it has placed the bar of entry to democratic politics at a sufficiently high level
to bar entry until a "reasonable" public can come into existence.

The rejection of the imperfectly rational citizenry is expressed aptly by
Stephen Macedo:

> I do not want to disparage the reasonableness of most citizens of advanced and
> stable democratic societies. Much of this book has been a discussion of the rea-
> sonableness that prevails in a successful modern democracy. Nevertheless, it would
> be foolish to regard the dangers of religious enthusiasm, or various forms of trib-
> alism, as problems that are superseded once and for all as a polity matures.[43]

Relying tacitly on a belief in moral progress—the "maturation" of a polity—
Macedo still acknowledges that some pockets of recidivist irrationality will
persist and require exclusion in the name of liberalism, if not democracy.
Calling for a rejection of "indiscriminate inclusion" and eschewing "the embrace of all differences, and a laissez-faire attitude to the civic dimensions of
liberal self-government," Macedo and other "deliberative democrats" invoke in the final instance the authority of the state, actualized primarily
through the judiciary, to "discriminate" between the rational and irrational,
between the "reasonable" and "unreasonable."

Apparent liberal "democratic faith" takes the form of belief in the growing "reasonableness" of the populace by means of moral progress but evinces
impatience with that progress in the form of arguments on behalf of exclusion of those people who evince less than perfect "reasonableness." In the
contest between liberalism's apparently equal embrace of faith in "reason"
and faith in a reasonable populace, there is finally no contest: actual political divisions can only be solved by appeal to reason, and where the people
evince imperfect reasonableness, liberal rationality—invoked in the defense
of personal autonomy, above all—will prove decisive. One finds an extensive "moral faith" underlying the democratic turn of "deliberative democrats." Where Locke (or Madison) lacked faith in fully rational justifications
of ethical precepts, there is substantial faith among "deliberative democrats"

in reason's ability, at the very least, to achieve, elucidate, and substantively resolve questions of self-governance; where Locke lacked faith in the "reasonableness" of fairness (without divine strictures), "deliberative democrats" assume the widespread existence of "reasonableness" as tacitly underlying most approaches to contemporary politics; where Locke lacked faith in the rational moral capacity of "the vast bulk" (especially the day-laborers and dairy-maids) owing concomitantly to the pressure of time and the lack of formal moral training as well as doubts about "capacity," "deliberative democrats" stipulate the existence of such rational moral capacity. Yet, by asserting the future existence of such full-blown deliberative capacities (ones that will exist when every citizen evinces a preliminary devotion to democratic "mutual respect"), liberal democratic faith is able to find in the countervailing evidence cause for a deeper undercurrent of democratic disillusionment—a disillusionment that lands them back to the dour assessment of deliberative capacities as expressed by Locke, without his initial kind of "realism." Contrary evidence to the expectations of human amelioration constitutes sufficient cause for rejection of such recidivist "unreasonableness."

Above all, "deliberative democrats" exhibit what Robert Adams terms "moral faith," or faith in morality itself. In the face of doubts about whether the morality might not be based on reason but, instead, "a massive socially induced delusion"—an echo of Thrasymachus's objection to justice—Adams suggests that such doubts can only be answered by a kind of circularity that reflects a core irrationality, if not a faith in morality:

> We shall not be able to answer without some essential reliance on the very inclinations to ethical belief that are being called into question. Of course, it does not follow that we should not rely on those inclinations . . ., but a certain level of rational discomfort with the situation seems to me appropriate.[44]

Despite rejecting any recourse to "comprehensive doctrines" in public discourse that rest on a basis other than "public reason," contemporary liberal democratic assumptions may themselves curiously rest just as fundamentally on grounds (if not "reasons") that are less than altogether "rational" or even "reasonable." The strong insistence that faith claims be excluded from the public sphere are presented in the guise of high reason, but may themselves rest more extensively on a basis of faith than could ever be willingly admitted.[45] Curiously the absolutism of this stance may reveal an unreflective and epistemologically prideful rigidity that otherwise underlies liberalism's suspicion toward "irrational" faith claims. Perhaps unconsciously, but revealingly, Stephen Macedo concludes his book—otherwise a sustained defense of "public reason" and a strong rejection of "irrational" forms of justification—with a call to "keep liberalism a 'fighting faith.'"[46]

The Bold Faith of Radical Democrats: Democratic Transformation

In contrast to liberalism's faith in the possibility of near-universal "reasonableness," as well as its longstanding belief in the prospect of human amelioration by means of progress and scientific advancement, one finds among modern radical democrats an even more robust and radical faith that underlies their democratic convictions. Contemporary antifoundational thinkers especially stress the need for unleashed *agonism* as a necessary prerequisite for the flourishing of true democracy; only by means of unconstrained democratic conflict can individuals be transformed into citizens, and thereby allow for the infusion of democratic activity into all aspects of human life.

This insistence on the necessity of political conflict, however, masks an important insistence on an even more fundamental form of agreement over the shared commitment to democracy itself, one that is, in fact, much akin to Gutmann and Thompson's appeal to "mutual respect." Antifoundationalist theories of democracy tempt the possibility that agonism will spill over from discrete political issues to the question of the legitimacy of democracy itself, thereby threatening the viability of democratic agonism. This self-contradicting potential has to be constrained in some manner to avoid negating the democratic potential of a wholly open, conflictual, even violent politics. In other words, even among the most committed agonistic democrats, there remains a prior unquestioned commitment to democracy itself, one confining arena which itself cannot be questioned. As such, the claims to thoroughgoing agonistic skepticism are undermined by this "foundational" commitment to democracy; yet, representing a form of faith, this commitment represents a belief not in "men as they are" but in a humanity transformed in wholly democratic directions by means of the alchemy of unrestrained agonism. To the extent that this outcome appears to be more a form of wishful thinking than readily realizable, one is not surprised to encounter expressions of democratic cynicism and even despair for the prospects of democracy among some radical democratic theorists.

In one breath the self-declared "agonistic" radical democratic theorist Chantal Mouffe, for example, criticizes the prior constraints on political conflict afforded by Rawlsian models that demand "reasonableness" from deliberating citizens, writing that "the very creation of consensus is the elimination of pluralism from the public sphere." Yet, in another breath, she notes that almost all pluralist views are acceptable in the public sphere except "those who do not accept the democratic 'rules of the game' and who thereby exclude themselves from the political community."[47] In this latter respect, Mouffe becomes almost indistinguishable from the broad position outlined by her liberal antagonists, sharing their perspective according to which certain voices that deny the "rules of the game" must in fact be excluded from the public sphere. Whereas for Rawls and deliberative democrats those who refuse to frame their arguments in "reasonable" terms are to be excluded, for Mouffe, those disallowed from democratic free play deny at the outset the need to preserve democratic openness. Each seeks to protect the sphere of democratic politics from ultimate disruption, albeit in a different register; each fears, above all, the "absolutist" who would, in turn, threaten an "absolute" commitment to democratic values.

From a Rawlsian perspective, this concession of the limits of agonism might seem sensible and expected; from an agonistic perspective, however, it is perhaps a pained and undesired admission of the limits of agonistic politics, and an implicit acknowledgment of prior "foundational" commitments that the embrace of agonism attempts to eschew.[48] One way of avoiding even this apparent concession follows, instead, that direction suggested by Nietzsche and Carl Schmitt, as well as, in a different register, Walt Whitman, John Dewey, and Benjamin Barber, who defend the transformational aspects of open democratic life. By this means, even virulent antidemocrats do not need to be constrained or muzzled prior to political conflict. Rather, by means of the very engagement in the open arena of agonistic political life, a democratic "self" will emerge concomitant with the flourishing of democratic activity— a self conditioned by the very activity of participation toward a more comprehensive consciousness that transcends mere individual desire and begins to apprehend a sense of the common good.

Mark Warren has aptly captured this widespread belief in the transformative powers of robust democratic participation held by antifoundational proponents of agonistic democratic theory, who propound what he calls an "expansive" view of democracy:

> On the expansive view, were individuals more broadly empowered, especially in institutions that have the most impact on their everyday lives (workplaces, schools, local governments, etc.), their experiences would have transformative effects: they would become more public-spirited, more tolerant, more knowledgeable, more attentive to the interests of others, and more probing of their own interests. These transformations would improve the workings of higher-level representative institutions, as well as mitigate—if not remove—the threats democracy is held to pose to rights, pluralism, and governability.[49]

The "transformation thesis" rests on a conception of selfhood that is to exhibit features both of autonomy and sociality, of deep commitment to felt interests (those derived from one's particular placement in the social setting), and, simultaneously, of openness to an expanded sense of what defines one's interests and what constitutes one's good—particularly in relation with, and transformed by (while oneself transforming), the interest and good of others.

It is through the practices of democracy, in its most ideal form, that such transformation is achieved. Benjamin Barber, among others, has emphasized this "transformative" nature of democratic participation: "democratic participation turns self-interested private beings into citizens with a concern for the community."[50] In *Strong Democracy*, Barber at once rejects liberal fears that unfettered democratic participation would result in the arbitrary rule of self-interested majority factions, as well as assumptions of "fraternity" that underlie "unitary" theories of democracy.[51] Instead, he stresses the extent to which, he believes—or hopes—that fully realized democracy can come about by means of

> a dynamic relationship among strangers who are transformed into neighbors, whose commonality derives from expanding consciousness rather than geographic

proximity. . . . They are united by the ties of common activity and common consciousness—ties that are willed rather than given by blood or heritage or prior consensus on beliefs and that thus depend for their preservation and growth on constant commitment and ongoing political activity. . . . Strong democracy promotes
reciprocal empathy and mutual respect, whereas unitary democracy promotes reciprocal love and fear and thin democracy promotes reciprocal control.[52]

The belief in individual democratic transformation posits at once an inviolable sense of selfhood that remains open to a kind of internal growth
achieved by means of external political interplay with other selves, remaining always "oneself" but not a self that is constant or unchanging.

Barber's vision of a "strong democracy" that requires neither assumptions
nor impositions of unity but rather rests on the hopes of a kind of "expanded" or "common consciousness" that arises from the activity of politics itself echoes a similar set of reflections by Hannah Arendt.[53] Indeed, perhaps more than any other single thinker, Arendt's version of this belief in
democratic self-transformation by means of participation in the agonistic
sphere of conflictual politics is frequently invoked and embraced by contemporary thinkers who claim the mantle "radical democratic theory."[54]
Called by Mark Reinhart "wildly transformative," Arendt's theory suggests
the possibility of "bringing new selves and relations into being," and at once
while constituting "common ground" also sustaining "difference-preserving
forms of distance between people."[55] Through an engagement with Kant's
Critique on Judgment, in various writings Arendt derived and developed a
theory of political judgment that described the transformative potential of
agonistic political encounters in the democratic sphere—the political realm
of "action," as described in her work *The Human Condition*.[56] As developed particularly in her essays "The Crisis in Culture" and "Truth in Politics," Arendt describes the acquisition of what Kant called an "enlarged mentality (*eine erweiterte Denkungsart*)," achieved by means of the faculty of
"imagination" which allows each member of a given society a kind of "liberation from one's own private interests."[57]

In the former essay especially Arendt stressed that the achievement of this
form of "enlarged mentality" required actual interaction within the political
sphere:

This enlarged way of thinking, which as judgment knows how to transcend its own
individual limitations, on the one hand, cannot function in strict isolation or solitude; it needs the presence of others "in whose place" it must think, whose perspectives it must take into consideration, and without whom it never has the opportunity to operate at all. . . . The capacity to judge is a specifically political
ability in exactly the sense denoted by Kant, namely, the ability to see things not
only from one's own point of view but in the perspective of all those who happen
to be present.[58]

While humans enter the public sphere initially as "agonistic" opponents
seeking there to make a name, or put their name into collective memory, and

carve out a space of immortality by means of "enacted stories," the effect of this interaction is to move each participant away from narrowly conceived self-interest and toward a form of "disinterestedness," resulting, as aptly characterized by Lisa Disch, in a form of "situated impartiality."[59]

Arendt maintained that this kind of "enlarged mentality" is achieved by the process of "representative thinking" via the faculty of "imagination." Individuals do not lose their self-identity through this practice but, rather, by "being and thinking in my own identity where I actually am not," each person expands the range of what he considers to be his own concerns, interests, and, finally, sense of good—now not only individually but in common.[60] Arendt insisted that this form of imaginative "visiting" was neither tantamount to losing one's own identity by means of "empathy" nor reducible to "counting noses"; rather, "the more people's standpoints I have present in my mind while I am pondering a given issue, and the better I can imagine how I would feel and think if I were in their place, the stronger will be my conclusions, my opinion."[61] The conclusions and opinions remain "mine" in an important sense; yet, at the same time, the "me" who began pondering these issues in isolation has been subtly transformed by the encounter with other minds, expanding how I think about those initial concerns, modifying what I consider to be my "own" interests, and, finally, changing the "I" through the interchange with other "I's" that now increasingly make a "we" without threat or loss of the "I" at any point.

While admirers of Arendt in particular are attracted by her insistence on the irreducible plurality of politics, and for its embrace of—in Susan Bickford's words—the inevitable "dissonance of democracy," these admirers in many cases implicitly accept Arendt's subtle argument that a transformed disposition is not only the *result* of political interplay and participation but, in a certain sense, necessarily *precedes* such interplay and makes democratic politics possible. Arendt—while cryptic and elusive—suggests in several instances that one cannot enter the public sphere without certain prior commitments to the prospects of compromise and agreement, thus suggesting a pre-political devotion to democratic openness itself. We cannot begin to engage in "representative thinking" unless we first believe in "potential agreement," a potential that we entertain by means of "anticipated communication with others."[62] Before we ever encounter "others" we must first prepare our minds to accept the possibility that we may alter our own view or that they will be willing to alter theirs or that together we will all arrive at a separate conclusion than the one with which we entered the public sphere. While Arendt emphasizes that "enlarged mentality" must occur in "the presence of others"—that it has an undeniably public and political dimension—in other registers she insists on the purely cognitive aspects of judgment to the extent that we "think in the place of everyone else" without literally or emotionally occupying that place. If our actual insertion into the public realm allows us to encounter the variety of different consciousnesses that populate the world, and thereby be in a better position to "represent" those "standpoints of those who are absent," there appears to be a key step that must occur *prior to or apart from entering the public sphere* that is implied in Arendt's normative description of the transformation of the "I" of limited perspective and finite interests (the "interested" self that Arendt implicitly counterposes with one who comes to be properly "disinterested") and the transformed "I" who now willingly "represents" and "re-presents" the minds of others in rendering political judgments. In short, the *agon*—which is not, or not necessarily, democratic—is transformed from potential violence into democratic contestation.[63]

Antifoundational democratic theorists like Chantal Mouffe, Bonnie Honig, William Connolly, Stanley Fish, and Richard Rorty must, in the first instance, assume a transformation of the self that in an important sense precedes the entrance of "agonistic" individuals into a pluralistic public realm. Whether Honig's "subject as multiplicity" or Rorty's "liberal ironists," each individual must become, or made to become, aware of the inherent limitations of his or her own limited worldview—to accept the "perspectival" epistemology as his or her own, indeed, from a "perspective" above his or her own limited set of beliefs or interests.[64] As argued by William Connolly, "the key is to acknowledge the comparative *contestability* of the fundamental perspectives you bring into public engagements," thereby achieving first what he calls "agonistic respect."[65]

The fact of pluralism—which we come to know presumably through our encounters with others in the public realm—leads to the desirable and even necessary acknowledgment of the limits of our own perspective.[66] Yet, that acknowledgment must precede our actual entrance into the public sphere, lest we encounter the "other" not with the presumed willingness to engage in "representative thinking" but rather with the hostility of an enemy who must be overcome through violence or repression. A fundamental common belief—one even more "fundamental" than those beliefs Connolly recognizes may divide us—must first exist, lest the *agon* in public life be manifested in undemocratic and antidemocratic forms. The *difference* of agonistic democracy rests on a more fundamental basis of *agreement* about the need to first "agree to disagree" (closely akin to the ideal of "mutual respect" that underlies democracy according to Gutmann and Thompson), to subject what are supposedly "fundamental beliefs" to interpretation, moderation, even outright rejection. In short, we must enter public life willing to reconsider every fundamental belief except our devotion to democracy itself: difference only seems to go "all the way down," in Stanley Fish's inimitable words—but, in fact, stops at the implied foundation of democratic faith. The democratic life that was assumed to "transform selves" in reality first requires that selves be transformed into appropriately "democratic selves" before democratic outcomes can be secured. There is a curious circularity at the core of Arendt's thought, and in the thought of those who adopt her to more explicit democratic ends: in order for the self to develop an "enlarged mentality," that self must enter the fray of the political world and encounter the full array of countervailing perspectives; yet, for this encounter to be successful in the first instance, one must enter the political sphere with a preliminary acknowledgment of one's own partiality, and thereby a willingness to reassess one's own "fundamental" views and to "represent" the views of others. On the one hand, such thinkers insist that democracy creates democratic selves; on the other, democratic selves are necessary for the creation of agonistic democracy that does not devolve into violence or repression.

That "radical" democracy can begin somewhere, either created by "skeptical" democratic selves or itself creating such selves, seems finally to be a conundrum that remains mysterious, even, it seems, to the democratic faithful.[67] Circularity allows for maintenance of faith in the face of disappointing evidence by means of which one can always assert that "strong" or "radical" democracy has not yet flourished because of the absence of a citizenry with appropriately "enlarged mentalities," and that such a citizenry cannot come into being in the absence of a truly agonistic democratic politics. Yet, the insistence that such an outcome is possible, regardless of the difficulty of assessing where its starting point might lie, with the successful overcoming of the liberal/capitalist modern state, remains a source of wishful thinking among the faithful who might otherwise be given over to despair.

Evidence of the possibility of such despair among even the most ardent radical democrats, whose "faith" goes unfulfilled to the point that democracy as imagined or dreamed seems an impossibility, is discernible in the later writings of, among the most renowned "radical democrats" of the late twentieth century, Sheldon S. Wolin. A despair for the future of democracy as an ongoing practice and form of self-rule is evinced especially in Wolin's late essay "Fugitive Democracy."[68] Democracy, according to Wolin, has always existed only as a series of discrete and momentary eruptions of popular self-rule waged against unequal distributions of power and wealth: democracy "seems destined to be a moment rather than a form."[69] Sporadic, revolutionary, and unpredictable, democracy emerges briefly and recedes once it is inevitably shackled within institutions, constitutions, and bureaucratic rationality. Democracy is to be hoped for, but only temporarily: those who support the eruptions of democracy must recognize its evanescent and impermanent quality. "Democracy needs to be reconceived as something other than a form of government: as a mode of being that is conditioned by bitter experience, doomed to succeed only temporarily, but is a recurrent possibility as long as the memory of the political survives."[70]

Admirers and critics of Wolin alike have noticed the aura of despair that accompanies recent essays like "Fugitive Democracy." William Connolly has noted the "mood of disappointment that seems to pervade the essay."[71] Astutely George Kateb has gone further to detect in Wolin's "pessimism" and "despair" the suggestion that "he wants the demos to be raised to a high level that is nothing aristocratic but rather the perfection of ordinariness."[72] His dream of "genuine democracy" suggests finally not only that "ordinary" democracy "would not be good enough for the people" but, further and most radically, that ordinary people may not be "good enough for democracy."[73] Ordinary democracy cannot exist: only fugitive democracy can occasionally and sporadically erupt, suggesting, therefore, that one can have little expectation that people can be made extraordinary enough to sustain an evanescent and idealized democracy, and thus that ordinary people are incapable or unworthy of all but the rarest forms of "fugitive" democracy. Wolin's very devotion to "radical democracy" has led him to despair of the prospects of real democracy: the unfulfilled dream of a people capable of ongoing practice of democracy has led him almost entirely to abandon hopes for ordinary democracy. "Democratic faith" in its purest and most ardent form leads almost inexorably to the willingness to consider radical forms of democratic transformation, on the one hand, or, failing that, to democratic despair, on the other. In either case, democratic faith may finally fail democracy. As worrisome as the democratic despair that so often accompanies the disappointment of democratic faith is, more troubling is the subsequent reaction by the most ardent democratic faithful, who call for a redoubling of our democratic faith and thus make likely a later (or perhaps current) moment of despair possibly deeper and more intractable. If the possibility of such despair seems unlikely to us in an age of democratic ascendancy, it may be because of the very airiness of our faith, and we would do well to be reminded of how easily such faith can be broken, and how fanciful subsequent calls to faith have been.

The Evidence of Things Seen: The Dangers of Democratic Disillusionment

This dynamic by which "democratic faith" contributes ironically to forms of democratic cynicism and even despair—one evident in the two leading forms of contemporary democratic theory, whether liberal or "radical—is more than "mere theory" but is evident in the near-demise of democracy in America at a time when democracy was under siege everywhere in the world. I turn to a near-forgotten crisis of democracy from the past century, the "American century."

Among the earliest American works devoted exclusively to an analysis of democracy is George Sidney Camp's 1845 book *Democracy*.[74] Inspired by an encounter with Tocqueville's *Democracy in America*, Camp at once sought to provide a native and more upbeat evaluation of democracy's prospects, and to refute some of Tocqueville's more critical assessments of the pathologies of democracy, especially the existence of a "tyranny of the majority."[75] Both describing the current state of affairs, and uncannily anticipating contemporary American devotions to democracy as the sole legitimate form of government, Camp wrote: "It is our common belief that our government is distinguished in principle from other governments. . . . If a man were seriously to propose for our adoption monarchical or aristocratical institutions, he would be overwhelmed with public obloquy. We should feel . . . as if he had been guilty of a moral delinquency on a moral question."[76]

Camp further anticipated contemporary approaches to political theory by rejecting as offensive to democratic devotion those forms of political analysis that treated varying political regimes—from democracy to monarchy—as morally equivalent and therefore distinguishable on practicable grounds. He rejected the academic prominence of such political theorists as Paley, Blackstone, Montesquieu, Burke, and Burlamqui, and, echoing Emerson's 1837 essay "The American Scholar," called for their substitution with American accounts of democracy's superiority.[77] What distinguished his analysis from those of more even-handed Europeans was a fundamental supposition that undergird his, and America's, belief in both the practicable and moral superiority of democracy, namely, a faith in democracy:

> Faith is as necessary to the republican as to the Christian, and the fundamental characteristic of both. We must believe in the capacity of man for self-government, or the framework of our Constitution will be altered. . . . The sacred ark of our liberties is kept in the temple of the human mind, and can only be preserved inviolate by gathering around it the forces of Truth, and intrenching it behind the deep and enlightened convictions of the moral sense. . . . The permanency and the excellence of self-government are our only motives to patriotic and self-sacrificing devotion; it behooves us, therefore, to be fully assured, not only of its immediate and practical value, but of its high moral rectitude and intrinsic propriety, its ennobling qualities, and its absolute capability of duration.[78]

Camp's is an early articulation of "democratic faith" that blended the religious and the political, the Christian and the republican, in an effort to suggest that the quality of "mutual respect" or "enlarged mentality" that is recommended by future democratic faithful—what he called the "self-sacrificing devotion"—was nothing more than a secular translation of religious ideals into democratic faith.

The term "democratic faith" itself was invented, to my knowledge, by one of the earliest American prophets of this belief, Walt Whitman, who coined the expression in a *Brooklyn Eagle* editorial written on November 7, 1846: "The leading spirits of the Democratic faith are always in advance of the age; and they have, therefore, to fight against old prejudices."[79] Almost entirely future-oriented and unmitigatingly optimistic, Whitman speaks throughout his corpus about democracy in terms resembling the language of sermon, proclaiming the secular apotheosis of democracy as a result of a redirection of faith away from old religious forms and toward mankind—a redirection accompanied by divine approbation. In another editorial, he writes,

> It is from Democracy that we are to expect the great FUTURE of this Western World! a scope involving such unparalleled human happiness and rational freedom, to such unnumbered myriads, that the heart of a true *man* leaps with a mighty joy to

think of it! God works out his greatest results by such means; and while each popinjay priest of the mummery of the past is babbling his alarm, the youthful Genius of the people passes swiftly over era after era of change and improvement, and races of human beings erewhile down in gloom or bondage rise gradually toward that majestic development which the good God loves to witness.[80]

In *Democratic Vistas* (1871) he writes of the impending third stage of American democracy, following the completed stages of political institutional fruition and material success, which he calls "a sublime and serious Religious Democracy," animated by an "essential faith in man" and thoroughly "democratizing society" through "higher progress."[81]

Yet, in those years following the Civil War, as mass democracy expanded and transformed, as its promise was praised and its shortcomings became more evident, the suspicion arose that the extraordinary ardent expressions of and calls for "democratic faith" were as much motivated by true belief as by desperation that "the evidence of things seen" was a daily affront to the faith. Writing in 1909, Herbert Croly averred that "if the American national Promise is ever to be fulfilled," then "the conduct of the affair demands more than anything else a hard and inextinguishable faith." The American promise—now a seemingly distant hope—"will be partly the creation of some democratic evangelist—some imitator of Jesus who will reveal to men the path whereby they may enter into spiritual possession of their individual and social achievements."[82] Or, as he wrote several years later in *Progressive Democracy*, "the assurance which American progressivism is gradually acquiring, and of whose necessity it is finally becoming conscious, is merely an expression of faith—faith in the peculiar value and possible reality of its own enterprise, faith in the power of faith. . . . Faith in things unseen and unknown is as indispensable to a progressive democracy as it is to an individual Christian. . . . The common faith sanctifies those who share it."[83]

Perhaps not unlike some early Christians who impatiently awaited the imminent Second Coming and millennium, the unfulfilled promise of democracy's apotheosis proved to be a source of disillusion and despair for some. One revealing account was provided anonymously by a college teacher writing in the *New Republic* in 1926. He describes the democratic faith he held as a young man in terms reminiscent of Whitman, Dewey, or Croly: "I left college in the late [eighteen] eighties. . . . I did share the general religion. Democracy was a younger and a brighter goddess in those days, worshiped with a pride and confidence of which our present Rotarian oratory is only the echo. Even the intelligent believed in democracy, and education was her sister deity."[84] Embracing his vocation as a teacher, he confidently believed "that only a little more change and amelioration was needed to bring in the millennium—a perfect democracy among perfected men."[85] After three years teaching in the secondary school system—an experience that left him with "my bitterest cynicism"—he moved on to teach in a public university system only to find the system riven with political machinations and inattentive students. While still feeling the obligation to proclaim his belief in democracy and the role of education in bringing about the perfection of democracy, he concludes his essay by admitting, "I have no such faith. . . . The one thing I still believe in is intelligence. It is a rare leaven, the capricious gift of God." He admits that he is, above all, "cynical" about the claim that he works on behalf of the betterment of mankind.[86]

Not only was the "democratic faith" being shaken based on the piecemeal experience with ordinary students in these early years of the twentieth century. Rather, belief in democracy was most severely if unexpectedly shaken from within the placid halls of America's universities on the basis of the most recent scientific findings. As unlikely as that may seem from the same locale where that faith is now a requisite feature of academic life—that which animates and undergirds the Inquisitorial condemnation of contemporary blasphemies that challenge core tenets of the democratic faith (i.e., "political incorrectness")—in years following the invocation of the democratic faith by Whitman and Croly there was a time of shaken faith. With the rise of behavioral sciences in the late nineteenth and early twentieth centuries, leading figures in sociology, political science, psychology, and anthropology, among other disciplines, as well as popularizing intellectuals such as H. L. Mencken and Walter Lippmann, increasingly questioned what seemed to be an unreasoned devotion to a radically insufficient political system. If faith is a belief in that which cannot be proven, reflecting emotional devotion or an act of will or simple wishful thinking, then the rise of a questioning unfaithful can be expected particularly with an increase of opposing hard evidence. Just as Darwinism and Freudianism resulted in an assault on traditional religious faith in the nineteenth century, for a time the intellectual movements they spawned led to an equally aggressive assault in the social sciences on American democratic faith that might have led to a similar "secularization" (i.e., undermining both religious and democratic faith) both within the academy and beyond but for the intervention of World War II.[87]

One notorious but not atypical example is illustrative. In his 1934 presidential address before the American Political Science Association, Walter J. Shepard began by noting a long line of political systems since superceded—from Greek city-states to feudal aristocracies to monarchy—each of which had rested on ideological belief structures that, despite their irrationality, were held to be true almost universally by people living under those systems. "Ideologies embody fundamentally ethical norms, which serve as guides, determinants, and motivation of social conduct. As such, they rest ultimately on faith. They are accepted without demonstration; they constitute the final and absolute postulates of life." Having established our shared belief that these belief systems, in retrospect, were based on flawed and irrational bases, Shepard set his sights on democracy: "For more than a hundred and fifty years, the western world has lived under the spell of the democratic idea. To the men of the mid-eighteenth century it came as a glorious vision, promising a new heaven and a new earth. . . . The ideals of political democracy and economic individualism have constituted the national faith of the American people from the time of Jefferson to our own day."[88]

Citing Graham Wallas's influential 1909 book *Human Nature in Politics*, as well as Walter Lippmann's books *Public Opinion* and *The Phantom Public*, Shepard noted that this faith in the individual capacity for self-governance so extensively departed from the best evidence as to be nothing more than a "myth." "Not the reason alone, but sentiment, caprice, and passion are large elements in the composition of public opinion. . . . We no longer believe that 'the voice of the people is the voice of God.'" While the gap between the "theory and practice" of democracy widened throughout the nineteenth century, "the American people retained their faith in the ideal of democracy. This faith was, however, a pathetic example of 'the substance of things looked for and the evidence of things not seen.'" Witnessing the despair of the American public amid the Depression, its disillusionment with market capitalism and cynicism about electoral democracy, as well as the rise of competitive alternative political systems, whether socialism, communism, or fascism, Shepard—not unhappily—observed that increasingly "there is little insistence on the time-worn principles of our traditional faith."[89]

Shepard saw this moment giving rise to "a new vision becoming the guiding faith of our people," one that would not clash too severely with lingering belief in democratic tenets such as free speech but, properly guided, would put America more in line with developments in social science. In addition to calls for a planned economy, Shepard recommended fundamental changes to the American political system. Among his proposed changes included the abolition of the Senate, a reduced role for the remaining unicameral chamber, and a central planning agency that would ensure permanent basic policy that was not subject to alterations by inconstant or incompetent political actors. The Supreme Court should become a "board of political censors" rather than a judicial tribunal. Whether the states should persist was an open question, although Shepard was critical of those who were defensive about their perpetuation. Finally, tackling the core tenet of the democratic faith, Shepard urged that the electorate "must lose the halo which has surrounded it. . . . The dogma of universal suffrage must give way to a system of educational and other tests which will exclude the ignorant, the uninformed, and the anti-social elements which hitherto have so frequently controlled elections." Admitting that this represented a fundamental break with traditional democratic faith, Shepard was defiantly unapologetic: "If this survey of a possible reorganization of government suggests fascism, we have already recognized that there is a large element of fascist practice that we must appropriate." In a poetic flourish, he "traversed the story of human evolution," picturing leaders—torch-bearers—who have alternatively inspired allegiance because of their strength or holiness or wealth or means. "And, as I followed through this long course of torch-bearing and finally arrived at the present world, I saw the runner fail; I saw his grip upon the torch loosen; I saw the torch grow dim. And then I heard the call: 'Seize the torch, men of brains!'"[90]

It might be easy in retrospect to dismiss Shepard as a bit of a crank or mis-guided authoritarian. Yet, he was a respected and influential figure in the American academy, and delivered this speech as president of the American Political Science Association (APSA), which was then and remains the main organization of the discipline. His sentiments were far from unrepresenta-tive of the views of leading figures in the behavioral revolution in the years preceding World War II. They reflected the logical conclusion of many then contemporary ideas about the insufficiencies of democratic institutions and its citizens. In addition to Graham Wallas and Walter Lippmann, prominent critics of democratic faith included respected scholars such as University of Chi-cago political scientists Charles E. Merriam, Harold F. Gosnell, and Harold Lasswell (later Yale), Harvard psychologists Elton Mayo and William S. Mc-Dougall, Columbia University sociologist Robert S. Lynd, and Smith College sociologist Harry Elmer Barnes.[91] Another APSA president, William F. Willoughby, declared in his 1932 presidential address that the leading re-search agenda of political scientists should be "Popular Government: A Re-examination of Its Philosophy and its Practical Operation in the United States." While less convinced than Shepard that democracy could not be de-fended, he nevertheless stated that "popular government, if it is to be justi-fied, must be justified by its results."[92]

While there were pockets of resistance to the leading scientific calls for democracy's demise, one might not have expected this besieged intellectual current to carry the day as in fact it did, albeit, it might be suggested, not al-together based on its scholarly merits.[93] The wholesale embrace of "demo-cratic faith" occurred not as a result of new scientific evidence that categor-ically disproved the findings based on currents of Darwinism, eugenics, and Freudianism in the social sciences but rather as a result of the external in-tervention of World War II. Scholars who had previously questioned the democratic faith came to embrace it. Charles E. Merriam published *The New Democracy and the New Despotism* in 1939, which began by setting forth his "Assumptions of Democracy," including "the essential dignity of man" and a "confidence in a constant drive toward the perfectibility of mankind," and called for "the validation of democratic assumptions by a comprehen-sive program vigorously directed toward the attainment of democratic prin-ciples."[94] The social sciences, in other words, were to be oriented toward proving the validity of the democratic assumptions; any failure to do so would no longer be attributed to the weakness of democracy but, instead, to the correctible imperfections of the social sciences.

The profession itself engaged in a series of soulful reflections on its past apostasy. Reporting on an APSA roundtable convened in 1940 to discuss "Teaching Political Science in a World War," Francis O. Wilcox defended the profession against accusations that "American college students . . . have no faith in democracy," and yet grudgingly admitted "we may have been *too* critical of our democratic institutions."[95] The roundtable concluded by drafting a resolution that was endorsed by participants and transmitted to the association. They resolved that "the American Political Science Association recognizes, in the present crisis, the unique responsibility resting upon its members for cultivating in the youth of this land an abiding faith in the democratic system of government," and concluded with Lincolnian echoes by affirming their collective "conviction that democracy is justified in calling upon its people everywhere to defend it by word and deed in whatever measure of devotion may prove necessary."[96] Peter H. Odegard framed the issue in the starkest possible terms: "Democracy must restore, revive, or win anew faith in its purpose and its destiny; for if such faith is lacking we face inevitable defeat."[97]

Under a broad consensus that is found almost nowhere else in the academy or beyond, contemporary research in the social sciences and humanities is now almost universally undertaken with the assumptions that democracy is the sole legitimate form of political governance.[98] While no less centrally concerned with abiding suspicions that the democratic public may not evince those rational features that are a core assumption of the democratic faith, scholars rarely draw "elitist" conclusions, and almost never arrive at antidemocratic ones, from research that may be less than encouraging. Instead, such evidence, where it exists, is used to invoke the necessity for correctives and reforms that will further the achievement of democratic ends. Thus, through the lens of democratic faith, the data are now always rendered amenable, rather than potentially hostile, to democracy. As stated explicitly in a recent work that combined empirical and theoretical approaches to democratic theory, this continuing effort

> involves a reconsideration of the evidence constituting the original indictment of the mass public—an exercise that is long overdue, in our opinion. If the evidence is found wanting, then the prospects for reform will certainly seem brighter, since the charge of utopianism will be removed, or at least reduced. And if the evidence withstands scrutiny, participatory democrats will be alerted to the need to bridge the "credibility gap" that now threatens their project.[99]

In effect, any data that might once have been interpreted as finally calling for the abandonment of the democratic faith now, instead, is made answerable to the "democratic creed." Thus Hanson and Marcus are able to write dismissively, if correctly, "Few people any longer subscribe to the extreme versions of elitism, and we feel no special obligation to answer their objections here."[100] Scholars, such as Shepard, who once believed that they were following the data to their logical conclusion are now deemed unworthy of response and are withheld academic respect. The data instead are now either harnessed on behalf of "reform"—a word that unavoidably contains a value judgment indicating prior commitments to democracy—or cited to fuel further efforts to justify democracy in light of challenging, but never damning, evidence.

Echoing the judgment of George Sidney Camp in 1845, it would be nearly inconceivable for a modern thinker to propose the abolition of democracy in favor of another form of governance.[101] Thus, almost unconsciously, we live in an "Age of Faith," even to the point that one finds explicit evocations of that faith less frequent and more scattered than heretofore. This is as sure a sign as any that the faith is now secure—so fundamental an assumption among contemporary people that the faith is no longer in need of being explicitly invoked. As H. Richard Niebuhr has pointed out, "we become aware of these primary questions of faith usually in those times when our confidence in the hitherto trusted is shaken or when we are moved to rely on the previously untried."[102] Those more frequent invocations of the democratic faith in the late 1930s and early 1940s reflect a moment of crisis in that belief, and in its willed invocation as a form of renewal. With the passing of that crisis the faith has become submerged, but it courses as an undercurrent in our daily interactions and only occasionally wells up to wash away any faint doubts that may arise. Even in an age of faith Niebuhr reminds us that questions of faith "are constantly addressed to us in all our daily encounters with our companions and our world. They accompany like an undertone all the transactions and communications between men and their dialogues of perception and conception with common objects. We are forever being asked and asking: Do you believe me? Do you trust me? Are you trustworthy and believable? Are you faithful to me and to our common cause?"[103]

SAVING FAITH

In response to this widespread loss of faith in democracy—and particularly the declining belief in the common man that rose as a result of recent scientific findings to the contrary—democratic theorists responded with a strong reassertion of "democratic faith." This was accompanied by calls that emphasized the need for "human transformation." Ironically these calls emanated not from wide-eyed utopians but rather from the philosophical school that drew its sustenance largely from American sources and whose very title seems to suggest a resistance to utopian tendencies: pragmatism.[104]

In his report to the American Political Science Association in 1941, Francis Wilcox noted that the renewed embrace of "democratic faith" presented a potential problem for the scientific study of politics given that such a form of faith represented an a priori value commitment which objective science otherwise sought to eschew. As such, some of the political scientists on the roundtable about which his report was written objected that "'the inculcation of moral virtues, ethical ideals, or social values is a matter beyond the scope of the science of politics.'" However, the predominant sentiment on the roundtable was that such value commitments in the teaching of political science were unavoidable: "education should be, to a very considerable extent, an exploration into the field of values. . . . Unless we expect this function to be carried out by philosophers or the humanist, whose knowledge of the field may be limited, we must operate in the classroom not only as political scientists, but as political philosophers as well."[105] Claims to objectivity were to be jettisoned with the re-embrace of democratic faith, and thus an implicit or explicit reliance on democratic political theory became essential with this new commitment by the faithful.

Political theory was largely accommodating. Much had changed since George Sidney Camp had lodged his complaints in 1845 about the "neutrality" that political theorists like Montesquieu and Burke exhibited in judging between the relative merits and disadvantages of democracy and other forms of government. American political theory in particular had come to embrace democracy as the sole legitimate form of rule—particularly in the nineteenth century under the influence of thinkers like Emerson and Whitman as well as currents from the increasingly democratic cultural milieu.[106] Figures like William James and John Dewey became among the most frequently cited and lionized thinkers amid the repudiation of antidemocratic implications of contemporary social science. Characteristic works like Jerome Nathanson's 1941 book *Forerunners of Freedom*—published by the American Council of Public Affairs—stressed this turn to the democratic traditions in American political thought.[107] Divided into four chapters on Emerson, Whitman, James, and Dewey, Nathanson concluded the latter chapter on Dewey with commentary on Dewey's belief in the prospects of unfolding human intelligence: "For in the last analysis, the faith in intelligence is nothing but the faith in a democratic society." Thereafter he quoted at length from Dewey's own embrace of this democratic faith, ending with Dewey's peroration, "For the faith [in intelligence] is so deeply embedded in the methods which are intrinsic to democracy that when a professed democrat denies the faith he convicts himself of treachery to his profession."[108] By 1940, when Dewey wrote these words, he could use not only the religious language of faith to describe and justify his belief in democracy—as he had throughout his career—but also the language of political and even religious persecution in denouncing those who were deemed faithless.

Are such invocations of "faith" oriented toward democracy to be understood as relying upon the strong forms of credence that are associated with religious belief or as a thinner form of belief that might more commonly be found in ordinary language, such as "have faith in me"? Arguably it is difficult to distinguish between the two, and it is the case that most proponents of "democratic faith" have done little to dissociate their call for democratic "faith" from the religious echoes that would inevitably accompany such language. "Faith" is finally a word perhaps as elastic as "democracy": combined as "democratic faith," it can be understood to mean "warranted belief" in the feasibility of a political system with which we have extensive experience; alternatively it can refer to "groundless belief" in the moral and psychic growth of humanity and a concomitant overcoming of human and physical limitations; or, finally, it might appeal to forms and intensity of belief at any point between these two poles. In all instances, however, "democratic faith" refers to a belief in a system of government based upon rule of the people about which we are finally not permitted full-blown certainty of its ultimate feasibility, or superiority, much less its final perfectibility. Expressions of democratic faith often implicitly aim to obfuscate the extent to which such faith is either "warranted" based upon best evidence, or "groundless" based upon radical uncertainty or even countervailing evidence of democracy's unfeasibility. Indeed, within a single piece of writing by the same author, both usages are often employed, slipping between an experiential belief in "men as they are" and an endorsement of "democratic men as they might be."

The opposite poles between "justified" and "unjustified" belief each represent an epistemic position that falls short of full and complete certainty, although the more extensive one's personal knowledge about the object of belief, the less "faith" is necessary to make up that gap of certainty. This difference itself has been explained by some to be one that rests between the difference in "faith in" and "faith that."[109] "Faith in" something or someone is a usage that is characteristically employed when the believer has a reasonably high level of confidence in the object, frequently based upon personal knowledge and experience. As such, "faith in" something or someone tends to be as close to certainty that most humans are likely to get in most circumstances in which absolute certainty cannot apply—that is, in most situations involving human interactions and even many matters of physical life. As argued in a clarifying article by Raziel Abelson, "'faith in,' unlike 'faith that,' often appears to be both serious and reasonable. Its seriousness is a function of the risk one commits himself to taking, while its reasonableness is a function of the degree to which one's personal experience of the object of faith justifies 'putting one's faith' in it or in him."[110] By contrast, "faith that" is "a more or less tentative truth claim."[111] The former "faith in" tends to be warranted belief in a known object, whereas "faith that" tends to be less justified belief in a proposition that cannot yet be said to have been proven beyond reasonable doubt.

Of course, these distinctions are artificially drawn to point out the distinctions employed in ordinary usage: most people would agree that "faith that the sun will appear in the east tomorrow morning" is more reasonable than "faith in leprechauns," in part because we have more experience with sunrises than with Irish pixies. More important than efforts to devise inflexible linguistic distinctions between faith "in" objects and faith in "that" propositions is the relationship of any such forms of belief to the "behavioral" dimensions of any such faith claims. Pointing to the intellectual legacy of "Bain, Peirce, James, and Dewey," Abelson notes that belief or "faith" commitments are most centrally important because of their tendency to prompt believers to "act in certain ways."[112] Thus, regardless of whether we would characterize our faith as one lodged "in" objects or persons, or "that" certain propositions are likely to be true, in Abelson's view the ultimate outcome of such beliefs is to commit us to a set of actions or activity that results from such belief. Such actions might be "negative" in form: if I believe that the ice on a nearby lake is thin, then I am likely not to lace up my skates. However, if I have "faith" in (trust, believe) the park rangers who have declared the ice safe for skating, I am more likely to go out on the ice.

These mundane examples stop short of elucidating the more radical aspect of faith-commitments. In the pragmatic tradition cited by Abelson, faith-commitments prompt us not so merely to act based upon the conditions and limitations imposed by such beliefs—either warranted or groundless—but rather to prompt activity and experimentation in an effort to reconcile our faith with those conditions in reality that give rise to the uncertainty—those very conditions that make our faith necessary in the first place. In short, such faith seeks to overcome its condition qua faith—belief that results from uncertainty—by motivating our activity to make into a fact and certainty what is now merely contingent and uncertain. Faith, so conceived, seeks to close the gap between uncertainty and certainty, thus making faith itself finally superfluous. Faith is a result of, and subsequently leads to, an act of will: we seek to change the external conditions of "reality" so that they begin to comport with our beliefs. "Belief is measured by action," writes William James, maintaining that our "will to believe" gives rise to the possibility and inclination to act on behalf of the realization of the object of our belief.[113]

James begins his justly famous essay by suggesting, in good pragmatic spirit, that such faith can neither alter mundane facts of reality nor act upon "dead wires" (that is, wholly falsified propositions) but, instead, can function only as a hypothesis. Defending now specifically religious faith in his preface, he writes: "If religious hypotheses about the universe be in order at all, then the active faiths of individuals in them, freely expressing themselves in life, are the experimental tests by which they are verified, and the only means by which their truth or falsehood can be wrought out."[114]

In nearly every aspect of human life, human beings must act with "practical faith": certitude is only rarely possible, meaning that most human activities are undertaken with a confidence that falls short of certainty to varying degrees.[115] Such "faith" is backward-looking, experiential, and seemingly the very definition of "pragmatic" faith. Yet, by the conclusion of his essay, James goes further in linking forms of riskier, seemingly groundless faith to such an experimental attitude: thus, by means of faith, we can actually bring into existence the objects of our faith.

> Wherever a desired result is achieved by the cooperation of many independent persons, its existence as a fact is a pure consequence of the precursive faith in one another of those immediately concerned. . . . There are, then, cases where a fact cannot come at all unless a preliminary faith exists in its coming. *And where faith in a fact can help create that fact*, that would be an insane logic which should say that faith running ahead of scientific evidence is the "lowest kind of immorality" into which a thinking being can fall.[116]

This slippage between "warranted" faith in past experience and faith as the source of future realization and even transformation informs and mirrors the kind of democratic faith that drifts between "men as they are" and "men as they might be." Pragmatic faith, then—remaining open to the possibility of alteration based on new practices and experiences—has an internal trajectory that leads it to view faith itself as a resource for the reconciliation of the real and the ideal. For James, "often enough our faith before-hand in an uncertified result *is the only thing that makes the result come true*."[117] Although James later suggested that the title "Will to Believe" was incorrect, in fact it is precisely the linkage between *will* and *belief* that is so centrally important to this pragmatic faith. As he would later write in "The Energies of Men," "our will [is] the manometer of our faiths. Ideas set free beliefs, and the beliefs set free our wills . . ., so that the will-acts register the faith-pressure within."[118] Perhaps more accurately still, he might have enti-tled his essay "The Belief to Will" or, further still, "The Will to Believe to Will," thus denoting the way in which our will fosters belief that in turn prompts our will into activity on behalf of the realization of that belief. This is finally a form of willing without limit, as James would have been the first to acknowledge: indeed, since faith itself can realize or create the object of its belief, one could easily conclude that it is humanity itself that creates the ultimate object of faith, namely, God. James acknowledged this trajectory toward human conceived and controlled divinity, thus at least implicitly rais-ing the question of whether God is finally created in the image of man: "I confess that I do not see why the very existence of an invisible world may not in part depend on the personal response which any one of us may make to the religious appeal. God himself, in short, may draw vital strength and increase of very being from our fidelity."[119] Divinity itself as the result of human intention, will, and, finally, faith is a theme that returns repeatedly in expressions of "democratic faith," and seems bound up in its trajectory of positing extensive human power and control in and over the world.

By means of faith in the known that we experience and the unknown that we potentially create, James sought to moderate between the twin tempta-tions of optimism and pessimism. Optimism, he wrote, is the unfounded be-lief that the salvation of the world is inevitable; pessimism is the equally un-justified belief that the salvation of the world is impossible. What is finally objectionable in both these views is their passivity: inevitability in either di-rection is tantamount to surrender by human beings, a final acknowledgment of human infirmity and the capitulation of human control. Instead, James recommended pragmatic "meliorism" between these two views of in-evitability as a means to preserving human power and control: "Meliorism treats salvation as neither inevitable nor impossible. It treats it as a possibil-ity, which becomes more and more a probability the more numerous the ac-tual conditions of salvation become."[120]

Nevertheless this belief in "meliorism" did not rest on a neutral view of the universe but rather on a belief that the universe was beneficent toward progressive human activity. Indeed, this was the most fundamental form of faith: a faith that human aims and ambitions were in perfect concord with the created existence that they are empowered to alter and control. James wrote: "Our faith in the seen world's goodness (goodness now meaning fit-ness for successful moral and religious life) has verified itself by leaning on our faith in the unseen world."[121] Humanity is at home in the world because our belief in God assures it. Religious belief ultimately supports human activity, and our faith in the divine functions to ensure our place in the world: our belief in God—which supports and strengthens his existence—in turn supports and strengthens our individual, social, and political endeavors. Yet, inasmuch as God himself "may draw vital strength and increase of very being from our fidelity," James begs the question whether our belief in creation's beneficence toward humanity has a source other than that selfsame belief.

For James, the past is substantially a prologue to the future, but the future is made real by means of faith that transcends the limitations born of the reality of the past. Democracy is a case in point: James could appeal to its superiority based upon past experience, on the one hand, or faith in its future realization, on the other. James evinced lucid moments when democracy was endorsed on grounds that were modest and justified by ordinary human experience. Among the most arresting democratic statements in James's corpus comes in the midst of an extraordinary speech that was given during the dedication of a monument to fallen Boston Civil War hero and colonel of the first black regiment Robert Gould Shaw. In that speech—delivered before numerous Civil War veterans—James extolled modest democratic virtues as more praiseworthy and rare even than those more obvious martial virtues of self-sacrifice that are displayed on the battlefield. Instead, James praised the "lonely" civic forms of civic courage by which democracy is sustained: "by acts without external picturesqueness; by speaking, writing, voting reasonably; by smiting corruption swiftly; by good temper between parties; by the people knowing true men when they see them, and preferring them as leaders to rabid partisans or empty quacks."[122]

Democracy is justified in part because of our experiences in the past—by the existence and cultivation of such "ordinary virtues"—but James, like Emerson before him, also was quick to exhibit discontent with "men as they are" because of his "will to believe" in men as they might and ought to be. One envisions a better humanity by projecting the best of present circumstance into the future: "Yet, little by little, there comes some stable gain; for the world does get more humane, and the religion of democracy tends towards permanent increase."[123] Yet, because the worst of the present tends to persist as an affront to this belief in human progress, one can be tempted to despair, to lose faith in democracy or to fall into bitter cynicism. Against such an outcome almost inevitably comes the religiously inspired call for democratic faith, one born of high hopes and fervent dreams culminating in the dream of "better men":

> Democracy is on its trial, and no one knows how it will stand the ordeal. . . . Nothing in the future is quite secure; states enough have inwardly rotted; and democracy as a whole may undergo self-poisoning. But, on the other hand, democracy is a kind of religion, and we are not bound to admit its failure. Faiths and utopias are the noblest exercise of human reason, and no one with a spark of reason in him will sit down fatalistically before the croaker's picture. The best of us are filled with the contrary vision of democracy stumbling through every error till its insti-

tutions glow with justice and its customs shine with beauty. Our better men *shall* show the way and we *shall* follow them.[124]

Faith in democracy is to be sustained even in the face of the contrary facts of reality, even to the point at which it must be defended and preserved by appeal to "the best of us." A kind of aristocratic elite is the necessary means to achieving future democratic ends.

In keeping with this expression of secular-minded pragmatism, almost unconsciously many contemporary proponents of democratic faith tend to speak of faith in these terms. Whether expressed as faith *in* an object, or faith *that* a certain proposition is true (or false), invocations of faith express our confidence (rather than an acknowledgment of our uncertainty) and foster an active and puissant stance toward the world. Faith is affirmative: its source is in our will, and its consequence is toward human activity, capacity, and power. The very nature of this faith tends to be obscured by otherwise more evident expressions of ranging pragmatism and even skepticism that otherwise appears to underlay democratic commitments of today's democratic faithful.

"Democratic faith" appropriately reflects a version of what philosopher Michael Oakeshott called the "Politics of Faith"—a form of political "faith" notable for the "absence of doubt" about itself, an unscrupulous belief "in the redemption of mankind in history and by human effort" aimed at the "perfection of mankind" and informed by a kind of "cosmic optimism."[125] Oakeshott contrasted this form of politics with the "Politics of Scepticism," a politics conducted under the assumption that humankind is not capable of its own perfection, one notable for "prudent diffidence" rather than "radical doubt," one hesitant about the claims of political rule and wary of despotism created in the name of progress or "the people."[126]

What is striking in Oakeshott's formulation is the extent to which those who maintain the "Politics of Faith" almost unanimously attack "faith" in its religious form (such as Machiavelli and Bacon or, by extension, Dewey and Rorty), whereas those whom Oakeshott identifies as maintaining the "Politics of Scepticism" include religiously "faithful" thinkers such as Augustine, Pascal, and Tocqueville.[127] Whereas a political form of faith, notably "democratic faith," appears innocuous because of its presence among so many religious "skeptics," the "politics of skepticism" is reinforced by the initial embrace of faith in redemption beyond the wholly human or political. In other words, it is the politics of "skepticism"—which Oakeshott noted included religiously "faithful" thinkers—that contains a degree of humility about the prospects of humanity securing its own earthly redemption through politics, in contrast to the absence of humility among religious "skeptics" and pragmatists. Democracy may, in the end, require faith in some form, but it remains contestable whether the "democratic faith" is finally the form of faith that best serves the cause and prospects of democracy.

Democratic Transformation

> The contest between the Future and the Past is one between Divinity
> emerging, and Divinity departing. You are welcome to try your
> experiments, and, if you can, to displace the actual order by that ideal
> republic you announce, for nothing but God will expel God.
>
> —Ralph Waldo Emerson, *"The Conservative,"* 1841

A CONUNDRUM EXISTS at the core of the democratic faith. On the one hand, it is a faith in human capacity for democratic self-governance that points to obstacles that stand in the way of the fruition of the faith, including such external obstructions as liberalism, capitalism, and the scale of the modern nation-state. On the other hand, given that human beings do not manifest the full democratic proclivities nor potential in the face of such obstacles—else such a faith would be utterly unnecessary—it is a faith that also, however implicitly, proves critical of the same people in whom the faith is otherwise lodged and points to the necessity of fundamental transformation not only of perceived obstacles but also of the people themselves.[1] Modern liberal democrats, on the one hand, who propound the use of reason in politics and antifoundational democratic theorists, on the other, who are unabashed in calling for the transformation of political life are simultaneously often loath to recommend outright efforts to transform the populace into true democratic beings. Often it is assumed that such transformation will occur automatically as a result of the disassembling of such external obstacles, either by removing obfuscating obstacles to the full-blown expression of rational discourse in the public sphere or, alternatively, by lifting the veil of false consciousness and giving rise spontaneously to full-blown democratic people.[2]

The largely shared contemporary eschewal to state in any explicit fashion the *means* of democratic transformation reflects an unwillingness to take recourse to any such means—whether private or public—that would suggest the manipulation or a propagandizing of citizens. Nevertheless a belief in a form of "transformation" by means of a kind of "invisible hand" is a tenet for many adherents to contemporary democratic faith (though not all) and itself rests on a foundation of more explicit and interventionist efforts at transformation that, if not shared by most contemporary democratic theorists, nevertheless is found in the work of earlier authors to whom modern democratic theorists appeal. This is particularly true of two methods of democratic transformation that are examined at greater length in this chapter: civil religion and scientific transformation.

The conundrum at the core of beliefs of contemporary "democratic faithful"—captured in the circularity of Gutmann and Thompsons's, Arendt's, and Arendtian arguments on behalf of "democratic transformation"—point to likely if not inevitable corollaries of democratic faith: not only toward the "what" in which one has faith but also the "how" by which the conditions of that faith are to be fulfilled. Historically, belief in the self-governing capacities of the people required not only similar "leaps of faith" but were also accompanied by statements about the means and methods of such transformation whose efficacy were themselves often as much infused with the spirit of faith as the ultimate goal of democratic transformation. Faith, in this sense, is not merely belief in the unseen and potentially unproveable, but, in the sense described by William James, is also a spur to the will to realize the conditions held as the object of that belief. Thus, in the history of political thought, one frequently witnesses recommendations of two methods of transformation:

1. A belief in the democratic efficacy of "civil religion"—for some an actual set of religious principles established by the city; for others a disposition to regard democracy as itself a secularized form of religion. In particular, such forms of "civil religion" are viewed as a means of creating a democratic polity and of fostering a spirit of collective or communal identification. This "religiously" infused form of democracy is seen as the best source of achieving widespread civic "mutual respect" lauded by Gutmann and Thompson, on the one hand, and "enlarged mentality" recommended by Arendt, on the other.

2. Optimism in the human ability of unbounded democratic amelioration by means of the conquest of nature, particularly as manifested in the equation of democracy and the modern scientific project, reflecting a belief in a fundamentally beneficent universe toward democratic ends. Linked to this method of transformation is a faith in the beneficent and democratic trajectory of historical progress—a progressive view that assumes human control over the flow and direction of history.[3]

Notably contemporary proponents of "democratic faith" are mistrustful of each "means" of achieving full democratic potential of the citizenry, particularly where there is any suggestion of hierarchical imposition or manipulation of belief. Nevertheless, to the extent that contemporary proponents of democratic faith resist devolution into despair suggests that echoes of these older beliefs in transformation persist, even if specific mechanisms for transformation have been jettisoned. The persistence of democratic faith raises the question as to whether such faith can be sustained in the absence of such optimistic "mechanisms" of transformation or whether, in the absence of discernible progress of moral sentiment, such faith is likely to tend toward disillusioned despair and cynicism.

Each method itself amounts to a form of democratic optimism, a confidence that humans are fated to democracy or, in the absence of "unnatural" or even natural barriers, a belief that the resulting condition will be the full flourishing of expansive democratic forms of life. This faith at once rests on the echoes of older religious forms of faith, yet transforms those traditional beliefs to ones that place humanity, and specifically human salvation by means of politics, at the very center of those beliefs. Based on a thoroughgoing belief in human ability to accomplish these democratic ends, this form of "faith" in democracy's flourishing appears at first blush to embrace the limitations on human activity in a world shorn of "truth" but, in fact, evinces moments of hubristic overconfidence in human capacities that resemble in some features the totalizing "discourses" of utopian politics that they otherwise claim to eschew. In the remainder of this chapter, I turn to a consideration of these two "methods" of transformation, in each instance first by considering early modern expressions of these forms of "democratic transformation," and then in turn considering in each case their subsequent American manifestation.

THE CIVIL RELIGION OF DEMOCRATIC FAITH

The transformation of selfhood from one that is narrow and incapable of mutual democratic self-governance to one that incorporates other "selves" by means of empathy, "mutual respect, or an "enlarged" and even "cosmic" consciousness has been seen by some among the democratic faithful as requiring cultivation by means of appeal to the sacred. This cultivation in the sacred arts of democracy can typically take the form of a recommendation to use the resources of religion, and religious belief, to effect the transformation of individuals into a whole; or, alternatively, by transforming democracy itself into a form of religion to which our devotions demand a willingness to open ourselves to other postulants. Both are a kind of civil religion, although the former takes the form of a religion that is instituted by the state or seeks the transformation of existing religions toward active support of democratic ends, whereas the latter seeks to displace traditional religion and to put in its stead the very worship of democracy, making civic life itself an object of worshipful regard. The first is a civic religion that uses "religion" for the purposes of civic life; the second is a form of civic life that itself is invested with qualities of the religious, even as religion in its traditional form is rejected for its antidemocratic aspects. If the first form represents a kind of "desacralization"—reflected, as discussed in the preface, by the transformation of the Cathedrale St.-Geneviève into the Panthéon—the second form reflects a kind of "resacralization"—reflected in the creation of the "Goddess of Democracy"—in which the political form that once displaced religion becomes itself a sacred practice and a truer object of faithful worship.

No thinkers saw more clearly the "religious" aspects of social and political cohesion than Emile Durkheim. Durkheim viewed the relationship between society, politics, and religion as intimate and inseparable, famously arguing that religion is a set of practices and beliefs that are "eminently social." Religion is at once the creation of social interaction and yet, in turn, is itself a form of organization that significantly supports, legitimizes, and even *creates* the fundamental conditions of that same society. Religion, conceived in its broadest possible form, is both a *reflection of* society and yet also, in important ways, *constitutive of* societies. Religion and society are born together, reflecting each other in interrelated beliefs of human significance and relationship to the divine and to nature, as well as celebrated and commemorated regularly in public festivals and symbolic rites and objects.[4] Society is thus inseparable from religion in the origin of its beliefs and the resonance of its practices. Thus Durkheim wrote that "the most diverse methods and practices, both those that make possible the continuation of the moral life (laws, morals, beaux-arts) and those serving the material life (the natural, technical and practical sciences), are either directly or indirectly derived from religion. . . . If religion has given birth to all that is essential in society, it is because the idea of society is the soul of religion."[5]

The origins of religion are at the same time profoundly individual and extensively social. Belief springs from the minds of individuals, but, to the extent it is "religious," this belief is itself conditioned and ultimately authorized by society by means of opinion, inculcation, sanction, and even outright suppression. On the other hand, collective belief, Durkheim acknowledges, remains invested in the minds of singular persons: "since society cannot exist except in and through individual consciousnesses, this force must also penetrate us and organize itself within us; it thus becomes an integral part of our being and by that very fact is elevated and magnified."[6] For Durkheim, religious belief "becomes the group incarnate and personified," whether one understands religion in its most primitive animistic form, as a kind of political belief and worship such as was manifested during the French Revolution, or as even the seemingly contradictory "faith in science."[7]

This intermingling between religion's operation on individual belief and social mores forms the essential bond that makes social collectivity possible. In the absence of religious belief, Durkheim contends, social bonds are impossible: human beings would be forever trapped in their own individual consciousnesses—otherwise "closed to each other"—without awareness or felt need to move toward "common sentiment." Religion makes possible "a fusion of all particular sentiments into one common sentiment," informing individuals "that they are in harmony and mak[ing] them conscious of their moral unity."[8] The interplay is mutually supportive between individual and society:

> Individual minds cannot come into contact and communicate with each other except by coming out of themselves; but they cannot do this except by movements. So it is the homogeneity of these movements that gives the group consciousness of

itself and consequently makes it exist. When this homogeneity is once established and these movements have once taken a stereotyped form, they serve to symbolize the corresponding representations. But they symbolize them only because they have aided in forming them.[9]

When Gutmann and Thompson speak of "mutual respect," and Arendt of "enlarged consciousness," according to Durkheim, they are using secular language to describe essentially religious phenomena. A profane script lies atop sacred text.

Religion makes "the part equal to the whole," both in relation to things human and divine, but, more important from Durkheim's perspective, in relation of human beings to the societies they create: "By the mere fact that [religion's] apparent function is to strengthen the bonds attaching the believer to his god, they at the same time really strengthen the bonds attaching the individual to the society of which he is a member, since the god is only a figurative expression of the society."[10] Religious belief, born of the human attempt to interpret and make "sensible," if not reasonable, the universe mankind inhabits, results in the creation of a sense of shared human solidarity, first as a mere concomitant effect of the division between the sacred and the profane, but ultimately as the primary significance and legacy of religious belief and practice.

The significance of this transformational potential of religion—turning "closed" selves into social beings engaged in common practices and inspired by shared commitments—has not been lost on many classical and contemporary democratic theorists. From Machiavelli and Rousseau to Emerson, Whitman, Bellamy, Croly, Dewey, as well as Robert Bellah, Amitai Etzioni, and Richard Rorty, the religious roots of solidarity have been recommended and newly reimagined, even when thinkers concerned primarily with the civic dimensions of religion no longer deem it necessary to make explicit appeal to the divine.[11] Among many "radical democrats"—many of whom evince a profound mistrust of all invocations of religion, either as explicit organization or implicit societal belief system, in spite of occasional appeals to "democratic faith"—there is explicit eschewal of invocations of "civic religion" even while there is extensive implicit reliance upon the thought of preceding thinkers who recognize the necessities of religion for the creation of democratic solidarity. Thus, for an antifoundationalist thinker like Benjamin R. Barber, who recommends solidarity and even "democratic faith" as necessary features of a "strong" democratic polity, not surprisingly there is no explicit recommendation of the role of "civic religion" in forming such a polity. Yet, one of Barber's formative influences in his conception of "strong democracy" is admitted to be Jean-Jacques Rousseau (as well as John Dewey), who dwells at considerable length on the necessary role of "civil religion" in forming the basic solidarity of a democratic polity.[12] Similarly, in the thought of radically "agonistic" theorists such as Bonnie Honig, Chantal Mouffe, and Stanley Fish—who go one step further by eschewing even

Barber's explicit recommendation of social solidarity as a constitutive feature of modern pluralistic democracy—one nevertheless but similarly encounters special sympathy to the "agonistic" features of Machiavelli's thought albeit without accompanying recognition of Machiavelli's recommendation of "civil religion" as a necessary system of belief that undergirds social stability.[13]

Agonistic theorists in particular embrace the arguments of Machiavelli for his recommendation of the "transformative power of politics."[14] Evidence for this "transformative" power of active and particularly combative, agonistic, and "ferocious" political conflict is interspersed throughout Machiavelli's writings but finds its most pristine expression early in the *Discourses* in which Machiavelli unqualifiedly praises the role of conflict in the creation of a good republic:

> I say that to me it appears that those who damn the tumults between the nobles and the plebs blame those things that were the first cause of keeping Rome free, and that they consider the noises and the cries that would arise from such tumults more than the good effects that they engendered. They do not consider that in every republic there are two diverse humors, that of the people and that of the great, and that all laws that are made in favor of freedom arise from their disunion, as can easily be seen to have occurred in Rome. . . . Nor can one in any mode, with reason, call a republic disorderly where there are so many examples of virtue; for good examples arise from good education, good education from good laws, and good laws from those tumults that many inconsiderately damn. . . . The desires of free peoples are rarely pernicious to freedom because they arise either from being oppressed or from suspicion that they may be oppressed. If these opinions are false, there is for them the remedy of assemblies, where some good man gets up who in orating demonstrates to them how they deceive themselves.[15]

As if anticipating the arguments of contemporary "agonistic" democrats, Machiavelli argues that from conflict itself springs the excellence of republicanism (and by some contemporary understandings, democracy), the source of liberty, and the potential for more broadly conceived common good beneficial not only—or not at all—to the ruling elite but rather also to the mass of ordinary people. Machiavelli on this reading appears to stand against attempts to create a monolithic or "foundational" politics based on antecedent understandings of what is commonly good, and thereby potentially threatening to the libratory project of antifoundational democracy.

This interpretation of Machiavelli's thought, however, stressing the "agonistic" and liberating aspect of Machiavelli's republicanism, must be accompanied by a studied neglect or even a willful misreading of Machiavelli's entire argument inasmuch as it overlooks the central role accorded by Machiavelli to a form of "civil religion" that underlies and restrains the "ferocious" conflict that he otherwise praises. Balancing Machiavelli's praise for the role of conflict among the various elements of the republic and the resulting liberty to the populace is his equally firm insistence upon the need for a common identity and source of restraint and even morality that is derived from a civically inspired and regulative religion.[16] Machiavelli argues that the laws of Rome were insufficient as initially created by Romulus—resulting in an excessively "ferocious" people—and required a second founding by Numa, who "turned to religion as a thing altogether necessary" to restrain this savagery, "to reduce it to civil obedience with the arts of peace" and create a unified people. "Whoever considers well the Roman histories sees how much religion served to command armies, to animate the plebs, to keep men good, to bring shame to the wicked."[17]

Indeed, Machiavelli goes further: such a form of foundational religion must have the prior position in a successful regime, forming the necessary condition in which subsequent beneficial conflict can unfold and *by which* such conflict is itself conditioned and restrained. "So that if the question were discussed whether Rome was more indebted to Romulus or to Numa, I believe that the highest merit would be conceded to Numa." The reason that he offers for this assessment is revealing: whereas in the *Prince* Machiavelli writes that "there cannot be good laws where there are not good arms," he concludes this thought with the completion of the above passage in the *Discourses* ("as if," in the words of Ronald Beiner, "in completion of a half-uttered thought"), writing "for where there is religion, arms can easily be introduced, and where there are arms and not religion, the latter can be introduced only with difficulty."[18] Ferocious conflict can exist without religion (as it did in the time after Romulus but before Numa), but in the absence of civic religion there can be no good law that acts as a restraint upon the conflict, no guiding spirit that promotes a sense of common good and that informs, restrains, and directs conflict, while also promoting obedience to law and inspiring sacrifice and patriotism for the sake of the polity among the military. As J.G.A. Pocock has argued, Machiavelli viewed such a form of religion to be necessary "to develop that dedication of oneself to a common good which was the moral content of pagan religion and the essence of civic virtue."[19]

For Machiavelli, all religions are not civically equal: Christianity, above all, had proven disastrous to the Italian city-states, promoting humility, other-worldliness, and expressions of excessive subordination among the populace.[20] For Machiavelli, new religions are "due to men," not "to heaven," and must be judged according to human standards—particularly political standards, especially with a view to whether that religion has beneficial civic effects.[21] Returning to the praiseworthy example of Numa, Machiavelli relates that the origins of the politically efficacious Roman religion were entirely fictional: "One sees that for Romulus to order the Senate and to make other civil and military orders, the authority of God was not necessary; but it was quite necessary to Numa, who pretended to be intimate with a nymph who counseled him on what he had to counsel the people. It all arose because he wished to put new and unaccustomed orders in the city and doubted that his authority would suffice." Machiavelli then asserts that this example reveals a general civic principle: "And truly there was never any orderer of extraordinary laws for a people who did not have recourse to God, because otherwise they would not have been accepted. For a prudent individual knows many goods that do not have in themselves evident reasons with which one can persuade others. Thus wise men who wish to take away this difficulty have recourse to God."[22]

Even as Machiavelli suggests that no excellent republic can come into being without the existence of politically beneficial religious belief, by the very fact of making this argument explicit it appears that Machiavelli may actually undermine the very efficacy of that religious belief that he otherwise recommends. By revealing to his reader that Numa's recourse to religion rested on wholly fictional grounds, the result of a "pretended" conversation with a nonexistent nymph, Machiavelli apparently undercuts the usefulness of his advice of how best to found an "ordered" regime.[23] Perhaps this accounts for Machiavelli's recommendation that new founders seek to ground a new city—and its accompanying religious belief—among an uncorrupt people "where there is no civilization," to avoid those sophisticated moderns who are apt to view cynically these efforts of a founder.

Machiavelli's apparently subversive description of a purely politically motivated religion is otherwise belied at the inception of his discussion of Numa's praiseworthy example. Curiously, and apparently in spite of his suggestion that all religion and the gods themselves are the invention of humanity, Machiavelli indicates a divine source of civil religion: "Although Rome had Romulus as its first orderer and has to acknowledge, as daughter, its birth and education as from him, nonetheless, *since the heavens judged* that the orders of Romulus would not suffice for such an empire, *they inspired in the breast of the Roman Senate* the choosing of Numa Pompilius as successor to Romulus so that those things omitted by him might be ordered by Numa."[24] Were Machiavelli writing to a wholly cynical audience—or one to be made thoroughly cynical by means of his teachings—this attribution of divine responsibility for the institution of civil religion might appear to be nothing other than thoroughgoing irony.

Yet Machiavelli may not in fact be assuming the existence of a wholly cynical audience at all, and further may not intend the creation of such an audience of "Machiavellian" readers. After all, he notes that his contemporary Savaronola was successful in persuading the Florentine populace that "he spoke with God"; this contemporary fact affords him ample evidence that his readership is apt to credit the divine source of political events.[25] Such a brilliant selection as Numa, ensuring the long-term existence of Rome at the moment of its very inception, may indeed have struck Machiavelli as a divinely inspired choice. And yet such an inference is curious, and certainly impious by many understandings. For Machiavelli suggests that "the heavens" themselves approve of the creation of a civil religion derived from a feigned pagan source—that the gods set in motion the selection of Numa in order to perpetrate the excellence of Rome's citizens by means of a religion whose excellence is judged in wholly civic and secular terms. As such, Machiavelli's is a cynical teaching designed to undermine cynicism itself: the gods approve of this form of religion, and piety itself calls for appropriate belief in politically beneficial religion. The heavens intend, above all, the perpetuation of excellent political regimes and recognize the need for feigned divine sanction for such an end. Therefore, by ensuring the choice of Numa as successor to Romulus, the heavens demonstrate the divine approbation of civil religion and indicate that a citizenry's own piety should be directed, above all, toward the city, if in the first instance by means of willing belief in the religion founded on behalf of that city. Reverence for the city reflects a citizenry's piety toward divine intentions; one's piety is manifested by a willingness to believe in a contrived religion. The religious and the secular become bound together more inextricably than a purely secular vision of religion could effect. We are directed by God himself to love the city more than our souls.[26]

Ironically this divine admonishment to revere the religious efforts of the founder results in the unleashing of a belief in human powers to transform the world in humanity's image. God orders his displacement by human religion for the end of the glorification of the city, and thus sanctifies a divinized conception of humanity. Revealingly, speaking of the "wisdom of the multitudes," Machiavelli suggests that this divinity extends to include all humans: "Not without cause may the voice of the people be likened to that of God; for one sees a universal opinion produce marvelous effects in its forecasts, so that it appears to foresee its ills and its good by a hidden virtue."[27] The Latin phrase *vox populi, vox dei* ambiguously combines two meanings: on the one hand, the phrase captures the sense that the "voice of the people" has the same power as the "voice of God"—that nothing can resist its force when it is unleashed; on the other hand, the phrase also suggests that the "voice of the people" is as unerringly true as God's, and shares the same features of omnicompetence. Machiavelli begins the tradition of combining a conception of civil religion as a cohesive social force with the idea, or ideal, that such cohesion lends itself to the increasing perfectibility of the multitudes. Civil religion becomes both a support for, and increasingly synonymous with, democratic faith.

Civil Religion in America

This combination of the sacred and the profane, of the divine and the political, while intimated by Machiavelli and further developed in Rousseau's conception of civil religion as both supportive and constitutive of "the General Will"—as is discussed at greater length in chapter 5—comes into greater focus in the American version of civil religion. A longstanding tradition in American political thought has bound together the conceptions of divine Providence, American nationhood, and democracy as an interwoven fabric.[28] From John Winthrop's 1630 speech "A Modell of Christian Charity" on the ship "Arabella," in which he suggested that the new settlements would

be as "a City upon a Hill, the eyes of all people . . . upon us," to Abraham
Lincoln's equation of the Union with "the last best, hope of earth"; from the
concluding prayer of John Quincy Adams's Inaugural Address ("knowing
that 'except the Lord keep the city the watchman waketh but in vain,' with
fervent supplications for His favor, to His overruling providence I commit
with humble but fearless confidence my own fate and the future destinies of
my country") to the concluding words of Reagan's Second Inaugural ("may
He continue to hold us close as we fill the world with our sound—sound in
unity, affection, and love—one people under God, dedicated to the dream of
freedom that He has placed in the human heart, called upon now to pass that
dream on to a waiting and hopeful world") America's democratic prospects
have been bound up with a firm belief in God's providential beneficence toward the nation and the nation's role in advancing the cause of democracy
in the world.[29]

In a seminal article published in 1967 Robert Bellah argued that America
has been marked throughout its history by a belief in a form of "civil religion."[30] Bellah's article was and continues to be a subject of discussion and
debate, often centering on questions such as whether the American form of
civil devotion—to the extent that such devotion exists—could be said to be
a form of religion or whether it was recognizably a form of "civil religion"
in keeping with traditional understandings of that term. Yet, to the extent
that Bellah's own account presented an arguably convoluted mixture of
mainline Protestantism, republican patriotism, and a quasi-religious devotion to democracy itself, Bellah, in fact, merely captured the convolution of
the secular and the sacred that has been a part of the discourse of republican and proto-democratic "civil religion" at least since Machiavelli's reflections. Focusing on inaugural addresses by Kennedy and Lincoln, Bellah
noted the "vestigal place" of religion in contemporary America, the implicit
and often explicit assumption of divine sovereignty over American politics
and America's destiny, the belief that America came into existence to "carry
out God's will on earth," and noted Tocqueville's description of the existence
of " a democratic and republican religion" in America.[31] The religious and
the political are seen as intimately connected, with the nation serving as
God's agent on earth and its citizenry charged with fulfilling God's divine
plan by means of simultaneously fulfilling the national destiny. The fruition
of democracy itself is viewed as part of that divine and national vision, with
democracy itself (as suggested in Tocqueville's words) becoming synonymous with the "religious," at once a means of worship of the divine political plan while also itself becoming increasingly the object of sacred devotion.

Although Bellah claimed in this early article that civil religion was "well
institutionalized" in America, he later came to approve of a set of typologi-
cal distinctions that stressed the "differentiation" of such a civic religion
from either of the institutions of church and state.[32] While many features of
the American civil religion echoed Machiavelli's description of the role of religion in a republic, the American example differed in one main respect, inas-

much as the civil religion itself was not claimed to have been founded or initiated by a single source or even several.[33] Because its sources are less identifiably secular (although many Founders and major American figures have been important players in the perpetuation of the national faith, without claiming to be its source or themselves the object of adulation), the American version of civil religion has also had about it an even greater sacral atmosphere than Machiavelli might have considered likely for a modern polity otherwise given over to corrupt forms of cynicism. The "legitimation" of the American national project, seen not as deriving from God by way of a figure such as Numa but instead solely from God alone, has resulted in the American belief not only in divine approval over its destiny but also a keen sense of its own role in fulfilling a higher moral calling among the world's nations, and particularly its part in making possible the realization of "the kingdom of heaven" on earth.

Yet, the overlapping combination of belief in divine Providence, national destiny, and democratic faith that has been part of America's particular and not easily reproduced inheritance has itself been seen at various points to be in precarious straits, in need of some form of intentional buttressing that would go beyond mere reliance upon "vestigal place of religion" and habitual faith commitments to the nation and its democracy. The idealism of the American creed makes it susceptible to profound disillusionment; in keeping with the "dynamics" of democratic faith, unrealized visions of democratic apotheosis can leave its adherents with the bitterness of lost faith. Bellah himself, in subsequent writings, has displayed despair over "the broken covenant": especially in the aftermath of the Vietnam War and Watergate, Bellah concluded that "today the American civil religion is an empty and broken shell."[34] In contrast to the brighter vision offered in his 1967 essay, he has since argued, "in a period like our own, when we [Americans] have lost our sense of direction, when we do not know where our goal is, when our myths have lost their meaning and comprehensive reason has been eclipsed by calculating reason," that "the main drift of American society is to the edge of the abyss."[35] Indeed, most recently he has suggested that the Protestant roots of the American civil religion lead necessarily to a form of self-serving, calculating, materialistic individualism, and has called upon religion proper (especially of non-Protestantism, and specifically Catholicism) to serve as a corrective to the self-destructive American "monoculture."[36]

Bellah's concern that the American civil religion—to be ultimately supportive of American democratic faith—may not persist without intentional support by means of specific persons or institutions taps into a long-standing concern that democratic belief must be created and maintained by purposive inculcation and direction. In some senses, inaugurating this concern in the American tradition is Walt Whitman, who, using "the words America and democracy as convertible terms," predicted that with the fate of America went the fate of democracy itself: "The United States are destined either to surmount the gorgeous history of feudalism, or else prove the most tremendous failure of time." To ensure the success of the American democratic enterprise, Whitman asserted that "democracy can never prove itself beyond cavil, until it founds and luxuriantly grows its own forms of art, poems, schools, theology displacing all that exists, or that has been produced anywhere in the past, under opposite influences." Above all, the poet must replace the priest, creating through language itself a sense of common collective purpose in the same fashion that was the provenance of a more directly sacral form of civil religion: "should some two or three really original American poets (perhaps artists or lecturers) arise, mounting the horizon like planets, stars of the first magnitude, that, from their eminence, fusing contributions, races, far localities, etc., together, they would give more compaction and more moral identity (the quality most needed today) to these States, than all its Constitutions, legislative and judicial ties, and all its hitherto political, warlike, or materialistic experiences."[37]

Whitman's insistence that the poet—and the medium of language itself—could supplant the previous role of religion has been more recently echoed in the work of Richard Rorty, who similarly has insisted on the transformative function of "poetry" and the political provenance of "strong poets," broadly defined to include everyone from writers of philosophy to literature, in the effort to create "liberal ironists" who nevertheless continue to be willing to die for that contingent and ironic belief, and evince an ennobling form of patriotism.[38] The poet creates new possibilities and unobstructed democratic vistas: "democracy is the principled means by which a more evolved form of humanity will come into existence. . . . Democratic humanity . . . has 'more being' than predemocratic humanity. The citizens of a democratic, Whitmanesque society are able to create new, hitherto unimagined roles and goals for themselves."[39] A secularized form of civil religion allows for the fashioning of a wholly new humanity, a more "evolved" form of mankind that is at once fervently individualistic and firmly communal.

Other thinkers have been less convinced that the American civil religion could be firmed up by so amorphous and unorganized a manner as reliance upon the appearance of strong democratic poets. Particularly in the wake of a "crisis in faith" following the Second World War and in the midst of the Cold War, an explicit concern with evangelizing the democratic faith not only abroad (by means of such institutions as the U.S. Information Agency [USIA]) but also at home rose to the level of pressing and explicit concern.[40] Among the most noteworthy efforts to persuade Americans of the need for purposive institutional proselytizing of the faith was J. Paul Williams in his 1952 book, *What Americans Believe and How They Worship*. In his concluding chapter, "The Role of Religion in Shaping American Destiny," Williams sounded a shrill alarm about the declining commitment of Americans to the "national faith," questioning whether "Americans have enough faith, courage, and stamina to preserve what democracy they possess, to gain more, and to play a democratic role on the world stage." He expressed fears that Americans increasingly reflected "a low rather than a high understanding of and faith in democracy," particularly as reflected in widespread public cynicism, corruption, and a "lack of attention to the spiritual core which is at the heart of her national existence."[41]

Williams went on to propose an explicit linking between religion and democracy by means of promoting democracy within the nation's churches. Arguing that democracy was no mere national ideal but rather a conception as universal as the sacred teachings of America's main religions, he insisted that "democracy is a way of life for all men, the truest vision of social ethics which mankind has dreamed." Indeed, as Williams proceeds in his defense of the active role that churches should take in inculcating the democratic faith, it becomes clear that faith in democracy is to *guide*, *correct*, and even in some cases, *replace* the fundamentals of the faiths of the various national sects. Inasmuch as some—and possibly all—religions at some level claim a unique access to true understanding of the divine, all forms of "religious exclusivism" threaten "American unity and American democracy," and therefore must alter their teachings appropriately. In situations in which there is a potential conflict between fundamental religious teachings within a particular religion and the universal tenets of democracy, the church should alter its teachings in order to accommodate the fullest inculcation of the democratic faith.[42]

If churches are to become more "secular" in their promotion of the democratic faith, Williams proposes that secular institutions become correspondingly more "religious," arguing that "governmental agencies must teach the democratic ideal *as religion*."[43] Rejecting the notion that such active inculcation of the democratic faith qua religious faith would contradict constitutionally mandated separation of church and state, Williams states that "it is a misconception to equate separation of church and state with separation of religion and state." Given that he has previously insisted—echoing Durkheim—that "culture is above everything else a faith, a set of shared convictions, a spiritual entity," in his view it is an unavoidable task of government to promote its own culture as a form of religious faith. Presaging the apparently more "secular" arguments of Stephen Macedo's call for an inculcation of "liberal faith," Williams also insists that, along with the nation's churches and its government, the public schools occupy a particularly valuable strategic role in "teaching democracy as a religion." Recommending "systematic and universal indoctrination" in "the values on which a society is based," Williams thereby believed that the freedom afforded by democracy could be preserved against the competing forms of totalitarian control evinced particularly by communism.[44]

Williams concludes on an interesting note by describing a more fundamental belief that must be inculcated *before* democratic faith can be embraced in full, namely, a widespread belief in "metaphysical sanctions" for democracy itself. "Open indoctrination" must teach that "the democratic ideal accords with ultimate reality, whether that reality be conceived in naturalistic or super-naturalistic terms."[45] Nature or God (or, Nature's God) is to be portrayed and perceived as sympathetic to and supportive of democracy. Echoing Machiavelli's suggestion that "the heavens" blessed the institution of civil religion in ancient Rome, Williams insists that democracy can only flourish amid a widespread belief in natural or divine sanction for democracy. Moreover, similar to Machiavelli, Williams's teaching at one level reflects cynicism about the presumptive credulity of the democratic populace (hence raising interesting paradoxical questions about their capacity for self-rule)—especially their willingness to embrace a first-order belief in "metaphysical sanctions," suggestively similar to the kind of "noble lie" that Numa tells about his pretended conversation with the nymph. However, at another level, Williams himself appears to believe that democracy can only flourish in a universe that sanctions democracy, but that such sanction is not sufficient without a concomitant popular belief in that sanction. Nature and God stand in ultimate need of human assistance for the fruition of democracy: humans at once require divine beneficence and yet are required themselves to fashion, by means of civil religion, the belief in this divine approbation. The success of such a belief—inculcated purely by human effort—paradoxically proves the divine blessing of that belief. The civil religion of democracy is both a worship of the divine beneficence toward mankind and of mankind's more preeminent role in bringing about God's plan.

Williams's concerns can perhaps be dismissed as animated purely out of Cold War fears of imminent communist conversion among American citizens, but, although extreme, his arguments are reflective of a long-standing and continued set of explorations about the possibility of and necessity for instruction in the democratic faith, particularly within the setting of schools and universities. Eldon J. Eisenach has recently argued for a renewal of American "political theology" that expresses, "within a national-spiritual horizon, a common democratic faith."[46] The source of renewal, in Eisenach's view, are the schools, and particularly within the locus of American universities. In a sensitive and compelling analysis, Eisenach revisits the origins of the modern American university and, in particular, its apparent transition from largely religious to secular institutions. However, by attending closely to the arguments of progressive democratic thinkers (such as Dewey) who were instrumental in shepherding this transition, Eisenach rightly concludes that what was accomplished by these leading "liberal evangelical Protestants" was "*not a secularization but a nationalization*, a relocation of God's spirit and revelation from particular churches to a unified American people through its most educated and morally serious leadership."[47] Citing a speech by University of Chicago president William Rainey Harper, Eisenach points out the widespread perception that the new role of the American university was to be the "prophet," "priest," "philosopher," and "Messiah" in advancing the mission of inculcating "the religion of democracy." Given that contemporary universities—notwithstanding their apparent widespread secular mission—nevertheless remain implicitly dedicated to this original motivating purpose, Eisenach concludes that it is the best site by which to ensure to future generations that "the national narrative [is] held sacred."[48]

Eisenach rightly places his own recommendations within the progressive tradition, broadly conceived to include, among others, Whitman, Croly, and especially Dewey. Dewey shared the concerns with which this discussion began, namely, Durkheim's fears that individuated human selves could not begin to interact without some form of socialization of a fundamentally religious form. Dewey dared to articulate the moral sources—even if translated as a secular religion—of the "mutual respect" or "expanded consciousness" deemed so central to democracy by Gutmann and Thompson, and Arendt, respectively. As Dewey began his succinct essay, "My Pedagogic Creed," "I believe that all education proceeds by the participation of the individual in the social consciousness of the race," and aims to prompt the individual "to emerge from his original narrowness of action and feeling and to conceive of himself from the standpoint of the welfare of the group to which he belongs."[49] While churches were once capable to some extent of achieving this aim, in modernity the torch had passed from more limited religious sects to democracy itself, and its main socializing institution, the schools.[50] However, the fundamental religious function of this democratic inculcation had not altered, in spite of its change in location:

> Our schools, in bringing together those of different nationalities, languages, traditions, and creeds, in assimilating them together upon the basis of what is common and public in endeavor and achievement, are performing an infinitely significant religious work. They are promoting the social unity out of which in the end genuine religious unity must grow . . . and articulated consciousness of the religious significance of democracy in education, and of education in democracy.[51]

According to Dewey, this conception of the religious nature of education and democracy, the active inculcation of the "democratic faith" among the American populace, pointed to the secular fruition of God's divine plan: "I believe that in this way the teacher always is the prophet of the true God and the usherer in of the true Kingdom of God."[52] Dewey prophesized (and rightly described his own thought as) a thoroughgoing conflation of the sacred and the profane, of the secular and the divine, by pointing toward a time "in which the distinction between the spiritual and the secular has ceased, and as in Greek theory, as in the Christian theory of the Kingdom of God, the church and state, the divine and the human organization of society are one."[53]

The word "religion" comes from the Latin *religare*, meaning "to bind." The idea that some kind of constitutive form of social cohesion is required in a democracy is at once an acknowledgment of democracy's valuation of the individual—reflected in the belief that each person's voice, and vote, counts the same as any other person's—and at the same time the reflection of deep concern that democracy requires "binding" of that individual to the society and, further, requires a preliminary dedication by each individual to democracy as a fundamental condition of his or her individuality.

Civil religion is often viewed as a wholly secular form of indoctrination that cynically employs the veneer of religion to inculcate obeisance and fealty amid a backward and credulous populace.[54] However, this view overlooks a constitutive feature of the civil religion of democratic faith: while civil religion is frankly admitted to be of human origin and propagation, and even among some to be a form of indoctrination (or, alternatively, "education"), the civil religion of democratic faith has been viewed as an outgrowth of God's will and a form of pious adherence to the plan of Providence. God has effectively passed his divine mission to humanity, and made humanity responsible for creating the "Kingdom of God" on earth by means of the culmination of democracy in the world. While seemingly a classic tale of secularization, the civil religion of democratic faith points rather to a kind of divination, a belief in the possibility of heaven on earth by means of a faith in democracy that ultimately accords with our faith in God's beneficence toward the political ends of humanity, and humanity's role in making ourselves gods on earth.

DEMOCRATIC OPTIMISM: SCIENCE'S BENEFICENT UNIVERSE AND THE PROMISE OF PROGRESS

Eisenach's embrace of Dewey and other progressive "religious" nationalists for the purpose of recommending a new "religious establishment" by means of, in particular, the nation's Universities, nevertheless neglects a core feature of the progressive agenda, and especially that of Dewey, namely the identification of *democracy* and *science*. For Dewey, "science, education, and the democratic cause meet as one," as he concluded in a 1944 essay entitled "Democratic Faith and Education."[55] This sentiment could serve as a capstone to his lifelong belief that science and democracy were largely equivalent in "methodology" inasmuch as both were animated by a spirit of investigation, constant reconsideration and revision, and a practical orientation toward solving discrete problems. More than such methodological similarities, however, for Dewey each project was imbued with the spirit of religion, now transferred from the churches jointly to near-identical scientific and democratic activities. "It is the part of men," Dewey wrote in 1908, "to labor persistently and patiently for the clarification and development of the positive creed of life implicit in democracy and in science, and to work for the transformation of all practical instrumentalities of education till they are in harmony with these ideas." Those "habits of mind" that he saw as essential in this mutually supportive pursuit of science and democracy through education were, above all, "honesty, courage, sobriety, and faith."[56]

Notwithstanding Dewey's linking of science and democracy as objects of a new "common faith," religion and science are famously, or infamously, perceived as dire antagonists, locked in eternal battle for the minds and souls of believers. From antiquity—in which, as some have argued, there was a movement from *muthos* to *logos*—to Galileo's forced recantation before the Pope in 1634 to the more familiar battles of modernity such as the 1925 Scopes "monkey trial" and contemporary battles over scientific and religious pedagogy, religion and science have been posed as dire and often fatal enemies.[57] Religion, based on faith, is regarded as the pure opposite of Science, which rests on skepticism, hypothesis, and provisional proof.

However, it has been also long observed that science itself rests on a form of faith, a "metaphysical" foundation that presupposes a certain order in the universe, that presumes human intelligence to be uniquely capable of discerning that order, and that contains an implicit assumption about the inevitability of progress in knowledge and, ultimately, for humankind generally.[58] Above all, if most implicitly, modern science in its earliest conception rests on the assumption that its findings will be largely benign for human beings, both in its theoretical implications and in its practical applications, resulting in the prospect and realization of the "relief of man's estate." The earliest formulations of the scientific project attest that the heavens themselves intend for mankind to pursue this theoretical and applied scientific enterprise, even if the existence of belief in the heavens is potentially shaken or displaced in the process, since heaven ultimately intends improvement in the human condition, liberation from drudgery, and human dominion of nature.[59] Eventually scientific faith becomes explicitly linked to democratic faith by some prominent thinkers who see a link between the ends of the two toward individual liberation, improvements to the human condition that come to resemble the human intervention in accelerating evolution, and ultimately the creation of the "kingdom of God," or heaven, on earth.

Often framed in the language of myth and invoking religious imagery and theological language, early proponents of the scientific enterprise sought to reformulate the conception of the "religious" away from the Augustinian or Calvinist belief in human depravity and the irredeemable nature of earthly domain. As such, scientific proponents sought to replace such perceived pessimistic beliefs with more optimistic faith in the prospects for human and natural amelioration by means of human endeavor and investigation, and ultimately the harnessing, manipulation, improvement, and even conquest of nature. Instead of posing this new (or, for some, renewed) enterprise of scientific inquiry as *antithetical* to religion, many prominent thinkers promoted scientific inquiry as a form of worship, a method of inquiry that sought to divulge God's presence in the world, and ultimately as an endeavor that would yield practical benefits which themselves would permit human ascent toward the status of divinity. This enterprise was viewed as both demanded and sanctioned by God—a practice undertaken out of piety rather than apostasy.[60]

David Noble has persuasively demonstrated the millenarian influence in the development of this "religion of technology," beginning with the controversial abbot Joachim of Fiore in the thirteenth century and continuing through subsequent centuries in the thought of such figures as Roger Bacon, Giordano Bruno, Francis Bacon, Robert Boyle, the "Cambridge Platonists," and Isaac Newton, and in the more secularized thought of the Freemasons and Karl Marx, and, in America, in such thinkers as Edward Bellamy.[61] Noble contends that contemporary scientific projects, such as space exploration, artificial intelligence, and the rise of genetic engineering, while "masked by a secular vocabulary," are, in fact, actually "medieval in its origin and spirit."[62] While long-standing religious doctrine held that humanity was created in the image of God and that, following Genesis, God granted humanity dominion over the earth and its creatures, following Augustinian influence these teachings did not mitigate belief in the fundamental imperfection of humanity stemming from the Fall and the primary role as "steward" amid nature rather than one who stood apart from nature.[63] The millenarian tradition, however, departed radically from these teachings, arguing that man's fallen nature was a temporary condition and that through his own efforts he could recapture not only the state of innocence but, by means of reading and manipulating the "text" of nature itself, man could actually also achieve a form of divinity. A representative statement, articulated by Giordano Bruno at the end of the sixteenth century, contends that such effort, in copying the creative activities of God, is sanctioned and ordained by God:

> Providence has decreed that man should be occupied in action by the hands and in contemplation by the intellect, but in such a way that he may not contemplate without action or work without contemplation. [And thus] through emulation of the actions of God and under the direction of spiritual impulse [men] sharpened their wits, invented industries and discovered art. And always, from day to day, by force of necessity, from the depths of the human mind rose new and wonderful inventions. By this means, separating themselves more and more from their animal natures by their busy and zealous employment, they climbed nearer the divine being.[64]

The millenarian and proto-scientific tradition—one that increasingly understood human activity as itself the necessary component to bring about the kingdom of God on earth—repeatedly emphasized three beliefs that constitute the "religion of technology": first, the belief in progress; second, the ideal of human self-transformation; and, third, the aspiration of human ascension to godliness. Each of these ends was to be achieved by means of mastery of "natural philosophy," the forerunner of science. If the story of the Fall had previously been understood to define strict limits on human aspirations and to deny the possibility of human perfectibility, millenarian interpretations increasingly understood the story of Adam's transgression to portray a temporary condition of ignorance that could be reversed by means of the development of human knowledge and applications of inventions and discoveries.[65] Thus progress, in effect, was a process of "rediscovery" of that which mankind had lost at its point of origin, but this second time not as an unearned gift from God's hand but rather as a divinely sanctioned result of human inquiry into God's creation. Reflecting this renewed confidence in human perfectibility was John Milton, who surmised that, "when the cycle of universal knowledge has been completed, still the spirit will be restless in our dark imprisonment here, and it will rove about until the bounds of creation itself no longer limit the divine magnificence of its quest. . . . Truly [man] will seem to have the stars under his control and dominion, land and sea at his command, and the winds and storms submissive to his will. Mother Nature herself has surrendered to him. It is as if some god had abdicated the government of the world and committed its justice, laws, and administration to him as ruler."[66]

Among the earliest and most celebrated calls for the prospects of near-infinite human self-improvement was Pico della Mirandola's 1486 "Oration on the Dignity of Man," which evinces this tripartite belief in progress, self-transformation, and the possibility of humanity ascending to divinity by means of science. Evoking a version of the Prometheus myth as purportedly related by Protagoras in Plato's dialogue *Protagoras*—which is discussed at greater length in chapter 4—Pico at once "updates" the ancient tale for a Christian audience and transforms the biblical story of creation as told in Genesis into one in which human beings avoid the Fall and become further defined by a very absence of fixed properties. God creates humankind as an afterthought, having fashioned all of existence but without any creature that could "ponder the plan of so great a work, to love its beauty, and to wonder at its vastness."[67] Since God had not initially planned to create mankind, he had already exhausted all the "archetypes" and there existed no model remaining in his "treasure-houses" upon which to base this new creature. "All was now complete; all things had been assigned to the highest, the middle, and the lowest orders" (224).

While Pico's portrayal of Divine oversight and limitation here runs the risk of blasphemy, he moves to affirm God's limitless powers of creation by describing the fashioning of a creature *without* fixed qualities or talents:

He therefore took man as a creature of indeterminate nature and, assigning him a place in the middle of the world, addressed him thus: "Neither fixed abode nor a form that is thine alone nor any function peculiar to thyself have we given thee, Adam, to the end that according to thy longing and according to thy judgment thou mayest have and possess what abode and what functions thou thyself desire. The nature of all other beings is limited and constrained within the bounds of laws prescribed by Us. Thou, constrained by no limits, in accordance with thine own free will, in whose hand We have placed thee, shalt ordain for thyself the limits of thy nature. We have set thee at the world's center that thou mayest from thence more easily observe whatever is in the world. We have made thee neither of heaven nor of earth, neither mortal nor immortal, so that with freedom of choice and with honor, as though the maker and molder of thyself, thou mayest fashion thyself in whatever shape thou shalt prefer. Thou shalt have the power to degenerate into the lower forms of life, which are brutish. Thou shalt have the power, out of thy soul's judgment, to be reborn into the higher forms, which are divine. (224–225)

Because of this unique and singular origin and destiny, humans exist at a "rank to be envied not only by brutes but even by the stars and by minds beyond this world" (223). Combined with his portrayal of God as limited to creating based on preexisting "archetypes" to which he cannot add (thus having only recourse to the fashioning of humans without qualities), this conception of humanity as entirely self-creating hints at a curious displacement and reversal of the divine and the human: God "creates" humanity to be self-creating, even "self-transforming," potentially growing into "a heavenly being (if rational)," "an angel and the son of God (if intellectual)," or one that "made one with God . . . shall surpass them all (if withdrawn 'into the center of his own unity')" (225). God is constrained in his creation of humanity by the prior existence of uncreated "archetypes," indicating a curiously limited deity who nevertheless negotiates these limits by means of the creation of a creature that does not appear, in the end, to be similarly limited. If God's limits force him to create mankind as a creature without qualities, humanity in turn becomes a creature who creates without limit, one that can even make itself into a divine being—something that God could not do, since the divine is itself uncreated, whereas humans are not limited to those same prior "archetypes."

While the necessity and these powers of self-creation come initially from God, they can only be exercised and realized by humans. God intends for human beings to make as much of themselves as they can—even to the point of transforming themselves into divine beings. Thus God sanctions and blesses human attempts at self-perfection. Pico makes this clear in his call for humanity to embrace "natural philosophy," the philosophical investigation of natural phenomena. Despite leaving mankind without qualities, God gives to humanity the script by means of which it can avoid a descent into depravity and instead attain a divine condition. Distinguishing a laudable form of "magic" from a form of deceptive conjuring (Pico praises the *magus* who is "the servant of nature and not a contriver" [248]),[68] he describes how the *magus* can become "ruler and lord" by "calling forth into the light as if from their hiding-places the powers scattered and sown in the world by the loving-kindness of God," and thus "does not so much work wonders as diligently serve a wonder-working nature." This investigator "brings forth into the open the miracles concealed in the recesses of the world, in the depths of nature, and in the storehouses and the mysteries of God, just as if she herself were their maker; and, as the farmer weds the elms to vines, even does the *magus* wed earth to heaven, that is, he weds lower things to the endowments and powers of higher things."[69]

This knowledge is not, however, the result of superficial investigation into the natural world. Rather, by undertaking to discern God's mysteries hidden throughout the earth and the heavens, finally to "wed earth to heaven," mankind ascends to a godlike status.

> Once we have achieved this by the art of discourse and reasoning, then, inspired by the Cherubic spirit, using philosophy through the steps of the ladder, that is, of nature, and penetrating all things from center to center, we shall descend, with titanic force rending the unity like Osiris into many parts, and we shall sometimes ascend, with the force of Phoebus collecting the parts like the limbs of Osiris into a unity, until, resting at last in the bosom of the Father who is above the ladder, we shall be made perfect with the felicity of theology.[70]

Human perfectibility is within its own power, achieved by means of "reading" and interpreting the text of nature wherein lie hidden God's hints of how to achieve a kind of divinity. If "theology" is needed to achieve final perfection, Pico suggests throughout that the most pious form of inquiry—the one intended by God at the time of humanity's creation—is the effort to understand divine intention through the scientific investigation of nature.

Pico's emphasis on God's hidden mysteries and the role of humanity in exposing and exploiting those clues is echoed in Francis Bacon's frequent invocation of Proverbs 25:2, "It is the glory of God to conceal a thing: but the honor of kings to search out the matter."[71] While Bacon's work is often cited for its influence on the modern belief in progress—especially the progress achieved by means of a scientific enterprise dedicated to the "benefit and use of men"—less often perceived is Bacon's accompanying belief in the possibility of human transformation by means of scientific advancement and, ultimately, the prospect of his "similitude" to the status of the Divine.[72] If Bacon is regarded as the progenitor of the secular modern scientific project, it is no less true that he perceived that project's secular aims to be wholly in keeping with divine strictures and ultimately undertaken under divine sanction and with an end to the greater glory of God and the eventual deification of humanity.

Echoing the belief of many millenarians, Bacon rejected the suggestion that mankind's fall from Eden indicated that human inquiry was forbidden or discouraged but concluded, in a spirit of piety, that such inquiry should not be undertaken as an effort to displace God. Bacon distinguished between the rightful form of human dominion in the earthly realm and the illegitimate attempt by mankind to free itself altogether from God's commandments.[73] Inquiry is to be limited by this outer boundary, to be undertaken at all times with piety and obeisance to divine majesty. Thus, Bacon writes, "all knowledge is to be limited by religion."[74]

Yet, these strictures are not as limiting as they might first appear. In *Valerius Terminus, or Of the Interpretation of Nature*, an early fragmentary work believed to have been written in 1603 in preparation for *The Advancement of Learning*, Bacon argued that mankind in Eden, like the rebelling angels, had sought to "ascend and be like unto the Highest," and instructively added, "not God, but the highest."[75] The transgression of Lucifer and the angels, like the transgression of Adam and Eve in the garden of Eden, was to seek to become *higher* than God rather than to be *like* God. While the attempt to gain "knowledge of good and evil" intruded into "God's secrets and mysteries," Adam's dominion over nature *before* the Fall—indicated especially by his naming of the animals—revealed that inquiry and knowledge was the proper provenance of prelapsarian humankind.[76] Bacon concludes that, "as to the goodness of God, there is no danger in contending or advancing towards a similitude thereof, as that which is open and propounded to our imitation."[77]

The "limitation" demanded by religion on scientific inquiry is revealed essentially to present no limitation at all. Piety requires thorough human investigation and the harnessing of all natural phenomena: "For that nothing parcel of the world is denied to man's inquiry and invention."[78] "Heaven and earth do conspire and contribute to the use and benefit of man," Bacon insisted, pointing to a confluence of sacred and secular grounds for the pursuit of knowledge.[79] Divine scripture "invite[s] us to consider and to magnify the great and wonderful works of God," an acknowledgment which leads Bacon to admonish his readers that "religion should dearly protect all increase of natural knowledge."[80]

By means of properly pursuing the advancement of learning—not in the manner of Adam in precipitating the Fall by seeking the knowledge of good and evil but rather in the manner of Adam *prior* to the Fall—mankind could hope to reverse the consequences of the Fall. Through investigation and artifice mankind could reachieve what was once its divine inheritance, and by means of inquiry it might restore the prelapsarian condition of plenitude, ease, peace, and even immortality.[81] The pursuit of this rightful form of inquiry could be expected to lead to

> a restitution and reinvesting (in great part) of man to the sovereignty and power (for whensoever he shall be able to call the creatures by their true names he shall again command them) which he had in his first state of creation. And to speak plainly and clearly, it is a discovery of all operations and possibilities of operations from immortality (if it were possible) to the meanest mechanical practice.[82]

Beyond those desirable if still "vulgar" ends of knowledge—which include "imperial and military virtue" as well as "power and commandment" over other humans—is the most sublime and final end of knowledge: by means of learning, "man ascendeth to the heavens" and achieves that to which "man's nature doth most aspire, which is immortality or continuance."[83]

Bacon unveils his confidence in human mastery of the universe, even beyond that of God, perhaps most suggestively, if subtly, in his retelling and interpretation of the myth of Prometheus in *The Wisdom of the Ancients*. Deploying the same tactic as Protagoras and Pico della Mirandola before him, and Percy Bysshe Shelley after him, the Promethean myth provides fertile ground in which to "rediscover" mankind's powers and restore human optimism of its central place in the natural and even divine order. While retaining enough elements of the tale to appear faithful to the original myth, Bacon, in fact, alters several familiar elements in order to permit an interpretation that is most sympathetic to mankind's capacity and points to the possibility of human transformation, even exhaltation, over the divine.

"Prometheus, or the State of Man (Explained of an overruling Providence, and of Human Nature)" is the longest of Bacon's thirty-one retellings of classic myths in *The Wisdom of the Ancients*, and is numbered twenty-six which corresponds to the number of the final letter of the English alphabet.[84] Bacon had cause to wish to call attention to the essay, for it is a subtly crafted exposition of humanity's place in the natural and divine order and, further, an exhortation for humanity to improve its position within that order (thus, to that extent, it resembles in more than subject matter Pico's "Oration"). As in the versions by Protagoras and Pico, Bacon relates that Prometheus created humanity and, at some point, stole fire from the gods and gave it to humanity. At this juncture, however, Bacon departs from known versions of the myth: mankind responds to this gift with *ingratitude* and arranges for Prometheus to be tried by Jupiter. Curiously Jupiter is delighted with humanity's efforts to prosecute Prometheus and by its possession of fire, and extends to humanity perpetual youth. Humanity foolishly gives away this gift to an ass, who then subsequently gives it to the race of serpents. Nevertheless (according to Bacon), Prometheus continues his "unwarrantable practices" (rather than, as the classic myth had it, protecting humanity) by deceiving Jupiter into choosing an unworthy sacrifice, and for his deception provokes Jupiter to fashion a punishment against humanity in the form of Pandora and a box of curses. Prometheus is also bound in chains to the side of a mountain where a vulture daily consumes his liver, and he is released from this punishment only when Hercules sails by upon the ocean, shoots the bird, and sets Prometheus free.[85]

In his explanation Bacon varies his account of the symbolic meaning of Prometheus, but at the outset he states that "Prometheus clearly and expressly signifies Providence" (394). By "providence" Bacon seems to suggest that Prometheus symbolizes mankind's divinely ordained destiny, the repository of God's plans for the universe (thus, he writes, "providence is implanted in the human mind in conformity with, and by the direction and the design of the greater overruling Providence" [395]). The "principal" ground for understanding Prometheus to signify Providence is because "man seems to be the thing in which the whole world centers, with respect to final causes" as explained at length by Bacon:

> So that if he [i.e.,mankind] were away, all other things would stray and fluctuate, without end or intention, or become perfectly disjointed, and out of frame; for all things are made subservient to man, and he receives use and benefit from them all. Thus the revolutions, places, and periods, of the celestial bodies, serve him for distinguishing times and seasons, and for dividing the world into different regions; the meteors afford him prognostications of the weather; the winds sail our ships, drive our mills, and move our machines; and the vegetables and animals of all kinds either afford us matter for houses and habitations, clothing, food, physic; or tend

to ease, or delight, to support, or to refresh us so that everything in nature seems not made for itself, but for man. (395)

Prometheus qua Providence would appear to be a worthy object of human gratitude and praise for this bounty of natural provisions and human dominion, but here Bacon surprises with his interpretation of *his own* departure from the traditional tale, in which, as Bacon relates, Prometheus receives instead *ingratitude* from humanity for his gifts. Calling it "a remarkable part of the fable" (which, clearly, it is, inasmuch as Bacon himself fashioned it), he recognizes that "it may seem strange that the sin of ingratitude to a creator and benefactor, a sin so heinous as to include almost all others, should meet with approbation and reward" (397). However, Bacon asserts that the fable teaches its perceptive readers that such ingratitude "proceeds from a most noble and laudable temper of the mind," namely, that those "who arraign and accuse both nature and art, and are always full of complaints against them . . . are perpetually stirred up to fresh industry and new discoveries" (397, 398). By contrast, those who stand in awe of humanity's place in the universe—and express gratitude for this position—are, in fact, subject to think themselves satisfied with their current state, and "rest, without further inquiry." This latter condition, Bacon avers, shows "little regard to the divine nature" (398).

In his interpretation of the preceding passage, Bacon subtly shifts the ground from his initial identification of Prometheus with "Providence" that directs mankind—a providence that affords men "mind and understanding" (395)—to one in which such providence is itself subject to a strenuous and accusatory form of human inquiry that it afforded in the first instance. Ingratitude only appears at first glance to be a sin: in fact, ingratitude— whether to "a creator and benefactor" (which only appears "heinous") or to "nature and art" (which is praiseworthy)—in both cases is curiously sanctioned and ultimately rewarded by "the divine nature." Echoing Pico's treatment, Bacon suggests that humanity is providentially given the necessary tools by which to "arraign and accuse" Providence, and can expect to be rewarded for these exertions by a higher power—even to receive the gift of immortality. Humanity has only unsuccessfully pursued the possibility of immortality because of impatience and unnecessary abstraction, but it is now within its reach—having now the example of the ancients both to emulate and to improve upon—to become, like the patient ass, "a useful bearer of a new and accumulated divine bounty to mankind" (400).[86]

As if to constrain the impious implications of his analysis, Bacon concludes with an interpretation of that section of the myth in which punishment is inflicted daily upon Prometheus by an eagle, suggesting that this image affords a warning against overweening and impious inquiries. "The meaning seems to be this," Bacon writes, "that when men are puffed up with arts and knowledge, they often try to subdue even the divine wisdom and bring it under the dominion of sense and reason, whence inevitably follows a perpetual and restless rending and tearing of the mind. A sober and humble distinction must, therefore, be made betwixt divine and human things, and betwixt the oracles of sense and faith."[87] Almost unnoticeably Bacon has replaced his initial interpretation identifying Prometheus with "Providence" with one that identifies Prometheus with humanity. Yet, it is a subtle transformation that has, in fact, been effected by means of the preceding "explanation" of the need to use the gifts of Providence to interrogate providence, and effectively make one's own new kind of "Providence" by means of those gifts. If humanity, in effect, makes itself into its own providential agent, then it now stands no longer at odds with Prometheus but, instead, against Zeus—the implied "higher power" that stands even above Providence. Bacon's warning seems to be, lest we tempt the kind of punishment visited upon Prometheus by Zeus—that daily "rending and tearing"—that we must humbly acknowledge the distinction between "divine and human things."

That might conclude matters but for the highly curious interpretive passage that has *preceded* this explanation of Prometheus's punishment which, in the original fable related by Bacon, in fact *follows* the description of Prometheus's daily torture. Bacon interprets the *freeing* of Prometheus *before* his interpretation of the punishment.[88] Thus, although his explanation *precedes* this apparently final warning about the need for human piety, in fact the prior interpretation of Hercules' role in Prometheus's liberation is the "final" lesson of the allegory in spite of its penultimate placement in the interpretation. As for the role of Hercules, Bacon writes,

> even Prometheus had not the power to free himself, but owed his deliverance to another; for no natural inbred force and fortitude could prove equal to such a task. The power of releasing him came from the utmost confines of the ocean, and from the sun; that is, from Apollo, or knowledge. . . . Accordingly, Virgil . . . account[s] him happy who knows the cause of things, and has conquered all his fears, apprehensions, and superstitions.[89]

Curiously Prometheus—who had provided humanity with the capacity to forge his own inquiries, even to the point of "arraigning" Prometheus, or "Providence"—does not now possess the abilities to free himself. He has not conquered all his fears—fears that he has not hitherto evinced in his willingness to combat Zeus—suggesting that his final fear is his unwillingness to possess the power that would forestall his punishment (or superstitious fear of punishment) and make his liberation at the hands of another unnecessary. Hercules represents the fearless scientist or discoverer—he who "supports and confirms the human mind"—who finally liberates the now humanized Prometheus from his final "fears, apprehensions and superstitions." The prospect of liberation at the hands of Hercules makes the fear of Zeus superfluous and apprehension of punishment nugatory, since, by emulating Hercules, humanity has no fear of any external form of bondage given that it possesses all the means of self-liberation. The final statement on the significance of Hercules—and hence of the parable itself—confirms that human transformation and ascendance to the status of human divinity is the true object of Bacon's teaching: "as if, through the narrowness of our nature, or too great a fragility thereof, we were absolutely incapable of that fortitude and constancy to which Seneca finely alludes, when he says: 'It is a noble thing, at once to participate in the frailty of man and the security of a god.'"[90] Bacon sought to remake humanity, by means of the advancement of learning and its resulting aim at "the glory of the Creator and the relief of man's estate," allowing humanity to achieve its due status, "not animals on their hind legs, but mortal gods."[91]

Bacon may be a curious and objectionable imputed background source for that variety of democratic faith that relies on an identification between advances in science and democracy, especially given that Bacon was a committed monarchist and frequently recommended secrecy in political matters.[92] Yet, Bacon advances arguments on behalf of the scientific enterprise that are easily assimilated to democratic ends and, indeed, may even lead logically and necessarily in that direction—a trajectory of which Bacon, in several moments, appeared himself to be well aware.

There is, of course, a potential tension between the scientific enterprise that emphasizes the role of expertise and elite knowledge, and democracy's expectation of the basic competence among, and widespread participation of, the citizenry. Even the most fervent democrats have recognized that informed elites play a role in the cultivation of intelligence and judgment among the populace. John Dewey, for example, readily recognized that "for most men, save the scientific workers, science is a mystery in the hands of initiates."[93] Modern democracy requires sufficient knowledge of complex issues, requiring not only the means of communication that adequately disseminate information and knowledge but also an adequately developed individual understanding of methods of inquiry and analysis. For Dewey, modern America had successfully achieved the former but was woefully insufficient in development of the latter. Answering Walter Lippmann's questioning of the political competency of the ordinary person, Dewey called for the "artful" presentation of the latest advances in scientific inquiry, likening the successful dissemination of knowledge of "enormous and widespread human bearing" to enticing forms of literary presentation. By means of such artistically rendered knowledge, Dewey believed that the creation of a "Great Community" was possible, one composed of "an organized, articulate Public." Here, Dewey acknowledges the central role not of a scientist or inventor but of democracy's "seer," Walt Whitman. He concluded that democracy would achieve a consummation when "free social inquiry is indissolubly wedded to the art of full and moving communication."[94]

In both these respects Bacon anticipates this "wedding" of scientific inquiry and democracy, particularly by linking the method of scientific inquiry to the concomitant amelioration of the human condition, brought about by the resultant practical applications and devices that would expand opportunities for leisure and universal communication. In several instances Bacon emphasized how his recommended form of scientific inquiry is based upon, and substantively promotes, a kind of equality. Denying that the scientific enterprise calls for a kind of specialized and elite knowledge, in the *Novum Organum* Bacon asserted that the form of inquiry he recommended was universally accessible:

> My method of scientific discovery leaves only a small role to sharpness and power of wits, but puts all wits and understandings more or less on a level. For just as drawing a straight line or a perfect circle simply by hand calls for a very steady and practiced hand, but little or no skill if a ruler or pair of compasses is used, so it is with my method.[95]

Bacon thus suggested that his method advances two forms of equality—one intrinsic to the method itself ("puts all wits and understandings more or less on a level"), and the other the result of practical applications deriving from the successful inquiry into natural causes ("little or no skill [is required] if a ruler or pair of compasses is used").

Bacon was keenly aware of the egalitarian, and even democratic, implications of the methodology itself. As he stated early in his writings, "howsoever governments have several forms, sometimes one governing, sometimes few, sometimes the multitude; yet the state of knowledge is ever a *Democratie*, and that prevaileth which is most agreeable to the senses and conceits of the people."[96] In seeking to employ the method of scientific inquiry—one that "puts all wits and understandings more or less on a level"—the expected result is the discovery of new applications that lighten the burdens of humanity, increase longevity, and promote social intercourse between citizens and people of varying nations. Writing in the *New Atlantis* about the final aim of the "Salomon's House," or "The College of Six Days," Bacon wrote that, "the End of our Foundation is the knowledge of Causes, and the secret motions of things; and the enlarging of the bounds of Human Empire, to the effecting of all things possible."[97] The discovery of "secret motions" and subsequent inventions that improve upon nature's bounty allows for the increased likelihood of practical human equality—such as the universal capacity offered by the "compass," when previously only a skilled hand could draw a perfect circle. Both the method of scientific inquiry, and its resultant applications, point to a democratic trajectory that was perceived even by Bacon, and became readily apparent to the full-blown democratic faithful.

Dewey, for instance, spared no praise for Bacon, calling him "the forerunner of the spirit of modern life," the "real founder of modern thought," and "the prophet of a pragmatic conception of knowledge."[98] In particular Dewey praised three aspects of Bacon's practical philosophy: first, his insistence that "knowledge is power," or that true knowledge leads to human empowerment over natural phenomena; second, his "sense of progress as the aim and test of genuine knowledge," the continual amelioration of the human condition by means of unceasing investigation and interrogation of nature; and, third, his insight that led to the perfection of the inductive method of experimentation, one that stressed activity and the constant "invasion of the unknown" based on the rejection of certainty and the embrace of ever constant doubt.[99] In *The Public and Its Problems*, Dewey articulated how this approach to human knowledge—one that aimed at practical amelioration of conditions as well as expanding circles of knowledge throughout the citizenry—was the essence of democratic life. Beyond mere suffrage or distant oversight over the activity of its representatives, *active* and *universal* inquiry and amelioration was the basis of a true democracy. In this sense, Dewey averred, "the cure for the ailments of democracy is more democracy."[100] If Bacon did not see the full implications of his own analysis, never "discovered the land of promise," Dewey insists that "he proclaimed the new goal and by faith he descried its features from afar."[101]

One sees the final aim of Baconian science in its original conception—namely, the transformation of humanity—continues to be articulated among proponents of democracy but often in less overtly religious tones as those employed by Bacon. Indeed, ironically, owing to the intervening history in which religion has been perceived to be more hostile than friendly toward the scientific enterprise, defenders of the scientific faith have advanced claims to human transformation as a prospect in spite of, and antithetical to, traditional religious belief.[102] Richard Rorty captures the dual religious and antireligious sense of this belief in the transformative powers of humanity by means of the interlinking of science—as the means of "relieving the human estate"—and democracy:

> In past ages of the world, things were so bad that "a reason to believe, a way to take the world by the throat" was hard to get except by looking to a power not ourselves. In those days, there was little choice but to sacrifice the intellect in order to grasp hold of the premises of practical syllogisms—premises concerning the after-death consequences of baptism, pilgrimage or participation in holy wars. To be imaginative and to be religious, in those dark times, came to almost the same thing—for this world was too wretched to lift up the heart. But things are different now, because of human beings' gradual success in making their lives, and their world, less wretched. Nonreligious forms of romance have flourished—if only in those lucky parts of the world where wealth, leisure, literacy, and democracy have worked together to prolong our lives and fill our libraries.[103]

For Rorty, the opportunities afforded by these contemporary advances—ones that he frequently and gratefully attributes to Bacon's proto-pragmatic arguments in favor of "knowledge as power"[104]—now allow us to be "carried beyond presently used language."[105] Humanity transforms itself by means of new uses and employment of language, according to Rorty's admonition of "liberal irony."[106]

For all the confidence in the prospect of democratic consummation and human transformation afforded by the modern scientific enterprise as expressed by such optimistic thinkers as Dewey and Rorty, there has persisted the misgiving that the scientific project may not be as seamlessly supportive of democracy's aims as might be hoped by the most faithful devotees. One only needs to consider those social scientists of the early twentieth century—such as APSA president Walter Shepard, whose scientific conclusions prompted him to call for a thorough reconsideration and revision of the prevailing "democratic faith"—to perceive the source of continued misgivings about the relationship between the scientific enterprise and democracy.[107] To the extent that each rests on a kind of faith in a better future, however, it is not surprising to find testaments of faith that endorse, promote, and even proselytize on behalf of a strengthened faith in the shared aims of science and democracy.[108]

One noteworthy document that affirms a firm connection between democracy and the ends of science (as against the more suspect forms of religious faith) is the Proceedings of a conference held in New York City in May 1943 entitled *The Scientific Spirit and Democratic Faith*.[109] Organized in part to combat the threat posed by the "closed society" of fascism, as well as to repudiate perceived authoritarian leanings of religious organizations within liberal democratic societies, the conference gathered together both prominent democratic theorists—such as Horace M. Kallen—as well as practicing scientists of different stripes, all with a common ambition to argue on behalf of "an essential interrelation" between science and democracy.[110] Most remarkable about the document is the extent to which the tension that the conference sought implicitly to dispel—the fear that the scientific project and democracy may not be altogether compatible enterprises—was in fact *deepened* by a curious disconnection between the vision of the conference's democratic theorists and its scientists. One might suspect that the participants at the conference became anxious as the meeting unfolded; yet, amid the shared optimism over the strong linkage of science and democracy, there was an absence of reflection upon the implications of the proceedings, and no self-conscious notes of caution during the conference.

Infused with the spirit of pragmatism and progressivism—one of the organizers explicitly states that the participants were "radical democrats" in the spirit of Emerson and belonged to the American philosophic tradition of William James and John Dewey—the papers of the first half of the volume strongly assert the essential connection between the freedom of inquiry required by science and the condition of open and ranging freedom that defines democratic politics at large.[111] Echoing Dewey, as well as the more distant echoes that Dewey attributed to Bacon, the organizers set forth several guiding principles of the conference, including the following:

- The scientific spirit is in essence the modern search for truth;
- The democratic faith is in essence the belief that human resources may become adequate for human needs wherever freedom of inquiry exists and cooperative techniques are developed;
- The scientific spirit is dependent upon the democratic faith in the sense that science cannot develop into an instrument for human welfare except in an atmosphere of freedom.[112]

Science requires democracy in order to fully engage in the search for truth without obstruction from authoritarian sources; democracy requires science to the extent that citizens must be afforded every opportunity for material advancement, as well as equipped with the tools of discernment provided by scientific inquiry, ultimately with an aim to making them capable of thinking and interacting by employing the same methodological approach as scientists. Thus another principle affirmed by the conference holds that "when the democratic faith becomes practice the resulting process is one in which all policy-making is an affair of participation. Policies which need to be 'lived out,' decisions which seek to represent the experience of the people, must be derived from the participating knowledge and experience of the people."[113]

Horace M. Kallen echoes these principles in his spirited attack on authoritarianism and a defense of the scientific enterprise and its essential connection to the democratic faith. Like democracy, science thrives on free inquiry and implies the equality of all reasonable participants:

> The sciences are preeminently the fields of free thought. No idea, no hypothesis, no technique that they consider is admitted to a privileged status. None is exempt from the competition of alternatives. None is denied the cooperation of its competitors in the tests of its validity. None enters the field as a truth revealed, self-evident, beyond the challenge of doubt, beyond the proofs of inquiry.[114]

For Kallen, as for Dewey, the phrases "scientific spirit" and "democratic faith" overlap to the point of being indistinguishable: both "convey an identical attitude in different but interacting undertakings of the human enterprise."[115] From the antifoundational, pragmatic point of view, all certainties—whether in natural sciences or politics—are, in fact, merely apparent, and must be subject to revision and potential rejection by unceasing inquiry and investigation. All beliefs are provisional, and "faiths" that maintain certainties are to be exposed and dismissed as forms of "spiritual fascism."[116] Kallen's certainty on the progressive nature of uncertainty derives from his democratic faith, the belief that open inquiry in the political and scientific realms will be forever mutually supportive in improving humanity's condition, and that all democratic citizens can be brought to a level of sufficient sophistication and interest to employ the methods of science in their own formulations of public policy.

This belief was fully shared by the practicing scientists who participated in the conference, several of whom strongly endorsed this "democratic faith" and viewed the full flourishing of science as affording the opportunity to move humanity to a condition that would justify this initial faith in their universal capacities. One scientist—Alfred Mirsky, an associate member of the Rockefeller Institute for Medical Research—distinguished between "those people who do not have the democratic faith" and thus who shared "a very low opinion of human nature" (here quoting, as an example, Alexander Hamilton) and those people "who do have the democratic faith" made possible by a "more optimistic point of view towards human nature."[117]

To demonstrate that this more "optimistic" faith in humanity is warranted, Mirsky launched into a lengthy analogy drawn from his close experience with laboratory rats. He noted that rats which are ill-treated—kept in dirty cages and not fed or handled sufficiently—are wild and uncontrollable. By contrast, those rats that are kept clean and well-fed are mild and gentle. "Petting" and encouraging laboratory rats to become accustomed to their "caretakers" is essential in this process of "gentling."[118] To further demonstrate his point, he described that ill-treated rats died with high frequency with the removal of the parathyroid gland, whereas "gentled" rats survived the operation at a much higher rate. Mirsky concluded that this comparison revealed the central importance of conditioning and pointed to its promise in the realm of genetic experimentation. In his peroration, he drew an explicit comparison between the more docile manner and better physical health of well-treated rats to human beings, calling for humans to be treated in a similar manner: "I think we know enough to say that if man were treated the way these rats have been in the laboratory, then . . . there are good grounds for the democratic faith; in other words, for the faith that there are some good potentialities in ordinary human beings."[119] While one can hardly gainsay the benefits of greater health—particularly necessary for laboratory animals in order to survive experimental surgery (a point which gives pause when Mirsky opines that "man should be studied in laboratories much more than he is")—one wonders if "gentling" is the highest democratic virtue that science can offer to humanity, and whether those purported "democratic" virtues of unceasing inquiry and participation—emphasized in the volume by Kallen—are aided by the experimental support of "responsible" scientists who count themselves among the democratic faithful. Characteristic disdain for "ordinary" humans who want "transformation," combined with solicitous "democratic faith," is evident in Mirsky's analysis.

Mirsky's vision of science that provides the means of transforming humans into more suitable democratic citizens was not a curious exception among the scientific participants at the conference, but a view shared by several others (all specially selected supporters of "democratic faith"), including Richard M. Brickner, an associate professor of clinical neurology at the College of Physicians and Surgeons. Brickner described his discovery, as a practicing psychoanalyst, that numerous apparently "normal" patients have extraordinarily "primitive" qualities, including "death wishes and hatreds and urges to aggression."[120] Psychotherapy brings these hidden pathologies to light, and, although Brickner did not contend that these aggressions can be alleviated, he argued that the awareness of their existence thereby alerts people to the imperative to avoid acting upon them. Echoing the sentiments of Albert Mirsky, Brickner stated that "it does seem to clear things up to know what is bothering you is that you are the same as a lion or a dog or an ungentleable rat in some ways." He concluded: "People get better, they get happier, when they have been through such a course of education."[121]

Again echoing Mirsky, Brickner argued that responsible scientists can offer their expertise to improve democratic conditions. Specifically Brickner proposed to prevent the onset of adolescent disillusionment by forestalling the initial implantation of illusions in young children. He insisted that he and other scientists should "teach some of the principles we find useful in adult psychotherapy to children as a sort of prophylactic psychotherapy."[122] As Mirsky suggested, wild rats cannot be easily "gentled," but laboratory rats, bred in captivity, and treated properly, can be conditioned to be gentle if one begins from the point of birth. Similarly "wild" humans can only with difficulty be "gentled" by means of extensive psychiatric intervention; better to avoid this eventuality by beginning gentling treatment from a very young age. As Mirsky argued, "genetically, [the gentled rat] is quite a different animal. His inherent germ-plasm or whatever you care to call it is different from that of the [wild] rats, and it really is impossible to gentle his variety of rat."[123]

These proposed "democratic" applications of science appear to be a long way from Bacon's belief that science allowed the realization of the proud declaration that humans are "not animals on their hind legs, but mortal gods." If anything, these attempts to use therapeutic science as a means of "gentling" humanity has more in common with the previously discussed ambitions of "civil religion," particularly its Machiavellian aim to quell the "ferocious populism" that threatened to tear the Roman republic asunder, and put in its place a more public-spirited citizenry. To this extent, the ambitions of "civil religion" and the "scientific spirit," linked to the "democratic faith," are essentially indistinguishable: both seek the transformation of human beings into fully realized democratic creatures; each provides a means to the fruition of the first and most essential tenet of democratic faith, self-transformation. If these expressions of democratic science appear to reduce humanity to the level of "mere" animals—laboratory rats—its aim is ultimately consistent with Bacon's belief that purely *material* amelioration, by means of inquiry into purely *natural* phenomena, was the route to a new form of divination (after all, Mirsky and Brickner each speak of the "gentled" rat as a signal improvement over its naturally "wild" alternative, and Mirsky points to the possibility of genetic improvement of the species). The linkage of this aim to a rarified democratic faith makes explicit the attempt to universalize this outcome for all citizens, to make common the transformation of imperfect creatures into—in Rorty's words—"a more evolved form of humanity," made possible by the "principle means" of democracy.[124]

One sees the way in which belief in scientific progress and a kind of "civil religious" belief in democracy combined especially among thinkers who ecstatically embraced the democratic promise of new communication technologies. Few thinkers come close to the unbridled enthusiasm of Marshall McLuhan in the 1960s (although at times John Dewey and Benjamin Barber come close, and fervent believers in the promise of internet technology may even exceed McLuhan's enthusiasm), who extolled the promise of modern communication technologies in familiar millenarian terms:

Our new electric technology that extends our senses and nerves in a global embrace has large implications for the future of language. Electric technology does not need words any more than the digital computer needs numbers. Electricity points the way to an extension of the process of consciousness itself, on a world scale, and without any verbalization whatsoever. . . . The computer, in short, promises by technology a Pentacostal condition of universal understanding and unity. The next logical step would seem to be, not to translate, but to by-pass languages in favor of a general cosmic consciousness which might be very like the collective uncon-sciousness dreamt of by Bergson. The condition of "weightlessness," that biologists say promises a physical immortality, may be paralleled by the condition of speech-lessness that could confer a perpetuity of collective harmony and peace.[125]

McLuhan's invocation of "cosmic consciousness" alerts one to the rela-tionship of his ambitions to those of Walt Whitman's friend and biographer, Dr. Richard M. Bucke, whose book, *Cosmic Consciousness*, argued that hu-mans (including Whitman, along with such figures as Christ, Buddha, and Emerson) were undergoing an evolution in which consciousness was be-coming universally perceptible and shared.[126] Bucke's book, in turn, was a central inspiration to Edward Bellamy's 1899 novel, *Looking Backwards*, which portrayed a utopian American future aided, in significant part, by technological advances such as a device that resembles the modern radio. Notably William James positively reviewed Bucke's book, and late in life ar-gued on behalf of "psychical research" (i.e., paranormal and post-death ex-periences) that would uncover the actual existence of such a form of consciousness:

Out of my experience, such as it is (and it is limited enough) one fixed conclusion dogmatically emerges, and that is this, that we with our lives are like islands in the sea, or like trees in the forest. The maple and the pine may whisper to each other with their leaves . . ., and the islands also hang together through the ocean's bot-tom. Just so there is a continuum of cosmic consciousness, against which our in-dividuality builds but accidental fences, and into which our several minds plunge as into a mothers-sea or reservoir. Our "normal" consciousness is circumscribed for adaptation to our external earthly environment, but the fence is weak in spots, and fitful influences from beyond leak in, showing the otherwise unverifiable com-mon connexion.[127]

Thus, James hoped, scientific research would reveal the existence of the "effect" of which democratic faith's "civil religion" had believed it must be the "cause." One cannot help but hear echoes to these progressive and quasi-religious be-liefs in human moral evolution in contemporary calls, such as by Benjamin R. Barber, for the inculcation of democratic "common consciousness."[128]

The Palimpsest of Democratic Transformation

Numerous democratic theorists of different ages combine the various meth-ods of democratic transfiguration in varying ways and degrees—or not at all—but to a common end, namely, democratic transformation of the individual into a human good enough for democracy. Resting in the background of apparently more modest efforts by contemporary theorists in defense of the democratic virtues of "mutual respect" or "enlarged mentality" are these translations of theologically informed efforts at human transformation. A lineage of thinkers combining forms of "civil religion" to democracy can be traced from Protagoras and Machiavelli and Rousseau to thinkers such as Dewey with his promotion of a "common faith," Rorty's "romance" and "strong poetry," and the "political theology" of Williams and Eisenach. Often overlapping, among those thinkers linking scientific progress to democratic faith, include Protagoras, Dewey, Rorty, Barber, as well as a significant number of liberal thinkers and countless scientists who view their work as advancing democratic ends. Many other contemporary democratic theorists—preeminent among them such "antifoundationalists" as Mouffe, Connelly, Honig, Dallmayr, Fish, and others—insist on the centrality of "democratic transformation" alone, and exhibit hostility both to religious and scientific belief as a source or helpmeet for this transformation, but curiously often credit their own "agonistic" thinking explicitly and alternatively to the thought of the pre-Socratics or specifically Protagoras (Fish, Wolin),[129] Machiavelli (Fish, Mouffe, Honig), Rousseau (Barber), James and Dewey (Barber, Rorty, Eisenach, and innumerable contemporary pragmatists), among others. Such thinkers claim that true democratic flourishing can only occur with the transformation of individuals by means of agonistic political activity, and simultaneously insist that such activity can only truly occur when this transformation has taken place. To the extent that their "democratic faith" apparently remains shorn of external support and thus the optimistic prospect of realization, they disavow any authoritative means to achieving fruition of their project and eschew describing a starting point for this transformation. However, to the extent that their faith points implicitly to the belief in its ultimate realization, they explicitly evoke a lineage that rests on nearly invisible "foundations" of belief, such as that afforded to them by predecessors like Protagoras, Machiavelli, Bacon, Rousseau, and Dewey. That belief—the "democratic faith" of their various predecessors—at once derives from religious and theological sources, but those sources have been subtly transformed to displace their original divine source with the prospect of a divinized humanity.

This "democratic faith"—like the French Panthéon—is a palimpsest of seemingly desacralized and wholly secularized belief that nearly obscures the subtle and not wholly erased sacred text beneath. It is a faith with sources outside humanity that nevertheless affirms thoroughgoing faith *in* humanity. It is a faith, initially blessed by God, that humanity should ultimately ascend to godlike status. It is a blasphemous faith of divine origin, a politicized faith with divine sanction, a secular faith aimed at human transformation into democratized divinity itself.

CHAPTER THREE

Democracy as Trial: Toward a Critique of Democratic Faith

> On waxen tablets you cannot write anything new
> until you rub out the old. With the mind it is not so;
> you cannot rub out the old until you have written in the new.
>
> —Francis Bacon, *Temporis Partus Masculus*, 1603

DEMOCRACY AS TRIAL

RESORTING AGAIN to the images with which this book began, the *desacralization* of a religious space such as the Panthéon reflects the implicit acknowledgment that the sacred remnants of such a space—suggested by the shape of the building, its history, the attenuated reverence its echoes still provoke—continue to confer sacral legitimacy on the new secular endeavor even as it succeeds in being only imperfectly secular. The paintings on the walls of the Panthéon reflect this incomplete secularization, portraying the life of Saint Geneviève, the supine protectress of Paris. Preserved perhaps out of purely secular appreciation for their artistic value, the presence of the wall frescoes depicting Saint Geneviève continue to recall the displaced devotions of the cathedral, dedicated to the worship of the divine and the simultaneous recollection of radical human imperfection. The palimpsest of the Panthéon preserves the echoes of that older faith, quietly but persistently calling attention to the transformation of that older faith to the democratic faith, at once standing in accusation against the newer faith while at the same time conferring on democratic faith a degree of legitimacy that it otherwise might not attain shorn of those ancient symbols, language, and narratives.

The Goddess of Democracy is also a palimpsest, reversing the apparent and partially erased scripts of the Panthéon. Instead of the newer secularized form of faith in divinized humanity in service of the republic that obscures the older sacred writing in praise of God—as in the case of the Panthéon—the Goddess of Democracy partially erases the visage and pose of an ordinary frail human being and replaces it with the divine embodiment of democracy itself. For reasons of exigency, the Goddess of Democracy was fashioned from an existing sculpture. The original sculpture portrayed a frail man, incapable of standing unaided. As described by Tsao Hsingyuan, the original sculpture from which the Goddess of Democracy was fashioned portrayed "a man grasping a pole with two raised hands and leaning his weight on it. It had been done originally as a demonstration of how the distribution of weight is affected when the center of gravity is shifted outside the body."[1] This portrayal of a man (the gender traditionally believed to be more "autonomous") revealed inevitable human frailty and the inevitable inability of any human to "stand" alone and unaided. This original image, if less "inspiring," by a certain understanding might best have served as a defining image of democracy—one instead conceived as that form of self-government that best recognizes universal human infirmity, the inability of humans to "stand alone." Instead, the dissidents, recognizing this as an "unlikely beginning from which the Goddess of Democracy was to grow," proceeded to "cut off the lower part of the pole and added a flame at the top to turn it into a torch; they leaned the sculpture into a more upright position; they changed the man's face into a woman's, added breasts and long hair, and otherwise made him into a her."[2] Altering the gender and pose of the statue, and most significantly discarding the staff on which the peasant leaned, an image of ultimate self-sufficiency is created from one that formerly portrayed frailty and mutual reliance. Divinized democracy is born by erasing the image of fragility.

In the first transformation of the Panthéon, traditional religion is desacralized; in the second transformation of the Chinese statue, democracy is resacralized. There appears to be a movement from secularization of the sacred to sacralization of the secular. Yet, the two motions are intimately connected, as both point in effect to a new religion of political democracy which requires, in the first instance, the obscuring of the divine (by desacralizing the Panthéon) and, in the latter instance, the erasure of the ordinary (the transformation of a traditional peasant farmer into a goddess). The two are linked in revealing ways: the need to divinize humanity requires both the partial erasure of the divine and the denial of traditional belief in the limits and imperfections of ordinary humanity.

Democratic faith is at once the attempt to sheer off traditional religious faith, even as it adopts the symbols, imagery, and language of religious faith albeit by reorienting the devotion they inspire toward human beings and human ends. Thus democratic faith is at once curiously similar to, yet in tension with, traditional religious faith. In its earliest forms, reflected in those antecedents to whom many contemporary democratic faithful resort—whether Protagoras in antiquity; in aspects of Machiavelli or Rousseau in early modernity; or Emerson, Whitman, Dewey, or Rorty, among many other American thinkers—there is often at once an explicit rejection of traditional religious belief as posing a hindrance to the full fruition of democratic faith, even as those traditional beliefs are themselves subtly transformed in order to undergird the "updated" faith in democracy. A form of legitimacy for democratic faith accompanies the adoption of the language and imagery of traditional religious belief—including the very language of faith itself—at once pointing to a continued if paradoxical awareness of the appeal of traditional religion even amid explicit condemnations of its obstacles to the full realization of democratic faith.

One sees this characteristic hostility to traditional religious faith and connected admonishment to embrace the democratic faith in numerous writings devoted to a discussion of democratic faith. Sidney Hook, for example, categorically rejected then contemporary arguments that democracy could only be distinguished from totalitarian regimes by dint of its basis on religious principles. "Insofar as civlization has a future," he wrote in a 1945 essay entitled "The Autonomy of the Democratic Faith,"

> it is contingent upon the growth of ideals of a universal, democratic humanism, which embraces what is morally best in religion, fortified by reliance not on supernatural dogmas but on the instruments of enlightened, scientific intelligence. Religion has had thousands of years to unify the world into a semblance of a just and cooperative world order. It has failed.[3]

Even as Hook strenuously rejected any role for "supernatural" religion in undergirding the democratic faith, he immediately recognized the challenge presented to an autonomous democratic faith and called for a transferral of that traditional belief to the human and specifically political realm. "Democratic humanism may fail too. That depends, in part, upon whether the ardor and devotion that have been expended on transcendent objects of faith can be transferred to the democratic heritage as a pattern for the reconstruction of social life."[4] Hook does not intend for us to examine too closely the apparent conundrum in his statement: if that ardor inspired by "transcendent objects" of faith has nevertheless failed to "unify the world in a semblance of a just and cooperative world order" (if that was indeed the object of that faith), Hook nevertheless maintains a confidence that a transformed faith— now "democratic faith"—will be more successful. If the religious believer's invocation of faith is to be rejected, Hook can only reply with a near-identical invocation of faith, albeit a faith transformed with its object of devotion as democracy, not God.

At the same time democratic faith "resacralizes" the democratic sphere, particularly by means of transposing the belief in the divine instead to a belief in the divinity in man. Democratic faith is at once apparently committed to the proposition that all men are created with equal democratic capacity, yet also frequently, if not almost always, suggests the need for some significant improvement in the current form of humankind to fulfill that potential. This belief often culminates in a recommendation for "transformation," a transformation particularly endorsed by contemporary democratic theorists who, in contrast to their theoretical predecessors, do not indicate how such transformation is to be effected. The possibility of transformation by means of "civil religion," on the one hand, or scientific progress, on the other, points not to confidence in *existing* human capacity understood as common-sense understanding of political phenomenon and the possibility of democratic dispositions that encourage civil exchange and political dialogue but, instead, understands "capacity" to be the potential for development, indeed—as reflected in works ranging from Pico and Bacon and Rousseau to Dewey and Rorty—the "capacity" to become something *more* than human, something more akin to god than man.

One sees such characteristic belief in human transcendence throughout the literature on democratic faith. J. Ronald Engel has argued, in an article entitled "Democratic Faith," that democratic faith should be institutionalized as a form of (civil) religion and that its object of faith be recognized as the only universally recognizable form of transcendence available to humankind. "Democratic faith affirms the locus of the transcendent to be in the public life only when that life takes a democratic form. . . . While agreeing to disagree about what kind of transcendence may or may not lie beyond the world, prophets of democratic faith agree in their view of the tangible world itself as a theater pregnant with the holy." Disputing that the "emergence of democracy in the world" should be construed to represent a form of "desacralization," Engel instead calls for "our adoption of the redemptive history of democratic faith as our ultimate identity."[5] Democracy itself needs to be seen as "redemptive" and "holy," the sole legitimate realm for "transcendence" available to humankind. The apparent devotion to the ordinary political experience of humans is belied by such transformational ambitions: the "ordinary" contains more than is otherwise apparent, and humanity is more divine than hitherto recognized. Echoing earlier arguments by Pico and Bacon, updated by Emerson, Whitman, Dewey, and Rorty, humanity is capable of achieving quasi-divine status if traditional religious forms are overthrown and human potential for infinite self-improvement is unleashed by means of a reoriented faith toward democratic ends. Democracy as apotheosis can be realized by the faith in and of ordinary people, and by means of that efficacious faith, a transformation of mere humans into ever more perfected democratic saints.

Democracy is often advanced as an alternative to the utopian ideologies of the twentieth century, the sole form of governance that recognizes the radical fallibility of human beings and instantiates this recognition through its commitment to discourse, debate, reassessment, and revision, and, at base, its commitment to a conception of equal human dignity. "Democratic faith" similarly advances democracy for all the same reasons but goes further by calling for "transformation" and "transcendence" through democratic politics. It should be worrisome that the most ardent proponents of democracy throughout time have similarly seen a necessary connection between "desacralization" of traditional religion and "resacralization" of democracy, and raise necessary questions whether there is a relationship between ardent democratic commitments and democratic faith. Might there be something inherent to democracy—or belief in democracy's sole claim to legitimacy—

that inclines its proponents toward excessive forms of democratic faith, which indeed demands such faith as a condition of admittance into the cult of democracy?

If so—and more is said on this relationship, below—then democracy's greatest trial may not arise from anything external to democracy but rather from democracy itself. While many commentators have suggested at various times that democracy is *on* trial—in need of proving itself before a skeptical world or in the midst of antidemocratic challenges that will test its plausibility in the future—it might be more accurate, instructive, and chastening to consider, instead, an alternative formulation: democracy *as* trial.[6] Democracy *as* trial suggests that there are inherent tendencies within democratic belief that tempt its true adherents to a utopian and immoderate form of "democratic faith." Such tendencies include the fervent belief that the displacement of traditional institutions and practices—institutions that represent various forms of constraint—allows for, even leads to, the fruition of human transformation. This unreflective faith also reflects a tendency to identify the realm of politics itself as the sole source of human redemption and meaning, simultaneously displacing the identification of redemption with the divine and denigrating the significance of nonpolitical forms of satisfaction and meaning.[7] All is permitted in the name of democratic apotheosis. As such, "democratic faith" reflects those dangers inherent to any faith, but perhaps most particularly to a faith in which the object of faith has been transferred from belief in the divine to the human. Faith is embraced, at some level, in spite of the evidence of one's senses. Faith can be a means of resisting despair or cynicism in the face of evidence to the contrary, a spur to action amid bleakness. But, as many proponents of democratic faith readily point out in regard to religious faith, faith also has the tendency to escape the bounds of moderation and tend toward excessive unquestioned belief, even forms of fanaticism. Proponents of democratic faith are unwilling, or more likely unable, to discern that this may be even more true of secular forms of faith.

Yet, if in one (earlier) visage "democratic faith" reflects the overweening belief in the possibility of human transformation, in another (later) guise it represents the fraying thread upon which growing despair about democracy's realization are now hung. In recent years, as expressions of "democratic faith" have moved away from an explicit reliance upon those "means" of transformation discussed in the last chapter—namely, inculcation and transformation by means of "civil religion" or by means of scientific progress and technology—the "democratic faith" has curiously begun to serve less as a spur to action toward the possible fruition of democratic apotheosis and more as a tenuous and residual belief in an indescribable democratic transformation, the belief in which is increasingly eroded by the brazen contradictory evidence of modern "post-democratic" society.[8] Indeed, many contemporary expressions of "democratic faith"—outside those more optimistic pronouncements by the likes of Richard Rorty and Benjamin Barber—instead reflect a deep pessimism toward the possibilities of even modest and imperfect forms of democracy, and even threaten to undermine those democratic commitments that currently exist.[9] Democratic faith is thus both relied upon and threatened in the midst of critiques of existing and imagined forms of political theory and practice, ones that point toward the insufficiency of any political creed that does not promote thoroughgoing openness and radical freedom. Faith in the possibility of such a transformed polity and citizenry, without concomitant belief in any "mechanism" for transformation other than a shared faith in this transformation, has led curiously to a thinning of explicit democratic commitments to equality. The claims of the most ardent "agonistic" democratic theorists ultimately threaten to undermine the selfsame faith in democracy that is otherwise advanced. Returning to the Nietzschean fount from which many have drunk deeply, even the claims of unquestionable or "self-evident" human equality must be subject to agonistic openness and opposition, and opponents to such egalitarian belief must be accorded "agonistic respect."[10] By means of the equation of "democracy" with complete plural openness, the grounds for democracy—human equality—effectively evaporate, and are retained only evanescently by means of a residual "democratic faith" as a bulwark against the threat to equalitarian commitments that the very openness of antifoundationalism threatens to dissolve. If anything, such a faith—while less apparently optimistic—in fact reflects greater optimism through its belief in self-generating societal transformation and self-sustaining democratic commitments than those forms of democratic faith that rely more explicitly on external "mechanisms" of transformation such as civil religion or scientific and technological progress. Yet, because the faith no longer directs us to particular means of transformation, it also moves the democratic faith increasingly toward the brink of democratic despair.

One way of restraining these twin tendencies of extreme "democratic faith" and the temptations to democratic despair among democracy's most ardent proponents is to look closely at the underlying "texts" of the twin palimpsests that inform the faith, namely, the significance of the icons that are obscured by the *desacralization* of the holy and by the *sacralization* of democracy. Just as the refurbishing of the Panthéon partially hides the example of St. Geneviève and her commitment to a divine order separate from, and superior to, the secular order, so, too, does the fashioning of the Goddess of Democracy obscure the ordinary, frail peasant beneath the resplendent divinity's robes. For the "democratic faith" that seeks the deification of humankind, a reminder that "Man is not God" is afforded by the palimpsest of the Panthéon. And for those who see democracy as a future promise rather than an inescapable condition necessitated by human frailty and imperfection, the image of the frail man beneath the Goddess of Democracy reminds us of our shared infirmities and our ultimate destiny. By reminding ourselves of what has been partially erased beneath the twin attempts to dethrone God and enthrone Man—in effect, what is already present, if obscured, in the fashioning of democratic faith—we can more easily become conscious of, and consequently see the need to temper, those tendencies of democracy toward extreme forms of faith in itself.

Reading the Palimpsest, Part 1: Faith and Doubt

When most people reflect consciously upon "faith," they associate it with particular forms of religious belief. However, many of its common usages refer to everyday phenomena, from the mundane to the significant albeit wholly unreligious. As entered in the *Oxford English Dictionary*, "faith" has a primary meaning of "belief, trust, [and] confidence"—a meaning that was intended, the entry notes, "in early use, only with reference to religious objects; this is still the prevalent application, and often colours the wider use."[11] Often, then, faith is used interchangeably with terms like "trust" or "belief," as found in such commonplace phrases as "I have faith in Frederick; he has never failed to complete an assignment before" or "Have a little faith! I won't let you down." One way of referring to the keeping of oaths and promises is to "keep faith"—to be true to one's word, echoing the idea that "faith" involves an act of trust or confidence. In this ordinary usage, even—as the *Oxford English Dictionary* rightly claims—when religious echoes of the word "faith" "colour" its invocation, there remains another feature that seems to depart from the religious echo, namely, that such faith can be undermined or altogether overthrown by empirical evidence to the contrary. If Frederick persistently fails to turn in his assignments, we rightly cease to "have faith" in him; if we do not keep our word, we have "broken faith" and people rightly cease to accord us their trust or confidence.

In all these usages, and in its more robust religious form, a common feature of faith emerges that is implied but never rendered explicit in the dictionary definition: faith is the belief in something unproven, unknown, uncertain, even unknowable. When we declare our faith in more mundane matters, it is a "faith" that more closely resembles those less robust forms of "belief" such as "confidence" or "trust" that thereby can be altered in the face of countervailing evidence. Moreover, often this is evidence that we rightly expect to encounter, either bearing out our initial faith and lending grounds for its continuity, or compelling us to withhold our confidence, trust, or faith in the face of countervailing evidence. Indeed, it is barely a form of "faith" in this sense of a belief in the unknown or unproven, or the unknowable or unproveable, since often it seems that such forms of faith qua "trust" or "confidence" are, in fact, based on some evidence—for example, reputation, personal experience with another person, or reasonable expectation based on similar encounters with other persons—and are subject to alteration based on contradictory experience. This is the faith that arises as the relatively simple response to incomplete knowledge that pervades all human interaction: no matter how well we might know someone and harbor strong expectations of certain outcomes, there is always the possibility that things can happen differently. We have faith, in such circumstances, but at best it is a tenuous and provisional faith that, whether by a singular or several occurances of betrayal, would appear subject to disbelief, mistrust, and lack of confidence.

This form of faith, then, implicitly contains seeds of doubt: we hold such faith in the absence of certainty, implying that the invocation of faith is required as a means of bridging the relatively small distance between expectation and belief. The bridge itself allows one to traverse that distance of doubt but never to ignore completely why the bridge of faith is necessary in the first instance. Indeed, in such seemingly innocent statements as the one above—"I have faith in Frederick; he has never failed to complete an assignment before"—it does not overstate the case to suggest that one can hear just as much trepidation about one's state of faith as confidence about one's reliance on past evidence. One does not *know* that Frederick will turn in the assignment, in spite of the best evidence that he will; one has confidence, perhaps even supreme confidence, but such supreme confidence is distinct from *certainty*. The small chasm of this distinction reveals an implicit acknowledgment of doubt. Faith, in this sense, both contains and momentarily overcomes doubt.

Some theologians have insisted that faith, properly understood, and against that conception of faith that permits no doubt about its fundamental tenets, rather necessarily contains elements of doubt that arise from the very dynamic of faith as a response to uncertainty. Since faith, whether in its more mundane commonplace form, or in its traditional and more robust sense of belief in God, the divine, the transcendent, the "Absolute," or some other conception of the supra-human or supernatural, reflects a belief in something (yet) unseen, unknown, or finally unprovable, even a faith directed to the divine partakes in and is implicitly conscious of its own relationship to doubt. Even religious faith that is embraced as a means of overcoming and conquering doubt about the nature and very existence of the divine reveals its own doubt as a condition of its faithfulness. Faith would be unnecessary if the divine were known: Abraham, in direct conversation with God, does not need a faith in the divine as such, although he does invoke faith in the face of God's promises about the generations that he will engender, and then faith in the rightness of God's command to sacrifice his son Isaac.[12] Faith is not the complete absence of doubt; it is, in a certain sense, a frank admission of its presence even as it is held at bay by faith. Such dual rejection and embrace of doubt amid faith is captured fruitfully in the following passage by theologian Paul Tillich from *Biblical Faith and the Search for Ultimate Reality*:

> Faith and doubt do not essentially contradict each other. Faith is the continuous tension between itself and the doubt within itself. This tension does not always reach the strength of a struggle; but, latently, it is always present. This distinguishes faith from logical evidence, scientific probability, traditionalistic self-certainty, and

unquestioning authoritarianism. Faith includes both an immediate awareness of something unconditional and the courage to take the risk of uncertainty upon itself. Faith says "Yes," in spite of the anxiety of "No." It does not remove the "No" of doubt and the anxiety of doubt; it does not build a castle of doubt-free security—only a neurotically distorted faith does that—but it takes the "No" of doubt and the anxiety of insecurity into itself. Faith embraces itself and the doubt about itself.[13]

In a similar vein Robert Merrihew Adams has written of faith as a belief in "something that a rational person might be seriously tempted to doubt," yet "is resistant to adverse experience, and is apt to revise itself before simply accepting refutation." At the same time he insists that such faith can and indeed should "include doubt, and a certain sensitivity to opposing reasons, as well as a certain resistance to them. In this way, the virtue of faith involves holding to a mean between vices of credulity and incredulity."[14] In both a theological register—in the case of Tillich—and regarding its more philosophical variant—in the case of Adams, among others—it is recognized that faith contains a constitutive component of doubt, even as faith entails resistance to doubt's full flourishing in relation to, in Tillich's words, "objects of ultimate concern."[15]

Yet, if the comments of Tillich and Adam give evidence that both theological and secular considerations of faith can evince such a profound "sensitivity" to doubt (in Adams's words), can it thus be suggested that there is no fundamental or constitutive distinction that needs to be drawn between the objects of faith themselves, and thereby to the character of the faith in those respective "objects of ultimate concern"? Is there no difference between a faith directed toward God as "object of ultimate concern," versus a more secular object, such as Annette Baier's "faith in a community of just persons"?[16] On the face of it, it would seem that the "objects of faith" would substantially influence one's relative inclination toward either faith as blind adherence or faith with a keen "sensitivity" to doubt. As the "object of ultimate concern" becomes less subject to empirical verification or disproof, it would seem that a greater intensity of faith would necessarily accompany one's belief. The greater the chasm between knowledge and uncertainty, the longer and more fragile the bridge, and the greater and more difficult (and less justified) the leap. On the other hand, to the extent that one's faith is directed at an object alternatively more comprehensible, provable, realizable, or subject to empirical consideration, it would seem that such faith—now much more akin to "trust" or "confidence"—would have a far greater inclination to actively consider any doubts that would arise as a result of such faith commitments.[17]

Adherents of democratic faith often implicitly and sometimes explicitly contrast their faith in a political and secular object as more "reasonable" and modest than the religious faith of which they are characteristically critical. It is not "faith" that is the bone of contention, but the *object* of faith. Yet, given the extent to which "democratic faith" is a "secular" translation of sacral language and narratives, it is altogether likely that the opposite is the case, that, in fact, faith in a conception of transcendent divinity results in a more "modest" form of faith. The very nature of such religious faith, in contrast to a political, profane, and "democratic faith," could and even should have the effect of engendering a keen sense of humility about the extent of human knowledge, including, but not limited to, accompanying questions about one's certainty regarding the defining characteristics of the divine object of faith. Thus the very faith in a divine "other" gives rise simultaneously to necessary doubts about that very faith, given the intrinsic recognition of the imperfection of human capacities to apprehend and comprehend the divine. Paradoxically the divine, perfect nature of such an object of faith can, and arguably ought to, lead a believer to question whether humans are capable of such faith. Such a moment of simultaneous belief and doubt is reflected in the response of a father of an afflicted child to Jesus' statement, "All things are possible to him who believes": "I believe; help my unbelief!"[18] The very belief in supra-human perfection renders human belief questionable in all its guises. One sees this paradox similarly expressed in Augustine's understanding of Scriptural interpretation. Believing the truth of Scripture thereby necessarily requires one to recognize one's insufficiency in correctly interpreting Scripture. The very source of one's faith—the revealed word of God—is recognized as being opaque to a significant degree by dint of one's very faith in that same text, one that necessarily requires a concomitant recognition of human imperfection.[19]

Alternatively it can be conversely argued that a faith solely invested in more "secular" objects lacks the paradoxically humbling realization that ought necessarily to accompany faith in the divine. Faith in human-centered activities may, on the one hand, be accompanied by the "sensitivity" to doubt recommended by Adams; yet, it is a faith that may also tend toward intrinsic *defiance* of any accompanying recognition of human insufficiency, a recognition that might in turn give rise to doubts about the intensity of one's faith. Curiously it is human-centered "objects of ultimate concern" that instead arguably give rise to the most intense forms and extremes of faith, inasmuch as such forms of faith lack the chastening feature that necessarily accompanies recognition of powers and perfection beyond human comprehension or possession.

One finds such observations forwarded equally by theological and secular thinkers. For example, Paul Tillich regarded nationalism as a dangerous "object of ultimate concern" inasmuch as it would comprehend all other objects of concern without allowing for any external grounds for opposition:

> If a national group makes the life and growth of the nation its ultimate concern, it demands that all other concerns, economic well-being, health and life, family, aesthetic and cognitive truth, justice and humanity, be sacrificed. The extreme nationalisms of our [twentieth] century are laboratories of what ultimate concern means in all aspects of human existence, including the smallest concern of one's daily life. Everything is centered on only one god, the nation—a god who certainly

proves to be a demon, but who shows clearly the *unconditional character* of an ultimate concern.[20]

Echoing these concerns, if writing from a more secular perspective and critical, above all, of the "secular religions" that arose during the twentieth century, Raymond Aron wrote that, "as long as men see politics as the vehicle of their fate, they will actively worship the regimes that, dangling before them an illusory future, reflect their desires and console them for their disappointments. As long as troubled masses think themselves betrayed or exploited, men will dream of liberation, and the image of their dream will be the face of their god."[21] Strikingly, unlike the paradoxically simultaneous embrace of faith as affirmation and as admission of human insufficiency that accompanies (or has, does, can, and indeed should accompany) a belief in the divine, there is no similar moment of self-limitation that accompanies the "faith" in human-centered creations or activities such as politics and the temptation to a worship of the state.

The suggestion that faith in the divine can act as a restraint upon secular "fanaticism" is perhaps on its face counterintuitive. A long-standing tradition in political theory argues that with the dethroning of religious faith as a guiding light in political affairs, one might rightly expect a rise in skepticism with accompanying toleration which are the marks of modern liberal democracy.[22] Faith—conceived almost exclusively as religious faith—is regarded as an unreasoned devotion to the unproveable and hence is unbounded in its potential for cruelty and impervious to rational persuasion. A forceful expression of this view has been made by one of liberalism's severest critics of religious faith, George Kateb, who relies upon Nietzsche for his contention that "much of religion is worthless":

> The criticism of religion is the premise of all criticism. . . . [Nietzsche] sees the convergence and mutual reinforcement of self-confidence, ignorance, self-deception, and mendacity. . . . No matter how thoughtful, complex, and seemingly attuned to human needs, religion is—or, say, religions are—usually based on unwarranted assumptions, which are always traceable to faith. Why should anyone have faith? Where is the starting place? A choice to accept is made but not always recognized as a choice; the line that separates faith from (Sartrean) bad faith is regularly crossed.[23]

For such liberal critics of religion, a kind of skepticism toward faith ought to be expected. Yet, such thoroughgoing skepticism is actually often resisted; religious faith is displaced in order to put a form of "democratic faith" in its stead. This "move" is not surprising inasmuch as, in many cases, "religion" qua "faith" was not in fact their actual target of critique. Many liberal thinkers of the late twentieth century who condemned the role of "certainty" and faith in politics—thinkers ranging from Judith Shklar and George Kateb to Isaiah Berlin and Karl Popper—were responding more to the "absolutisms" of twentieth-century secular fascism and communism than the radically different forms of "certainty" evinced by medieval and early-modern Christianity. For many liberal thinkers, the two forms of "absolutism"—secular political and religious—were seen as inspired and motivated by the same underlying causes and beliefs.[24] Rightfully seeing in such fanatic devotions and worship of the state the specter of religion (albeit in a secular translation), many mid-century thinkers explicitly criticized religion as a source of such modern fanaticisms. Because both species of "certainty"—sacred and profane forms of "religious" belief—resulted in manifest forms of political repression, they have been viewed as equally threatening; indeed, since religiously inspired "certainty" has had a longer historical life, is focused on the other-worldly, and even today retains its legitimacy in the wake of the defeat of many secular forms of political absolutism including fascism and communism, religious faith has come under withering scrutiny and criticism by many contemporary liberal thinkers.

Yet, at the same time, because of democratic devotions held by these liberal thinkers, they have sought to retain a claim on "faith" that could continue to be oriented toward the secular sphere. Even among such "skeptical" thinkers, belief does not and cannot cease: democratic faith remains necessary even for those most suspicious political thinkers, revealing the extent to which such faith remains essential to a democratic age, albeit often going undetected by the most relentlessly skeptical thinkers. Others have been more clear-eyed about the necessity for "faith" even in an apparently skeptical age: one well-known "skeptic," Judith Shklar, recognized both the potential extremism and the limits of skepticism. In discussing the portrayal of radical nihilism in Orwell's 1984, she commented that the book "forces its readers to recognize that even doubters and skeptics can be just as dogmatic as the most besotted believers."[25] Alternatively she painted a sympathetic portrait of Emerson's "democratic faith," a faith upon which democracy "depended," a faith which, for Emerson, depended in turn upon "an Eternal Cause, a supersensible Nature, an intimation of another world."[26]

Even so aggressively an antireligious a thinker as George Kateb, in speaking of democracy, echoes even more robustly this Emersonian faith. He writes, "There are moments, moods, and episodes in which one experiences a democratized understanding of all reality, an understanding which goes beyond self and society, but does not (necessarily) aspire to the supernatural or the more-than-human. This is democratic transcendence."[27] In pointing to the expression of this form of "transcendence" in the writings of his intellectual heroes—Emerson, Whitman, and Thoreau—Kateb rightly places his qualifying word "necessarily" in parentheses, since he knows only too well the extent to which these thinkers—and especially Emerson and Whitman—equated democracy itself with the approbation of the divine order, the earthly unfolding of a divine plan, and as an expression of ultimate worship of the divine in man. The faith may appear in more secular garb, but it remains a form of faith—appealing to the language and resonances of traditional religious faith through the invocation of such words as "transcendence," "redemption," and "hope"—and one that, in the end, may be less subject to doubt than the religious faith it supercedes. As Kateb has written elsewhere, "constitutional democracy itself is a political embodiment of a certain kind of moral absolutism. . . . The Law is divinized, and, by extension, the laws are reverenced."[28]

The strong insistence upon the secularized form of faith in democracy, of "democratic transcendence" in purely human terms, of "divinization" in the political realm, both obfuscates the religious lineage of such belief and also discloses the secular aspirations of the faith. Democratic faith imports aspects of religious belief—including belief in human transformation and the aspiration for human apotheosis in the "City of God"—and places them wholly within the secular realm, at once retaining the aura of divine sanction for such aspirations while making humanity the sole agent of their realization.

In spite of the religious origins and resonant overtones of "democratic faith" that have been explored in the preceding chapters, the explicit hostility of most democratic faithful toward "traditional" religion opens the door to temptations toward inherently excessive forms of secular faith in spite of the mantle of skepticism and openness. Believing itself secure amid its apparent grounding in a belief in "mere" or "common" man, "democratic faith" has frequently expressed an unreflective and unconscious zeal on behalf of the transformation of "common" man into an "uncommon," even godlike creature. Believing itself finally free of the passions and certainties formerly associated with the excesses of religious fanaticism, "democratic faith" has instead sought to divinize humankind and justify at various junctures the superior place of humanity in the natural order. Believing itself shorn of extreme belief, in contemporary times it has justified the most extreme belief in unbelief as the core "antifoundation" of democracy—incoherently concluding that, in the openness toward inegalitarian arguments, one cannot advance arguments on behalf of equality as "true" or "self-evident." Instead, faith in the culmination of a universal embrace of "openness" and "agonistic respect" will result in (infinitely pliable) democratic forms, (still contestable) democratic beliefs, and self-transformative (democratic? or Nietzschean?) citizens.

In its hostility to "traditional" religion—often provoked by pointing rightly to those moments of "traditional" religion's unarguable failings, its own shameful manifestations of fanaticism, its own blinkered unwillingness to open itself to those who differ in belief and tradition—the democratic faithful have overlooked, even blinded themselves unnecessarily to, those resources afforded by religious belief that are most helpful in raising the level of consciousness (and even thereby preventing) democratic faith's own slide into excessive ardor, and its flirtation with concomitant despair. In particular, religious faith can serve as a witness to the democratic tendency to divinize itself. In being reminded, in the words of Vaclav Havel, that "man is not God," we thereby implicitly acknowledge human imperfection, including the ultimate imperfection of democracy itself. There can be no secular apotheosis, no "Kingdom of God" on earth, no singular transformation of humanity into divine godhead. Democratic aspirations which rest on that implicit faith are born of a less reflective faith than the religious faith they attack, and actions taken in their name can be revealed for their fanaticism and hubris. The witness of religious faith reminds us that perfection is not the lot of humankind, that democracy is a hard discipline even as its ideal serves at once as an unreachable but necessary aspiration but also as an alluring temptation in our willingness to believe in its immanent realization. As Tocqueville sought to remind an increasingly democratic world, the fervent embrace of religious disbelief—undertaken in the belief that it reflected considered modesty—in fact represented a betrayal of fundamental humility. For, he wrote of "materialists," "when they believe they have sufficiently established that they are only brutes, they show themselves as proud as if they had demonstrated they were gods."[29]

A belief in the potential divination of humanity reflects, ironically, a fundamental mistrust of democracy that is no less severe than that wariness of earlier "reactionary" antidemocratic thinkers who are condemned by the democratic faithful for a lack of faith in the people. All that differs between proponents of democratic faith and the democratic incredulous is a belief in man's transformative potential. Yet neither position should be attractive to a moderate supporter of democracy—the democratic realist. A constant and conscious recognition of human insufficiency can, in fact, be supportive of democracy (contra antidemocrats) and can constrain the excesses of "democratic faith." Such recognition can serve as the basis for a modest, if potentially far more robust, belief in human equality, while forestalling temptations to believe that only when man can aspire to divinity can democracy flourish.

The recognition that "Man is not God" serves as a witness to, and protection from, temptations of excessive and optimistic forms of democratic faith. Democracy inevitably requires faith in some form—at the very least, "faith" must exist as a belief in, trust for, and confidence toward human ability and capacity for self-rule. Yet, our survey of belief in democratic transformation suggests that this same faith has inherent tendencies to go beyond this initial modest belief. In the absence of accompanying reminders of human frailty and insufficiency—such as those offered in the submerged "texts" embedded within the palimpsests of the Panthéon and the Goddess of Democracy—this tendency reflects a utopian vision as precarious as those ideological utopias that democratic faith fervently rejects. It is a faith with tendencies to be unaware of the extent and intensity of its own faith commitments, even, for many, of the fact that it is a faith. And in its long-standing hostility to traditional religious forms of faith—ones from which, curiously, it arises and upon which it relies (albeit in an altered form) for its own legitimacy—makes it all the more likely to reject those teachings of religious belief that point to human insufficiency, imperfection, and the undermining of the belief in human equality that arises from such a recognition. Instead, democracy becomes the promise of things to come rather than an imperfect form of governance of, by, and for frail human beings. We await the perfection of wished-for human capacity to godlike status—the fullest form of equality—rather than rest democracy upon our common and shared imperfections. We await the coming of the Kingdom of God on earth while we neglect the limited and imperfect polity of humans on earth.

Reading the Palimpsest, Part 2: "Wisdom of the Multitude"

It is arguable that fear, even despair, underlies "democratic faith," especially fear over the democratic capacity of ordinary citizens. For example, on the one hand, one finds innumerable nineteenth-century American optimistic expressions of belief in the common man. Yet, in spite of growing belief in democratic capacity of the citizenry, one also finds such expressions to be stated often in the midst of deep doubts about the democratic project. The existence of such doubts suggests that the language of democratic faith is resorted to as a means of holding at bay a potential state of democratic despair. Perhaps, surprisingly, one of the thinkers most fearful about the capacity for self-governance among ordinary citizens was America's most acclaimed prophet and defender of democracy, Walt Whitman: "I will not gloss over the appalling dangers of universal suffrage in the United States. In fact, it is to admit and face these dangers that I am writing. To him or her within whose thought rages the battle, advancing, retreating, between democracy's convictions, aspirations, and the people's crudeness, vice, caprices, I write this essay. . . . Genuine belief seems to have left us . . ., nor is humanity itself believed in."[30]

In the face of cynicism, even despair, about the possibility of genuine and transformed democratic life, Whitman wrote in large part to renew and deepen the democratic faith, indeed to declare that he would be the first among its new secular prophets.[31] Whitman sought to persuade his fellow citizens to avoid despair and believe (again) in his or her fellow humans, to acknowledge the advance of democracy in the world, and its slow fruition into full-fledged secular apotheosis within America:

> Advancing visibly, it still more advances invisibly. Underneath the fluctuations of the expressions of society, as well as the movements of politics of the leading nations of the world, we see steadily pressing ahead and strengthening itself, even in the midst of immense tendencies toward aggregation, this image of complete separateness in separation, of personal dignity, of a single person, whether male or female, characterized in the main, not from extrinsic acquirements or position, but in the pride of himself or herself alone; and, as an eventual conclusion or summing up (or else the entire scheme of things is aimless, a cheat, a crash), the simple idea that the last, best dependence is to be upon humanity itself, and its own inherent normal, full-grown qualities without any superstitious support whatever. This idea

of perfect individualism it is indeed that deepest tinges and gives character to the idea of the aggregate.[32]

Humanity is at once to be seen as utterly self-dependent without need to resort to "superstition" and yet simultaneously viewed as the embodiment of "perfect individualism" that will accompany this rejection of encrusted religious institutions and embrace of human-centered political perfectibility. If this is not borne out, then we rightly feel betrayed by the universe—it's all just "aimless, a cheat, a crash." One senses that Whitman's faith, confronted with his own disillusionment in the aftermath of the Civil War, moved him to ever more fervent expressions of his confidence in humanity's democratic capacities, ultimately moving him to declare the need for "divine pride of man in himself (the radical foundation of the new religion)."[33]

Democratic faith requires a new conception of humankind, one altogether shorn of tradition and yet at the same time devoted to some remnant of traditional belief in human equality. It is a humanity of unlimited potential yet necessarily cognizant of its political devotions, resulting in a concomitant allegiance to radical freedom and radical democracy. Human beings are at once conceived as individualists and "species beings," the two seemingly incommensurable existences forged together through the alchemy of democratic faith.[34] Whitman echoes this Emersonian theme that democratic individualism is made possible by, and encompassed within, a greater whole which transcendental discernment allows us to see in glimpses and occasionally by means of epiphany and quasi-religious revelation.[35] Belief in the wholeness of creation once afforded by a belief in God is replaced by a belief in the "oversoul," the "common mind," or "cosmic consciousness."

In an effort to resist earlier grandiose expressions of faith in democracy, as well as inclinations to forms of democratic despair, rare articulations of "democratic faith" by contemporary thinkers (ones who recognize the quasi-religious origins of so much of democratic discourse) have sought to render more modest articulations of their faith. Characteristically traditional religious faith continues to be rejected, but, among some, the calls for human transformation are muted. Yet, the very modesty of such contemporary defenses reveals that democratic faith cannot finally escape an assertion of fundamental human goodness of the kind earlier endorsed by Rousseau, Emerson, Whitman, and Dewey. This "utopian" sentiment remains detectable even within the modest and compelling account of "radical democracy" by C. Douglas Lummis.[36]

Confronting the thorny question of the basis for faith of any kind, Lummis suggests four possible "moves": sentimentalism, cynicism, despair, and religious faith. He rejects all these in favor of democratic faith, but not before discussing at greatest length his reasons for rejecting religious faith in terms that are more generous and sympathetic than most proponents of democratic faith, such as the dismissive tones of Sidney Hook. Lummis appreciates that religious faith offers a "realistic view of the world," a conclusion that most committed secularists are unable to discern given their assumption that religious belief acts as a balm or assuaging fantasy. "There is no trace of sentimentalism in the great heroes of faith, Abraham or Job, or in the great theologians such as Augustine and Aquinas. On the contrary, faith in the Absolute gives one a chillingly clear picture of how far humankind has Fallen" (148). While such faith prevents the prospect of sentimentalism, it also holds at bay the temptation to despair. One maintains the ability to act in a world that one recognizes to be riven with imperfection and at an unbridgeable distance from perfection.

Nonetheless, Lummis rejects religious faith as a plausible candidate for belief in modernity. "After Ludwig Feuerbach—and after Marx, after Kierkegaard, after Nietzsche—we know that faith is, indeed, a 'move.' We know, that is, that if we want to understand faith we must look at it as an act taken in this world, not as something provided us from outside the world. This view includes understanding that the object of faith is also a human construction and a human choice" (148–149). While attracted to the religious disposition that at once resists sentimentalism, cynicism, and despair, Lummis concludes that "we" modern humans are all too aware of the falsity of religious belief and thus cannot "in good faith" any longer place any real credence in so obviously a human-contrived object of belief. We exist in a world shorn of transcendent objects of belief, permitted only to believe now in the original contriver of such objects, humanity. Lummis admits that there is danger to replacing God with man as an object of faith but only because of the distance between one's hopes for humanity and the sad evidence of one's senses: "it can cause one to pass rapidly through the stages of sentimental humanism to disillusion and despair and finally to cynicism" (150). Faith remains necessary, but not a self-deceiving faith nor a faith that induces disillusionment. The faith based both in reality and which is reality-resistant, which acts as a prod to action but stops short of calling for brutalizing "true belief" is democratic faith—"the true faith of which all other faiths are evasions; the faith of which all other faiths are imitations or indirect expressions or distorted forms; a *radical* faith, at once the most natural and the most difficult" (153).

Lummis's realism about humanity's capacities is refreshing in the midst of so many expressions of democratic faith that posit a transformed or divinized form of humankind. Lummis argues that such a faith is possible because it rests on commonsense identification that trust, at some level, underlies all human relations. In contrast to those tales of bloody civic foundings captured in tales about Romulus and Remus, or nearly undertaken by Abraham as he prepared to sacrifice Isaac, democratic faith rests instead on a fundamental belief in, and widespread evidence of, human trustworthiness. "Democratic faith, common-sense faith, is founded differently, by people who do *not* kill their brothers and children" (152).[37]

Lummis's is an attractive statement of "democratic faith" in the ordinary decencies of human beings. However, Lummis may himself be too sanguine about these decencies in the absence of hard thought about what goes into creating, cultivating, and sustaining such decencies. "Democratic realism" resists equally the millenarian belief in transformation, as well as the complacent belief that humans are "good enough" without due consideration of the viciousness and even evil of which all humans are capable. While Lummis resists interventionist attempts to initiate "democratic transformation" by means of "changing, as it were, human nature itself," in the words of Rousseau, whether through "civil religion" or scientific amelioration or the assumption of historical or evolutionary progress, Lummis instead asserts a certain sanguine view of preexisting human beneficence. He assumes that human beings are fundamentally well intentioned, even "good" by nature, and that, shorn of obstacles to its realization, democracy is the most "natural" condition suited to humankind—the "truest" object of faith.

The very rejection of "democratic transformation" amid an assertion of "democratic faith" points to the horns of the dilemma on which contemporary democratic theorists uneasily reside. Either humanity must be made good enough for democracy—therefore calling for transformation—or humanity is currently good enough, leading potentially to disillusionment when humankind fails to exhibit the democratic virtues dreamed of by the faithful. Lummis's basic claim about human decency—the care we exhibit to those closest to us—might be considered a dubious or debatable basis for more extensive "democratic faith," and potentially leads to democratic cynicism. A cycle of faith in human goodness can too easily bring on disillusionment, and then in turn lead to a reassertion of even greater democratic faith that, recognizing contemporary shortcomings, points instead to future possibility. By contrast, "democratic realism" recognizes at once the fundamental imperfection of humans—their tendency to self-aggrandizement, overestimation of their own powers, and viciousness—and yet also a limited potential for democratic virtue that can be nourished and cultivated. Such a "mixed" picture has its beginnings at the very origins of political philosophy, especially in the thought of Aristotle, where one encounters a wholly different portrait of humankind—one which is not conceived in hostility toward democracy nor toward human potential but which recognizes limitations on the easy assumption of the fruition of either because of the inescapable viciousness of humankind. Indeed, addressing the question of whether humankind's natural decency is to be detected in our unwillingness "to kill our brothers and children," as suggested by Lummis, Aristotle echoes his long-standing analysis that human nature is fundamentally "mixed"— even, or especially, in light of that most evident sign of human decency, that is, the love we express toward our own. For, he writes, "[one's] spirit is more stirred up against relatives and friends when it thinks it has been slighted than against strangers. . . . For, in the case of those from whom people suppose a debt of kindness is due, they consider that, in addition to the harm inflicted, they have been deprived of this debt as well. Hence the sayings 'harsh are the wars of brothers' and 'those who love to the limit hate to the limit'" (1328a).[38] It is no less true in our own time than in Aristotle's that more often than not murder is committed by and against relatives and lovers, and wars are fought between neighbors and "brothers."

Nevertheless, Aristotle would seem to be a natural ally to the "democratic faithful" in sharing Lummis's faith in the capacities of ordinary citizens. Evidently alone among the ancients, he expresses the greatest confidence in the capacity of ordinary people to govern themselves justly, even arguing at one point that rule by the multitude is in certain respects superior to any other form of rule.[39] In Book 3 of *Politics*, Aristotle famously defended the possibility that the multitude may collectively evince more wisdom and good judgment than even the expert few. While some have understood his defense of the "wisdom of the multitude" as problematic at best, others have asserted that Aristotle's argument should be understood as one of the singular and persuasive defenses of democracy in antiquity.[40] While position taking is to be expected, however, what tends to be overlooked is the typically "mixed" quality of Aristotle's analysis—one that at once both endorses and qualifies his stated confidence in democracy.

Aristotle offers a varied set of justifications for the superiority of the rule of the many. His first set of justifications provides the strongest argument on behalf of the greater wisdom of the multitude. He writes that "the many, each of whom is not a serious man [*spoudiaos*], nevertheless could, when they have come together, be better than those few best—not indeed individually but as a whole" (1281a). Three analogies are advanced in order to demonstrate the superior judgment of the many:

- First, "meals furnished collectively are better than meals furnished at one person's expense";
- Second, "for each of them, though many, could have a part in virtue and prudence, and just as they could, when joined together in a multitude, become one human being with many feet, hands, and senses, so also could they become one in character and thought";
- Third, "that is why the many are better judges of the works of music and the poets, for one of them judges one part and another and all of them the whole." (1281a–b)

Many commentators have rightly noted that each of these is a curious and debatable analogy, none of which is, by itself, self-evident. The first and third do not seem to reflect the realities of perceived culinary or artistic/critical excellence and, upon cursory reflection, do not by themselves convincingly refute the claims of the superiority of expertise.[41] The second has struck a number of commentators as advancing a grotesque image, one that more reflects the likelihood of clumsiness and disorganization, and suggests the need for leadership and organization.[42]

Yet, Aristotle seems to choose these analogies with care, since in each case he seeks to stress, above all, the collective nature of good judgment. The apparent excellence of experts is rendered more dubious by means of the specific analogies inasmuch as Aristotle here is not only stressing the deficiencies of individuals within the mass—those people who are not "serious"—but the deficiencies of *all* individuals, including experts. Thus Aristotle emphasizes the importance of shared participation not by means of an analogy of a gourmet meal prepared for a single individual (for whom an expert may indeed be better able to make recommendations) but rather a large shared meal in which the many diners will bring to the table different tastes, backgrounds, and inclinations. An artistic expert may be able to give an impressive account of the historical context or the technical specifics of a work of art but might easily overlook aspects of the artwork that fall outside the domain of artistic expertise (a farmer may be able to tell us something quite different and interesting about Monet's haystacks than perhaps an expert on impressionism could). By means of these analogies, Aristotle seeks to point to the shared insufficiencies common to *every* human being—even experts, who, by definition can only be an expert in one particular area of knowledge. Once the analogies are extended into the political arena, they become even more evidently sound: there are no comprehensive political questions that can be solved by recourse to expertise (assuming, as Aristotle does, that by "political" one means questions or issues that require political—that is, deliberative, contested, and prudential—solutions).

These analogies—particularly the first and third—also point to the superiority of shared participation in deliberation regarding *human* things. As Aristotle points out in his *Nicomachean Ethics* (*NE*), "exactness" is not to be expected in all disciplines. In matters related to human sciences one can only achieve inexact solutions subject to "much difference of opinion and uncertainty," in contrast to the natural sciences in which a greater degree of certainty and exactness can be expected (*NE*, 1094b, 1104a). Given the "inexactness" of human-centered inquiries, "expertise" is not comparably applicable as it is in the natural sciences. Indeed, it is arguable that the very inexact nature of human-centered inquiry renders the very concept of "expert" suspect and dubious. Given the multivalenced, complex, inexact, and permanently unsettled nature of political phenomena, no single individual can claim a uniquely knowledgeable perspective from which singular solutions can be derived. Aristotle's second analogy to a many-limbed body—while seemingly grotesque to some commentators—reflects, in fact, the cumbersomeness of political life itself: its occasional ungainliness and even outright ugliness, its desire to grasp at different goals and to lurch in contradictory directions, and its multiple ways of seeing any one (or seemingly one) issue or phenomenon. Yet, Aristotle's analogy to a human body—however unsettling and uncanny—nevertheless stresses the *commonality* of political life. However ungainly, politics is a common undertaking and necessarily benefits from the multiple perspectives and contributions of its many parts.[43]

None of this would be in any way objectionable, nor possibly even distinguishable, from the arguments and beliefs of the "democratic faithful." Yet, Aristotle is also remarkably circumspect, even cautious, about the likelihood of such a well-governed democracy coming to pass. While not disallowing the possibility of such self-governed excellence, he holds it to be difficult and even unlikely:

> Now whether this superiority of the many relative to the few serious can exist in the case of any populace and any multitude is unclear, though, by Zeus, it is perhaps clear that it cannot in the case of some of them. Otherwise, the same argument could also be made to fit beasts, and how, practically speaking, do some people differ from beasts? But nothing prevents what has been said from being true of *some* multitude. (1281b16–22 [emphasis added]; also 1283b33–35)

Perhaps many, even most, "multitudes" are comparable to "beasts" by Aristotle's estimation, and thus no more capable of just self-rule than irrational brute creatures. Far from suggesting that the shared political life necessarily results in superior judgment by the multitude to that of the "serious" few, Aristotle departs here quite radically from the "democratic faithful" in suggesting that such shared excellence is only achieved with difficulty and, indeed, is not a virtue that arises naturally from the inherent features of shared democratic life. Virtues appropriate to democracy must "precede" democracy and thus can exist apart from democracy (just as democracy can exist apart from such civic virtue).[44] "Mutual respect" or "enlarged consciousness"—in the language of Gutmann and Thompson or Arendt, respectively—is not a result of democracy but arguably is its necessary but not sufficient cause.

Aristotle seems to take away grounds for faith in the multitude even as he has just moments before extended such confidence. While entertaining the possibility that rule by the multitude may be a more excellent basis of governance due to collective wisdom and the combination of individually insufficient but collectively wise plurality, Aristotle quickly notes that such a possibility is available to a limited number of "multitudes"; indeed, by not specifying what multitude might qualify as superior to mere "beasts," Aristotle even hints that the superiority of the many may be true in theory but not, as far as he can tell, in practice. Aristotle, then, contemplates and even accepts the sorts of arguments made on behalf of the "wisdom of the multitude" that one might expect to be advanced by the "democratic faithful" without concluding either that mere recognition of such potential excellence allows for its easy fruition or that its fruition is contingent on a radical transformation of humanity. By suggesting that many "multitudes" do not rise even to the level of "humanity," Aristotle suggests that democracy is the regime of human beings—indeed, the regime that, by definition, would arise when most or all of its citizens had "become" fully human—and not a regime of either humans "as they are" by nature nor what can be expected when humanity rises above the human condition and approaches divinity. Aristotle's sights are considerably lower than those who profess a "democratic faith."

How, then, do we distinguish those multitudes that are "beastly" from those that rule with judiciousness, prudence, and virtue? Indeed, how do we make such a polity come into being? How do we differentiate a vicious democracy from one of excellence? Aristotle first suggests that human beings only "become" fully human within political communities, stating famously in Book 1,

> The man who first united people in such a partnership was the greatest of benefactors. For as human beings are the best of all animals when perfected, so they are worst when divorced from law and right (*nomou kai dikes*). The reason is that injustice is most difficult to deal with when furnished with weapons, and the weapons a human being has are meant by nature to go along with prudence and virtue, but it is only too possible to turn them to contrary uses. Consequently, if a human being lacks virtue, he is a most unholy and savage thing." (1253a30–37)

His argument that humans are "by nature" political beings does not prevent humans from falling short of that natural *telos*: indeed, he suggests throughout *Politics* and *Ethics* that the full flourishing of human beings is accomplished only with great difficulty and a good deal of luck. Most important, what distinguishes Aristotle from the "democratic faithful" is his insistence that democracy is a regime best suited to ordinary (albeit, in practice, exceptional) human beings who have flourished by means of a fulfillment of their nature, not a transformation of their humanity. Democracy is the realm of the ordinary made common and the common made extraordinary, of the virtuous made general, and of the natural fulfilled.[45]

Yet, even a teleological explanation does not tell us enough. For throughout *Politics* Aristotle describes regimes that could be described as acceptable—sufficient in virtue and justice—that fall well short of being considered democratic. One surmises, at the very least, that these regimes are governed with sufficient justice not to permit the conclusion that its multitudes are less than entirely human. Even full participation in a regime is not sufficient to conclude that such rule is in itself praiseworthy. Indeed, aside from his brief praise of the potential "wisdom of the multitude," Aristotle consistently spares no criticism for the greater likelihood of viciousness manifested in democracy (e.g., 1280a; 1291b–1292a). Democracy is most typically a mere "partiality" of the political whole, better conceived as the collected interest of the poor (who happen to be more numerous) than representing the rarified collective views of all (1279b20–35). When Aristotle describes the potential "wisdom of the multitude" in Book 3, he is engaging in a fundamental redefinition of democracy.

Throughout this section of *Politics* in which Aristotle entertains the possible superiority of "the rule of the many," Aristotle constantly uses language of commonality. Though individually not "serious" (*spoudaios*), the many can judge better "when they have come together" (*sunelthontas*) and "collectively" decide (*sumpantas*; 1281b1–4). "When joined together" (*sunel-*

thontas; 1281b5) the various separated parts of virtue and prudence are combined, whereas "in separation, however, each man lacks the completeness necessary for passing judgment" (1281b37). Since Aristotle has previously critically described the form of "democracy" typically arising from the combination of the many *poor* who seek to advance only their partial political interest, we have to conclude that here Aristotle is investing these characterizations of "coming together" with special significance that distinguishes this "many" from the partiality of typical democracies. Aristotle essentially appears to be delineating two forms of democracy, a distinction he only explicates in fuller detail in a (too brief) discussion in Book 6.

While apparently distinguishing between four different kinds of democracies, Aristotle, in fact, opens his discussion of the various features of democracy by describing two fundamental forms of democracy. Departing from his usual assumption that democracy's key feature is simple numerical equality, he begins by noting that "freedom (*eleutheria*) is the supposition of the democratic regime" (1317a40–41). He then describes the two forms that this fundamental supposition of liberty can take in democracy. The first form of freedom "is to rule and be ruled in turn" (*archesthai kai archein*; 1317a41–1317b2). This is his famous definition of citizenship (1275a22): yet only here, within the context of a discussion about democracy in Book 6, does Aristotle associate the activity of "ruling and being ruled in turn" with *eleutheria*, or "freedom." Indeed, in discussing how one best exercises rule among others who are "similar in birth and free," Aristotle stresses that freedom is premised upon the necessity of learning the discipline of *being* ruled, above all:

> This rule we call political rule, and the ruler must learn it by being ruled, just as one learns to be a cavalry commander by serving under a cavalry commander, or to be a general over an army by serving under a general and commanding a regiment and a company. Hence it was nobly said that one cannot rule well without having been ruled. And while virtue in these cases is different, the good citizen must learn and be able both to be ruled and to rule. This is, in fact, the virtue of a citizen, to know rule over the free from both sides. (1277b7–15)

Moreover, Aristotle continues, it is precisely this combination of different and seemingly opposite virtues that also distinguish "the good man" (*andros de agathou*; 1277b17), combining both "moderation" and "justice" of a ruler and a subject. The meeting point of the good citizen and good man is precisely in this ability to rule others with a thought to their welfare, one that has been cultivated and deepened by means of a training in being well ruled by others. This is not reciprocity in theory but rather mutual governance in fact, a set of learned practices that results in democratic habituation.

Such shared governance requires at once a subordination of our immediate inclinations, our narrow interests, and our partial desires by means of an education in being ruled. Democracy defined according to this first supposition of "ruling and being ruled in turn" in fact militates against a Hobbesian definition of freedom as the ability or capacity to achieve what one desires. Freedom is achieved through the activity of mutual rule, not by dint of self-fulfillment or self-satisfaction. Indeed, by Aristotle's lights, only in such a political setting is one's whole humanity allowed its full fruition. As described by Delba Winthrop,

> the partisan of democracy demands political equality because he believes that the exercise of freedom is a worthy choice for man. The defense of the democratic principle of equal participation is not made in terms of governmental efficiency or stability or the psychic satisfaction it provides, but rests on the belief that being a whole human being means being a political participant of this sort. Democracy is demanded not for the sake of a right to do my own thing, but because of an obligation to live as a man ought.[46]

Aristotle then offers a second, contrasting definition of the "supposition" of democratic government:

> Another sort of freedom is to live as one likes, for they say this is the work of freedom since to live as one does not like is characteristic of the slave. This, then, is the second defining mark of democracy. From it has come the feature of not being ruled, by anyone at all but preferably, failing that, of being ruled in turns; and that is how this defining mark contributes to freedom based on equality. [1317b11–17]

According to this second definition of freedom one sees that democratic governance is only accepted as a second-best choice in the absence of the opportunity not to be ruled "by anyone at all." The desire "to live as one likes"—seen in contrast to the constraints of slavery—leads to the most cherished if secret wish to act as tyrant, even if the less attractive option imposed by political reality forces one to act merely as a grudging democrat.

Lest one think this characterization of "two democracies" is a curious and dismissible Aristotelian anachronism, consider a more recent formulation of this problem. In a much-discussed article entitled "A Paradox in the Theory of Democracy," published in 1962, the political theorist Richard Wollheim pointed out the difficulty that democracy posed to modern assumptions. On the one hand, he wrote, as a citizen of a democracy one can believe that "Policy A" ought to be enacted and thereupon try to articulate that preference by means of one's vote. However, it may come about that a majority of one's fellow citizens vote instead for "Policy B," thereby defeating the enactment of one's preference. As an individual, I continue to prefer Policy A—its electoral defeat has not persuaded me otherwise—but as a democratic citizen, I am also in a position now of thinking Policy B ought to be enacted, since, as a democrat, I defer to the will of the majority. Wollheim poses the apparent paradox thus: "How can the citizen accept the [democratic] machine's choice, which involves his thinking that B ought to be enacted when, as we already know, he is of the opinion, of the declared opinion, that A ought to be enacted?"[47]

Of course, this is only a paradox to the extent that a priority is placed upon individual self-interest as in much modern liberal and democratic theory.

Wollheim rightly notes that one might, in a democratic age, merely *appear* to prefer Policy B while in fact harboring the secret wish to parlay that appearance into a position of power within the democracy. A person motivated at every point by self-interest would merely use the machinery of democracy to achieve power, at which point "he would probably try to end the democratic process" (thereby altogether resembling the Aristotelian democrat who craves "not to be ruled at all"). The problem, states Wollheim, "arises how we are to distinguish such a man from the genuine believer in Democracy."[48] Yet, given Wollheim's basic premise—that democracy is defined by citizens fundamentally motivated by self-interest—it remains unclear whether there could truly exist a "genuine believer in Democracy" in the first instance. Democracy so understood is a means to power.

Wollheim concludes by attempting to suggest that both conditions can apply—one can genuinely prefer Policy A without thereby necessarily repudiating Policy B—without adequately being able to express how this can be so, and why fundamentally self-interested individuals ought to give any credence whatsoever to the preference of the majority. The empty formalism of Wollheim's articulation of the problem of democracy is revealed when we reconsider whether democracy can truly be based most fundamentally upon self-interest. Moving from philosophic abstraction, we might pose the question: If I detest slavery and vote against it, but come up short in a majority vote, what prevents me from being a "believer in democracy" and endorsing Policy A (i.e., slavery) inasmuch as the majority would demand my compliance with this law? In short, why become a "believer in democracy"? A belief in democracy—as in the case of Stephen Douglas's position in defense of "popular sovereignty" on the question of slavery—must rest on a set of assumptions that are preliminary to majoritarianism and thus, when opposed by a majority, can easily resist such an antidemocratic outcome. One is a believer in democracy *not* because one believes in the superiority of majority rule in the first instance but because one initially embraces an unassailable belief in human equality. Democracy must have a foundation, or it is a house of cards.

For Aristotle, the all-too-common transformation of the ideal of "political" freedom—resulting in a democracy of mutually self-governing citizens—into an ideal of freedom "to do as one likes" lies at the crux of the "trial of democracy." Once the ideal of individual freedom is allowed to undermine the commitment to equal governance, democracy becomes either the exercise of raw political power by one "partiality" over another or devolves into the outright rejection of any rule at all. At base, the distinction between these two forms of democratic freedom underlies Aristotle's alternating high regard for, and deep mistrust of, democracy. Unlike the democratic faithful, Aristotle does not assume that the two forms of freedom are easily reconcilable by means of a transformation of human nature.[49] Instead, the two tend toward being mutually exclusive, and depending upon democracy's respective embrace of one or the other form of freedom, so, too, depends Aristotle's assessment of whether the "many" are likely to act out of mutual regard and respect or out of partial interest and personal aggrandizement. Democracy properly conceived, he argues, must be based on the principle of rule for the benefit of the whole, not for the advantage of the (poor) many. Thus, as if anticipating the cry that "the cure for the ailments of democracy is more democracy," Aristotle suggests that properly constituted democracy ought to resist its own proclivities. A democracy should "always seem to be speaking on the behalf of the well-off," just as a well-governed oligarchy should "always seem to be speaking on behalf of the populace" (1310a). The corrective for any regime is to act less like "itself," to avoid extremes toward which it is inherently inclined. Democracy must avoid defining itself as the system that allows each citizen "to do as one likes" and instead promote the more ambiguous ideal of freedom that results from considerable mutual- and self-restraint. One cannot intend tyranny over other citizens, just as a majority cannot intend tyranny over a minority.[50] In short, one must rule out of regard for those one rules, an outcome best achieved by means of a training in, and expectation of, being ruled by others.

Aristotle thus appears both to regard democracy highly and also to deeply mistrust it—and, indeed, any form of political rule, but in all events avoid excessive faith and pessimism. For politics, Aristotle ultimately recognizes, is a sphere of imperfection—the realm of governance that arises from human insufficiency, even assuming the unlikely possibility of the full flourishing of human capacity. While many readers perceive Aristotle as an alternative to Plato in his insistence on preserving politics as a realm of plurality and prudential compromise, throughout his work Aristotle also warns his readers that humans are too easily tempted to think of the realm of politics as sufficient and autonomous in itself. From such a proclivity comes the nearly unavoidable but democratically undermining belief that one should "live as one likes." In a revealing analogy, Aristotle reminds his readers of the temptation to think that "medical science is in authority over health," just as they might be tempted to say that "political science (*ten politiken*) governs the gods, because it gives orders about everything in the state (*polis*)" (*NE*, 1145a6–12). Just as there is a condition called "health" that is not created by humans—an ideal to which the medical sciences are oriented but which it does not initially create—Aristotle suggests that political science is subordinate to considerations beyond even the city it arguably governs. Humans need to be reminded of their createdness, the givenness of an existence they do not create and to which they are subject, and, by extension, the extent to which thoroughgoing autonomy is a false ideal. This lesson is as true for individuals as it is for polities. Thus, when speaking of the first sets of exchange that form partnerships, Aristotle again resorts to a reminder of the presence of the divine as a standard by which we remind ourselves of the extent to which we rely upon others: "It is by their mutual contribution that men are held together. That is the reason why [the state] erects a sanctuary of the Graces [*Charis*] in a prominent place, in order to promote mutual exchange.

For that is the proper province of gratitude; we should return our services to one who has done us a favor, and at another time take the initiative in doing him a favor" (*NE*, 1133a). By means of such reminders—that the virtues central to democracy are learned with difficulty, discipline, and often not at all—Aristotle points out humanity's inextricably mixed and imperfect nature. Among the foremost of human imperfections is the inclination to overlook our partiality and imperfection, and thereby to think of ourselves as self-sufficient—a temptation that makes democracy at once necessary, dangerous, and almost insuperably difficult to achieve. Democracy is a trial as much as a possibility.

CREATING A "WE"

Hannah Arendt's recommendation of a form of "enlarged mentality" appears largely to echo many of Aristotle's reflections on the distinction between potentially virtuous and observably vicious forms of democracy. Democracy requires of its citizens, perhaps above all, the ability to think outside one's immediate perceived self-interest, to aim toward a comprehension of the good of the whole, even if limits to human perception, sympathy, and understanding require recognition that such a comprehensive vision can only be imperfectly achieved. Arendt recommends this "faculty of judgment" in preference to a purely rational and internal "dialogue between me and myself" undertaken to determine, by means of the Kantian categorical imperative, the right principles for action.[51] While Arendt argues that such "enlarged mentality" can be reflectively undertaken—that it "finds itself always and primarily, even if I am quite alone in making up my mind, in an anticipated communication with others with whom I know I must finally come to some agreement"—she goes on to insist that it cannot be fully achieved in the absence of contact with other people, with fellow citizens and varied interlocutors. "This enlarged way of thinking," she continues, "which as judgment knows how to transcend its own individual limitations, on the other hand cannot function in strict isolation or solitude; it needs the presence of others 'in whose place' it must think, whose perspectives it must take into consideration, and without whom it never has the opportunity to operate at all."[52]

Contemporary "agonistic" democratic theorists—ones who stridently dismiss "foundational" limits on democracy in the name of democratic openness—frequently advance such claims in Arendtian terms, promising the flourishing of expanded mentalities by means of the interplay of individuals in a political mêlée. Only through the rough and tumble of politics itself can such "enlarged mentalities" come into being. Liberal constitutional, cultural, religious, and other constraints actually undermine democracy, creating cramped and narrowly self-interested calculators instead of expansive and agonistically respectful citizens. Ironically, only through the absolute unleashing of every potential conflict in politics can one arrive at a truly consensual democratic polity—now not imposed a priori by means of abstract "contractual" consent but rather *in* and *through* politics itself, arrived at unmediated and hence fully embraced and realized.[53]

The persistence of democratic belief amid the embrace of thoroughgoing openness is reflected perhaps most strikingly in the terms of Arendt's explicit rejection of "foundational" claims that many otherwise assert undergird the American regime and democracy itself.[54] Arendt dismisses the notion that America's Declaration of Independence has attained its long-standing and permanent significance by dint of its self-declared universality. Its greatness, she asserts, "owes nothing to its natural-law philosophy."[55] In a stunning insight Arendt instead highlights the *consensual* aspect of the Declaration's most "self-evident" claims by focusing on the phrase "we hold." The presence of these two words, she contends, reveals the dubious relevance of even "self-evident" truths in political matters:

> There is perhaps nothing surprising in that the Age of Enlightenment should have become aware of the compelling nature of axiomatic or self-evident truth. . . . The fallacy of this position . . . was to believe that these mathematical "laws" were of the same nature of the laws of a community, or that the former could somehow inspire the latter. Jefferson must have been dimly aware of this, for otherwise he would not have indulged in the somewhat incongruous phrase, "*We hold* these truths to be self-evident," but would have said: These truths are self-evident, namely, they possess a power to compel which is as irresistible as despotic power, they are not held by us but we are held by them; they stand in no need of argument.[56]

Arendt rejected the "despotic power" of philosophical truth as fundamentally "unpolitical by nature."[57] "Self-evidence" is irrelevant in political affairs if such principles are not recognized and agreed upon by the citizenry. By stressing the importance of the words "we hold" that preceded the Declaration's axiomatic claims, Arendt pointed to Jefferson's recognition, however unconscious, that in public life such "truths" become politically relevant only when they enter into the sphere of "opinion." Thus "the statement 'All men are created equal' is not self-evident but stands in need of agreement and consent—that equality, if it is to be politically relevant, is a matter of opinion, and not 'the truth.'"[58]

Arendt acknowledges an almost heretical possibility that equality itself is nothing more than "opinion." Equality is a widely held but finally unproveable belief dressed in the clothing of "political truth," but its actual legitimacy comes from the fact that it is widely *held* to be true and not from its inherent truthfulness. A polity that operates on the assumption that humans are by nature "unequal" is no more "right" or "wrong" than one devoted to Jefferson's "self-evident" proposition. In a world of open, agonal, antifoundational contestation, even this supposed "truth" must be open to revision and outright rejection, and there are no unshakeable grounds or knockdown reasons for its permanent preservation. Thus the apparent desirability of "agonal respect" is also contestable, since it, too, appears to rely implicitly on a willing acknowledgment among all contesting parties of a form of basic, precedent moral equality. The recommendation for equality, for mutual respect, for basic recognition of human dignity are all "contestable," open to continuous revision and finally subject to rejection. Thoroughgoing democratic openness requires the willingness to permit the refutation of democracy, and its defense can only be made in the name of a partial and partisan devotion to an opinion that humans are political equals.

On one level Arendt's striking observation is irrefutable: the "self-evidence" of equality will have as little effect in a regime based on a belief in human inequality as the self-evidence of 2 + 2 would have in a regime that insisted on the presence of a miracle which required the answer to be 5. Only by means of argument and persuasion would both regimes be moved to give up their respective beliefs in inequality or mathematical absurdity. Equality's "self-evidence" is not tantamount to its instantaneous embrace, much less its political realization, a fact that must have been all too obvious to the writers and signers of the Declaration (facing an impending war with Britain and amid an acceptance of chattel slavery) as much as it is to equality's sometimes despairing proponents today. Lincoln's subtle but revealing change of language eighty-six years after the Declaration also reflects this recognition: equality is a "proposition" more than anything else, a belief that must be tested and proven and continually defended in the hard reality of a political world often resistant to this core democratic assumption.[59]

Yet Arendt's insight demands further reflection: by concluding that the phrase "we hold" reveals human equality to rest most fundamentally on opinion, Arendt implicitly places more emphasis on the verb "hold" than on the pronoun "we." Equality is the result of our active belief, a willed agreement between minds. Political belief of any form, finally, must be forged by pure exercise of will. By means of "holding" a belief in equality, Arendt implies, "we" create a "we" of equal citizens. Yet, obviously, an implicit emphasis on the verb "hold" begs an unavoidable question: who is the "we" who "hold" this belief in the first place? How does a mass of separate and agonistic "I's" come to "hold" a shared belief, even come to a preliminary willingness to engage in the political dialogue necessary to develop, inculcate, and instantiate this belief?

This question of "creating a 'We'" occupied Arendt in her last spoken and published work, in particular the intended middle volume of her planned three-volume work, *The Life of the Mind* (Arendt never completed the third volume, "Judgment," leaving behind two volumes, *Thinking* and *Willing*, and voluminous attempts by scholars to speculate on the main outlines of her unfinished last volume based on lectures and other notes).[60] In *Willing*, Arendt sought to disassociate "philosophical willing" from the forging of a political "we," noting that "willing" construed as the ability to forge a new and distinct self could lead to a wholly divisive form of self-differentiation and mutual antagonism:

> The individual, fashioned by the will and aware that it could be different from what it is (character, unlike bodily appearance or talents and abilities, is not given to the self at birth) always tends to assert an "I-myself" against an indefinite "they"—all the others that I, as an individual, am *not*. Nothing indeed can be more frightening than the notion of solipsistic freedom—the "feeling" that my standing apart, isolated from everyone else, is due to free will, that nothing and nobody can be held responsible for it by me myself.[61]

In contrast to this "frightening" form of philosophical willing, Arendt highlighted a "We" that arises "wherever men live together" and "is always engaged in changing our common world."[62] *How* this "We" comes into being remains a mystery for Arendt, entirely subject to a "predicament of not-knowing": it is enough to offer its existence as a fact and to reflect on the foundational myths and legends that serve as narratives of collective self-understanding.[63] The "darkness and mystery" that shroud the origins of a "We" point to "the abyss of nothingness that opens up before any deed that cannot be accounted for by a reliable chain of cause and effect."[64] Also "an abyss of pure spontaneity," the creation of a "We" appears equally in Arendt's allusive description to be an exercise and result of willing but one aimed at political constitution rather than philosophical individuation.[65] A "We" apparently arises "wherever men live together," but nothing more can be said about this fact. The "we" of the Declaration's "we hold" can no more be explained than any other "We" that owes its origins to some shrouded past.

This conclusion seems to evince unwarranted absence of simple curiosity. Does not the fact of the existence of a "we" that necessarily precedes the "holding" of a belief already imply the existence of some fundamental equality that had to exist before the "holding" of a belief in equality? Moreover, does not the very possibility of conceiving of a "we" already point to the "self-evidence" of equality, inasmuch as a "we" is unthinkable unless "we" is based on a form of commonality at the outset? In short, does not even Arendt's assumption that equality rests necessarily on an opinion that "we hold" build in a certain assumption about the prior existence of equality's presence by dint of the acknowledgment of the existence of a human "we"?

Of course, a "we" can be limited and view itself in exclusive and exclusionist terms. Nevertheless, such a claim to the equality of our "we" points to the persistent challenge that such a preliminary and incomplete acknowledgment of equality entails. Such a "we"—equal if limited—by necessity must create narratives, fictions, and an array of justifications as to why such recognition of equality should and must be withheld from equally human "others." Arguments finally excluding others from our "we" must be devised on the basis of another's nonhumanness.

Arendt concludes *Willing* in an Augustinian vein, observing that humans exist in a realm of freedom by dint of their "natality"—the fact of being born. "[W]e are *doomed* to be free by virtue of being born, no matter whether we like freedom or abhor its arbitrariness, are 'pleased' with it or prefer to escape its awesome responsibility by electing some form of fatalism."[66] "Natality" necessarily implies "createdness": our existence as human beings is unchosen, unbidden, and fundamentally inescapable. Natality also implies mortality: between the beginning and end point of our lives we encounter humans whose lives were also equally unchosen. Our existence with them—*these* particular humans at *this* particular moment of history—was also unchosen. The purported realm of freedom between unchosen natality and mortality is also a realm of inescapable constraint, especially the constraint imposed by the necessity of politics amid a world of other humans. The fact of "We" arises from the inescapability of being human: equality is a "self-evident" truth *not* because we "hold" it to be true but because all men are *created* and, because of that common condition, are a "we" of equals.

Needing a "We"

Arendt, and many democratic "antifoundationalists," seek to avoid inquiring too extensively into the origins of human political life, one must surmise, in order to avoid confronting the liberal assumptions of a State of Nature and the voluntarist, contractarian tradition they largely deplore. By leaving the question of human origins in primeval obscurity, one can avoid questions of origins and instead focus one's energies on the possibilities of transformative new or re-foundings.[67] Yet, this avoidance arguably betrays the very project of political theory and neglects the wellspring behind its most basic motivation, namely, the inquiry into the origins of human political life and its implications for the possibility of justice. It is precisely this exploration that marks the beginning of the first explicitly sustained examination of political philosophy in the Western tradition, namely, the origins of political philosophy in Plato's *Republic*. It is Plato's earliest investigation into the origins of politics and helps to shed light on precisely the point of "darkness and mystery" otherwise avoided by Arendt.

While the most obvious lesson of Plato's *Republic* appears to involve either the recommendation, or perhaps the implausibility, of the inegalitarian rule of philosopher-kings, in Socrates' description of the origins of the human city, it is surprisingly owing to our equal insufficiency, not our inequality, that Socrates locates as the source of the initial definition of justice. Much of the *Republic*'s justification of the inegalitarian rule is famously based upon the necessity of a radical division of labor that is itself the result of distinctive capacities of human beings. Justice, it is concluded, consists of "the minding of one's own business" (*to ta hautou prattein*).[68] However, this understanding of justice, while indeed central to the dialogue, itself follows upon and is developed out of an earlier and provisional definition of justice that tends to be overlooked in most treatments of the *Republic*. An earlier definition of justice resting upon an understanding of humanity as lacking self-sufficiency points to a radically different understanding of justice and near-opposite implications of the division of labor both from this apparent later definition within the *Republic* and, further, from contemporary understandings of the division of labor and autonomy that arise famously from Adam Smith.

Often neglected is the very first definition of justice that precedes the development of the "feverish" city in speech (372e). This first definition occurs at the conclusion of a regrettably brief initial description of the "first" city that occurs between Socrates and Adeimantus in Book II. This first city, described by Socrates as "the city of utmost necessity" (369d), is marked by a very rudimentary division of labor. Socrates begins with the observation that "a city, as I believe, comes into existence because each of us isn't self-sufficient but is in need of much" (369b). However, nature or providence has fortunately assured that we are equal in our need and fortunately diverse: "each of us is naturally not quite like anyone else, but rather differs in his nature; [and] different men are apt for the accomplishment of different work" (370a).For this reason, Socrates suggests, it would be *selfish* for those of us with specific talents *not* to undertake that profession in a relatively exclusive fashion. Socrates says, "Must each of [these men] put his work at the disposition of all in common—for example, must the farmer, one man, provide food for four and spend four times as much time and labor in the provision of food and give it in common to the others; or must he *neglect* them and produce a fourth part of the food in a fourth of the time and use the other three parts for the provision of a house, clothing, and shoes, not taking the trouble to share in common with others, but *minding his own business for himself (ta hautou prattein)*?" (369e–370a; emphasis mine).

While Socrates describes an economic system that rests as thoroughly on a "division of labor" as that recommended by Adam Smith in *On the Wealth of Nations*, the *motivations* for our engagement in work is fundamentally different: whereas in Smith we should only consult our *interests*, in Plato we engage in our particular form of work out of a kind of *generosity* to those with whom we live.[69] We are to engage in that form of work for which we have special talent explicitly to avoid *neglect* of our fellow citizens, and out of a *rejection* of the idea that justice consists most fundamentally in "minding one's own business." We do so because no one is capable of providing the entirety of our sustenance—"because each one of us isn't self-sufficient but in need of much" (369b)—and, beyond that, because no one of us is capable of creating the good things of life by ourselves alone. Thus the too brief conversation with Adeimantus concludes with Socrates asking where one can locate justice in such a city. Adeimantus responds, haltingly, that it must rest in a recognition of our common "need" (372a).[70] Reflecting the necessity to acknowledge that lack of self-sufficiency, among the few nonsubsistence activities in which citizens engage in the rudimentary city is worship: "After [their work] they will drink wine and, crowned with wreaths, sing of the gods. So they will have sweet intercourse with each other, and not producing children beyond their means, keeping an eye out for poverty or war" (372b). Such worship reflects ultimate acknowledgment that "each of us isn't self-sufficient but is in need of much" (369b).

Adam Smith's conception of the "division of labor," emphasizing above all our self-interest, is made possible by a background assumption imported from liberal political theory and the social contract tradition that human beings are, by nature, "free, equal, and independent" in John Locke's words, and that we enter society only on the basis of an appeal to calculated self-interest.[71] Self-interest is the natural, "default" mode of human life: any appeal to "benevolence" toward humanity or generosity to one's fellow citizens is unnatural. Plato offers us an alternative conception, not one that begins with a portrait of human self-sufficiency nor one with an unrealistic call to benevolence achieved by means of "transformation" but rather one with a strong acknowledgment of human *insufficiency*, one that stresses the human inability to supply our needs and wants through our own efforts alone. Even if we conclude this rudimentary city to be "a city of pigs"—as it is accused of being by Adeimantus's brother, Glaucon—we should not forget that more sophisticated and intricate societies, even the "feverish city" whose citizens come to believe that justice lies in "minding one's own business," still rest on this first acknowledgment of human *insufficiency* rather than self-sufficiency.[72]

The ideal city governed by "philosopher-kings" is thus built on the foundations of a city "of utmost necessity" in which justice is acknowledged to be based upon need. Human cities exist as an acknowledgment of such need, no matter what our apparent difference of position in the shadow of gleaming skyscapers and in spite of the vast distance we have seemingly traversed from those swinish origins. Equality's self-evidence is demonstrated every day by the simple existence and permanent persistence of politics. Democracy is not premised upon the eventual perfection of our imperfect city nor the citizens who reside therein but precisely upon the permanent presence of imperfect humans who must, by dint of their equal insufficiency and the permanency of need, inhabit, and govern together, cities of men.

PART TWO

Voices of the Democratic Faithful

CHAPTER FOUR

Protagoras Unbound: The Democratic Mythology of Protagoras's "Great Speech"

> Man is the measure of all things.
>
> —*Protagoras of Abdera*

SOPHISTIC DEMOCRACY

THE MOST PREEMINENT Sophist of his age, Protagoras of Abdera, is reported by Plato to have made one of the great declarations of relativism: "man is the measure of all things: of the things which are, that they are, and of the things which are not, that they are not."[1] Because of this extreme denial of any measure or standard upon or by which to judge human actions outside relative human perceptions, as most accounts have it, the Sophists drew the attacks especially of Socrates, Plato and Aristotle, who assured that future generations would think only negatively about sophists and their philosophy. As captured by a commentator on Sophistry more than a century ago,

> the old view of the Sophists was that they were a set of charlatans who appeared in Greece in the fifth century, and earned ample livelihood by imposing on public credulity: professing to teach virtue, they really taught the art of fallacious discourse, and meanwhile propagated immoral practical doctrines. They gravitated to Athens . . ., they were there met and overthrown by Socrates, who exposed the hollowness of their rhetoric, turned their quibbles inside out, and triumphantly defended sound ethical principles against their plausible pernicious sophistries. That they thus, after a brief success, fell into a well-merited contempt, so that their name became a byword for succeeding generations.[2]

This standard view of the moral poverty of the Sophists, and the philosophic eminence of Socrates, Plato, and Aristotle has been almost altogether reversed in recent years. With the rise of skepticism, postmodernism, and value pluralism in Anglo-American and continental philosophical schools in the past several decades, the reputation of the Sophists has undergone considerable rehabilitation, particularly at the hands of liberal, antifoundationalist, and postmodern scholars. Once abhorred as presenting a form of proto-nihilism, in recent years there has been an embrace of the wide-ranging skepticism and the epistemic relativism of Sophists such as Protagoras, Gorgias, Antiphon, Prodicus, among others. Scholars such as G. B. Kerferd, Mario Untersteiner, Jacqueline de Romilly, Eric Havelock, Cynthia Farrar, and

Susan Jarrett, following the earlier rehabilitation by George Grote, have each undertaken lengthy examinations of the Sophists, and have found compelling recommendations for skepticism, empiricism, progressive anthropology, agnosticism, and political liberalism.[3] Notable voices in philosophy and politics have embraced the Sophists for providing a desirable alternative to the philosophical tradition dubbed by Dewey as the "Quest for Certainty" attributed to Plato.[4] Indeed, one finds explicit linkage of pragmatists like Dewey to the Sophists by thinkers such as Eric Havelock, who wrote that "the pragmatism and empiricism of Protagoras would have won sympathy from Hume, James, and Dewey."[5] Claiming the lineage of both the Sophists and Dewey, the philosopher Richard Rorty, in his arguments against a turn to "foundations" in philosophical and political thought, has sought to dethrone the "Platonic Principle" by suggesting that, in doing so, "we shall, in short, be where the Sophists were before Plato brought his principle to bear and invented 'philosophical thinking.'"[6]

In political thought some thinkers have turned to the Sophistic tradition, and specifically the fragments of Protagoras as the first, and in many cases among the most compelling, examples of democratic thinking in the Western tradition. As stated baldly by Cynthia Farrar, "Protagoras was, so far as we know, the first democratic political theorist in the history of the world."[7] While one does not find in Protagoras's remaining fragments specific arguments in support of democratic governance, with particular attention to elections, office holding, citizenship, and the like, in certain passages, especially in Plato's *Theaetetus* and *Protagoras*, commentators have identified a series of arguments that suggests a democratic epistemology confirming the legitimacy of collective judgment and civil equality.[8] Further elaborating his "man/measure" theory in *Theaetetus*, Socrates' Protagoras builds from his analysis of the differences in our individual perceptions (e.g., wind or rain) and extends them to judgments that are rendered by political communities.[9]

> Consider political questions. Some of these are questions of what may or may not fittingly be done, of just and unjust, of what is sanctioned by religion and what is not; and here the theory may be prepared to maintain that whatever view a city takes on these matters and establishes as its law or convention, is truth and fact for that city. In such matters neither any individual nor any city can claim superior wisdom. (172a)

Appealing to this view that community judgment *is* enacted truth, against authoritative or transcendent appeals to "principle" or "truth," commentators sympathetic to "strong" versions of democratic self-governance have viewed Protagorean defense of community judgment as embodying an early argument in favor of participatory democracy. According to Cynthia Farrar, in both Plato's *Protagoras* and *Theaetetus* Protagoras (the character) defends

> the beneficent socializing effect of *polis* life and democratic political action. The man-measure doctrine conceives of the experience and understanding attained by ordinary men as the touchstone of social values. Protagoras's measure is a man who no-

tices his neighbor and who moves through life and interacts with others as a human being, with all that implies about basic needs, responses and capacities. In a democracy, indeed in response to democracy, epistemology and political ethics coincide.[10]

This view reflects contemporary versions of "antifoundationalism" found in writings by scholars ranging from John Dewey, Hannah Arendt, and Benjamin Barber to Richard Rorty and Stanley Fish. Almost echoing the Protagorean defense of communal political judgment absent the availability of independent or "true" grounds for judgment offered by Socrates (on Protagoras's behalf) in *Theaetetus*, Benjamin R. Barber has written in defense of his conception of "Strong Democracy" that,

> strong democracy relies on participation in an evolving problem-solving community that creates public ends where there were none before by means of its own activity and of its own existence as a focal point of the quest for mutual solutions. In such communities, public ends are neither extrapolated from absolutes nor "discovered" in preexisting "hidden consensus." They are literally forged through the act of public participation, created through common deliberation and common action and the effect that deliberation and action can have on interests, which change shape and direction when subjected to these participatory processes.[11]

In effect, community judgment rendered through legitimate "strong" democratic practices creates justice, rather than conceptions of justice creating justifications for and subsequent constraints on democracy. By this "strong democratic" account, conceptions of right and of a just society can only arise from the universal interactions of a community of equals, and not from what are regarded either as Platonic or liberal assumptions such as appeals to preexisting "truth" or predetermined principles of justice.

By turning to the greatest, indeed, according to some, the *only* positive account of democracy in the ancient Sophistic tradition, attributed by Plato to Protagoras in the dialogue *Protagoras*, it may be possible to locate the origin of some of this modern antifoundational, even "Sophistic" confidence in democracy, in the capacity of democratic citizenry for self-rule not in spite of but because of the absence of preexisting standards of "justice" or "right." We may begin to locate there the origin of what many contemporary theorists time and again refer to as their "democratic faith," a faith in democracy that accompanies their rejection of a form of faith in any transcendent source of truth, a faith, indeed, in some paradoxical form, born of a thoroughgoing epistemology of skepticism.[12] By turning to the words attributed to Protagoras by Plato, we seek the origins of a "democratic faith" far older than the phrase itself.

The Great Speech

Protagoras's status as "the first democratic theorist" is based most extensively on the arguments made in the lengthy speech by Protagoras in Plato's

Protagoras.[13] In this speech Protagoras attempts to justify his view that virtue can be taught, against Socrates' contention that virtue is not teachable (320c–328c). Socrates decides to visit the home of Callias to meet Callias's guest, Protagoras, at the behest of young Hippocrates, who has awoken Socrates with the exciting news that Protagoras has returned to Athens.[14] Responding to Socrates' question of what he claims to be able to teach Hippocrates, Protagoras is not humble in his claims: he declares, "on the day when you [Hippocrates] join my class you will go home a better man, and on the day after it will be the same; every day you will constantly improve more and more" (318a–b). Protagoras signals his belief in the infinite amelioration of humans by means of education. When asked to be more specific about what matters he teaches, Protagoras replies: "he will learn . . . good judgment (*euboulia*) in his own affairs, showing how best to order his own home; and in the affairs of the city, showing how he may have the most influence on public affairs (*poleōs dunatōtatos*) both in speech and action (*prattein kai legein*)" (318e–319a). Protagoras confirms that he proposes to teach "political skill" (*politikēn technē* [319a], at which point Socrates raises what becomes the central point of contention by asserting that he does not believe such a skill can be taught.

Socrates gives a sociological and political (and not epistemological) reason why *politikēn technē* cannot be taught by giving specific evidence based on the behavior of his contemporary Athenians. He poses two arguments in support of his view that political skill cannot be taught. First, he observes that Athenians (whom he, along with the rest of Greece, regards as wise— *sophous* [319b]) call upon experts to give testimony in the Assembly when the matter at hand is technical in nature, whereas when the matter is a general public issue, anyone is allowed to offer testimony without any objection from the other listeners. He concludes, "obviously it is because they hold that here the thing cannot be taught" (319d), which, by extension, suggests that the "wise" Athenians act on the assumption that "political skill" is already dispersed among the citizen population, without need of further transmission or instruction.

The second argument offered by Socrates in support of his view that "political skill" cannot be taught does not wholly accord with the first argument. He contends that "in private life our best and wisest citizens are unable to transmit this excellence of theirs to others," offering the example of Pericles' children, who are given instruction on all subjects except the one in which their father "is himself a master" (319e–320a). Here again there is the suggestion that "political skill" is simply known—not learned—in this case by the generation of Pericles, but there is a further indication (one that exists in some tension with the previous one) that the subsequent generation *does not* know this political skill but, like ignorant beasts, "must graze like sacred oxen, on the chance of their picking up excellence here or there for themselves" (320a).

By combining the two arguments, one arrives at the substance of Socrates' argument as follows: there is no explaining how any given generation might happen upon political skill (assuming the generation possesses it, about which Socrates appears skeptical), and the people are fortunate when they do, but they are thereafter incapable of transmitting that knowledge to subsequent generations and instead throw that skill to the winds without ensuring that it be passed along and become a permanent legacy of a given city. Thus the generation of Pericles possesses a kind of wisdom but is incapable of giving an account, or explaining the content, of that wisdom since it has not arrived at that wisdom through its own efforts. The first part of Socrates' position contends that, where virtue exists, there is no accounting for how it came to be possessed; his second position holds that, where virtue exists, it is practically assured to die within a generation since it cannot be transmitted. The first argument concerns the origins of virtue; the second, whether virtue attained by happenstance can be passed on to subsequent generations.

Based on his response to Socrates' claim that political skill cannot be taught, Protagoras offers a sustained defense of a kind of general and egalitarian education that has persuaded generations of scholars that Protagoras understands and appreciates Athenian democracy more than the native sons of Athens, such as Socrates and Plato, do. Protagoras famously offers to defend his position by means of either a "*muthos*" or "*logos*"—a myth (or story or fable or tale) or a discourse (or exposition or logical analysis or speech). After declaring a willingness to hear either, Protagoras proceeds to tell his famous version of the Prometheus etiology, as it will prove "more pleasing" (*chariesteron* [320c]), followed thereafter by a *logos*—a rational argument—justifying as well Protagoras's position that virtue is learned and accessible widely if not universally in any polity.

According to Protagoras's telling (320c–324d), there was a time when the gods existed but mortal creatures did not. At a "destined time" the brothers Prometheus and Epimetheus were charged with distributing equipment and faculties to the yet undefined creatures. Epimetheus, prevailing on Prometheus to allow him to do the distribution, successfully portions out qualities to the beasts so that some have strength while others excel in defensive qualities, but, as might be expected, Epimetheus ("Afterthought") does not adequately plan his distributions: human creatures are left without special talents or defenses. Prometheus, attempting to discover some device for humanity's preservation, steals from the Olympians Hephaestus and Athena "wisdom of the arts" (*entechnon sophian*) as well as fire of the gods. Distributing these arts to mankind, they develop "the wisdom of daily life" (*bion sophian*) but continue to lack "civic wisdom" ([*sophian*] *politikēn*).

The stolen arts allow humanity to develop forms of worship of the gods—since humanity, opposed to the beasts, now "partakes of a divine portion" (*moiras*)—as well as speech and various artifacts like clothing and homes. However, humans continue to dwell separately, subject to destruction by beasts since they were still lacking "civic art" (*politikēn technē*). Despite attempts to band together, lacking this *politikēn technē*, humans immediately began to wrong one another, leading them again to scatter and perish in the wild. "Fearing that our race was in danger of utter destruction," Zeus intervenes by calling Hermes to distribute "Justice" (*dike*) and "Shame" (*aidos*) to humanity.[15] Hermes asks whether he is to distribute these qualities to just a few humans, as was done with the other arts (those that were distributed by Prometheus); Zeus instructs him to distribute *dike* and *aidos* to all humans, as without universal partaking in these qualities "cities cannot be formed."

Thus, by means of the Promethean *muthos* and its explication, instead of contradicting Socrates' observation about the belief in the universal political capacity of the Athenian assembly, Protagoras confirms that Socrates is altogether correct about the general distribution of political wisdom throughout the populace. Moreover, Protagoras's etiology addresses the implied challenge of Socrates' first objection regarding the teachability of virtue, namely, to locate its origin and, by extension, its availability to all human beings. All humans minimally have the capacity for *aidos* and *dike*, yet it may be more or less realized in particular individuals. As Protagoras further clarifies, in spite of the universal distribution of the virtues, there is an indication that humans will not similarly manifest or embody those qualities: Zeus states: "he who cannot partake of shame and justice shall die the death as a public pest" (322d). Although all humans will apparently have *aidos* and *dike* available to them as a divine inheritance, some will either willfully or unknowingly neglect to perfect or manifest those qualities and hence be subject to punishment. Such punishment indicates that virtue—of which some have in fuller measure—can be transmitted to future generations. By means of the story of human origins, Protagoras devises a set of assumptions about human nature based on thefts of certain arts by Prometheus and gifts of others by Zeus that require certain conclusions about the expectations of universal justice and the nature of punishment qua instruction. Rather than the former being a kind of enforced conformity and the latter being purely retributive, each is seen to reflect the universal distribution of *dike* and *aidos* at least as accessible qualities that thereafter require development and education within political communities.

At this point (324d) Protagoras invokes the use of *logos* rather than *muthos* to refute (rather than confirm) at least part of Socrates' second argument, namely, to demonstrate that virtue can be transmitted purposively from one generation to the next. The explication of the myth had already begun to state this case: that is, virtue's transmissibility inheres in the nature of the distribution of virtue itself as related in the *muthos*. Protagoras argues that the fact cities exist proves that these virtues exist distributed widely throughout the city, just as the myth suggests they must. Again, Protagoras invokes the use of punishment as a fundamental form of instruction in all cities: "we should instruct and punish such as those who do not partake of it, whether child or husband or wife, until the punishment of such persons has made them better, and should cast forth from our cities or put to death as incurable whoever fails to respond to such punishment and instruction" (325a–b).

Protagoras goes on to describe a form of communal education that contrasts starkly with Socrates' accusation against the likes of Pericles. At the outset of a child's life, his "nurse, mother, tutor and the father" all seek to educate the child in the ways and virtues of the city. If he does not obey, "they treat him as a bent and twisted piece of wood and straighten him with threats and blows" (325d). After this familial education, children are educated more formally by teachers in various disciplines such as writing and music. After one's formal education, Protagoras evokes the role of the full community in the education of the individual, compelling each person to live according to the laws of the country—in effect, teaching each person justice as defined by each respective city by an education in the city's laws—and punishing anyone "who steps outside these borders" (326d).

Thus, by means of a "fable and argument" (*muthon kai logon*), Protagoras claims to prove that virtue can be taught, given every person's god-given inheritance from Zeus, dependent on further cultivation through the customs and laws of the city and instruction like that offered by the Sophists themselves. In a manner remarkably similar to contemporary views on human potential—often unstated—Protagoras affirms a kind of fundamental equality of all persons in principle without precluding the possibility of individual distinction. Little wonder that many readers have often concluded that Protagoras's "Great Speech" represents an incipient democratic theory.

ORIGINS OF PROTAGORAS'S MYTH: HESIOD'S PROMETHEUS

The myth appears to be an updating of the Prometheus legend, but comparisons with earlier versions of the myth suggest that, rather than simply retelling the myth, Protagoras is engaged in a fundamental redefinition of the relationship between gods and man as originally expressed in the Promethean mythology, a redefinition that proves favorable to humankind generally and allows Protagoras to justify a plastic and infinitely ameliorable human capacity that he might not have been able to do without resorting to the resonance of the Prometheus myth. As is often the case with versions of "democratic faith," the myth he tells is a palimpsest, a newer form of an ancient story that nevertheless cannot escape the hidden resonances and lessons of the older stories, particularly ones by Hesiod and Aeschylus. Indeed, rather than attempting to efface altogether the older versions of the Prometheus story, Protagoras's version evokes echoes of particular elements of those older versions throughout his own retelling, thus calling our attention to the alterations he has made to the ancient *muthos*. Of course, here it is worth pointing out that Protagoras is a "character" in a dialogue by Plato;

whether the historical Protagoras would himself have sought to evoke those older stories as an encouragement for our comparison remains unanswerable. What is certain is that *Plato* formed the *muthos* in such a manner to call our attention to it, and thus calls upon us implicitly to compare Protagoras's new form of storytelling with the lessons of older versions.

The oldest version of the Prometheus myth is found in the poems of Hesiod. *Works and Days* begins with Hesiod telling his brother that there are two causes of Strife—one due to warfare, the other to the burdens of work placed by the gods on humankind. He proceeds to tell the origins of this latter strife by means of the tale of Prometheus. Notably he has promised to "describe the true way of existence" to his brother, Perses, *etētuma muthē saimēn* (WD, 10).[16] The "tale" of Prometheus is related using the language of song and poetry, *muthēomai*. Following the tale of Prometheus, Hesiod offers a second description of the source of mankind's burdens: "I will outline it for you in a different story (*logon ekkoruphōsō*), well and knowledgeably" (WD, 106). This second version of humanity's sorrows, "outlined" now as a "*logos*," departs from his earlier promise to tell his brother the source by means of song and poetry. The second tale, the "*logos*," is also a mythological tale about the five ages of humankind but cleaves closer to our understanding of the analytic aspect of a *logos* by relating the five ages to the particular qualities of the humans who dominated in that period. By evoking Hesiod's earlier use of two tales to tell of humanity's origins and the sources of its travails, (Plato's) Protagoras invites us to compare both the two versions of Hesiod's tale to each other, one a *muthos*, the other a *logos*, and subsequently the two versions to his own *muthos* and *logos*.

Hesiod begins his story of Prometheus by revealing that humanity might have once escaped lives of hard labor had not "devious-minded Prometheus" cheated Zeus (WD, 43–49; cf. 90–93). Without stating how Prometheus cheated Zeus, Zeus responds by punishing humanity (not Prometheus) through the confiscation of fire. Prometheus steals the fire back, hiding it in a hollow fennel stalk, calling greater vengeance down upon humanity (not Prometheus). Zeus orders Hephaestus to make the figure of a female human out of clay; instructs Athene to "teach her skills"; directs Aphrodite to make her tempting to men; and, finally, orders Hermes to give her "a treacherous nature" (WD, 54–68). She is named Pandora and is brought as a gift to Prometheus's brother, Epimetheus, who "did not remember to think how Prometheus had told him never to accept a gift from Olympian Zeus" (WD, 86–87). Pandora brings a jar filled with "gifts" from all the gods; releasing the lid of the jar, she unleashes innumerable troubles that have plagued mankind ever since, leaving only hope trapped inside the jar (WD, 94–104). Voicing a sorrowful determinism, Hesiod concludes his tale by stating that "there is no way to avoid what Zeus has intended" (WD, 105).

Jean-Pierre Vernant has observed that the two versions of the Prometheus myth, one appearing as described in *Works and Days*, the other in *Theogony*, almost perfectly complement each other, since valuable information in the latter is only supplied in the former, and vice versa.[17] *Works and Days*, for instance, does not tell us the nature of Prometheus's original deception, and leaves us also uninformed as to why Zeus would punish humanity and not Prometheus. The story of Prometheus in *Theogony* provides many of those answers. The original deception is described as a result of a dispute at Mecone (Sicyon) in which Prometheus "matched wits" with Zeus (*T*, 534). Two portions of an ox were laid out, one for humanity, one intended for sacrifice to the gods. In one pile, Prometheus arranged the meatiest portions to be hidden inside the ox's stomach; in another pile, Prometheus hid the bones in a layer of white fat. Prometheus invited Zeus to choose the pile he preferred, clearly suspecting that Zeus would choose impetuously guided solely by his sense of sight.

The poet surprises us by describing Zeus's decision in the following terms:

[Prometheus] spoke, with intent to deceive, and Zeus, who knows imperishable
counsels, saw it, the trick did not escape him, he imagined
evils for mortal men in his mind, and meant to fulfil them.
In both hands he took up the portion of the white fat. Anger
rose up about his heart and the spite mounted in his spirit
when he saw the white bones of the ox in deceptive arrangement.

(550–555)

The evidence suggests that Zeus knowingly chooses the meager sacrifice in order that he will be able to justify his own desire to "fulfill" his "imagined evils for mortal man." Zeus, for an inexplicable reason, intends to torment humanity, and desires (as well as apparently needs) a justification to do so.

Zeus does not punish humanity directly for Prometheus's offense but rather uses the offense (of which he was aware even before he chose the sacrifice consisting of bones) in order to carry out a desired calamity upon humanity. At this point Zeus withdraws fire from humanity, only to have it stolen by Prometheus (*T*, 560–569). As described in *Works and Days*, Zeus then commands the creation of woman (this time not mentioning her name, and only noting her endowments by Hephaestus and Athene, not Aphrodite or Hermes). The woes visited on humanity by woman are described in terms more specific to the perceived ruinous role of women (not as the bearer of general woe, as in the tale of *Works and Days* (*T*, 586–611). He goes on to note that Prometheus also was visited with a punishment for his role, now being confined by "force and mighty chain" (*T*, 616). Again, as in *Works and Days*, Hesiod draws the moral that "it is not possible to hide from the mind of Zeus, or escape it" (*T*, 613).

The "true things" that Hesiod seeks to tell (*etētuma muthēsainmēn*) result in a radically different portrait of humanity's relation to the gods, Zeus especially, than that which *muthos* offered by Protagoras to defend the proposition that virtue can be taught, and further is taught, by each city. In Hesiod's versions Zeus's anger at humanity plays a prominent role, initially the anger at Prometheus for his deception (*cholos*, *WD*, 47; *T*, 561) and then the anger at the theft of fire that motivates the creation of Pandora (*WD*, 53). Prometheus, like mankind, does not escape Zeus's anger (*T*, 615) but can only be released from his bonds by Heracles, son of Zeus: Zeus's pride in his son's deed does not assuage his anger, but he allows Prometheus to be released from his wrath (*T*, 533).

The initial animus of Zeus toward humanity arises, it would appear, as a result of an initial "dispute" or "separation" between humanity and the gods (*T*, 535: "*kai gar hot ekrinonto theoi thnetoi t' anthrōpoi*"). The source of this dispute or separation is uncertain: Hesiod's text suggests that, before the "separation" between the gods and mortals, each lived together without dispute or division. It is unclear what divides humanity and the gods; in any event, it appears that there is an attempt afoot to bring the two sides together through the dividing of the ox, in what is intended to be the origins of worship of the gods. Human worship, to be initiated at the feast of Mecone (Sicyon), seeks to assuage the division that separates the "undying gods" and "humanity": if a fair division of the beast can take place, humanity and the gods will be brought together. This plan is undermined by Prometheus, "eager to try his wits," who uses deception to unevenly separate the remains of the ox. Often viewed as humanity's great benefactor against the anger of Zeus, Prometheus here, in fact, appears to *undermine* what might have become a rapprochement between humanity and the gods by attempting to trick Zeus into choosing a meager portion. Humanity's implication in this trick is unclear and unstated, but Hesiod does stress that humanity continues to keep the meatier portions of the sacrificed beast. Yet, at the same time, that fact suggests a willingness to maintain the original bargain (albeit a self-interested one, to be sure) indicating a continued goodwill on the part of humanity to keep its initial promise during the meeting at Mecone. Worship of divinity becomes a double-edged activity in Hesiod's estimation: if it represents a form of concord between humanity and the gods, in its current form it serves also as a constant reminder of the origin of humanity's woes.

Despite the widespread reputation of Prometheus as mankind's savior, Prometheus appears to act at Mecone out of a concern for glory and self-aggrandizement.[18] True, his trick does result in humanity's greater share of the ox for all perpetuity. However, the exposure of the trick—which was inevitable, since Zeus would discover his meager portion as soon as he picked it—resulted as well in the perpetual woes of humanity. If Prometheus goes on to steal fire for the sake of humanity, it is not altogether out of the question that he does so in realization that it was his own actions that precipitated Zeus's animus. At the same time, that Zeus chooses the meager share *in full knowledge* of Prometheus's trick modifies this account somewhat. It is apparent that Zeus has little intention to allow humanity to persevere without torment: he chooses the meager portion *in order that he can punish* humanity, notwithstanding Prometheus's primary role in the charade. The result of the actions of both Prometheus and Zeus at Mecone suggests that humans have no friends among the gods. Zeus seeks the suffering of humanity, and Prometheus—despite, or worse, perhaps because of, his "fore-sight"—only aids him in his animus. The "gift" of Zeus—the creation of woman, who brings woes to humanity—represents the opposite of the gifts of *dike* and *aidos* that are the result of Zeus's beneficence in Protagoras's *muthos*.

The *logos* that follows the myth of Prometheus in *Works and Days* does not resemble the *logos* in *Protagoras* either in its form or content. Hesiod's second version of the origins of human woe is mythological in quality, although with less dramatic intervention of the gods as in the Prometheus legend. Hesiod tells of five ages of man, from the ages of gold, silver, bronze, and the heroic age to his own age of iron, an age of which he states, "I wish that I were not any part" (*WD*, 174). As in the Prometheus myth humanity begins its existence without toil or worries, and only over time (not now owing to the machinations of Prometheus but to the subsequent creation of generations by Zeus) does humanity come to suffer the woes in their current form. An even worse fate awaits humanity: if, in the age of iron, "some good things [are] mixed with the evils," in coming years a time of even greater woes will arrive.

> But Zeus will destroy this generation of mortals also,
> in the time when children, as they are born, grow gray on the temples,
> when the father no longer agrees with the children, nor children with their father,
> when guest is no longer at one with host, nor companion to companion,
> when your brother is no longer your friend, as he was in the old days.
> Men will deprive their parents of all rights, as they grow old. . . .
> Not even to their aging parents will they give back what was once given.
> Strong of one hand, one man shall seek the city of another. . . .
> Shame will not be (*aidōs ouk estai*). . . .
> The spirit of Envy, with grim face and screaming voice, who delights
> in evil, will be the constant companion of wretched humanity,
> and at last Nemesis and Aidos, Decency and Respect, shrouding
> their bright forms in pale mantles, shall go from the wide-wayed
> earth back on their way to Olympos, forsaking the whole race
> of mortal men, and all that will be left to mankind
> will be wretched pain. And there shall be no defense against evil. (*WD*, 180–201)

As in the case of the two *muthoi*, this Hesiodic *logos* stands in stark contrast to Protagoras's version. If the central tenet of Protagoras's *logos* is the demonstration of virtue's educability by means of reflection of the role of generational inheritance of justice and shame (initially the gift of Zeus in the *muthos*), Hesiod tells an opposite story of the inevitable divide separating children from their parents, and demonstrates that cities are not the repositories of a sense of justice but rather are prizes to be fought over by the strongest seeking conquest. Witnessing this parade of wantonness, *aidos* will cease to exist, and the deified forms of *Aidos* and *Nemesis* will retreat back to Olympos leaving only sorrows and pain for humanity. If Protagoras's *logos* follows "logically" from the premises of his *muthos*—that is, given a widespread sense of *dike* and *aidos*, children honor their parents, cities teach all its residents a capable form of justice because all its residents are receptive to its lessons (except those who require punishment or "correction")— Hesiod's *logos* follows just as "logically" from his mythological premises, which assumes a hostility of the gods toward humanity and an accompanying decline of respect between children and parents, brothers, friends and citizens.

Aeschylus's Prometheus

If Hesiod's version of the Prometheus myth stresses, above all, the animosity of Zeus toward humanity, Aeschylus's tragedy, *Prometheus Bound*, deepens this theme, assigning motivations for the respective actions of Zeus and Prometheus, as well as initiating a new stress on Prometheus's name and special talent, "foresight."[19] Aeschylus portrays Zeus as the newly settled ruler of the universe, recently having defeated Cronos and his supporters, the Titans. The arbitrary and cruel new rule of Zeus is stressed: not only does he mercilessly punish Prometheus for his assistance to humanity, but also revealed in far starker terms than in Hesiod's version is the complete animus Zeus bears against humanity. According to Prometheus,

> As soon as [Zeus] ascended to the throne that was his father's, straightaway he assigned to the several gods their several privileges and portioned out the power, but to the unhappy breed of mankind he gave no heed, intending to blot the race out and create a new. (230–235)[20]

Apparently unwilling to permit the persistence of any creatures from the old regime of whose loyalty is not wholly certain, or simply deciding in a completely arbitrary and unjust fashion to obliterate the existing race of humans in order to allow the creation of a new set of creatures, Zeus's motivation appears to be some combination of political prudence and arbitrary cruelty.

The viciousness of Zeus's new rule is established at the play's outset. The tragedy opens with Prometheus being bound to a mountain crag by Hephaestus, who, while not altogether willing to torment Prometheus, is being directed by *Kratos* (Power) and *Bia* (Force) at the behest of Zeus. Zeus's new dominion has no relationship to justice (he is often described as being unjust) but instead rests wholly on the same "power" and "force" that allowed him to triumph over Cronos. Prometheus reveals that the reason for his punishment is wholly owing to his desire to come to humanity's aid (106–110). His aid has taken two forms: first, he has caused humans "no longer to foresee their doom" (*moron*—fate, or destiny, most specifically knowledge of their own deaths; 250) and, instead, has given them "blind hope" (*elpidas katokisa*). This first gift echoes that "gift" brought by Pandora, the collection of miseries she unleashes from a chest leaving only "hope" trapped inside. In Hesiod's version "hope" is ambiguous inasmuch as it is included among humanity's miseries but remains trapped inside its container. In Aeschylus's version, Prometheus's gift of "hope" is presented as an unmitigated good inasmuch as humans are shielded from the painful knowledge of the time and place of their own deaths and, instead, affords them an unspecified hope for good things in their future, presumably allowing humanity to live in the shadow of death without abandoning the will to action.

The second boon brought to humanity is the traditional Promethean gift of fire (254). This second gift, however, also proves to be more extensive and positive than that first presented by Hesiod, inasmuch as the gift of fire comes to represent the whole of human progress from undifferentiated beasts to a creature of *logos*. As Prometheus describes the full extent of his bounty,

> But hear what troubles there were among men, how I found them witless and gave them the use of their wits and made them masters of their minds. . . . They lived like swarming ants in holes in the ground, in the sunless caves of the earth. For them there was no secure token by which to tell winter nor the flowering spring nor the summer with its crops; all their doings were indeed without intelligent calculation until I showed them the rising of the stars, and the settings, hard to observe. And further I discovered to them numbering, preeminent among the subtle devices, and the combining of letters as a means of remembering all things, the Muses' mother, skilled in craft. It was I who first yoked beasts for them. . . . It was none other than I who discovered ships, the sail-driven wagons that the sea buffets. Such were the contrivances I discovered for men. (441–469)

Prometheus literally *creates* humanity, not merely serving as protector from Zeus's animus but arming humanity with the tools, disciplines, and artifacts that make it possible for humans to cease being creatures of a day and, instead, to begin living meaningfully into the future. If, as Timothy V. Kaufman-Osborn has suggested, "instead of claiming that human beings make artifacts, we should say that artifacts make human beings," here Prometheus claims credit for the creation and dissemination of those human-creating artifacts.[21]

Furthermore, beyond making human beings future-oriented creatures, he has also made them god-worshiping: "It was I who arranged the ways of seercraft. . . . It was I who set in order the omens of the highway and the flight of the crooked talon birds, which of them were propitious or lucky by nature. . . . It was I who burned thighs wrapped in fat and long shank bone and set mortals on the road to this murky craft" (483–498). Here echoing the lessons of Prometheus at Mecone in *Works and Days*—when he taught humanity that, in addition to worshiping the gods, he might cheat them—Prometheus reveals that he taught humanity to recognize the divine signs in dreams, the flights of birds and their entrails, and to make appropriate sacrifices to the gods. In all respects, Prometheus lays claim to introducing humanity to those arts that put human beings in control of their world and, indeed, their *cosmos*. By recognizing the movement of the sun and stars, they can count days and plan the future; by tethering beasts, they can minimize their own labor while extending dominion over nature; by curing illness, they delay death and have further control over human biology; by correctly reading divine signs, they simultaneously bow to necessity but also bring necessity into their own circle of knowledge, allowing people to act accordingly in order to minimize or avert what might be portended. Even sacrifice takes on this quality of control: while most obviously a sign of human worship, at the same time it suggests a bargain that can be struck between humans and the gods who are otherwise so hostile toward them, a curious form of human control over divine arbitrariness. Thus, while we are given no reason why, once Zeus has bound Prometheus, he should not proceed to obliterate humanity according to his original plan, at least suggested is the transformation that occurs between god and man once humanity has been introduced by Prometheus to the practices of worship. If the worst aspects of Prometheus's "trickery" in devising human worship of the gods are dropped in this new version, one aspect remains inasmuch as Prometheus again teaches humanity how to "trick" the gods into a form of nonhostile toleration and, perhaps, even reliance upon their worship for a sense of meaning.

Prometheus's most positive aspects are emphasized in Aeschylus's version of the myth, while any outright negative aspects are dropped. Nowhere mentioned is the reason for Zeus's confiscation of fire in the first place, which, according to Hesiod, is the result of Prometheus's trickery at Mecone. If Prometheus admits to teaching humans how to worship in *Prometheus Bound*, it is nowhere implied that he does so through a form of chicanery intended to preserve the better sections of the ox for humanity.[22] Furthermore, just as Zeus's motivation is only implied by Hesiod—his animus against humanity is only suggested in his choice of the meager sacrifice despite his knowledge of the trick—but brought out explicitly in *Prometheus Bound*, so, too, is Prometheus's implied motivation in Hesiod—the demonstration of his wits and cleverness—also altered by Aeschylus, now replaced instead by a thoroughgoing love and affection for humanity. While Prometheus stresses repeatedly that he cares for humanity, the basis for that affection is curious, given what he has told us about the state of humanity before his introduction of the useful arts and sciences. Humanity was bestial, inarticulate, unknowing of its past or its future; indeed, by comparison, Zeus's intention to destroy humanity is more sensible if only because he has some cause, given his interest in creating a new race of beings. Considering humanity's animal-like existence, it is as if Zeus had stated his intention to destroy the slug, and Prometheus had come to its aid and made what was the slug into what we now regard as uniquely human. Why Prometheus should have expressed such admiration and affection for this creature is beyond curious, unless we take into account the new stress upon Prometheus's foresight in *Prometheus Bound*.

Hesiod does not make much of Prometheus's name, "foresight." If anything, his foolish gambit at Mecone results in great misfortune both for himself and for the humanity that he otherwise appears interested in assisting (although it is unclear whether his motivation is primarily to assist humanity or to test his own wits against Zeus). In *Prometheus Bound*, examples of Prometheus's foresight litter the text, and form the fundamental premise of the play's action. Prometheus is bound to the mountainside as punishment for his assistance to humanity but quickly divulges that he knows a secret about Zeus's future that he will reveal only when he is freed. Otherwise, he declares, Zeus's reign will come to an end (167–179, passim). Prometheus knows of a future sexual coupling in which Zeus will conceive a child more powerful than he; unless Zeus is warned of this potential offspring, his reign will end (clearly this suggests that Zeus is incapable of understanding the true lesson of this warning, that he should avoid activities that will result in potentially competitive progeny). At the end of the play, infuriated at the withholding of this information, Zeus sends Hermes to force Prometheus to reveal his secret or, instead, to increase the magnitude of his punishment by burying Prometheus beneath the mountain for a time, then raising him up, and again bounding him to the mountainside where an eagle will feast daily on his liver (1018–1029). Prometheus "knows" he will not divulge this secret, just as he knew he would be punished for helping mankind. Part of his tragedy is that he acts in full knowledge of the dire consequences he calls upon himself. Although he has prevented humanity from knowing of their own tragic fate by giving them "blind hope," he is himself only too able to see the horrors in his own future.

His "foresight," in fact, allows him to see clearly how his actions led to his punishment from the earliest point in the conflict between the gods. Prometheus—one of the Titans whose race Zeus and the new gods have just defeated—had initially fought against the Olympians until he was told by his mother that the outcome of the battle was to favor the side that employed "crafty schemes." After initially trying, but failing, to persuade the Titans to pursue this crafty strategy, Prometheus switched sides after prevailing upon Zeus to accept this advice. He reveals that, "thanks to my plans the dark receptacle / of Tartarus conceals the ancient Kronos, / him and his allies. These were the services / I rendered to this tyrant [Zeus] and these pains / the payment he has given me in requital" (222–226).

One wonders about Prometheus's foresight here. Had he not switched sides, he admits, Zeus could not have won. The prediction that the side employing "crafty schemes" would win only applied if one side knew this was the case and pursued this advice. Otherwise, an entirely different outcome of the battle might have occurred. Prometheus rather callously and opportunistically switches sides by offering his secret to the most likely (and most underhanded) victor. The prediction becomes a classic example of the "self-fulfilling prophecy": the side that wins is the side that employs crafty schemes, and can only discover the necessity of fighting dirty by means of Prometheus's willingness to apply this knowledge himself in a prior kind of crafty scheme by offering to become a traitor, if necessary.

Prometheus also claims that he foresees all the punishments for his actions that will be forthcoming from Zeus. Why, then, does he switch sides in the first place? Why, returning to our earlier question, does he "create" mankind through the introduction of the useful arts and sciences? Prometheus's motivations seem clear at the outset—"Power" twice notes Prometheus's "man-loving disposition," and Prometheus admits to harboring "an excessive love for man" (11, 28, 123). Yet, he might never have had to intervene on humanity's behalf at all (the beastlike creature at this point, not the creature that Prometheus eventually creates) had he not sided with Zeus, and hence permitted his victory over Kronos. Kronos appeared to have no such animus for humanity. Given his ability to foresee these events, why has Prometheus acted in this fashion?

Here one perceives remarkably "Hesiodic" aspects of Prometheus's character in Aeschylus's version: if Prometheus attempts to trick Zeus in *Works and Days* in order to test and prove his wits, one almost unavoidable conclusion in *Prometheus Bound* is that Prometheus acts so that he can eventually become humanity's savior and martyr. He establishes the conditions under which his intervention will become necessary, and, as he extensively described in his great speech about educating humanity, he afforded humanity the knowledge of worship that would ultimately redound to his own favor. Prometheus exhibits classic aspects of self-interested *eros*—if he loves humanity, it is in large part because he appears to desperately crave their love and adoration in return. He craves fame, reputation, and worship, as was precisely the case in Hesiod's version, although significantly less so.

PROTAGORAS'S PROMETHEAN PALIMPSEST

Each of these three versions of the Prometheus myth, appearing, respectively, in Hesiod, Aeschylus, and Plato's *Protagoras*, provide a different account of human origins as well as varying descriptions of humanity's relationship with the gods. The character Protagoras in Plato's dialogue appears to self-consciously fashion his own version of the myth out of the raw materials provided by his predecessors, both utilizing elements of previous myths when supportive of his own intended effects and notably departing, in an equally self-conscious manner, when the objects of his own mythology require. Yet, as should be obvious from the rehearsal of the preceding myths, Protagoras's version, if not made out of new cloth, still fundamentally alters older material in ways that leave the garb nearly unrecognizable despite the appearance of easy recognition.

Neither Hesiod's nor Aeschylus's versions of the myth expressly give Prometheus (or Epimetheus) responsibility for "creating" humanity as Protagoras implies, although clearly Aeschylus relates that Prometheus took an existing, animalistic creature and, by introducing artifacts, "created" humanity. However, Aeschylus's account provided a motivation for this act of creation quite distinct from the one suggested by Protagoras. Whereas in Aeschylus's tragedy, humanity is to be obliterated by Zeus (whose own motivation remains unclear, beyond the suggestion that he is an arbitrary and cruel tyrant) and this act is prevented by Prometheus by means of the theft of fire (although, again, the reason Zeus desists is only implied), in Protagoras's retelling there was a destined time when the gods were compelled to create humanity. Human existence, on this telling, arises out of neutral circumstances and the gods' actions are compelled by fate, not arbitrary machinations. All mortal creatures are formed out of earth and fire beneath the earth by the gods, and then Prometheus and Epimetheus are charged with providing each creature its requisite equipment.

Despite his apparent talents, Prometheus proves remarkably ineffective twice in Protagoras's tale, in each case apparently belying his vaunted "foresight." In the first instance, he allows Epimetheus to assign the faculties, presumably at the very least suspecting Epimetheus's shortcomings (just as in Hesiod's version, Epimetheus is warned not to accept gifts from Zeus—which he is unable to heed when offered Pandora—suggesting that Prometheus knows his shortcomings, just as events prove). Second, his theft of fire and the "wisdom of the arts," meant to make up for Epimetheus's mistake, prove insufficient to the task of saving humanity. By this telling, compared to the clever and combative Prometheus of Hesiod's version and the defiant and brilliant Prometheus of Aeschylus's, Protagoras's Prometheus appears a rather bumbling, ineffective, and finally pathetic shadow of his former self.

Yet, a further possibility might be entertained, one more in keeping with past versions and, indeed, suggested by aspects of the Aeschylus account especially. Assuming for a moment that Protagoras's Prometheus is indeed the deity of foresight, then his behavior from the outset to the conclusion can be seen as setting into motion a series of actions that result purposively, even victoriously, in the morally equal human creature of *dike* and *aidos*. Had Prometheus declined Epimetheus's request to distribute the talents of mortal creatures, one could have hardly credited "foresight" with the inability to appropriately distribute the assigned faculties to *aloga* creatures. Only Epimetheus's mistake justifies Prometheus's theft of fire and the "wisdom of the arts." Protagoras relates that Prometheus was unable to steal the "political arts"—for presumably he would have stolen them as well, thus suggesting that he knew at the outset that his theft would be insufficient to save humanity—because the "political arts" were kept securely in the citadel of Zeus. Protagoras reveals that "Prometheus could not make so free as to enter the citadel . . ., and moreover the guards of Zeus are terrible" (*phoberai* [321d]). Zeus's singular retention of the "political arts," guarded in the secure citadel by fearsome sentinels, suggests how unlikely it would have been for any creature to receive it freely as among the original faculties that Prometheus and Epimetheus are charged to distribute. No creature is intended to be the "political animal," just as no creature was intended to speak or to worship. And yet, after witnessing the likelihood of human extinction, Zeus decides to unlock the citadel and distribute the "political arts" to humanity.

Again, an apparent inconsistency presents itself: if humanity was left bereft of any means of self-defense after Epimetheus's faulty distribution, why didn't Prometheus simply ask Zeus to give humanity the "political arts" since Zeus eventually proceeds to distribute them anyway? The notable security surrounding the "political arts" suggests the answer: Zeus would not lightly give away this supremely prized possession, presumably the art (now rendered exclusive to him alone) that secures his own rule. Instead, Prometheus steals the arts from Athena and Hephaestus—both lesser gods— and secures for humanity all those same accomplishments that Aeschylus described except *politikēn technē*. And among those notable activities that he secures is worship, a practice that arises because—owing to Prometheus's theft—humanity is now "a partaker of a divine portion" (*ho anthropos theias metaske moiras* [322a]). Only after this intermediary stage is achieved, at which point humanity is able to provide for its own survival but for the absence of the "political arts," does Zeus decide to save humanity from imminent destruction by the beasts by distributing *aidos* and *dike* generally among humanity, "to the end that there should be regulation of cities and friendly ties to draw them together" (322c).

By this latter understanding, Zeus does not in any way pick up the pieces after an incompetent Prometheus but, rather, acts according to a well-conceived, "foresightful" plan to open the citadel and provide to the human creature the well-guarded "political arts" hitherto reserved only for the gods. If Zeus is not portrayed as hostile toward humanity, as in both Hesiod and Aeschylus, then he appears to be altogether neutral at least until humanity partakes of a "divine portion" by means of Prometheus's theft. As it is similarly suggested in Hesiod's and Aeschylus's versions (although in different ways), Prometheus intervenes in order to establish the worship of the gods and, subsequently, the relationship between humanity and the gods (in Hesiod's version, one of hostility; in Aeschylus's, one that is transformed from hostility to at least forbearance). Protagoras pushes this connection further: if Zeus is not initially hostile in Protagoras's version (as opposed to Aeschylus's), he seems to be indifferent. Only by means of Protagoras's intervention—especially, it is implied, because of the introduction of "a divine portion" and the practice of divine worship—is Zeus prompted to move from indifference toward being humanity's benefactor.

LOGOS AS MUTHOS: PROTAGORAS'S DEMOCRATIC FAITH

In the view of many contemporary readers of *Protagoras*, the mythic elements of Protagoras's "Great Speech" are largely ornamental—"pleasing" in Protagoras's description—and serve primarily to set the table of the more analytic justification of the acquisition of virtue in Protagoras's *logos*. W.K.C. Guthrie characteristically states, "Protagoras's view on whether virtue is natural or acquired can be extracted from his long and brilliant speech in *Protagoras* when its mythical elements are thought away."[23] However, a close reading of the mythic sources of Protagoras's *muthos* suggests that the opposite may in fact be the case: the analytic justification of the acquisition of virtue derives most extensively from the mythic underpinnings in Protagoras's first telling. In the case of Protagoras's "Great Speech," the simple assumption that Protagoras himself leaves behind the mythic bases of his story, or that contemporary interpreters can simply extract the analytic portions without regard for the mythic justifications for the acquisition of *dike* and *aidos* in the *muthos*, is more wishful thinking than textually permissible. Rather than seeking to extract the *logos* from the *muthos*, given the mythical antecedents that are implicitly part of Protagoras's tale of the origins of political virtue, we are better advised to acknowledge the *muthos* in the *logos*—or, as stated in more contemporary terms, the metaphysics in the epistemology.

Indeed, an attempt such as Guthrie's to "think away" the mythic or divine aspects of the "Great Speech" results, in fact, in a portrait of politics far more troubling and even potentially horrific than if those elements are included. Most admirers of Protagoras's justification of the educability of virtue focus on the transformation of punishment as one of Homeric retribution to one of rehabilitation, and also focus on the aspect of moral and civic equality that the tale suggests.[24] Each of these aspects of Protagoras's *logos*, however, derives from the presuppositions of the *muthos*, which in turn derive most fundamentally from Protagoras's "description" of human origins. Without the gifts of *aidos* and *dike*, Protagoras's confidence that punishment would implicitly and necessarily represent rehabilitation would be without foundation. Without the presupposition of Zeus's general dispersal of these virtues, the claim of a fundamental equal virtue (strongly stated) or equal potential to realize *dike* and *aidos* (more weakly stated) would be as evident as it was when Socrates observed the behavior in the Athenian assembly, but without a kind of imprimatur of legitimacy that its basis in divine origins gives to it. Once Protagoras establishes that it is part of the inherent human legacy granted by the gods that humans are both just and subject to shame, the problem of human educability has been largely solved on a metaphysical, divine basis. The *muthos* does not limit itself to answering the charge that virtue cannot be taught but, rather, implicitly makes the challenge moot by locating the features of *dike* and *aidos* in human origins, and thereby makes its transmission no longer problematic on the basis of divine inheritance.[25]

As noted at the outset, Socrates poses two challenges to Protagoras, the first regarding the question of human acquisition of virtue—especially the political virtues—and the second, its transmissibility. The emphasis of the *logos* particularly concerns the latter, and it is this aspect that has particularly attracted the admiration of self-declared "antifoundational" democratic scholars. Mario Untersteiner has written that Protagoras's "Great Speech" provides "an optimistic representation of human evolution, starting from the primitive condition and rising to a rational ordering of human affairs."[26] Eric Havelock confidently asserts that Protagoras's speech "documents the hopefulness, the pragmatic satisfaction with the present shape of things characteristic of Periclean liberals."[27] Pushing this argument in a more philosophical and participatory direction, Cynthia Farrar has suggested that Protagoras's speech can be understood to be recommending "interaction [that] would lead to social order—and perhaps even to prudence and justice—because the citizens were constantly being shaped and tempered by that social interaction even as they controlled it."[28] A sense of confidence reminiscent of Protagoras's own infects these and many such assessments of Protagoras's democratic faith.

In each case there is a confidence placed in a form of pragmatic human development through experience, a progressive assumption based in an understanding of human anthropology.[29] Yet, this assumption partakes extensively and implicitly in an optimistic view of human responses to that experience, one that not only results in material improvement and progress but, moreover, results in moral and ethical progress as well. The much-admired Protagorean view of punishment as *educative* rather than *retributive* assumes at base that polities will have adequate ethical resources to impart positive lessons through the practice of punishment. Confidence in adequate human development of ethical political qualities imports many of Protagoras's "mythic" explanations of the *origin* of a uniquely human virtue, which—if my analysis of the *muthos* is correct—is, to a large extent, explicable because of assumptions derived initially from the human practice of worship and the kindly response of the gods. The universe is implicitly friendly toward human endeavors, just as the gods endorse the progressive future of the democratic project. Thus a form of religious belief is transformed quietly but ineluctably into democratic faith. As Donald Kagan has suggested, "like all basic assumptions in the political realm it was not, in spite of Protagoras, demonstrable. It was an article of faith, one of those 'truths' which must be self-evident in order to be effective. It was a boundary stone which separated democratic thought from all shades of political theory."[30]

At the same time Protagoras hides the relationship between the two forms of belief by appearing to regard the *muthos* and the *logos* as fundamentally imparting the same lessons, thereby obfuscating the resources that the etiology provide to the *logos*. In this sense he invites secular-minded current listeners and future readers to discount the role of humanity as the "worshiping creature" by seeming to allow for and even encourage the "thinking away" of the mythic elements. By allowing us the impression that we can "detach" the *muthos* from the *logos*, Protagoras allows for an interpretation of his "Great Speech" that stresses the wholly secular, anthropological, progressive sources of human political virtue.

Even as we recognize this feature of Protagoras's speech, it is necessary to recall that this is *Plato's* version of a Protagorean justification of universal political virtue. By subtly pointing to this tendency in a democratic thinker like Protagoras, Plato, in effect, sets a "trap" for future readers, who accept Protagoras's invitation to "think away" the relationship between the two forms of faith, and deceives them into finding an endorsement of antifoundational democratic thinking. Plato shows quite how fond a wish it is to "think away" the faith born of human worship qua control of the gods, when at the same time seeking to presuppose an extensive faith in human political virtue allowing for full confidence and even optimism in democratic self-governance. Plato's version is, then, a subtle warning for future democrats who might be tempted to endorse the Protagorean view without adequate reflection on the extent and implicit basis of his—and their—democratic faith. Contemporary readers who are deeply sympathetic to Protagoras's project are altogether correct to suspect Plato of opposing Protagoras's views, but he does this not, as they suppose, by making his arguments on behalf of democracy weaker but, in fact, by making them stronger than they appear on first blush. By allowing us the belief that the gods are wholly our friends, even as democratic proclivities lead increasingly to a replacement of those gods with human capacities, Plato through Protagoras subtly reveals the excesses of human self-overestimation endemic to the democratic faith.

CHAPTER FIVE

Civil Religion and the Democratic Faith of Rousseau

> Comedy is an escape, not from death but from despair,
> a narrow escape into faith.
>
> —*Christopher Fry*

JEAN-JACQUES ROUSSEAU is the first great modern articulator of "democratic faith." As discussed in the introduction to this book, it was Rousseau's claim at once to be content with "men as they are," yet his ambition to fashion humanity as they *might* be, that oriented his faith toward human political potential. His faith led him to view human contrivances that might otherwise serve to effect humanity's corruption—such as arts, laws, even religion—as potentially manipulable artifices that could be employed toward the end of realizing a democratic humanity. Rousseau rejected the Calvinism of his Genevan youth—one which held that humanity was corrupt and could do nothing to earn redemption but could only be redeemed through the unearned grace of God and his redeemer Son. Instead, Rousseau saw humanity, and in particular the philosopher/legislator, as the source of mankind's own redemption. Rousseau's thought is steeped in a profound faith, one that only apparently rejects traditional forms of religious faith, even as it orients now human-centered faith toward an effort to realize the capacity of human perfectibility. Rousseau effectively redefined the meaning of "optimism"—until Rousseau, a theodicy that commended acceptance of a created world that is the best possible in spite of its attendant evils—to its more recognizable contemporary form, namely, optimism as a belief in the human ability to effect near-infinite improvement of the world. "Optimism" thus begins not with an impulse of "acceptance" but, instead, seeks "transformation" arising from an initial dissatisfaction with the world and with humanity. Human beings are believed to be endowed with godlike powers of re-creation, and, by means of a reoriented faith in humanity's capacity to realize its own perfectibility, a refashioning of the world and of humanity itself can be undertaken and effected.

THE PROMETHEAN INHERITANCE — RELIGION AND CONTROL OF THE GODS

In its published form, Rousseau's *First Discourse* features a frontispiece that depicts Prometheus about to hand a blazing torch to a naked human standing next to and slightly below him, while a hirsute satyr moves toward the fire on the other side of and slightly lower than the human. The inscription of the frontispiece reads, "Satyr, tu ne le connois pas"—"Satyr, you do not know it" (*FD*, 30) (see Figure 5.1).[1] The first image of Rousseau's initial and still most powerful indictment of the corrupting power of the arts and sciences—of the deleterious effects of so-called progress on the natural virtue of the human creature—portrays the gods giving a gift to humanity which, according to popular myth, will in the first instance allow humanity to survive and lead further to the development of myriad arts and sciences, and which in turn will give rise to prosperity, leisure, knowledge, and just political rule. The satyr—half-man, half-goat—appears to grasp unwisely for the fire, and the warning is directed toward him, not toward the noble human form between the divine and the bestial.

The frontispiece anticipates the opening lines of the second part of the "First Discourse," in which Rousseau writes, "It was an ancient tradition, passed from Egypt to Greece, that a god who was hostile to the tranquility of mankind was the inventor of the sciences" (*SD*, 47). Here Rousseau places the following footnote:

> The allegory in the fable of Prometheus is easily seen; and it does not seem that the Greeks who riveted him on the Caucasus thought any more favorably of him than did the Egyptians of their god Thoth. "The satyr," an ancient fable relates, "wanted to kiss and embrace fire the first time he saw it; but Prometheus cried out to him: Satyr, you will mourn the beard on your chin, for fire burns when one touches it." This is the subject of the frontispiece. (*SD*, 47–48)

Here a convoluted set of references is touched upon: the Egyptian god Thoth (or Theuth), who gives to humanity the knowledge of writing, is described, and decried, in Plato's *Phaedrus*; Prometheus, who gives fire to humanity and is subsequently punished, is described in several ancient sources, including Hesiod's *Works and Days*, *Theognis*, Aeschylus's *Prometheus Bound*, and Plato's *Statesman*; and the "ancient fable" that Rousseau cites in his note refers to Plutarch's discourse, *How to Profit from One's Enemies*.

Through these brief references, Rousseau appears to reverse the prevailing view of the benefits that the arts and sciences, bestowed as gifts of the gods, brought to humanity. However, this apparent reversal rests on an overstatement of the opposition of ancient man to these divine gifts, most evidently in his claim that it was the "Greeks" who bound Prometheus to the Caucasus, when, in fact, it was the *gods*—Zeus, in particular—who enchained Prometheus for stealing divine fire and permitting the survival of humanity against the divine will.[2] Nowhere in Rousseau's implicit sources of the Prometheus myth—not in Hesiod, Aeschylus, or Plato—nor in the explicitly cited source of Plutarch is it stated that humanity viewed the gift of fire or the various arts and sciences arising from that source with disapproval. In each case, before Prometheus's intervention, humanity stands at the verge of extinction, most often at the vindictive hands of Zeus. Only Prometheus's assistance prevents imminent wholesale destruction of the

Figure 5.1. "Satyr, you do not know it." Frontispiece to Jean-Jacques Rousseau's *Discours qui a remporté le prix a l'Academie de Dijon en l'année 1750 : sur cette question proposée par la même académie: si le rétablissement des sciences & des arts a contribué à épurer les moeurs. Par un citoyen de Genéve* (Geneva: Chez Barillot & fils, 1750). Reprinted with permission from Princeton University Firestone Library, Department of Rare Books and Special Collections.

species. Indeed, in Plutarch's essay, "How to Profit by One's Enemies," Plutarch describes how fire can be regarded as the "enemy" of the satyr—or presumably any "beastly" creature who does not use it properly—but that, for the more prudent among humanity, "it furnishes light and heat, and is an instrument of every craft for those who have learned to use it."[3]

Plutarch begins the subject by considering the relationship of primitive humanity to the beasts, noting that, whereas mankind was first merely the prey for more successful wild animals, eventually humanity was able "by learning" to hunt their erstwhile hunters and put their "enemies" to good use as food, clothing, shelter, and medicine. Were man to revert back to his previous condition and become incapable of "using" animals (Plutarch speculates here what would happen if the supply of animals were to be depleted), man would then revert to his original condition: "his life would become bestial, helpless, and uncivilized."[4] Like Rousseau, the classical sources view original humanity as naturally more "bestial" than human. People lack the arts and sciences by which to thrive and are barely capable of continuing life in a more extreme portrayal of a hostile nature than presented by Rousseau in his *Second Discourse* but find themselves equally ignorant of the means by which to achieve leisure and those conveniences that permit a contemplative life. However, Rousseau's explicit source, Plutarch, differs in his judgment of this condition, which he views in a wholly negative light, in stark contrast to the stance of Rousseau, who laments humanity's embrace of the arts and sciences as the cause of the corruption of morals and mankind's natural goodness.

Perhaps most significant, considering that each of these ancient sources touch upon the relationship of god and man, is that several of these ancient versions of "the state of nature" portray mankind as creatures wholly unaware of the time, death, or presence of the divine. As discussed in the previous chapter, Aeschylus's *Prometheus Bound* portrays a world in which, prior to Prometheus's gifts of the arts and sciences, humanity is no different than the least developed and weakest beast. Prometheus describes the extensive gifts granted to humanity that make humans more recognizably like the gods than the beasts:

> But hear what troubles there were among men, how I found them witless and gave them the use of their wits and made them masters of their minds. . . . For men at first had eyes but saw to no purpose; they had ears but did not hear. Like the shapes of dreams they dragged through their long lives and handled all things in bewilderment and confusion. They did not know of building houses with bricks to face the sun; they did not know how to work with wood. They lived like swarming ants in holes in the ground, in the sunless caves of the earth. For them there was no secure token by which to tell winter nor the flowering spring nor the summer with its crops; all their doings were indeed without intelligent calculation until I showed them the rising of the stars, and the settings, hard to observe. And further I discovered to them numbering, preeminent among the subtle devices, and the combining of letters as a means of remembering all things, the Muses' mother, skilled

in craft. It was I who first yoked beasts for them. . . . It was none other than I who discovered ships, the sail-driven wagons that the sea buffets. Such were the contrivances I discovered for men. (441–469)

Prometheus literally *creates* humanity not merely by serving as their protector from Zeus's animus but by arming them with the tools, disciplines, and artifacts that make it possible for humanity to cease being creatures of a day and instead to begin living meaningfully into the future.

Furthermore, beyond making human beings future-oriented creatures, he has also made them god-worshiping: "It was I who arranged the ways of seercraft. . . . It was I who set in order the omens of the highway and the flight of the crooked talon birds, which of them were propitious or lucky by nature. . . . It was I who burned thighs wrapped in fat and long shank bone and set mortals on the road to this murky craft" (483–498). Prometheus reveals that he taught humanity to recognize the divine signs in dreams, the flights of birds and their entrails, and to make appropriate sacrifices to the gods. Similarly, in Plato's *Protagoras,* Protagoras describes in his celebrated "Great Speech" how Prometheus steals the arts, including fire, from Athena and Hephaestus—both lesser gods—and secures for humanity all those same accomplishments that Aeschylus described except *politikē technē*—the political arts. Among those notable arts he secures is *worship*, a practice that arises because—owing to Prometheus's theft—humanity is now "a partaker of a divine portion" (*ho anthropos theias metaske moiras* [322a]). Only after this intermediary stage is achieved, at which point humanity is a worshiping creature but remains unable to provide for its own survival because of the absence of the "political arts," does Zeus decide to save humanity from imminent destruction from the beasts by distributing *aidos* and *dike*—shame and justice—generally among humanity, "to the end that there should be regulation of cities and friendly ties to draw them together" (322c). Protagoras appears to suggest that it is only because of Zeus's continued craving for worship that he permits the survival of humans by distributing those political arts he had formerly withheld.

In all respects, in the traditional versions as told by Aeschylus and Plato's *Protagoras,* Prometheus lays claim to introducing humanity to those arts that put them in control of their world and, indeed, their *cosmos.* By recognizing the movement of the sun and stars, they can count days and plan the future; by tethering beasts, they can minimize their own labor while extending dominion over nature; by curing illness, they delay death and further their control over human biology; by correctly reading divine signs, they simultaneously bow to necessity but also bring necessity into their own circle of knowledge, allowing people to act accordingly in order to minimize or avert what might be portended. Even sacrifice takes on this quality of control: while most obviously a sign of human worship, at the same time it suggests a bargain that can be struck between humanity and the gods who are otherwise so hostile toward them, a curious form of human control over divine arbitrariness. Thus, in Aeschylus's well-known telling, although we are given no reason why, once Zeus has bound Prometheus, he does not proceed to obliterate humanity according to his original plan. Aeschylus hints that the reason for humankind being spared Zeus's arbitrary anger lies in the very transformation that occurs between god and man once Prometheus has introduced humanity to the practices of worship. By this reading, Prometheus appears to teach humanity how to "trick" the gods into a form of nonhostile toleration and, perhaps, even reliance upon their worship for a sense of divine meaning. Religion for humanity is not "natural" but rather one of the semidivine inheritances of Prometheus's gift. If that gift is potentially an "enemy" for those bestial among us, such as the satyr, then, at least according to those very ancient sources Rousseau cites or to which he alludes, the boon of the divine inheritance has been an unmitigated good for humanity, particularly inasmuch as worship gives humanity a measure of control not only over the earthly but apparently also over the divine will. The question is whether humanity can be brought to transcend the level of satyrs and "become" fully human.

In a subsequent letter defending the thesis of the *First Discourse*, Rousseau offered a further interpretation to the frontispiece in spite of his stated belief in the clarity of the allegory's meaning:

> I would have thought I insulted my readers and treated them as children if I interpreted for them such a clear allegory; if I told them that the torch of Prometheus is that of the sciences, made to animate the great geniuses; that the Satyr, who seeing the fire for the first time, runs to it and wants to embrace it, represents the vulgar men who, seduced by the brilliance of letters, indiscreetly give themselves over to study; that the Prometheus who cries and warns them of the danger is the Citizen of Geneva.[5]

Roger Masters, along with others who have paid the letter some attention, with some justification interprets this passage as an articulation of Rousseau's inegalitarianism and elitism (which he finds unobjectionable): "There is no question that the sciences and arts can be useful to man; Rousseau is primarily concerned with their effects on 'vulgar men' who study without having the genius necessary to succeed."[6] Much of Rousseau's work was undertaken explicitly in an attempt to protect simple people from the corruptions of sophisticates and city manners.[7]

Nevertheless, taking into account particularly the background sources to which Rousseau was implicitly or explicitly appealing (and to which he directed his sophisticated reader), Rousseau's apparent "elitism" may, in fact, hide a deeper aspirational egalitarianism. If the "Citizen of Geneva"— namely, Rousseau—qua Prometheus must warn away the "vulgar" satyr, as Prometheus he is also charged with *fashioning* human creatures for whom fire (and the arts and sciences generally) are rightly intended. Thus Rousseau states that "the torch of Prometheus is that of the sciences, made to animate [*animer*] the great geniuses" (*OC*, III.102).[8] Prometheus is charged with two tasks: first, to prevent the arts and sciences from falling into the hands of the vulgar, namely, creatures who are portrayed as not fully human; and, second, based upon ancient mythology and hinted by Rousseau, to fashion a fully developed humanity *by means of* those same arts and sciences, and human contrivances generally. A vast gulf separates the human from the satyr, like one that distinguishes two radically different species. However, once fashioned into humans, all people are equal by dint of their divine "portion" and the greater fulfillment of their perfectibility. Equality, thus, is "created" by a Promethean artisan such as Rousseau; equality is explicitly not a divine inheritance from humankind's inferior original creation. This suggestion, only a passing hint in the *First Discourse*, becomes the basis of Rousseau's understanding of human malleability and the possibility of democratic transformation in the *Second Discourse*. This is seen especially by the role that religion plays in forming a more perfect humanity.

The Second Discourse: On the Unnaturalness of Religion

For Rousseau's ancient sources, religion is not part of man's "natural" inheritance but rather represents a beneficent acquisition that permits humanity to communicate with, if necessary to importune, and, when fortunate, to influence the gods. This ancient genealogy of the human acquisition of religion is superficially similar to Rousseau's portrayal of humanity's movement from a "bestial" state in "the state of nature" to the civilized creature of modernity, at least inasmuch as both versions portray humanity as naturally a creature that does not worship. However, this superficial resemblance dissolves when the implications of the later acquisition of religion are compared, which, in Rousseau's reckoning, are considerably more ambivalent, even negative, than suggested in ancient versions of the Prometheus myth.

Rousseau concludes the "Preface" to the *Second Discourse* with a Latin citation to Persius's *Satires*, which reads, "Learn whom God has ordered you to be, and in what part of human affairs you have been placed."[9] As Rousseau enters the Discourse proper, namely, the wholly naturalistic explanation of the origin of inequality among humans, he invokes the intentions of God as justification of his potentially heretical examination. Immediately in the next sentence he states that, "it is of man I am to speak" (*SD*, 101; "C'est de l'homme que j'ai à parler," *OC*, III.131), although in the next sentences it is rather of God he speaks. There, Rousseau offers justification for the departure of his subsequent analysis from traditional accounts of human creation in the biblical tradition:

> It did not even enter the minds of most of our philosophers to doubt that the state of nature had existed, even though it is evident from reading the Holy Scriptures that the first man, having received enlightenment and precepts directly from God, was not himself in that state; and that giving the writings of Moses the credence that any Christian philosopher owes them, it must be denied that even before the

flood men were ever in the pure state of nature, unless they fell back into it because of some extraordinary event: a paradox that is very embarrassing to defend and altogether impossible to prove. (*SD*, 102–103)[10]

Rousseau acknowledges the unorthodoxy of his examination, admitting at the outset that he tempts persecution of the powers, and thereby seeks to disarm hostile clerical and political critics through express acknowledgment of the departure from traditional religious explanations for the human creature.[11] Notably he points to Adam's original intimacy with God, thereby acknowledging that the biblical explanation described humanity as originally and often in contact with God. Rousseau's version of human development in history will expressly reject this version.

Rousseau proceeds to give his defense of his unorthodox approach as follows:

> Let us therefore begin by setting all the facts aside, for they do not affect the question. The researches which can be undertaken concerning this subject must not be taken for historical truths, but only for hypothetical and conditional reasonings better suited to clarify the nature of things than to show their true origin, like those our physicists make every day concerning the formation of the world. Religion commands us to believe that since God Himself took men out of the state of nature immediately after the creation, they are unequal because He wanted them to be so; but it does not forbid us to form conjectures, drawn solely from the nature of man and the beings surrounding him, about what the human race might have become if it had remained abandoned to itself. (*SD*, 103)

These sentences represent one of the more tortured explanations one can find in Rousseau's writings. Rousseau proposes to "put all the facts aside," comparing his activity to that of physicists who presumably also base their investigations of the origins of the universe on the basis of pure, nonfactual speculation. Does Rousseau here suggest that his activities are as innocent and unworthy of clerical suspicion as those of Galileo or Newton? Moreover, although Rousseau has warned his readers to disregard the footnotes during their first reading of his text ("Notice on the Notes" [*SD*, 98], anyone curious enough to delve into the notes Rousseau provides will discover that Rousseau does not give the slightest pretense of "putting all the facts aside," at least not those based on the most contemporary scientific and anthropological data available at his time.[12] Perhaps most important, while seeming to avoid apostasy by observing that God took humanity from the state of nature "immediately after creation," Rousseau suggests that God was unable to create original humanity according to any plan other than the dictates of nature. In this brief statement, far from suggesting that his treatment can be understood to be wholly in accord with the biblical understandings of human origins, in fact Rousseau indicates that nature is the most fundamental standard by which to judge subsequent human development and behavior, although nature is clearly malleable by the intervention of God—at least initially—and God's inheritors, humanity.[13]

As in the ancient genealogy of human development depicted especially in the Prometheus myth, humanity is portrayed by Rousseau as existing originally in a state comparable to animals, foraging for food individually, occasionally coupling without remaining to raise offspring beyond the absolute minimal time necessary for survival, incapable of speech beyond basic gestures, and unable to plan into the future or preserve discoveries for generations that follow. This latter feature is of particular significance, for without the ability to communicate accidental, intentional, or experimental discoveries to others, any possibility of learned or preserved knowledge is lost. Humans in their natural state are so wholly unaware of the passage of time that they have no knowledge of their own eventual deaths (*SC*, 116).

As in the ancient genealogies, then, human beings by Rousseau's telling are also notably by nature *not* god-worshiping creatures. As he describes, in his summary, the natural condition of humanity that appears toward the close of the first part of the *Second Discourse*,

> Let us conclude then that wandering in the forests, without industry, without speech, without domicile, without war and without liaisons, with no need of his fellow-men, likewise with no desire to harm them, perhaps never even recognizing anyone individually, savage man, subject to few passions and self-sufficient, had only the sentiments and intellect suited to that state; he felt only his true needs, saw only what he believed and had an interest to see; and his intelligence made no more progress than his vanity. If by chance he made some discovery, he was all the less able to communicate it because he did not recognize even his children. Art perished with the inventor. There was neither education nor progress; the generations multiplied uselessly; and everyone always starting from the same point, centuries passed in all the crudeness of the first ages; the species was already old, and man remained ever a child. (*SD*, 137)

Man in his natural state has no ability for abstract thought, and thus, in addition to obliviousness about philosophy, is also ignorant of "the known will of his creator" (*SD*, 119). While Rousseau acknowledges the Divine source of humanity, he denies that humanity would have any natural inclination to know or understand that Creator, to speculate on the state of existence after death—since that is unknown—or to establish religious institutions or practices as a means to understanding the divine.

Alternatively Rousseau also denies that the Creator is concerned with human affairs, instead portraying created humans existing wholly in accordance with a natural order—one Rousseau implies exists separately from God—and whose development occurs as a result of accident rather than divine intention.[14] The primary cause of human "development," Rousseau suggests, is "perfectibility" (*SD*, 114–115). However, this inherent feature of humanity might never have altered man's natural condition but for "the chance combination of several foreign causes which might never have arisen and without which he could have remained eternally in his primitive condition" (*SD*, 140). Among chance causes for the "activation" of the dormant feature of "perfectibility" are lightning, volcanoes, floods, and earthquakes, which draw people together and lead to the formation of societies (*SD*, 143, 148). It is noteworthy that the first instance of human memory preserving a discovery, as related by Rousseau, occurs when "lightning, a volcano, or some happy accident [*quelque heureux hazard*; *OC*, III.165] introduced them to fire, a new resource against the rigor of winter. They *learned* to *preserve* this element, then to *reproduce* it, and finally to prepare with it meats they previously devoured raw" (*SD*, 143; emphasis mine). Thus Rousseau suggests that this first instance of human *memory*, *learning*, and the *transmission of knowledge* occurs with the discovery of fire, echoing the gifts of Prometheus but now portrayed as a "happy accident." By means of these arguments, in a departure from ancient genealogies, Rousseau denies that such developments—now wholly natural and not the result of divine intervention such as that of Prometheus—are signs of moral corruption nor manifestations of human progress or nobility nor even—in the words of Plato's Protagoras—the result of a "divine portion" introduced in the human creature.

As in the ancient genealogies, in Rousseau's view the development of religion is a later acquisition by humans. Yet, rather than explaining its origins as providing a means of communicating with the gods, or even trying to influence or govern their activities as it bears on humanity, Rousseau twice mentions the development of religion as a result of its connection with purely *political* contingencies, and each time with largely negative connotations. The movement away from man's natural condition and into civilization leads inexorably to the partitioning of property. The creation of private property represents *the* central feature of civilization and the primary cause of human inequality, if the first sentences of the second part of the *Second Discourse* are any indication: "The first person, who, having fenced off a plot of ground, took it into his head to say *this is mine* and found people simple enough to believe him, was the true founder of civil society. What crimes, wars, murders, what miseries and horrors would the human race have been spared by someone who . . . uproot[ed] the stakes" (*SD*, 141–142). Along with this creation of private property arises the first necessity for religion in order to provide justification for this new, unjust, and unnatural division:

> As men began to look to the future, and as they all saw themselves with some goods to lose, there was not one of them who did not have to fear reprisals against himself for wrongs he might do to another. . . . When the ancients, says Grotius, gave Ceres the epithet of legislatrix, and gave the name Thesmaphories to a festival celebrated in her honor, they thereby made it clear that the division of lands produced a new kind of right: that is, the right of property, different from the one which results from natural law. (*SD*, 154)

The division of land into private parcels is initially an act of injustice against the credulous or the weak, perpetrated by the more clever or powerful. The possessors of property, fearing reprisals at the hands of those they have conquered or deceived, therefore create a deity and a religious practice to legitimate their original act of fraud. Thus, while property necessarily results in "the first rules of justice" (*SD*, 154), these positive laws do not prove powerful enough to obscure the unjust foundations of private property. Religion first appears as a support for unjust laws but, in fact, more than supplementing them, in turn gives them legitimacy and force through the structure of belief underlying society, and gives a status to laws that derive from a source other than nature and natural law.[15]

In its earliest appearance religion serves to defend and to obscure the original injustice committed at the moment of the division of private property. Rousseau complicates this relatively straightforward explanation for the civic uses of religion in a later passage, where he suggests that religion can serve a dubiously more beneficial function, utilized still as a means of duping the weak but evidently for their own benefit as a way of preventing disorder in society. Explicating the origin of polities from a social contract, Rousseau writes:

> Now to consider, as we are doing, only what is of human institution, if the magistrate who has all the power in his hands and who appropriates for himself all the advantages of the contract, nonetheless had the right to renounce his authority, there is all the more reason that the people, who pay for all the faults of the chiefs, ought to have the right to renounce their dependence. But the frightful dissensions, the infinite disorders that this dangerous power would necessarily entail demonstrate more than anything else how much human governments needed a basis more solid than reason alone, and how necessary it was for public repose that divine will intervened to give sovereign authority a sacred and inviolable character which took from the subjects the fatal right of disposing of it. If religion had accomplished only this good for men, it would be enough to oblige them all to cherish and adopt it, even with its abuses, since it spares even more blood than fanaticism causes to be shed. (*SD*, 170–171)

This curious and deeply ambivalent observation appears more to damn the use of religion as a support for oppressive regimes than to praise it for permitting a perverse kind of peace secured by deception and the protection of illegitimate sovereignty.[16] The two explicit references to religion, in both instances portraying religion as an artificial acquisition of "civilized" man that is created to justify "civilized" injustice, both point to religion's deep implication in the injustices upon which civilization is based. Indeed, as these two references suggest, the illegitimate division of property and subsequent development of laws, government, and civilization itself could not persist *but* for the existence of religion as a form of legitimation, since laws would have proved insufficient (cf. 154) and reason, too, would have failed as justification (170). Perhaps Rousseau speaks truthfully when he regards the costs of confrontation against illegitimacy as too steep for those it would apparently benefit, and genuinely praises the role that religion can play in maintaining the fiction that thereby maintains the peace. In this sense he reverses the Augustinian argument that *politics* are necessary to secure peace for the sake of *religious* believers. Yet, one is perhaps justified to believe that Rousseau harbors deep reservations about this arrangement, and even whether he views the arrangement as having successfully achieved what it purports, inasmuch as he expresses misgivings in the phrase "if religion had only accomplished this good for man." It is unclear whether we are to understand that religion has accomplished many *other* goods in addition to this one, or whether it has in fact succeeded in providing even this one purported good for which it was evidently invented.

Yet, elsewhere in the *Second Discourse*, in a significant note exploring the possibility of returning to the pristine "state of nature," Rousseau invokes religion as a reason that would prevent such a return, and indeed appeals to a "divine voice" that, while not actively intervening, nevertheless "called the whole human race to the enlightenment and happiness of celestial Intelligences" (*SD*, 202 n. i). While Rousseau declares in this note that humanity in its original bestial state was "naturally good" (*SD*, 193), in the body of the text he suggests a different understanding of man's original moral condition:

> It seems at first that men in that state, not having among themselves any kind of moral relationship or known duties, could be neither good nor evil, and had neither vices nor virtues: unless, taking these words in a physical sense, one calls vices in the individual the qualities that can harm his own preservation, and virtues those that can contribute to it; in which case, it would be necessary to call the most virtuous the one who least resists the impulses of nature. (*SD*, 128)

The physical "virtue" centered on mere survival that comes automatically to natural man is of a baser sort than that of humans like Rousseau who are no longer capable of "nourishing themselves on grass and nuts," who "endeavor, through the exercise of virtues they obligate themselves to practice while learning to know them, to deserve the eternal reward they ought to expect from them" (*SD*, 202). Rousseau suggests here a legitimate kind of religion that can correspond to a moral and virtuous condition *outside* the state of nature.

When Rousseau describes the lost happiness he might have achieved at a turning point of his own life, he does not describe an existence like that of "natural man" of the *Second Discourse* but rather a life lost when the gates of Geneva closed upon him and he began a life as a citizen/wanderer divorced from his city. This lost life, captured in the closing lines of the first book of his *Confessions*, describes an existence of interlocking identities from the most general to the most specific, and features in the first instance his identity as co-religionist to his fellow citizens:

> In the bosom of my religion, my fatherland, my family and my friends, I would have passed a peaceful and sweet life, such as my character needed, in the uniformity of a labor to my taste, and of a society in harmony with my heart. I would have been a good Christian, good citizen, good father of a family, good friend,

good worker, good man in everything. I would have loved my station; perhaps I would have honored it, and after having passed a simple and obscure, but even and sweet life, I would have died peacefully in the bosom of my own people. Doubtless soon forgotten, at least I would have been missed for as long as I might be remembered. (C, 36–37)

Although now defined by multiple identities ranging from the religious to the civic to the familial to the occupational, this idyllic description of the life Rousseau *might* have lived shares a notable similarity to that radically different one of "mere life" and singular identity that marks the existence of "natural man." Each form of life is "self-contained," in Christopher Kelly's estimation, bordered by limits either natural or civil that contain the multiplication of desires and internal divisions that mar civilized life, and thereby preserve "wholeness and self-sufficiency" and avoid "the tendency of corrupt civilized humans to live outside themselves."[17]

If the role of religion in the *Second Discourse* is portrayed primarily in opposition to humanity's natural state, in its first and most prominent manifestation as the necessary accompaniment to illegitimate laws, there are also these other suggestions that religion can serve a legitimate role in the civilized state that follows mankind's abandonment of his natural state. In his opening dedication, "To the Republic of Geneva," he praises the clerics of that city for "their wisdom and recognized moderation," for their "zeal for the prosperity of the State [on which] I ground hope for its eternal tranquility" (*SD*, 88). Yet, given the condemnatory tones of the subsequent descriptions of the role of religion in supporting legally sanctioned injustices, how does Rousseau reconcile these seemingly contradictory portraits? How can religion—an unnatural acquisition that is originally an invention of a state deployed to support illegitimate rapacity—be placed in the service of legitimacy, and become itself legitimate?

BENEFICIAL RELIGION

In Plutarch's essay, "How to Profit by One's Enemies"—a treatise Rousseau consulted both in his earliest work as well as his last[18]—Plutarch argues that one must learn to use to one's own advantage those very obstacles that initially obstructed the achievement of one's desired ends: "So look at your enemy, and see whether, in spite of his being in most respects harmful and difficult to manage, he does not in some way or other afford you means of getting hold of him and of using him as you can use no one else, and so can be of profit to you."[19] If religion is created at the moment when one human perpetrates injustice on another, then, like the laws themselves, these artifices of repression can be turned to good use in the refashioning of civic virtue in the state of civilization.

Based on Rousseau's discussions of religion in both the concluding chapter of *On the Social Contract* ("On Civil Religion," IV.8) and, more generally, throughout his writings, one can identify three distinguishable conceptions of religion: civil religion, "natural" religion, and Christianity.[20] Civil religion is a concoction of the state, whether legitimate or not, a necessary cement that binds together separate humans and points them toward a greater civic whole, even to the point that they will sacrifice their lives for the good of the state. As Rousseau wrote in his *Geneva Manuscript*, echoing what has already been discussed in the *Second Discourse*, "As soon as men live in society, they must have a religion that keeps them there. A people has never subsisted nor ever will subsist without religion, and if it were not given one, it would make one itself or would soon be destroyed" (*GM*, 195). Civil religion involves practices, worship, customs, and outward signs that exist for the ultimate support of the state and are approved exclusively through its auspices.

"Natural religion" is described at length by the Savoyard Vicar in book IV of *Emile* based wholly on mankind's natural sentiments. It is a minimalist religion, building exclusively on a few certain truths that are perceptible by means of one's "inner light" (*E*, 269) or "inner sentiment" (*E*, 294), and discerned through the sincere examination of one's conscience. "Natural religion," based upon the application of rational deduction of natural phenomena, demonstrates the existence of God, the immortality of the soul, the probability of reward and punishment in the afterlife, and prohibits intolerance of other beliefs, albeit also requires external adherence to the laws of the regime.[21] "Natural religion" tends toward deism: while one worships a divine and beneficent God, worship is expressed more through a sense of gratitude than through visible practices directed to the divine (*E*, 278).[22] Indeed, "natural religion" precludes prayer as an appropriate form of worship, since one should and must be content with the natural order established by God and avoid seeking special suspension of some element of that natural order on one's own behalf.[23] "Natural religion" rejects popularly conceived notions of religion as an organized, institutional form of worship, or as portrayed by Rousseau in the *Second Discourse*, in which religion exists as an extension of the state.

Christianity, famously or notoriously, receives Rousseau's unmitigated hostility in his discussion of "civil religion" in *On the Social Contract* (IV.8, 126–130). Christianity introduces a requirement of loyalty outside the state or even one's own natural sentiments, dividing the human soul between demands of two cities, in Augustine's well-known metaphor. Christianity draws men's attention away from the city, draining it of fervent devotion and leaving its citizens indifferent to its prospects. Christians can go through the motions of citizenship, but this indifference actually invites the ruin of the state, either at the hands of invading armies that they care not to repel, or domestic hypocrites who take advantage of their goodwill and charity—in effect, their naïveté (*SC*, 129). Christianity is antithetical to the principles of self-rule, in Rousseau's view: "I am mistaken when I speak of a Christian republic; these two words are mutually exclusive. Christianity preaches noth-

ing but servitude and dependence. Its spirit is so favorable to tyranny that
tyranny always profits from it. True Christians are made to be slaves" (*SC*,
130).[24]

In the description of "civil religion" in *On the Social Contract* Rousseau
depicts an ideal form of religion that follows in broad outlines those aspects
of "natural religion" that were developed in "The Profession of Faith" in
Emile:

> The dogmas of the civil religion ought to be simple, few in number, stated with
> precision, without explanations or commentaries. The existence of a powerful, in-
> telligent, beneficent, foresighted, and providential divinity;[25] the afterlife;[26] the
> happiness of the just; the punishment of the wicked;[27] the sanctity of the social
> contract and the laws.[28] These are the positive dogmas. As for the negative ones,
> I limit them to a single one: intolerance.[29] (*SC*, 131)

Similarly, in the "Profession of Faith of the Savoyard Vicar," the Vicar requires even one who has arrived at the minimal articles of faith by himself
still to act wholly in accordance with the laws of the state:

> As for the dogmas which have an influence neither on actions nor on morality, and
> about which so many men torment themselves, I do not trouble myself about them
> at all. I regard all the particular religions as so many salutary institutions which
> prescribe in each country a uniform manner of honoring God by public worship.
> These religions can all have their justifications in climate, the government, the ge-
> nius of the people, or some other local cause which makes one preferable to an-
> other according to the time and place. I believe them all to be right as long as one
> serves God suitably. (*E*, 308)

In Rousseau's ideal regime both "natural" and "civil" religions work in concert, the former prompting the individual to moral action by means of his
own "inner light," the latter creating necessary bonds between citizens by
means of laws and the threat of punishment, even the specter of death (*SC*,
131).

Arthur M. Melzer argues persuasively that the "internal" and "external"
forms of religion represented by "natural" and "civic" religion work seamlessly together toward the goal of both strengthening the political role of religion while limiting religion's independent power:

> Seeking to restore forceful political unity to the Christian world, [Rousseau] wants,
> on the one hand, to preserve and even strengthen the political role of religion and
> yet, on the other, to prevent it from ever becoming a force separate from the state.
> The religion of sincerity, if accepted, would accomplish this double goal. By mak-
> ing "orthodoxy," for the first time, completely internally defined and individual,
> by thus draining every public ceremony of its relevance for salvation, it frees up
> the public world for complete political control.[30]

These two religious forms are combined, creating a religion both of "man"
and the "city" (as Emile is to be both a "man" and a "citizen" [*E*, 40–41]),

a single religious form that combines both internal and external compulsion to virtue and thereby unites humans back to the original whole that was shattered when it moved from its natural condition.

However, having identified the form religion must take to make man whole again, a key clause in Melzer's analysis remains troubling, certainly to Rousseau: "if [it is] accepted." For Rousseau, beyond the necessity of arriving at the proper solution, there remains the nearly insuperable difficulty of bringing humanity to act on the implications of his analysis. When inquiring what must be done to make Emile simultaneously "a citizen" and "a man," Rousseau observes "very much, doubtless" (E, 41). Rousseau leaves little doubt that, having arrived at a form of religion that might make social man, like natural man, "entirely for himself . . ., a numerical unity" (E, 39), it does not suffice to rest with the self-satisfaction of true analysis. A form of persuasion beyond demonstration is necessary.

Indeed, Rousseau elsewhere holds out little hope that the general population of mankind will come to accept the prescriptions of his analysis, notwithstanding the arguments demonstrating the accessibility of "natural religion" to every human in "The Profession of Faith." In the *Geneva Manuscript* Rousseau again points out the necessity of religion for securing political order, particularly for ensuring that men in political settings will not break the contractual and legal obligations and duties as self-interest inclines them naturally. Yet, departing from his apparently more sanguine view of the beneficial role religion can play in support of the polity that he explicates in his discussion of "civil religion" in *On the Social Contract*, here Rousseau suggests that even religion will not adequately suffice to guide humans to moral action and civic devotion:

> The sublime concepts of a God of the wise, the gentle laws of brotherhood He imposes upon us, the social virtues of pure souls—which are the true cult He desires of us—will always escape the multitude, which will sacrifice worthless things in honor of these Gods in order to indulge in a thousand horrible, destructive passions. The whole earth would be covered in blood and the human race would soon perish if philosophy and the laws did not hold back the furies of fanaticism and if the voice of men was not louder than the voice of the Gods. . . . Let us, therefore, set aside the sacred precepts of the various religions, whose abuse causes as many crimes as their use can avoid, and give back to the philosopher the examination of a question that the theologian has never dealt with except to the detriment of the human race. (*GM*, 160–161)[31]

Here, in a turnabout from what has previously been suggested, Rousseau argues fervently against the beneficial role for religion in society, turning instead to the philosopher and the laws as checks upon the abuses to which religion inclines humanity. Exercising a kind of restraint, even control over the influence of religion, philosophy promises the possibility of turning humanity, now bereft of its natural "goodness," toward a consideration of its duties to the whole, a commitment to a life of virtue, and a repudiation of its

inclination toward selfishness and rapacity. Under the influence of philosophy, man "will become good, virtuous, sensitive, and finally—to sum it all
up—rather than the ferocious brigand he wished to become, the most solid
support of a well-ordered society" (*GM*, 163).

Philosophy, of course, needs also to admit its own limits. Part of its wisdom is the acknowledgment of the insufficiencies of reason to persuade. Indeed, ironically, given his condemnation of the role of religion in securing
political order in the *Geneva Manuscript*, Rousseau nevertheless argues that
philosophy must eschew the aim of the modern enlightenment project to persuade humanity to deny the existence of God and embrace atheism as a tenet
of a rational and materialist life.[32] Given the requirements that religion be
prevented from extending its inherent abuses and yet nevertheless be permitted in some form to offer consolation to the masses; given that the state
both requires religion as part of the social bond and yet must be wary of its
tendency to tear humans apart; given that religion is at once derived from
principles in keeping with the natural order and yet remains an unnatural
acquisition of the human creature after leaving the state of nature; given that
humanity, to be made whole in this state of civilization, must come to acquire a "second nature" that both differs from man's existence in civilization
and yet at the same time cannot hope to resemble that semi-bestial existence
in the state of nature; given all these apparently contradictory undercurrents
that inform Rousseau's project, not only as a true analysis of the cure for the
ailments of modern man but as an attempt to offer a remedy to those ailments, to what recourse can Rousseau avail himself?

THE TRUE CIVIL RELIGION: ROUSSEAU'S DEMOCRATIC FAITH

A prior condition must first be achieved that will allow the reconciliation of
these apparent contradictions. Mankind must be made whole within civilization, freely creating a new legitimate state but in a manner wholly different from that first state described in the *Second Discourse*—that illegitimate
state established through the unjust establishment of private property in
which self-interest and rapaciousness governed, rather than a cultivated concern for commonweal. Religion must accompany this founding moment in
order to provide a necessary bond to society, but not a religion that can potentially divide, or even be recognized as a form of civil religion, but instead
one that can be accepted with the same intuitive ease with which the new citizens accept the will of all as their own. Philosophy points to the need for a
legislator to create the conditions that resolve the paradoxes of the human
condition in its unnatural state.

This legislator faces the most daunting task of all—to reconcile the contradictions dividing the soul of modern man. Describing the requirements of
such a lawgiver, Rousseau begins his analysis by suggesting that "Gods
would be needed to give laws to men" (*SC*, II.vii, 68). Yet only men can give

laws, and a uniquely extraordinary human might aspire to such a role if he properly understands the challenge.

> One who dares to undertake the founding of a people should feel that he is capable of changing human nature, so to speak; of transforming each individual, who by himself is a perfect and solitary whole, into a part of a larger whole from which this individual receives, in a sense, his life and his being; of altering man's constitution in order to strengthen it; of substituting a partial and moral existence for the physical and independent existence we have all received from nature. He must, in short, take away man's own forces in order to give him forces that are foreign to him and that he cannot make use of without the help of others. (*SC*, 68)

This description accords with Rousseau's standing analysis of what modern man requires to be made self-sufficient and whole; yet, he goes further by providing a description, however sketchy, of the means by which this remedy can be achieved, here quoted at length:

> In order for an emerging people to appreciate the healthy maxims of politics, and follow the fundamental rule of statecraft, the effect would have to become the cause; the social spirit, which should be the result of the institution, would have to preside over the founding of the institution itself; and men would have to be prior to laws what they ought to become by means of laws. Since the legislator is therefore unable to use either force or reasoning, he must necessarily have recourse to another order of authority, which can win over without violence and persuade without convincing.
>
> This is what has always forced the fathers of nations to have recourse to the intervention of heaven and to attribute their own wisdom to the Gods; so that the peoples, subjected to the laws of the State as to those of nature, and recognizing the same power in the formation of man and of the City, might obey with freedom and bear with docility the yoke of public felicity.
>
> It is this sublime reason, which rises above the grasp of common men, whose decisions the legislator places in the mouth of the immortals in order to convince by divine authority those who cannot be moved by human prudence.[33] But it is not every man who can make the Gods speak or be believed when he declares himself their interpreter. The legislator's great soul is the true miracle that should prove his mission. . . .
>
> One must not conclude from all this, as Warburton does, that politics and religion have a common object for us, but rather that at the origin of nations, one serves as an instrument of the other. (*SC*, 69–70)

In this extraordinary passage Rousseau recognizes the nearly insoluble puzzle at the core of his analysis: how to overcome modern humanity's internal divisions, to lead people to recognize the good of the whole despite their inclination to see only their own interests, to create a legitimate state in which one is governed by laws of one's own making but which does not oppress anyone whose personal interests might cause them otherwise to withhold assent. Rousseau recognizes that truly republican institutions can create republican characters over time, but simultaneously realizes that such institutions can only be legitimately formed by a republican people in the first instance. The question of origin lingers unresolved: "the effect would have to become the cause; the social spirit, which should be the result of the institution, would have to preside over the founding of the institution itself; and men would have to be prior to laws what they ought to become by means of laws." Recognizing the circularity of this conundrum, Rousseau invokes the legislator as one capable of *creating* the effect that the institutions themselves aim to form, of *originating* a social character that over time would otherwise be the result of social practices, of *instituting* the laws that, legitimately, must be the voluntary creation of the general will.[34]

The legislator is a being of extraordinary talent, power, subtlety, and artfulness; one suspects that such a being could hardly exist. As Rousseau has suggested at the beginning of his discussion of what is needful to change "human nature, so to speak," "Gods would be needed to give laws to men." Yet, this exceptional being is human: the Gods do not change human nature in the state of society any more than they did in the state of nature. Human malleability permits this singular human being to perform what might otherwise be regarded as a divine act. Because this transformation of the modern human creature requires "sublime reason" that is not readily comprehensible to those "who cannot be moved by human prudence," the legislator, in fact, attributes his precepts and actions to the Gods even as he produces them solely through his own craft. Attributing "his own wisdom to the Gods," placing "in the mouth of the immortals" his wisdom "in order to convince by divine authority" those who might otherwise bridle at a perceived act of human manipulation intended to point them away from their narrow interests and toward a willingness to "obey with freedom and bear with docility the yoke of public felicity," the Legislator in the first instance creates a new humanity. This new humanity, in turn, will prove capable of creating a legitimate state. This legitimate state, in turn, will perpetuate a form of civil religion subsequent to that *first* usage of religion upon which the legislator relied in his creation of the new humanity. The legislator's recourse, it is suggested, in fact *precedes* the later form of civil religion described toward the conclusion of *On the Social Contract*.[35]

In order for the legitimate regime described in *On the Social Contract* to arise, a fundamental transformation of our inherited understanding of human nature must be achieved. Rousseau is not a naïve believer in an easy form of natural goodness that simply erupts from humans with little cause; humanity, at least now constituted outside the original conditions of the state of nature, is now "naturally" vicious and self-interested: "It is false that in the state of independence, reason leads us to cooperate for the common good out of a perception of our own interest. Far from there being an alliance between private interest and the general good, they are *mutually exclusive* in the *natural order of things*, and social laws are a yoke that each wants to impose on the other without having to bear it himself" (*GM*, 160; emphasis mine). Yet, because this "nature" is not itself fixed—because this is a "later" nature that itself was an alteration on humanity's original "nature"—there is the prospect, however slim, of transforming this "new" nature toward the ends of a cohesive civil society.

Contemporary philosophers who plumb the early parts of *On the Social Contract* in order to "appropriate" Rousseau's theory of a legitimate social contract based on unanimous self-rule often struggle to explicate, or even explain away, some of the curious features that accompany Rousseau's depiction of the formation of the general will.[36] Rousseau describes a form of collective self-sacrifice that seems "inhuman," or superhuman, requiring by most estimations a wholly unrealistic neglect toward even the *consideration* of one's own interests in the act of forming the "general will." In forming "the social compact," each individual "gives his entire self . . . without reservation" toward the aim of "the total alienation of each associate" in the formation of a union that is "perfect," that itself in turn becomes a "common self," a "public person" (*SC*, 53). The general will, while unanimous, is not mere unanimity, since "there is a great difference between the will of all and the general will" owing to the latter's underlying basis in complete sacrifice of self-interest and the overcoming of alienation (*SC*, 61). Indeed, the citizens achieve such a state of shared understanding that the general will can be formed "without communication" (*SC*, 61). In order to adequately understand this fundamental transformation of modern human "nature," one must account for the *prior* transformation of that nature, its replacement with a *new* nature, achieved at the moment of founding by the Legislator.

Most important, by means of this reliance upon the Legislator's art, Rousseau both relies upon the necessary support of religion in forging the bonds of the polity, yet avoids the potential dangers of religion (as described, and previously cited, in *GM*, 160), since the inculcation of this new nature at the hands of the Legislator *appears* to be a religion without in fact *being* religion. Unlike Rousseau's later description of "civil religion" in which the religion is *defined* as requiring certain articles of faith, both positive and negative, in this *prior* use of religion by the Legislator Rousseau tells us that the appeal to religion, in fact, merely affords persuasive force to the true teaching of the Legislator. Religion is the vehicle by which the Legislator promulgates his "own wisdom" and his "sublime reason," when, indeed, it is his own "great soul" that is the "true miracle" (*SC*, 69, 70).

The legislator is the new Prometheus. He takes a malleable creature, as in the ancient myths of Prometheus, and creates a creature capable of achieving the political arts.[37] He introduces humanity to worship of the gods, but, in fact, it is his own efforts that achieve this transformation. He takes a creature incapable of self-rule and makes one capable of governing the earth. The first legislator is akin to the figure of Orpheus portrayed in an illustration to book IV of *Emile*, who introduces fur-wearing savages to the "music" of civilization and raises them from the comparable level of bestial "satyr" to that of human being.[38] The image, as Rousseau described in the accompanying caption, "represents Orpheus teaching men the worship of the gods" (*E*, 36) (see Figure 5.2). Interspersed with the images of terrified primitive humans are various species of animals who also appear to listen to the discourse of the toga-clad (and hence civilized) Orpheus. This juxtaposition suggests that humans are akin to the animals in their state of savagery but differ from the beasts to the extent to which they can be "made" human by means of their capacity to worship the gods. This particular illustration, notably, appears in the book in which the "Profession of Faith of the Savoyard Vicar" unfolds: religion, which had initially been used to "sanctify" the inequality within nations, is eventually employed by a godlike Legislator with the aim of creating a new humanity.[39] "Satyr, you do not know it."

Yet, unlike Prometheus, who in pointing to the gods showed humanity how to worship, the Legislator points humans away from worship of the true source of their political redemption, not now the uncaring and unresponsive gods but a human being, the promethean Legislator. While religion itself is not "natural," it remains available for humans to use for the purpose of *changing* human nature. Rather than an acknowledgment of human insufficiency, this first appearance of a wholly "civil religion"—employed by the Legislator to alter the human creature—demonstrates the complete control of humanity over that most recalcitrant part of nature, namely, *humanity itself*, the only creature capable of departing from its original nature and thereby the only one able by its own efforts to create a new nature for itself. Such a conclusion gives added significance to Rousseau's declaration that "the most general will is also the most just, and that the voice of the people is indeed the voice of God" (*PE*, 8).[40] One might rephrase Rousseau's statement in light of the fact that the voice of the people is created by the art of the Legislator by means of the purported voice of God, that, in effect, the voice of God is the voice of perfected humanity.

Rousseau's Optimism: Solving the Theological-Political Problem by Faith Alone

Rousseau's "democratic faith"—his belief in the malleability and infinite perfectibility of humanity—rests, much as the case for Protagoras, upon an implicit set of metaphysical assumptions. Rousseau's "theodicy" reflects the optimism of the philosopher Leibniz or the poet Alexander Pope in accepting ours as the best of all possible worlds, yet at the same time it rejects the very passivity to which philosophical optimism was originally inclined. His own form of self-declared "optimism" thus, in fact, rejects the first premise of optimism—that the world as created is fundamentally good—while endorsing, if indirectly, that the world is "the best possible" precisely because of the inherent human ability to alter the evident imperfections of the world to humanity's liking. Rousseau's activist political optimism is developed with a backdrop of "cosmic optimism," an optimism that is articulated in its greatest succinctness in a letter to Voltaire dated August 18, 1756. In this let-

Figure 5.2. Orpheus teaching men the worship of the gods. Frontispiece to Jean-Jacques Rousseau's *Émile, ou De l'éducation,* Vol. 3, Book IV (Amsterdam: Jean Néaulme, 1762). Reprinted with permission from Princeton University Firestone Library, Department of Rare Books and Special Collections.

ter one sees in bold relief the metaphysical and theological assumptions that undergird his form of "democratic faith."

Optimism, as developed by Leibniz and Pope, held that God could have only created the best world possible: given an infinite number of possible choices of worlds He might have chosen to create, God necessarily created the one with the fewest imperfections.[41] Optimism was developed as a response to the rise of naturalist, or "materialist," beliefs which held that the universe was not governed by a providential plan or beneficent power. "Optimism" was developed as a theology aimed at reconciling the existence of evil and imperfection with the belief in God's perfection and beneficence— albeit one that departed from traditional understandings of "Providence" inasmuch as it dismissed the redemptive promises of Christ's presence in human history. It was thus a deistic "theodicy" that sought to reject the prospect of a random and meaningless universe. While "optimism" had gained adherents in the eighteenth century, it was severely tested by the devastating earthquake in Lisbon, Portugal, in 1755. Voltaire's own sense of optimism was shattered by the earthquake, and in its wake he wrote a poem entitled "The Lisbon Earthquake: An Inquiry into the Axiom 'Whatever Is, Is Right.'"[42] Thereafter he wrote the anti-optimist novel *Candide* which featured a caricature of the Leibnizian optimist Dr. Pangloss. Rousseau's 1756 letter was written in response to Voltaire's seering poem about the earthquake.

Rousseau begins the letter by asserting his own inclination toward the optimist worldview, above all, because it provides "solace" rather than "distress" (*LV*, 233). Given a choice between Pope and Voltaire, he prefers to have his fears allayed than to be left with "shaken hope" that "reduces me to despair" (*LV*, 233). Yet, in setting forth the two choices that appear to be offered and embracing the one he prefers—the optimism of Leibniz and Pope against the pessimism of Voltaire—Rousseau describes two positions each equally unattractive (as well as equally blasphemous), ones that he recognizes as "errors," and both of which he effectively rejects.

His rejection of Voltaire's position is obvious. He takes the following from Voltaire's poem:

> Suffer forever, unhappy man. If there is a God who has created you, no doubt he is omnipotent; he could have prevented all your evils: hence do not hope that they will ever end; for there is no understanding why you exist, if not to suffer and to die. (*LV*, 233)

If God is omnipotent as is supposed, then he is malevolent: the evidence of evil in the world is evidence of an omnipotent God's unmerciful cruelty and inhumanity. Rousseau rejects this possibility for the "distress" it causes, by means of embracing the "optimist" position and its concomitant rejection of the idea of an omnipotent God.

Thus he writes that optimists tell him the following:

> Man, have patience. Your evils are a necessary effect of your nature and of the constitution of this universe. The eternal and beneficent Being who governs you would have wished to safeguard you from them. Among all possible economies he chose the one that combined the least evil with the most good, or (to say the same thing even more bluntly, if need be), if he did not do better, it is that he could not do better. (*LV*, 233)

Rousseau sees directly to the blasphemous implication of Leibniz's "optimism": its assertion of the fundamental goodness of this world is only made sensible by a claim that limits God's omnipotence, such that He is incapable of creating an entirely perfect world. It applies the principle of noncontradiction to creation—that a perfect God could only create an imperfect universe, because the universe is separate from and different than God—but such an application does not entertain the possibility that God is not subject to those very laws (such as noncontradiction) that seem to govern the universe He created. Rousseau's attraction to this position is because of the solace it provides—particularly because it is effected by interpreting the world in light of the human desire to comprehend its attendant evils—but that solace is bought at a price of the optimist's resignation to those very evils of an imperfect universe, ones against which even God cannot combat.

Rousseau claims to find Voltaire's position crueler than "Manicheanism" inasmuch as Voltaire seeks to "justify [God's] power at the expense of his goodness." Given a choice between the "two errors" committed by Voltaire or Leibniz, respectively, Rousseau prefers the "error" of the optimist over that of the pessimist, because the idea of a weaker but still beneficent God is more conducive to assuaging his fears and taming his despair (*LV*, 233). The very articulation of the two choices reveals, in fact, his understanding of optimism as a form of "Manicheanism": forced to choose between an omnipotent but apparently indifferent or even cruel God and a beneficent but limited God—that is, one much closer to a Manichean worldview which supposes that God is opposed by an equally powerful and separate force of evil—Rousseau admits his greater attraction to the Manichean understanding. Notably Rousseau does not entertain the possibility (and an obvious one at that, given its existence as the reigning Christian orthodoxy) that God is *both* omnipotent *and* beneficent. Of the four possible options one may apparently entertain—Christian, materialist (both implicit in Rousseau's analysis), and the two named "errors" of the optimist and pessimist—Rousseau rejects out of hand the Christian and materialist options, and expresses greater attraction to the theodicy of the "optimists" than that of the "pessimists." He does this, however, not finally to endorse the conventional optimist's position—one that results in resignation to the existence of the world's evil—but rather to alter it in such a way that it makes a human-centered optimism possible, one that rejects the resignation of traditional optimists. In short, Rousseau advances the idea that we live in the best of all possible worlds *not* as a result of God's omnipotence, nor arguably even his beneficence, but rather because God's beneficence and lack of complete omnipotence allows the possibility of *man's* power to fill the creativity gap opened by God's weakness. Given a choice between the "errors," Rousseau will cleave more closely to the error that accords with a more flattering vision of the universe—one, notably, that posits the idea of a limited God—in order that he might subsequently correct the "errors" inherent in that vision. Optimism is embraced only to be fundamentally redefined.

Rousseau elaborates his own "theodicy" through an analysis of the Lisbon earthquake and, in so doing, reveals the radicalism of his "Manichean" perspective: the external force that "creates" evil is not a distinct God or Devil but rather humanity itself. Man, not God, is the source of evil and, as the source, also has the potential ability to cure the very evil man creates. As he writes quite plainly, "I do not see that one can seek the source of moral evil anywhere but in man, free, perfected, hence corrupted." Physical "evil" is a simple consequence of the interaction between "sentient and insentient" matter, but even the threat of physical harm presented by the world must be reconsidered inasmuch as "most of our physical evils are also of our own making" (*LV*, 234). Here Rousseau delivers his conclusive analysis by means of a consideration of the earthquake's damage: "You must admit, for example, that nature had not assembled two thousand six- or seven-story houses there, and that if the inhabitants of that great city had been more evenly distributed and more simply lodged, the damage would have been far less, and perhaps nil" (*LV*, 234). Rousseau compares the damage of the earthquake on such unnatural human habitations to its irrelevance to dispersed beasts in the natural state, and concludes that humanity "creates" the evils that it falsely attributes to an otherwise beneficent God. Again following Plutarch's advice, the very "enemy" of humanity—human ingenuity—can be reevaluated to humanity's advantage. Thus, by means of an awareness of the human source of "evil," we can be appropriately armed in considering how such evils can be extirpated.

While Rousseau clearly enjoins the dream of returning to a presocial condition, he also suggests that humankind misdirects its efforts if it attempts to "subjugate nature" to human convenience (*LV*, 234). Instead, a "second nature" must be fashioned for mankind, one that will make the potentially deleterious effects of indifferent natural causes irrelevant to a reconceived humanity.[43] Rousseau thus demands a belief in a beneficent if not omnipotent God—much like the "optimists"—but he rejects the notion that the universe is irredeemably imperfect. God's beneficence is not one that promises redemption by divine intervention: rather, divine beneficence is deduced through a preliminary belief in thorough human agency. While God creates a creature that potentially can become human, it is in fact humankind that creates itself. Further, humanity is the true source of the knowledge of Good and Evil: evil is most fundamentally the cause of ill-conceived human contrivance, and can be alleviated and even overcome by means of better-conceived human contrivance. Much of Rousseau's writing describes various forms of refashioning human "nature": through education, laws, political institutions, family, and even a re-creation of the individual by means of a tutor (in *Emile*) or a Legislator (in the *Social Contract*).

It is unsurprising that, in an effort to support his view of such a beneficent if otherwise indifferent God, Rousseau concludes his letter to Voltaire describing the basic outlines of a "civil religion" much akin to the one he describes in the *Social Contract* (*LV*, 245–246). If humanity is to be brought to the point at which man will believe in a form of Providence that recommends man's mastery of his own condition by means of artifice—thus, recommending at once a belief that humanity is the cause of, and potentially the solution to, evil—then a religious "artifice" must serve as the first source of a renewed human belief in its own potential. A human-based religion gives rise to a belief in a beneficent but not all-powerful God, which in turn gives rise to the belief that evil is caused and potentially eliminated by humans. Human needs dictate the shape of our God, and the limits of that God dictate the compensating power of human creation.

Such belief—one that finally undergirds Rousseau's democratic faith, his belief in political transformation by means of human self-fashioning—is finally a matter of chosen faith: "I believe in God just as strongly as I believe in any other truth, because to believe and not to believe are the things that least depend on me, because the state of doubt is too violent a state for my soul, because when my reason wavers, my faith cannot long remain in suspense, and decides without it; and finally because a thousand things I like better draw me toward the more consoling side and add the weight of hope to the equilibrium of reason" (*LV*, 242–243). In the first instance, Rousseau recognizes that as a human he cannot escape the condition of believing: it comes down, simply, to what belief he will embrace. Rousseau freely admits that his faith comes about as a result of his desire for solace: his faith is an expression of pure will and the result of a human-centered calculus of preference. Reason—poised at a point of equilibrium on a scale—cannot choose between optimism and pessimism. Human will to power tips it toward the optimistic side. Yet, to conclude by elaborating on Rousseau's own image, a finger already tilts the balance of the scale—the weight of human preference, human will, and human self-flattery. The resulting faith reflects the assumptions that went into its formulation. Rousseau thus endorses and recommends a human-centered faith that follows when humanity's view of the universe is assumed to be a simple matter of individual choice between faith that consoles and faith that leads to despair. In either case, faith is endorsed for the sake of human needs and ends, primary among which is a faith in a perfectible democracy, one whose necessary accompaniment is the potential for despair in the face of unrealized democratic faith, and this suggests why Rousseau, that "dreamer of democracy," entitles his final work "Reveries of a Solitary Walker."

CHAPTER SIX

American Faith: The Translation of Religious Faith to Democratic Faith

> While I cannot understand or argue it out, I believe in a clue
> and purpose in Nature, entire and several; and that invisible
> spiritual results, just as real and definite as the visible,
> eventuate all concrete life and all materialism, through Time.
>
> —*Walt Whitman, "A Backward Glance o'er Travel'd Roads"*

IN LIGHT OF THE individual excellences that democracy calls upon—in Santayana's words, even requiring that "the common citizen must be something of a saint and something of a hero"—it is not surprising to encounter expressions of the need to promote *belief* in democracy, and indeed to see such belief as a requisite feature of democracy's fruition.[1] One unavoidably encounters the language of "trust," "belief," "hope," and even "faith" in the prospects of democratic self-governance, in the capacities of democratic citizens, and in the possibility of a democratic ideal. Democracy takes on the characteristics of a community of the faithful: as William James would write, "democracy is a kind of religion, and we are not bound to admit its failure."[2]

A characteristic call for such democratic belief is expressed by the Transcendentalist Edward Everett, who, during an address at Harvard University in 1824, raised the question of whether the people could be considered to be good enough, or possessed adequate capacity, for democracy: "It rests with us to solve the great problem in human society, to settle, and that forever, the momentous question—whether mankind can be trusted with a purely popular system?" Surveying the history of human efforts toward liberation, Everett waxed into a prophetic voice, invoking our common faith, a faith that would itself act as a spur to the realization of the object of that faith: "[The departed] exhort us, they adjure us to be faithful to our trust. They implore us by the long trials of struggling humanity, by the blessed memory of the departed; by the dear faith, which has been plighted by pure hands, to the holy cause of truth and man."[3] Combining the belief that the past justified what pragmatists would later call "warranted belief" with a prospective belief, or hope, in the future trajectory of the examples of the past, Everett characteristically combined backward-looking and "experiential" piety with forward-looking faith, or hope, in the future.

Even one nearly thoroughly disillusioned with democracy as Henry Adams could speak of democracy in terms of faith—or at least could put such words in the voice of one of his characters in a novel anonymously published. Although his novel, *Democracy*, ends with seeming bitterness toward democracy and its tendency toward corruption and self-interest, at least one character—Nathan Gore—resists this predominant mood and expresses his enduring (and perhaps self-admitted futile) faith in democracy:

> These are matters about which I rarely speak in society; they are like the doctrine of a personal God; of a future life; of revealed religion; subjects which one naturally reserves for private reflection. But since you ask for my political creed, you shall have it. I believe in democracy. I accept it. I will faithfully serve and defend it. I believe in it because it appears to be the inevitable consequence of what has gone before it. Democracy asserts the fact that the masses are now raised to a higher intelligence than formerly. All our civilisation aims at this mark. We want to do what we can to help it. I myself want to see the result. I grant it is an experiment, but it is the only direction society can take that is worth taking. . . . I have faith; not perhaps in the old dogmas, but in the new ones; faith in human nature; faith in science; faith in survival of the fittest.[4]

Particularly in the face of suspicion and skepticism, if not outright disbelief in its feasibility, democracy has been discussed as frequently in "religious" terms as it has been understood in purely secular terms. This is true as well when democracy is considered in purely "pragmatic" terms: often those thinkers who insist most fervently upon the secular and nonmetaphysical nature of democracy are the most likely to employ religious terms to describe democracy's legitimacy or to recommend its improvement. While this is frequently the case with respect to nineteenth- and early-twentieth-century American thinkers such as Emerson, Whitman, Dewey, William James, and Sidney Hook (among others), it is no less true today among late-twentieth and early-twenty-first century thinkers such as Richard Rorty, Richard Bernstein, and Benjamin Barber—scholars who otherwise understand themselves as thoroughly secular.[5] The language of "Religious Democracy" extolled by Walt Whitman, far from being a historical curiosity, is with us today even among insistently secular thinkers.[6]

Contemporary thinkers valorize "secularized" religious conceptions such as *caritas* (charity), reverence, piety, faith, redemption, forgiveness, and hope as necessary underpinnings, even essential civic ingredients, for flourishing democracy.[7] In so doing, such thinkers at once retain the power and conceptual force of the religious concepts (just as the building of the Panthéon maintained the sacral atmosphere of the Cathedrale St.-Geneviève) while deploying these respective conceptions explicitly toward secular ends and purposes. Democracy calls upon a form of "naturalized" belief, but it is a belief expressed frequently in terms of religious discourse, and therefore appears to be a secularized version of theological language. This is both half-correct, given that the call for "faith" in democracy retains and invokes religious echoes and traditions, and half-false, given that the object of belief is no longer a divine or transcendent deity but, instead, human beings and political forms. On the one hand, such invocations seem a "tamer" version of full-blown religious (theological) concepts, as democracy would appear to be less an object for excessive or fanatical belief; on the other hand, since the "naturalized" object now is subject to "deification" in its own right—particularly a belief in the possibility of thoroughgoing human transformation—such invocations can often take the form of immodest claims in our ability to transform human nature or political society.

Frequently a central aim of these religiously derived recommendations for contemporary democratic citizens is an effort to negotiate the civic relationships between individuals, at once seeking to preserve the central value of individual autonomy while recommending such religious sensibilities as a means of bridging individual interest, of containing destructive selfish impulses and pointing citizens outward beyond narrowness of self. Durkheim's contention that, at base, human community is "religious" is echoed in these secularized yet sacral evocations.[8] If originally these conceptions were invoked in a religious setting to point individuals beyond their earthly moorings and toward a transcendent existence beyond our immediate ken—therefore reflecting a faith beyond what we can currently know for certain and a belief in the existence of a universal fabric in which all humanity is sewn together in spite of our apparent disparateness—these conceptions are now recommended to move individuals toward a "dance with community," either toward a strong embrace of the "whole" that calls for a chastening of individual interest, or at least minimally recommending a dialogic stance of openness and a willingness to conceive of the self as expansive and near-infinite in its capacity for receptivity and engagement.[9] It is at the point of practical intractableness, theoretical difficulty, and even human mystery, in which thinkers attempt to reconcile the ancient conundrum—the relationship of the many and the one—that one witnesses this religiously derived language so often invoked.[10] "Democratic faith" is commonly conceived as the "saving faith" that will foster transcendence of individual identity within a more comprehensive human whole while simultaneously resisting the absorption of the ego into an undifferentiated collectivity, thereby allowing us to retain our claims to inviolable individuality.[11]

Especially in nineteenth-century America many thinkers turned to a secularized narrative of redemptive human history that had been imported by various admirers of Hegel, a narrative that gave special stress upon the ways in which there was no fundamental dualism between the actual and the ideal, and that developing historical consciousness made possible the reconciliation of god and man, man and society, and man and man.[12] Hegel's theory held forth the possibility of a universal community of humans and a reconciliation between spirit and matter, a future apotheosis that would unfold in spite of what might appear to be the contradictory evidence discernable in our discrete actions and efforts. History was viewed as a progressive force that was bringing into existence the reconciliation of individual selfhood and "cosmic consciousness." The ultimate object of such faith was the overcoming of human alienation.

Such transplanted "religious" views represented a rejection of traditional Augustinian doctrine that posited the existence of a vast expanse between humanity and the divine, and even the inescapable alienation of humans from one another—a distance that had opened as a result of the sin of Adam and which could be narrowed but not closed by human effort, and might be repaired solely through the grace of God. A rejection of this Augustinian, Jansenist, or Calvinist view for one that saw history itself as a process by which seemingly permanent alienation could be overcome made it possible for thinkers to promote the human ability to effect the progress of human consciousness and the achievement of divine attributes formerly deemed to be the sole provenance of God alone.[13] The ideal of perfectible humanity suddenly seemed not only to be no longer impious but an achievable goal. According to William Henry Channing in 1840, "We seek to conceive and realize an Ideal of Humanity. The temple in which the Holy Spirit loves to dwell is a true man; the acceptable worship is a pure character, manifested in acts of dignity and love. The end of existence is growth; progress is the vital law of the soul; hope will admit no limit but perfection. . . . Again; we see a progress in the past history of our race; we feel that a mighty power of good is stirring now in society; we believe in the coming of the kingdom of God."[14]

The belief in the possibility of such reconciliation arrived amid already fertile soil, prepared, perhaps somewhat unexpectedly, by the explicitly religious thought of, in particular, the colonial Calvinist theologian Jonathan Edwards. Writing about the nature of "true virtue," Edwards famously asserted that "true virtue most essentially consists in benevolence to Being in general. Or, perhaps to speak more accurately, it is that consent, propensity and union of heart to Being in general, that is immediately exercised in a general good will."[15] Edwards contrasted such generalized benevolence to "Being in general"—one that takes "the most comprehensive view" and is "related to everything that it stands in connection with"—with a more particularistic "benevolence toward a private circle or system of beings, which are a small part of the whole" (540, 541). For Edwards, such generalized love of being was one that permitted, even made possible, the fullest flourishing of love directed toward specific objects, since "from such a disposition may arise exercises of love to particular beings . . . [inasmuch as] he who is of a generally benevolent disposition should be more disposed than another to have his heart moved with benevolent affection to particular persons, whom he is acquainted and conversant with, and from whom arise the greatest and most frequent occasions for exciting his benevolent temper" (541–542). The development of this disposition, while reinforced and strengthened by benevolence toward particular persons and things, derived ultimately from our love of the being with "the greatest share of universal existence": therefore, "'tis evident that true virtue must chiefly consist in love to God; the Being of beings, infinitely the greatest and best of beings" (550).

While providing an uplifting portrait of the possibility of achieving the "consent, propensity and union of heart to Being in general," Edwards emphasized that the fallen condition of human beings put such complete self-lessness finally out of our reach. Humans are instead inclined toward partiality of vision, tending to prefer private interest and self-aggrandizing pursuits against the general or common good (555).[16] Indeed, humans tend to mistake their own partial vision for one that encompasses totality, mistaking their own selfish sight for the "benevolence" toward all being. Even in the love of a parent for a child, or most forms of seemingly generous charity, such apparent forms of virtue "are essentially defective . . . [because] they are private in their nature; they do not arise from any temper of benevolence to being in general. . . . These private systems are so far from containing the sum of universal being, or comprehending all existence to which we stand related, that it contains but an infinitely small part of it. The reason why men are so ready to take these private affections for true virtues, is the narrowness of their views; and above all, that they are so ready to leave the Divine Being out of their view. . . ."[17] Having described the nature of "true virtue," Edwards nonetheless concludes that such true virtue is all but inaccessible to inveterately fallen human beings. Humans tend always toward aggrandizement of the self, toward concern for their own happiness and rebellion toward the necessary attitude of submission and abasement before God: "Man is naturally exceeding[ly] prone to exalt himself, and depend on his own power or goodness; as though from himself he must expect happiness."[18] As Christopher Lasch has summarized Edwards's thinking on the subject of human happiness, "the secret of happiness lay in renouncing the right to happiness."[19]

While many leading lights in the nineteenth century rejected this latter exhortation to recognize the inescapability of our sinfulness, and hence the permanence of our selfish inclinations, the former aspect of Edwards's praise of the possibility of a kind of generalized "benevolence," the comprehension of the whole qua "Being," the reconciliation between God and man, and the final overcoming of human alienation were not similarly rejected but instead viewed as imminently (and immanently) possible.[20] In spite of a rejection of reigning theology—even, for many in political theory, of theology altogether—religious language persisted, and persists, unabated: exhortations to achieve this now accessible form of comprehensive vision and coexistence are not rejected as mere superstition but rather continue to take the form of religious invocation, even if now God is not separate and sovereign but resides within each individual's soul or in the mysterious interstices between people.

Ralph Waldo Emerson exemplifies the rise of "democratic faith" as a "translation" of religious into civic and political language in the American context. One sees this "religious" expression especially in Emerson's lifelong efforts to describe and promote a reconciliation between the individual and the collective whole. While many recent commentators understand Emerson as a thinker, who, more than any other in the American context, set forth an ideal portrait of "democratic individualism," such a reading should be accompanied by a recognition of Emerson's firm insistence that the unleashing of individuals from the strictures of tradition and, in particular, from ossified religious organizations would make it possible for all people to perceive the whole of which they were merely parts.[21] Individualism is a means to universality, not an end in itself. In his less-read essay "The Over-Soul," Emerson acknowledges that our diurnal human reality is fragmented and discrete, just as our lives are led separately to seemingly different ends and attracted to seemingly distinct objects: "We live in succession, in division, in parts, in particles."[22] Our scattered experience of life is finally too limiting, and too easily leads to a dismissal of further possibilities: "The argument which is always forthcoming to silence those who conceive extraordinary hopes for man, namely, the appeal to experience, is for ever invalid and vain. We give up the past to the objector, and yet we hope. . . . We grant that human life is mean; but how did we find out that it was mean?"[23] An ideal whole lies barely outside our field of awareness, but we perceive it nonetheless by hints, by glimpses, and surmise:

> That Unity, that Over-soul, within which every man's particular being is contained and made whole with all other; that common heart, of which all sincere conversation is the worship. . . . Within man is the soul of the whole; the wise silence; the universal beauty, to which every part and particle is equally related; the eternal ONE. . . . We see this world piece by piece, as the sun, the moon, the animal, the tree; but the whole, of which these are the shining parts, is the soul. Only by the vision of that Wisdom can the horoscope of the ages be read, and by falling back on our better thoughts, by yielding to the spirit of prophecy which is innate in every man. . . . I desire, even by profane words, if I may not use sacred, to indicate the heaven of this deity, and to report what hints I have collected of the transcendent simplicity and energy of the Highest Law.[24]

Individualism is the way station to comprehending this more universal whole, permitting the necessary attitude of reverence and piety. Indeed, for Emerson, such an outlook becomes the very definition of the act of worship, as expressed in his essay of that title: "For, though the new element of freedom and an individual has been admitted, yet the primordial atoms are prefigured and predetermined to moral issues, are in search of justice, and ultimate right is done. Religion or worship is the attitude of those who seek this unity, intimacy, and sincerity; who see that, against all appearances, the nature of things works for truth and right forever."[25] The "profane" words that Emerson claims to deploy in describing the ascent of the individual into an apprehension of the collective whole is altogether "religious," albeit translated for secular purposes and ends.

Man's nature is indivisible from the natural whole, and the whole is itself part of the larger divine whole: "Ineffable is the union of man and God in every act of the soul. The simplest person, who in his integrity worships God, becomes God." By overcoming limiting "facts" that nature appears to present to us, we open the possibility of infinite improvement: "When we have broken our god of tradition and ceased from our god of rhetoric, then may God fire the heart with his presence. It is the doubling of the heart itself, nay, the infinite enlargement of the heart with a power of growth to a new infinity on every side. It inspires in man an infallible trust."[26] On the one hand, a divinized nature assures that every action and reaction in the natural world is infused with divine meaning and ultimate significance; on the other, a naturalized—or humanized—divinity places humanity on a par with the divine and makes nature itself subject to our mastery. The universe is finally beneficent, arranged, and organized for human comprehension and ultimately human control. All that has existed and will exist are marks of final progress, with a culmination promising full liberation of the human will and concomitant perception of the universal whole:

> No statement of the Universe can have any soundness, which does not admit its ascending effort. The direction of the whole, and of the parts, is toward benefit, and in proportion to the health. Behind every individual, closes organization: before him, opens liberty,—the Better, the Best. The first and worst races are dead. The second and imperfect races are dying out, or remain for the maturing of the higher. In the latest race, in man, every generosity, every new perception, the love and praise he extorts from his fellows, are certificates of advance out of fate into freedom. Liberation of the will from the sheaths and clogs of organization which he has outgrown, is the end and aim of the world.[27]

Emersonian "democratic faith" frees belief from the constraints and limitations of Edwards's more chastened view of human potential. Instead, our faith acts as a spur to action in realizing what does not yet exist. We do not need a reduction of faith in the face of reality (as the "secularization thesis" would hold), but "naturalism" permits greater and deeper faith *as a spur to action* and as a prompt to the realization of shared democratic ideals. In "New England Reformers" Emerson chides "doubt," the "destitution of faith," and our "infidelity" to man. Those who proclaim the fundamental depravity, or irredeemability, of mankind are possessed of "skepticism and atheism."[28] What is needed instead is not piecemeal reform but the infusion of faith itself: "The disease with which the human mind now labors is want of faith." Emerson endorses a "faith in man" discernible in and expressed through the "divine sentiments in man." If men as they are seem to fall short of justifying this faith, we must nevertheless believe that "men in all ways are better than they seem."[29] Even as Emerson acknowledges that democracy requires us to believe that individual voters standing in line at the polls "mean to vote right"—thus seemingly accepting men as they are—quickly, unsurprisingly, he goes on to envision still higher and more perfect humans (in Messianic tones) from these modest men at the polls. "If the auguries of the prophesying heart shall make themselves good in time, the man who shall be born, whose advent men and events prepare and foreshow, is one who shall enjoy his connexion with a higher life, with the man within man."[30]

Characteristic of those who believe in a higher and more perfect eventual development of human capacities, Emerson combines seemingly ordinary and modest expectations from democracy with soaring expectations of democratic "perfectionism" that most people fail to meet. Democracy is endorsed even as its citizens want improvement. In a late address entitled "The Fortune of the Republic"—one more expressly about American democracy than many of his essays—Emerson at once praises "men as they are" yet slides almost inevitably into visions of democratic man as he might be. In his more realistic mien, Emerson captures the manner in which democracy succeeds in keeping the ambitions of the few "great" men in check and advancing the firm common sense of the people:

> The lodging of the power in the people, as in republican forms, has the effect of holding things closer to common sense; for a court or an aristocracy, which must always be a small minority, can more easily run into follies than a republic, which has too many observers—each with a vote in his hand—to allow its head to be turned by any kind of nonsense: since hunger, thirst, cold, the cries of children and debt are always holding the masses hard to essential duties.[31]

Taking "men as they are," Emerson extols democracy's very ordinariness in the manner Rousseau would similarly claim—and, just like Rousseau, a short space later, in the same essay, he calls for a different kind of person than the ordinary citizens he seemingly extolled in the previous passage. "We want men of original perception and original action, who can open their eyes wider than to a nationality,—namely, to considerations that benefit the human race,—can act in the interest of civilization; men of elastic, men of moral mind, who can live in the moment and take a step backward. . . . The new times need a new man, the complemental man, whom plainly this country must furnish."[32]

Emerson rested considerable hopes of the progress of the human species on material and technological development, anticipating a similar faith as that of Whitman, Dewey, Barber, and Rorty. While individual "self-reliance" would assist in the creation of self-confident and anticonformist individuals, this emphasis upon individual competence was combined in his thought with a belief that such individualism would eventually make possible a greater awareness of, and identification with, the human whole. In the line of Emerson's attack were all *partial* identifications that served, at once, to obscure a true apprehension of each person's individuality and simultaneously the extent to which each individual was part of a more comprehensive "over-soul." The ability to discern our "self-reliance" made it possible to perceive our human wholeness. To this end, partial identifications and identities needed dissolution, and technological progress could assist in the greater "globalization" of human identity.

In his confident essay, "The Young American," Emerson lauds the progressive spirit of America that advances, almost unbeknownst to its actors, as a result of the impersonal forces of commerce and technological development. He celebrates the evaporation of local and particular identities that is being effected by means of the "assimilation" of a national commercial republic:

> This rage for road building is beneficent for America, where vast distance is so main a consideration in our domestic politics and trade. . . . Not only is distance annihilated, but when, as now, the locomotive and steamboat, like enormous shuttles, shoot every day across the thousand various threads of national descent and employment, and bind them fast in one web, an hourly assimilation goes forward, and there is no danger that local peculiarities and hostilities should be preserved.[33]

Emerson's praise of the "mechanistic" nature of human progress, one that brings humanity into closer national consanguinity, anticipates similar contemporary belief in the role of global commerce and technological progress in effecting a global community and international sense of commonweal. This dream continues to evoke the religious-tinged language of Emerson. In this same vein, Richard Falk has recently written that efforts to realize a future global community is "an essentially religious and normative undertaking based on faith in the unseen, salvation in a world to come."[34]

Commerce and technological advances that increase human interaction through such inventions as the locomotive and steamboats confirm that humanity contributes to its own moral progress. Human inventiveness points to the future self-directed evolutionary advance of humanity: "The population of the world is a conditional population; these are not the best, but the best that could live in the existing state of soils, gases, animals, and morals: the best that could *yet* live; there shall be a better, please God."[35] Human inventiveness is woven into the fabric of existence: thus our own efforts blend seamlessly with the Providential progressive course intended by Nature. "Men are narrow and selfish, but the Genius or Destiny is not narrow, but beneficent. . . . Only what is inevitable interests us, and it turns out that love and good are inevitable."[36] Emerson is the new prophet of the Good News.

FAITH, OLD AND NEW: DEWEY'S TRANSLATION OF RELIGION TO DEMOCRACY

In his magisterial study of American views of progress, *The True and Only Heaven*, Christopher Lasch reminds us to be wary of accusing nineteenth-century thinkers of "secularizing" the religious theme of progress, since traditional Christian conceptions sought to avoid materialistic explanations of progress and, instead, viewed with great caution any idea of a final culmination, even given the promise of the Second Coming. As described by Lasch, this traditional conception of human history was "much more the record of moral failure than a promise of ultimate triumph. It put less emphasis on the millenium to come than on the present duty to live with faith and hope, in a world that often seemed to give no encouragement to either."[37] The idea of progress as both a moral and material amelioration of the human condition,

Lasch contends, decidedly departs from this darker view of human history. The call for "faith" by Emerson—the belief that "believes in itself"—or, later, the "will to believe" of James, and similar invocations of "democratic faith" by John Dewey and contemporary thinkers such as Benjamin Barber and Richard Rorty, does not represent a form of "secularization" if we understand that phrase to imply "the disenchantment of the world." Rather, "faith" is retained, albeit without any external limits on what it might hope, and attempt, to achieve.

The "secular" form of faith does not necessitate any ideal of culmination or final securing of human perfection. Nothwithstanding even Hegel's contention for "the end of history," modern conceptions of progress have largely eschewed any transformative "end game" in favor of a more incrementalist understanding of human activity.[38] Lasch comments, "what was so original about the [modern conception was] not the promise of a secular utopia that would bring history to a happy ending but the promise of steady improvement with no foreseeable ending at all." What is ultimately attractive about this open-ended conception is the resilience with which such an approach could confront the more obvious contradictions and setbacks that both ancient and contemporary history pose to any fixed progressive view. The aim is not utopia but rather a progressive view of history's halting motion, a scientific view of hypothesis and skepticism, a "self-perpetuating inquiry" whose only outcome, Lasch assures, is the certainty that the future holds a "sophisticated contempt for the rudimentary quality of our present ways."[39]

That increasingly secular-minded thinkers did not indiscriminately reject the massive apparatus of religion, including its evocative language, is revealing of the extent to which progressive democratic theorists realized that "religious" belief could not be jettisoned. This recognition is seen with utter clarity in the work of John Dewey, whose work evinces the fact that, at base, the appeal to "faith" must be understood as a necessary and inescapable component of progressive assumptions. Dewey was explicit about the role of faith in his reconstruction of philosophy. As he described it, his project was not simply to seek the dissolution of old faiths but rather the creation of new ones. Addressing those who felt "a conflict between loyalty to the past and faithfulness to new truth," Dewey argued:

> The responsibility now upon us is to form our faith in the light of the most searching methods and known facts; it is to form that faith so that it shall be an efficient and present help to us in action, in the cooperative union with all men who are sincerely striving to help on the Kingdom of God on earth.[40]

Notwithstanding the frank acknowledgment of faith intertwined in modern theories of progress, even Dewey was finally unwilling to consider the implications of this new form of faith and its relationship to the old. Like the old forms of faith, the new secular faith in progress rested on a certain degree of "trust," even "hope," that the object of faith would fulfill the expectations of its believers. Yet, if this "trusting" aspect of faith reveals a continuity with religious antecedents, another element suggests a radical break with the past. Inasmuch as the modern conception of faith relies on secular means to a secular end of progress, and insofar as those means reflect a reliance upon rationality and science, there is an implicit assumption among the modern faithful that the formerly "irrational" element of old faith drops away; that is, because the *object* of faith changes, the *quality* of that faith changes as well. If anything, this transformation made it possible for adherents of progressivism to hold their faith with much greater robustness and certainty than that permitted by the old faith. Ironically the very faith in progress that is given rise by a kind of skepticism toward the "quest for certainty" results in a much more fundamental kind of certainty than older forms of faith allowed.

Dewey is rightly renowned for his skepticism in the service of pragmatism. In works like *The Quest for Certainty*, he criticizes ancient philosophic conceptions of a fixed human nature and the attempts by traditional philosophy to separate the "real" from the "true." For Dewey, that which exists is necessarily "true": there can be no separation of "knowledge" from "doing." Only through experience can one gain a foothold of knowledge about the world, and only in the world can any real form of knowledge be acquired. Anything less stands accused of what he called the "spectator theory of knowledge," a false attempt to contemplate some eternal verity on high which willfully ignored the necessary realities of current existence.[41]

Above all, what should be avoided is a "quest for certainty." Solutions to existing problems arising from human affairs are always provisional and tentative. As Dewey stated in *Quest for Certainty*, "no mode of action can give anything approaching absolute certitude; it provides insurance but not assurance. Doing is always subject to peril [and] to the danger of frustration."[42] Rather than prompting us to avoid such precariousness in our knowledge, Dewey suggests that such an attitude is the necessary and desirable consequence of adopting a kind of knowledge that is constantly and rightly in danger of obsolescence. We should avoid reaching the conclusion that the opposite of uncertainty is knowledge. Calling this the "commonest fallacy," he urges a kind of patient willingness to submit to doubt, noting the undesirable tendency by which "thought hastens toward the settled and is only likely to force the pace."[43] The attempt to secure knowledge about any aspect of human life or natural phenomena is always discrete and tentative, and any resulting answer to questions about human affairs is always limited and momentary. Not only can our experience change in such a manner as to render the old solutions moot, but new applications of human ingenuity and questioning can easily overthrow temporarily "settled" beliefs.

The proper method of investigating apparent truths, of constantly improving them through outright rejection or incremental adjustments, Dewey called the "method of intelligence." As he described,

> Some of its obvious elements are willingness to hold belief in suspense, ability to doubt until evidence is obtained; willingness to go where evidence points instead

of putting first a personally preferred conclusion; ability to hold ideas in solution and use them as hypotheses to be tested instead of as dogmas to be asserted; and (possibly most distinctive of all), enjoyment of new fields for inquiry and of new problems.[44]

The openness and provisionality of this approach lends itself most appropriately to the democratic temperament, given its willingness to entertain disagreement and variety of opinions. Dewey perceived the "method of intelligence" and democracy as intimately bound together: the "method of intelligence" could only fully find expression in an appropriately open society like a democracy, whereas democracy could only be improved from within by the application of the "method of intelligence." The "method," then, had explicitly democratic and progressive applications:

> The purpose [of the method of intelligence] is to set free and to develop the capacities of human individuals without respect to race, sex, class or economic status. . . . Democracy has many meanings, but if it has a moral meaning, it is found in resolving that the supreme test of all political and industrial arrangements shall be the contribution they make to the all-around growth of every member of society.[45]

Dewey's confidence in the ability of the "method of intelligence" to create conditions of moral and material growth is almost unbounded: nature holds an incalculable bounty for human use, if only its secrets can be unlocked by the proper attitude of inquisitiveness and the development of certain technical adeptness. Noting his indebtedness to Francis Bacon in this regard, Dewey wrote that "scientific laws do not lie on the surface of nature. They are hidden, and must be wrested from nature by an active and elaborate technique of inquiry."[46] The job of the modern, and especially of modern science—a realm of inquiry that extends to the human sciences as well as to the natural sciences—is to extract the secrets of nature by whatever means possible, even if these methods at times evoke ominous overtones. Indeed, again echoing Bacon, Dewey reveals the severity with which the modern scientist must approach his task:

> [He] must force the apparent facts of nature into forms different to those in which they familiarly present themselves; and thus make them tell the truth about themselves, *as torture may compel an unwilling witness to reveal what he has been concealing.*[47]

Only through such a ruthless and single-minded manner has humanity begun to achieve the "conquest of physical nature"; and only by extending this method of inquiry to the "social-moral" realm can humanity hope to achieve an equilibrium between the physical and social sciences, the latter permitting true "social or humane knowledge and human engineering."[48]

At no point does Dewey suggest what the conclusions of such inquiries either *will* entail nor what they *should* conclude. The *ends* of scientific inquiry are determined entirely by the facts the method will uncover: no "values" need be introduced a priori into the inquiry itself.[49] Nevertheless, Dewey remains confident that the conquest of nature, both human and social, will result in an opening of technological, biological, and political vistas. Nature is a bountiful source, and the administration of a scientific "inquisition" will "open up marvelous possibilities in industry and commerce, and new social conditions conducive to invention, ingenuity, enterprise."[50] If any end of human activity can be suggested at all, it is an open-ended one, described often by Dewey as "growth." Noting that "growth" is the only "moral 'end,'" Dewey leaves the aim or object of growth as entirely undefined, concluding solely that "growth, or growing [is] developing, not only physically but intellectually and morally."[51]

Dewey's view that human ends are "defined" through a process of intelligence that will constantly make previous conclusions obsolete relies ultimately on a kind of secular faith in two respects: the ability of humans to adequately uncover, or "torture," nature to disclose its truths; and, second, the belief that the secrets of nature, once disclosed, will prove exclusively beneficial to human moral ends. Dewey's "democratic faith" is bound up in a belief in the beneficent trajectory of scientific inquiry and the promise held forth by the correct application of scientific technique in politics.[52] Indeed, notwithstanding Dewey's reliance on rationality, scientism, and praise of "uncertainty," he would nonetheless be the first to acknowledge that his confidence in the prospects of science, and especially science in the service of democracy, contained an element of faith that derived from a kind of "reconstruction" of religious tenets. This project of "reconstruction" began quite early in Dewey's career but continued throughout his life and served as a constant well of hope for Dewey.

Dewey's Democratic Faith

Dewey described his early project of reconstruction of religion as

> devoted to making explicit the religious values implicit in the spirit of science as undogmatic reverence for truth in whatever form it presents itself, and the religious values implicit in our common life, especially in the moral significance of democracy as a way of living together.[53]

From the outset Dewey considered democracy to be a modern incarnation of the religious spirit, and he effectively sought to transfer the faith, once directed toward the divine, instead toward the prospects and promise of democracy. In his earliest writings (often dismissed as immature neo-Hegelian attempts), Dewey insisted that faith was an essential component of human experience.[54] In 1884 he uncharacteristically adopted the traditional religious language of faith in God but, in an entirely consistent manner with his later writings, insisted that faith is a matter of *attitude* and *will*, with strong emphasis upon human control over both: "man's knowledge or lack of knowledge depends wholly upon this original attitude of his will and desires toward God; and because *these* are under his control, because these express his moral tendency, his knowledge does also."[55] Even more central than our belief in God per se is the importance of our own *control* over our will and desires. Faith, as conceived in this early essay, is not in some crucial regard a *release* of control or an admission of human insufficiency but, rather, a moment of mastery over our own will, and hence, for Dewey, is comparable to the control we can exert over the external world through our knowledge. Even framed in the traditional language of sin and moral culpability, Dewey is already engaged in a reconstruction of the idea of faith that would support his democratic aspirations.

This reconstruction becomes quite explicit in Dewey's 1892 essay, "Christianity and Democracy." Dewey sought to equate the role religion once played—before its institutionalization—and the role democracy must now play. The common feature each shares, he argues, is revelation—understood now not as the unveiling of true doctrine from divine sources but, instead (in a Hegelian manner), as a process of "unfolding." Christianity, in its original form, reflected a "continuously unfolding, never ceasing discovery of the meaning of life."[56] By suggesting that revelation is a process of unfolding, Dewey argues that the truest agent of religious faith available to modern man is *not* organized religion, which has crystallized into a defender of unbending doctrine, but instead the more open-ended activity of democratic life. Rather than a revelation from on high, democracy "enables us to get our truths in a natural, everyday and practical sense."[57] Since one of the guiding principles of democracy is freedom—and it is not presupposed in democratic societies that one way of life or system of belief must be the sole road to truth—democracy is most suitably said to be the contemporary incarnation of the process of revelation.

> Democracy thus appears as the means by which the revelation of truth is carried on. It is in democracy, the community of ideas and interest through community of action, that the incarnation of God (man, that is to say as organ of universal truth) becomes a living, present thing, having its ordinary and natural sense. This truth is brought down to life; its segregation removed; it is made a common truth enacted in all departments of action, not in one isolated sphere called religious.[58]

Dewey, in effect, is able to equate democracy and religion not by making politics "religious" per se but by suggesting that religion (and even here, while speaking of Christianity, he notes that this analysis might apply to any religion) in its most *authentic* incarnation seeks to encourage an open-ended search for truth. Dewey comes close here to associating "true" Christianity with the broad process of education he was to embrace in coming decades. Forty years later Dewey would still write that "the future of religion is connected to the possibility of developing a faith in the possibilities of human experience and human relationships that will create a vital sense of the solidarity of human interests and inspire action to make that sense a reality."[59] Religion is to be transformed to serve the ends of democratic politics.

Democracy also proves the most promising manifestation of this religious "unfolding" in modern life since, quite in contrast with most organized religion, it remains open and even sympathetic with the scientific pursuit of knowledge. Indeed, Dewey explicitly accuses the churches of "faithlessness" for their opposition to the rise of science. Arguing that the example of Jesus truly exemplifies openness toward human innovation, Dewey criticizes organized religion for disregarding the parable of the two sons, the younger of whom "went out into the vineyard of nature and by obedience to truth revealed the deeper truth of unity of law, the presence of one continuous living force, the conspiring and vital unity of all the world."[60] The churches have assumed the role of those who seek to hold back revelation rather than allow it to unfold through the modern auspices of democracy and science. Dewey admonishes the churches to "remember Lot's wife, who looked back, and who, looking back, was fixed into a motionless pillar."[61]

Alternatively Dewey enthusiastically (and in almost Whitmanesque tones) celebrates the rise of the scientific era coincident with the rise of democratic society:

> Here then we have democracy! On its negative side, the breaking down of barriers which hold truth from finding expression, on its positive side, the securing of conditions which give truth its movement, its complete distribution or service. It is no accident that the growing organization of democracy coincides with the rise of science, including the machinery of telegraph and locomotive for distributing truth. There is but one fact—the more complete movement of man to his unity with his fellows through realizing the truth of life.[62]

Here Dewey explicitly links the scientific development of human capacities, the conquest of nature, the process of "growth" that occurs in a democratic setting, and subsumes all these elements into a grand new reconstruction of faith—one that holds for a transformation of human life in the wholly secular sphere. Dewey echoes Emerson's faith in the benefits of technology, represented here by the telegraph and locomotive. Both permit for wider dissemination of knowledge, of greater movement of people and ideas, and of greater overall "growth" of the restless American spirit. Dewey trusted implicitly that these and other developments always promised an unconditional boon to the human condition. Indeed, it is striking that Dewey retains and develops many of these themes in the most notable "religious" work of his later period—*A Common Faith*, published in 1934—in which he would return explicitly to the example of the telegraph and locomotive as exemplars of human progress and tools of the democratic faith.

A COMMON FAITH

In his "definitive" work on religion and politics, *A Common Faith*, the result of three Terry Lectures at Yale University in 1933–34, Dewey revisits and expands on many of the themes he advanced in his earlier writings. The first lecture of *A Common Faith* is devoted almost entirely to an attempt to distinguish between "religion" as organized institutions, largely explicable through anthropological and historical references, and "the religious," by which Dewey means a sentiment or attitude toward the world, one of openness and a willingness to discover the meaning through whatever available means.[63] One could view the world in two possible ways, neither one rejecting the possibility of God per se, but one leading to the stultifying approach of organized religion and the other more sympathetic to the project of democracy and science. He describes these two attitudes in this way:

> We begin to select, to choose, and say that some present ways of thinking about the unseen powers are better than others; that the reverence shown by a free and self-respecting human being is better than the servile obedience rendered to an arbitrary power by frightened men; that we should believe that control of human destiny is exercised by a wise and loving spirit rather than by madcap ghosts or sheer force—when I say, we begin to choose, we have entered upon a road that has not yet come to an end. (*CF*, 7)

At some points Dewey calls the belief in "madcap ghosts" nothing other than simple superstition and dismisses it because of the sense of *fear* it creates, a fear that prevents an adequate approach toward control of seemingly uncontrollable forces inherent in nature, and not some inaccessible "sheer force."[64] But elsewhere Dewey recognizes this to be a form of faith, however imperfect, calling it "religious faith" (here meaning the faith associated with organized religions), describing it as "a kind of anticipatory vision of things that are now invisible because of our finite and erring nature" (*CF*, 20). Because this form of faith denigrates human knowledge, it lends itself to control by authorities—and hence the creation of "systematic propositions" and doctrine. Moreover, it sets forth an unprovable ideal end to human activity, an end, however, which remains outside our ability to achieve. Such "conviction" implies "being conquered, vanquished, in our active nature by an ideal end. . . . The authority of an ideal over choice and conduct is the authority of an ideal, not a fact, of a truth guaranteed to intellect, not of the status of the one who propounds the truth" (*CF*, 20–21). Such faith, born of fear and superstition, reminds Dewey of "the old saying, [that] fear created the gods" (*CF*, 24).

By contrast, Dewey asserts a different kind of faith, one that does not first pose an ideal and then formulate doctrines arising from any stipulated or preformulated end. He seeks "to reverse the ordinary statement and say that whatever introduces genuine perspective is religious, not that religion is something that introduces it" (*CF*, 24). If the old faith assumed a hostile nature over which people could exert little control, the new faith presumes a more tractable nature over which humans can exert control and from which they can extract support and sustenance. Echoing Emerson's sentiments of humanity's relationship with nature, rather than viewing humans as wholly subject to, or indivisible parts of, nature, we should rather assume a kind of "natural piety" that rests on the "just sense of nature as a whole of which we are parts, while it also recognizes that we are parts that are marked by intelligence and purpose, having the capacity to strive by their aid to bring conditions into greater consonance with what is humanly desirable" (*CF*, 25). Returning to the definition of Christianity from his earlier essay, "Christianity and Democracy," Dewey described this attitude as the preferable form of faith: "Faith in the continued disclosing of truth through directed cooperative human endeavor is more religious in quality than is any faith in completed revelation" (*CF*, 26).

Since human beings can exercise a choice over how they view the universe and its controlling spirits, it is preferable that our faith assume the universe is benign, controllable, nonarbitrary and malleable to human will. Not only is the object of our faith chosen but that it is chosen because it is subject to human control means, in effect, that all aspects of faith—its content, object, and human relation to that object—are essentially under human command. As Dewey stated in response to Reinhold Niebuhr's withering critique in *Moral Man and Immoral Society*, we must choose the "illusions" we will embrace:

> The situation is such that it is calculated to make one look around, even if from sheer desperation, for some other method, however desperate. And under such circumstances, it also seems as if the effort to stimulate resort to the method of intelligence might present itself as at least one desperate recourse, if not the only one that remains untried. In view of the influence of the collective illusion of the past, some case might be made out for the contention that even if it be an illusion, exaltation of intelligence and experimental method is worth a trial. Illusion for illusion, this particular one may be better than those upon which humanity has usually depended.[65]

Dewey seeks to reject at every turn the notion that faith somehow implies a loss of human control, a surrendering to real or potentially intractable forces, or an admission of human insufficiency. Faith is an affirmation of human power and the possibility of "growth" in every instance.

Nor does Dewey's faith in human control—in the successful manipulation of the mechanisms that result in human progress—dismiss the doubt so central to the scientific project. Noting that his position might be misconstrued with a kind of "agnosticism," Dewey finally rejects the notion that we should be occupied at all with any concerns about the existence or nonexistence of any supernatural being or that our lack of knowledge on this front should have any deep significance. "Generalized agnosticism is only a halfway elimination of the supernatural. Its meaning departs when the intellectual outlook is directed wholly to the natural world. When it is so directed, there are plenty of particular matters regarding which we must say we do not know; we only inquire and form hypotheses which future inquiry will confirm or reject" (*CF*, 86). From our doubts we are able to fashion creations of control—again Dewey notes the invention of the telegraph and locomotive as concrete manifestations of human imagination and creativity (*CF*, 49)—innovation that can only be created from a kind of productive doubt over which human agency and creativity can work to overcome. The doubt remains as a general motivator toward action and scientific analysis but is never about the ultimate trajectory of human undertakings: conundrums and unsolved problems, both in nature and politics, are ultimately subject to a benificent solution arising out of human grappling with doubt.

This is finally Dewey's democratic faith: that through the human ability to confront all specific problems by the "method of intelligence," a progressive tendency of history resulting in ever greater human "growth" and capacities for democratic self-governance can be achieved. Democracy is a condition into which humanity will grow, a culmination we can yet come to achieve. Dewey was persuaded by Walter Lippmann that contemporary citizens evinced too little democratic capability—reflecting the characteristicly low estimation that most "democratic faithful" have regarding "current" humanity's capacities; he contended, however, that democracy was a condition that could yet be achieved through a combination of purposive human action in the areas of education and social engineering, and by an uncontrolled movement in history which he argued was resulting in "democratic convergence."[66] By means of education, for example, democratic citizenship could undergo a process of "continual reorganizing, reconstructing, transforming."[67] Because of his belief in the possibility of human transformation into beings capable "in the long run" of democratic citizenship, Dewey was able to retain his "democratic faith":

> Democracy is an educative process. . . . This educational process is based upon faith in human good sense and human good will as manifests itself in the long run when communication is progressively liberated from bondage to prejudice and ignorance. It constitutes a firm and continuous reminder that the process of living together, when it is emancipated from oppressions and suppressions, becomes one of increasing faith in the humaneness of human beings; so that it becomes a constant growth of that kind of understanding of our relations to one another that expels fear, suspicion, and distrust.[68]

AFFIRMING DEMOCRATIC FAITH

A Common Faith is more concerned with distinguishing religion from "the religious," and affirming the place of the "method of intelligence" in the unfolding of revelation than it is with reaffirming Dewey's faith in democracy as the best political organization in which this unfolding can occur. Late in life—following Dewey's struggles with pacifists in World War I and interventionists in World War II—he again returned to the theme that had concerned him since his days teaching at the University of Michigan in the 1880s and 1890s: affirming his faith in democracy and science as mutually supportive and progressive enterprises.[69] In a 1944 essay entitled "Democratic Faith and Education," Dewey at once condemns one version of what he considers to be the "old" democratic faith, namely, a progressive, even Marxist, version in which history will result in universal peace and the withering away of the state. Notably one article of this "old faith" he dismisses is the creed that "enlightenment and rationality were bound to follow the increase in knowledge and the diffusion which would result from the revolution of science that was taking place."[70] While at first glance it might appear that Dewey is rejecting a fundamental tenet of his own faith, in fact he objects to the "finished" quality of this assumption, *viz.*, the belief that "enlightenment" would be a "condition" rather than an ongoing process. Dewey never believes that "enlightenment" is or can be final, asserting only that if humanity takes on the endless task of improvement and progress can a fundamental if ongoing transformation result. He objects to any conception of the "end of history."

There cannot be exclusive reliance upon history to solve the human puzzle; history's trajectory must be set into motion by human effort and creativity.

> Refusal to accept responsibility for looking ahead and for planning in matters national and international is based upon refusal to employ in social affairs, in the field of human relations, the methods of observation, interpretation, and test that are matters of course for dealing with physical things, and to which we owe the conquest of nature.[71]

By 1944 Dewey, although still confident in the ability of democracy and science to extend this "conquest" to the social and political sphere, nevertheless was deeply shaken in his confidence. Calling for "courage" by defenders of democracy, he insisted that "successful maintenance of democracy demands the utmost in use of the best available methods to procure a social knowledge that is reasonably commensurate with our physical knowledge, and the invention and use of forms of social engineering reasonably commensurate with our technological abilities in physical affairs."[72]

If Dewey's confidence in the prospects of democracy at this late date apparently wavered at times, this essay seems to call forth an almost superhuman attempt to overcome any such doubts (now about the ability of doubt, democracy, and science to fill the breach). To the end, Dewey maintained his faith in the combination of democracy and the "method of intelligence" that animated his early writings. At the conclusion of "The Democratic Faith," he affirms his "new" faith in democracy and science, writing that "the task can be executed in the concrete only as it is broken up into vital applications of intelligence in a multitude of fields to a vast diversity of problems so that science and technology may be rendered servants of the democratic hope and faith. . . . In this achievement science, education, and the democratic cause meet as one."[73] Dewey's attempt to transfer a concept of faith in the "supernatural" from the domain of religion to the secular entities of science and democracy remained consistent throughout his life. Even if that faith was shaken, it was never broken; only by proceeding under the assumption that everything would improve by the application of the "method of intelligence" in a democratic setting, one surmises, was it at all possible for Dewey to accept the seeming doubt upon which his philosophy insisted in the first instance. Rejecting the "quest for certainty" required a kind of assurance born of a reconstructed faith that Dewey time and again acknowledged and to which he returned for sustenance against the grim reality of the twentieth century.

Dewey scholar Charles Frankel has observed that "Dewey's trust in science gives a bit of the feeling of listening to a Strauss waltz, a melody from the time when the world was young."[74] This observation seems partly true: Dewey's faith in science—indeed, his unique attempt to link faith to the secular ends of science and democracy—does have about it the restless and perhaps understandable optimism akin to that trust in the future exhibited by one of the favorite books of his youth, Edward Bellamy's *Looking Backward*.[75] Yet, by 1944, Strauss's waltz is increasingly played out of tune: what allows Dewey to overcome the perceptible obstacles to progress is not empirical evidence to the contrary but rather his continued faith in the progress arising from doubt.

A curious paradox arises out of this faith, one rarely commented upon either by inheritors of Dewey's position or critics of his brand of skepticism.[76] Admirers of Dewey embrace his skepticism as a healthy rejection of any kind of "foundationalism" in politics, a willingness to throw politics open to the mutual exploration of citizens and experts in the attempt to discover the best possible answer to existing problems at any given time.[77] Few modern commentators, however, acknowledge Dewey's reconstruction of faith as applicable to secular ends. Herein lies the paradox: Dewey, and those like Dewey who embrace "doubt" as the fundamental "antifoundation" of modern politics, ultimately rest that doubt on a deeper foundation of faith in the capacity of humanity to fundamentally master its environment (natural, social, and political) and alter it in appropriate ways that can permit answers to seemingly intractable problems. The embrace of "doubt," the rejection of "certainty," rests on a curious absence of doubt about human abilities and the potential for politics to resolve all challenges. Of course, no resolution may be assumed to be final or complete; provisionality remains the watchword of Deweyan skepticism. Nevertheless, the assumption underlying the embrace of doubt is not a kind of even-sided showdown with the problems confronting humanity; rather, it is a process of continual improvement and mastery, a process with no necessary culmination but one in which even acts of horrible barbarism are viewed solely as "setbacks," not as intractable manifestations of human depravity.

In the older faith, belief in an omniscient and supreme being necessarily involved the simultaneous acknowledgment of human fallibility and incompleteness. No activity in the secular sphere—not science, not politics, not worship—can overcome this knowledge of radical uncertainty. Martin Luther King claimed to have hope without optimism; this is the approach to life that accompanies the "old faith."[78] Reinhold Niebuhr (with whom King studied at Boston University) seemed to express the same sentiment when he wrote, "There must always be a religious element in the hope of a just society. Without ultra-rational hopes and passions of religion no society will ever have the courage to conquer despair and attempt the impossible; for the vision of a just society is an impossible one, which can be approximated only by those who do not regard it as impossible."[79] Acknowledgment of human insufficency does not result in a form of desperate resignation, in this view, but a tempered approach to the project of realizing justice—however imperfectly—in the *saeculum*.[80]

Dewey's was an optimistic hope, a "faith" perhaps as unreasoned as any, but in whose name he believed might be accomplished substantial acts of human transformation. One of his primary objections to "supernaturalism" is precisely Niebuhr's view that justice could only be imperfectly achieved: instead, Dewey saw the need to eliminate this belief and hence liberate ambitions toward fundamental transformation in political and social life:

> The objection to supernaturalism is that it stands in the way of an effective realization of the sweep and depth of the implications for natural human relations. It stands in the way of using the means that are in our power to make radical changes in these relations.[81]

The object of Dewey's faith—democracy and science wholly under human control—permits a kind of hopeful optimism that a faith which acknowledges human infirmity finally resists. Such is the curious "certainty" that Dewey's "doubt" ultimately allows, and one which he—unlike many—was willing to acknowledge as finally nothing more or less than faith.

RORTY'S "COMIC FRAME"

Among those willing to embrace democracy as a form of faith is Dewey's greatest contemporary inheritor, Richard Rorty. For Rorty, our faith can and should be transferred to democratic practice and contingent narratives which articulate our hopes and through which we act.[82] Rather than place our hopes in external or transcendent objects, Rorty urges us to look more toward the potentials and possibilities of human creatures and creations in the present and the future. "The kind of religious faith which seems to me to lie behind the attractions of both utilitarianism and pragmatism is, instead, a faith in the future possibilities of mortal humans, a faith which is hard to distinguish from love for, and hope for, the human community. I shall call this fuzzy overlap of faith, hope and love 'romance.' "[83]

This is especially true of modern societies for which secularism has become increasingly possible owing to material amelioration and technological progress. "Nonreligious forms of romance have flourished—if only in those lucky parts of the world where wealth, leisure, literacy, and democracy have worked together to prolong our lives and fill our libraries. Now the things of the world are, for some people, so welcome that they do not have to look beyond nature to the supernatural and beyond life to an afterlife, but only beyond the human past to the human future."[84] Echoing the sentiments of both Emerson's essay, "The Young Americans," and Dewey in the first part of *A Common Faith*, the superstitions of our primitive forebears can be left aside with the modern amenities of literature, television, and the Internet to comfort and divert us instead. Our fears can be explained by modern methods, by scientific inquiry, by uncovering or—in Dewey's language—by torturing the nature that hides its answers from us. What fears cannot be explained or fully accounted for—bad luck, inevitable unexpected consequences, and finally death—can at least be assuaged by material comforts.

More than mere self-satisfaction, however, Rorty echoes Dewey's confidence that a new era continues to dawn in which accustomed human forms can be transformed by sheer human will alone—that by our own efforts and willingness to *believe* in the optimistic narratives we might weave, we can bring to fruition any of our most cherished "social hopes." "Modern, literate, secular societies depend on the existence of reasonably concrete, optimistic, and plausible *political* scenarios, as opposed to scenarios about redemption beyond the grave. To retain social hope, members of such a society need to be able to tell themselves a story about how things might get better, and see no insuperable obstacles to this story's coming true."[85] Like Dewey after World War II, Rorty admits that "social hope has become harder lately," but elsewhere he insists that we must "think of our sense of community as having no foundation except shared hope and the trust created by such sharing."[86] At base, this hope is as wholly unfounded as the more traditional religious faith that Rorty rejects; it simply presents a more appealing narrative, one that is simultaneously contingent yet optimistic, resting only on the human ability to both will the narrative into existence and will its hopes into reality.

With the unshackling of humanity from diverting narratives that direct us toward an unseen and unreachable transcendent beyond, Rorty optimistically expects not merely that we will continue to improve our condition materially and expand our leisure opportunities but, further, that as we throw off older forms of superstition humanity will have the opportunity to wholly alter its composition, its very existence. Democratic humans, Rorty states at one point, have "more being" than all previous human beings that have passed their lives in nondemocratic regimes: thus "the citizens of a democratic, Whitmanesque society are able to create new, hitherto unimagined roles and goals for themselves."[87] Rorty argues that "it does not greatly matter whether we state our reason to believe—our insistence that some or all finite, mortal humans can become far more than they have yet become." Such belief "carries us beyond argument, because beyond presently used language."[88] Part of the Deweyan faith in human transformation rests in a hope in our development into an entirely different species at some point in the future.[89] Our technology in part frees us from the wretchedness of the past; in turn, our imagination—or "romance"—can be unleashed to conceive new forms and wholly new ways of being that cannot even yet be expressed, described, or debated, since language cannot do the work of capturing a wholly new human reality. Democracy is a future prospect, a yet unachieved political condition that awaits human transformation.

In a frank moment Rorty admits the appeal of Dewey's attempt to transmute "early religious belief into a belief in the human future, [and] come to think of God as Friend rather than as Judge and Savior." Yet, as an atheist, he admits wavering between "romance" and "needy, chastened humility. Sometimes it suffices to trust the human community. . . . Sometimes it does not."[90] However, it is not surprising that elsewhere he has rejected humility as an inappropriate stance or disposition for such forward-looking humanity.[91] Given his profound optimism in the human ability to conceive of new forms of life beyond present language, his belief that modern democratic citizens possess "more being" than all previous humanity, and finally his confidence in our ability to realize that new, yet undefined, existence, one is hard-pressed to accept the proposition that humility is the appropriate stance for Rortyean men and citizens. Indeed, the inescapable danger of assuming the mantle of religious sanctification in the name of transformative democracy is that humility is the one and only "religious" virtue that likely cannot be retained nor adequately translated into the vocabulary of those who would commend "social hope." Humility, to "translate" the legend of Pandora's box, is the only virtue to remain locked and inaccessible to the democratic faithful.

PART THREE

Friendly Critics of Democratic Faith

CHAPTER SEVEN

"A Pattern Laid Up in Heaven": Plato's Democratic Ideal

> God is the measure of all things.
>
> —Plato, *Laws*

CRITICS OF democratic faith—that is, critics of the belief in democracy that is premised upon "transformative" efforts aimed at fulfilling the godlike capacities of potential democratic citizens—are, more often than not, most easily served simply by rejecting democracy as a viable political system. This has been the obvious conclusion of many thinkers throughout the Western tradition. A hardheaded civic realism results in an antidemocratic temper, and in the current age of democratic ascendancy such thinkers are largely vilified for their fundamental inegalitarianism and, more, their lack of democratic faith.

Some have undertaken a different form of critique of democratic faith not by rejecting the possibility of democracy but, instead, by maintaining a profound sympathy with democratic aspirations. We might understand such thinkers as "democratic realists"—friendly critics of democratic faith who seek to remind the most idealistic and even utopian of democracy's supporters that their own "faith" can actually serve to undermine democratic commitments. Such "friendly critics"—ranging from, as I argue in the next several chapters, Plato (a candidate that will surprise most) and Aristotle in antiquity, Tocqueville and Abraham Lincoln in early modernity, and Reinhold Niebuhr (if inconsistently) and Christopher Lasch in modern America—have at once sought to chasten their idealistic democratic counterparts while defending democracy not in the name of human potential for "perfectibility" but rather on opposite grounds, namely, based on fundamental and inescapable human imperfection, insufficiency, and frailty. Their endorsement of human equality underlying their devotion to democracy rests upon our current shared condition of imperfection and not on a projected future condition of fulfilled human promise.

"Democratic realism" holds at bay the disillusionment typical of so many disappointed "democratic faithful," but at the same time its representative thinkers do not assert thoroughgoing contentment with "men as they are." Recognizing that humankind rarely evinces the most ideal forms of democratic virtue, such as those described by Aristotle in outlining his view of the "wisdom of the multitude," "democratic realists" are as likely to call for the cultivation of democratic virtues as are the "democratic faithful." However, rather than positing the possibility of a form of human "transcendence" or "transformation" as the desired means or end of the democratic ideal, "democratic realists" instead firmly insist that the development of democratic virtue requires a concentrated emphasis upon those very imperfections that are most fundamentally constitutive of our human equality. Our "improvement" as democratic citizens is premised upon our continued recognition of our insufficiency and not upon a transcendence of that condition. If "democratic realists" retain the language of religion as fully as the "democratic faithful" (particularly inasmuch as they often lack the hostility toward "traditional" forms of religious belief), they eschew the discourse of "redemption," "transformation," and "transcendence." Instead, the theological virtues emphasized are humility, hope, and charity. Humility is the democratic virtue par excellence, the requisite disposition that results from the constant attentiveness to our shared imperfections. Hope is at once a rejection of its more confident counterpart, "optimism," a positive disposition toward the future that nonetheless contains and does not contradict humility. Charity is the resultant call to action of the "democratic realist." Recognizing the fundamental human condition as one of need—reminiscent of Plato's understanding of the fundamental nature of justice—we are more likely to recognize a reality to which individual humans are otherwise deeply resistant: that our own fates are bound together with those of our fellow citizens. The resultant disposition from our democratic humility and our democratic hope is not one of condescension or resentment but rather one of democratic charity born of the conscious recognition of the inescapability of our partiality and not based on superhuman "transcendence" of our limited perspective. If "transcendence" or "enlarged mentality" is the ideal of the "democratic faithful," in the view of "democratic realists," charity is the bond that can be forged between inescapably alienated citizens and humans. We can act from charity *because of*, not in spite of, our inevitable alienation.

WITH FRIENDS LIKE PLATO . . .

Plato is undoubtedly a curious choice as a "friendly critic" of "democratic faith." He is obviously a critic of democracy, one hostile toward unrealistic expectations of universal human transformation that are likely to result in an ideal democracy. What is deeply dubious is whether he can, in any way, be considered a "friendly" critic. Yet, as I argue in the remainder of this chapter, Plato not only posits a potential for democratic self-governance that is more radically egalitarian than the defense of democracy advanced by Protagoras, but he envisions an ideal of democracy that may in some respects outstrip the most idealistic visions of the "democratic faithful." What holds at bay the potential democratic utopianism of Plato, however, is his firm insistence that our equality is most fundamentally premised not on a common shared divine inheritance—as was articulated by Protagoras—but instead by a common and shared condition of insufficient knowledge of virtue. Our equality is most profoundly defined by a *lack* or *want* of knowledge rather than its actual or likely attainment. The recognition of this lack of knowledge is intended to prompt all citizens alike to pursue its attainment; yet, that same recognition forces upon every citizen the awareness that each individual cannot lay claim to a greater form of political wisdom. Our equal insufficiency prompts us to pursue the ideal of the "philosopher-king" even as it forces upon us the recognition that we are, of necessity, inescapably equal citizens. Plato describes a condition of philosophic ignorance that is at once inspiring and chastening.

Although a subject of ongoing contention in recent years by students of ancient political thought, it is safe to say that many if not most commentators agree that Plato was a deeply antidemocratic thinker. Such views range from earlier post–World War II condemnations by Karl Popper and Sheldon Wolin for Plato's totalitarian proclivities, criticisms anticipated by R.H.S. Crossman who considered the city described in Plato's *Republic* to be "a polite form of Fascism," to more contemporary critiques such as those advanced by Jean Bethke Elshtain, Benjamin R. Barber, and Cynthia Farrar, the latter considering Plato to be an "undemocratic and politically alienated thinker."[1]

Nevertheless, in spite of Plato's explicit criticisms of democracy, a number of other recent thinkers have found in Plato's dialogues what is oftentimes a subtle and mostly indirect endorsement of democracy. In particular, there have been two notable contemporary attempts to demonstrate Plato's sympathy with democracy: those originated by Leo Strauss and defended by a myriad of his students, and the other a loose school informed by postmodern sensibility articulated by J. Peter Euben.

The first, originated by Strauss, suggests that Plato's sympathy with democracy comes about simply by default, owing primarily to the implausibility of the "city in speech." As Strauss wrote in his seminal essay, "On Plato's Republic,"

> The just city is then impossible. It is impossible because it is against nature. . . . It is against nature that rhetoric should have the power ascribed to it: that it should be able to overcome the resistance rooted in men's love of their own and ultimately in the body.[2]

According to Strauss's interpretations of the *Republic*, the dialogue is less about founding the ideal regime—since such a regime is self-evidently impossible to realize—than about how best to secure the possibility of a superior life in imperfect regimes, namely, a life of philosophy. The impossibility of the city in speech—both because of its unnaturalness and the unwillingness of the philosopher to rule—leads Strauss and his students to conclude that democracy is the only realizable regime in which the philosopher could survive. As Strauss writes,

> Democracy itself is characterized by freedom which includes the right to say and do whatever one wishes: everyone can follow the way of life which pleases him most. Hence democracy is the regime which fosters the greatest variety: every way of life, every regime can be found in it. Hence, we must understand, democracy is the only regime other than the best [regime] in which the philosopher can lead his peculiar way of life without being disturbed.[3]

The criticisms leveled against democracy by Plato, rather than utterly condemning its inadequacies, point out democracy's greatest strength vis-à-vis philosophy: only through the freedom democracies afford can philosophy hope to flourish. Thus democracy is not valued as a regime in itself. Its citizens remain tenuously close to a descent into tyranny, but the philosopher may pursue his search for knowledge so long as he does not disclose his subversive activity too publicly—as was the unfortunate case for Socrates. Democracy, by default is the best possible regime, not for its citizens but for philosophers.

The second, less organized "school" that has sought to rehabilitate Plato's status as a democratic thinker shares Strauss's subtle textual approach, including the latter's inclination to find a submerged meaning that stands in opposition to the explicit text, but ultimately finds in the Platonic corpus a subtle endorsement of democracy qua democracy, and not simply a default support for democracy because of the benefits it affords the philosophic life. Such interpretations find Platonic democratic sympathies *not* in Plato's explicit writings but in the interstices of the text, more in the *way* that he writes rather than in anything he might explicitly say. One of the foremost proponents of this approach is J. Peter Euben.[4]

Euben has produced a series of intriguing interpretations of Plato that adopts certain postmodernist hermeneutic tools and by means of these, he finds in the dialogic form an implicit endorsement of a Platonic democratic theory.[5] For Euben, Plato's decision to write dialogues, not treatises, indicates his acknowledgment that the tensions between ideal and real cannot be surmounted, and that the philosophic enterprise—like the democratic enterprise—rests at some level on conversation, dialogue, deliberation, and, ultimately, uncertainty. Euben argues that the claim of the philosopher's direct knowledge of unchanging, transcendent "Forms" outlined in the *Republic* is substantially undermined by the dialogic form itself. According to Euben, "justice requires reciprocity between content and form, which is another way of saying it requires an active complementarity between opposed understandings of philosophy, of politics, of the relations between them, and of the *Republic itself*."[6] Thus, by extension, the dialogic form ever undermines Plato's purported distaste for democracy. The dialogues are an example of how to "politically educate a democracy democratically, even if, as I would not deny, [Plato] remains skeptical of certain practices we regard as essentially democratic."[7] For Euben, even though Plato is critical of democratic regimes, a Platonic endorsement of democracy is perceptible more in his dialogic stance to the world, his willingness to entertain dissension, disagreement, and alternative voices, and his ultimate distrust of the philosophic endeavor.[8] While Plato's explicit *words* attack the plausibility of a democratic regime, those words are in turn undermined by the dialogic form which offers us an alternative understanding to existing democratic deficiencies. Thinkers of this loose school of "democratic Platonists" insist at the very least that we recognize a tension between the word and the form, and moderate what they admit are the explicitly antidemocratic statements of Plato.

In the cases of Strauss and Euben, in spite of their strenuous efforts to read the Platonic texts "against the grain," they agree that there is finally no getting around certain fundamental antidemocratic aspects of Plato's thought. Neither denies the explicit Platonic critique of democracy. For each of these defenders, to a greater or lesser extent, the *Republic* can only be understood to render a "democratic theory" in direct contradiction to its stated claims of democracy's inferiority.

These, then, are some of the leading modern interpretations attempting to justify or minimize the critique of democracy in Plato's *Republic*. Each recognizes the severity of the criticisms of democracy: one largely embraces them (Strauss); the other finds in the Platonic form an implicit sympathy with democracy through its more "tragic" or dialogic dimensions (Euben). However, it is possible to locate a Platonic endorsement of democracy not by indirection but more directly through Plato's identification of the just city and the just soul. If the ideal city in speech indeed proves to be nearly impossible to establish in reality—here I largely accept the argument of Strauss and Bloom—it is the case that the *just soul*, one notable for self-rule, is in fact the actual object of inquiry of the *Republic*, and indeed a somewhat more realistic goal in its realization than the "just city." Further, a regime composed of just souls suggests a democratic alternative to the deficient democratic regime described in Book VIII. The possibility of a regime composed of just souls points to an ideal democratic regime—one in which individuals would practice a form of moderate self-rule while avoiding the kinds of excesses, omissions, and abuses that lead to the downfall of democracy and the rise of tyranny. Although such a regime is neither suggested nor explored by Plato, by reading the *Republic* as a work primarily about the soul, the possibility, even plausibility, of such a regime is inescapably intimated.

In other words, Plato introduces the possibility of a "self-ruling" soul to counterbalance what he perceives to be the flaws of democracy, and further suggests that the just soul may be more universally achievable than the city in speech. By giving more credence to Socrates' claim that he explores the components of the just *city* as a means to his primary purpose of describing the just *soul*—thus giving less weight to the wholly undemocratic depiction of the explicitly political city in speech of the *Republic*—a surprisingly positive project of democratic self-rule arises more directly from Plato's criticisms of democracy than has been credited by most other interpretations. This understanding of the *Republic* can be reinforced by reconsidering the question of the "teachability" of virtue in the *Meno*, in which Plato allows for a much more extensive, indeed universal, conception of human capability than is commonly acknowledged. At the same time Plato resists the Protagorean vision of a "transformed" humanity in that dialogue by dint of his argument that humans imperfectly "recollect" what they have already known. Humans do not become new creatures; they merely "become" what they already were, albeit incompletely. In combination with the reevaluation of the *Republic*'s teaching, it will be shown that Plato has a considerably more positive—if challenging and elusive—theory of democracy than otherwise believed, while at the same time holding at arm's length the more transformative tendency of the "democratic faithful."

An Alternative Case for Platonic Democracy: Reconsidering the *Republic*

Most cursory as well as profoundly knowledgeable understandings of the *Republic* largely if not completely neglect that it is explicitly a work that seeks to define and locate justice in the city and the soul. Indeed, to take Socrates literally at his word, the *Republic* is clearly about the composition of the just *soul*, and the extensive discussion of the just *city* is intended in fact to serve as a means of better perceiving the internal organization of the soul. The *Republic* begins its examination of justice within the individual soul, and only after some consideration of the question does Socrates suggest that one should search for justice by "enlarging" the soul, in effect expanding the soul's dimensions to the size of a city, searching there for where justice might be found.[9] Of course, most of the text of the *Republic* examines the question of political justice, and, perhaps rightly, the vast bulk of scholarly attention has been focused on this subject when considering Plato's political philosophy. However, often overlooked in this concentration of attention on Plato's examination of the ideal city in speech is that throughout the *Republic* the assumption persists that the interlocutors are searching for justice in the composition of the individual soul, and that the examination of the ideal city in speech is serving metaphorically as eyeglasses for people "who don't see very sharply to read little letters" (368d). Accordingly Plato returns in the latter part of the dialogue to consider the kinds of souls that would be equivalent to the various regimes he has explored; moreover, the dialogue culminates with a story related by Er about how souls choose new lives in the afterlife, strongly indicating that throughout the dialogue the question of the excellent or virtuous soul was Plato's overriding concern.

In an important and richly suggestive article published more than twenty-five years ago, Bernard Williams explored the "analogy" of the city and the soul in the *Republic* with particular attention to the tension between the constituent virtues of each.[10] Although at several points Socrates claims that the virtues of the city and of the soul are identical (e.g., 435e), and indeed that the just city must be composed of just souls each of which "minds its own business," Williams pointed out that the analogy did not quite hold up under scrutiny. While Socrates maintains that both the city and the soul consist of three components—the "appetitive" or "desiring" (*epithumetikon*), the "spirited" (*thumeides*), and the "rational" (*logistikon*)—and are hence "tripartite," Williams raises the question as to whether the city and the soul can be understood to be "composed" of these elements in quite the same way. If both the just city and the just soul require that the more numerous "desiring" classes must be ruled by the "rational" with support of the "spirited," it is evident that there is no equivalence between the souls of the people of the just city and the requirements of the just soul. In other words, the just city does not require a populace of just souls, properly ordered with "reason" governing "desire" with the assistance of "spiritedness." Instead, the only class of the just city that exhibits the just soul is that of the guardians, who—themselves governed by reason in the arrangement of their own soul—in turn govern the more numerous among the population whose souls are either governed by an excess of *thumos* or *epithumos*. As Williams suggests, a grim picture results: "We come back once more across the bridge to the analogy to the city, we shall find not a *dikaios* [just] and logistically cooperative working class, but rather a totally logistic ruling class holding down, with the help of a totally thymoedic military class, a weakened and repressed epithymetic class; a less attractive picture."[11]

Justice in the city in speech is found in the relations *between* the classes and not in the souls of individual citizens. As Socrates explains, "courage and wisdom . . . resides in a part [of the city], the one making the city wise and the other courageous" (432a). Spiritedness in the city comes from those in the population whose souls are dominated by *thumos* (535e), just as the greater number of citizens who are least capable of governing their appetites comprise the vast mass of citizens who will be subject to governance of the wise. Only the philosopher-kings, whose "rational" faculties order their own souls, appear to present an equivalence between the just soul and the just city. However, that very fact prevents their own happiness, as Glaucon discovers when he objects to the extent to which they appear to sacrifice their own good for the good of the whole (420 b). Happiness—which is later revealed to be the accompanying condition of the just soul (580b)—is not promised to the individual classes making up the city, even those whose souls are most just. Rather, justice consists of each class "minding its own business," and *sophrosyne*—"moderation" or "self-rule"—"stretches throughout the whole, from top to bottom of the entire scale" (432a). However, if we are to understand this form of "self-rule" as a kind of "self-governance" of the rational part of the individual soul over the "desiring" part, then in the context of the just city it is the self-ruling *logistikon* class that rules over the *epithemetic* class whose souls are *ungoverned* and, by definition, by themselves ungovernable.

The just city is predominantly composed of unjust souls, including the most numerous "desiring class" and the "spirited" auxiliary class. Plato portrays a just city which, because of its willingness to accept the extensive repression of what are viewed as irredeemably ineducable masses, has seemed to many modern readers to be fundamentally *unjust*. If Glaucon's reaction was to pity the unhappiness of the guardians in this situation, contemporary readers are wont to condemn Plato for being thoroughly inattentive to the potentials of all human individuals, as well as overestimating the potential of a select few to discern unchanging forms by which to govern. Standard readings of the *Republic* dutifully note that Plato does not hold a very exalted view of the masses, consigning most of them to a life of obscurity and subservience under the luminous rule of the guardians (the wise) and the auxiliaries (the courageous). After discussing the three parts of the city and the soul in book IV, the "desiring" class of artisans and workers are largely neglected for the remainder of the *Republic*, presumably because all they can hope for is that they be governed by the philosopher-kings, requiring foremost the creation of such an educated class (books V–VII) and the willingness of the "desiring" class to be governed by the philosophical guardians (an assumption that proves problematic, of course, and threatens the actualization of the just city in speech).

Given the thoroughly antidemocratic character of the city in speech, and in spite of the best efforts of commentators ranging from Strauss to Euben, it remains implausible to many, if not most, of Plato's contemporary readers that one can hope to retrieve a positive democratic teaching from the *Republic*. Yet, if we take Socrates at his word—one that is constantly reiterated throughout the *Republic* despite the dominant emphasis on the city in speech—that the dialogue is *foremost* and most explicitly about the formation and composition of the *just soul*, a different portrait than the customary understanding of the political teaching of the *Republic* arises. For if the bulk of the dialogue implicitly concludes that the city in speech—requiring both the exceedingly difficult formation and the even more unlikely rule of philosopher-kings—is itself thereby implausible, if not impossible, to establish in reality, one might question whether there is the equivalent suggestion in the *Republic* that the "just soul" is equally unlikely.

At the conclusion of the lengthy discussion which moves from the question of the just soul, its relation to the just city, to the question of the plausibility of the just city (in each case moving seemingly further away from the original question about the just soul, as Socrates seems to admit at the outset of book V [450a–c]) in which the "three waves" are successively proposed, culminating in Socrates' declaration of the need for "philosopher-kings" in order for the just city to come into existence, Socrates finally admits that the "theoretical" enterprise (472e) in which they have been engaged seems unlikely to prove realizable. Thus, at the conclusion of the conversation at the close of Book IX, in response to Glaucon's supposition that the city they have been "founding" exists only in speeches, Socrates responds, "But in heaven . . . perhaps a pattern is laid up for the man who wants to see and found a city *within himself* on the basis of what he sees. It doesn't make any difference whether it is or will be somewhere. For he would mind the things of this city alone, and no other" (592b; emphasis mine). Here, confirming the Strauss/Bloom thesis that the *Republic*'s political teaching must be understood as a warning *against* attempts to establish in reality the city in speech and instead to serve as a "model" (*paradeigma*) of the ideal city, at the same time Socrates affirms that this "model" can be used as a guidance for *actual* souls in the attempt to achieve a form of internal justice. If the *Republic* appears, on the one hand, to be a warning against a form of political utopianism, does Socrates here simultaneously recommend a more realizable ideal for all people to attain just souls?

Strauss and Bloom both believe this to be the case, although they conclude that the just soul can only be the philosophic soul, and is therefore reserved to very few fortunate individuals who are capable of achieving a form of philosophic wisdom. Yet, if we follow this explicit statement that the just soul is to be viewed as more likely to be realized than the just city, then might this argument be understood to recommend the actualization of just souls more universally? Why conclude that the just soul is only possible to an exclusive few when Socrates seems, at the conclusion of Book IX, to indicate that the achievement of the just soul is more possible in reality?

Of course, there is much evidence to support the embrace of the more "exclusive" understanding of Strauss and Bloom, and the condemnation of this "elitism" by the likes of Popper and Crossman (among many others). Socrates may not afford a definitive statement that all souls are equally capable of a just internal arrangement. The most explicit statements that would seem to contravene a more universal moral and pedagogic understanding of the *Republic* occur in the discussion of those souls that are deemed as naturally capable of a form of internal justice or self-rule. Such naturally just souls, according to Socrates' discussion in Book IV, are exceedingly few in number. As Socrates says to Glaucon, "It is therefore, from the smallest group and part of itself and the knowledge in it, from the supervising and ruling part, that a city founded according to nature would be wise as a whole. And this class, which properly has a share in that knowledge which alone among the various kinds of knowledge ought to be called wisdom, has, as it seems, the fewest members by nature" (429a). As a description of the city, Socrates portrays a small number of people naturally suited to ruling as guardians and eventually philosopher-kings, that is, possessing the requisite "rational" faculty by which to exercise wise rule over the more numerous "spirited" and "desiring" classes in the city. It is based on this, and similar passages, that both admirers and critics conclude that the just soul (and hence a ruling position in the city) is possible only to a select few.

However, as a description of the individual soul, the analogy becomes less clear and less easily transferable. It is evident that, even among members of the guardian class, the "rational" faculty will always be the "smallest" and the "desiring" element with the individual souls will always be the most "numerous" or comprise the greatest portion of the soul. Only in combination with the "spirited" part of the soul can the "rational" portion maintain rule over the greater "desiring" part. Yet, this can only be accomplished—at least in the description of the city—with the active cooperation of the "desiring" class. It is somewhat unclear in the text by what means the active cooperation of the "desiring" class is secured. In the first instance, the subordinate condition of this most numerous class is elucidated by means of the "Noble Lie" which establishes that those in the "gold" and "silver" classes are designated by the gods to rule over the "bronze" class (415a–c). However, if this Noble Lie makes some sense—even while straining credulity—within the context of a city's founding, it seems altogether implausible as the necessary motive underlying the ignoble portion of the soul's willingness to submit to the rule of the better classes.

In considering the composition of the soul it is more sensible to follow the explicit directions of Socrates—the city analogy is meant to help us see more clearly the composition of the soul. If all cities have a small but at most times ineffectual "rational" element that can only rule in combination with the "spirited" element over the cooperating "desiring" element, then—notwithstanding Socrates' claim that only a few people in the city are capable of rational self-rule—a literal transference of the analogy would require the interpretation that *all* souls, like all cities, have a "smaller" rational faculty and respectively "larger" spirited and desiring elements. We cannot transfer the purported composition of the souls of *each class* in the city back into the analogy of the soul. This would result in the senseless and absurd notion that the "desiring" element itself has a smaller but nondominating "rational" element. This is precisely the point raised by Bernard Williams in his analysis of the city/soul analogy:

> Now if the epithymetic ["desiring"] class has in this way to exercise some *logistikon*, and this helps it stick to its tasks, recognize the rulers and so forth, and if we read this result back through the analogy to the individual soul, we shall reach the absurd result that the *epithumetikon* in a just soul harkens to *logistikon* in that the soul through itself having an extra little *logistikon* of its own. Recoiling from this absurdity, we recognize that in the individual soul, the *epithumetikon* cannot really harken; rather, through training, the desires are weakened and kept in their place by *logistikon*, if not through the agency, at least with the co-operation of *thumoeides*.[12]

The analogy of the city, rather than prompting us to the absurd conclusion of "mixed" elements *within* the soul, points instead to an understanding that each element within the soul is purely itself—for example, the "spirited" part of an individual's soul is exclusively spirited and not mostly spirited mixed in with some "desiring" and "rational" elements—and that justice is achieved through the proper arrangement of those elements within each soul. Thus the just soul requires governance of the rational, with the spirited, over the desiring. Yet, since the desiring element *in all souls* is more "numerous" or preponderant, it is only by means of "weakening" that element, in Williams's words, that the less dominant rational element can gain rule over the "many." This is achieved—resorting again to Williams's observation—*through training*. The idea that only a few in any city are capable of self-rule seems as implausibly transferable back through the analogy to the soul as the idea that the soul will govern itself by resort to a self-told Noble Lie. When the analogy becomes strained or threatens to break down, we are directed by Socrates' intention of discovering the just soul to let the incongruities of the city help clarify our understanding of the soul and not abandon our understanding of the composition of the just soul to contemporary assumptions that the establishment of the city is the main or primary aim of the *Republic*.[13]

The *Republic* confirms the essential nature of "training" earlier in the conversation. Discussing the kind of education necessary for the city's rulers, Socrates indicates that those lacking in the proper education will be incapable of self-governance: "Don't you think it's a disgrace, and a sure sign of poor education, to be forced to rely on an extraneous justice—that of masters or judges—for want of a sense of justice on one's own?" (405b).[14] Those lacking proper education—even guardians—will be incapable of proper self-rule and, instead, will require rule from outside themselves. Thus no one is "naturally" capable of self-rule but rather requires an extensive education, at the very least in music and gymnastics, to arrive at proper governance of one's dominantly natural inclination toward *epithumia*.

While most commentators understand Socrates' statements emphasizing the "small" number of those who will be guardians—that is, capable of being governed by *logistikon* in contrast to the far greater number who will be governed entirely by *epithumia* (e.g., 429a)—to be an expression of irremediable Platonic elitism, if again we adhere strictly to the stated ambition of looking at a city in speech in order to discern the arrangement of the just soul, we are led to conclude that Socrates' overarching aim is to portray the "smallness" of the "rational" element in any given soul. Training, above all—and especially in music and gymnastics—fortifies this rational faculty against the more "numerous" desires that threaten to overwhelm rational calculation. Since education is the key to securing the rule of the "smallest" element over the greatest, then the central question facing the reader of the *Republic* becomes whether this form of virtue—the just arrangement of the soul—is available to all humans or only to a select "well-bred" few who exhibit an innate capacity of self-rule. While the *Republic* appears definitively to embrace the former, it is entirely plausible—given the dialogue's stated exploration of the *arrangement* of the just soul rather than the *acquisition* of the necessary virtues for self-rule—that, in fact, the *Republic* is not the final word on the question it is typically interpreted to answer. If we wish to understand the Platonic understanding of human learning—the *acquisition* of virtue, of which the just soul would be the culminating manifestation—then

it is instructive toward these ends to turn to a dialogue that is directly dedicated to the exploration of this question, namely, the *Meno*.

The Myth of "Recollection" in the *Meno*: On Human Equality

Meno begins abruptly, without the framing story that is common in many
other Platonic dialogues such as the *Republic* or *Protagoras*, with an un-
usually direct question by Meno: "Can you tell me, Socrates, can virtue be
taught? Or is it not teachable but the result of practice, or is it neither of
these, but men possess it by nature or some other way?" (70a).[15] Meno poses
the question that a reader of the *Republic* rightly wishes to have answered:
whether virtue can be learned, and, if so, how it is learned, and, implicitly,
since Meno raises the question of some who might possess virtue "by nature," who, if anyone, is capable of learning it.

In accordance with his famous declaration in the *Apology* to be knowledgeable only of his own ignorance (23a–b), Socrates claims that the entire
citizenry of Athens, including himself, is ignorant not only as to how virtue
is acquired but, in the first instance, what virtue is (71a–b). Meno is encouraged to answer the question himself and offers an initial response that differentiates the virtues of men (rulers, particularly), women, the elderly, free men,
slaves, and children. He concludes, "There are very many other virtues, so
that one is not at a loss to say what virtue is. There is a virtue for every action and every age, for every task of ours and every one of us" (71e–72a).
Socrates responds with ironic joy that they have gone from searching for the
meaning of virtue *simpliciter* and have instead discovered "a whole swarm of
them" (72a).[16] However, Socrates points out that that the word "virtue" must
refer to some common feature of the many "virtues," just as the word
"bee"—alluding here to the image of a swarm—refers in general to a particular kind of insect notwithstanding the specific differences that may differentiate individual bees. Eventually Socrates leads Meno to share the conclusion that all humans, regardless of individual distinctions such as age, gender,
or political position, at least potentially possess the same general form of
virtue: "so all human beings are good in the same way, for they become good
by acquiring the same qualities" (73c). Neither natural nor conventional distinctions mitigate or effect the commonness of this singular human virtue.

As the conversation continues, Meno is increasingly frustrated by Socrates' *elenchus* —the careful refutation of stated positive definitions—and
eventually resorts to a proclamation of his own ignorance of the definition
of virtue that echoes Socrates' earlier claim (80a–e). Socrates insists that they
persist in their search, and the following exchange unfolds in which Meno
suggests a famous "paradox":

> Meno: How will you look for [virtue], Socrates, when you do not know at all what
> it is? How will you aim to search for something you do not know at all? If

you should meet it, how will you know that this is the thing that you did not know?

SOCRATES: I know what you want to say, Meno. Do you realize what a debater's argument (*eristikon logon*) you are bringing up, that a man cannot search either for what he knows or what he does not know? He cannot search for what he knows—since he knows it, there is no need to search—nor for what he does not know, for he does not know what to look for. (80d–e)

Meno first poses, and Socrates succinctly restates, a major and recurring problem in the Platonic corpus—the question of whether, even assuming virtue might be learned, humans are capable, first, of identifying and acquiring virtue and, second, whether, after having learned of and acquired virtue themselves, they can thereafter transmit that knowledge to other human beings.[17] It is the same question and problem that animates the dialogue in *Protagoras*: the problem of virtue's origins and transmissibility. If Protagoras in that dialogue offers a *muthos* and *logos* to explain the origins of human virtue and the method of its transmission, Socrates notably follows similar steps in the demonstration of human knowledge of virtue in *Meno*—first by an appeal to a kind of story and then to a more "logical" demonstration of *muthos*. However, in contrast to Protagoras's *muthos* in the "Great Speech," in which all human beings are initially "transformed" into fully capable political creatures by eventually being given an equal share of *aidos* and *dike* by Zeus, Socrates suggests that all humans are similarly equal, albeit in their *lack* of knowledge of virtue. Our equality is best understood as a deficiency and not—as propounded by Protagoras—as fulfilled capacity.

Socrates tells Meno of an "account" (*logon* [81a]) that he has heard from "men and women who talk of divine matters (*andrōn kai gunaikōn sophōn peri ta theia pragmata*)," namely, "priests and priestesses (*hiereōn ka hiereiōn*)" as well as "Pindar . . . and many others of the divine among our poets (*polloi tōn poiētōn, hosoi theioi eisin*)" (81a–b). From these sources Socrates relates a supernatural thesis:

They say that the human soul is immortal; at times it comes to an end, which they call dying, at times it is reborn, but it is never destroyed, and one must therefore live one's life as piously as possible:

> Persephone will return to the sun above in the ninth year
> the souls of those from whom
> she will exact punishment for old miseries
> and from these come noble kings,
> mighty in strength and greatest in wisdom (*sophia*),
> and for the rest of time men will call them sacred heroes

As the soul is immortal, has been born often and has seen (*heorakuia*) all things here and in the underworld, there is nothing which it has not learned; so it is in no way surprising that it can recollect the things it knew before, both about virtue

and other things. As the whole of nature is akin, and the soul has learned everything, nothing prevents a man, after recalling one thing only—a process men call
learning—discovering everything for himself, if he is brave and does not tire of the
search, for searching and learning are, as a whole, recollection (*anamnēsis*). We
must, therefore, not believe in that debater's argument, for it would make us idle,
and fainthearted men like to hear it, whereas my argument makes them energetic
and keen on the search. I trust (*pisteuōn*) that this is true (*alēthei*), and I want to
inquire with you into the nature of that virtue. (81c–e)

Thus Socrates briefly outlines and also provides the mythical background
to what has come to be known as the "Theory of Recollection" or the "Doctrine of Recollection."[18] Meno asks Socrates to "prove" or "demonstrate"
to him the truth of this myth, and Socrates agrees and proceeds with the famous demonstration of inductive reasoning through the exploration of a
geometric problem with one of Meno's slaves. Precisely what Socrates
demonstrates in his questioning of the slave's knowledge has long been the
subject of dispute among philosophers, particularly those interested in
Plato's theory of epistemology, and many conclude that Socrates demonstrates the existence of a kind of reasoning that rests on a priori knowledge.[19]
This may be the case, although it remains disputed, and is challenged in a
way that—much like debates about Socrates' discussion of the city in Plato's
Republic, which detract from a consideration of his own emphasis on the
just soul—in turn detracts from Socrates' larger intention in raising the Theory of Recollection in the first place. While nearly every commentator responds at great and detailed length on the dimensions of this theory, utterly
neglected is the identity and significance of the interlocutor with whom
Socrates speaks—Meno's slave.

In order to demonstrate the claim that learning is a process of *anamnēsis*,
Socrates requests that Meno call one of his "attendants"—one of his
slaves—and then crucially adds, "whichever you like" (82b). We know exceedingly little about this slave other than he is Greek, speaks Greek, and
was born in Meno's house. His name is never given, and he is implicitly
deemed utterly unimportant—an interchangeable "prop" of sorts. He is, in
short, a truly anonymous character in the Platonic corpus, arguably more
anonymous and certainly less significant than the several "strangers" that
appear in dialogues like the *Sophist* and *Laws*. The demonstration of the accessibility of knowledge and learning (or "recalling") is notably undertaken
under conditions in which the identity of the individual "recalling" knowledge is entirely irrelevant—with the sole exception that the person is able to
speak the language of the interlocutor. Whether Socrates in fact proves the
truth of "recollection" in his conversation with the unnamed and interchangeable slave, what he indeed demonstrates through this conversation, if
one accepts his assertion of the existence of prior knowledge and its availability through "recollection," is that virtue is equally available to every
human being.

Moreover, Socrates does not stop short by claiming that such knowledge is limited solely to geometrical subjects. Upon concluding his demonstration of the slave's knowledge of geometry, Socrates declares that this proves existing knowledge in all human beings: "he [the slave] will perform in the same way about all geometry, *and all other knowledge (kai ton allon mathēmaton)*" (85e). Knowledge through "recollection" extends beyond the narrow demonstration of the validity of the Pythagorean theorem, according to Socrates, and could be proven through subsequent demonstrations presumably using similarly interchangeable people from any walk of life, even that of the least noticeable or natively intelligent slave from the household of a gentleman. An important point is that Socrates does not go on to prove this but rather asserts it as a self-evident truth that relies implicitly on the previous demonstration of *anamnēsis* with the slave.

However, shortly after settling with apparent certainty and clarity the existence of *anamnēsis*, the eternal presence of a priori knowledge and the possibility of demonstrating this and any form of "knowledge" in the soul of any person, Socrates casts doubt on what has transpired. He states:

> I do not insist that my argument is right in all other respects, but I would contest at all costs both in word and deed as far as I could that we will be better men, braver and less idle, if we believe that one must search for all things one does not know, rather than if we believe that it is not possible to find what we do not know and that we must not look for it. (86b–c)

After all the ink is spilled by commentators attempting to determine the key features and claims of Plato's Doctrine of Recollection, Socrates proceeds to announce his own uncertainty about its correctness, and thus, at some level, he undermines the idea of certainty of knowledge that the doctrine seems to suggest. This stated uncertainty should not surprise readers, however: by means of several hints at the beginning of the discussion of the so-called Doctrine of Recollection Socrates indicates that the theory is not without substantial difficulties.

In the first instance, Socrates bases his belief in the "truth" of *anamnēsis* on what he has heard from "prophets" and "poets." For any reader of Plato, this should raise alarm bells and a quizzical pause. After all, this is the same Socrates, as portrayed by Plato in the *Apology*, who questions the wisdom of poets and finds them wanting, and who, in Book X of the *Republic*, charges that poetry is unable to demonstrate true knowledge because of its mimetic qualities. Second, as many commentators have observed (although some have tried to minimize its troublesomeness), Socrates does not strictly prove the human ability to gain original knowledge through the "theory of *anamnēsis*."[20] In order to recall knowledge from past lives, at some point humans must have been able to acquire knowledge. As Socrates describes it, the immortal soul "has *seen* all things, here and in the underworld, [and] there is nothing which it has not learned; so it is in no way surprising that it can recollect the things it knew before, both about virtue and other things"

(81c–d; emphasis mine). Since the doctrine purports to "prove" that humans have this knowledge from some past life, it never answers how we gain that original knowledge—one cannot "recall" what one does not already know. At some time people would have had to have "learned" something, but Socrates claims that humans do not "learn" but only "recall."

Given these problems of the Doctrine of Recollection, it should be no less surprising, but equally problematic, that Socrates ends his description of *anamnēsis* by declaring: "I trust (*pisteuōn*) that this is true" (81e). *Pistis* means "trust" or "faith," a belief one can maintain with relative degrees of confidence depending on one's knowledge of a person's character or comprehension of a thing or situation, but something about which one cannot maintain with utter certainty. In the division of kinds of knowledge in the image of the "divided line" of Book VI of the *Republic*, *pistis* is the more elevated of the two forms of "lower" "intellection"—*pistis* is the kind of "intellection" one has of visible "things."[21] By Socrates' own reckoning, it is an inferior form of intellection. Thus, by claiming to "trust" the tales of prophets and poets, Socrates implicitly admits that his "theory of knowledge" rests on an imperfect manner of knowing. Nevertheless, Socrates insists on the utmost importance of maintaining this "faith."

The reasons for this declaration of belief, or faith, have almost everything to do with the reasons for wanting to believe in *anamnēsis* and less to do with the legitimacy of the actual theory. Socrates' main objection to the "debater's argument" that Meno has posed regarding the possibility of "learning" is not, at base, the validity of Meno's paradox—which the Theory of Recollection only dubiously refutes since it has noticeable problems—but, rather, the *effects* an argument such as Meno's paradox has on a credulous listener, namely, that such a *logon eristikon* would make its hearer "idle, and fainthearted men like to hear it" (81d). This central concern is highlighted at the conclusion of the examination of Meno's slave, when Socrates states his uncertainty about the specifics of the theory and instead insists, in the most strenuous terms, that "faith" in *anamnēsis* will "make us better men, braver and less idle, *if we believe that one must search for the things one does not know*" (86c; emphasis mine). Whether "recollection" actually takes place is less important than our *belief*—our trust, even *faith*—that this is the manner by which we come to apprehend knowledge. Otherwise, with the exception of a very few people like Socrates, most people might be inclined toward a lazy acceptance of the inaccessibility of knowledge—a condition of lethargy, a total absence of courage and "spiritedness."[22]

This latter reason is also why the Theory of Recollection is important, why it deserves the "faith" Socrates accords it, and why it is resistant to the transformative temptations of the "democratic faithful" such as Protagoras. When considering the actual effect of this belief, one is forced to realize that the theory gives us no greater insight into true "knowledge" than we might have had before the assertion of the theory. The theory does not provide us with any specific kind of "knowledge" about virtue nor any kind of epistemological advantage by which knowledge of virtue suddenly becomes easily apprehended. In effect, Socrates' theory leaves us as bereft of true "knowledge" as before it was introduced.[23] Instead, what the theory succeeds in doing is to change our view toward the knowledge of virtue and our relative enthusiasm in its pursuit, because we now inquire into the nature of knowledge and *aretē* under the assumption (or belief or faith) that through *anamnēsis* our persistence will uncover what is already known, and, more important, that which no human "possesses." The theory brilliantly affords us the belief in the *existence* of comprehensible knowledge and *aretē* while at the same time denying us its easy apprehension. By contrast, Meno's paradox threatens to leave us truly stunned, unable to begin the inquiry, since we are left with the belief at the outset that we will be incapable of recognizing knowledge or virtue even if we encounter it or alternatively, that we already possess it. In this sense, it is Meno who is more akin to the "torpedo fish" that stuns its prey than Socrates, whom Meno accuses of resembling the fish; indeed, Socrates is just the opposite, a being who stuns us into activity from a state of torpor and lethargy (80a–b), more a gadfly than a "torpedo fish."

In this respect it is worth contrasting Socrates' solution—his "theory" or, better stated, his *muthos* or "story" of *anamnēsis*[24]—to the *muthos* of the origins of human virtue according to Protagoras, which throughout the dialogue appears to be the implicit competitor to Socrates' account. According to Protagoras, humanity acquires the virtues of *aidos* and *dikē*—"shame" and "justice"—as a divine gift from the gods. It is the gift of original humanity, and its transmission is thereafter ensured by the everyday teaching within the city, much like each person learns language through everyday interaction, as Protagoras relates in his subsequent *logos*. In short, we possess virtue—particularly that of *dikē*—as a matter of divine inheritance, and its transmission proves wholly unproblematic as long as humans live in cities. This teaching is thereafter echoed in the *Meno* by Anytus (and later by Meletus in the *Apology*), who, while condemning the teachings of the Sophists in the harshest terms, nevertheless, in the course of correcting Socrates' claim that he has never met a teacher of virtue, insists that the teachers of virtue are none other than the citizens of Athens. In each case Protagoras and Anytus (and Meletus) insist that the acquisition of original knowledge and virtue has been achieved by some prior transformation of humanity, and also insist that its transmission is accomplished without difficulty by means of the unconscious and unexamined daily interactions within the city. Upon consideration, each exhibits the kind of complacency and laziness which Socrates seeks to thwart by means of his *muthos* of *anamnēsis*.

The defeat of complacency has the effect of making us "spirited." We become "energetic and keen on the search" (81e), despite the fact that we do not "know" any more, now that we seek to "recollect," than we knew when we tried to "learn." By means of this "spirited" activity, the inquirer is prompted to question inherited wisdom, even superficially "true opinion" (*orthē doxa*), in the attempt to "secure" this fleeting kind of perception with "knowledge."[25] What one makes "fast" by means of "recollection" is "an account of the reason why" or "reasoning out the explanation" (*aitias logismos* [98a]). It is, then, only by means of the "energetic" or spirited inquiry that we come to a knowledge of things through *logismos*—that "higher" part of the soul that rules the more numerous "desiring" elements. *Meno* demonstrates if not the "truth" of *anamnēsis* then the need to kindle one's *thumos* to engage in the energetic search for knowledge that results in *aitias logismos*. And by means of his demonstration of this theory on Meno's unnamed, interchangeable slave, Socrates points out how this activity can and indeed must be pursued by every human being who deservedly can and should become "self-ruled."

KALLIDĒMOKRATIA

In the *Republic*'s description of the just "city in speech" depicted by Socrates in conversation with Glaucon and Adeimantus, there are few inhabitants who possess just souls aside from the small ruling class of "guardians." This has suggested to most readers that, for Plato, only few souls are *capable* of achieving a just soul. Yet, considering both the difficulties posed by the "city/soul analogy" and the more egalitarian conclusions to be drawn from *Meno* (Plato's dialogue about the education of the soul), it is difficult to avoid concluding that the *Republic* seeks not to propound the establishment of the just city—as is so often assumed by many of its readers—but rather the more plausible training and proper disposition of the just soul. This understanding follows Socrates' explicit claim that the "city in speech" is a means of better understanding the composition of the just soul, and not, as the dialogue is more often read, that the discussion of the "soul" is merely a pretext for engaging in an examination of the just city in speech. The city/soul analogy presents many challenges, but, by accepting Socrates' claim that the discussion is *foremost* about the creation of the just soul, and by testing the claims of the just city *against* those of the just soul (rather than vice versa), one cannot automatically conclude that Socrates justifies limiting a ruling "just soul" to a few guardians. Rather, to read the analogy in the strictest sense, Socrates describes instead the soul in which the "ruling" rational element will always represent the "smaller" portion, and thereby requires training in order to weaken the natural dominance of the "larger" desiring element. The object, as is also suggested in the *Meno*, is to encourage the participation of the "spirited" element in the service of the ruling rational element.

By concentrating more explicitly on the analogy that animates the *Republic*, we are thus forced to question one of the most long-standing assumptions about the dialogue, namely, that Plato seeks to reserve only to a few naturally capable souls the role as either guardians (or philosopher-kings) in the just city, or simply philosophers in the less-perfect city in which they are constantly under threat of persecution. Nearly all readers of the *Republic*—ones either sympathetic with such a conclusion, as in the case of Strauss and Bloom, or critical of such elitism, as in the case of Popper and Farrar—share this common assumption about a small ruling class of just souls. However, emphasis on the priority of the just soul raises questions about the validity of this assumption and, instead, points to a dual teaching of the *Republic*: even as the "political" portion of the analogy—and especially the introduction of the "three waves" in Books V–VII—undermines the conviction that the city in speech can plausibly be regarded as realizable, the leading portion of the analogy about the just soul attempts to bring the reader to the opposite conclusion, namely, that the just soul can be realized and ought to be the proper aim of one's ameliorative efforts. Thus the city in speech, as Socrates insists, serves as a "pattern laid up in heaven" for one who rightly seeks to found "a city within himself." The proper object of our activities is the founding of a "city" *within* the soul, not an actual political organization. Moreover, "it does not make any difference whether [the city] is or will be somewhere. For he would mind the things of this city alone, and of no other" (592b). The creation of the just soul is in no way reliant on the prior existence of the just city other than its exploration "in speech" in support of understanding the proper and just composition of the soul.

On the one hand, Socrates recommends the "establishment" of the just city exclusively within the soul—that is, the arrangement of the various elements in pursuit of a "self-ruled" psyche. On the other hand, however, he also appears to recommend a new form of "minding one's own business," namely, that one's proper "business" should solely consist of achieving this proper arrangement and should altogether avoid attempting to found a just city in the diurnal world. This conclusion would seem to reinforce the interpretation of readers like Strauss and Bloom who understand the *Republic* to recommend a portrait of the philosopher who hides under "a little wall" in Book VI (496a–e), weathering the storm of politics, perhaps hopeful of the existence of a just city but altogether resigned to the unlikelihood of such a city coming into being.

This interpretation is only the most plausible if we automatically conclude that the education of the just soul is possible only to a select few fortunate or naturally endowed humans. This conclusion, however, appears to import and apply assumptions incorrectly about the arrangement of the "just city" into the arrangement of the "just soul," concluding wrongly that only a small portion of the *people* are capable of achieving a just soul and thence ruling, when, in fact, acknowledging the force of the analogy leads us instead to find that only a small portion of the *soul* is capable of governing. The *Republic* points us to a consideration of how the just soul might be properly arranged, and additionally—like the *Meno*—insists, by means of an emphasis on the "achievability" of the just soul, that such a pursuit should be a common undertaking and not solely the province of a select few. Like the *Meno*, the *Republic* aims to make us "courageous" and "eager" in the pursuit of the soul's education in virtue. This is evidently the case, since it is precisely through the dialogue itself that Socrates moves Glaucon and Adiemantus away from their initial attraction to Thrasymachus's position and, by the end of the dialogue, guides them toward an embrace of the "pattern laid up in heaven," not by means of seeking its institution on earth but rather within their own souls.

Such a conclusion raises new perplexities about the culmination of the exploration of the city/soul analogy in Books VIII and IX. Socrates continues to maintain that the analogy between the soul and the city holds together seamlessly, but the problem of noncommensurability continues to be in evidence. This, above all, is the case as a result of Socrates' discussion of democracy in which he describes a regime notable for the variety of its citizenry:

> "[Democracy] is probably the fairest of regimes" I [Socrates] said. "Just like a many-colored cloak decorated in all hues, this regime, decorated with all dispositions, would also look the fairest. . . . And what's more . . . it's a convenient place to look for a regime. . . . Because, thanks to its license, it contains all species of regimes, and it is probably necessary for the man who wishes to organize a city, as we were just doing, to go to a city under a democracy. He would choose the sort that pleases him, like a man going into a general store of regimes, and, once having chosen, he would thus establish his regime."
>
> "Perhaps," he [Adeimantus] said, "he wouldn't be at a loss for patterns at least." (557c–e)

If the city in speech contains three "types" of citizens, that is, three classes whose souls are each arranged so that one virtue dominates in each, in democracy there appears to be no arrangement that dominates nor even a concatenation of arrangements that can be said to predominate. Democracy is notable for the absence of any kind of predominant arrangement of souls. One finds there any and all kinds of regimes by encountering the variety of souls that inhabit the democratic regime. If "justice" is the result of the "arrangement" of the just city, then it appears that "freedom" results in the disarray of such various and unorganized souls, the very absence of arrangement that characterizes democracy.

The democratic soul is completely distinct from the other souls that correspond to particular regimes—namely, the just, timocratic, oligarchic, and tyrannical souls—all of which feature one predominating virtue or vice, be it reason, honor, greed, or *eros*. In contrast to these other souls, the democratic soul is defined by its very lack of definiteness: it is a jumble of elements containing every possible species of regime within it, every conceivable virtue and vice in no particular order or ranking. Its freedom comes from a lack of "self-rule": no single element rules or predominates, and thus "freedom" is the result of this absence of a dominant feature or virtue, and not owing to the presence of some virtue that inclines the soul to a love of freedom. If any single "element" rules, it is only for a brief time, since the "equality" of all the conflicting elements within the democratic soul precludes any one from asserting permanent rule:

then [democratic man] lives his life in accord with a certain equality of pleasures he has established. To whichever one happens along, as though it were chosen by the lot, he hands over the rule within himself until it is satisfied; and then again to another, dishonoring none but fostering them all on the basis of equality. . . . He also lives along day by day, gratifying the desire that occurs to him, at one time drinking and listening to the flute, at another downing water and reducing; now practicing gymnastics, and again idling and neglecting everything; and sometimes spending his time as though he were occupied with philosophy. Often he engages in politics and, jumping up, says and does whatever chances to come to him. . . . And there is neither order nor necessity in his life, but calling this life sweet, free, and blessed he follows it throughout. (561b–d)

Here one discerns the incommensurability of the democratic soul and the democratic regime. Whereas in a democratic regime one can find any kind of soul—including that of a timocrat, an oligarch, a tyrant, or even a just soul—because, in the case of the democratic soul, no single element is dominate, one cannot hope to find *any* of these "souls" within the democratic soul. One will find these elements in disarray but will never find a predominating element as one would find *in the soul of that nondominant element within the democratic city*. Thus, while in a democratic city one can hope to find a philosopher, one could not be a philosopher with a democratic soul, since the former is defined by a just and ordered soul and the latter is wholly unordered. At best, one with a democratic soul can merely spend some time "*as though* he were occupied by philosophy." Even if philosophers do not rule in the democratic city, reason rules within the soul of the philosopher who lives in a democracy. By contrast, reason can never rule in the soul of the democratic man, just as no element can rule for any continuous period of time. One sees incommensurability between the city and soul, as one detects throughout the dialogue.

A question arises: what would it mean if there *were* such a commensurability between city and soul? In particular, what kind of regime would arise in a city in which its citizens were able to achieve a just internal organization of each person's respective soul, following upon Socrates' recommendation that the achievement of such souls should be a common endeavor and practicable goal? If the *Republic* is a book about achieving a just soul, and Socrates resorts to a description of the city in speech in order to clarify the composition of that soul, then what would be the resulting regime of a city composed of such just souls? The question comes up of necessity when we conclude that a city of just souls would not correspond to the description of the "just city," since the "just city" of the analogy requires the existence of the many "unjust souls" that comprise it.

A regime composed of a citizenry of just souls represents an unexplored and implied option in the Platonic panoply of regimes, one that goes unnamed in the description of cities. It is neither *kallipolis*, where only a select few guardians rule over spirited and desiring classes by means of a founding deceit, nor "democracy," in which an endless variety of conflicting souls stake equal claim to rule. However, such a regime would combine elements of each—it would combine the rule of just souls with the numerousness of democratic rulers; the self-rule of the just soul with the ideal political self-rule of democracy; the self-discipline of the guardian class with the freedom of the democratic regime—since "rule" would not have to be exerted on those incapable of, or unwilling to accept, the rule of the just.

This regime would be democratic—ruled by the people—but in a manner wholly at odds with that democracy in which rule is disorganized and souls are varied and equal. Instead of either *dēmokratia* or *kallipolis*, a self-ruled city of self-ruled souls might be called a *kallidēmokratia*. Such citizens would not seek out rule or power, since they would not have an excessive love of honor or influence. However, such souls—organized like those of philosopher-kings—would recognize a good outside one's own immediate happiness, and mutually rule for those reasons. Yet, that recognition would derive less from the stated belief in universal apprehension of the "forms" and more from the suggestion, in the *Meno*, that all are equally deprived of a certain knowledge of virtue. A kind of egalitarian self-rule is forged, grounded on equal if permanently unfulfilled capacity for virtue, and forms the ground for legitimate rule acknowledged in the just city (419a–421c). Moreover, since there are no separate classes that must be enticed into accepting such rule, there is no need to resort to a "Noble Lie"—grounds for mutual self-rule are understood by appeal to reason and commonweal.

If this is a plausible conclusion based on an understanding of the *Republic* that follows Socrates' emphasis on the creation of the just soul, why, then, did Socrates not *state* that this regime was the ultimate aim of his endeavors? Why divert generations of readers by his description of *kallipolis*? Was he such a bad teacher?

The questions are unavoidable, and one might wish—if this interpretation has merit—that Socrates had stated this aim explicitly. However, in keeping with the humility and avoidance of rashness that characterized Socrates' teachings, one can also conclude that he was most hesitant above all to expressly state such a "positive" teaching given his awareness of the manner in which any positive teaching could be misused, misread, misinterpreted, and malevolently implemented in the world of politics. Instead, upon further reflection, one can see that the entirety of Socrates' life and teachings *is* the positive demonstration of his aim of creating such a chastened and egalitarian democratic polity.

In a justly famous pronouncement in the *Apology*, Socrates states that he would not cease to practice his manner of philosophy, even if the city were to implore such cessation. The reason he gives accords entirely with the aim of *anamnēsis* in the *Meno* of provoking everyone toward the achievement of a just soul, and with the *Republic*'s aim of creating a city self-governed by justly self-governed souls:

"As long as I draw breath and am able, I shall not cease to practice philosophy, to exhort you and in my usual way to point out *to any one of you* whom I happen to meet: Good Sir, you are an Athenian, a citizen of the *greatest city* with the greatest reputation for both wisdom and power; are you not ashamed of your eagerness to possess as much wealth, reputation and honors as possible, while you do not care for nor give thought to wisdom or truth, *or the best possible state of your soul?*" Then, if one of you disputes this and says he does care, I shall not let him go at once or leave him, but I shall question him, examine him and test him, and if I do not think he has attained the goodness that he says he has, I shall reproach him because he attaches little importance to the most important things and greater importance to inferior things. I shall treat in this way *anyone I happen to meet*, young and old, citizen and stranger, and more so the citizens because you are more kindred to me. (29d–30e; emphasis mine)[26]

In this declaration of his vocation Socrates emphasizes the *generality* of his mission: the attempt to induce *everyone* and *anyone* he meets toward achievement of the best possible soul, and the special need of this mission in the city of Athens, one close to him but also "the greatest city." While potentially ironic, given his suggestion that the "great reputation" of Athens is wholly undeserved, its greatness may also lie in its form of regime, at that point a deeply flawed democracy but potentially, given the presence of Socrates, also the finest.

Socrates emphasizes this potential excellence of democratic Athens shortly thereafter in his *Apology* when he compares himself to a "gadfly" who seeks to awaken "a great and noble horse which was somehow sluggish because of its size" (30e). Athens is "great and noble" by its nature but betrays that nature by laziness induced by lack of training and curiosity, much like the condition afflicting those who accept the "debater's argument" offered by Meno and refuted by means of "recollection." Socrates, as "gadfly," represents the opposite of a "torpedo fish"—like the torpedo fish he stings but not to induce torpor but rather to awaken others from their torpor. He seeks the awakening of the entire city by means of an awakening of each citizen to the potential excellence, and current insufficiency, of his or her own soul. The greatest obstacle to the achievement of virtue is not an insufficiently excellent nature or an inability of some souls to achieve this excellence but rather the *laziness* of most, if not all, souls, a laziness that makes even the "greatest and noblest" regime fall far short of its potential excellence. It is that laziness from which Plato would shake us in all his dialogues, including, and especially, in both the *Meno* and the *Republic*, just as Socrates would awaken all whom he encounters in his imperfect democratic Athens in an effort to ennoble, without encouraging excessive faith in, democracy.

CHAPTER EIGHT

The Only Permanent State:
Tocqueville on Religion and Democracy

> When the old God leaves the world, what happens
> to all the unexpended faith?
>
> —Don Delillo, *Mao II*

CONTEMPORARY DEBATES about the presence and role of religion in the liberal-democratic polity tend to take extreme sides on the ancient controversy about the proper place and role of religion in political life. Some claim that religion poses too great a danger to the liberal polity to be allowed entrance into the public sphere; others insist that democracy cannot survive without a religious basis, that the continued civic health of the polity requires the moral underpinnings and ethic of self-sacrifice that religion alone provides.[1] It is a truism perhaps to acknowledge that both positions have certain merits: religion is indeed not altogether without its dangers to a liberal-democratic polity (as we see in its most extreme forms by some contemporary expressions of religious fundamentalism); yet corrosive individualism, crass material hedonism, high levels of lawlessness, and widespread loss of civic responsibility suggest to many that only the broader inculcation of religious values can forestall these perceived threats to the polity.[2] While this debate has brought forth many persuasive and valuable observations, it is perhaps time to acknowledge that proponents of these positions have staked claims that make them unlikely to hear the persuasive arguments of their opponents, and that the extreme positions each side has taken makes it difficult for each to admit the merits of the other given the significant investment each side now has in its own stance.

Such an acknowledgment would force us to consider anew the potential benefits and threats of religion for a *democratic* polity without the impetus to dismiss the profound tension in that approach. Democracy places special demands on the governing capacities, and moral decencies, of each citizen; absent those decencies, even virtues, democracy has the potential to devolve into the most vicious of regimes if the citizenry is itself vicious and entirely lacking in self-rule and respect for the claims of the minority. Although it was Plato who first argued that democratic regimes had the greatest tendency to become tyrannical, Alexis de Tocqueville was preeminent in articulating the tendency of modern democracy toward a destructive form of peculiarly democratic despotism. In describing the potential of a "tyranny of the majority" and of "democratic tyranny," as well as the different but related threats posed by excessive individualism and materialism, Tocqueville analyzed the internal logic of democratic equality and individualism to its theoretical denouement. At the same time, however, he believed that democracies should, and America did, avail themselves of the moral resources of religion as a counterweight to those more virulent tyrannical leanings that inhered in the "rule of the people." Most of all, unlike many contemporary liberal theorists, Tocqueville believed that religion not only was compatible with democratic polities but, indeed, that religion was *necessary* for the continued flourishing of a democratic regime. Yet, Tocqueville also held that democracy tended, over time, to undermine those necessary democratic virtues that religion could best support, and that when such deterioration occurred, those who would turn to religion as a support would likely invoke it only for utilitarian reasons which would just contribute to the further subversion of democratic virtues. This conviction was based not only on his experience in America but also on certain theoretical insights he had into the religious underpinnings of contemporary belief in equality and human dignity, and on implications of his very analysis of the internal dynamics of democracy itself.

Much of today's (largely, but not exclusively, academic) hostility toward religion in the public sphere is premised on assumptions remarkably similar to Tocqueville's own assessment of the hostility of European liberals toward, in particular, the Catholic Church.[3] By demonstrating the deficiencies of this understanding—both by pointing to the example in America but, more important, by highlighting the dangers of this hostility and the necessary influence of religion to the flourishing of a democratic regime in a more philosophical register—Tocqueville hoped that he might disabuse his contemporary antireligious liberals of their prejudice.

Tocqueville's recognition of the central importance of religion to democracy, however, did not tempt him to endorse a form of "civil religion" of the kind defended by Jean-Jacques Rousseau. Religion could not be viewed most fundamentally as a support for any political regime. Tocqueville's similar concern for the role of religion in forming and sustaining democracy firmly departs from Rousseau's understanding when considering whether the state should be involved in some way in shoring up democracy by means of a civically devised religion. At the same time, while Tocqueville rejects arguments on behalf of a mixing of religion and the state, he also holds at bay extreme "separationist" positions by asserting that religion ought to influence the citizens of a democracy, if largely "indirectly." Tocqueville presents a strong alternative to the two camps arrayed against each other in America today— one seeking to erect "a wall of separation" and the other to reclothe the "naked public square" in the vestments of religion.

Yet, important as the acknowledgment is of the beneficial aspects of religion for democracy, equally essential is the recognition that Tocqueville was himself troubled by the plausibility of his own suggestions. Thus his is a form of chastened analysis that even the most ardent enthusiast of his views must heed. While acknowledging that what was needful in modern democracy was the countervailing force of religion, he was not sanguine about the possibility of religion remaining influential in a democratic age. He even appeared, at times, to succumb to the temptation of recommending a kind of "civil religion," a form of religion that, by his own analysis, would be insufficient to the task he set for religion in democracy. Yet, he ultimately resisted such recommendations, precisely because, in his view, a "civil religion" would simply exacerbate the self-destructive tendencies of democracy. His analysis, then, should be the cause of reflection for those concerned with the future of democracy but at the same time hardly reason for celebration by those who would find there an ardent recommendation of school prayer and biblical wall decorations. Tocqueville concludes that religion is most useful to democracy when it is not valued for its usefulness, and, in times when democracy is most imperiled, Tocqueville suggests that perhaps the most dangerous impulse would be to try to recommend the inculcation of religion as a necessary support for democracy. Nevertheless, he does not despair for the possibility of religion playing a significant role in democratic life, although his chastened hopes suggest that religion's greatest apparent friends may, in fact, be the potential foes not only of democracy but, curiously enough, of religion as well.

Tocqueville's "Religious Terror" — The Problem of Equality

Tocqueville explained in the introduction to the first volume of *Democracy in America* that he was inspired to write about the promise and dangers of modern democracy, and particularly about what he regarded as the inevitable spread of "equality of conditions," because of "a kind of religious terror (*d'une sorte de terreur religieuse*) inspired by contemplation of this irresistible revolution [of democratic equality] advancing century by century over every obstacle and even now going forward amid the ruins it has itself created" (12).[4] His sense of "religious terror" is curious at best, since, in the following paragraph, Tocqueville asserts that it is the will of divine providence that this universal spread of equality occurs: "God does not Himself need to speak for us to find sure signs of His will; it is enough to observe the customary progress of nature and the continuous tendency of events" (12). Tocqueville concludes, "In that case effort to halt democracy appears as a fight against God Himself, and nations have no alternative but to acquiesce in the social state imposed by Providence" (12). In Tocqueville's view, the spread of democracy is a result of the irresistible divine plan of God.

Why, then, does Tocqueville express "religious terror" at the prospect of God's divine will coming to pass? For Tocqueville, it is one of the eternal paradoxes of human existence that the greatest legacy of the Christian tradition—the universal belief in human equality and equal human dignity—

simultaneously represents one of the greatest threats to that tradition at the moment of its fruition in the world of politics. Tocqueville held that one of the most pernicious effects of democracy would be to turn humanity away from considerations of the divine, and hence an appreciation of the ultimate source of human equality, and instead credit human efforts alone for equality's triumph. If equality was in the first instance the result of God's divine plan—the inheritance of the belief that all humans are created from the same divine source—the paradoxical result of equality was to create the possibility of a tyrannical form of democracy based on the widespread acceptance of human equality. Thus equality ultimately threatened to undermine the capacity of humanity to acknowledge the divine source of equality, and thereby unleash a range of pernicious effects resulting from disbelief, including materialism, individualism, selfishness, and political indifference.

For Tocqueville, "equality of conditions" meant not the literal equality of material resources—although he recognized that material conditions had become more equal in the democratic America of the 1830s—but primarily a psychological condition in which no person is recognized as having any claims to superiority over or deference toward any other person.[5] This view was a direct inheritance of the Christian tradition, in which all human beings are equal in the eyes of God, regardless of their social situation, wealth, accomplishments, even claims to moral worth. It is an equality, in part, at once deriving from an implicit insufficiency of all humans in relation to the divine, a recognition of shared imperfection, and at the same time, in Tocqueville's view, an ennobling form of equality inasmuch as each person is equally part of God's creation. As Tocqueville observes, this religious conception of equality inevitably leads to a political conception: "Christianity, which has declared all men equal in the sight of God, cannot hesitate to acknowledge all citizens equal before the law" (16).[6]

However, this form of equality, in spite of contributing fundamentally to the development of democratic equality, is threatened by another more debased type of equality. If every system of government operates on certain unquestioned assumptions (lest its legitimacy be constantly called into question), in democracy that assumption of equality was transformed into "the dogma of the sovereignty of the people" (58). A legitimate government must respect the sustained will of the people, Tocqueville suggests; however, in democracies this principle is raised to a dogma, meaning that the sovereignty of human opinion goes all but unquestioned and thereby threatens to become a potentially tyrannical force. Tocqueville maintains that it is "an impious and detestable maxim that in matters of government the majority of people has the right to do everything, and nevertheless I place the origin of all powers in the will of the majority" (250). A government based on decisions of the majority is animated by fundamental *egalitarian* assumptions, since each person's vote, and, by extension, each person's view and opinion, is deemed to be absolutely equal to any other person's. But Tocqueville distinguishes two forms of majority rule that mirror the two forms of equality he has identified. In its debased form, majority rule is a reflection of a level-ing democratic equality in which the majority is comparable to "an individ-ual with opinions, and usually with interests" (251), a collective of interests against which a minority has no recourse or appeal (252). Tocqueville con-trasts this limited sense of democratic majority with "the majority of all men," whose single law is justice, and which "forms the boundary to each people's right" (250).

Equality of conditions produces an unwillingness to defer to the view of any other human, a condition of complete but misguided self-reliance aris-ing from assumptions of equal worth in its most debased sense: "There is a general distaste for accepting any man's word for anything" (431). This un-willingness to submit to another's judgment, however, does not result in a strong sense of self-regard nor confidence in the validity of one's own posi-tion. Rather, the unwillingness to defer to the judgment of anyone else is ac-companied by the unwillingness to judge anyone or anything in turn, and leads to an ironic abandonment of judgment to a perceived majority opin-ion. The result of this inability to judge based on standards outside prevail-ing opinion allows for the creation of a tyranny of the majority, one of Tocqueville's original and counterintutitive analyses of the potential perni-ciousness of democratic equality.

Tocqueville believes that all regimes have an inclination toward tyranny when a given regime's guiding principle ceases to have any check to restrain that principle. He explicitly rejects the classical conception of mixed gov-ernment as a "chimera," since all governments must place "somewhere one social power superior to all others" (251). In a democracy, then, "freedom is in danger when that power [of the majority] finds no obstacle that can re-strain its course and give it time to moderate itself" (251–252). Tocqueville worries that there will be no political recourse or remedy when a democracy has committed an injustice, since all the levers of government are inevitably subject to majority control (251).[7]

This is only the most obvious form of democratic tyranny, and its struc-tural form says little about the psychological features that Tocqueville has described as emanating from a combination of majority rule and equality of conditions. Indeed, a person slighted or abused by a democratic majority is not *convinced* by that majority but retains a willful defiance toward it even if he or she is powerless in the short term to remedy the majority's actions. The more powerful critique that Tocqueville levels at the tyranny of the ma-jority concerns the power the majority exerts over freedom of thought itself: people will avoid even the possibility of thinking in contradiction to a per-ceived widespread majority consensus for fear of a thoroughgoing social os-tracism. Ironically, despite the social controls that exist in aristocratic Eu-rope, Tocqueville sees more allowance for widely disparate views on political theories in Europe than in democratic America: "I know of no country in which, generally speaking, there is less independence of mind and true free-dom of discussion than in America" (254–255). In Tocqueville's view, Americans effectively internalize the fear of social rejection and avoid even the possibility of nonconformity to the perceived agreements of the democratic majority. Tocqueville contrasts the respective kinds of freedom that characterize aristocracies and democracies, and expresses reservations toward the view that democratic freedom is to be preferred to aristocratic constraints if the price of democratic "freedom" is an even more insidious form of enslavement:

> Formerly tyranny used the clumsy weapons of chains and hangmen; nowadays, even despotism, though it seemed to have nothing more to learn, has been perfected by civilization. Princes made violence a physical thing, but our contemporary democratic republics have turned it into something as intellectual as the human will is intended to constrain. Under the absolute government of a single man, despotism, to reach the soul, clumsily struck at the body, and the soul, escaping from such blows, rose gloriously above it; but in democratic republics that is not at all how tyranny behaves; it leaves the body alone and goes straight for the soul. (255)

The individual, without recourse against the actual machination of the majority, and bereft of resources external to the "dogma of the sovereignty of the people," is in gravest peril not of being strengthened by participation in the greater whole of humanity of which the majority is only a part but rather from a thoroughgoing enervation as he or she retreats from the seeming omnipotence of the faceless and nameless democratic majority. The ironic result of conformity that is engendered by a tyranny of the majority is not the creation of a collectivist majoritarian nightmare but, instead, an exacerbation of the other effect of equality—individualism.

Thus Tocqueville concluded that equality of conditions did not lead to mass conformity per se (not as a final end but as an intermediary result) but rather, in response to the perception of individual weakness in the face of a perceived tyranny of the majority, that it led to a kind of virulent individualism. "Individualism is a calm and considered feeling which disposes each citizen to isolate himself from the mass of his fellows and withdraw into the circle of his family and friends. . . . Individualism is of democratic origin, and threatens to grow as conditions grow more equal" (506–507). In response to perceptions of his individual weakness, democratic man retreats further from the public sphere that might otherwise sustain his sense of individual strength. While people in democracies are individually weak amid a large and faceless majority, they sense potency when left to themselves and a small private circle: "They form the habit of thinking of themselves in isolation and imagine that their whole destiny is in their own hands" (508). This perceived potency, born of withdrawal from conditions that otherwise confirm their individual weakness, in fact leaves them weaker than before as they have no influence on public affairs, and each person's voice—made more singular in the absence of a wider circle of associates—is altogether drowned out. The response, ironically in Tocqueville's view, is not to seek out fellowship that would strengthen the individual but instead to retreat further from the perceived indignity of public life: "Thus, not only does democracy make men forget their own ancestors, but also clouds their view of their descendents and isolates them from their contemporaries. Each man is forever thrown back on himself alone, and there is danger that he may be shut up in the solitude of his own heart" (508).

The combination of this withdrawal in the face of perceived insignificance and the equality of conditions that led to it creates a kind of thoroughgoing materialism that is singular to the democratic age. The same unwillingness to judge or to be judged that results in a tyranny of the majority also leads to a form of willful self-reliance. From this simple effect of equality, Tocqueville deduces an iron law of materialism and democratic optimism that borders on overconfidence. When equality of conditions becomes widespread,

> each man is narrowly shut up in himself, and from that basis makes the pretension to judge the world. This American way of relying on themselves alone to control their judgment leads to other mental habits. Seeing that they are successful in resolving unaided all the little difficulties they encounter in practical affairs, they are easily led to the conclusion that everything in the world can be explained and that nothing passes beyond the limits of intelligence. Thus they are ready to deny anything which they cannot understand. Hence they have little faith in anything extraordinary and an almost invincible distaste for the supernatural. (430)

Through the internal logic of equality's implications, Tocqueville wryly observes that "of all the countries of the world, America is the one in which the precepts of Descartes are the least studied and best followed" (429). The tendency of equality—itself born of the Christian tradition, in Tocqueville's view—is to undermine all religions, and put in its place the radical skepticism of Descartes, derived not from study but from democratic practice.

Tocqueville's "religious terror" points to the likely decline of religion that, ironically, is born of the legacy of Western Christianity. Christianity's insistence that all men are created equal in the eyes of God moves humankind providentially toward the ascendance of democracy and the accompanying equality of conditions. This very equality, however, in its most virulent manifestation, actually undermines the religious basis from which it derived and which in fact offered the best obstacle to equality's tendencies toward skepticism, individualism, and materialism. At some level one can understand Tocqueville's "*terreur religieuse*" to be both a dread for religion and, at the same time, a dread of what religion has wrought.

TOCQUEVILLE'S CRITIQUE OF MATERIALISM AND THE DEMOCRATIC FAITH

In Tocqueville's view, there is a nearly unavoidable inclination in egalitarian societies toward doctrines of materialism. Tocqueville understood such doctrines not to offer a more modest conception of humanity as part of a natural order but rather to release human ambitions in directions hitherto restrained by religious admonitions of humility. Speaking directly of the need for religion to serve as a corrective for this tendency toward materialism, Tocqueville wrote, "when [materialists] think they have sufficiently established that they are no better than brutes, they seem as proud as if they had proved that they were gods" (544). If "faith is the only permanent state of mankind" (297), Tocqueville feared that in a materialistic, egalitarian democracy, faith would manifest itself as a belief in human perfectibility resulting in an unbounded human restlessness.

It is not in spite of the materialist bent of democratic man that he is restless; it is because of his materialism.[8] At its most mundane level, this materialism is expressed by the hedonistic pursuit of worldly success. Despite their comparative wealth and success, Tocqueville finds it curious "with what feverish ardor the Americans pursue prosperity and how they are ever tormented by the shadowy suspicion that they may not have chosen the shortest route to get it" (536). He wonders at the drivenness of Americans, their constant desire for more abundance, more security, more possessions, even as one might judge them as successful by some comparative or even objective basis. Tocqueville accounts for their restless anxiety by pointing to a more fundamental kind of materialism, a submerged but evident desire to outrun death through the accumulation.[9] This leads to a rushing from thing to thing, from sensation to sensation, and results in a loss of any sense of true human permanence, exacerbating, instead, the feeling of impermanence that pervades the material age:

> Americans cleave to the things of this world as if assured that they will never die, and yet are in such a rush to snatch any that come within their reach, as if expecting to stop living before they have relished them. They clutch everything, but hold nothing fast, and so lose grip as they hurry after some new delight. . . . A man who has set his heart on nothing but the good things of the world is always in a hurry, for he has only a limited time in which to find them, get them, and enjoy them. Remembrance of the shortness of life continually goads him on. Apart from the goods that he has, he thinks of a thousand others which death will prevent him from tasting if he does not hurry. This thought fills him with distress, fear, and regret and keeps his mind continually in agitation, so that he is always changing his plans and his abode. (536–537)

In contrast to aristocratic ages, when man was neither a materialist—believing in a good beyond the material world—nor endowed with the freedom to make himself wholly new in whatever direction he wished, the democratic age is marked by a kind of endless motion that ceases only in death. These two new conditions—democratic materialism and the decline of restraining social roles that hold one to a particular status—combine to create a universally restless nation (537): "At first there is something astonishing in this spectacle of so many lucky men restless in the midst of their abundance. But it is a spectacle as old as the world; all that is new is to see

a whole people performing in it" (536). Yet, rather than leading to a strengthening of the individual's confidence in the unlimited freedom to remake oneself, Tocqueville concludes that the democratic citizen's restlessness in fact
leads to a peculiar condition of enervation. "The same equality which allows
each man to entertain vast hopes makes each man by himself weak. His
power is limited on every side, though his longings may wander where they
will" (537). One finds this noteworthy paradox repeated in different per-
mutations in Tocqueville's analysis: the appearance of individual puissance
in fact reveals a more subtle form of individual weakness. Thus, whereas the
equality of conditions leads to the appearance of individual political
strength, in fact Tocqueville's analysis of the effects of the "dogma of the sovereignty of the people" leads him to conclude that the result of the democratic dogma is an individual weakness that arises from a tyranny of the majority. So, too, in analyzing the consequences of materialism and the
unleashing of human potential from restraints of the aristocratic past,
Tocqueville similarly concludes that this apparent confidence—located in an
increasingly weakened and solitary individual—ironically also results in a
condition of individual enervation.

   This form of restlessness, the perception of a fluid new world shorn of traditional limits even as it contributes to a sense of individual weakness, also
encourages a new form of belief in human perfectibility. Perfectibility,
Tocqueville notes, is not new to democratic times; perfectibility, like the restless pursuit of material abundance, is likely "as old as the world" (452).
However, in contrast to the freedom that marks a democratic age, under aristocracies "citizens are classified by rank, profession, or birth . . . , everyone
thinks he can see the ultimate limits of human endeavor quite close in front
of him, and no one attempts to fight against an inevitable fate" (452–453).
Democratic ages, by contrast, present new social arrangements that encourage perfectibility not as a distant ideal but as more immediately realizable
through striving and achievement. While aristocratic ages did not deny the
possibility of improvement, in democratic ages that legitimate pursuit is
thought to be "unlimited" (453).

   Like those simultaneous conditions of political power and political weakness, like the opportunity and enervation created by restlessness, with the belief in human perfectibility engendered by democratic equality, so, too, there
is a concomitant resulting disappointment that is inescapably intertwined
with the belief in unlimited improvement. Democratic man "concludes that
man in general is endowed with an indefinite capacity for improvement. . . .
Thus, searching always, falling, picking himself up again, often disappointed, never discouraged, he is ever striving toward that immense grandeur
glimpsed indistinctly at the end of the long track that humanity must follow"
(453). What was once a goal thought to be achievable only in the afterlife is
now, in a materialist age, thought to be realizable within man's lifetime.
Tocqueville notes that this belief is no less a form of faith than the faith it
displaced: the constant and inevitable setbacks to human perfection present

a cause for "disappointment" if not "discouragement," solely owing to the secular faith in perfectibility that results from the new and wholly open social conditions. Democracy fosters extreme expectation for imminent perfectibility and extreme disillusionment when that vision goes unachieved. By contrast, aristocracy—which does not entertain the possibility of radical amelioration—is prone to an opposite vice of complacency and resignation. In Tocqueville's view, neither the conditions of aristocratic limitation nor democratic openness is ultimately desirable; both represent extremes that seem to abandon a form of moderate and chastened striving toward material and moral improvement. So, Tocqueville concludes, "aristocratic nations are by their nature too much inclined to restrict the scope of human perfectibility; democratic nations sometimes stretch it beyond reason" (454).[10]

These political and social conditions resulting from the equality that undergirds "the dogma of the sovereignty of the people" describe most fully what can be regarded as Tocqueville's view of democratic faith. Faith in the "dogma" of democracy, unmediated by those institutions that Tocqueville saw as affording some corrective to the worst ravages of this democratic faith—family, civic associations, and, above all, religion—resulted in a curious and yet unseen condition in which democratic man thought himself at once both thoroughly omnipotent but still found himself to be utterly isolated and powerless. Democratic faith transfers faith from divine objects to human endeavors, a result of the materialism which Tocqueville thought was the consequence of democratic equality. If democratic faith was as "unreasoned" as the divine faith it displaced, its results were widely divergent, in large part owing to the *object* of the faith itself—now not a divine Creator whose very perfection required the recognition of human fallibility but, instead, a belief in democratic capacities and human perfectibility. If a religious faith necessitated the admission of human imperfection—leading citizens to acknowledge a condition of mutual insufficiency that encouraged endeavors undertaken in common—that recognition also involved a concomitant acknowledgment of human *dignity* that resulted from humanity's participation in, and guidance from, the divine, thereby serving as a potential source of moral strength for each individual in a democratic setting. By contrast, the "democratic faith," premised on human perfectibility, ironically resulted in a condition of radical *indignity* as it placed human life on an ultimately unsatisfying material basis, contributed to the shattering of human associations, and thereby rendered individuals politically and socially ineffectual.

As Tocqueville pointed out when speaking of perfectibility, there was no more cause for regarding earthly perfection as any more realizable than our likely heavenly redemption, but that human beings were now regarded as thoroughly responsible for the realization of their own perfection had the effect of altering humanity's view of perfection. Democratic man becomes at once more optimistic, thinking that human efforts alone will suffice; yet, the almost inevitable frustration of those efforts leaves him dissatisfied, restless, and impatient. Democratic faith increasingly sees democracy itself as the source of its own corrections, thus exacerbating those worst aspects that derive from that faith in the first place. Tyranny of the majority becomes more firmly entrenched the more completely people believe in democratic equality and the "dogma of the sovereignty of the people"; the materialism resulting from this thoroughgoing belief in equality deepens and magnifies democratic restlessness and the idea of perfectibility; and, as these ambitions are frustrated, more emphasis is placed on *democratic* correctives, further deepening the simultaneous senses of democratic omnipotence and weakness. The democratic citizen is simultaneously overconfident and overwhelmed:

> Since in times of equality no man is obliged to put his powers at the disposal of another, and no one has any claim on the right to substantial support from his fellow man, each is both independent and weak. These two conditions, *which must be neither seen quite separately or confused*, give the citizen of a democracy extremely contradictory instincts. He is *full of confidence and pride* in his independence among equals, but from time to time his *weakness* makes him feel the need for some outside help which he cannot expect from any of his fellows, for they are both impotent and cold. (672; emphasis mine)

Tocqueville thus suggests two apparently contradictory conditions arising from democratic equality. On the one hand, tyranny of the majority leaves democratic man individually weak, unable to render judgments or to resist the perceived tide of majority consensus and only drives him further into "the solitude of his own heart." On the other hand, his unwillingness to render judgment, or to view any other person's judgment as potentially superior (or inferior) to his own, creates a form of individualism that devolves into a form of materialism, a thoroughgoing restlessness, an unwarranted belief in human capacities, even a faith in the possibility of human perfectibility.[11] The logic of the equality of conditions places democratic man simultaneously in the position of enervated isolation and overweening self-confidence. Tocqueville, quite startlingly, sees these conditions as compatible, not contradictory, and, moreover, as extremes which democratic humanity is likely to simultaneously and perpetually manifest.[12] Both conditions—beliefs in excessive weakness and excessive strength—are a result of democratic equality, the former in combination with the "dogma of the sovereignty of the people," and the latter a result of equality of conditions. Further, both conditions result in a form of virulent individualism, simultaneously a result, and a cause, of additional isolation from other citizens who might help in shoring up the enervated self and moderate the overambitious claims of the prideful self.

From the dynamics of democratic equality Tocqueville perceives a resulting democratic man who exists simultaneously at a version of both Aristotelian extremes and increasingly lacks the resources to reach, by moving simultaneously in opposite directions, a form of the virtuous Aristotelian mean. This belief in excessive and deficient personal significance—held at the same time—suggests that democratic man is wholly a new creature. While Aristotle describes an "extreme" as *either* an excess or deficiency of a particular quality,[13] by contrast, democratic man *at the same time* exhibits both an excess and a deficiency of felt personal significance, and thus exists simultaneously at two extremes. Whereas according to Aristotle one could correct an excess or deficiency by "drawing away [from the extreme] in the opposite direction,"[14] democratic man must be charged with moving *simultaneously* in opposite directions—both by restraining his overconfidence and overcoming his sense of enervation—thereby attaining an equilibrium that resembles a version of the virtuous Aristotelian mean. However, with the full fruition of democracy, he increasingly lacks the resources for doing either, no less both.

This seemingly contradictory condition of individual weakness and over-confidence is a result of consequences that Tocqueville adduces from the equality of conditions that marks the new democratic age. Yet, it is precisely this belief in equality that is a result of the divine plan that now brings the world toward this democratic age. The selfsame religion that made equality the accepted order now stands threatened by the logic of that equality. Moreover, in Tocqueville's view, the paramount way of combating what he regarded as these most corrosive effects of equality was religion itself. Tocqueville effectively describes a vicious circle: the Christian religion bequeaths to the modern age a belief in equality and a new democratic form that manifests this belief most fully; the equality of conditions, placed now in this democratic context, results in forms of subtle tyranny, materialism, restlessness, and a belief in perfectibility that were formerly precluded by older aristocratic forms and religious belief; now what is most needful to combat these tendencies is not a return to aristocratic forms—our age of equality precludes this possibility[15]—but a strengthening of the religious beliefs that stand to mitigate these vicious outcomes of the belief in equality that arose in the first place from the same religious tradition. Religion, indirectly the cause of the democratic faith, is paradoxically needful as its corrective.

The Utility of Religion

Tocqueville believed he had described the unperceived weakness that would undermine his highest hope for the democratic age: equality is both the greatest boon and the insoluble problem of modernity. As described in his complex analysis of equality's tendencies, equality at once derived from Christianity but also undermined the same religious basis that otherwise might restrain its worst effects. In a chapter entitled "Why in Ages of Equality and Skepticism it is Important to Set Distant Goals for Human Endeavors" (II.i.17), Tocqueville explained why religion was most for necessary for a democratic age marked especially by materialism, restlessness, and a belief in human perfectibility:

In ages of FAITH the final aim is placed beyond life. . . . Religions instill a general habit of behaving with the future in view. In this respect they work as much in favor of happiness in this world as of felicity in the next. That is one of their most salient political characteristics.

But as the light of faith grows dim, man's range of vision grows more circumscribed, and it would seem as if the object of human endeavors came daily closer. When once they have grown accustomed not to think about what will happen after their life, they easily fall back into a complete and brutish indifference about the future, an attitude all too well suited to certain propensities of human nature. As soon as they have lost the way of relying chiefly on distant hopes, they are naturally led to want to satisfy their least desires at once; and it would seem that as soon as they despair of living forever, they are inclined to act as if they could not live for more than a day. (547–548)

In order to combat this tendency, one "suited to certain propensities in human nature," Tocqueville argued that another propensity, one possibly stronger than unbelief but less supported in a democratic age, should be encouraged as a counterforce to excessively short-term, materialistic thinking. This "propensity" was the wellspring of religion itself, the longing for a continuation of one's existence beyond the short time allotted to humans upon this planet:

The short span of sixty years can never shut in the whole of man's imagination; the incomplete joys of this world will never satisfy his heart. Alone among all created beings, man shows a natural disgust for existence and an immense longing to exist; he scorns life and fears annihilation. These different instincts constantly drive his soul toward contemplation of the next world, and it is religion that leads him thither. Religion, therefore, is only one particular form of hope, and it is as natural to the human heart as hope itself. (296–297)

It seems contradictory that Tocqueville should declare that humans should have as much a propensity for *disbelief* in religion, and a concentration on things of this life, as they have a propensity for *belief* in religion. Yet, Tocqueville believed that the condition of belief could be redirected, if not altogether thwarted, at the cost of tremendous psychological and social damage: "It is by a sort of intellectual aberration, and in a way, by doing moral violence to their own nature, that men detach themselves from religious beliefs; an invincible inclination draws them back. Incredulity is an accident; faith is the only permanent state of mankind" (297).

In a skeptical and materialist age, this faith could too easily be reborn not as supportive of democracies or, more important in Tocqueville's view, as a necessary response to the human confrontation with finitude, but in a perverse and fanatical form:

If ever the thoughts of the great majority came to be concentrated solely on the search for material blessings, one can anticipate that there would be a colossal reaction in the souls of men. They would distractedly launch out into the world of

spirits for fear of being held too tightly bound by the body's fetters. . . . If their social condition, circumstances, and laws did not so closely confine the American
mind to the search for physical comfort, it may well be that when they came to
consider immaterial things they would show more experience and reserve and be
able to keep themselves in check without difficulty. But they feel imprisoned within
limits from which they are apparently not allowed to escape. Once they have broken through these limits, their minds do not know where to settle down, and they
often rush without stopping far beyond the bounds of common sense. (535)[16]

In another of Tocqueville's paradoxes, skeptical and material ages are wont
to exhibit the most "enthusiastic" and even fanatical forms of spirituality,
precisely because the widespread materialism of the age does not give rein to
any human desires, including the desire for eternity. Democratic materialism
coincides comfortably, even necessarily, with religious fanaticism in Tocqueville's view, not as contradictory but as necessary consequences of humanity's two "propensities"—the desire for material satiation and the longing
for life after life.[17] Yet, this form of unleashed spirituality, rather than tending to correct or balance the excesses of democratic materialism, in fact only
further supports the kind of restlessness and boundlessness that is its
inheritance.

Thus it was not simply religion that could serve to combat democracy's
self-destructive dynamics; Tocqueville suggested that religion itself might
simply become one more expression of, and response to, democratic materialism. In his view, religion could best support democracy by resisting
democracy's prevailing tendencies. Religion could point beyond the present
in two ways: first, by taking democratic man beyond the confinement of narrow self-interest and solitude; and, second, by lifting the democratic purview
past its own horizons, toward a contemplation of the transcendent and final
things beyond fleeting opinion. By resisting democracy's claim to universal
rule, religion best served the cause of democracy. Religion, in Tocqueville's
view, was most supportive of democracy when it moderated democracy's
claims while strengthening the resolve of individual democratic citizens to
seek a standard outside the democratic will. Where democracy simultaneously contributed to illusions of perfectibility and undermined the individual's sense of dignity, religion could offer antidotes for each condition, at
once chastening and strengthening. Above all, religion could teach democratic man to arrive at Pierre Manent's precept, "to love democracy well, it
is necessary to love it moderately."[18]

In the first instance, religion is the primary source of resistance to the
specter of a tyranny of the majority. Tocqueville begins his discussion of that
new tyranny by noting that no form of rule, not even majority rule, can make
exclusive claim to justice. While an informed and judicious majority could
arrive at conclusions that would ensure greater justice for all its participants,
thereby following the theories of Rousseau, Tocqueville held that majority
rule was ultimately as subject to human failing and limiting interests as any

form of rule. He contrasted rule of the majority to a universal rule of justice: "There is one law which has been made, or at least adopted, not by the majority of this or that people, but by the majority of all men. That law is justice. Justice therefore forms the boundary to each people's right" (250).

While all human forms of rule can aspire to justice, no form can claim to attain it: "only God can be omnipotent without danger because His wisdom and justice are always equal to his power" (252). Human rule that does not recognize its insufficiency is tempted to claim an omnipotence that is not its due, and leads inevitably toward tyranny. "There is no power on earth in itself so worthy of respect or vested with such a sacred right that I would wish to let it act without control and dominate without obstacles" (252). Tocqueville regards religious belief as affording a transcendent law, a standard outside the shifting and temporary opinion of majorities, "beyond the ebb and flow of human opinion" (298), an alternative code of morality to which a citizen can appeal even when a vast majority opposes him or her. Tocqueville concludes,

> When I see the right and capacity to do all given to any authority whatsoever, whether it be called people or king, democracy or aristocracy, and whether the scene of action is a monarchy or a republic, I say: the germ of tyranny is there, and I will go look for other laws under which to live. (252)

Democracy stands to be corrected and guided by such laws, and perhaps, if those laws are willfully ignored, knowledge of them outside the majority opinion can shore up the individual soul as in the case of the believer whose soul was impervious to the inquisitor. In a democracy informed by such a religious view, both the body and soul have the potential to be free, rather than one or the other enslaved by the omnipotent claims of a particular regime.

Yet, even a tyranny of the majority can be advantageous in a democratic regime that is constituted with such an indirect governing force of religious belief. In an ironic twist, Tocqueville describes how, in America, widespread religious belief creates after a fashion a "beneficent" form of tyranny of the majority, guiding even nonbelievers to credit the tenets of religious belief, and thereby restraining them from the worst excesses of their materialistic disbelief. In contrast to the boundless ambition and ideas of perfectibility that tend to inform a materialistic democratic age, Tocqueville suggests that a democracy suffused with religious belief serves to restrain such dangerous optimistic tendencies and a thoroughgoing form of secular consequentialism.

> Nature and circumstance have made the inhabitant of the United States a bold man, as is sufficiently attested by the enterprising spirit with which he seeks his fortune. If the spirit of the Americans were free of all impediment, one would soon find among them the boldest innovators and the most implacable logicians in the world. But American revolutionaries are obliged ostensibly to profess a certain respect for Christian morality and equity, and that does not allow them easily to break the laws when those are opposed to the executions of their designs; nor

would they find it easy to surmount the scruples of their partisans even if they were able to get over their own. Up till now no one in the United States has dared to profess the maxim that everything is allowed in the interests of society, an impious maxim invented in the age of freedom in order to legitimize every future tyrant. Thus, while the law allows the American people to do everything, there are things which religion prevents them from imagining and forbids them to dare. (292)

Such a "benevolent" tyranny of the majority actually serves as a counter-force to the doctrine that "everything is allowed" but is itself resistant to the most tyrannical aspects of majority rule, inasmuch as such a view does not begin with the assumption that the opinion of the majority is the sole reigning source of political legitimacy and justice. Distrustful of wholly secular claims to justice, such a "benevolent" religiously informed majority exerts an indirect control over the disbelieving minority, who, ironically, do not have a similar appeal beyond that religious majority, since that disbelieving minority lacks the religious source of appeals outside the claims of majority rule. Tocqueville implies that a religiously informed form of majority rule is the only legitimate kind, since it does not credit the wholesale legitimacy of majority rule in the first instance.[19]

Religion conditions democratic man's inclination toward self-interest, restrains the tendency to retreat within his own private circle and regard all decisions, personal and political, as pure expressions of utility or economic calculation. Elaborating on the Americans' praise of the concept of "self-interest properly understood," Tocqueville observes that Americans often claim to be acting in accordance with liberal assumptions of self-interest, but, in fact, "in this they often do themselves less than justice, for sometimes in the United States, as elsewhere, one sees people carried away by the disinterested, spontaneous impulses natural to man" (526). Despite having earlier asserted that Americans tend to be Cartesians without ever having read Descartes (429), here he implies that Americans claim to be Lockeans but in fact occasionally act in accordance with an entirely different motivation of benevolence. He wryly comments, "They prefer to give the credit to their philosophy rather to themselves" (526). "Self-interest properly understood," in fact, in Tocqueville's view, has as its wellspring a religious sentiment deriving from the inescapable concern with the afterlife: "however hard one may try to prove that virtue is useful, it will always be difficult to make a man live well if he will not face death" (528). Even the "official" liberal doctrine of America, an Enlightenment liberal philosophy that posits self-interest as the animating feature of human action, needs and receives moderation by a more fundamental and benevolent influence of religiously inspired self-sacrifice.

Stating most explicitly how religion moderates the harmful dynamics of democratic equality and individualism, Tocqueville points to the aspect of religion that draws men outside themselves, outside their times, and points them toward a concern for the eternal and the place of all human beings in that order:

The usefulness of religion is even more apparent among egalitarian peoples than elsewhere. One must admit that equality, while it brings great benefits to mankind, opens the door . . . to very dangerous instincts. It tends to isolate men from each other so that each thinks only of himself. It lays the soul open to the inordinate love of material pleasure.

The greatest advantage of religions is to inspire diametrically opposed contrary urges. Every religion places the object of man's desires outside and beyond worldly goods and naturally lifts the soul into regions far above the realm of the senses. Every religion also imposes on each man some obligations toward mankind, to be performed in common with the rest of mankind, and so draws him away, from time to time from thinking about himself. (444–445)

This is the core of Tocqueville's belief in the "usefulness" of religion. Neither contradicting nor damning human equality or liberty—both of which are endorsed and perfected by religion, in Tocqueville's view—by exerting a contrary force against extreme expressions of each, religion protects democracy from itself. Without *being* democratic, religion supports democracy more thoroughly and better than could any expressly "democratic" doctrine. The cure for the ills of democracy is not more democracy, in Tocqueville's view; such a "cure" only worsens the underlying disease. Instead, if democracy is to thrive it requires the support and chiding of religion. Chastening humans where they become too prideful and giving them support when they become too enervated, religion pulls democratic man away from the extremes toward which equality of conditions thrusts him, back toward a version of the "Aristotelian mean," neither immobile from fear of the majority's tyranny nor restless amid discontent; neither fearful of democracy's omnipotence nor hubristically holding to the view of human perfectibility. Religion is most useful for democracy, Tocqueville concludes, when it points us away from doctrines of utility and toward a conception of the self and humanity as part of a greater and comprehensive order.

THE UTILITY OF RELIGION?

Tocqueville expressly saw the *utility* of religion in democracies as among the most promising means of correcting democracy's self-destructive tendencies. Yet, even while acknowledging that religion's utility relies on moving democratic man away from an embrace of utility as the basis of all judgment, Tocqueville often suggested that it was precisely because of religion's utility that it needed to be subtly promoted by temporal powers. In the view of many scholars, Tocqueville actively sought to *promote* a form of beneficent religion for a democratic age, effectively engaging in a project similar to that of Montesquieu and Rousseau, the creation of a *civil religion*.[20] Indeed, at several points in *Democracy in America*, Tocqueville appears to recommend that democratic governments should actively seek to promote a salutary form of religion to support the continued survival of democracy. In one of his baldest statements to this end, Tocqueville wrote,

> I think that the only effective means which governments can use to make the doctrine of immortality of the soul respected is daily to act as if they believed it themselves. I think that it is only by conforming scrupulously to religious morality in great affairs that they can flatter themselves that they are teaching the citizens to understand it and to love and respect it in little matters. (546)

Several of Tocqueville's otherwise admiring students have found this aspect of Tocqueville's thought troubling. Jack Lively accuses Tocqueville of wishing to correct democracy's defects by appeal to "social myths," and finds it "difficult to see how Tocqueville's basic plea for liberty as recognition of the morally responsible individual can be reconciled with his acceptance of a deliberately manipulated myth designed to enforce or sustain a particular pattern of moral response."[21] More pointedly, Marvin Zetterbaum suggests that such form of "social myth" is ultimately destructive of religious belief itself, and leads Tocqueville back to the impasse he seeks to overcome by means of religion: "What [Tocqueville] recommends to ensure the well-being of democratic regimes is little more than the propagation of spiritualistic myths designed to answer the question of immortality. Propagating such salutary myths cannot but weaken genuine religious belief rather than strengthening it, for by propagating them men are emboldened to consider religion from a functional point of view."[22] Tocqueville seems to confirm these suspicions with lines that appear to recommend the mere *existence* of belief against the importance of the *content* of belief, such as when he states:

> Though it is very important for man as an individual that his religion should be true, that is not the case for society. Society has nothing to fear or hope from another life; what is most important for it is not that all citizens should profess the true religion but that they should profess religion. (290)

While scholars such as Lively and Zetterbaum have been sensitive to aspects of Tocqueville's thought that seem to lead toward the recommendation of a wholly functionalist view of religion in the service of politics, and democracy particularly, other scholars have sought to defend Tocqueville from this charge by pointing out Tocqueville's stress on the necessarily transcendent nature of the religion he recommends.[23] Prominent among these scholars is Pierre Manent, a French scholar who has tried to reacquaint the French with a native thinker hitherto more embraced by Americans. In his work, *Tocqueville and the Nature of Democracy*, Manent stresses Tocqueville's assertion that religion is the inescapable fact of human existence, a part of man's nature as a self-aware dying creature. Given the naturalness of religion, Manent asserts that,

> [religion] does not need the help of human conventions to make its voice heard and its influences felt. In particular, it does not need the support of political insti-

tutions. . . . To want to aid religion by fusing it to the political order is in fact to weaken it, especially in democratic centuries when political institutions are so fragile and subject to such frequent changes. In order to give religion its full force, it is necessary to leave it to its own force alone. On preserving its purity, one assures its greatest social utility.[24]

In volume 1 of *Democracy in America*, more expressly drawing on his experiences in America, Tocqueville briefly examines the direct role of religion on democratic life but spends the greatest portion of his discussion on the support religion gives to American democracy by emphasizing its "indirect effects." Indeed, Tocqueville writes that religion's "indirect action seems to me much greater still, and it is just when it is not speaking of freedom at all that it best teaches the Americans the art of being free" (290).

Religion is best kept separate from the apparatus of the state in Tocqueville's view. This is not primarily out of liberal concern for the likelihood of religious repression (although Tocqueville believed that Europe's Enlightenment thinkers rightly denounced religion because of the church's alliance with the temporal powers, a condition he regarded nevertheless as "accidental and particular" [300–301]). Rather, it emanates from his concern that religion should maintain its independent legitimacy and force. Tocqueville expressly rejects the concept of a civil religion inasmuch as a religion that adapts itself to the requirements of a specific regime "sacrifices the future for the present" and adopts "maxims which apply only to certain nations" (297). By allying itself with a particular regime, religion ceases to appeal to transcendent norms and calls down upon itself all the suspicion and obloquy associated with a particular regime. Moreover, given the fluctuating fortunes of political life, a religion endangers its long-term appeal by aligning itself with the inherently changeable status of regimes and their leaders: "when a religion chooses to rely on the interests of this world, it becomes almost as fragile as all earthly powers. Alone, it may hope for immortality; linked to ephemeral powers, it follows their fortunes and often falls together with the passions of a day sustaining them" (298).

Religion must reject identification with any government to be the greatest support to democracy; at the same time, however, in order to be democracy's benefactor, it must point democratic man beyond the earthly and, in some regards, challenge the foundations of democratic government itself. It is difficult to deny that Tocqueville apparently endorses a form of "civil religion" in some instances, and yet, at other times, expressly rejects any identification of a religion with a specific state. However, as in many other instances in his thought, his beliefs only appear to be paradoxical.

Pierre Manent has suggested that one needs to distinguish the different perspectives of Tocqueville qua observer and the beliefs of the democratic citizens he regards. Manent notes that religion's force as a corrective to democracy's excessive claims to rule rely upon

the authentic and purely religious attachment of each man to his religion. This utilitarian assessment is brought by an outside observer who takes into consideration the natural and universal characteristics of men and the needs of society—in particular democratic society. When this utilitarianism becomes that of the citizens themselves, the argument of the observer, far from being strengthened is to such an extent undermined. For religion to have its proper force, it is necessary for men to be devoted to it for itself and not for social utility or by love of the political institutions to which it can be fused.[25]

This would seem to be the only view that can be maintained through a full appreciation of the source of religion's force, in Tocqueville's own view, as a corrective for democracy's inclinations. He notes that "the unbeliever, no longer thinking religion true, still considers it useful. Paying attention to the human side of religious beliefs, he recognizes their sway over mores and their influence over laws" (299).

In short, the unbeliever recognizes what Tocqueville himself has observed, often prefacing his observations with variations of the very phrase, "looking at the human side of religion."[26] However, although few unbelievers, or an observer like Tocqueville, might make such an evaluation without undermining the belief of the broader citizenry, once democracy's materialist tendency has itself undermined belief, and all or most people begin to view religion as useful to democracy, at that point it altogether loses its effectiveness. Religion no longer governs democratic man's excessive impulses because its precepts are no longer believed. The utility merely becomes that which is good for others, for society at large, and not that by which an individual governs his or her own actions and intentions. If religious belief restrains thoroughgoing utilitarian calculation, once this central tenet of religions is undermined everything is allowed, even the attempt to use religion for the benefit of democracy. Belief in religion is advanced without regard to whether its actual precepts are embraced, thereby altogether undermining its corrective potential. Rather than offering a corrective to democracy, religion merely becomes one more weapon in the utilitarian arsenal.

When Tocqueville describes the way that religion can become useful to a democratic regime in volume 2 especially, one must read these recommendations in light of what he has revealed about democratic thought in volume 1. In volume 2 Tocqueville states that in a democracy, faced with the likely and perhaps inevitable inclination to materialism leading democratic man to "lose the use of his sublimest faculties and that, bent on improving everything around him, may at length degrade himself,"

> it is ever the duty of lawgivers and of all upright educated men to raise up the souls of their fellow citizens and turn their attention toward heaven. There is a need for all who are interested in the future of democratic societies to get together and with one accord to make continual efforts to propagate throughout society a taste for the infinite, an appreciation of greatness, and a love of spiritual pleasures. (543)

Tocqueville calls upon the lawmakers and educated elite to act as a counterforce to democracy's inclinations by invoking religious sentiments that, in turn, will act as a counterforce.

The question arises, on what basis does Tocqueville conclude that law-givers can act in opposition to the prevailing materialism of democracy, once manifested? One wonders, what is the impetus for governments or elite society to act in support of a religion that serves as a counterforce to the democratic mores that form and undergird that government and society? As Tocqueville points out in his discussion of tyranny of the majority in volume 1, a democratic government *is* ultimately an expression of the will of the people, just as the society is the collective expression of the underlying beliefs of the people. Lawmakers, in most cases, will not act in opposition to the majority sentiment but rather in its image: the "legislative body . . . represents the majority and serves as its passive instrument" (252). Even assuming that Tocqueville intends that governments or society must propagate a form of belief which disrupts the destructive dynamic of democratic individualism, he is fully aware that such a recommendation could have little hold in a thoroughgoing democratic era.

Tocqueville reiterates this sentiment in an important chapter entitled "Why in Ages of Equality and Skepticism It Is Important to Set Distant Goals for Human Endeavor" (II.ii.17). He begins by noting that religion by its nature points humanity beyond the temporal and earthly toward a consideration of eternity, which in turn tempers the human inclination to think in the short term. However,

> as the light of faith grows dim, man's range of vision grows more circumscribed, and it would seem as if the object of human endeavors came daily closer. . . . In skeptical ages, therefore, there is always a danger that men will give way to ephemeral and casual desires and that, wholly renouncing whatever cannot be acquired without protracted effort, they may never achieve anything calm or lasting. If, with a people so disposed, social conditions become democratic, this danger is increased. (547–548)

In such a setting, Tocqueville argues, it falls upon "philosophers and men in power" to "set a distant aim as the object of human efforts" (548). The "upright educated men" of a prior chapter (543) becomes here the "philosopher" who acts to point democratic man's sight beyond the immediate toward a contemplation of the eternal. However, as in the case of the lawgivers (or "men in power"), Tocqueville has previously warned that it is unwarranted to place much hope in this particular resource—namely, philosophy—in a democratic age. The first chapter of the first book of the volume 2 discusses "the philosophical approach of the Americans," in which Tocqueville remarks upon the hidden influence of Descartes as the guiding philosophic spirit of the Americans (429). As if almost anticipating the pragmatic philosophy of the likes of John Dewey and Richard Rorty, Tocqueville writes that the Americans' philosophical method consists of using "tradition as valuable for information only and to accept existing facts as no more than a useful sketch to show how things could be done differently and better; to seek by themselves and in themselves for the only reason for things, looking to results without getting entangled in the means toward them and looking through forms to the basis of all things" (429).

Tocqueville does not evince any more confidence in the role of philosophers toward correcting the excesses of democracy's dangerous tendencies than he does, in the long run, to religion or associations or families, all of which he views as subject to the irresistible wave of atomism and materialism that accompanies a democratic age. Yet, of these corrective possibilities, Tocqueville mentions philosophy in only the briefest way, and does not examine the possible corrective role that such a resource might play beyond the passing comment cited above, in contrast to his more lengthy treatments of the "arts of association" and the beneficial role of religion. Is Tocqueville justified in placing some, or even more, hope in the ameliorative role that a philosopher might play in a democratic setting, given what he has previously said about the likelihood of a peculiarly democratic form of philosophy that does not challenge democracy's tendency toward utilitarian calculus in all regards? Tocqueville suggests that even philosophers are likely to have to accept many of the prevailing precepts of their age, inasmuch as human beings cannot function without an extensive degree of "dogma" in their assumptions about daily life: "No philosopher in the world, however great, can help believing a million things on trust from others or assuming the truth of many things besides those he has proved" (434). This is especially true during democratic times, when even philosophers are inclined to accept the fundamental aspects of the democratic faith: "Thus men who live in times of equality find it hard to place the intellectual authority to which they submit, beyond and outside humanity. Generally speaking, they look into themselves or into their fellows for the sources of truth" (435).

Yet, Tocqueville elsewhere describes a dynamic that comports with a certain understanding of philosophy which is not extinguished in a democratic age, or any age, but would appear to be, in Tocqueville's view, a human possibility at all times—as much in democratic Athens as in democratic America. He appears to describe a form of philosophic ignorance that echoes the famous Socratic declaration that "one of you, O human beings, is wisest, who, like Socrates, has become cognizant that in truth he is worth nothing with respect to wisdom."[27] As Tocqueville describes this encounter with human ignorance,

A great man has said that *ignorance lies at both ends of knowledge.*[28] Perhaps it would have been truer to say that deep convictions lie at the two ends, with doubt in the middle. In fact, one can distinguish three distinct and often successive states of human understanding.

A man may hold a firm belief which he has adopted without plumbing it. He doubts when objections strike him. Often he succeeds in resolving those doubts, and then he again begins to believe. This time he does not grasp the truth by chance or in the dark, but sees it face to face and is guided forward by its light. (186–187)

Tocqueville seems to echo the Platonic description in the *Republic* (514a–521b) of the philosopher's ascent from the cave of opinion, toward the confusion and uncertainty that his ascent renders, and finally culminating in a form of knowledge through an encounter with the "light" above the cave. Yet, Tocqueville, in a footnote at the end of the above-cited passage, suggests that the form of knowledge at the other end of doubt is not the same as before the "journey": "Nevertheless, I doubt whether this deliberate and self-justified conviction ever inspires the same degree of ardor and devotion as do dogmatic beliefs" (187). A belief without dogmatism reflects a kind of Socratic ignorance, a belief in knowledge that undermines the claims of that very belief.

Tocqueville suggests that this last condition is rare and even as unexpected as the existence of a Socrates in Athens might be: "One may count on it that the majority of mankind will always stop short in one of these two conditions: they will either believe without knowing why or will not know precisely what to believe. But only a few persevering people will ever attain to that deliberate and self-justified type of conviction born of knowledge and springing up in the very midst of doubt" (187). The first two conditions, even simultaneously, appear to capture Tocqueville's assessment of the viewpoint especially of a democratic age, an age both of profound faith in democracy itself—an "unlimited confidence in the judgment of the public" (435)—but one also marked by an overarching doubt in the correctness of one's own convictions, as "when he compares himself with his fellows and measures himself against this vast entity, he is overwhelmed by a sense of his insignificance and weakness" (435). Only one who can combine the conditions of belief in doubt toward a kind of "self-justified" conviction is left immune from this dynamic. If Tocqueville eschews the democratic faith, he seems to embrace a kind of philosophic faith, or hope, that for all of democracy's irresistible tendencies, the possibility of philosophic knowledge *that can exist outside the democratic dogma* will not be extinguished. Like faith itself, philosophy may be a permanent state of mankind.

If Tocqueville's hope is warranted, he maintains the possibility that philosophers may be able to exert a guiding and corrective influence on democratic governments, somehow contravening both the tendencies of democratic governments and democratic philosophy. He thereby gives an altogether different picture of what would be needful for promoting a more widespread corrective for democracy's tendencies that does not wholly comport with a traditional view of "civil religion":

> Governments must study means to give men back that interest in the future which neither religion nor social conditions any longer inspire, and without specifically saying so, give daily practical examples to the citizens proving that wealth, renown, and power are the rewards of work, that great success comes when it has been long desired, and that nothing of lasting value is achieved without trouble. Once men have become accustomed to foresee from afar what is likely to befall them in this world and to feed upon hopes, they can hardly keep their thoughts always confined within the precise limits of this life and will always be ready to break out through these limits and consider what is beyond. (549)

As such, governments, philosophically informed, should promote not a civil religion per se but rather should seek to promote long-term thinking through secular means, means that comport with the restlessness and materialism of democratic man but that in fact serve ends which are not wholly secular. As Tocqueville concludes this remarkable chapter,

> I have therefore no doubt that, in accustoming the citizens to think of the future in this world, they will gradually be led without noticing it themselves toward religious belief. Thus the same means that, up to a certain point, enable men to manage without religion are perhaps the only means we still possess for bringing mankind back, by a long and roundabout path, to a state of faith. (549)

In a culminating Tocquevillian paradox, Tocqueville suggests that the promotion of long-term thinking in secular affairs will in fact redound favorably to a reinvigoration of religious belief that can then exert a beneficial indirect effect on the democratic polity. The government, guided by philosophy's more considered form of "doubt," can indirectly seek to moderate democracy's excesses, and thereby subtly promote a return to a form of religious belief that will, in effect, undergird such efforts by the government and perhaps make those efforts unnecessary. In contrast to the positions of most scholars, Tocqueville then appears neither to recommend a civil religion—as such a recommendation merely plays upon the tendency of a democratic age to measure all good by a utilitarian calculus, thus undermining the nonutilitarian aspect of religion—nor does he suggest that a noncivil religious sentiment can be simply and directly supported by the state. In both instances, democracy's prevailing tendencies only serve to undermine each effort, rendering such efforts either fruitless or dangerous. Friends of democracy must act with the recognition of democracy's inherent inclinations, working to moderate tendencies such as materialism and restlessness not by extinguishing them but through democratic man's adoration of material life, promoting beneficial long-term thinking through circumspect and indirect education. Only by means of such acceptance (and not hostility), Tocqueville suggests, can democracy find its way back to a "state of faith" that originally placed a priority on human equality and thereby made democracy possible, and which, in the long term, is the only basis on which a belief in democratic equality, and hence the pursuit of democratic justice, can rest.

However, while Tocqueville's arguments in favor of the role of religion in democracy often afford encouragement to those who would like to see the reinvigoration of religious belief among a democratic citizenry, he was more wary than many of today's most fervent proponents of the restoration of religion's preeminent place. Tocqueville's stern warning that the temptation to "use" religion for the express purpose of supporting democracy by offering a counterforce to democracy's internally destructive logic—thereby further undermining religion's potential power as democratic antidote—is often studiously ignored by Tocqueville's most ardent admirers. Far from offering confirmation to put religion back in the public square for the purpose of strengthening democracy, Tocqueville himself appears to advise a form of chastened faith in the ability of religious faith to act as a corrective to the dangers of the democratic faith.

Tocqueville's analysis of modern democracy is complex and elaborate, and we are right to view his recommendations with a degree of hesitancy and skepticism. However, Tocqueville himself recognizes the daunting nature of the task at the very outset of his project, in the introduction to volume 1:

> The first duty imposed on those who now direct society is to educate democracy; to put, if possible, new life into its beliefs; to purify its mores; to control its actions; gradually to substitute understanding of statecraft for present inexperience and knowledge of its true interests for blind instincts; to adapt government to the needs of time and place; and to modify it as men and circumstance require. A new political science is needed for a world itself quite new. (12)

The various components that Tocqueville describes as the requirements of "educating democracy" are, in fact, those very elements that mark the vast remainder of his book. His own work, *Democracy in America*, is perhaps the paramount example of philosophic education that works indirectly in support of democracy; for, by posing as a work of description and not a text of philosophic education, it is one more likely to be read and reread by a democratic people averse to the philosophic approach that Tocqueville views as most needful as a critical vantage on democracy, chiding its excesses while leaving intact its admirable democratic hopes.

Hope in America: The Chastened Faith of Reinhold Niebuhr and Christopher Lasch

> "The assumption of [the optimist and the pessimist] is that a man criticises this world as if he were house-hunting, as if he were being shown over a new suite of apartments. . . . But no man is in that position. A man belongs to this world before he begins to ask if it is nice to belong to it. . . . My acceptance of the universe is not optimism, it is more like patriotism. It is a matter of primary loyalty. The world is not a lodging house at Brighton, which we are to leave because it is miserable. . . . The point is not that this world is too sad to love or too glad not to love; the point is that when you do love a thing, its gladness is a reason for loving it, and its sadness a reason for loving it more.
>
> —G. K. Chesterton, *Orthodoxy*

HOPE AGAINST OPTIMISM

I HAVE ARGUED at the beginning of the last part of this book that "friendly critics" of "democratic faith" lay claim in particular to the religious language and accompanying theological and political concepts of humility, hope, and charity. The former two, in particular, might seem to fit together only fitfully: humility would appear to coexist, if at all, in considerable tension with hope. Hope, oriented toward a belief in a better, even ideal, future, would seem to necessitate the abandonment of humility in favor of a kind of boldness. Yet, as I argue in this penultimate chapter, hope and humility are virtues that are conceptually and by definition bound together. This close relationship, however, might be easily missed given the unjustified appropriation of the language of hope by the most passionate of today's democratic faithful, Richard Rorty. I propose to "reappropriate" the language of hope by insisting upon its close kinship with humility.

In a series of essays culminating in his recent book, *Achieving Our Country*, Rorty has advised the Left to become more modest with regard to revolution and more fervent with regard to reform. Revolution, he suggests, in the twentieth-century Marxist version, assumes a vision of transcendent perfection which alone can justify the complete transformation of existing social structures, even at the cost of untold human misery and death. Con-

demning this version of transcendent history in his essay, "The End of Leninism, Havel, and Social Hope," Rorty asks that his fellow philosophers realize that "we have reached a time at which we can finally get rid of the conviction common to Plato and Marx that there *must* be large theoretical ways
of finding out how to end injustice, as opposed to small experimental
ways."[1] Rather, in *Achieving Our Country*, he urges the Left to adopt the
poetic patriotism of Whitman and the pragmatic patriotism of Dewey, to
love America enough to wish to change it for the better not by attempting to
make it into utopia but rather to improve it in "small, experimental ways."
Urging the Left to abandon its foray into "cultural politics" and, rather, to
reengage in "real politics" of reform in imitation of Progressivism, Rorty
seeks to move the Left from its flirtation with Germanic pessimism and instead renew its origins as the "party of hope."[2] The two figures Rorty cites
as guiding his own thoughts in his critique of historicism and as exemplars
of "social hope" are, first, his accustomed hero, John Dewey, and the newer
entrant Václav Havel.

The surface similarities between the two are compelling. Dewey's universe
is one in which human beings function without any belief in a transcendent
answer to all questions or philosophical insight into the true nature of reality or essences. Rorty also lauds the thought of Václav Havel for similar reasons: Havel's writings appear to offer a similar condemnation of certainty as
that offered by Dewey, and also hold the appeal of "substituting groundless
hope for theoretical insight."[3] Yet, while Rorty correctly contends that
Dewey and Havel share a fundamental distrust for culminating historical
narratives, upon further reflection not on the apparent similarities between
Dewey and Havel but rather on certain central differences, one is led to question whether Rorty hasn't blurred those differences in a way that itself obscures fundamentally different approaches to politics and democratic theory.
For while, in essence, Dewey's commendation of "uncertainty" (the accompanying doubt that arises from his criticisms of the "quest for certainty")
seems to resemble Havel's advice that "we have to be very careful about coming to any conclusions about the way we are, or what can be expected from
us," in fact the *source* of those doubts are substantially and irreconcilably
different. Whereas Dewey's doubt is skeptical in origin, arising from his refusal either to place his faith in, or even attempt to discover, any ultimate or
transcendent "truth" or "being" that might afford final insight into the
human condition, Havel's doubt emerges from a different source: not, like
Dewey, as the complete *absence* of any transcendent objective Truth but,
rather, as an acknowledgment of the human inability to wholly comprehend
the transcendent, an acknowledgment that requires Havel to embrace a view
of human insufficiency. Given this feature of Havel's thought, Rorty's appeal
to Havel is, in fact, quite surprising. While Rorty's very brief and selective
citations of Havel's interviews appear to substantiate a sketchy theory of "social hope"—that is, hope qua optimism that arises solely from discrete

human endeavors devoid of appeals to "a philosophy of history and without being placed in the context of an epic or tragedy whose hero is Humanity"[4]—much of Havel's writing generally, and especially those dealing with "hope" specifically, appears to contradict Rorty's characterization.

Rorty is attracted to Havel's use of the word "hope" and designates this form of "groundless hope" as the only form of positive aspiration that should be available to the post-Marxist Left. He further defines this form of hope as "social hope" (as indicated in his later title), a phrase that Havel in fact does not use. Instead, one finds a significantly different conception of hope in Havel's various discussions of hope, explored most extensively in Havel's work *Disturbing the Peace* in response to the question, "Do you see a grain of hope anywhere in the 1980s?" While Havel's response cannot be said to finally afford an altogether satisfying account of hope (although no less satisfying than Rorty's), nevertheless what is revealing is the extent to which his ruminations appear to *resist* Rorty's conclusion that Havel's hope is finally "social hope."

The first part of Havel's response to the interviewer's question seems to accord with Rorty's interpretation. Describing what he refers throughout as hope in the "deep sense," he replies:

> The kind of hope I often think about (especially in situations that are particularly hopeless, such as prison) I understand above all as a state of mind, not a state of the world. Either we have hope within us or we don't; it is a dimension of the soul, and it's not essentially dependent on some particular observation of the world or estimate of the situation. Hope is not prognostication.[5]

This passage is particularly appealing to Rorty, and he cites the concluding sentence with approval. According to this formulation, hope is appropriately internal, relying not on any belief in inevitability through history or transcendence outside it. It is likely that Rorty also concludes that such hope is "social," since our efforts can only be directed at the improvement of society within and by society, not its transformation according to any "objective" measure, nor the transformation of the human soul according to a preconceived notion of what is good or virtuous.

However, Havel continues (in a passage not cited by Rorty):

> [Hope] transcends the world that is immediately experienced, and is anchored somewhere beyond its horizons. I don't think you can explain it as a mere derivative of something here, of some movement, or of some favorable sign in the world. I feel that its deepest roots are in the transcendental, just as the roots of human responsibility are, though of course I can't—unlike Christians, for instance—say anything concrete about the transcendental.[6]

While Havel's modesty about claiming any knowledge about the composition of the "transcendent" would undoubtedly remain appealing to Rorty, in fact the very affirmation of the existence of the transcendent as the *source* for hope (and not, therefore, solely "social hope") presents a distinctly different perspective than that for which Rorty contends in his essay, "The End of Leninism, Havel, and Social Hope."

This amorphous "hope," deriving from the transcendent and informing human actions even against the greatest of odds, Havel quite clearly distinguishes from a different kind of positive response to the world—optimism. "Hope is definitely not the same thing as optimism. It is not the conviction that things will turn out well, but the certainty that something makes sense, regardless of how it turns out."[7] While optimism results from tangible or assumed success *in the world*, hope informs human aspirations regardless of the current composition of the world, and, as Havel contends, is derived from a source *outside* or *beyond* the world. As he concludes his discussion of this form of hope, "I think that the deepest and most important form of hope, the only one that can keep us above water and urge us to good works, and the only true source of the breathtaking dimension of the human spirit and its efforts, is something we get, as it were, from 'elsewhere.'"[8]

In more recent writings Havel has become more explicit and even less hesitant about his invocation of the "transcendent" nature of hope (as opposed to what he considers to be the more "internalized" aspects of optimism). Speaking before "The Future of Hope Conference" in Hiroshima, Japan, in December 1995, Havel stated ("to the delight of some and the astonishment of others," he admitted):

> I have always come to the conclusion that the primary origin of hope is, to put it simply, metaphysical. By that I mean that hope is more, and goes deeper, than a mere optimistic inclination or disposition of the human mind, determined genetically, biologically, chemically, culturally, or otherwise. . . . Somewhere behind all that, acknowledged or unacknowledged, and articulated in different ways, but always most profound, is humanity's experience with its own Being and with the Being in the world. . . . Without the experience of the transcendental, neither hope nor human responsibility has any meaning.[9]

Havel remains mostly silent about what he means by the "transcendent": while he refuses to clarify, one can conclude that he might mean any variety of "entities," "beings," "Being," or "ideas" that transcend purely human experience in the world. While he refuses to identify explicitly "hope" with the divine, at some level he appears to recognize its theological origins, since "hope" is one of the three theological virtues of Christianity, *fides, spes*, and *caritas*—faith, hope, and love (or charity). It is through that tradition, especially, that one recognizes the great appeal of "hope" over "optimism" in Havel's estimation—not only to the extent that hope affords the basis for political action and resistance but also to the degree that hope, in its classical conception, offers a defense of an accompanying attitude of humility, cautiousness, and even, at some level, uncertainty.

While both faith and hope are obviously distinguishable from *caritas* so as not to invite extensive comment on any apparent similarity, many commentators have been forced to acknowledge that faith and hope themselves seem to resemble each other extensively. In his *Enchiridion on Faith, Hope and Love* Augustine acknowledges the similarity of the two concepts, addressing the question in the eighth section as to whether there is a "distinction between faith and hope."[10] He admits that it is possible to have *faith* in something for which we may nevertheless not hope. "What true Christian, for example, does not believe in the punishment of the wicked? And yet such a one does not hope for it." Thus Augustine continues, "faith may have for its object evil as well as good; for both good and evil are believed, and the faith that believes them is not evil, but good." A further significant distinction for Augustine is the *temporal* nature of faith and hope, respectively. Faith is directed toward beings and events in the past, the present, and the future. Thus Christians are asked to have faith not only in redemption in the future but also to believe in the life, words, and deeds of Jesus as described in the Bible. By contrast, hope "has for its object only what is good, only what is future." While both faith and hope are directed toward that which is not seen (i.e., known definitively through our senses), they differ in these two fundamental regards according to Augustine. However, each of these claims, upon close examination, suggests not that the two are "essentially different," as Augustine contends, but rather that hope seems to be a subset of faith. Faith represents the belief in that which exists in any temporality and which has as its object things that may be either good or bad; hope represents only the belief of a happy outcome in the future. Hope is a form of faith, finally, but assumes only certain features of faith—those that are most positive and, because they are oriented toward the future, least provable from the standpoint of sensory evidence.

Yet, for Augustine, hope cannot be extended to inappropriate objects. Hope is directed toward the eternal: as the aspiration for good things beyond sensory evidence, hope, by Augustine's estimation, cannot be accorded purely to human attempts to achieve the object of hope. Accordingly, of the "true objects of faith, those only pertain to hope which are embraced in the Lord's prayer. For, 'cursed is the man that trusteth in man' is the testimony of holy writ; and, consequently, this curse attaches also to the man that trusteth in himself."[11] Of the few things Augustine writes about hope in the *Enchiridion*, worth noting is this immediate emphasis on the *limitations* of the object of hope—hope is oriented ultimately toward the divine, not the secular. There is a suggestion that a danger accompanies the pious belief in hope, namely, a form of confidence in the human potential for the realization of hope within the earthly sphere. Augustine's immediate and stern reminder of the simultaneous infinite extent of hope and yet its limitations to human endeavors appears as a consistent rebuke to the overweening ambitions of a humanity longing for mastery.

Aquinas echoes this understanding in several discussions of the "theological virtues." He writes in his work "On Hope" ("*De Spe*") that hope must be distinguished from "fear, because its object is good; from joy, because *fu-*

ture; from desire, because *difficult*; and from despair, because *possible*."[12] Because hope necessitates faith, and the object of our faith is the divine, Aquinas holds that hope contemplates the *possible* but that, at the same time, the possible is only attainable through the divine in which we hope, not purely through human efforts. As he states, "No man is able of himself to grasp the supreme good of eternal life; he needs divine help. Hence there is here a twofold object, the eternal life we hope for, and the divine help we hope by."[13]

Aquinas distinguishes this final hope in eternal life from more realistic hopes that can be attained through our own efforts. This latter kind of hope is less perfect than that directed toward divine ends; for "to have faith and hope about things which are subject to human power falls short of the nature of virtue."[14] Thus "hope goes wrong and is mistaken when you rely on your own strength."[15] However, while hope should be directed toward ultimate objects, Aquinas praises the *shared* attempt to seek hope's realization, since, when we pursue our aspirations in combination with others, we are reminded of our own insufficiency in its pursuit, even as our resolve is strengthened through a shared undertaking. He writes, "although our hope rests on divine help, be mindful how we should lean on one another in order to gain the more readily what we seek."[16]

Theological understandings of hope, then, appear consistently to recommend *humility* as an appropriate accompanying attitude of hope. The modern Thomistic scholar, Josef Pieper is quite explicit in this regard. He argues that two virtues must accompany hope: magnanimity and humility. Magnanimity necessarily joins with hope, since "it is the aspiration of the spirit to great things." Yet, taken alone, magnanimity tends toward overconfidence, leads one both to attempt too much and to crave more than human infirmity justifies. Thus he writes that "humility is the protective barrier and restraining wall of this impulse [of hope]."[17] Humility for Pieper naturally joins with the magnanimity of hope, since the object of hope (as with Augustine)—the divine—implicitly reveals humanity's fundamental limits. "Humility, with its gaze fixed on the infinite distance between man and God, reveals the limitations of these possibilities and preserves them from sham realization."[18]

The explicit distinction between the humility born of faith in a transcendent existence in contrast to the confidence born of faith in human abilities— those two attitudes denoted by Havel as *hope* and *optimism*—derive from an ancient theological tradition that finds continued resonance well into modernity and to our day. Yet, while "hope without optimism" implies humility, just as often its modern proponents have turned to this concept of hope—one that continues to be replete with its ancient theological resonance—in order to combat quiescence or resignation in the face of injustice or overwhelming obstacles, or simply to reject the overwhelming temptation for pessimism in this most brutal age.

Hope motivates, if humility moderates. Martin Luther King evoked the distinction between hope and optimism both early in his career in his rejec-

tion of the "unwarranted optimism concerning man . . . [that] leaned unconsciously toward self-righteousness" and late in life, after many triumphs
and setbacks, when he declared in his Montgomery sermons that he was not
an optimist, but he still had hope.[19] Neither wishing to succumb to the temptations of optimism evinced around him by those attracted to Marxist stories of historical culmination or some religious stories of imminent redemption and the establishment of the kingdom of heaven on earth, nor to the
temptations of pessimism born of a too slow and difficult process of achieving recognition and true equality, King returned constantly to the theme of
hopefulness as distinct from optimism in his sermons and speeches.[20]

More recently, asking whether "the tradition of struggle can be preserved
or expanded," Cornel West has evoked this language of King in his own exploration of our "moral obligations" as democratic citizens. Noting that "we
are living in one of the most terrifying moments in the history of this nation,
[that] we are experiencing a lethal and unprecedented relative economic decline, cultural decay and political lethargy," West nevertheless concludes this
otherwise pessimistic essay with an invocation of tempered hope understood
in a similar way to that of Augustine, King, and Havel:

> Hope has nothing to do with optimism. I am in no way optimistic about America,
> nor am I optimistic about the plight of the human species on the globe. There is
> simply not enough evidence to infer that things are going to get better. That has
> been the perennial state and condition of not simply black people in America, but
> all self-conscious human beings who are sensitive to the forms of evil around them.
> We can be prisoners of hope even as we call optimism into question. To be part of
> the democratic tradition is to be a prisoner of hope. And you cannot be a prisoner
> of hope without engaging in a form of struggle in the present moment that keeps
> the best of the past alive. To engage in struggle means that one is always willing
> to acknowledge that there is no triumph around the corner, but that you persist
> because you believe it is right and just and moral.[21]

In praising democracy for its singular aspect of according all citizens "mutual respect, personal responsibility, and social accountability," West concludes that such values can only be cultivated, maintained, and deepened by
recognizing their "spiritual dimension." Echoing Havel's view in this regard,
he notes that "spirituality requires an experience of something bigger than
our individual selves that binds us to a community." Absent this dimension,
West fears, the bases of democratic virtues succumb all too readily to con-
sumer excess and market-driven "gangsterization of culture."[22]

I think we do better to understand Havel's understanding of "hope" in the
context of this background, not as "social hope," as Rorty's more optimistic
understanding would suggest. To conclude this point with one final observation about the more tragic nature of Havel's hope in contrast to Rorty's
praise of "the comic frame," one should consider a speech that Havel delivered at Stanford University in 1994, which was published under the title
"Forgetting We Are Not God." There, Havel firmly resists the notion that

his belief in the transcendent sources of democratic legitimacy should result in a heightened level of certainty or fanaticism often associated with religion, instead evoking the connection of hope and humility. As he concluded in his speech,

> Obviously, this is easy to say but hard to bring about. Unlike many ideological utopians, fanatics, and dogmatists, and a thousand more or less suspect prophets and messiahs who wander around this world as a sad symptom of its helplessness, I do not possess any special recipe to awaken the mind of man to his responsibility to the world and for the world. . . . Given its fatal incorrigibility, humanity will probably have to go through many more Rwandas and Chernobyls before it understands how unbelievably shortsighted a human being can be who has forgotten that he is not God.[23]

While hope longs for a day when humans will eradicate the worst of our violent and technological evils, there is little optimism of an imminent solution here. Notable about this rejection of easy optimism is not only Havel's assumption that human barbarity will continue indefinitely but also that human confidence in science, technology, and progress is a comparable phenomenon. Such a view repudiates the common assumption that Western confidence in its own mastery of nature represents purely *rational* expression that is fundamentally opposed to ethnic or nationalist or any particularistic fanaticism.[24] Moreover, Havel insists that human mastery in one domain always involves "unintended consequences" in another, revealing, in fact, that "mastery" is always incomplete.[25] Suggesting that these forms of confidence represent a form of unjustified "optimism," Havel attempts to distinguish a more modest form of hope that at once allows for aspirations of political improvement and democratic self- and mutual-respect, and finally for communities based on shared experiences (what Rorty calls "contingency") and yet at the same time is attentive to claims of justice, without concluding that the culmination of such a hope is entirely likely through any optimistic engineering on the part of humanity.

Through a reminder of the original theological resonances of the language and concept of hope and its close kinship to humility, we can begin to recapture an understanding of "hope" as a core virtue of the "democratic realist." While America has been a land given in particular to optimistic forms of "democratic faith," we can also find there robust articulations of bracing "democratic realism." For the remainder of this chapter I consider two of the greatest modern American defenders of this chastened faith, humility, and hope against optimism—Reinhold Niebuhr during the mid-twentieth century and Christopher Lasch at its twilight.

REINHOLD NIEBUHR'S DARKNESS AND LIGHT

Reinhold Niebuhr towers as perhaps the most influential figure in America's mid-twentieth century for his opposition to the widespread optimism shared

by many of his country's leading intellectuals, and, most notably, John
Dewey. For this opposition he is now alternatively excoriated by Dewyans
and progressives either as overly dour or as insufficiently attentive to
Dewey's own less optimistic articulations, and lionized by political "realists"
of various kinds for his fulsome critiques of Soviet Communism and his un-
remitting insistence upon the inescapability of human fallibility. His theological emphasis upon the relevance of "original sin"—the only empirically
verifiable aspect of the biblical tradition according to Niebuhr—led him to
a full embrace of the Christian virtues, including a strong insistence upon the
essential presence of love in justice, the priority of hope over optimism, and,
finally, forgiveness over the impatience or disillusionment that can too easily accompany the dashed expectations of human perfectibility.[26] His endorsement of the Christian virtues is stated with typical Niebuhrian brevity
and profundity in the following passage:

> Nothing that is worth doing can be achieved in our lifetime; therefore we must be
> saved by hope. Nothing which is true or beautiful or good makes complete sense
> in any immediate context of history; therefore we must be saved by faith. Noth-
> ing we do, however virtuous, can be accomplished alone; therefore we are saved
> by love. No virtuous act is quite as virtuous from the standpoint of our friend or
> foe as it is from our standpoint. Therefore we must be saved by the final form of
> love which is forgiveness.[27]

Yet, Niebuhr's insistence upon humility, and his strong opposition to a version of "democratic faith" that stressed the transformative potential of humanity, was curiously made in the service not only of a chastened sense of
political possibility but also arguably and ultimately in support of a vision
of democracy as fully utopian as that advanced by the progressive opponents
he otherwise excoriated. Niebuhr's case is particularly noteworthy inasmuch
as it reveals the extent to which his very "realism" could serve as a source
for, and support of, that democratic faith that he otherwise criticized. His
thought is both a valuable resource in its cautionary stance toward the progressive—and, in his view, particularly American—tendency to overestimate
human power and base an unrealistic politics upon faulty assumptions, and
simultaneously an important cautionary note to those whose "realism" can
end up serving in the very unrealistic cause against which they otherwise see
themselves arrayed.

First, however, I begin with a sympathetic consideration of his critical
stance toward optimistic "democratic faith." Niebuhr is well known for his
opposition to Dewey's optimistic worldview, beginning with the book that
thrust Niebuhr into national prominence and continuing throughout his long
career.[28] In that first work that brought him attention and notoriety—*Moral
Man and Immoral Society* (1932)—Niebuhr broke with his own early liberal and optimistic worldview (as well as with thinkers in the "Social
Gospel" movement and most explicitly with Dewey) and articulated sustained disillusionment with the optimism that inclined contemporary
thinkers to attribute fundamental goodwill and the possibility of achieving

morality in politics.[29] Finding in Dewey a "typical and convenient example," Niebuhr excoriated the belief that humans could be morally improved by means of better education or greater material support, and insisted upon the need to recognize "the power, extent and persistence of group egoism in human relations."[30] Confronting him by name, Niebuhr rejected Dewey's faith in progressive accumulation of knowledge and "intelligence" in the social and humanistic spheres. "The most persistent error of modern educators and moralists is the assumption that our social difficulties are due to the failure of the social sciences to keep pace with the physical sciences which have created our technological civilisation. The invariable implication of this assumption is that, with a little more time, a little more adequate moral and social pedagogy and a generally higher development of human intelligence, our social problems will approach solution."[31]

This work sounded a theme that continued throughout Niebuhr's career: that the belief in human perfectibility was misguided, naïve, and even politically calamitous. Such a worldview insisted that human moral potential had gone largely unrealized because of external factors and limiting obstacles that could be reversed by the relatively simple application of modern scientific and progressive technique and method. As Niebuhr stated in a late summary of the origins of his thought,

> The faith of modern man contains two related articles: the idea of progress and the idea of the perfectibility of man. The latter is frequently the basis of the former article. Man is regarded as indeterminately perfectible because it is not understood that every growth of human freedom may have evil as well as virtuous consequences. . . . This essential religion of modernity is no less "dogmatic" for being implicit rather than explicit, and it is no more true for being arrayed in the panoply of science.[32]

Niebuhr was a fierce critic of modern "idolatries," most obviously of the twin twentieth-century totalitarianisms of Nazism and Marxism but even against some of America's most admired thinkers such as Dewey, willing to direct his skeptical eye upon the modern "faith" in democracy.[33]

Because modern man exhibited increasing levels of self-confidence owing to a growing sense of mastery over nature and social phenomena, Niebuhr observed a marked decrease not only in moral "realism" that informed a recognition of the ineradicability of force and coercion in political affairs but also a growing neglect of the brute fact of unintended consequences of which "moral realists" were more likely to be cognizant. Optimists were inclined to concentrate only upon the best-case scenarios and preferred outcomes, whereas "realists"—while hopeful about improved conditions—were insistently conscious of likely setbacks, negative and (more often) worst-case consequences of well-intended actions. Pacifists were admirable for their sentiments but blameworthy to the extent that they invited malevolent forces to take advantage of such goodwill and gain ascendancy in the absence of a credible and forceful response and resolve. Similarly modern educators were praiseworthy for their efforts to improve the morality and reasonableness of their students—and might even succeed in improving individuals—but were naïve in their neglect of social institutions and practices that could restrain the ineradicable immorality of people thrown into competitive social situations.[34]

Informed by biblical anthropology that insisted upon the ineradicability of human self-interest and sinfulness, Niebuhr rejected facile assumptions of human progress. Nowhere did Niebuhr state more forcefully the theological basis for his belief in human finitude and the ineradicability of evil than in his Gifford Lectures, collected in two volumes as *The Nature and Destiny of Man* (1941–43). Modern man's overestimation of his capacities derived from an unwillingness to recognize his inherent sinful nature. "The fact that modern man has been able to preserve such a good opinion of himself, despite all the obvious refutations of his optimism, particularly in his own history, leads to the conclusion that there is a very stubborn source of resistance in man to the acceptance of the most obvious and irrefutable evidence about his moral qualities. This source of resistance is not primarily modern but generally human. The final sin of man, said Luther truly, is his unwillingness to concede that he is a sinner."[35] Referring to this as the "easy conscience of modern man," Niebuhr located in such belief the unbounded optimism of modernity's belief in the near-infinite malleability of humans. "The modern man is . . . so certain about his essential virtue because he is so mistaken about his stature. . . . He is consequently unable to understand the real pathos of his defiance either by some accidental corruption in his past history or by some sloth of reason. Hence he hopes for redemption, either though a program of social reorganization or by some scheme of education."[36]

Human beings tend necessarily to overestimate their powers. Without denying human freedom and creativity—the very sources of the dynamism and alterability of human circumstance that Niebuhr identified as history—human nature stubbornly seeks nevertheless to escape its finitude and imperfection by an assertion of will and an attempt to attain God-like status. In short, humanity inescapably is subject to the sin of pride:

> Man is insecure and involved in natural contingency; he seeks to overcome his insecurity by a will-to-power which overreaches the limits of human creatureliness. . . . Man is ignorant and involved in the limitations of a finite mind; but he pretends he is not limited. He assumes he can gradually transcend finite limitations until his mind becomes identical with the universal mind. All of his intellectual and cultural pursuits, therefore, become infected with the sin of pride. Man's pride and will-to-power disturb the harmony of creation. The Bible defines sin in both religious and moral terms. The religious dimension of sin is man's rebellion against God. . . . The moral and social dimension of sin is injustice. The ego which falsely makes itself the center of existence in its pride and will-to-power inevitably subordinates other life to its will and thus does injustice to other life.[37]

Sin lies in the fact of humanity's finitude and our simultaneous desire and attempt to escape finitude. One could even say that human overestimation derives as much from our finitude as does the inevitable failure to achieve the ambitions born of that overestimation: our finitude obscures from us (or inclines us to the self-deception to obscure from ourselves) the fact of our finitude. We see ourselves through a glass darkly, and that obscurity inclines us not to requisite humility but, instead, to hubris, pride, injustice, the will-to-power and domination.

Niebuhr's insight revealed that, for modern man, the Christian alternative was reviled not because—as was often claimed—Christianity was based upon false illusion that led to fanatical self-righteousness but, rather, precisely because it disallowed the certitude and optimism upon which modern faiths—such as those in progress and perfectibility—were based. As such, Niebuhr insisted that Christianity provided a more penetrating and ultimately more sustained form of probing self-examination of, even skepticism toward, self-deception (one based upon its initial faith) than the resultant impervious faith that was endorsed as a result of apparent modern forms of (e.g., scientific) skepticism.[38]

> Christianity rightly regards itself as a religion, not so much of man's search for God, in the process of which he may make himself God; but as a religion of revelation in which a holy and loving God is revealed to man as the source and end of all finite existence against whom the self-will of man is shattered and his pride abased. But as soon as the Christian assumes that he is, by virtue of possessing this revelation, more righteous, because more contrite, than other men, he increases the sin of self-righteousness and makes the forms of a religion of contrition the tool of pride.[39]

Niebuhr was among the first twentieth-century American critics, and certainly the most forceful voice, to articulate the now more acceptable view that modern scientific "skepticism" was in fact premised upon so much faith, and that it was a faith that lacked the more profound sense of self-suspicion of Christian faith. Indeed, Niebuhr's insistence upon the juvenile "wishful thinking" of liberal optimists prompted Dewey to admit that his own progressive beliefs were so many "illusions," albeit ones that were preferable, in his view, because they were more flattering to humanity than illusions of the Christian variant.[40] Niebuhr insisted that Christianity resulted in the severest form of realism—far more so than the "illusions" permitted by modernist faiths—precisely because of its unflattering and open-eyed perspective on the inherent sinfulness of human nature.

If Niebuhr's Christian anthropology provides a chastening resource in contrast to the optimist's belief in fundamental human goodness or the view that modern technique would contribute inexorably to material and moral progress, nevertheless that same anthropology is also a concomitant source of hope.[41] Human pride and the will-to-power require the "realist" to see all human actions tinged inescapably with the motives of self-interest. Optimists who believe that humanity can transcend such self-interest seek to deny the fallen condition of humankind. Nevertheless, if Christianity has its "realist" face—emphasizing the fall of Adam—it also has its "idealist" face, focused on the redemptive and sacrificial words and deeds of Christ. Thus Niebuhr also argued forcefully against pessimists who insisted that *all* human motivations were to be understood solely in terms of self-interest. "Realism" requires taking into account the full scope of human limitations *and* possibilities, thus calling simultaneously upon humility and hope. As articulated by Robin Lovin, "Niebuhr's aim, consistent with the Realist's admonition to take *everything* into account, is to show how self-interest is limited by an equally fundamental sense of mutuality and obligation."[42]

Christian realism seeks to hold at bay both optimism and pessimism about human nature, insisting simultaneously upon the fact of human finitude and the possibility of human transcendence. For the Christian *realist*, humility is our appropriate response to the recognition of human creatureliness and finitude, while contrition is the fitting disposition in light of our inevitable tendency toward pride and injustice. For the *Christian* realist, *faith* in the redemptive and sacrificial presence of Christ leads to the *hope* in the possibility of *love* moving individuals beyond self-adoration. Thus, for the *Christian realist*, love is perpetually an "impossible possibility."[43] For Niebuhr, love was more often an aspiration than a likelihood: even if love of family, friends, and neighbors could become a reality, Christ had admonished humankind above all to love those most impossible to love, one's enemies (Matthew 5:43–44). Extraordinary self-criticism and self-chastisement was the necessary precursor to this hardest of loves and attendant forgiveness: "Genuine forgiveness of the enemy requires a contrite recognition of the sinfulness of the self and the mutual responsibility for the sin of the accused." The supreme difficulty of widespread goodwill made such love an "impossible possibility": "The ideal in its perfect form lies beyond the capacities of human nature."[44] Humans could only hope to approximate, to greater, and more often, lesser extent, this "relevant" ethical ideal.

Niebuhr contrasted the difficult and self-abasing faith of the Christian realist that led him to conceive of love as an "impossible possibility" to the "simple" faith of the optimist who held higher regard for human potential to transform, or altogether overcome, self-interest: "The faith which regards the love commandment as a simple possibility rather than as an impossible possibility is rooted in a faulty analysis of human nature which fails to understand that though man always stands under infinite possibilities and is potentially related to the totality of existence, he is, nevertheless, and will remain, a creature of finiteness."[45] This recognition does not permit the abandonment of "simple faith" for easy pessimism but rather clears space for "ultimate hope": "In such faith Christ and the Cross reveal not only the possibilities but the limits of human finitude in order that a more ultimate hope may arise from the contrite recognition of those limits. . . . It insists, quite logically, that this ultimate hope becomes possible only to those who no longer place their confidence in purely human possibilities."[46] The relinquishing of optimism—particularly belief in the human capacity to overcome human limitations and imperfection—and the resistance to pessimism as a consequence of our emulation, however imperfectly, of the sacrificial example of Christ point to the path of "ultimate hope." Love is an aspiration, of which justice is an imperfect approximation.[47] Our presence in the world with other humans forces us to strive for the latter in the name of the former, all the while recognizing the insufficiency of justice compared to the ultimate if unachievable ethical ideal of Christlike human love.[48]

Niebuhr was a critic of optimism in the name of optimism; that is, he was a critic of the form of optimism that posited *human* control over events, and especially a belief in historical progress, in the name of Christian optimism that assumed the ultimate goodness of creation without donning blinders that obscured the inability of humans to overcome evil or alienation solely through their own efforts. He sought to counteract the progressive optimism of the modern era with the "ultimate optimism" of Christian religion. Modern optimism, although typically aligned against traditional religion, is itself a form of religious belief, according to Niebuhr:

> The religion of modern culture [is] a superficial religion which has discovered a meaningful world without having discovered the perils to meaning in death, sin and catastrophe. History [according to modern optimists] has an immediate, if obvious, meaning because it spells progress. Progress is guaranteed by increasing intelligence because human sin is attributed to ignorance which will be removed by proper pedagogy. It is surprising how little modern culture has qualified the optimism upon this point.[49]

Against such modern optimism, Niebuhr argued on behalf of the "ultimate optimism" of the Christian faith: "Christian faith is . . . a type of optimism which places its ultimate confidence in the love of God and not the love of man."[50] Such optimism—while an object of belief held by humans—does not see its ultimate fruition as a result of human efforts nor even assisted by that belief. The final transcendence of human finitude, sin, evil, injustice, self-love, and alienation is only possible by the gift of divine grace, not as the result of human efforts. Yet, this recognition does not permit release from the hard efforts of working toward this unachievable ideal. Recognition of the "relevance" and "unachievablity" of the ethical ideal at once tempers blithe assumptions that intractable human nature can be wished away and inclinations to despair wrought by the inevitable failure of efforts to achieve the unachievable. "Ultimate optimism" thereby breaks the reinforcing cycle of optimism and pessimism: "When . . . optimism is not qualified to accord with the real and complex facts of human nature and history, there is always the danger that sentimentality will give way to despair and that a too consistent optimism will alternate with a too consistent pessimism."[51]

For all the persuasive force of Niebuhr's realism, a cautionary note needs to be sounded. The chastened form of realism defended by Niebuhr cannot finally obscure the extent to which he sought to put such realism in the service of political idealism, and even raises the question of whether Niebuhr's realism was finally as attractive an alternative to the optimism he otherwise criticized. Certain aspects of Niebuhr's realism serve as a warning to the realist, namely, the extent to which the realist view inclines not to pessimism or cynicism (as one might naturally suppose) but, instead, to chastened and therefore less obvious optimism. Niebuhr sought to articulate and defend a worldview that occupied a middle position between excessive overestimation and depressive underestimation of human powers and capacities, holding out hope while dismissing despair, excoriating optimism while defending human capacity for justice, even love. His was a prophetic voice at a time when much of the world, and America especially, was inclined toward untroubled idealism.[52]

Yet, perhaps surprisingly, Niebuhr's darker and complicating moral suasion was the starting point for the articulation of a different kind of worldly optimism that in certain respects (particularly because of its comparative lack of obviousness) even outstripped that of the secular optimists whom he criticized. For, Niebuhr's more realistic worldview was ultimately put in the service of an idealistic politics, and his more circumspect judgment about human capacity for goodness in some senses allowed him more ultimate confidence in the ability of humanity to control, if not expunge, its tendencies toward immorality and injustice. It was by means of the very self-awareness of our capacity for evil, and our resultant clearsightedness, that made it possible for Niebuhr to argue that a "realist" could better arrive at the same idealistic destination as that envisioned by the optimists he criticized. His "anti-optimism" was articulated in the name of the goals of the optimists, in particular a rearticulated belief in the possibility of overcoming human alienation and the achievement of worldwide democracy. In this sense, Niebuhr's very critique of optimism opened an avenue to a more pervasive if submerged optimism about the potential for human perfectibility. Niebuhr's case is thus complex and instructive not only for his extraordinary and persuasive stance against Pollyannaish optimism but also as a cautionary tale regarding the tendencies to optimism to which even—or perhaps especially—a "realist" can be tempted.

This counterintuitive aspect of Niebuhr's thought is nowhere better demonstrated than through his views on democracy. One sees a pristine articulation of Niebuhr's "idealism" and "realism" in the book most explicitly focused on democratic politics and democratic theory, *The Children of Light and the Children of Darkness* (1944). Niebuhr wrote this book as a "vindication of democracy" that necessitated a "critique of its traditional defense." Democracy's "traditional defense," in fact, was antitraditional: in Niebuhr's sights was his long-standing nemesis, the optimists who believed in moral amelioration, in the progressive trajectory of history, in the ability of humans to master their environment, and, finally, in the inherent goodness of humanity. Niebuhr rejected a belief in democracy that was premised upon the likelihood, or even plausibility, of human perfectibility or historical culmi-nation.[53] At its best—and Niebuhr, at his best, was better than most—Niebuhr's understanding of democracy rested fundamentally on a recogni-tion of human equality born of the shared recognition of our insufficiency, and hence of our mutual humility. There are few more arresting justifications of democratic equality than a passage in which Niebuhr identifies democrat-ic humility with the long tradition of religious humility, thereby calling both to task for the overestimation of their own sense of righteousness:

> Religious humility is in perfect accord with the presuppositions of democratic so-ciety. Profound religion must recognize the difference between divine majesty and human creatureliness; between the unconditional character of the divine and the conditioned character of all human enterprise. According to the Christian faith the pride, which seeks to hide the conditioned and finite character of all human en-deavor, is the very quintessence of sin. Religious faith ought therefore to be a con-stant fount of humility; for it ought to encourage men to moderate their natural pride and to achieve some decent consciousness of the relativity of their own state-ment of even the most ultimate truth. It ought to teach them that their religion is most certainly true if it recognizes the element of error and sin, of finiteness and contingency which creeps into the statement of even the sublimest truth.[54]

Niebuhr recognized that democratic faithful, no less—and perhaps more—than religious believers, were inescapably inclined to overestimate human powers, and thereby to move faith away from the "fount of humility" and toward the intransigency of true belief.

Among Niebuhr's primary targets, then, were the "children of light," whom he excoriated for their "naïve form of the democratic faith" which sought to forge "an identity between the individual and the general inter-est."[55] Recognizing a gap between their wishes in human reconciliation and the reality of human divisiveness, the children of light demonstrated their "stupidity" in their "evolutionary hope" that "human history is moving to-ward a form of rationality which will finally achieve a perfect identity of self-interest and the public good" (29, 30). Such belief—far from supporting widespread devotion to, and efforts on behalf of, democratic ideals—was likely to result in disillusionment in light of the shortcomings of actual democracy: "The excessively optimistic estimates of human nature and of human history with which the democratic credo has been historically asso-ciated are a source of peril to democratic society; for contemporary experi-ence is refuting this optimism and there is danger that it will seem to refute the democratic ideal as well" (xii).

The solution, however, is not a rejection of the democratic faith of the chil-dren of light in favor of the thoroughgoing cynicism of the "children of dark-ness." Unlike the children of light, who have certain redeeming qualities—especially their support for and belief in democracy—Niebuhr considered the children of darkness to be malevolent, if knowingly so: "The children of darkness are evil because they know no law beyond the self. They are wise, though evil, because they understand the power of self-interest. The children of light are virtuous because they have some conception of a higher law than their own will. They are usually foolish because they do not know the power of self-will. They underestimate the peril of anarchy in both the national and international community" (11).[56] This passage reveals that Niebuhr's counsel is ultimately intended for the children of light. His ambition is to inject some of the "wisdom" of the children of darkness into the children of light without altering the ultimate ambitions of the latter: "The children of light must be armed with the wisdom of the children of darkness but remain free of their malice. They must know the power of self-interest in society" (41). The children of light are democrats—"our democratic civilization has been built, not by children of darkness but by foolish children of light"—whereas the children of darkness Niebuhr identifies at one point with Nazism (11, 123–124). By recognizing the ineradicability of self-interest that so thoroughly informs the "moral cynicism" of the children of darkness, the children of light can thereby prepare appropriately for the persistence of self-interest even as their ambitions for democratic perfectibility do not undergo radical revision. With full awareness of human inclination toward self-interest, a "realist's" means can result in the "idealist's" ends. Democracy's grandest ambitions can be fulfilled—especially the creation of a global order in which individuals and the common good are reconciled—but only when politics is placed on a firmly realistic footing.

This dual quality of democracy—one of liberating promise based on our "lightness" and, alternatively, one of necessary restraint as a result of our "darkness"—is captured by Niebuhr's famous "definition" of democracy: "Man's capacity for justice makes democracy possible; but man's inclination to injustice makes democracy necessary" (xiii). The first clause is an expression of "democratic faith"; the second, an assertion of liberal realism. Jefferson, Emerson, Whitman, and Dewey, among others, implicitly lie behind the first; Hobbes, Locke, Madison, and Hamilton stand guard behind the second. Although I have more to say about the first part of the statement—particularly as it touches on the optimistic aspect of Niebuhr's thought—it is the latter part of Niebuhr's formulation that, arguably, has received the most attention from Niebuhr's admirers and critics alike. Niebuhr's Madisonianism has long been recognized.[57] He especially admired Madison's recognition of the "inevitability of factions."[58] Governments, he recognized, existed to a significant extent based upon a recognition of the human proclivity to self-interest and factional conflict. To this extent, Niebuhr shared early-modern liberalism's suspicion of humankind's tendency to depravity and saw the essential need for restraint through law, thus echoing the sentiment expressed in the words of Thomas Hobbes: "For the use of laws (which are but rules authorized) is not to bind the people from all voluntary actions, but to direct and keep them in such a motion as not to hurt themselves by their own impetuous desires, rashness, or indiscretion; as hedges are set, not to stop travellers, but to keep them in the way."[59] Niebuhr believed that the

"Christian attitude" toward government—one that stressed human depravity—demanded a conception of "political order as a vast realm of mutually dependent and conflicting powers" that in turn called for "the specific equilibria of forces" to achieve the "relative character" of justice.[60]

Above all, Niebuhr shared Madison's belief that humans, if decent individually, tend to exhibit irrationality and excessive self-interest when gathered in groups, factions, and parties. Factions, like nations and all collectivities, are inevitably immoral. Constituted in opposition to other groups, drawing upon our partial attachments, our reason-obscuring passions, and our love-dimming interests, groups reinforce the worst aspects of the human tendency toward self-interest while negating our *individual* capacity for morality, justice, and love. Niebuhr's lifelong belief in *sometimes* moral man, *always* immoral society, is strikingly Madisonian, echoing the sentiment expressed by Madison in *Federalist 55* that, "in all very numerous assemblies, of whatever character composed, passion never fails to wrest the scepter from reason. Had every Athenian citizen been a Socrates, every Athenian assembly would still have been a mob."[61] The rationality and potential other-regarding quality of the individual in isolation, contrasted to the irrationality and self-interest of those *same individuals* when brought into contact with others, is captured in its pristine form in the opening sentences (if not simply the title) of *Moral Man, Immoral Society*:

> Individual men may be moral in the sense that they are able to consider interests other than their own in determining problems of conduct, and are capable, on occasion, of preferring the advantages of others to their own. They are endowed by nature with a measure or sympathy and consideration for their kind, and breadth of which may be extended by an astute social pedagogy. . . . But all these achievements are difficult, if not impossible, for human societies and social groups. In every human group there is less reason to guide and to check impulse, less capacity for self-transcendence, less ability to comprehend the needs of others and therefore more unrestrained egoism than the individuals, who compose the group, reveal in their personal relationships.[62]

By recognizing the inevitable immorality of groups and nations, the children of light—taking into account the wisdom of the children of darkness—can suitably manipulate institutions and structures to channel self-interest and thereby achieve social concord that optimistic mechanisms (e.g., Deweyan education) cannot. The children of light "must have this wisdom [of the children of darkness] in order that they may beguile, deflect, harness, and restrain self-interest, individual and collective, for the sake of the community."[63]

Because of the human tendency to ungovernability when drawn together, strong and controlling governments are necessary; but because of the existence of multifarious governments, irrationality and conflict persist *between* those governments. In order to minimize conflict between *citizens*, conflict between *nations* is rendered inevitable. The degree of conflict is, in a sense, moved up a level, from that between subnational groups and factions to that between nations. While nations lead to an advance in making justice—an approximation of love—possible for modern humans, the greater scope and power of modern nations makes worldwide conflict a horrific reality.[64] The implications of Niebuhr's analysis naturally and inevitably led him to consider whether conflict itself might finally be overcome through the simple transcendence of all partial organizations. While Niebuhr resisted the idea that this ambition would be quite feasible given current world reality—particularly the bipolar world of the Cold War—nevertheless his assumption of a fundamental (even if infrequently displayed) *individual* human goodness and a socially induced corruption attracted him throughout his career to the possibility of overcoming all partial associations, thereby giving rise to "moral individual man within one moral society." While Niebuhr recognized that achieving a version of the "social contract" between nations, giving rise to world government, was unlikely, still he argued that "to call attention to this fact does not mean that all striving for higher and wider integration is vain."[65] Characteristically realism is put in the service of the idealism that he otherwise criticizes.

One witnesses Niebuhr's continuous attraction to the possibility of worldwide earthly redemption from his earliest writing to his work late in life. At the conclusion of *Moral Man and Immoral Society* Niebuhr writes in a redemptive tone that appears to depart from the hard-headed analysis that preceded it, but that—in light of his lifetime belief that "realism" could inform "idealism"—becomes a benchmark first statement of a refurbished optimism. Having "rid [ourselves] of some of our illusions," he sounds a Deweyan note:

> We can no longer buy the highest satisfactions of the individual life at the expense of social injustice. We cannot build our individual ladders to heaven and leave the total human enterprise unredeemed of its excesses and corruptions.
>
> In the task of that redemption the most effective agents will be men who have substituted some new illusions for the abandoned ones. The most important of these illusions is that the collective life of man can achieve perfect justice. It is a very valuable illusion for the moment; for justice cannot be approximated if the hope of its perfect realization does not generate a sublime madness in the soul.[66]

Niebuhr held that, whatever the contributions of Christian anthropology in describing the limits to human perfectibility on earth, nevertheless the most "realistic" Christian assessment of human limitations was flawed for its rejection of limitless human agency. Niebuhr's assessment of Augustine's realism, in this regard, is revealing: while admiring of Augustine in some particulars, his overall assessment results in a rejection of Augustine's "excessive" form of realism—in part because of the latter's dour view of the possibility of world government.[67] According to Niebuhr, "excessive realism" overlooked the extent to which numerous human civilizations (including Christianity) have rightly recognized that "there are no limits to be set in history for the achievement of more universal brotherhood, for the development of more perfect and more inclusive human relations." Augustine—and any thinker, Christian or otherwise, who is "excessively realistic"—would deny the utopian promise of infinite human freedom afforded by our participation in dynamic history. "For the freedom of man makes it impossible to set any limits of race, sex, or social condition upon the brotherhood which may be achieved in history."[68]

It is further revealing that the concluding chapter of Niebuhr's book on democratic theory—*The Children of Light and the Children of Darkness*—is entitled "The World Community." The culminating consideration of democracy demands an evaluation of whether world democracy is possible; indeed, Niebuhr suggests that it is "the most urgent issue" of our time.[69] Unsurprisingly Niebuhr begins on a cautionary note: while technological progress has increased humanity's sense of proximity and resulted in greater interdependence, Niebuhr cautions against the optimistic view that this technological globalization is unambiguously supportive of the moral imperative to moral universalism. "Simple universalists" neglect the extent to which the very technology that results in greater human interdependence—what Niebuhr calls the "armament of universality"—is also inevitably employed by "the egoistic forces of history" to advance perceived national self-interest.[70] He rejects the belief of those optimists who see the world community as a "practically inevitable achievement"; yet, by contrast, rather than concluding that realism demands devotion to more limited forms of democratic self-governance, Niebuhr indicates his belief in the possibility of democracy's fruition by insisting that its achievement is "more difficult than commonly assumed."[71] By starting from a realistic and skeptical standpoint, the goal advanced by the optimists is more likely to be achieved.

His recommended solution should now be familiar, namely, that a "union" of the world's nations can be achieved *not* by assuming the best intentions of nations, their leaders and citizens, but rather by controlling their worst inclinations. "The world community must be built by men and nations sufficiently mature and robust to understand that political justice is achieved, not merely by destroying, but also by deflecting, beguiling and harnessing residual [rather than endemic!] self-interest and by finding the greatest possible concurrence between self-interest and the general welfare."[72] Having warned for much of his life against Dewey's overly secular, even profane faith in human capacity, scientific method, and historical progress, Niebuhr concludes with a resounding call to a faith that one unmistakably recognizes as "democratic faith": "Since all political and moral striving results in frustration as well as fulfillment, the task of building a world community requires a faith which is too easily destroyed by frustration." Democracy's fulfillment—the overcoming of alienation through the achievement of "world community," itself a resounding echo of Dewey's endorsement of the "Great Community" (if more expansive than even Dewey's more nationalistic conception)—is defended as the result of historical processes largely controlled by human will and achievement. Liberal realism supports and finally cedes into liberal idealism, endorsing the very ambitions toward human perfectibility that its realism only apparently appears to caution against.[73]

Niebuhr's political realism was finally placed in the service of nearly thoroughgoing worldly idealism. In this regard, he is more Madisonian than most observers realize: Madison himself articulated a proto-Kantian argument on behalf of international "perpetual peace" three years before the publication of Kant's well-known essay. Like Niebuhr after him, Madison begins by stating firm reservations about the plausibility of such "universal peace" (explicitly against Rousseau's optimistic position) given the reality of national self-interest; yet, Madison (akin to Niebuhr) goes on to state, in support of overcoming the "folly" and "wickedness" of war, "if any thing is to be hoped, every thing ought to be tried."[74] Again much like Niebuhr, Madison arrives at a similar conclusion to that goal articulated by Rousseau, albeit by explicitly more "realistic" means, namely, through the harnessing of self-interest in the cause of avoiding future war.[75] Madison writes that the likelihood of war between nations could be averted when the populace was engaged in consideration of whether the benefits of war would outweigh its costs; thus "avarice would be sure to calculate the expense of ambition."[76] By means of more modest "realistic" means that recognize and harness self-interest—in contrast to Rousseau, who calls for humans to supersede narrow interest—Madison concludes in an "unrealistic" flourish that, "were all nations to follow the example, the reward would be doubled to each; and the temple of Janus might be shut, never to be opened more."[77]

This returns us to the first part of Niebuhr's definition of democracy: "Man's capacity for justice makes democracy possible." Like the relationship between the children of light and the children of darkness, Niebuhr does not in fact describe a "balanced" or even "mixed" human anthropology. He stands firmly on the side of the children of light, identifying them as the source of democracy yet viewing their unalloyed optimism as an obstacle to the fruition of their utopian vision. Niebuhr does not repudiate the utopian vision as such but, rather, believes that the route to its achievement is through an embrace of the insights of the children of darkness. By means of the constitutional and institutional mechanisms designed by the realist, the "possibility" of democracy can be more fully realized. In other words, the "injustice" of humanity that makes democracy "necessary"—here the mechanisms that restrain human self-interest and lead to the rise of nation-states—actually leads to a greater possibility of realizing the "human capacity for justice" that optimists otherwise assume will come about by means of proper education and as an inevitable expression of natural human goodness. Our "capacity for justice" is realized not by a faith in the best in humanity but, instead, by controlling the worst. Echoing Whitman, who held that the final "stage" of democracy—"Religious democracy"—could not be achieved without first securing the first stage of "Political [i.e., Constitutional] democracy," Niebuhr suggested that the children of light would fail to achieve their idealized vision of democracy until they have adequately recognized the need for restraining political institutions and the "hedges" created by ever growing nation-states.

Arthur Schlesinger Jr. revealed perhaps more than he realized when he wrote that Niebuhr's work evinces a "penetrating reconstruction of the democratic faith."[78] Niebuhr's Christian realism is at once a bracing alternative to then contemporary optimisms of the early twentieth century (and, indeed, all human history, including, but not limited to, more recent optimism that America could, in an age of terror, "change the world") and also—in light of its own optimistic conclusions—a necessary reminder that all human philosophy, even the most "realistic," is subject to the prevailing forces of "democratic faith." As such, Niebuhr's generous assessment of the "Social Gospel" theology of Walter Rauschenbush might apply equally to him: "One reads this capitulation of a great theologian and a great Christian soul to the regnant idea of progress of his day with some dismay because it proves how vulnerable we are to the illusions of our generation."[79] It is also a cautionary note to beware of the hubris that can accompany the belief in one's own humility: perhaps the least discernible pride is that held by one who insists upon the inescapable pridefulness of human beings. Because of our pride, it is difficult to escape from our illusion, trapped within a prism of reflecting illusions—even ones that can entrap the most realistic of Christian realists— that the fruition of democracy awaits us in our perfected future rather than persists because of our imperfect "ever present" present.

Christopher Lasch's Democracy of "Limits and Hope"

A forceful "Niebuhrian" corrective to Niebuhr's "realistic optimism" is, perhaps surprisingly, not to be found (only) in an even more orthodox religious believer but rather in a heterodox, predominantly secular intellectual.[80] In recent years, the American thinker whose writings perhaps most directly (if not explicitly) opposed the optimistic sensibility of Dewey and Rorty, and even holds at arm's length Niebuhr's sanguine if more bracing brand of liberalism, and who appealed likewise to "hope" in contrast to "optimism" (or Rortyean "social hope"), was the historian and social critic Christopher Lasch. It is ironic, but somehow fitting, that while Niebuhr was an explicit critic of Dewey who nevertheless ultimately exhibited many of Dewey's assumptions about democracy, Lasch was an admirer of Dewey who otherwise leveled many criticisms toward the progressive assumptions that are particularly pronounced in Dewey and even ultimately embraced by Niebuhr. Especially in the two books published shortly before his untimely death in 1995, *The True and Only Heaven* and *The Revolt of the Elites and the Betrayal of Democracy*, Lasch most fully elaborated on this distinction between "hope" and "optimism."[81]

In particular, Lasch sought to persuade his American readers that the "party of hope" was not, as Emerson had argued, identical with the "Party of Innovation" and arrayed in opposition to the "Party of Conservatism" and its fidelity to "memory" and the past.[82] Most often only implicitly appealing to the long theological tradition that sought to reveal the connection between hope and humility, Lasch argued on behalf of a number of "conservative" cultural positions—even while condemning the inequalities, loss of individual liberty, and social instability bred by modern capitalism—in the name of, and not in spite of, democratic devotions.[83] Lasch sought to disassociate the widespread modern and liberal American assumptions that commonly identified democracy with progress, individualism, and secularism. Instead, Lasch wrote of hope's connections to and reliance upon memory, virtue, limits, and humility, and, finally, hope's resource in the spiritual discipline of religion.[84] He sought to reclaim hope in America from those who had lifted it from its theological context, and who had thereby liberated hope from any conception of limitation or humility (and permitted a thinker like Rorty to employ a conception of "social hope" in *opposition* to limits and humility). Instead, Lasch sought to return to a tradition of hope that recognized limits, tragedy, and, most fundamentally, a conception of human equality arising from a shared sense of human frailty upon which, in his view, democracy ultimately rested.

Lasch observed that populist forms of democratic equality, promoted most fervently at the turn of the nineteenth to the twentieth century, had been almost entirely routed by a victorious liberalism that advanced in its stead progress, meritocracy, cosmopolitanism, scientism, the "therapeutic" regime, and secularism. By overcoming the natural sense of human limits, liberalism sought to open up endless possibilities for advancement and individual cultivation, but it had done so at the expense of democratic virtues that had once been inculcated in local communities and relied upon "middle-class" virtues of moderation, a sense of limits, and an acknowledgment of the inescapability of tragedy in human life. In the name of leftist populism and egalitarianism, Lasch found himself siding with the "conservative" critics of liberalism against the progressive assumptions of Left liberals.

Modern progressives identified democracy with radical individualism, on the one hand, and global interdependence, on the other. The result of this simultaneous narrowing and near-infinite expansion of the human horizon resulted in modern individuals who resisted the intermediary position of "citizenship"—one that insisted on the necessity of common undertakings and yet resisted the dissolution of local forms of life in the name of opportunity and progress. Lasch recommended concrete rather than abstract recognition of our "interdependence," insisting that an "interdependence" personally encountered would more readily lead to the recognition of the reality of our common fate.[85] Instead, modern liberals justified the "secession of the successful" in the name of individual liberty, the abandonment of the less fortunate in favor of "lifestyle enclaves" in which all expenses were to be borne solely by its inhabitants on behalf of its inhabitants.[86] Even the fading sense of "noblesse oblige" among an older set of aristocrats was preferable to the widespread sense of self-congratulation and accompanying evaporation of generosity among contemporary liberals for whom prevailing notions of individual entitlement to the fruits of one's own superior labor meant that one owed no duty or obligation to those who had not succeeded.[87] Moral and civic equality had been effectively replaced by "equality of opportunity"— a form of equality that resulted in more radical forms of material inequality than the world had ever witnessed and which had given rise to a new "aristocracy of talent" that, quite ironically, claimed to have arisen as a result of the increasing perfection of democracy (now understood as progressive market-based liberalism).[88]

For Lasch, these developments represented a betrayal of democracy: citizenship had been replaced by individualism; civic virtue had been substituted for an ethic of material success; the priority of equality and attendant belief in civic obligations had given way to that of individual liberty and its emphasis upon autonomy. Curiously, while the spirit of aristocratic generosity (shorn of a sense of libertarian entitlement) had all but ceased, in its place arose an even more inegalitarian form of attention to the less fortunate: "compassion" and its attendant therapies. On the one hand, the ethic of self-creation gave rise to a widespread sense that one was solely and singularly responsible for the outcomes of one's own choices, whether good or ill. At the same time, in order to comprehend the existence of those who had made inadequate choices—since it could hardly be credited that equality of opportunity could so radically fail to produce a more equal set of outcomes— failings were attributed instead to various pathologies that were curable by recourse to therapeutic intervention.[89] A simultaneous and pernicious condition of self-congratulation for one's own success accompanied by all-too-easy compassion for those who had fallen behind was the resulting combination—one that permitted elites to believe that their enviable position was the singular result of superior effort while at the same time insisting that "second-class citizens" had failed by dint of social, psychological, or physical circumstances beyond their control. A curious paternalism was the result: releasing individuals of responsibility to one another, duty was translated into the impersonal helping professions and an underlying notion of commonality was subverted in favor of health and illness.[90] Most important, democracy ceased to be defined as a system of self-governance based upon the assumption of common competence. As Peter Lawler has described Lasch's understanding of the rise of the therapeutic state, "The self-indulgence of compassion allows both classes to shy away from the hard work really required to raise the competence of everyone. Compassion-based toleration is really a form of apathetic indifference for the characters or souls of our fellow citizens."[91]

In its place Lasch recommended a populism that aimed at a more "strenuous and moral definition" of human excellence, with the particular democratic goal of "universal competence."[92] In *The True and Only Heaven*, Lasch repeatedly praised those thinkers in the British and American tradition who recommended lives and economies of *independence* rather than *interdependence*. Democracy did not literally rest upon the ability of every person to produce his or her means of survival but did rest on the beneficial forms of psychic independence that resulted from such populist and local economies, thereby voiding the creation of a society of consumers and the mentality of dependence exhibited by wage laborers.[93] Such forms of basic economic self-sufficiency pointed to Lasch's conception of democratic equality. Lasch rejected the linkage of democracy to contemporary liberal economic notions that highly advanced economic development would extend equality—understood as "equality of opportunity"—by means of economic "interdependence," since, in fact, the predictable result of such theories was economic and social stratification of elite "symbolic analysts" from ordinary manual laborers. Liberalism aimed at "liberation" but only for those few highly successful "meritocrats" who thereafter successfully ceded from the common life of democratic society.

Strenuous "self-sufficiency," Lasch argued, was the only actual means to ensure requisite self- and mutual respect among equal citizens and, in turn, was the basis upon which a vibrant democracy rested. Far from seeing their lives as separate and unconnected, "self-sufficient" populist democrats were keenly aware of human limits and the need for self-governance undertaken in common. Modest "populist" economies tended to be more local, and within such circumscribed civic dimensions one could more readily perceive the links that were forged between citizens who were considerably more self-reliant than contemporary "interdependent" liberal individualists.[94] On behalf of democracy Lasch insisted upon the superiority of visible local interchange rather than abstract global interdependence. As Lasch firmly stated, "Humans, not humanity, inhabit the earth."[95]

Such local forms of life also afforded the spaces for more than merely economic interchange. Called by Ray Oldenburg "third places" between the private sphere of home and the public spaces of official life, such settings were the wellspring of vital informal civic practices.[96] Offering dignity and equality, such spaces inculcated the "art of conversation." Lasch expressed disagreement with "communitarians" who, in his view, assumed that community was a space of automatic unanimity and comfortable conformity.[97] Lasch praised such localities not for their easy production of agreement (a condition that never existed) but rather for offering opportunities for heated exchange and disagreement—the "art of conversation" that had been "lost" as those spaces had given way to increasingly privatized existence in suburbs and "lifestyle enclaves," on the one hand, and the bloodless international market, on the other.[98] In contrast to liberal thinkers who advanced a form of "democracy" qua "decision making" by which elites and "experts" forged appropriate policies that were approximately guided by the inchoate "opinions" of otherwise unbothered and apathetic citizens, Lasch praised democratic dialogue because of its *inefficiency* and its resultant civic benefits:

> If we insist on argument as the essence of education, we will defend democracy not as the most efficient but as the most educational form of government, one that ex-

tends the circle of debate as widely as possible and thus forces all citizens to articulate their views, to put their views at risk, and to cultivate the virtues of eloquence,
clarity of thought and expression, and sound judgment.[99]

Democracy deserves our embrace not, as such, for enabling governmental
stability or efficient production of goods and information but rather as the
best form of government toward the end of fostering more complete, if permanently flawed, human beings. Underlying Lasch's conception of local, dialogic, civic if combative, egalitarian democracy of independent and yet engaged citizens is an anthropology not altogether distant from Aristotle's:
human beings are by nature "political animals" that achieve full faculties of
judgment and civic virtue by means of participation in ruling and being ruled
in turn.

In advancing this alternative conception of "populist" democracy to its
predominant liberal conception, proponents of which Lasch located in such
sources as Jonathan Edwards, Thomas Carlyle, Orestes Brownson, Abraham
Lincoln, Reinhold Niebuhr, and Martin Luther King, Lasch sought to rein-
troduce a link between democracy and *limits* that had been disassociated by
liberalism's promise of near-infinite economic, material, and even moral
progress.[100] For Lasch, the attempt to overcome the local ecology in which
democratic life flourished was tantamount to the destruction of the very conditions that sustained democracy. Liberalism, while advancing in the name
of democracy for reasons of legitimation, was disassembling the very moral
sources on which it relied. Even while speaking in the name of equality and
liberty, liberalism advanced political (qua expert) and economic (qua meritocratic) beliefs that corroded the necessary virtues on which democracy ultimately rested. Its influence into the modern era was akin to that of a poi-
soned river emptying into a healthy ocean, over time destroying its own
inhabitants by its promise of controlling nature, releasing individuals from
all forms of necessity and limitation, and, finally, overcoming human alienation. For Lasch, liberalism was supremely dangerous precisely because it
was premised upon an infantile psychology.[101]

Lasch believed that democracy was imperiled by liberalism's adherence to
a voluntarist conception of human relationships. For Lasch, an inescapable
limitation upon human beings was their *givenness*: one could not escape
one's condition as created being, and the effort to do so would likely resort
in both internal psychological damage as well as dangerous implications for
other humans who might come to be regarded as obstacles to the fulfillment
of one's individual happiness. One sees a microcosm of Lasch's defense of
democracy as primarily premised upon an attitude of "acceptance" rather
than "transformation" in his many discussions of family.[102] This "givenness" is especially a feature of the relationship between parents and children:
each child is a surprise, a gift, a unique and unpredictable adventure as well
as a visible sign of one's willingness to sacrifice much of one's own personal
preference and freedom. For Lasch, the modern embrace of no-fault divorce

and abortion policies justifying unlimited infanticide was concrete and horrific evidence of the modern effort to subject all human and natural phenomena to *control* and *planning*. The modern abortion regime was but one
reflection of "an unquestioning faith in the capacity of the rational intelligence to solve the mysteries of human existence, ultimately the secret of creation itself" and the desire to engage in "the conquest of necessity and the
substitution of human choice for the blind workings of nature."[103]

For Lasch, the prospects for democracy, if not the soul of humanity, lay in
the balance. Arrayed on one side are modern elites who claim the mantle of
democracy in the name of personal and economic autonomy, mobility, meritocracy, and cosmopolitanism. They seek the mastery of necessity and the
overcoming of accident by means of the awesome controlling power of science and technology. In the background is a vision of overcoming tragedy—
of never having to choose between incommensurable goods or, even better,
never having to choose between largely bad options—and ultimately escap-
ing all limitations, finally death itself. In the foreground is the condemnation
of various parochialisms, patriotism, and unchosen loyalties that limit personal autonomy and voluntarism. This elite threatens to "betray" democracy, to leave behind (under the care of attendant therapeutic experts) those
undereducated and less-mobile losers in the meritocratic stakes and to abandon a shared conception of universal "democratic competence."[104] "Democratic faith" as a belief in the ability of some, if not all, to make themselves
wholly at home in the world by means of scientific mastery and the overcoming of human alienation has as its likely result an utter disdain for ordinary people—a "betrayal of democracy." One can expect to find (as one
commonly does) among the cultural, intellectual, and economic elite a
"snobbish disdain for people who lack formal education and work with their
hands, an unfounded confidence in the moral wisdom of experts, an equally
unfounded prejudice against untutored common sense, a distrust of any expression of good intentions, a distrust of everything but science, an ingrained
irreverence, a disposition (a natural outgrowth of irreverence and distrust)
to see the world as something that exists only to gratify human desires."[105]

On the other side are ordinary citizens in the "populist" tradition, mistrustful of various forms of progress, willing to assume obligations that arise
from family, community, and nation (thus more likely to enlist in its armed
forces), and less liable to be open to cosmopolitan yearnings and the attractions of mobility.[106] Such "populists" are far more likely to accept, even embrace, human limitation. Embeddedness in daily life, the willingness to forgo
immediate pleasures and even long-term personal happiness (narrowly conceived) for the sake of others, and the cultivation of common "democratic
competence" rather than exclusionary expertise are more likely to lead to an
endorsement of "democratic realism," even as cultural elites are likely to regard such "realism"—born of limitations and imperfection—as fundamentally antidemocratic. Counterintuitively it is those who are less "individualist"
who recognize the inescapability of human alienation, and those who are more

voluntarist and individualistic who endorse modern efforts to overcome forms of human alienation in the name of democracy.[107] Those who readily acknowledge human limitation, the limits upon progress and any easygoing optimism of the prospects for solving the "mysteries" of existence, are most apt to recognize that "alienation is the normal condition of human existence."[108]

Perhaps contributing most profoundly to the recognition of the inescapability of human alienation—and hence the need for loyalty and limits rather than "escape" and "progress"—is the persistence of religious belief among most ordinary citizens. This persistence rankles, offends, and even fosters anxiety and dread among the cultural, intellectual, and economic elite, because it flies so baldly in the face of the Enlightenment creed that religious faith would be overcome with the advent of scientific progress, economic development, and political liberalization. Seen by elites as superstitious and unwarranted belief in the unknown and unknowable, religious belief is derided as pabulum and false security, and policy implications that arise from such religious traditionalism—including limits upon divorce, abortion, and efforts to protect the cohesion of local communities—are viewed as irrational, inegalitarian, illiberal, and arbitrary efforts at oppression.[109]

Lasch wrote with particular vehemence in an attempt to dispel this particular portrayal of religious belief, arguing instead that religion is profoundly misunderstood by its liberal opponents, on the one hand, and, arguably, by some—even many—religious adherents, on the other.[110] Religious belief (properly understood, including by the believer) is neither a source of complacent self-righteousness nor easygoing comfort and security but, rather, a profound challenge to any sense of self confidence, belief in one's own independent power, or any settled confidence of certainty of one's own position. Against the disparaging view of religion by its liberal opponents, Lasch wrote that such a false understanding

> misses the religious challenge to complacency, the heart and soul of faith. Instead of discouraging moral inquiry, religious prompting can just as easily stimulate it by calling attention to the disjunction between verbal profession and practice, by insisting that a perfunctory observance of prescribed rituals is not enough to ensure salvation, and by encouraging believers at every step to question their own motivations. Far from putting doubts to rest, religion has the effect of intensifying them. It judges those who profess faith more harshly than it judges unbelievers. It holds them up to a standard of conduct so demanding that many of them inevitably fall short. For those who take religion seriously, belief is a burden, not a self-righteous claim to some privileged moral status. Self-righteousness, indeed, may be more prevalent among skeptics than believers. The spiritual discipline against self-righteousness is the very essence of religion.[111]

Lasch's theological understanding—drawn from a variety of sources but prominently dependent upon a tradition of Augustinianism qua Calvinism that found an American voice in Jonathan Edwards—advances a complex interplay of belief and doubt, faith and anxiety, affirmation and renunciation.[112] Belief in a beneficent divinity does not result in the easygoing conclusion that God's creation is aligned in humanity's favor nor that His will exists in seamless accord with human desires. Indeed, the immediate and chastening consequences of such belief is the unavoidable acknowledgment, in the words of Leszek Kolakowski, that "God owes us nothing."[113] Rather than suggesting humanity's centrality in divine creation or lending support to a view of humanity that endorses efforts to conquer nature and render fortune and tragedy altogether tractable, such religious belief forces the religious penitent to acknowledge human dependence and weakness, and to regard temptations toward mastery as forms of sinful and hubristic pride.

Lasch endorses Jonathan Edwards's view that most forms of belief in thoroughgoing human agency are born of fundamental rebellion against a religious view that begins with an acknowledgment of human createdness and dependency: "Rebellion against God, according to Edwards, was simply the normal condition of human existence. Men found it galling to be reminded of their dependence on a higher power."[114] Such belief combines acknowledgment of the inescapability of sin, pride, and attendant evils in the created world, all the while acknowledging the universe as essentially good, having been created by a loving God: "Religious faith asserts the goodness of being in the face of suffering and evil."[115] With such renunciation of the expectation that, from created existence, humanity has a "right" or entitlement to happiness there arises the possibility of a truer form of happiness—one earned by a heightened sense of human dependency and contingency: "the secret of happiness lay in renouncing the right to be happy."[116] A condition of resignation along with faith in the goodness of creation, acceptance combined with searching self-examination, and a kind of lowered expectation for the human potential of mastering all outcomes, including those that are tragic, accidental, or evil, in concert with a keen sense of *all* human dependence, gives rise to those accompanying theological virtues—and, quite arguably, profoundly *democratic* virtues—hope and charity.

Hope is that "middling" form of belief in the possibility of amelioration and attendant activity toward that end, all the while eschewing any optimism that such efforts will bear immediate benefit or even any fruit at all. Simultaneously hope also holds at bay the likely retreat into despair or hopelessness that such apparently fruitless efforts can prompt. Hope chides our impatience and frustration, lessens our sense of self-righteous expectation (without betraying a chastened belief in righteousness), and moderates our insistence that all injustices be overcome immediately "though the world perish," while maintaining our belief that justice is a worthy common civic mission. Hope looks to the future without belief in near-term culmination and yet holds firm to the belief that the goodness of creation will, in the end, resolve what we ourselves may be incapable of effecting. For Lasch, "hope without optimism" is the necessary disposition in achieving the "spiritual discipline against resentment":[117]

> Hope is the rejection of envy and resentment and all that invites them. It's not difficult to see why those would always seem to be compelling moral postures, be-

cause we live in a world that doesn't seem arranged for human convenience. It's a world in which human happiness is not the overriding goal, and our plans go awry, and there are terrible limitations on what we can know and understand and control. And in any case our lives are very short. The fact of death is always there, haunting our imagination. All of which seems to justify a renunciation of any belief in the possibility that the world, in spite of these facts, is good, just, beautiful. None of this, of course, implies that this is the best of all possible worlds or that the struggle against injustice ought be suspended on the grounds that whatever is, is right.[118]

As these last lines suggest, hope rejects the easy complacency of optimism. Hope is the primary disposition of the "democratic realist": we share innumerable miseries together in the *saeculum* with little expectation that we can exert control over final sorrow and suffering, and *because of this* shared condition of suffering, dependency, and weakness, democracy is the regime most fully in accord with our shared human condition. Democracy, so understood, arises out of mutual *need*, and demands at once the ongoing recognition not of the possibility of human *transformation* but, instead, of the inescapability of human dependence and limits, and finally points to the overarching necessity of fostering a shared sense of democratic *caritas*, or charity.

Lasch's argument was counterintuitive according to the contemporary political orthodoxy in which "liberals" are more attendant to the suffering of the weak and "conservatives" more likely to call for bootstrapping self-reliance. Lasch—eschewing the easy consignment to any political party or sect—embraced classically "conservative" arguments, with their strong emphasis upon human limitation and their profound mistrust of the optimistic belief in the promise of progress, albeit with an aim that ultimately embraced "liberal" sympathy with the plight of those most apt to be abandoned or overlooked, ironically because contemporary liberal creeds of meritocracy, cosmopolitanism, and optimism folded so seamlessly into "conservative" endorsements of self-reliance, if assuaged (but ultimately strengthened) by misguided reliance upon "therapeutic" solace. "Limits and hope"—the central theme of Lasch's final work—is a combination that points to our shared condition of frailty and imperfection, and thereby exhorts us to be keenly attentive to the suffering and alienation under which we all live and die, the recognition of which impels us to act with generosity and charity. The "spiritual discipline against resentment" chastens our impatience with injustice precisely by emphasizing the necessity for love. This emphasis upon "mercy" was, Lasch concluded, perhaps the most difficult virtue for humans generally—and modern man especially—to sustain. And yet, in Lasch's view, it was a message needing repetition and renewal, even in the face of likely failure. Hope demands nothing less. For Lasch, history did not justify optimism but rather was a standing reminder of the simultaneous challenge to and utter necessity for mercy: "In the history of civilization . . . vindictive gods give way to gods who show mercy as well and uphold the morality of loving your enemy. Such a morality has never achieved anything like general popularity, but it lives on, even in our own enlightened age, as a reminder both of our fallen state and of our surprising capacity for gratitude, remorse, and forgiveness, by means of which we now and then transcend it."[119]

A Model of Democratic Charity

"Pride is perverted imitation of God. For pride hates a fellowship
of equality under God, and seeks to impose its own domination
on fellow men.

—Augustine, *City of God*

ON JANUARY 20, 2001, President George W. Bush waxed uncharacteristically
poetic in the midst of his Inaugural Address, invoking a faith different from
that Christian faith he often professed during the campaign. While frequent
allusions to his Christianity caused alarm and consternation among committed secularists, the invocation of a "democratic faith" in his Inaugural
Address created no ripples and set off no figurative alarm bells, but appeared
a seamless part of the traditional language of the secular sermon that such
speeches traditionally resemble. Indeed, his mention of democratic faith ele-
cited all but no remarks. He invoked this faith as follows:

> Through much of the last century, America's faith in freedom and democracy was
> a rock in a raging sea. Now it is a seed upon the wind, taking root in many na-
> tions. Our democratic faith is more than the creed of our country, it is the inborn
> hope of our humanity; an ideal we carry but do not own, a trust we bear and pass
> along.[1]

Given the deep suspicion that accompanied candidate Bush's invocation of
faith throughout the campaign, it is perhaps surprising that no attention was
paid to this particular passage. In the absence of any significant reaction to
the invocation of this form of faith—recognized by President Bush as a core
feature of American devotions and increasingly a part of international belief
as well—it appears that nearly all listeners dismissed the phrase as a meaningless or innocuous rhetorical trope. Yet, as I have argued throughout this
book, I think it is necessary to raise questions about the seeming invisibility
of the phrase and its apparent insignificance. In light of the potential excesses
of democratic faith—that very faith to which democracy is inclined—exactly
what does the absence of attention to the new president's invocation of democratic faith reveal about ourselves and about the presuppositions of those
who criticized the president's invocations of religious faith? Might democratic faith be a form of faith that many accept, if only implicitly, and hence
view as uncontroversial not because of its meaninglessness but rather for its
very significance in our deepest political assumptions?

Particularly in light of the president's reaction to 9/11 and his stated belief that, by invading Iraq, America seeks to "change the world," it is now perhaps easier to see the fearful portents some listeners heard when the new president endorsed the "democratic faith." Still, many of the president's critics neglect the deep current of Pelagian dualism, Gnostic optimism, and humanistic messianism that the president shares with such "secular" thinkers as John Dewey and Walt Whitman, and instead insist that his flawed policies are a direct result of his stated Christian belief. To this extent, critics echo the long-standing suspicion of the baleful role of religious faith such as that expressed by John Dewey in *A Common Faith*—a superstition that needs to be overcome by enlightenment and democracy—without entertaining the likelier possibility that it is the president's "democratic faith" that most profoundly drives his actions in the post–9/11 world.

It is undoubtedly jarring to have the name George W. Bush placed in juxtaposition with the likes of Emerson, Whitman, Dewey, and Rorty. Yet, they share a characteristic American belief in "progressivism," historical optimism, and faith in human mastery, one that tends toward an overestimation of human powers and toward a glorification of American democracy.[2] This curious combination of overconfident belief about the rightness of one's own cause and one's own position, apparently in spite of the apparent skepticism of the progressive viewpoint of thinkers like Dewey and Rorty, can otherwise mask a secular and thus likely limitless faith. Indeed, believing they have thrown off the superstitious "certainty" of traditional religious—and, more generally, metaphysical—forms of faith, progressives typically have no compunction or self-awareness in invoking "pragmatic" faith. They overlook the ways in which that form of faith may lack the inherent humbling features of the Augustinian faith they eschew. Such progressives are less likely to be made aware of the existence, much less the excesses, of "democratic faith" than even as true a believer in democracy's divine destiny as a Christian claimant such as George W. Bush.

By viewing America as the paragon of democratic openness, one often encounters strong chauvinistic statements about America's superiority, at times coupled with justifications of aggressive imposition of American values in the world. Characteristic is a set of sentiments advanced by Sidney Hook in his book, *Pragmatism and the Tragic Sense of Life*. Hook collected the essays in order to combat the view that pragmatism lacked a "tragic" sense or any kind of internal or inherent sets of limitations upon the ambitions, activities, and confidence of human beings. In his introduction, in particular, Hook sought to dispel common misconceptions about pragmatism, beginning with the assertion that the very word "pragmatic" tended to be misapplied to describe utilitarian or "self-serving expediency." Instead, Hook suggested that a better word would be "experimentalism," which stresses "the reference to action, empirical control, and the test of consequences inherent in the pragmatic tradition."[3] Yet, in arguing against the notion that pragmatism was equivalent to a form of skepticism, or that it was willing to subject every "warranted belief" to a version of scientific testing, Hook also insisted that pragmatism could be certain about some things—and, notably, sought to demonstrate such certainty by reference to the superior American understanding of what it takes to "build a good country." Comparing such an undertaking to the knowledge of what it takes to build a "good house," Hook dismissed as "silly" the hesitation expressed by some Americans (now in the wake of the Vietnam War) that the American understanding of "a good country"—"one in which citizens live in freedom, justice, prosperity and peace"—qualified it to dismiss any doubt or uncertainty.[4] Leaving aside the rather thorny issue of how one is to define such contested concepts as "freedom" and "justice," or at what cost and in what manner "prosperity" is to be secured, or whether "peace" can be assumed to coexist at ease with justice or prosperity, Hook's cavalier dismissal of such concerns is striking not only for its apparent lack of experimentalism but finally for its overweening confidence that all the problems of the political realm could be definitively solved through pragmatic methods. The very "faith" in experimentalism here leads curiously to the kind of overconfident certainty that pragmatism claims to eschew.

The absence of the tragic sense—even when one is claimed—is strikingly consistent among thinkers in the "pragmatic" tradition. The most visible modern defender of Dewey's and James's pragmatism, Richard Rorty, speaks of modern belief in religion and "truth" as a form of "poetry," yet is strikingly incapable of discerning the cautionary lessons from even poetry that he otherwise embraces. For example, echoing sentiments in Emerson's "American Scholar" address, Rorty contrasts the tired metaphysical philosophy of Europe ("Old Europe," one might say) with the "new metaphysic" of democracy in the New World:

> Just as Mark Twain was convinced that everything bad in European life and society could be corrected by adopting American attitudes and customs which his Connecticut Yankee brought to King Arthur's Court, so Dewey was convinced that everything that was wrong with traditional European philosophy was the result of clinging to a world picture which arose within, and met the needs of, an inegalitarian society.[5]

This is, to say the least, a surprising understanding of Twain's novel from a professor of comparative literature at Stanford University. While it is true that Hank Morgan, the "Yankee," skewers aristocratic and religious traditions in medieval England, by the end of the novel he proves to be more brutal and murderous than the knights he ridicules. Using the technologies of the Gatling gun, modern explosives, and electricity generated from coal, he succeeds in killing thirty thousand of Arthur's knights and, in the process, defeats himself as he and his band of modernist allies succumb to the pestilence that the piled corpses create. Twain's novel hardly stands as a morality tale about the corrupt evils of Europe as opposed to the decencies of America but rather—in addition to deriding the inequalities of English aristocratic society—even more fiercely condemns the smug superiority of American optimism that refuses to see the ways that its own democratic faith both overlooks, and may itself contain, seeds of deadly unintended consequences and the persistence of inescapable human tragedy and cruelty. In light of this oversight, Rorty's sympathy for an "Americanized humanity" is all the more alarming.[6]

The certainty of Hook and Rorty (and, for that matter, George W. Bush) about America's leading role in remaking the world in its image is an echo of the confident nineteenth-century sources of contemporary American optimism, especially found in the work of Emerson and Whitman. In his "Fortune of the Republic," Emerson writes that with America's destiny lies the destiny of the world. "At every moment some one country more than any other represents the sentiments and future of mankind. None will doubt the position that America occupies in the opinion of nations."[7] America's special role in the world is to lead as a vanguard to the fruition of humanity—the more fully human, or divinized humanity, that finds expression throughout Emerson's corpus.[8] "The Genius or Destiny of America is no log or sluggard, but a man incessantly advancing, as the shadow on the dial's face, or the heavenly body by whose light it is marked."[9] Like Dewey, Hook, and Rorty after him, Emerson chastised his countrymen for seeking God in the Heavens, and sought to bring their eyes down—both inward, and concentrated, upon the world. In doing so, the will of God and the will of man were combined, leading to the possibility of a sense of national righteousness and even providential fate.

Against such assumptions about the psychic immaturity of the religious believer, Christopher Lasch has argued that religious belief (in contrast to "democratic faith"), far from representing comforting tales born of childlike credulity, rather, in its most strenuous form, forces a harrowing recognition of the vast chasm that exists between humanity's self-flattering ambitions and God's intentions. Religious belief, by this reckoning, holds that the "comforting belief" belongs to that of modernity, with its stress upon human mastery, progress, and the possibility of overcoming alienation. It is precisely this "comfortable belief that the purposes of the Almighty coincide with our purely human purposes that religious faith requires us to renounce."[10] Democratic faith—holding an optimistic view of human transformation, scientific-driven progress, and the reconciliation of the individual and the global by an overcoming of human alienation—too easily inclines to the illusion of national mission undertaken in the name of democratic universalism and crusading self-righteousness.

It is against this belief that friendly critics of democratic faith have sought to warn us, in the words of Václav Havel, to avoid "forgetting we are not God." By keeping in view our condition as partial, frail, incomplete, and insufficient creatures, one's initial stance is one of cautious self-appraisal of one's own motives at precisely the moment one is tempted to advance the superiority of one's own way of life. Such cautiousness is not to be misinterpreted as moral relativism or even moral complacency: its source is immanently a *democratic* ethic, given its derivation as a recognition of human partiality and frailty. It is a strongly egalitarian ethic—particularly with its stress on our common insufficiency—yet is resistant to the egalitarian claims of those who posit the possibility of a future form of equality conditional upon the overcoming of human imperfection. It is a democratic ethic at once capable of the boldest defense against those who would deny its source (that is, those who hubristically deny our fundamental equality) and yet simultaneously is an ethic that demands a high degree of self-examination of one's own motives and, ultimately, because of its stress on human insufficiency, calls upon charity toward our own and others.

To better describe this ethic, and particularly to place it within the context of new (but certainly recurring) American adventurism and even hubris abroad, I conclude this book with a brief consideration of America's greatest defender of democracy, the most eloquent articulator of democracy's egalitarian basis, and the most seering critic of the tendency of democratic faith to overestimate its own power: Abraham Lincoln. Cornel West has written that pragmatism lacks a "tragic sense" and, to be complete, must combine the optimism of Jefferson, Emerson, and Dewey with the tragic sensibility of Abraham Lincoln.[11] I agree with West that pragmatism lacks a sufficient "tragic" sense, but I firmly disagree that Lincoln can comfortably be brought within the orbit of pragmatism or progressivism generally. Rather, Lincoln's vision is a standing accusation against the progressive and "transformative" dreams entertained by the pragmatist. In contrast to the sense of righteousness expressed by the likes of Hook, Rorty, Emerson, and George W. Bush, one can find no greater articulation of a caution against national self-aggrandizement, no more moving endorsement of our common human equality based not on our perfectibility but rather on our insufficiency, and no more poignant call for mercy born of the recognition of our shared frailty than the Second Inaugural Address of Abraham Lincoln.

LINCOLN'S RADICAL DEFENSE OF DEMOCRACY

Many interpreters of Lincoln's political thought read his earliest work *forward*, finding in such early speeches as the "Address to the Young Man's Lyceum" of 1838 or the "Address to the Washington Temperance Society" of 1842 the blossoming seeds of Lincoln's full-blown mature thought.[12] These treatments stress Lincoln's rationalism, and particularly his strong Lockeanism, that presumes government is based purely on consent and that consent is derived through the agreement of rationally self-interested parties. Such interpreters argue that Lincoln's understanding of equality is fundamentally *liberal*—that is, that we are all equally free in the State of Nature and that, by means of our mutual agreement to bind ourselves under a legitimate government, our equality is retained in the form of equal treatment under law and through equal opportunity in the sphere of economics.[13] The Calvinism, even Augustinianism of the Second Inaugural is, by contrast, thought to be the culmination of a series of reflections late in Lincoln's life that were prompted by the awful carnage and unexpected duration of the Civil War. An unpublished fragment entitled "A Meditation on the Divine Will," as well as several religious-themed letters to his occasional Quaker correspondent Eliza P. Gurney, point to Lincoln's growing sense of providential and divine meaning lying behind the discrete actions of the war (2:359, 627).[14]

Of course, there is considerable overlap between social contract theory and Protestantism, particularly Calvinism: in the previous chapter's discussion of Niebuhr, it was Niebuhr's Protestantism that attracted him to the Calvinist "realism" of Madison in the first instance, and in part Madison's training at the hands of Princeton University's Calvinist president John Witherspoon that laid the groundwork for his understanding of the ineradicability of human self-interest and hence the need for institutional controls of depravity.[15] Nevertheless, there is also profound tension and even outright disagreement between the liberalism of Locke and Madison, on the one hand, and Augustinianism in its various forms, on the other. Liberals begin by assuming that government, and politics generally, is an unnatural condition; Calvin, by contrast, does not.[16] Liberals advance the ideal of our equal natural liberty; Augustinians and Calvinists instead stress our equal subordination, our status as brothers and sisters under a common Father. Liberals posit that self-interest can be channeled productively for the greater good of society and thus need not be restrained; Augustinians seek not only to "abridge" self-interest and reprimand the inclination to concentrate upon the "self" in general but also reject individualism and individual autonomy as an ideal of human life. Liberals regard justice as the highest, and an achievable, political ideal; Augustinians regard love—*caritas*, or "charity"—as the highest yet likely unachievable ideal, and justice as an imperfect and second-best approximation of love. Liberals believe that religion is a source of strife and division and is therefore best left to the individual conscience in the private sphere; Augustinians regard both the public and private spheres as ultimately subordinate to divine law, and therefore eschew a simple division between religion and the state, although, at the same time, they resist the notion that theocracy or a full mixing of the sacred and profane would be in any way desirable (mostly because this would draw religion too fully within the sphere of the political and too deeply immerse it in inessential considerations that are best left to temporal powers).[17] If, according to one approach, Lincoln begins his career as a secular liberal but ends on a note of somber Augustinianism, might we conclude that there is a fundamental break in his thought and a contradiction between his early and late articulations?

Without being able to answer this question at the length and with the detail it deserves, I propose that we best understand Lincoln not by reading his early "rationalist" and apparently liberal speeches *forward*—as obvious and correct as that might seem—but rather by reading the import of his last words *backward*. In particular, we would do best to understand his lifelong critique of slavery and his conception of human equality, his defense of government as natural and democracy as superior, and finally his endorsement of "charity" as a fitting response to his belief in human equality *because of* this understanding of human equality, in essence foreshadowed throughout his written record and finding its culmination in the Second Inaugural. I conclude with a brief reflection on this alternative understanding of, and justification for, democracy.

In the Second Inaugural Lincoln describes briefly the causes of the war, attributing it foremost to the one cause—slavery—that even he at times studiously avoided naming as the source of the Southern secession and the Northern efforts to maintain the Union. After all, he states, "Neither anticipated that the *cause* of the conflict might cease with, or even before the conflict itself should cease. Each looked for an easier triumph, and a result less fundamental and astounding" (2:686). The resulting war was longer and more brutal than either side expected and yet, throughout its prosecution, each side appealed to the ultimate source in justifying its cause: "Both read the same Bible, and pray to the same God; and each invokes His aid against the other." Yet Lincoln expresses his (apparently mild) disapproval of the South's attempt to harness God on the side of slavery in the subsequent line: "It may seem strange that any men should dare to ask a just God's assistance in wringing their bread from the sweat of other men's faces; but let us judge not lest we be judged" (2:687). One might think that Lincoln was entitled here to a tone of far harsher and more seering denunciation. Nevertheless, in spite of the apparent mildness of this one criticism of the South that finds expression at the end of a harrowing war, Lincoln is, in fact, articulating a profound critique of the South and is further engaged in a form of theological education—not only of the South but for all Americans.

The Bible is a constant resource for Lincoln in his speeches and writings. While many scholars and amateurs alike have long debated Lincoln's piety, there is no contending that he was not only knowledgeable about the Bible but about much Christian and particularly Calvinist theology as well.[18] For all of Lincoln's apparent impiety, he nevertheless gave testimony to the central truth of the Bible's teachings. Upon being presented with a Bible in 1864 by the "Loyal Colored People of Baltimore," Lincoln responded that the Bible was "the best gift God has given to man" and further asserted that, "but for it we could not know right from wrong" (2:628). Nevertheless, the Bible is equally a work he could seemingly dismiss for its elusive meaning. One sees this, in particular, in Lincoln's response to what was termed the "pro-slavery theology," namely, the biblically grounded attempt to justify slavery. Responding to the view of some that slavery was in accordance with the will of God in a fragment entitled "On Pro-slavery Theology" tentatively dated 1858, Lincoln averred that, "certainly there is no contending with the

Will of God; but there is some difficulty in ascertaining, and applying it, to particular cases. . . . For instance . . . , [if] the question is 'Is it the Will of God that Sambo shall remain a slave, or be set free?' The Almighty gives no audible answer to the question, and his revelation—the Bible—gives none, or at most, none but such that as admits of a squabble, as to it's [*sic*] meaning" (1:685). At first glance this statement appears to be nothing other than a cheeky dismissal of any actual applicable "wisdom" in the Bible—a work that, six years later, he locates as the source of human morality. Can one square these sentiments?

In fact, there is good reason to believe that the sentiments of these two statements are in perfect accord. In his fragment on "pro-slavery theology" Lincoln acknowledges that "there is no contending with the Will of God" and yet simultaneously recognizes that the will of God can only be imperfectly discerned in that very text where the infallibility of His will is revealed. The imperatives of God's will are conveyed in a written work the meaning of which imperfect humans inevitably contest. By this understanding, God wills at once that we know His will to be incontestable and yet that we are not equipped with sufficient knowledge or discernment to know with certainty all the particulars of His will. This recognition forces upon the devout an acknowledgment of the need for *interpretive humility*.

"Interpretive humility," as articulated by Augustine, was based on an initial acknowledgment of the truth of Scripture and, because of the implications of that recognition of God's perfection and attendant human frailty, simultaneously insisted that we recognize the manifold ways in which the Bible can be read and understood.[19] As understood and developed by Lincoln, this situation of *interpretive humility* necessitates as well an acknowledgment of *subordinated equality*. Because no one among us has a privileged or definitive understanding of Scripture, a practical implication is that no one among us is endowed with superior knowledge that can serve as the basis of a claim to rule. As Lincoln contends again and again, theocracy and slavery are both equally ruled out. Those who would enslave another *on the basis of a reading of the Bible* engage in a heretical activity of claiming an unavailable superiority. Lincoln does not hesitate to frame the debate with defenders of slavery in the starkest political and theological terms: "It is the eternal struggle between these two principles—right and wrong—throughout the world. They are the two principles that have stood face to face from the beginning of time; and will ever continue to struggle. The one is the common right of humanity and the other the divine right of kings. It is the same principle in whatever shape it develops itself. It is the same spirit that says, 'You work and toil and earn bread, and I'll eat it' " (1:810–811; "Lincoln-Douglas Debate at Alton").

The political distinction between "divine right" and democracy has deeper theological roots in Lincoln's thought. Those who would claim the food produced by the sweat of another man's brow are effectively succumbing to the same temptation by Satan to eat from the Tree of the Knowledge of Good and Evil in the Garden of Eden: "This argument of the Judge [Douglas] is the same old serpent that says you work and I eat, you toil and I will enjoy the fruits of your labor" (1:457; "Speech at Chicago," 1858). Ironically Douglas confirmed Lincoln's suspicions: at one point Douglas justified the doctrine of "popular sovereignty"—which should be given every opportunity to accept or reject slavery according to the will of the majority—based on his reading of the second chapter of Genesis, in which (Douglas argued) God placed good and evil before Adam and Eve and gave them the freedom to choose. In effect, Douglas used the Bible to defend what he admits to be the choice of evil. Lincoln responded in his "Peoria" speech that "God did not place good and evil before man, telling him to make his choice. On the contrary, he did tell him that there was one tree, of the fruit of which, he should not eat, upon pain of certain death" (1:342). As Harry Jaffa correctly assesses Lincoln's riposte, "the condition of man under a free government, according to Lincoln, resembled that of man in the Garden of Eden. His freedom was conditional—conditional upon denying himself a forbidden fruit. That fruit was the alluring pleasure of despotism."[20] Slavery, in effect, was a commission of yet another version of original sin, a form of disobedience against the divine will.

Returning to the Second Inaugural, in light of the theological understanding of the basis of subordinate human equality, one is forced to reassess the initial suspicion that, in differentiating the two sides that have otherwise fought in a prolonged and savage war, Lincoln only appears conciliatory when he states: "It may seem strange that any men should dare to ask a just God's assistance in wringing their bread from the sweat of other men's faces; but let us judge not lest we be judged." Instead, particularly regarding the first of two biblical passages Lincoln cites in this sentence, one sees that he is engaged in a radical and far more sweeping critique of the South. If one can have sufficient reason to assert the wrongness of American slavery (given the various legitimate interpretations that can be drawn from the biblical source), it is surely on the ground of the outrageousness of asking "God's assistance in wringing their bread from the sweat of other men's faces." Here, by referring to the expulsion of mankind from Eden (Genesis 3:19), Lincoln points out that the slaveholding South—by attempting to overcome the burden God places on humanity in punishment for the commission of the original sin—is, in the first instance, engaged in an attempt to resist humanity's fallen condition in direct contradiction to God's will. Further, resistance to God's will in the name of God is a reenactment of the original sin inasmuch as it is the claim by fallible humanity to the infallible knowledge that is at once based upon, and used to justify, the assertion of human superiority over other humans. The effort to enslave an inferior humanity based on a superior reading of Scripture denies our common and equal "enslavement," in the words of John Calvin in his interpretation of the third chapter of Genesis.[21] The effort to resist God's burden points more broadly to the attempt to deny man's fallen nature. If the North can claim "superiority" in its cause against the South, it is not because of its greater "righteousness" but rather because the North's denial of the rightness of slavery reflects a greater humility in abiding by the will of God and a greater acceptance of the condition of human fallenness.[22]

Lincoln's seering condemnation of the South appears superficially all the more bland because of the second biblical passage: "but let us judge not lest we be judged" (Matthew, 7:1). Lincoln appears to retreat from a condemnatory judgment against the South, and even the ability to render any judgment, at precisely the moment when it appears most justified. Again, the biblical context is revealing: drawn from the Sermon on the Mount in Matthew, Jesus is not rejecting the capacity of judgment in favor of relativist uncertainty but, instead, is insisting that any judge must first judge himself by the same standard that he intends to use in the judgment of others. As the biblical passage continues, "For with the judgment you make you will be judged, and the measure you give will be the measure you get. Why do you see the speck in your neighbor's eye, but not notice the log in your own eye ... ? You hypocrite, first take the log out of your own eye, and then you will see clearly to take the speck out of your neighbor's eye" (Matthew, 7:2–5). Far from being an encouragement to avoid judgment (we are still admonished to take the speck out of our neighbor's eye), Scripture first demands that we engage in a searching self-examination of our own inclination to the similar kinds of sin. Lincoln's passive tone disguises not only his strong condemnation of the heretical assumptions underlying the South's justification of slavery but partially obscures a strong suggestion that even the righteous judge is tempted to avoid probing self-scrutiny of his own inevitable failings through an exclusive effort to cast blame upon the failings of others. With these words Lincoln echoes one of his earliest statements against a condemnatory stance precisely because such a stance can obfuscate recognition of our own imperfections. Speaking before the Washington Temperance Society in 1842, Lincoln recommended instead that one seek to reveal to another man his wayward actions "in the accents of entreaty and persuasion, diffidently addressed by erring man to an erring brother" (1:82).[23] The attempt to escape the discernment of one's own sinfulness—the very assertion of superiority even in the name of one's greater humility—is no less subject to "judgment." By means of this one sentence in the Second Inaugural, Lincoln at once condemns the South's justification of slavery and yet places the North firmly within the scrutiny of God's judgment

Slavery was particularly heinous—indeed, likely among the worst sins humanity could commit—because it was motivated by a self-deceptive belief in our thorough independence. Traditional Augustinian doctrine held that God had differently endowed humanity with a multiplicity of talents so that humans would readily perceive the extent to which they were, by themselves, insufficient. An effort to escape from the necessity of work—the burden placed upon humanity for their transgression against God—could be understood as nothing less than an effort to "declare independence," now from the necessary interdependence of all humans for each other and of all humans upon the ultimate beneficence of God.

This understanding of the role work is intended to play in fostering our understanding of each person's insufficiency is captured with particular force in John Winthrop's famous 1630 address aboard the ship *Arabella*, sometimes called "A Model of Christian Charity." Indeed, there are such strong structural and thematic similarities between Winthrop's *Arabella* speech and Lincoln's Second Inaugural that it is likely Lincoln based his later speech if not directly on Winthrop's address then almost certainly on a closely shared theological vision.[24] Counterintuitively, Winthrop begins his address with an apparent statement of human *inequality*: "God Almighty in His most holy and wise providence hath so disposed the condition of mankind as in all times some must be rich, some poor; some high and eminent in power and dignity, others mean and in subjection."[25] If one read no further, one could perhaps rightly conclude that Winthrop endorses hierarchy and the permanent control of some by others as facts of life. Yet, Winthrop continues by attempting to understand such diversity in light of God's purposes: the fact of pluralism, in current parlance, exists "that every man might have need of other, and from hence they might be all knit more nearly together in the bond of brotherly affection."[26] Our differences are not an indictment against others whom we might regard as comparatively on a lower standing from a terrestrial standard but rather evidence of *every* person's radical insufficiency. Nor can we claim or blame our position—whether inferior or superior— thoroughly as a result of our own agency: "From hence it appears plainly that no man is made more honorable than another or more wealthy, etc., out of any particular and singular respect to himself, but for the glory of his creator and the common good of the creature, man."[27] Augustinian and Calvinist doctrine did not permit the impious claim of ultimate human responsibility for a person's respective position and accomplishments: all outcomes are the result of divine providence. The fact of radical human imperfection, fallenness, even depravity, does not permit claims of superiority over any element of society—since, in the eyes of God, all humans are equal in their insufficiency and sinfulness—nor, of course, does it permit the claim of ultimate human agency in the world, given the fact of thoroughgoing human dependence on divine beneficence and grace.

Government, for this reason, is natural to human beings. We are, in the first instance, insufficient, and therefore needful of organized society; second, we are also given to viciousness, and thus need law and the administration of justice. Following Calvinist teaching, Lincoln recognized this dual rationale for the naturalness of government, even reasoning at one point (1854?) in an unpublished fragment that government would still be necessary even if humans were naturally "just" and no longer subject to original sin:

The legitimate object of government, is to do for a community of people, whatever they need to have done, but can not do, *at all*, or can not, *so well do*, for themselves—in their separate, and individual capacities. . . .

The desirable things which the individuals of a people can not do, or can not well do, for themselves, fall into two classes: those which have relation to *wrongs*, and those which have not. Each of these branch off into an infinite variety of subdivisions.

The first—that in relation to wrongs—embraces all crimes, misdemeanors, and non-performance of contracts. The other embraces all which, in its nature, and without wrong, requires combined action, as public roads and highways, public schools, charities, pauperism, orphanages, estates of the deceased, and the machinery of government itself.

From this it appears that if all men were just, there still would be *some*, though not *so much*, need of government. (1:301)

Notably, because of our shared insufficiencies (even imagining away human propensity to injustice), nevertheless government is necessary in order to extend "charity" to those who are less fortunate.

Likewise, for Winthrop, the recognition of our shared insufficiency demands, above all, the Christian virtue of charity. God intends us to understand our diversity as evidence of a whole of which we are necessarily a part, and which we must actively work to build: "we must be knit together in this work as one man. We must entertain each other in brotherly affection; we must be willing to abridge ourselves of our superfluities, for the supply of others' necessities; we must uphold a familiar commerce together in all meekness, gentleness, patience and liberality."[28] In light of our insufficiency and imperfection, and the resulting humility that results from that recognition, individuals are called upon to discern and accept their dependency upon others, to eschew viewing their positions as the result of their own efforts or as entitling them to exclusive enjoyment of the benefits accruing from that position.[29]

Our equality is not necessarily evident to the senses in the most obvious way—some will still enjoy positions of higher rank and greater wealth—but rather is evinced in the very fact of our difference. Instead of the existence of difference leading to a stress upon individual autonomy—pluralism as evidence of the priority of our right to the individual pursuit in fulfillment of our individual capacities—Winthrop insists that those very differences exist as a chastening reminder of the insufficiency and ultimate dependence of *all* humans, and as a call to view one's position as a contingent blessing that demands of us strenuous efforts on behalf of those who are not so well positioned. At the same time it is a reminder to those who are less well positioned that they are neither at fault for their station nor should their first instinct be toward resentment of others (though they are given good grounds for critique of those elites who give any hint of self-congratulation). Winthrop's is a strenuous reminder of what Timothy P. Jackson has called an "ethic of care." Belief in personal independence, in this view, is severely moderated inasmuch as such individuality can only arise meaningfully as the result of the cultivation that takes place in light of a recognition of prior dependence (cf. Lincoln's defense of the natural need for public schooling): as stated by Jackson, "relatively 'independent' persons do not just happen; they require cultivation and protection, especially when very young. Any society that cannot attend to this dependency will treat autonomous persons like 'manna from heaven' and thereby fail to support the necessary conditions for the emergence of its own citizenry."[30] Gratitude and charity, not a belief in our self-creation, are the appropriate responses to this recognition of our shared frailty.

Lincoln echoes these very sentiments articulated by Winthrop in the Second Inaugural, albeit now in light of the American national community, in the shadow of the existence of the Civil War, and the persistence of slavery and its legacy in American history. Like Winthrop, Lincoln begins with a chastening of American pretensions to independence—Southern and Northern alike. He insists that human efforts take place in light of God's purposes, not vice versa. Alluding to his earlier reference to the now abandoned shared belief in an "easier triumph," Lincoln broods—as he did throughout the course of the war—upon the significance of the war's duration and carnage:

> The Almighty has His own purposes. "Woe unto the world because of offenses! for it must needs be that offenses come; but woe to the man from whom the offence cometh!" If we shall suppose that American Slavery is one of those offenses which, in the providence of God, must needs come, but which, having continued through His appointed time, He now wills to remove, and that He gives to both North and South, this terrible war, as the woe due to those by whom the offence came, shall we discern therein any departure from those divine attributes which the believers in a Living God always ascribe to Him? Fondly do we hope—fervently do we pray—that this mighty scourge of war may speedily pass away. Yet, if God wills that it continue, until all the wealth piled by the bond-man's two hundred and fifty years of unrequited toil shall be sunk, and until every drop of blood drawn with the lash, shall be paid by another drawn with the sword, as was said three thousand years ago, so still it must be said, "the judgments of the Lord, are true and righteous altogether." (2:687)

In spite of the justness of the North's cause against the willful denial of original sin committed by the South, the war had continued for so long, and with such enormous suffering on both sides, that Lincoln increasingly concluded that even the North—and he personally—could not be certain of God's intentions in allowing a righteous war to continue. Without casting into doubt his belief that the North should continue to prosecute the war "with firmness in the right," he did open space between his belief in that rightness— born of itself of humble acknowledgment of human limits and imperfect equality of perception—and God's understanding of those like actions. Thus he qualified his call for "firmness" with an acknowledgment, "as God gives us to see the right."

In a series of reflections, including his "Meditation on the Divine Will" and his correspondence with Eliza P. Gurney, Lincoln increasingly came to view the war itself as a glass through which the will of God could be discerned only darkly. He strongly acknowledged his belief in the righteous Providence of God in 1864 to Eliza Gurney, "the purposes of the Almighty are perfect, and must prevail, though we erring mortals may fail to accurately perceive them in advance" (2:627). These latter sentiments echo his 1862 words in his "Meditation on the Divine Will" that God's and man's intentions were likely distinct: "In the present civil war it is quite possible that God's purpose is something different from the purpose of either party—and yet, human instrumentalities, working as they do, are of the best adaptation to effect His purpose" (2:359). Lincoln's sense of a divide between God and man throws into stark relief human insufficiency: even so awesome an undertaking as the American Civil War, resulting in the death of more than six hundred thousand men and untold destruction, may not mean quite what its actors believe it does. At the same time Lincoln tentatively concludes that God may once again—as he did after the original sin in the Garden of Eden—be placing a terrible burden upon America, even all humanity, because of the sin of *American* slavery. After having briefly (and seemingly mildly) chastised the South's attempt to justify slavery on biblical grounds, Lincoln thereafter insists that slavery was a *national* sin, one that will be repaid by the whole country, perhaps for as long as it exists.

Too often Lincoln's acknowledgment that God had laid a terrible burden upon the North and South alike is understood to be a reflection of Lincoln's belief in a vengeful God. Such a view was the very opposite, however, of that held by Calvinists. According to Calvin's interpretation of God's curse of Adam and Adam's sons, the burdens placed upon humanity are not the result of God's vindictive will to punish but rather are a harsh but necessary kind of teaching to an obdurate and recalcitrant sinful humanity. As Calvin writes of Genesis 3,

> They who meekly submit to their sufferings, present to God an acceptable obedience . . . that knowledge of sin which may teach them to be humble. . . . But they who imagined that punishments are required as compensations, have been preposterous interpreters of the judgments of God. For God does not consider, in chastising the faithful, what they deserve; but what will be useful to them in future; and fulfils the office of a physician rather than of a judge. . . . If we duly consider how great is the torpor of the human mind, then, how great its lasciviousness, how great its contumacy, how great its levity, and how quick its forgetfulness, we shall not wonder at God's severity in subduing it. If he admonishes in words he is not heard; if he adds stripes, it avails but little; when it happens that he is heard, the flesh nevertheless spurns the admonition. That obstinate hardness which, with all its power opposes itself to God, is worse than lasciviousness.[31]

Harsh as it sounds, Lincoln came to accept the view that the Civil War was a horrible reenactment of God's curse on Adam as a constant and necessary reminder to sinful humans—ones inclined to repeat original sin in their effort to escape the burden of work, in denying their dependence, and in claiming false self-sufficiency through the enslavement of other human beings. It was a lesson being meted out to North and South alike, since both had benefited from the sin of slavery, and both were equally inclined to view their position as in thorough accordance with the will of God.

That the North by the end of the war had come to believe that God was on its side and that God's favor upon America was evident in the North's victory was itself a further reminder of humanity's inclination to sinful overestimation of its own powers. The belief that God smiled upon the North—widely held by America's leading theologians at the culmination of the Civil War—has been characterized by Mark Noll as "a morally juvenile view." Such a self-flattering view is contrasted to Lincoln's more mature and subtle injection of doubt whether Americans should understand themselves as God's chosen people and whether such belief does not, in fact, reenact the first sin of humankind.[32] Horace Bushnell, for instance, celebrated the Northern victory in familiar terms of the "democratic faithful" by declaring that "the sense of nationality becomes even a kind of religion."[33] Noll rightly differentiates most theologians from Lincoln on two grounds:

> Almost universally they maintained the long-treasured axiom that the United States had enjoyed, and would continue to enjoy, a unique destiny as a divinely chosen people. The war, they held, had decisively reconfirmed this calling. Second, the theologians continued to speak as if the ways of providence were transparent, as if it were a relatively easy matter to say what God was doing in the disposition of contemporary events. Moreover, what was clearly seen could also be controlled. . . . On these points, the chorus of theologians sang with one voice.[34]

Using the platform of the presidential inaugural podium, Lincoln gently but firmly reprimanded not only the sinful hubris of the South but also the growing and disturbing sense of triumphalism of the North.

Having leveled human belief in its thorough agency and ability to control events—much as Winthrop razes human pretensions and self-deception of its own accomplishments—Lincoln, like Winthrop, begins his peroration with a call for charity:

> With malice toward none; with charity for all; with firmness in the right, as God gives us to see the right, let us strive to finish the work we are in; to bind up the nation's wounds; to care for him who shall have borne the battle, and for his widow, and his orphan—to do all which may achieve and cherish a just, and lasting peace, among ourselves, and with all nations. (2:687)

Lincoln's is more than a statesmanlike call to move beyond the bitterness of the war—although it is certainly that. Rather, it retraces the movement, followed in Winthrop's speech as well, from the bitter fruit of humanity's fall, and the accompanying situation of insufficiency and depravity, to the possibility of redemption through love. The call for charity, in Lincoln's theological understanding, follows intimately and necessarily upon the recognition of our universally shared insufficiency. Our primary condition is one of *need*. The weakest and most forlorn—widows and orphans—are clearly most in need, and charity is our fitting response. But in Lincoln's more encompassing theological understanding, we are all roughly in the same position as widows and children—we are all equally bereft of the ability to fend for ourselves, equally deprived of any true form of self-sufficiency. We are all, like children, created and frail, and, like widows, ultimately bereft of those we love most. From a God's eye view—to which the Second Inaugural at times aspires, even while recognizing that such a perspective is unattainable by any human—humans are radically equal in their insufficiency. To attain the conditions of life, to make possible a decent society and the flourishing of human beings individually and collectively, to make peace and even the aspirations for justice a reality, society must, in the first instance, be suffused with a spirit of charity. It is through the very chastening of the allurement of belief in our thorough agency, our ability to transform ourselves, our insistence that humanity individually or collectively controls its own destiny, even that redemption is possible through politics if it can only be arranged in a manner compatible with human potential for perfection that the priority of sacrificial love can take its rightful place. On those grounds true human equality, and democratic endurance, are rendered possible.

In a fragment tentatively dated in 1858, Lincoln stated his "idea" of democracy: "As I would not be a *slave*, so I would not be a *master*. This expresses my idea of democracy. Whatever differs from this, to the extent of the difference, is no democracy" (1:484). While apparently a hidden syllogism, and clearly stating a principle of reciprocity, politically it is far from obviously true. The first impulse of one who would not be a slave is not necessarily that he would instead refuse to be a master, but, rather, it might well be concluded that mastery would be the best protection against enslavement. While it is possible that a Hobbesian calculus lies in the background of this statement—that it might be in the ultimate interest of all parties to eschew slavery, lest one be so unfortunate as to be enslaved by a stronger party—in light of the preceding discussion it is revealing that Lincoln's assessment is undertaken purely in reference to himself alone. For one thing, it does not reflect Lincoln's ultimate fear that a stronger human is potentially capable of mastering him but, instead, is a refusal to become a master in light of his unwillingness to be a slave. Here master and slave are brought closely into alignment: to be a slave is to be subject to powers one cannot control. In classical and Christian conceptions, to be a slave is not merely to be subject to the domination of another human; internally it is possible to be subject to one's instinctual appetites, such as pleasure, sloth, the will to tyranny. To seek to be a *master* is to be a *slave* to one's will to mastery; to assert one's unwillingness to be a slave to one's worst appetites is to refuse the possibility of mastery: it is to master the will to master, and to thereby reject the inclination to enslave others. Democracy, by this understanding, is not justified as a contractual arrangement in which we avoid mastery out of fear of our own enslavement—yet internally remain attracted to mastery in theory, if not in fact—but, rather, consists more fundamentally as a mastery of our internal propensity to believe ourselves to be unequal and as the rejection of our will to mastery. Lincoln's "idea" of democracy is a belief in the "proposition" of "the capability of the people to govern themselves" that is itself ultimately premised upon the capability of each individual to govern the ineradicable human inclination to inequality based on a false belief in our individual self-sufficiency (1:34).

Lincoln's culminating speech seeks to temper the impious belief in personal or national superiority, and thereby chasten the human temptation toward individual or national self-glorification. While Lincoln called the United States "the last, best hope on earth," it was in light of his recognition that Americans were an "almost chosen people."[35] His high estimation of America—one held throughout his life—was not because, in his view, America was superior to other nations owing to its greater approximation to God's will, but because, as a democracy, it was organized politically in recognition of the fact that man was not, nor could become, God. Even at his most patriotic and triumphal moments, Lincoln was cognizant that the "superiority" of democracy rested most fundamentally upon the humble recognition of human imperfection. Thus, even in his earliest speech—"Address to the Young Man's Lyceum"—Lincoln proclaims America's greatness in the context of acknowledging the division between God and man: "Let the proud fabric of freedom rest, as the rock of its basis; and as truly has been said of the only greater institution, *the gates of hell shall not prevail against it.*" (1:36). Citing Matthew 16:18, in which Jesus "establishes" his Church on earth, Lincoln acknowledges that America is subordinate to "the only greater institution," the rule of God. American democracy is superior to the world's monarchies and tyrannies because of its basis in equality, and that basis in equality is grounded upon a shared understanding of our common subordination and the concomitant call for charity born of a humble acknowledgment of our shared lack of self-sufficiency.[36]

Following his second inauguration Lincoln wrote to an admirer that "men are not flattered by being shown that there has been a difference of purpose between the Almighty and them. To deny it, however, is to deny that there is a God governing the world. It is a truth that needed to be told, and as whatever humiliation there is in it, falls most directly on myself, I thought others might afford for me to tell it" (2:689). His "humiliation" is a result of his recognition of a divide between humanity and God: that acknowledgment is the source of his own humility, a reminder of his own human, all-too-human inclination to believe himself to be in control of human destiny. From the starting point of that acknowledgment arises the source of humility that animates and justifies democracy. The rejection of that recognition, at its most extreme, underlies the Southern practice of enslaving "inferiors": shorn of an appropriately "humiliating" understanding of its own frailty, slave-holding America denied the wellspring of democratic belief.

Lincoln indicates that the necessary source of this "humiliation" is an acknowledgment that "God governs the world." By this Lincoln strongly asserts that the acceptance of the revealed existence of God is the fundamental premise upon which democracy rests. This understanding of democracy—while sometimes advanced by some among the more vociferous religious and even secular figures in today's culture wars—will, for many, be as unwelcome coming from the modest and reasonable Lincoln as from self-righteous Bible-thumping preachers. And rightfully so; I, too, would not like to think or argue that democracy rests upon an orthodox religious belief. Yet, those who resist the ground premise of Lincoln's assumption, as expressed in this late letter, should feel compelled at the very least to ask themselves, in the absence of a shared religious understanding as that expressed by Lincoln, if they share implicitly or explicitly a different faith in its place—a democratic faith that implicitly raises humanity to the position of God and understands democracy as a vessel of salvation and redemption. Further, do the democratic faithful have the resources of chastening self-introspection, the rejection of personal and national self-aggrandizement, and the strong endorsement of charity all of which are articulated in Lincoln's understanding of democracy? Today's democrats of all stripes, of all sects and all churches, of all creeds and all faiths, must subject themselves equally to the same question Lincoln asked: Do we harbor a sense of democratic self-satisfaction that is closely aligned to a belief in the possibility of mastery and dominion—whether of other humans, nature, or even ourselves—and does not such a belief ultimately threaten to undermine democracy? If we ask that of ourselves, then the chastening words of friendly critics of democratic faith such as Lincoln will have been enough, without demanding the last full measure of devotion.

NOTES

PREFACE
WORSHIPING DEMOCRACY: THE PANTHÉON AND THE GODDESS OF DEMOCRACY

1. See the various reports of the removal and transportation of Rousseau's remains in R. A. Leigh, ed., *Correspondance complète de Jean-Jacques Rousseau* (Geneva: Banbury, 1965–95), 8217–8224. See also Maurice Cranston, *The Solitary Self: Jean-Jacques Rousseau in Exile and Adversity* (Chicago: University of Chicago Press, 1997), 186–187.

2. As Allan Bloom summarizes the history of the *Encyclopédie* entry on Geneva against which Rousseau was writing, "Voltaire persuaded D'Alembert [author of the article] to insert a passage (which Rousseau insists Voltaire himself wrote) in an otherwise laudatory presentation suggesting that Geneva should have a theatre" (Bloom, Introduction to *Politics and the Arts* [Ithaca: Cornell University Press, 1960], xv).

3. Jean-Jacques Rousseau, *Politics and the Arts: Letter to M. D'Alembert on the Theatre*, trans. Allan Bloom (Ithaca, N.Y.: Cornell University Press, 1960), 58–59.

4. For background on the religious and political history of the building, see Roger-Armand Weigert, *Le Panthéon* (Paris: Éditions du Cerf, n.d.); and *Le Panthéon: Symbole des revolutions. De l'Eglise de la Nation au Temple des Grand Hommes* (Montreal: Canadian Centre for Architecture, 1989).

5. Jean-Jacques Rousseau, *On the Social Contract*, trans. Victor Gourevitch (New York: Cambridge University Press, 1997), book 4, chap. 8. See also my discussion in chapter 5, below.

6. Linda Zerilli comments critically on this mistaken connection, given that the Chinese students themselves sought to avoid the identification of the Goddess of Democracy with the Statue of Liberty. See Linda Zerilli, "Democracy and National Fantasy: Reflections on the Statue of Liberty," in *Cultural Studies and Political Theory*, ed. Jodi Dean (Ithaca: Cornell University Press, 2000), esp. 167–171, 185–188.

7. Han Minzhu, ed., *Cries for Democracy: Writings and Speeches from the 1989 Chinese Democracy Movement* (Princeton, N.J.: Princeton University Press, 1990).

8. The juxtaposition of calls to worship the Goddess of Democracy and renditions of *The Internationale* is jarring, to say the least. The verses of *The Internationale* call for the overthrow of superstition and unjustified faith:

> Arise ye workers from your slumbers
> Arise ye prisoners of want
> For reason in revolt now thunders
> And at last ends the age of cant.
> Away with all your superstitions
> Servile masses arise, arise
> We'll change henceforth the old tradition
> And spurn the dust to win the prize.
>
> So comrades, come rally
> And the last fight let us face
> The Internationale unites the human race.
> So comrades, come rally

And the last fight let us face
The Internationale unites the human race.
No more deluded by reaction
On tyrants only we'll make war
The soldiers too will take strike action
They'll break ranks and fight no more
And if those cannibals keep trying
To sacrifice us to their pride
They soon shall hear the bullets flying
We'll shoot the generals on our own side.

No saviour from on high delivers
No faith have we in prince or peer
Our own right hand the chains must shiver
Chains of hatred, greed and fear
E'er the thieves will out with their booty
And give to all a happier lot.
Each at the forge must do their duty
And we'll strike while the iron is hot.
(Eugene Pottier, 1871)

INTRODUCTION

Dynamics of Democratic Faith

1. Ian Shapiro writes that "the democratic idea is close to nonnegotiable in today's world" (*The State of Democratic Theory* [Princeton, N.J.: Princeton University Press, 2003], 1).

2. "I want to inquire whether in the civil order there can be some legitimate and sure rule of administration, taking men as they are, and the laws as they can be" (*Of the Social Contract*, trans. Victor Gourevitch [New York: Cambridge University Press, 1997], book 1, preface, 41). As my subsequent discussion and chapters suggest, it may very well be that Rousseau's implicit answer to this guiding question is decisively no.

3. On Rousseau's democratic "dreams," see James Miller, *Rousseau: Dreamer of Democracy* (New Haven: Yale University Press, 1984).

4. On the antidemocratic thought of the ancients, see Josiah Ober's treatment of Thucydides, Plato, and Aristotle in his *Political Dissent in Democratic Athens: Intellectual Critics of Popular Rule* (Princeton, N.J.: Princeton University Press, 1998). Few contemporary political theorists bother to consider, much less read, the medieval thinkers, in large part owing to the concurrence of antidemocratic and theological aspects of their thought. For a powerful modern restatement of Augustinian and Thomistic suspicions toward democracy, see Robert P. Kraynak, *Christian Faith and Modern Democracy: God and Politics in the Fallen World* (Notre Dame, Ind.: University of Notre Dame Press, 2001). On critics of "democratic individualism," both ancient and modern, see George Kateb, "Democratic Individualism and Its Critics," *Annual Review of Political Science* 6 (2003): 275–305, which focuses on the work of two "not completely hostile" critics of democracy, Plato and Tocqueville, both of whom are treated as friendly critics of "democratic faith" later in this book.

5. George Santayana, *The Life of Reason, or The Phases of Human Progress*. 1 vol. (London: Constable, 1954), 148 (chaps. 5, *"Reason in Society"*).

6. Rousseau, *Social Contract*, book 2, chap. 7, 71.

7. While I contend that the perception of the gap between men as they are and men as they might be is perceived with keenness and dissatisfaction by democratic theorists in particular, it is likely the case that dissatisfaction with this gap is endemic to the activity of the political theorist. As Sheldon S. Wolin has explained, "most political thinkers have believed that precisely because political philosophy was 'political,' it was committed to lessening the gap between the possibilities grasped through political imagination and the actualities of political existence. . . . This more comprehensive vision was provided by thinking about the political society in its corrected fullness, not as it is but as it might be" (*Politics and Vision: Continuity and Innovation in Western Political Tradition*, exp. ed. [Princeton, N.J.: Princeton University Press, 2004], 20).

8. A prescient treatment of the democratic inclination toward "perfectibility" can be found in Alexis de Tocqueville, Democracy in America, vol. 2, book 1, chap. 8, ("How Equality Suggests to the Americans the Idea of the Indefinite Perfectibility of Man"). See also my discussion of Tocqueville in chapter 8, below.

9. Richard Rorty, "Faith, Responsibility, and Romance," in *The Cambridge Companion to William James*, ed. Ruth Anna Putnam (New York: Cambridge University Press, 1997), 97. The phrase "democratic perfectionism" is adapted from Stanley Cavell's pathbreaking interpretations of "Emersonian perfectionism," which, as a source of inspiration, similarly posits infinitely improveable human selves. See Stanley Cavell, *Conditions Handsome and Unhandsome: The Constitution of Emersonian Perfectionism* (Chicago: University of Chicago Press, 1990).

10. For a contemporary theological exploration of these themes, see Miroslav Volf, *Exclusion and Embrace: A Theological Exploration of Identity, Otherness, and Reconciliation* (Nashville, Tenn.: Abingdon, 1996); see especially his account of human relationality as one of "separating and binding" (66). A classic nineteenth-century "translation" of this theological theme can be found in the title essay in Edward Bellamy, *The Religion of Solidarity* (New York: Concord Grove, 1984), 5–26. This particular theme will be elucidated at much greater length in the chapters that follow.

11. For a representative contemporary example of the kind of recommendation one is likely to encounter, see, for instance, Fred Dallmayr, "Beyond Fugitive Democracy: Some Modern and Postmodern Reflections," in *Democracy and Vision: Sheldon Wolin and the Vicissitudes of the Political*, ed. Aryeh Botwinick and William E. Connolly (Princeton, N.J.: Princeton University Press, 2001), 58–78. See especially, the concluding section, "Toward Transformative Democracy" (69–75), in which Dallmayr recommends "ongoing self-transformation," the "decentering of the ego" by means of "self-transcendence and transformation" (72). On "transformative constitutionalism," see, alternatively, Stephen Macedo, "Transformative Constitutionalism and the Case of Religion: Defending the Moderate Hegemony of Liberalism," in *Constitutional Politics: Essays on Constitution Making, Maintenance, and Change*, ed. Sotirios Barber and Robert P. George (Princeton. N.J.: Princeton University Press, 2001), 167–192; and George Kateb, *The Inner Ocean* (Ithaca, N.Y.: Cornell University Press, 1992), chap. 1.

12. "Democratic cynicism" is increasingly recommended as the preferable dispo-

sition for democrats. While it would appear that we have, in contemporary democracy generally, more than our fair share of cynicism, it is the view of a number of theorists that "cynicism" can clear away our illusions. In fact, "democratic cynicism" is often recommended precisely so that *false* illusions can be overcome and a purified democratic faith can arise in its place. See William Chaloupka, *Everybody Knows: Cynicism in America* (Minneapolis: University of Minnesota Press, 1999), esp. chaps. 15, 16; and Denise E. Dutton, *Holding Out Hope: Cynicism in Democracy*, (Ph.D. dissertation, Princeton University, 2003).

13. This dynamic was noted long ago by Reinhold Niebuhr: "An optimism which depends on the hope of the complete realization of our highest ideals in history is bound to suffer ultimate disillusionment" ("Optimism, Pessimism, and Religious Faith," in *The Essential Reinhold Niebuhr: Selected Essays and Addresses*, ed. Robert McAfee Brown [New Haven: Yale University Press, 1986], 12). The likely outcome of such disillusionment for many is to "try desperately to avoid the abyss of despair by holding to credos which all the facts have disproved" (9). See also Jean Bethke Elshtain's wise caution that "optimism may drive us but it invites unwarranted certainty and, over the long run, is a recipe for cynicism" ("Limits and Hope: Christopher Lasch and Political Theory," *Social Research* 66 [summer, 1999], 542).

14. As Ian Shapiro divides the main camps of democratic theory, there is first a more cynical "aggregative tradition," which is drawn from an incomplete understanding of Rousseau's theory of the "General Will" (as discussed in chapter 5 below), in which "the challenge for democratic theorists as they conceive it is to come up with the right rules to govern the contest"; and, second, a "deliberative" model, which is based on an equally incomplete understanding of Aristotle (as discussed in chapter 3) "in taking the transformative view of human beings," particularly in seeking to "transform interests rather than aggregating them" (*The State of Democratic Theory*, 3, 21). Similarly Margaret Canovan has identified two approaches to democracy that she broadly characterizes as "pragmatic" and "redemptive" and that line up closely to Shapiro's distinction, in her essay "Trust the People! Populism and the Two Faces of Democracy," *Political Studies* 47 (1999): 2–16. In both cases, each neglects the reinforcing dynamic that arises as a result of the interaction between the two extremes, rendering a "realistic" mean increasingly untenable. Arguably the "cynical" (or "pragmatic") and "ideal" (or "redemptive") function as a mutual reinforcing mechanism in which the low expectations, and resulting bleak picture of democratic politics of the "aggregative" model give rise to a roseate view of humanity that informs the "transformative" (or "redemptive") model, the disappointment of which reinforces the cynicism of the "aggregative" model. Shapiro attempts to depart from the implicit dynamic of these two models (which he does not explore) by appealing to a democratic theory of "non-domination," which, in my view, remains rather firmly, albeit with modifications, in the "aggregative" camp.

15. William F. May, President's Council on Bioethics discussion of "The Birth-Mark" by Nathaniel Hawthorne, at http://bioethicsprint.bioethics.gov/transcripts/jan02/jansession2intro.html. This distinction was called to my attention by Michael J. Sandel, "The Case against Perfection," *Atlantic Monthly*, April 2004, 51–62. These discussions center on the ethical issues raised by the possibility of human biological perfectibility by means of genetic manipulation; May and Sandel both object on grounds that this enterprise is driven by the hubristic attempt to overcome the gift of "givenness" by means of complete human mastery over nature. As expressed by May, speaking here of the love of parents for children:

Attachment becomes too quietistic if it slackens into mere acceptance of the child as he is. Love must will the well-being and not merely the being of the other. But attachment lapses into a Gnostic revulsion against the world, if, in the name of well-being, it recoils from the child as it is. Ambitious parents, especially in a meritarian society tend one-sidedly to emphasize the parental role of transforming love. We fiercely demand performance, accomplishments, and results. Sometimes, we behave like the ancient Gnostics who despised the given world, who wrote off the very birth of the world as a catastrophe. We increasingly define and seize upon our children as products to be perfected, flaws to be overcome. And to that degree, we implicitly define ourselves as flawed manufacturers. Implicit in the rejection of the child is self-rejection. We view ourselves as flawed manufacturers rather than imperfect recipients of a gift. Parents find it difficult to maintain an equilibrium between the two sides of love. Accepting love, without transforming love, slides into indulgence and finally neglect. Transforming love, without accepting love, badgers and finally rejects.

16. Canovan, "Trust the People! Populism and the Two Faces of Democracy."

17. Aristotle, *Nicomachean Ethics*, trans. Martin Ostwald (New York: Macmillan, 1962), book 2. See, especially, Aristotle's discussion of the "mean" as comparable to the course taken by Odysseus between the Scylla and Charybdis at 1109: "The first concern of a man who aims at the median should, therefore, be to avoid the extreme which is more opposed to it, as Calypso advises: 'Keep clear your ship of yonder spray and surf.' For one of the two extremes is more in error than the other, and since it is extremely difficult to hit the mean, we must, as the saying has it, sail in the second best way and take the lesser evil; and we can best do that in the manner we have described" (50) (note that Aristotle mistakes Circe's advice as Calypso's). Aristotle recalls that Odysseus does not set sail directly in the middle of the two dangers but rather sails closer to Scylla—who will kill "only" six men—rather than Charybdis, who will destroy the whole ship and whose current is stronger. See Homer, *The Odyssey*, trans. Richmond Lattimore (New York, Harper Collins, 1965), 12.201–259.

18. In this sense, there is an undeniable connection between my conception of "democratic realism" and various articulations of "Augustinian," "Thomistic," or, more generally, Christian realism. For helpful articulations of these theological forms of "realism," see Reinhold Niebuhr, *Christian Realism and Political Problems* (New York: Scribner, 1953); Jean Bethke Elshtain, *Augustine and the Limits of Politics* (Notre Dame, Ind.: University of Notre Dame Press, 1995); James Wetzel, *Augustine and the Limits of Virtue* (New York: Cambridge University Press, 1992); Charles T. Mathewes, *Evil and the Augustinian Tradition* (New York: Cambridge University Press, 2001); and Peter Augustine Lawler, *Postmodernism Rightly Understood* (Lanham, Md.: Rowman and Littlefield, 1999).

19. Plato, *The Republic of Plato*, trans. Allan Bloom (New York: Basic Books, 1968), 369b-372a (Socrates: "a city, as I believe, comes into being because each of us isn't self-sufficient, but is in need of much" [369b]; Aristotle, *Politics*, trans. Peter L. Phillips Simpson (Chapel Hill: The University of North Carolina Press, 1997), 1252a1–1253b40; idem, *Nicomachean Ethics*, 1132b21–1134a16.

20. C. S. Lewis makes the connection between Original Sin and democracy (as the regime that arises from a belief in human equality) explicit: "I am a democrat because I believe in the Fall of Man." See his essay "Equality," in *Present Concerns*, ed. Walter Hooper (New York: Harcourt Brace Javanovich, Publishers, 1986), 17.

21. G. K. Chesterton, *Orthodoxy* (San Francisco: Ignatius, 1908), 52.

22. For a defense of democratic "charity," see Timothy P. Jackson, *The Priority of Love* (Princeton, N.J.: Princeton University Press, 2002); and "Liberalism and Agape: The Priority of Charity to Democracy and Philosophy," *Annual of the Society of Christian Ethics* 13 (1993): 47–72; as well as my discussion in the conclusion of this book.

23. This aspect of the project overlaps considerably with the ambitions of Jeffrey Stout in his recent book *Democracy and Tradition* (Princeton, N.J.: Princeton University Press, 2004), esp. chap. 1. However, Stout writes firmly in the Emersonian "democratic perfectionist" tradition and does not sufficiently appreciate the (in his view, likely unwelcome) chastening resources that might be the result of a more robust engagement with the religious tradition that he hopes to engage in order to revivify a religious Left. In this regard, Stout is overly sanguine that even a religious Left will endorse his form of Emersonian perfectionism. To take one example, David L. Chappell's recent revisionist history of the Civil Rights movement, *Stone of Hope: Prophetic Religion and the Death of Jim Crow* (Chapel Hill: University of North Carolina Press, 2004), suggests that the prime movers in the southern efforts to achieve racial equality were driven by overarching religious and prophetic convictions—ones that rejected any easy acceptance of liberal norms of autonomy—and also suggests that, even where the religious Left and liberal aims overlap, there may continue to be considerable tensions if not outright disagreements. A review critical of Stout's argument on this general point is made by Gilbert Meilander, "Talking Democracy," *First Things* (April 2004): 25–30.

Nevertheless, while Stout correctly acknowledges in passing the potential for a vast chasm between his own Emersonian commitments and less optimistic views of human transformation held by Augustinians, at the same time he also rightly recognizes areas of extensive overlap between the two positions, particularly in their mutual rejection of complacency and their recognition of the "limits of politics" (*Democracy and Tradition*, 39–41).

CHAPTER 1
FAITH IN MAN

1. Nathan Rotenstreich, *On Faith* (Chicago: University of Chicago Press, 1998), 6.

2. I am grateful to Colleen Sheehan for helping me to see this relationship between the ideas and careers of Madison and Hamilton. See her article, "Madison v. Hamilton: The Battle over Republicanism and the Role of Public Opinion," *American Political Science Review* 98 (2004): 405–424.

3. Alexander Hamilton, James Madison, and John Jay, *The Federalist Papers*, ed. Clinton Rossiter (New York: Mentor, 1999), no. 31, 161.

4. *Federalist* 31, 162. It is not surprising that it is Hamilton who endorses the role of reasoned deliberation by the Supreme Court in *Federalist* 78, which was invoked in support of a doctrine of judicial supremacy in *Marbury v. Madison* (1 Cranch 137; 1803).

5. *Federalist* 37, 195–196.

6. Ibid., 195.

7. Ibid., 197. In these passages Madison reveals most clearly the influence of John Witherspoon, in particular, and, more generally, of Calvinism refracted through Scottish Enlightenment theology. On Witherspoon's influence, see Garrett Ward Sheldon, *The Political Philosophy of James Madison* (Baltimore, Md.: The Johns Hopkins Uni-

versity Press, 2001), 10–15, 20–26. See also Jeffry Morrison, "John Witherspoon and 'The Public Interest of Religion,'" *Journal of Church and State* 41, no. 3 (summer 1999): 551–573.

8. *Federalist* 49, 283.

9. Ibid., 55, 310.

10. John Gray, *Two Faces of Liberalism* (New York: New Press, 2000). Gray writes, "Liberalism has always had two faces. From the one side, toleration is the pursuit of an ideal form of life. From the other, it is a search for terms of peace among different ways of life. In the former view, liberal institutions are seen as applications of universal principles. In the latter, they are a means of peaceful coexistence. In the first, liberalism is a prescription for a universal regime. In the second, it is a project of coexistence that can be pursued in many regimes" (2).

11. Ibid., 2. Gray further writes, "For [John] Rawls, as for Ronald Dworkin, F. A. Hayek and Robert Nozick, political philosophy is a branch of the philosophy of law—the branch which concerns justice and fundamental rights. The goal of political philosophy is an ideal constitution, in principle universally applicable, which specifies a fixed framework of basic liberties and human rights" (*Two Faces of Liberalism*, 14).

12. *Federalist* 1, 1.

13. Ibid., 78, 437. Hamilton further notes that courts will be no better than legislatures should they exercise "WILL instead of JUDGMENT" (437). In general, then, the people and their representatives are perceived by Hamilton as a swirling mass of unreflective wills that need the restraining judgment of reflective men. His conception of the polity is akin to an unhealthy version of the Platonic city, in which the "will," or *thumos* ("spirit") is aligned with mere appetites (*epithumetic*), rather than *logistikon* (rationality). In a properly aligned Hamilton regime, the rational rules over the will and the appetites. While Madison dismisses the prospect of a "nation" of philosophers, Hamilton retains a Platonic vision of ideal rule through the courts, a sense that was echoed by Learned Hand when he rejected the idea of judges who would rule as "philosopher-kings." Interestingly Hannah Arendt would alter these senses of "Willing" and "Judging" by means of Kantian emphasis in judgment as a *shared activity* leading to "enlarged mentality," in contrast to the secluded practice stressed by Hamilton.

14. These phrases occur, of course, in Madison's famous *Federalist* 10, pp. 46, 47, 51.

15. See, for example, Hamilton's June 3, 1802, letter to Rufus King, in which he writes "the prospects for our Country are not brilliant. The mass is far from sound. At headquarters a most visionary theory presides. . . . [Yet,] among Federalists old errors are not cured. They also continue to dream though not quite so preposterously as their opponents. 'All will be very well (they say) when the power once more gets back into Federal hands. The people convinced by experience of their error will repose a *permanent* confidence in good men.'" See also Hamilton's July 10, 1804, letter to Theodore Sedgwick, in which he despaired of the current Jeffersonian rule, writing "that Dismemberment of our Empire will be a clear sacrifice of great positive advantages, without any counterbalancing good; administering no relief to our real Disease; which is DEMOCRACY, the poison of which by a subdivision will only be the more concentered in each part, and consequently more virulent" (Hamilton, *Writings* [New York: Library of America, 1979], 993, 1022).

16. Madison to Thomas Jefferson, October 17, 1788. See also "Speech in Con-

gress Proposing Constitutional Amendments," in which he calls them "paper barriers," in James Madison, *Writings* (New York: Library of America, 1999), 420, 446.

17. Madison to Thomas Jefferson, October 17, 1787, in Madison, *Writings*, 421–422.

18. Dworkin's confidence in individual judicial decision making as the most reasonable form of deliberation is expressed most forcefully in his *Law's Empire* (Cambridge, Mass.: Harvard University Press, 1986), particularly in his discussion of the imaginary judge and Justice, Hercules (239–413).

19. See, for instance, Amy Gutmann and Dennis Thompson, *Democracy and Disagreement* (Cambridge, Mass.: Harvard University Press, 1996); John S. Dryzek, *Discursive Democracy: Politics, Policy, and Political Science* (New York: Cambridge University Press, 1990), esp. chap. 1 ("Democratizing Rationality").

20. Gutmann and Thompson write in *Democracy and Disagreement*:

> When Rawls considers how to make the principles of justice more specific, he does not propose that citizens or their representatives discuss moral disagreements about these principles in public forums. Although his theory of constitutional democracy leaves room for such discussion, it emphasizes instead a solitary process of reflection, a kind of private deliberation. He suggests that each of us alone perform an intricate thought experiment in which a veil of ignorance obscures our own personal interests, including our conception of the good life, and compels us to judge on a more impersonal basis. (37)

In my view, Gutmann and Thompson overstate even Rawls's commitment to the idea that *each individual* is expected personally to undergo the thought experiment behind "the veil of ignorance." Just as Locke does not believe that each of us has "consented" to a government in which we happen to be born or even find ourselves traveling through (and hence arrives at a thorny theory of "tacit consent"), so, too, does Rawls's depiction seem to function largely as a justificatory theory by which the "reasonableness" of the conclusions that any person *would* draw from the "original position" are sufficient to legitimate the resulting regime without requiring each individual to undergo the "thought experiment."

21. See Stephen Macedo, *Diversity and Distrust: Civic Education in a Multicultural Democracy* (Cambridge, Mass.: Harvard University Press, 2000), 28–39, for a discussion of Locke's *Letter Concerning Toleration*; see also 173–174 for an endorsement of consent-based social contract theory as "central to liberalism." This view is equally shared by Peter Berkowitz, otherwise a severe critic of liberal "deliberative democrats." See Berkowitz's discussion of Locke's influence on contemporary liberal democratic thinkers in "John Rawls and the Liberal Faith," *Wilson Quarterly* 26 (spring 2002), 60.

22. See Robert Faulkner, "The First Liberal Democrat: Locke's Popular Government," *Review of Politics* 63 (2001): 5–39. See also Michael P. Zuckert, *Natural Rights and the New Republicanism* (Princeton, N.J.: Princeton University Press, 1994), 187–319; and the republican reception of Locke, especially in the *Declaration of Independence*, in Michael P. Zuckert, *The Natural Rights Republic* (South Bend: University of Notre Dame Press, 1996), 10–55, 202–243. While Faulkner and Zuckert speak respectively of democracy and republicanism, each points to a constitutional system of limited government (liberalism) based on ultimate popular sovereignty (democracy). Hence each understands Locke as the originator of liberal democratic thought.

23. John Locke, *The Reasonableness of Christianity as Delivered in the Scriptures*, ed. John C. Higgins-Biddle (Oxford: Clarendon, 1999), chap. 14, 156–157.

24. Ibid., chap. 14, 150, 153, 154. For further analysis of the insufficiency of reason in the thought of Locke (and several other early modern political thinkers), see Joshua Mitchell, *Not By Reason Alone: Religion, History, and Identity in Early Modern Political Thought* (Chicago: University of Chicago Press, 1993), esp. chap. 3 ("Locke: The Dialectic of Clarification and the Politics of Reason"). Based on the state of contemporary ethical theory, one might conclude that Locke was correct, in particular, about reason being insufficient to prevent arguments in favor of infanticide. See the utilitarian arguments in defense of such practices in Peter Singer, *Unsanctifying Human Life* (London: Blackwell, 2002); Helga Kuhse and Peter Singer, *Should the Baby Live?* (New York: Oxford University Press, 1988); and Singer's earlier work, *Practical Ethics* (New York: Cambridge University Press, 1993).

25. Locke, *Reasonableness of Christianity*, chap. 14, 157–158 (emphasis mine).

26. Ibid., chap. 14, 158.

27. John Locke, *A Letter Concerning Toleration*, ed. James H. Tully (Indianapolis: Hackett, 1983), 51.

28. Locke, *Reasonableness of Christianity*, chap. 11, 108–109; chap. 14, 157 n. 2. This view that only a religious or "faithful" people can be trusted extensively with democratic self-governance is hardly one that lacks further articulation. See, for example, Gregory Vlastos, *Christian Faith and Democracy* (New York: Association Press, 1939); Yves Simon, *Philosophy of Democratic Government* (Chicago: University of Chicago Press, 1951); John Hallowell, *The Moral Foundation of Democracy* (Chicago: University of Chicago Press, 1954); Claes Ryn, *Democracy and the Ethical Life* (Washington, D.C.: Catholic University Press, 1990); Christopher Wolfe, *Essays on Faith and Liberal Democracy* (Lanham, Md.: University Press of America, 1987); Tage Lindom, *The Myth of Democracy* (Grand Rapids, Mich.: Eerdmans, 1996).

29. Stephen Macedo, who otherwise readily endorses the "partialities" of Locke that are viewed as necessary supports to a liberal regime (and potentially as objectionable to libertarians, who believe that the state should be impartial in all matters, including toward liberalism itself), revealingly rejects Locke's exclusion of atheists *in a footnote*:

> Locke also argues, famously but not convincingly, that atheists should not be tolerated because they cannot be trusted to abide by "promises, covenants and oaths, which are the bonds of human society." Nearly everyone in Locke's day, and many thereafter, believed that divine punishment was a crucial motive for good conduct. (*Diversity and Distrust*, 287 n. 44)

(Curiously Macedo does not mention Locke's accompanying exclusion of Catholics, since much of Macedo's book is directed toward excluding Catholic arguments as objectionable to "public reason." Since Macedo at least does not call for the exile of Catholics, in this respect as well, Macedo—if only tacitly—also "liberalizes" Locke.) But rejecting solely this one element of Locke's argument, namely, the exclusion of atheists, as mere historical epiphenomenon, Macedo—and deliberative democrats generally—avoid the sticky issue of motivations and obligation, and hence permit themselves more extensive faith in the domain and effectiveness of reason than even Locke permits himself.

30. Gutmann and Thompson approvingly cite Mill, among other places in *Democracy and Disagreement* on page 42.

31. Gutmann and Thompson, *Democracy and Disagreement*, 16.

32. Stephen Macedo, "Transformative Constitutionalism and the Case of Religion: Defending the Moderate Hegemony of Liberalism," in *Constitutional Politics:*

Essays on Constitution Making, Maintenance, and Change, ed. Sotirios Barber and Robert P. George (Princeton, N.J.: Princeton University Press, 2001) 167–192. Macedo speaks of the "transformative" nature of liberalism on pages 167–169, 171–174. In a different register, but with similar assumptions, see George Kateb, *The Inner Ocean: Individualism and Democratic Culture* (Ithaca, N.Y.: Cornell University Press, 1992).

33. Gutmann and Thompson, *Democracy and Disagreement*, 79.

34. Macedo, "Transformative Constitutionalism," 179.

35. See Stephen L. Carter, *The Culture of Disbelief: How American Law and Politics Trivialize Religious Devotion* (New York: Basic Books, 1993).

36. Stephen Macedo is more forceful than most "deliberative democrats" in his insistence that the arguments of some groups should be politically marginalized on the basis of the strictures of "public reason": "Some groups have been pushed to the margins of society for good reason, and the last thing we want is a politics of indiscriminate inclusion." Among those groups he names as meriting possible exclusion are "Nazis, fundamentalists, even the Amish," although lurking implicitly on this list are Catholics, about whom much of the book is written and whose educational justifications of the last century he rejects. Common to all these groups to which he would not extend political recognition or legal accommodation is a rejection of at least some fundamental liberal credos that are deemed incontrovertible to "reasonable" people, including "broad individual freedoms, the rule of law, constitutionally limited government, representative democracy, and capitalism." See Macedo, *Diversity and Distrust*, 24, 25, 276. Substantial portions of Gutmann and Thompson's *Democracy and Disagreement* and Macedo's *Diversity and Distrust* are devoted to discussions of court cases. See also Christopher H. Schroeder, "Deliberative Democracy's Attempt to Turn Politics into Law," *Law and Contemporary Problems* 65 (summer 2002): 95–132.

37. Stanley Fish has perceptively analyzed how liberalism defines "public reason" and reasonableness in ways that privilege liberal priorities of autonomy, choice, and a profound mistrust of religious believers in *The Trouble with Principle* (Cambridge, Mass.: Harvard University Press, 1999).

38. See Christopher Eisgruber's argument that constitutional restrictions upon majoritarianism are to be understood as "democratic," in *Constitutional Self-Government* (Cambridge, Mass.: Harvard University Press, 2001).

39. John Rawls, *Political Liberalism* (New York: Columbia University Press, 1993), 217 (emphasis mine).

40. Madison writes that representation will "refine and enlarge the public views by passing them through a chosen body of citizens, whose wisdom may best discern the true interest of their country" (*Federalist* no. 10, 50).

41. Discussing Amy Gutmann's preference for elite-imposed desegregation policies over local control of school districts, Christopher Lasch observed that Gutmann "chooses liberalism over democracy, while clinging to the hope that it is unnecessary to make that choice." Given the preponderance of evidence of the juridical bent of elite liberal rule, Lasch may have overstated the apparent ambivalence of thinkers like Gutmann. See Christopher Lasch, *The True and Only Heaven: Progress and Its Critics* (New York: Norton, 1991), 567. See also Peter Berkowitz, "The Debating Society," *New Republic,* November 25, 1996, 36–42. Discussing Gutmann and Thompson's *Democracy and Disagreement*, Berkowitz writes: "What remains curious, though, is just how much of their own deliberation—the refinement of com-

monly held opinions, the intricate reasoning from distilled moral principles, the sifting and weighing of the latest social science research—takes place without the actual involvement of fellow citizens, in the comfort of the study and the congenial climate of the seminar room; and to what extent the legitimacy of the substantive conclusions Gutmann and Thompson reach is, from the perspective of their own principles, independent of whether their fellow citizens can be persuaded to endorse them" (36).

42. It can be positively chilling to hear the constant use of "we" when "deliberative democrats" deliberate together about the fate of the polity. Presumably the "we" is intended to encompass all reasonable people who are implicitly engaged in an effort to forge the guiding principles of a "reasonable" liberal polity, but its constant use—often invoked in the explicit effort to exclude the "unreasonable"—appears to encompass only the academic elite who are participating in that particular conversation. For a characteristic example of this usage of the liberal "we," see Macedo, "Transformative Constitutionalism." For example, "when the consequences [of decisions by the moderate liberal hegemony] are unhappy, we may have grounds for accommodation" (186). "We" will decide.

43. Macedo, *Diversity and Distrust*, 276.

44. Robert Merrihew Adams, "Moral Faith," *Journal of Philosophy* 92 (February 1995): 77.

45. Peter Berkowitz perceptively reminds us of the extent to which such contemporary deliberative theorists rest on Kantian assumptions but stop short of recognizing Kant's insistence that morality is inconceivable without the existence of a belief in God. See Immanuel Kant, *Critique of Practical Reason*, trans. Lewis White Beck (New York: Macmillan, 1956), chap. 2, esp. sec. 4. See also Kant's *Religion within the Limits of Reason Alone* (New York: Harper and Row, 1960). In his "Preface to the First Edition," Kant writes: "For its own sake morality does not need a religion at all . . .; by virtue of pure practical reason it is self-sufficient" (3). Yet, when considering the *end* toward which such morality is undertaken, Kant maintains that one must conceive "the idea of a highest good in the world for whose possibility we must postulate a higher, moral, most holy, and omnipotent Being which alone can unite the two elements of the highest good. . . . Viewed practically, this idea is not an empty one, for it does meet our natural need to conceive of some sort of end for all our actions and abstentions, taken as a whole, an end which can be justified by reason and the absence of which would be a hindrance to moral decision" (4–5). In other words, Kant, even more strongly than Locke, suggests that reason would be sufficient to determine moral behavior but of itself would be insufficient to justify acting in such a manner in the absence of a more comprehensive and divine conception of ends. Christine M. Korsgaard has sought to show the rational basis of Kant's conception of the ends of morality but has revealingly concluded that even such a "religion of reason" needs to rest on "an optimism based on a moral faith in humanity" (*Creating the Kingdom of Ends* [New York: Cambridge University Press, 1996], 27, 35).

46. Macedo, *Diversity and Distrust*, 279. Rogers Smith also concludes his magisterial study of American citizenship with an invocation of the same phrase, in *Civic Ideals: Conflicting Visions of Citizenship in U.S. History* (New Haven: Yale University Press, 1997), 502. Both draw the phrase from John Stuart Mill, *On Liberty*, in *Utilitarianism, On Liberty and Considerations on Representative Government*, ed. H. B. Acton (London: J. M. Dent, 1972).

47. Chantal Mouffe, *The Democratic Paradox* (New York: Verso, 2000), 49;

idem, *The Return of the Political* (New York: Verso, 1993), 4. Cf. also Bonnie Honig, *Political Theory and the Displacement of Politics* (Ithaca: Cornell University Press, 1993), 15; Bickford, *The Dissonance of Democracy: Listening, Conflict, and Citizenship* (Ithaca, N.Y.: Cornell University Press, 1996), 38, 41 (dissonance resembles more a symphony by Ives than the cacophony of a high-school band before the band teacher enters). Honig, for example, describes action as "boundless, excessive, uncontrollable, unpredictable and self-surprising" (119). Elsewhere, however, she notes that conflict ultimately occurs "within an ordered setting," thus, in a typical move, setting democratic boundaries around the threatening features of Arendtian "action" (15).

48. Mouffe writes that "for democracy to exist, no social agent should be able to claim any mastery of the *foundation* of society" (*The Democratic Paradox*, 21).Yet, she also writes that democracy is a "passionate commitment to a system of reference. Hence, although it's *belief*, it is really a way of living, or of assessing one's life" (98; emphasis mine).

49. Mark Warren, "Democratic Theory and Self-Transformation," *American Political Science Review* 86 (March 1992): 8.

50. Benjamin R. Barber, "Reductionist Political Science and Democracy," in *Reconsidering the Democratic Public*, ed. George E. Marcus and Russell L. Hanson, 65–72 (University Park: Pennsylvania State University Press, 1993), 69.

51. Benjamin R. Barber, *Strong Democracy: Participatory Politics for a New Age* (Berkeley: University of California Press, 1984), 93–98; 221–222.

52. Ibid., 223.

53. Several thinkers seek to differentiate Barber from Arendt on the grounds that Barber's version of strong democracy appears to result in a greater sense of common good than Arendt's version suggests; for example, Lisa Jane Disch, *Hannah Arendt and the Limits of Philosophy* (Ithaca, N.Y.: Cornell University Press, 1994), 218–219; Bickford, *The Dissonance of Democracy*, 12–14. While this may be the case, in my view this is more a difference of emphasis than significant disagreement. For example, critics who note that Barber recommends the role of "empathy" in politics whereas Arendt explicitly rejects it otherwise overlook Barber's insistence that the self is not lost (Barber, *Strong Democracy*, 224, 225–229, 232), just as they also overlook their common recommendation of the role of "imagination" in the transformation of selves. Indeed, it seems to me that Barber's critics overstate the extent to which Arendt appears to embrace thoroughgoing agonism (here I agree with Dana R. Villa, *Politics, Philosophy, Terror: Essays on the Thought of Hannah Arendt* [Princeton, N.J.: Princeton University Press, 1999], chap. 5) and overlook even those occasions when Barber has been critical of Arendt's temptations for "Kantian" purity in politics. See Barber, *The Conquest of Politics: Liberal Philosophy in Democratic Times* (Princeton, N.J.: Princeton University Press, 1988), chap. 8, esp. 198.

54. In addition to Lisa Jane Disch, *Hannah Arendt and the Limits of Philosophy* (Ithaca, N.Y.: Cornell University Press, 1994) and Bickford, *The Dissonance of Democracy*, see, especially, Honig, *Displacement of Politics*, chap. 4 (notably Honig states that her discussion of Arendt represents "the spiritual and conceptual center of this book" [10]), as well as Mark Reinhart, *The Art of Being Free: Taking Liberties with Tocqueville, Marx and Arendt* (Ithaca, N.Y.: Cornell University Press, 1997), chap. 5. Unsurprisingly, while Arendt is admired in certain respects by George Kateb, he is finally critical of her commendation of the Greek concept of "action" as well as her lack of estimation for representative democracy. See Kateb, *Hannah*

Arendt: Politics, Conscience, Evil (Totowa, N.J.: Rowman and Allanheld, 1983), chaps. 1, 4.

55. Reinhart, *The Art of Being Free*, 143.

56. See the following works by Arendt: *Lectures on Kant's Political Philosophy,* ed. Ronald Beiner (Chicago: University of Chicago Press, 1992); "The Crisis in Culture" and "Truth and Politics" in *Between Past and Future: Eight Exercises in Political Thought* (New York: Penguin, 1977); "On Humanity in Dark Times: Thoughts about Lessing," in idem, *Men in Dark Times* (New York: Harcourt, Brace and World, 1968); and *The Human Condition*, 2nd ed. (Chicago: University of Chicago Press, 1998). See also Ronald Beiner, "Interpretive Essay," in Arendt, *Lectures on Kant's Political Philosophy;* and *Political Judgment* (London: Methuen, 1983).

57. Arendt, "The Crisis in Culture," 220; idem, "Truth and Politics," 242.

58. Arendt, "The Crisis in Culture," 221.

59. Arendt, "Truth and Politics," 242; Disch, *Hannah Arendt and the Limits of Philosophy*, 161–171. Arendt confirms that her conception of "impartiality" is not to be confused with a decontextualized form of impartiality defended in liberal thought, one in which decisions are held to be universally valid and always reproducible regardless of circumstance or specific persons rendering judgment. Instead, in Arendt's view, "judgment is endowed with a certain specific validity but is never universally valid. Its claims to validity can never extend further than the others in whose place the judging person has put himself for his considerations" ("The Crisis in Culture," 221).

60. Arendt, "Truth and Politics," 241.

61. Disch nicely characterizes Arendt's theory of judgment to be analogous to a form of mental "visiting" (*Hannah Arendt and the Limits of Philosophy*, chap. 5); Arendt, "Truth and Politics," 241.

62. Arendt, "The Crisis in Culture," 220.

63. Arendt, "Truth and Politics," 241, 242.

64. Honig, *Displacement of Politics*, 65; Richard Rorty, *Contingency, Irony, and Solidarity* (New York: Cambridge University Press, 1989), 61.

65. William E. Connolly, *Why I Am Not a Secularist* (Minneapolis: University of Minnesota Press, 1999), 8, 10. See also idem, *The Ethos of Pluralization* (Minneapolis: University of Minnesota Press, 1995).

66. This assumption is quite extraordinary. As Dana Villa notes, "the problem is that this version of agonistic politics presupposes a culture in which no individual's or group's 'fundamental position' is *fundamental* in the sense that it is a truth which stands in irreconcilable conflict with other ultimate values." Conflict over such fundamentals, which seems to be the core activity of human life to be defended by "agonistic" democrats, rather oddly "ceases to be a problem." See Dana R. Villa, "Democratizing the Agon: Nietzsche, Arendt, and the Agonistic Tendency in Recent Political Theory," in idem, *Politics, Philosophy, Terror: Essays on the Thought of Hannah Arendt* (Princeton, N.J.: Princeton University Press, 1999), 121.

67. Among Arendt's last writings she notes that the creation of a "We" is "shrouded in darkness and mystery" and results in "the predicament of not-knowing." See Arendt, *The Life of the Mind, Willing* Vol. 2 (New York: Harcourt, Brace, Jovanovich, 1978), 202.

68. Sheldon S. Wolin, "Fugitive Democracy," in *Democracy and Difference*, ed. Seyla Benhabib (Princeton, N.J.: Princeton University Press, 1996): 31–45. It is undoubtedly problematic to place Wolin among the company of self-professed "ago-

nistic democrats," particularly inasmuch in this essay Wolin puts himself at distance from postmodernist sensibility with its stress on "difference" and diversity, instead defining "the political" as "a free society composed of diversities [that] can nonetheless enjoy moments of commonality when, through public deliberations, collective power is used to promote or protect the well-being of the collectivity" (31). While some self-professed "agonistic democrats" take issue with Wolin's emphasis upon the "common" and "collective" in his definition of "the political," even those critics seek to elucidate how Wolin's conception shares fundamental likenesses with the "agonistic" model. See, for instance, William Connolly, "Politics and Vision," in *Democracy and Vision: Sheldon Wolin and the Vicissitudes of the Political*, ed. Aryeh Botwinick and William E. Connolly (Princeton, N.J.: Princeton University Press, 2001), 3–22. Wolin still maintains that democracy is arrayed against various other collective interests (oligarchic and aristocratic) within the polity, and thus has an inescapably "agonistic" feature (even if there seems to be the suggestion that by means of struggle *against* antidemocratic forces, differences between and among the *demos* are overcome. Democracy based implicitly upon a commonness forged of the consensus that "the enemy of my enemy is my friend" suggests further reason why democracy is unsustainable in Wolin's view).

69. Wolin, "Fugitive Democracy," 39.

70. Ibid., 43.

71. Connolly, "Politics and Vision," 13.

72. George Kateb, "Wolin as a Critic of Democracy," in Botwinick and Connolly, *Democracy and Vision*, 39, 40, 47. In particular, Kateb reflects that "I cannot help thinking that the death of the student movement of the 1960s has sharpened Wolin's despair lastingly" (40).

73. Ibid., 47, 48.

74. George Sidney Camp, *Democracy* (New York: Harpers and Brothers, 1845).

75. Chapter 1 of part 2 of Camp's *Democracy* is entitled "The Alleged Tyranny of the Majority in America."

76. Camp, *Democracy*, 11. It is peculiar that a study which culminates in an attempted refutation of a "tyranny of the majority" should begin with a frank acknowledgment of its existence.

77. Ibid., 12–13.

78. Ibid., 20.

79. Walt Whitman, "Perpetuity of the Democratic Spirit," in *The Gathering of Forces*, ed. Cleveland Rogers and John Black, 2 vols. (New York: Putnam's Sons, 1920), 1:7.

80. Walt Whitman, "American Democracy," in Rogers and Black, *The Gathering of Forces* (April 20, 1847), 1:4–5.

81. Walt Whitman, *Democratic Vistas*, in *The Portable Walt Whitman*, ed. Mark Van Doren (New York: Penguin, 1973), 365. Elsewhere Whitman cites the need for democratic poets to restore "Faith . . . with new sway, deeper, wider, higher than ever." This ambition, he states, is in keeping with "Hegelian formulas" (376).

82. Herbert Croly, *The Promise of American Life*, ed. Arthur M. Schlesinger Jr. (Cambridge, Mass.: Harvard University Press, 1965 [1909]), 451, 452, 453, 454.

83. Herbert Croly, *Progressive Democracy* (New Brunswick, N.J.: Transaction, 1998 [1914]), 168, 191.

84. Anonymous, "The Confession of an Educator," *New Repubic*, April 18, 1926, 356.

85. Anon., "The Confession of an Educator," 356.

86. Ibid., 358.

87. For a superb examination of the assault of behavioralism on democratic "ideology," see Edward A. Purcell Jr., *The Crisis of Democratic Theory: Scientific Naturalism and the Problem of Value* (Lexington: University Press of Kentucky, 1973), esp. chap. 6. Many of the following references came to my attention through Purcell's meticulous scholarship. Purcell, however, does not particularly attend to or emphasize the continual invocation of "democratic faith" and its wider significance to democratic theory. Also helpful is Bernard Crick, *The American Science of Politics: Its Origins and Conditions* (Berkeley: University of California Press, 1964); David Ricci, *The Tragedy of Political Science: Politics, Scholarship, and Democracy* (New Haven: Yale University Press, 1984); Robert B. Westbrook, *John Dewey and American Democracy* (Ithaca, N.Y.: Cornell University Press, 1991), 275–318; and Roderick Nash, *The Nervous Generation: American Thought, 1917–1930* (Chicago: Rand McNally, 1970), chap. 3 ("Intellectuals: A Lost Generation?"), esp. 55–67.

88. Walter J. Shepard, "Democracy in Transition," *American Political Science Review* 29 (February 1935): 2, 3–4.

89. Ibid., 7, 9, 12.

90. Ibid., 16–17, 18–19, 20.

91. Charles E. Merriam's *New Aspects of Politics* (Chicago: University of Chicago Press, 1925), although measured, concludes by raising questions about the nature of "mass rule" in light of social scientific findings that indicate widespread irrationality (345–349); Harold F. Gosnell, "Some Practical Applications of Psychology in Government," *American Journal of Sociology* 28 (May 1923); Harold D. Lasswell, in *Psychopathology and Politics* (New York: Viking, 1930), writes that "the findings of personality research show that the individual is a poor judge of his own interest" (194); Elton Mayo, "The Irrational Factor in Human Behavior: The 'Night-Mind' in Industry," *Annals of the American Academy of Political and Social Science* 110 (November 1923); William McDougall's *Is America Safe for Democracy?* (New York: Scribner's, 1921) begins, "As I watch the American nation speeding gaily, with invincible optimism, down the road to destruction, I seem to be contemplating the greatest tragedy in the history of mankind" (v), and concludes, "Our aim in general must be to favor increase of the birth-rate among the intrinsically better part of the population, and its decrease among the inferior part" (192); Robert S. Lynd, in *Knowledge for What? The Place of Social Science in American Culture* (Princeton, N.J.: Princeton University Press, 1939), questions the strength and basis of American democratic forms in the face of the threats of fascism and communism (and finds Stalin more attractive than Hitler or American democracy (212 n. 4), and states "our present culture's false reliance upon the rational omni-competence of the adult tends to cramp the deep, vital spontaneities by institutionalizing superficial whims, and to institutionalize reckless irrationality in the name of rationality as 'the American Way'" (235); Harry Elmer Barnes, *History and Social Intelligence* (New York: Knopf, 1926); and idem, "Some Contributions of Sociology to Modern Political Theory," in *History of Political Theories*, ed. Charles E. Merriam and Harry Elmer Barnes (New York: Macmillan, 1924). In the latter, Barnes argues that social science has proven "the old Aristotelian dogma that some men are born to rule and others to serve" (373). In this same work, see the discussion by Malcolm M. Willey of Dartmouth College, which concludes, "an embalmed democracy deserves burial" (79). For an extensive description of these and similar claims throughout the social scientific profession, see Purcell, *The Crisis of Democratic Theory*, chap. 6.

92. William F. Willoughby, "A Program for Research in Political Science," *American Political Science Review* 27 (February 1933): 3–4.

93. While influential, rejection of the democratic faith was not universal, and found one center of resistance in the Department of Politics at Princeton University. Edward Corwin—himself a past president of the APSA who preceded Willoughby—repudiated these attacks on democratic faith and urged a recommitment to "democratic dogma." Defending especially "the most fundamental assumption of the democratic dogma," namely, that the people "know their own good and act upon their knowledge, and so know the most widely spread public good," Corwin rejected the most negative interpretations concerning American voting behavior. Apparent disinterestedness or apathy among American voters was not a sign of their indifference to democracy but rather a high compliment to their satisfaction with the system. Corwin insisted on these conclusions because of his adherence to the most fundamental article of "democratic dogma": the overarching rationality of individual citizens. Accusing the new social science's "disparagement of reason" as nothing more than a "species of religion," Corwin implied that, given a choice between contemporary dogmas, he would profess democratic faith. See Edward S. Corwin, "The Democratic Dogma and the Future of Political Science," *American Political Science Review* 23 (August 1929): 570, 571, 576–577. See also the resistance to contemporary social science by Corwin's Princeton colleague Alpheas T. Mason, "Politics: Science or Art? *Southwestern Social Science Quarterly* 16 (December 1935): 1–15.

94. Charles E. Merriam, *The New Democracy and the New Despotism* (New York: Whittlesey House, 1939), 11, 8.

95. Francis O. Wilcox, "Teaching Political Science in a World at War," *American Political Science Review* 35 (April 1941): 325, 327.

96. Ibid., 333.

97. Peter H. Odegard, "Book Reviews and Notices," *American Political Science Review* (December 1941): 1161.

98. There have been only a few isolated instances in which scholars in the post–World War II era have claimed explicitly to lose faith in democracy, although such doubts take less the guise of older accusations against democracy's insufficiencies or inescapable flaws than accusations against democracy for failing to live up to its own promise. As such, they resemble more the critiques of Maritain than the attacks of Nietzsche (both regarding the legitimacy of religion and democracy) and, instead, take the form of accusations that seek to be proven wrong. For example, see Susan Mendus, "Losing the Faith: Feminism and Democracy," in *Democracy: The Unfinished Journey, 508 B.C. to A.D. 1993*, ed. John Dunn (New York: Oxford University Press, 1992). Mendus differentiates between the promise of equality in democratic theory and shortcomings in reality, and argues that "democratic faith" has always been manifested in the belief that the latter could be brought to conform to the former. However, echoing many feminist critiques of prevailing forms of democratic theory, Mendus questioned whether even the theory deserved the "faith" that was accorded it. While she claims that "the faith is giving out" for many feminists, she concludes by suggesting feminist revisions to democratic theory that can thereby renew "the faith to which feminists now cling" (208, 219).

99. Russell L. Hanson and George E. Marcus, "Introduction: The Practice of Democratic Theory," in *Reconsidering the Democratic Public*, ed. George E. Marcus and Russell L. Hanson (University Park: Pennsylvania State University Press, 1993), 5.

100. Marcus and Hanson, *Reconsidering the Democratic Public*, 2.

101. An exception proves the rule. Robert P. Kraynak has recently taken modern democratic suppositions to task in his book *Christian Faith and Modern Democracy: God and Politics in a Fallen World* (South Bend: University of Notre Dame Press, 2001). Writing explicitly as a Catholic political theorist, he proposes a return to the guiding Augustinian doctrine of the "Two Cities" which recognizes justice to be the object of the City of God, not the City of Man. Given that stability and piety, and not justice, is the appropriate goal of earthly regimes, he proposes the return of a form of aristocratic constitutionalism. One suspects that Kraynak will find few sympathizers in contemporary America or elsewhere, a suspicion Kraynak ruefully shares. See my review in *Commonweal* (October 26, 2001): 26–28.

102. H. Richard Niebuhr, *Faith on Earth: An Inquiry into the Structure of Human Faith*, ed. Richard R. Niebuhr (New Haven: Yale University Press, 1989), 22.

103. Ibid., 22.

104. Margaret Canovan's article "Trust the People! Populism and the Two Faces of Democracy," *Political Studies* 47 (1999): 2–16, is largely enlightening on the distinction that can be drawn between the "pragmatic" and "redemptive" schools of democratic theory but, in reference to American pragmatism properly, proves unfortunately obfuscatory. This is because, as this chapter and book go on to argue, American "pragmatism"—as one expression of Progressivism more generally—consistently articulates a strong version of "redemptive" democratic faith. Indeed, it is precisely to the same somewhat "secularized" religious language to which American pragmatists consistently appeal in their own defense of a "faith in secular redemption" (Canovan, "Trust the People!" 11).

105. Wilcox, "Teaching Political Science in a World at War," 329.

106. On the "democratization" of American culture, roughly from the Jacksonian period—including the Civil War period—until the Progressive era, see, inter alia, Robert H. Wiebe, *Self-Rule: A Cultural History of American Democracy* (Chicago: University of Chicago Press, 1995); Russell L. Hanson, *The Democratic Imagination in America: Conversations with Our Past* (Princeton, N.J.: Princeton University Press, 1985); James A. Morone, *The Democratic Wish: Popular Participation and the Limits of Government* (New York: Basic Books, 1990); Andrew Burstein, *Sentimental Democracy: The Evolution of America's Romantic Self-Image* (New York: Hill and Wang, 1999); and Kevin Mattson, *Creating a Democratic Public* (University Park: Pennsylvania State University Press, 1998). Louis Menand, in *The Metaphysical Club* (New York: Farrar Strauss and Giroux), describes the concomitant rise of pragmatism during this time.

107. Jerome Nathanson, *Forerunners of Freedom: The Re-creation of the American Spirit* (Washington, D.C.: American Council on Public Affairs, 1941). An explanatory note at the front of the book about the American Council on Public Affairs reads:

> Dedicated to the belief that the extensive diffusion of information is a profound responsibility of American democracy, the American Council on Public Affairs is designed to promote the spread of authoritative facts and significant opinions concerning contemporary social and economic problems.

Here one sees displayed the assumption that "facts" are seamlessly supportive of democratic ends.

108. Nathanson, *Forerunners of Freedom*, 151. The citation of Dewey is from *The*

Philosophy of the Common Man: Essays in Honor of John Dewey to Celebrate His Eightieth Birthday. (New York: Putnam's, 1940), 224 [cited in Nathanson, *Forerunners of Freedom,* 151], subsequently republished as "Creative Democracy—The Task ahead of Us."

109. I am grateful to Jeffrey Stout for elucidating the importance of this difference, in a conversation.

110. Raziel Abelson, "The Logic of Faith and Belief," in *Religious Experience and Truth: A Symposium,* ed. Sidney Hook (New York: New York University Press, 1961), 125.

111. Ibid., 123.

112. Ibid., 120.

113. William James, "The Will to Believe," in *William James: Writings 1878– 1899,* ed. Gerald E. Myers (New York: Library of America, 1992), 477 n. 4.

114. W. James, preface to "The Will to Believe," 450. See James, "The Will to Believe," 457–458, for a further emphasis on the hypothetical nature of faith.

115. This is also Alexis de Tocqueville's point in *Democracy in America,* trans. George Lawrence, ed. J. P. Mayer (New York: Harper and Row, 1969), II.1.i, in which he states than even most philosophers must base most of their daily actions upon faith.

116. James, "The Will to Believe," 474.

117. W. James, "Is Life Worth Living?" in Myers, *William James: Writings, 1878– 1899,* 500.

118. W. James, "The Energies of Men," in *William James: Writings, 1902–1910,* ed. Bruce Kuklick (New York: Library of America, 1987), 1236. While James often was prone to deny the influence of Hegel, one nevertheless cannot but help to detect a certain Hegelianism in a subsequent statement: "Our philosophic and religious development proceeds thus by credulities, negations, and the negating of negations" (1236).

119. James, "Is Life Worth Living?" 502.

120. W. James, "Pragmatism," in Kuklick, *William James: Writings, 1902–1910,* 612.

121. James, "Is Life Worth Living?" 502.

122. William James, "Robert Gould Shaw: Oration by Professor William James," in *The Works of William James: Essays in Religion and Morality* ed. Frederick H. Burkhardt (Cambridge, Mass.: Harvard University Press, 1982).

123. W. James, "What Makes A Life Significant," in Myers, *William James: Writings, 1878–1899,* 868

124. W. James, "The Social Value of the College-Bred," in *William James: Writings, 1902–1910,* 1245–1246.

125. Michael Oakeshott, *The Politics of Faith and the Politics of Scepticism* (New Haven: Yale University Press, 1996), 26, 55, 23. Oakeshott attributes the origins of the "politics of faith" to Francis Bacon (52–57), much as Dewey recognizes Bacon's formative influence in his own thought in *Reconstruction in Philosophy,* and Rorty as a fundamental source in, among other places, *Consequences of Pragmatism (Essays: 1972–1980)* (Minneapolis: University of Minnesota Press, 1982), xvii.

126. Oakeshott, *The Politics of Faith and the Politics of Scepticism,* 30–38. Oakeshott refers briefly to a contemporary faith in democracy as one form of "the politics of faith," although he does not consider its particular manifestation or implications at any length (130–132).

127. Oakeshott composes an "ill-assorted gallery" of the "politically skeptical,"

which, in addition to including the likes of Augustine and Pascal, also includes Spinoza, Hobbes, Bentham, and the Federalists. See Oakeshott, *The Politics of Faith and the Politics of Scepticism*, 80–81, 129.

CHAPTER 2
DEMOCRATIC TRANSFORMATION

1. A characteristic simultaneous expression of "faith" in the people, coupled with severe disillusionment with people as they are and confidence in the prospects for full-scale societal transformation, is expressed by Walt Whitman in "Democratic Vistas," in *The Portable Walt Whitman*, ed. Mark Van Doren (New York: Penguin, 1973). On this apparent conundrum, see Richard J. Ellis, *The Dark Side of the Left: Illiberal Egalitarianism in America* (Lawrence: University Press of Kansas, 1998), 73–80.

2. Such assumptions echo those of Thomas Paine, who held that natural "society" was the locale of "natural democracy," in contrast to the repression that humans experienced by the "State." See Sheldon S. Wolin, *Tocqueville: Between Two Worlds* (Princeton, N.J.: Princeton University Press, 2001), 53.

3. Despite the many invocations of "democratic faith" that one can locate, especially in the American setting, few dwell at any length on what are the core tenets of that faith. Of those few there is one notable example that affords a more explicit investigation of the contours of democratic faith that, upon reflection and analysis, hold up remarkably well as a preliminary description of the faith. Completed in 1939—the same year the democratic faith found renewed devotion among social scientists in the wake of the Nazi invasion of Poland—and published in 1940, with subsequent editions published in 1956 and 1986, Ralph Henry Gabriel's introductory text, *The Course of American Democratic Thought*, is centrally devoted to an explicit exploration of the American democratic faith, and represents one of the more sustained analyses of the elusive concept.

Gabriel offers three basic features of "democratic faith," which I have revised somewhat so that they may be applied more broadly and even universally to manifestations of "democratic faith" both within and outside the American setting. Thus my distillations were initially drawn from, and continue to resemble, Gabriel's three "doctrines" of American democratic faith in their broad outline. The third "tenet" is drawn from Gabriel's conclusion of how his three doctrines culminate in an optimistic portrait of human potency, reflected especially in the scientific enterprise. His explicit renderings are:

1. "the free individual," supremely capable of self-governance owing to "the progress of men in apprehending and translating into individual and social action the eternal principles which compromise the moral law"
[This first feature echoes my own discussion of the first tenet of "democratic faith" in the previous chapter, the belief in human democratic potential];

2. a "frank supernaturalism derived from Christianity": "The basic postulate of the democratic faith affirmed that God, the creator of man, has also created a moral law for his government and has endowed him with a conscience with which to apprehend it. Underneath and supporting human society, as the basic rock supports the hills, is a moral order which is the abiding place of the eternal principles of truth and righteousness";

2_2. related to this last is a belief in "the mission of America": "the belief that democracy will give life to an oppressed and suffering world . . . [and] that it is the mission of the United States to cherish and to hold steadfastly before the peoples of the earth the ideal of the free and self-governing individual";

[These combine and anticipate my discussion of one "means" of democratic transformation, namely, the means of "civil religion"]; and

3. "The democratic faith . . . proclaims that, within broad limits of an ordered nature, man is the master of his destiny."

[This last feature anticipates my discussion of the role of science—an inheritance of a beneficent deity or universe—in contributing to the democratic transformation of individuals.]

See Ralph Henry Gabriel, *The Course of American Democratic Thought: An Intellectual History since 1815* (New York: Ronald Press, 1940), 19, 14, 22, 24, 418.

4. Emile Durkheim, *The Elementary Forms of the Religious Life*, trans. Joseph Ward Swain (New York: Macmillan, 1915), 10, 1–20.

5. Ibid., 223, 419. See also Michael W. Hughey, *Civil Religion and the Moral Order* (Westport, Conn.: Greenwood, 1983), 15.

6. Durkheim, *The Elementary Forms of Religious Life*, 209.

7. Ibid., 210. Cf.: "It may be objected that science is often the antagonist of opinion, whose errors it combats and rectifies. But it cannot succeed in this task if it does not have sufficient authority, and it can obtain this authority only from opinion itself. If a people did not have faith in science, all the scientific demonstrations in the world would be without any influence whatsoever over their minds" (208; see also 427–439).

8. Ibid., 230.

9. Ibid., 230–231.

10. Ibid., 229, 226.

11. For an example of this transformation of the language of civil religion in a political direction, see Edward Bellamy, *The Religion of Solidarity* (New York: Concord Grove, 1984), 5–26. Durkheim notes that many of the world's religions do not require a belief in the "divine" as such but rather rest most fundamentally on the distinction between and the separation of the "sacred" and the "profane" (*The Elementary Forms of Religious Life*, 37, 40–41).

12. See, for example, Benjamin R. Barber, "How Swiss Was Rousseau?" *Political Theory* 13 (1985): 475–495.

13. Bonnie Honig, *Political Theory and the Displacement of Politics* (Ithaca: Cornell University Press, 1993), 16, 71–75; Chantal Mouffe, *The Return of the Political* (New York: Verso, 1993), 19–21, 35–38; Stanley Fish, *The Trouble with Principle* (Cambridge, Mass.: Harvard University Press, 1999), 13–14 (in which he lists his antecedents to be, among others, the pre-Socratics, James, Dewey, and Rorty, in addition to Machiavelli). John P. McCormick has also argued for recognition of "ferocious populism" in the thought of Machiavelli, and suggests that the suspicion directed toward elites should be understood to be a form of "Machiavellian democracy" ("Machiavellian Democracy: Controlling Elites with Ferocious Populism," *American Political Science Review* 95 [June 2001]: 297–314).

14. Honig, *Displacement of Politics*, in which she refers to "Machiavelli's faith in the transformative power of politics," 75.

15. Niccolò Machiavelli, *Discourses on Livy*, trans. Harvey C. Mansfield and Nathan Tarcov (Chicago: University of Chicago Press, 1996), Book I, chapter 4, 16–17.

16. John C. McCormick, for example, while praising "ferocious" conflict in Ma-

chiavelli's thought, does not discuss Machiavelli's equally evident recommendations for the foundations of a unifying form of religion in such a republic ("Machiavellian Democracy"). Similarly contemporary recommendations of "republicanism" that stress liberty and "non-domination" also equally neglect Machiavelli's insistence for the presence of a form of civic religion, an omission—while helpful to arguments that insist upon the preeminence of liberty in republican thought—that points to historical and theoretical inaccuracies in this interpretation. Among those who neglect this aspect of Machiavelli's work are Quentin Skinner, *The Foundations of Modern Political Thought* (New York: Cambridge University Press, 1978), 113–193 (in which there is no entry in the index for "religion" but an extensive entry on "liberty" on page 297), idem, *Liberty before Liberalism* (New York: Cambridge University Press, 1998); and Philip Pettit, *Republicanism: A Theory of Freedom and Government* (New York: Oxford University Press, 1997) (which has extensive entries in its index on "civil liberty" and "freedom" on pages 297 and 299 but none on "religion" or "civil religion"). Maurizio Viroli has been more explicit in his attempt to forge a theory of modern republicanism that does not rely upon "cultural or ethnic or religious homogeneity." He asserts that "civic virtue can also easily do without religion, though classical republicans [such as Machiavelli] thought differently." Whether republican civic virtue can ever exist "easily," with or without recourse to religion, is a debatable proposition. See Maurizio Viroli, *Republicanism*, trans. Antony Shugaar (New York: Hill and Wang, 2002), 90. For a more nuanced understanding of Machiavelli's employment of religion as a means to civic unification, see Vickie B. Sullivan, *Machiavelli's Three Romes: Religion, Human Liberty, and Politics Reformed* (Dekalb: Northern Illinois University Press, 1996), esp. 9, 157–171. Sullivan rightly recognizes the ultimate secular purposes of Machiavelli's transformation of traditional religion, writing of Machiavelli's "faith in human abilities" that leads to the crafting of a religion "that recognizes only earthly sins and offers only earthly salvation" (189).

17. Machiavelli, *Discourses*, I.11, 34–35.

18. Ibid., I.11, 35; Machiavelli, *The Prince*, trans. Harvey C. Mansfield, 2nd ed. (Chicago: University of Chicago Press, 1998), chap. 12, 48; Ronald Beiner, "Machiavelli, Hobbes, and Rousseau on Civil Religion," *Review of Politics* 55 (fall 1993): 622.

19. J.G.A. Pocock, *The Machiavellian Moment: Florentine Political Thought and the Atlantic Republican Tradition* (Princeton, N.J.: Princeton University Press, 1975), 202. Machiavelli elaborates on these necessary and beneficial aspects of a civil religion in *Discourses*, I.12–15. See also J. Samuel Preus, "Machiavelli's Functional Analysis of Religion: Context and Object," *Journal of the History of Ideas* 40 (June 1979): 171–190.

20. See, for example, his criticisms of Christianity in *Discourses*, II.2, although there Machiavelli also suggests that Christianity has been falsely interpreted "according to idleness (*l'ozio*) and not according to virtue (*virtù*)" (II.2, 132). Machiavelli appears to call for a new "founding" based upon a new "interpretation" of Christianity, one that will more closely resemble the civically virtuous religion of paganism.

21. Machiavelli, *Discourses*, II.5, 139: Some changes "come from men, part from heaven. Those that come from men are the variations of sects and of languages." Beiner calls this "a kind of first-order politics" ("Machiavelli, Hobbes, and Rousseau on Civil Religion," 623).

22. Machiavelli, *Discourses*, I.11, 35. Machiavelli continues: since mankind does not live in such religiously credulous times, a modern legislator seeking to found a republic would best work among "mountain men, where there is no civilization." Yet, he concludes the chapter by offering the contemporary example of Savaronola, who, he pregnantly suggests, also led people to believe that "he had spoke with God" (I.11, 36). Machiavelli deems himself incapable of judging the veracity of this claim, but by dint of such a statement suggests his deep suspicion of, if also admiration for, Savaronola's abilities to inculcate this belief in modern, sophisticated Florence.

23. This is apparently similar to the manner in which Machiavelli seems to undermine the efficacy of his lessons to the Prince, particularly the manner in which the deceptive practices of the Prince are "revealed" to the very populace that the Prince otherwise seeks to deceive. Some interpreters have argued that this practice is intended by Machiavelli to undermine his apparent teachings, in effect inoculating the populace against such deceptive practices by increasing cynicism among the populace. See Mary G. Dietz, "Trapping the Prince: Machiavelli and the Politics of Deception," *American Political Science Review* 80 (September 1986): 777–799.

24. Machiavelli, *Discourses*, I.11, 34; emphasis mine. Preus points out that "only at this point of his entire account of Rome's early history did Machiavelli refer to a divine causality, almost as if he were offering an alternative to Christian *Heilgeschichte*" ("Machiavelli's Functional Analysis of Religion," 178).

25. Machiavelli, *Discourses*, I.11, 36.

26. Thus Machiavelli's apparently impious statement, "I love the city more than my soul," suggests paradoxically that, for Machiavelli, this is a statement of profound piety—that care for his soul demands that his first allegiance lie with the city (Machiavelli, letter to Vettori, April 16, 1527).

27. Machiavelli, *Discourses*, I.58, 119; the chapter title is "The Multitude Is Wiser and More Constant Than a Prince" (115).

28. See, especially, Andrew Delbanco, *The Real American Dream: A Meditation on Hope* (Cambridge, Mass.: Harvard University Press, 2000). While Delbanco explores the American dream as a series of transitions that emphasize, alternatively, God, Nation, and Self, the portrait he draws is, in fact, a complex interrelationship between the three. See also Sacvan Bercovitch, *American Jeremiad* (Madison: University of Wisconsin Press, 1978); Ernest Lee Tuveson, *Redeemer Nation: The Idea of America's Millennial Role* (Chicago: University of Chicago Press, 1968); Conor Cruise O'Brien, *Godland: Reflections on Religion and Nationalism* (Cambridge, Mass.: Harvard University Press, 1999); Eldon J. Eisenach, *The Next Religious Establishment: National Identity and Political Theology in Post-Protestant America* (Lanham, MD: Rowman and Littlefield, 2000).

29. John Winthrop, "A Modell of Christian Charity," in *The Puritans: A Sourcebook of their Writings*, ed. Perry Miller and Thomas H. Johnson, 2 vols. (New York: Harper and Row, 1963), 1:199; Abraham Lincoln, "Annual Message to Congress," December 1, 1862, in *Abraham Lincoln: Writings, 1859–1865* (New York: Library of America, 1989), 415. Inaugural addresses for the presidents are available at http://www.bartleby.com/124/. For an exploration of America's belief in its democratic mission in the world, see Walter A. McDougall, *Promised Land, Crusader State: The American Encounter with the World since 1776* (New York: Houghton Mifflin, 1997). On the presidency and civil religion, see Robert V. Pierard and Robert D. Linder, *Civil Religion and the Presidency* (Grand Rapids, Mich.: Academie Books, 1988). The *locus classicus* of America's providential place in the world is Ernest Lee Tuveson, *Redeemer Nation* (Chicago: University of Chicago Press, 1968).

30. Robert N. Bellah, "Civil Religion in America," *Daedelus* 66 (1967): 1–21; reprinted in *Beyond Belief: Essays on Religion in a Post-traditional World* (New York: Harper and Row, 1970), and in *American Civil Religion*, ed. Russell E. Richey and Donald G. Jones (New York: Harper and Row, 1974). Citations to the essay are drawn from the latter collection. For further discussion, see also Robert N. Bellah, *The Broken Covenant: American Civil Religion in Time of Trial*, 2nd ed. (Chicago: University of Chicago Press, 1992); and Robert N. Bellah and Phillip E. Hammond, eds., *Varieties of Civil Religion* (New York: Harper and Row, 1980).

31. Bellah, "Civil Religion in America," 23, 24, 25, 34.

32. Bellah, introduction to *Varieties of Civil Religion*, xi. Bellah cites a typology suggested by John A. Coleman, who contrasted "undifferentiated" forms of civil religion—namely, Church-sponsored and State-sponsored forms, as well "secular nationalism," which is a secularized variant of the latter—and "differentiated" civil religion—namely, that variety found especially in the United States and Western Europe which finds sponsorship neither through Church nor State but emanates from various voluntary social institutions and organizations. Coleman helpfully noted three main tenets of the American civil religion:

1. "The nation is the primary agent of God's meaningful activity in history";
2. "The nation is the primary society in terms of which individual Americans discover personal and group identity";
3. "The nation also assumes a churchly function as the community of righteousness."

As I have suggested above, these main tenets are ones that Machiavelli would find familiar. See John A. Coleman, "Civil Religion," *Sociological Analysis* 31 (summer 1970): 67–77, esp. 74.

33. One should not overstate the implications of this difference, however. Marcela Cristi stresses a distinction between Durkheim's description of the "integrative" form of spontaneous civil religion and Rousseau's depiction of a more "coercive" form of civil religion aimed at "legitimation and social solidarity." Yet, this distinction overstates the differences between the two, inasmuch as Durkheim recognizes the "coercive"—or normative role—of religion in society, whereas Rousseau or advocates of "republican" and even "democratic" civil religion see such normative function as essential toward the end of freedom. Rousseau is quite earnest when he stresses that one must be "forced to be free." See Marcela Cristi, *From Civil to Political Religion: The Intersection of Culture, Religion, and Politics* (Ontario, Canada: Wilfrid Laurier University Press, 2001), 1–13.

34. Bellah, *The Broken Covenant*, 142.

35. Ibid., 153, 158.

36. Bellah, "The Protestant Structure of American Culture: Multiculture or Monoculture?" *Hedgehog Review* 4 (spring 2002): 7–28. Bellah's argument echoes the gentler recent writings by Charles Taylor, who insists upon the importance of institutional forms of religion as a corrective to modern individualism, both secular and religious. See Charles Taylor, *A Catholic Modernity?* ed. James. L. Heft (New York: Oxford University Press, 1999); and idem, *Varieties of Religion Today: William James Revisited* (Cambridge, Mass.: Harvard University Press, 2002).

37. Whitman, "Democratic Vistas," 319, 320, 323.

38. Richard Rorty, *Contingency, Irony, and Solidarity* (New York: Cambridge University Press, 1989), esp. chaps. 3, 4, 9; and idem, *Achieving Our Country: Leftist Thought in Twentieth-Century America* (Cambridge, Mass.: Harvard University Press, 1998), which begins with an appreciation of Whitman and Dewey, particularly

the extent to which "Whitman and Dewey were among the prophets of this [American] civil religion" (15). For a fuller discussion, and alternatively aggressive and appreciative critiques of Rorty's political thought, see Sheldon S. Wolin, "Democracy in the Discourse of Postmodernism," *Social Research* 57 (spring 1990): 5–30; and Richard J. Bernstein, "Rorty's Liberal Utopia," *Social Research* 57 (spring 1990): 31–72.

39. Rorty, *Achieving Our Country*, 142–143 n. 12.

40. Here, a personal admission: I worked as Special Adviser and Speechwriter to the director of the U.S. Information Agency from 1995 to 1997. On the role of the USIA in "telling America's story to the world," see, for example, Robert E. Elder, *The Information Machine: The United States Information Agency and American Foreign Policy* (Syracuse, N.Y.: Syracuse University Press, 1968); John W. Henderson, *The United States Information Agency* (New York: Praeger, 1969); and Leslie Lisle, *United States Information Agency, 1953–1983* (Washington, D.C.: USIA, 1984). More generally, see Joshua Muravchik, *Exporting Democracy: Fulfilling America's Destiny* (Washington, D.C.: AEI, 1992); and David Fromkin, *In the Time of the Americans: The Generation That Changed America's Role in the World* (New York: Knopf, 1995). The USIA (now a part of the State Department) was officially barred from disseminating its materials and programs within the United States, thus reflecting the belief that the American citizenry should not be subjected to what might be construed as propaganda.

41. J. Paul Williams, *What Americans Believe and How They Worship* (New York: Harper and Brothers, 1952), 366, 367.

42. Ibid., 368–369, 370.

43. Ibid., 371.

44. Ibid., 373, 372.

45. Ibid., 373–374.

46. Eisenach, *The Next Religious Establishment*, 110.

47. Ibid., 86.

48. Ibid., 149. On the original religious mission of America's institutions of higher education and the rise of "established nonbelief," see George M. Marsden, *The Soul of the American University: From Protestant Establishment to Established Nonbelief* (New York: Oxford University Press, 1994).

49. John Dewey, "My Pedagogic Creed" [1897], in *The Early Works of John Dewey, 1882–1898* ed. Jo Ann Boydsten, 5 vols. (Carbondale: Southern Illinois University Press, 1967–72), 5:84.

50. See John Dewey, "Christianity and Democracy," *Early Works*, vol. 1; and my discussion of this essay in chapter 6, below.

51. John Dewey, "Religion and Our Schools" [1908], in *John Dewey: The Middle Works, 1899–1924*, vols. (Carbondale: Southern Illinois University Press, 1976–1983), 4:175.

52. Dewey, "My Pedagogic Creed," 95.

53. Cited in Eisenach, *The Next Religious Establishment*, 123. In her first commencement address as president of Princeton University, Shirley Tilghman echoed this awareness of the "religious" role of the modern university, despite being Princeton's first avowed atheist president. She quoted from the 1910 commencement address of Woodrow Wilson: "There is a sense, a very real sense, not mystical but plain fact of experience, in which the spirit of truth, of knowledge, of hope, of revelation dwells in a place like this" (Shirley Tilghman, Presidential Commencement Address,

June 4, 2002, Princeton University (available at: http://www.princeton.edu/pr/news/ 02/q2/0604-tilghmanspeech.htm).

54. See Cristi, *From Civic to Political Religion*; and Christopher Flood, *Political Myth: A Theoretical Introduction* (New York: Garland, 1996).

55. John Dewey, "The Democratic Faith and Education," in *Philosophy of Education (Problems of Men)* (Totowa, N.J.: Littlefield, Adams, 1975 [1944]), 33.

56. Dewey, "Religion and Our Schools," 168.

57. Wilhelm Nestle, *Vom Mythos zum Logos* (New York: Arno, 1978 [1942]). Cf. F. M. Cornford, *From Religion to Philosophy: A Study in the Origins of Western Speculation* (Princeton, N.J.: Princeton University Press, 1991 [1912]), who finds far greater interdependence between the ancient religion and philosophy.

58. See, especially, E. A. Burtt, *The Metaphysical Foundations of Modern Science* (Garden City, N.Y.: Doubleday, 1954).

59. Francis Bacon wrote that "a little or superficial knowledge of [natural] philosophy may incline the mind of man to atheism, but a further proceeding therein doth bring the mind back again to religion" (*The Advancement of Learning* [New York: Modern Library, 2001], 9–10).

60. The "religiosity" of the early proponents of the scientific enterprise is explored at greater and more exhaustive length by a number of studies, all of which have been of great assistance in elaborating on this "method" of realizing "democratic faith," although none of these authors themselves draw this historical or intellectual connection. Among the most helpful have been Norman Cohn, *The Pursuit of the Millennium: Revolutionary Millenarians and Mystical Anarchists of the Middle Ages* (New York: Oxford University Press, 1970); Amos Funkenstein, *Theology and the Scientific Imagination from the Middle Ages to the Seventeenth Century* (Princeton, N.J.: Princeton University Press, 1986); Eugene M. Klaaren, *Religious Origins of Modern Science: Belief in Creation in Seventeenth-Century Thought* (Grand Rapids, Mich.: Eerdman's, 1977); David F. Noble, *The Religion of Technology: The Divinity of Man and the Spirit of Invention* (New York: Knopf, 1998); Ernest Lee Tuveson, *Millennium and Utopia: A Study in the Background of the Idea of Progress* (Berkeley: University of California Press, 1949); Charles Webster, *The Great Instauration: Science, Medicine and Reform, 1626–1660* (London: Duckworth, 1975).

61. Noble, *The Religion of Technology*, 3–100.

62. Ibid., 104, 9.

63. See R. G. Collingwood, *The Idea of Nature* (Oxford: Clarendon, 1945).

64. Giordano Bruno, "The Expulsion of the Triumphant Beast," quoted in Noble, *The Religion of Technology*, 39–40. Bruno's suggestion that humanity comes to know the mind of God by means of "emulation of the actions of God" is within the "maker's knowledge tradition" that deeply informs the thought of Francis Bacon. See Antonio Pérez-Ramos, "Bacon's Forms and the Maker's Knowledge Tradition," in *The Cambridge Companion to Bacon*, ed. Markku Peltonen (New York: Cambridge University Press, 1996), 99–120; and Pérez-Ramos, *Francis Bacon's Idea of Science and the Maker's Knowledge Tradition* (New York: Oxford University Press, 1988).

65. Webster, *The Great Instauration*, esp. 8, 15–16, 100–103, 324–335, 516; Klaaren, *Religious Origins of Modern Science*, 85–126; Noble, *The Religion of Technology*, 43–87.

66. John Milton, "Prolusions," in *Complete Poems and Major Prose*, ed. Merritt Y. Hughes (Indianapolis: Bobbs Merrill, 1957), 625.

67. Pico della Mirandola, "Oration on the Dignity of Man," in *The Renaissance*

Philosophy of Man, ed. Ernst Cassirer, Paul Oskar Kristeller, and John Herman Randall Jr. (Chicago: University of Chicago Press, 1948), 224.

68. The first aphorism of Francis Bacon's *Novum Organum* similarly calls man "the servant and interpreter of Nature"; in the third aphorism he further states, "we can only command Nature by obeying her." See Bacon, *Novum Organum*, trans. Peter Urbach and John Gibson (Chicago: Open Court, 1994), 43.

69. Pico della Mirandola, "Oration on the Dignity of Man," 248–249.

70. Ibid., 230.

71. Webster, *The Great Instauration*, 341. The citation is to be found, for example in Bacon, *The Advancement of Learning*, 41.

72. Bacon, *The Advancement of Learning*, 36.

73. Ibid., 6, 39.

74. Bacon, *Valerius Terminus*, "Of the Interpretation of Nature," in *The Works of Francis Bacon*, ed. James Spedding, Robert Leslie Ellis, and Douglas Denon Heath, 14 vols. (London: Longmans, 1870), 3:218.

75. Ibid., 217. The conjecture of its 1603 composition is justified in an introductory note on pages 207 and 208.

76. Ibid., 217.

77. Ibid., 218.

78. Bacon, *The Advancement of Learning*, 7.

79. Ibid., 37.

80. Bacon, *Valerius Terminus*, 221.

81. Perez Zagorin also explores Bacon's fascination with the possibility of prolonging life, and even overcoming death, by means of reversing the original Fall, in *Francis Bacon* (Princeton, N.J.: Princeton University Press, 1998), 44–51.

82. Bacon, *Valerius Terminus*, 223.

83. Bacon, *The Advancement of Learning*, 56, 58, 60. Here, Bacon is careful to suggest that by "heavens" he means the contemplation of outer space, and "immortality" is that sort achieved by lasting achievements, such as the epics of Homer (60–61). Nevertheless the invocation of the language of "ascent," "heaven," and "immortality"—here contrasted to "vulgar" ends of knowledge—unmistakably echoes arguments, such as those by Pico, Bruno, and Bacon himself, that mankind should seek ultimately to "reinstate" his former state of immortal and even quasi-divine innocence prior to the Fall.

84. Robert K. Faulkner has argued that Bacon was attentive to the numerical ordering in his *Essays*. It is perhaps nothing more than suggestive, but interesting nonetheless, that in a work devoted to the "Wisdom of the Ancients," the longest essay (on the "State of Man") should be the same number as the final letter of the English alphabet, which may allude to the practice of dividing the Homeric epics into twenty-four roughly equal books to correspond with each letter of the Greek alphabet. See Robert K. Faulkner, *Francis Bacon and the Project of Progress* (Lanham, Md., Rowman and Littlefield, 1993), 27–56. The significance of the myth and its interpretation does not, however, rest on this tenuous numerical relationship but rather is self-evident on the basis of its content.

85. Bacon, "Prometheus, or the State of Man," in *Lord Bacon's Essays* (Boston: Little, Brown), 391–394.

86. Bacon was confident that mankind had reached a stage at which it could overcome past errors and achieve new and transformative forms of power and dominion by means of the advancement of knowledge:

This is a thing which I cannot tell whether I may so plainly speak as truly conceive, that as all knowledge appeareth to be a plant of God's own planting, so it may seem the spreading and flourishing or at least the bearing and fructifying of this plant, by a providence of God, nay not only by a general providence but by a special prophecy, was appointed to this autumn of the world: for to my understanding it is not violent to the letter, and safe now after the event, so to interpret that place in the prophecy of Daniel where speaking of the latter times it is said, *Many shall pass to and fro, and science shall be increased*; as if the opening of the world by navigation and commerce and further discovery should meet in one time or age. (Bacon, *Valerius Terminus*, 221)

87. Bacon, "Prometheus," 405.

88. Bacon calls attention to this curious displacement by explaining that he sought not "to break the connection of things," and thus "designedly omitted the last crime of Prometheus" ("Prometheus," 404).

89. Ibid., 403–404.

90. Ibid., 404.

91. Bacon, "Refutation of Philosophies," in *The Philosophy of Francis Bacon*, ed. Benjamin Farrington (Chicago: University of Chicago Press, 1964), 106. Thomas Hobbes—who served for a time as Bacon's personal secretary—used the phrase "Mortall God" to describe his "Leviathan." See Thomas Hobbes, *Leviathan*, ed. Richard Tuck (New York: Cambridge University Press, 1991), chap. 17, sec. 87, 120.

92. Markuu Peltonen has argued interestingly that Bacon should be understood as belonging to the republican tradition because of his frequent reliance on the thought of Machiavelli and his influence on James Harrington ("Bacon's Political Philosophy," in *The Cambridge Companion to Bacon*, ed. Markku Peltonen [New York: Cambridge University Press, 1996], 283–310). However, Zagorin rightly notes that Bacon's resemblance to republicanism stops well short of endorsing popular rule, and explores at greater length his commitment to monarchy and political secrecy (*Francis Bacon*, 147–174). On Bacon's insistence on the necessity of secrecy in government affairs, see, for instance, *The Advancement of Learning*, 208–211.

93. John Dewey, *The Public and Its Problems* (Athens, Ohio: Swallow, 1985 [1927]), 164.

94. Ibid., 183, 184. Thus, like Whitman, Dewey recommended the role of the poet as final proselytizer of democracy, although his text would be considerably more "scientific" than Whitman likely supposed.

95. Bacon, *Novum Organum*, I.61, 66. See also Zagorin, *Francis Bacon*, 85.

96. Bacon, *Valerius Terminus*, 227.

97. Bacon, *New Atlantis*, ed. Jerry Weinberger (Wheeling, Ill.: Harlan Davidson, 1989), 71.

98. John Dewey, *Reconstruction in Philosophy* (Boston: Beacon, 1957 [1920]), 28, 38.

99. Dewey, *Reconstruction in Philosophy*, 28–38. Bacon articulated the need for doubt (though not skepticism) in a felicitous phrase in *The Advancement of Learning*: "if a man will begin with certainties, he shall end in doubts; but if he will be content to begin with doubts, he shall end in certainties" (35).

100. Dewey, *The Public and Its Problems*, 146; cf. 144.

101. Dewey, *Reconstruction in Philosophy*, 28.

102. One can only survey the vast and expanding recent literature on the human implications of the genome project to see this is the case. On a more sanguine pro-

jection of human transformation, see Lee M. Silver, *Remaking Eden: Cloning and Beyond in a Brave New World* (New York: Avon, 1997). For a criticism of the implications of the genome project on both religious and secular grounds, see Francis Fukuyama, *Our Posthuman Future: Consequences of the Biotechnology Revolution* (New York: Farrar, Strauss and Giroux, 2002); and Peter A. Lawler, *Aliens in America* (Wilmington, Del.: ISI Books, 2002); see also Noble, *The Religion of Technology*, 103–228.

103. Richard Rorty, "Religious Faith, Intellectual Responsibility and Romance," in *Philosophy and Social Hope* (New York: Penguin, 1999), 162.

104. See, for example, Rorty, "A World without Substances or Essences," in idem, *Philosophy and Social Hope*, 50; and "Heidegger, Contingency and Pragmatism," in *Essays on Heidegger and Others: Philosophical Papers*, Vol. 2 (New York: Cambridge University Press, 1991), 27.

105. Rorty, "Religious Faith, Intellectual Responsibility and Romance," 161.

106. Rorty, *Contingency, Irony, and Solidarity*, esp. 73–95. For a criticism of Rorty's belief in "self-creation" that points out the ways that language is not easily thrown off or wholly transformed in the manner Rorty suggests, see Sheldon S. Wolin, "Democracy in the Discourse of Postmodernism," *Social Research* 57 (spring 1990): 21–26.

107. Contemporary misgivings in "faith in science" have been expressed by Philip Kitcher, *Science, Truth, and Democracy* (Oxford: Oxford University Press, 2001). For instance, Kitcher revealingly writes, "Behind the often evangelical rhetoric about the value of knowledge stands a serious theology, an often unexamined faith that pursuing inquiry will be good for us, even when it transforms our scheme of values. It's time to abandon that theology, too. We need agnosticism all the way down" (166).

108. For an insightful reflection on Bacon's own scientific and political faith, and its continued if less sanguine adherence in contemporary times, see Howard B. White's elegant study, *Peace among the Willows: The Political Philosophy of Francis Bacon* (The Hague: Martinus Nijhoff, 1968), esp. chap. 1 ("Political Faith and Utopian Thought"). See also Jerry Weinberger, *Science, Faith, and Politics: Francis Bacon and the Utopian Roots of the Modern Age* (Ithaca, N.Y.: Cornell University Press, 1985).

109. *The Scientific Spirit and Democratic Faith* (New York: King's Crown, 1944).

110. Edward C. Lindeman, introduction to *The Scientific Spirit and Democratic Faith*, ix.

111. Ibid., xi.

112. Ibid.

113. Ibid.

114. Horace M. Kallen, "Freedom and Authoritarianism in Religion," in *The Scientific Spirit and Democratic Faith*, 3.

115. Ibid.

116. Ibid., 10; see also 6. In this context, Kallen is discussing several works by then prominent Catholic thinkers, and comparing the arguments to those of Hitler in *Mein Kampf* (7–10).

117. Alfred Mirsky, "The Democratic Responsibilities of Science," in *The Scientific Spirit and Democratic Faith*, 58.

118. Ibid., 59.

119. Ibid., 60, 61.

120. Richard M. Brickner, "The Democratic Responsibilities of Science," in *The Scientific Spirit and Democratic Faith*, 63.

121. Ibid.

122. Ibid., 64.

123. Mirsky, "The Democratic Responsibilities of Science," 60.

124. Rorty, *Achieving Our Country*, 142 n. 12. Actual scientific development ironically suggests that democracy is the least likely outcome of "evolutionary" advances. As Lee M. Silver chillingly describes in his book, *Remaking Eden*, the prohibitive cost of genetic "enhancements" will likely result in an increasing distinction between two classes of people, and even eventually result in a differentiation of the human species between those who can afford to "improve" themselves and those who cannot. As he describes this difference from the perspective of the twenty-second century, "although these [former] beings can trace their ancestry back directly to *homo sapiens*, they are as different from humans as humans are from the primitive worms with tiny brains that first crawled on the earth's surface" (292–293). Strikingly, if unconsciously evoking the early modern belief that science would allow humans to attain godlike capacities, Silver concludes his book by suggesting that such enhanced creatures will discover that their "creator" is no one other than themselves (293). Silver is a direct descendent of the "transformational" dreams that motivated Mirandola and Bacon, a lineage that is highlighted by the book's title, *Remaking Eden*.

125. Marshall McLuhan, *Understanding Media: The Extensions of Man* (New York: McGraw-Hill, 1964), 80.

126. Richard M. Bucke, *Cosmic Consciousness: A Study in the Evolution of the Human Mind* (New Hyde Park, N.Y.: University Books, 1961 [1901]).

127. William James, "Confidences of a 'Psychical Researcher,'" in *Essays in Psychical Research* (Cambridge, Mass.: Harvard University Press, 1986), 374. On the dustjacket of my copy of *Cosmic Consciousness*, a "blurb" reads: "Professor William James read *Cosmic Consciousness* soon after it first appeared, and wrote to the author: 'I believe that you have brought this kind of consciousness "home" to the attention of students of human nature in a way so definite and inescapable that it may be impossible henceforward to overlook it or ignore it.'"

128. Benjamin R. Barber, *Strong Democracy: Participatory Politics for a New Age* (Berkeley: University of California Press, 1984), 223.

129. Sheldon Wolin, notably, begins his magisterial study *Politics and Vision*— which includes a chapter deeply critical of Plato's political philosophy for its reliance on an elite philosophical group who claim access to "truth"—with a lengthy quote from Protagoras's "Great Speech" in which Zeus distributes to all humans, and not merely some, the necessary political virtues of "justice" and "shame" (*aidos* and *dike*) (*Politics and Vision: Continuity and Innovation in Western Political Thought* [Boston: Little, Brown, 1960], 10). See also Stanley Fish's endorsement of the sophists, in his *Trouble with Principle*, 13, which also acknowledges the influence of Dewey, Rorty, and, at greater length, Machiavelli.

CHAPTER 3
DEMOCRACY AS TRIAL: TOWARD A CRITIQUE OF DEMOCRATIC FAITH

1. Tsao Hsingyuan, "The Birth of the Goddess of Democracy," in *Cries for Democracy: Writings and Speeches from the 1989 Chinese Democracy Movement*, ed. Han Minzhu (Princeton, N.J.: Princeton University Press, 1990), 343–344.

2. While the Goddess of Democracy was not fashioned in the image of the Statue of Liberty (ibid., 343), numerous commentators have inevitably compared the God-

dess of Democracy to her American counterpart—inevitably because of the similar pose, and particularly the shared iconography of torch bearing. Nevertheless, no commentator has observed the significance of the singular difference between the two icons: the Goddess of Democracy does not hold a book, in contrast to the book (one indicating the date July 4, 1776) that is held pressed to the body of the Statue of Liberty. If America's constitutional order rests on documents that seek to limit the role and extent of government, the Goddess of Democracy is notable for the absence of any such limiting documents. I am grateful to James Stoner for helping me to see the significance of this difference between the two icons.

3. Sidney Hook, "The Autonomy of the Democratic Faith," *Philosophy and Public Policy* (Carbondale: Southern Illinois University Press, 1980), 273.

4. Ibid.

5. J. Ronald Engel, "The Democratic Faith," *American Journal of Theology and Philosophy* 6 (1985): 153, 154–155.

6. The most significant recent treatment of democracy's trial is Jean Bethke Elshtain, *Democracy on Trial* (New York: Basic Books, 1995). The phrase, however, has long pedigree in American thought. For example, William James's oration commemorating the memorial to Robert Gould Shaw in Boston Commons in 1897:

> Democracy is still upon its trial. The civic genius of our people is its only bulwark, and neither laws nor monuments, neither battleships nor libraries, nor great newspapers nor booming stocks; neither mechanical invention nor political adroitness, nor churches nor universities nor civil-service examinations can save us from degeneration if the inner mystery be lost.

See "Robert Gould Shaw: Oration by Professor William James," in *The Works of William James: Essays in Religion and Morality* ed. Frederick H. Burkhardt (Cambridge, Mass.: Harvard University Press, 1982), 76.

7. For a recent work that understands democratic politics as the sole sphere of possible "redemption," see, generally, J. Peter Euben, *Platonic Noise* (Princeton, N.J.: Princeton University Press, 2003).

8. Sheldon S. Wolin argues that we are moving into a time of "post-democracy" (*Tocqueville: Between Two Worlds* [Princeton, N.J.: Princeton University Press, 2001], chap. 26). One also detects a sense of disillusionment with "postmodern" power in the recent additions to Wolin's classic work, *Politics and Vision, Expanded Edition* (Princeton, N.J.: Princeton University Press, 2004), chaps. 11–17.

9. For an expression of concern over such a form of democratic cynicism, see George Kateb's piercing critique of Sheldon S. Wolin's recent democratic theory, "Wolin as Critic of Democracy," in *Democracy and Vision*, ed. Aryeh Botwinick and William E. Connolly (Princeton, N.J.: Princeton University Press, 2001), 39–57. In particular, Kateb points to Wolin's "despair" over the possibility of democracy as a form of governance, instead pinning his hopes on momentary and fleeting "eruptions" of "fugitive democracy." Further, Kateb concludes that Wolin appears to suggest that, in the final estimation, "the people are not good enough for genuine democracy" (39, 40, 50).

10. William Connolly recommends "agonistic respect" in *Why I Am Not a Secularist* (Minneapolis: University of Minnesota Press, 1999), 10. He calls for a resistance to "generic cynicism" which is the result of "residual faith" that many on the Left nevertheless claim to have lost—a residual faith that thus subtly informs and frustrates the democratic hopes of the Left. Alternatively Connolly embraces and recommends a "nontheistic faith in the plurovocity of being"—a faith, on the one hand,

for which he does not expect all to trade in their own faith commitments but, on the other, in which he insists, at a more fundamental if implicit level, all must believe in order to achieve due measure of "agonistic respect" (16, 8). A chastening voice on the democratic Left, at once appealing to progressive commitments to democracy and warning that our own democratic articulations cannot take on the same optimistic hue as the earlier Progressives, is that of Jeffrey C. Isaac in *The Poverty of Progressivism: The Future of American Democracy in a Time of Liberal Decline* (Lanham, Md.: Rowman and Littlefield, 2003).

11. "Faith," *The Compact Edition of the Oxford English Dictionary*, 2 vols. (Oxford: Oxford University Press, 1971), 1:952.

12. Of course, the *locus classicus* on Abraham's "leap of faith" is Søren Kierkegaard, *Fear and Trembling* (Princeton, N.J.: Princeton University Press, 1983). For example, Kierkegaard writes, "What is omitted from Abraham's story is the anxiety, because to money [that one may give away as an act of faith] I have no ethical obligation, but to the son the father has the highest and holiest" (28). The source of Abraham's anxiety must have been the doubt he experienced about the truth of his faith, even in spite of its direct and unmediated source from a personally known God.

13. Paul Tillich, *Biblical Religion and the Search for Ultimate Reality* (Chicago: University of Chicago Press, 1955), 60–61. See also idem, *Dynamics of Faith* (New York: Harper and Brothers, 1957).

14. Robert Merrihew Adams, "Moral Faith," *Journal of Philosophy* 92 (February 1995): 75, 86. See also idem, *The Virtue of Faith and Other Essays in Philosophical Theology* (New York: Oxford University Press, 1987), esp. 9–47.

15. Tillich, *Dynamics of Faith*, 1–2.

16. Annette Baier, "Secular Faith," *Canadian Journal of Philosophy* 10 (March 1980): 131–148. Here she defends the thesis "that the just must live by faith, faith in a community of just persons," and rests her argument substantively on William James's claim that "confidence can produce its own justification" (133, 134).

17. See Wilson Carey McWilliams, "In Good Faith: On the Foundations of American Politics," in *Humanities in Society* 6 (1983): 19–40, for a helpful discussion that distinguishes between "trust" and "faith" based on their respective reliance upon, or eschewal of, empirical (particularly visual) evidence.

18. Mark 9:23–24. See the gloss on this passage by Miguel de Unamuno, *The Tragic Sense of Life*, trans. J. E. Crawford Flitch (New York: Dover, 1954), 133, in which he concludes that "his faith is a faith based on uncertainty."

19. This is particularly true given Augustine's emphasis on the fallenness—and hence radically imperfect apperception—of humans. See Peter Brown, *Augustine of Hippo: A Biography* (Berkeley: University of California Press, 1967), 260–269. Of course, one's "faith" in the truth of the human Fall derives from the Bible and hence reflects faith as the belief in the Bible's certain truth even as it informs one of the uncertainty of human knowledge. Curiously, however, the faith both required by this pious approach to the Bible and also encouraged by the text at the same time calls upon a recognition of radical insufficiency of human endeavor, including even that faith itself. As such, Augustinian faith, acknowledging the limits of its own faith, stands in stark contrast to William James's limitless "will to believe."

20. Tillich, *Dynamics of Faith*, 1–2; emphasis mine.

21. Raymond Aron, "The Future of Secular Religions," in *The Dawn of Universal History: Selected Essays from a Witness of the Twentieth Century*, trans. Barbara Bray, ed. Yair Reiner (New York: Basic Books, 2002), 192–193.

22. A classic statement of this view is Judith N. Shklar, "The Liberalism of Fear," in *Liberalism and the Moral Life*, ed. Nancy L. Rosenblum (Cambridge, Mass.: Harvard University Press, 1989), 21–38, esp. 23, 25: "The cruelties of the religious wars had the effect of turning many Christians away from the public policies of the churches and to a morality that saw toleration as an expression of Christian charity. . . . There is a real psychological connection between [liberalism and skepticism]. Skepticism is inclined toward toleration, since in its doubts it cannot choose among the competing beliefs that swirl around it, so often in a murderous rage."

23. George Kateb, "Freedom of Worthless and Harmful Speech," in *Liberalism without Illusions: Essays on Liberal Theory and the Political Vision of Judith N. Shklar*, ed. Bernard Yack (Chicago: University of Chicago Press, 1996), 225.

24. See Ian Buruma and Avishai Margalit, "Occidentalism," *The New York Review of Books*, January 17, 2002, 4–7. Both religious fundamentalism of various forms and totalitarianism are identified as common enemies of reason, science, progress, equality, and democracy. Contrast their assessment to a contemporaneous article that appeared in the *New York Times* noting the extreme *contrast* between totalitarianism and religion. In an instructive article entitled "The Case against the Nazis: How Hitler's Forces Planned to Destroy German Christianity" in the January 13, 2002, *New York Times*, Joe Sharkley pointed to apparent resemblances—and ultimately the more fundamental differences—between Christianity and Nazism. While Christianity and Nazism both shared a conservative outlook toward modernization, Hitler realized that the Christian churches "could not be reconciled with the principles of racism, with a foreign policy of unlimited aggressive warfare, or with a domestic policy involving the complete subservience of Church to State," and hence sought its long-term destruction (sec. 4, 7). One would be unable to make such a distinction from a reading of *Occidentalism*, which includes sentences such as: "Worshipers of tribal gods, or even of allegedly universal ones, including Christians, Muslims, and Orthodox Jews, sometimes have a tendency to believe that infidels either have corrupt souls or have no souls at all" (5). Given the evidence from Nazism, would it be equally fair to state that "secular thinkers sometimes have a tendency to kill millions of people"?

25. Judith N. Shklar, "Nineteen Eighty-Four: Should Political Theory Care?" in *Political Thought and Political Thinkers*, ed. Stanley Hoffmann (Chicago: University of Chicago Press, 1998), 349. For a fuller treatment of the "limits of skepticism," see Petr Lom, *The Limits of Skepticism* (Albany: State University of New York Press, 2001).

26. Judith N. Shklar, "Emerson and the Inhibitions of Democracy," in *Redeeming American Political Thought*, ed. Stanley Hoffmann and Dennis F. Thompson (Chicago: University of Chicago Press, 1998), 60–61. Dennis Thompson notes in his foreward to this book that Shklar "paints a sympathetic and vivid portrait of [Emerson's] democratic faith" (xii). Many of Shklar's admirers noted that Shklar ultimately entertained democratic hopes that went beyond her stated liberal fears. As Michael Walzer has suggested, "liberalism is a particular social-historical construction, and it isn't made by throwing up bulwarks around a piece of social space. . . . Insofar as this work is intentional, it will be driven by a positive vision of its purpose. So the liberalism of fear depends on what we might call the liberalism of hope." (Michael Walzer, "On Negative Politics," in *Liberalism without Illusions*, ed. Bernard Yack [Chicago: University of Chicago Press, 1996], 19). Similarly, while John Dunn writes that Shklar rejected at every turn "emotionally eager and cognitively gratuitous hope," he also insists that a kind of chastened hope remained integral even to the

"liberalism of fear." While such liberals reject membership in "the party of hope," yet "that did not mean that they were committed to denying themselves hope," but rather, "for her, hope as it should be, appropriate hope, was a category of the will, not a refuge for (or from) the intelligence" (John Dunn, "Hope over Fear: Judith Shklar as Political Educator," in Yack, *Liberalism without Illusions*, 53). Shklar herself, while firmly committed to the liberalism of fear that categorically rejects utopianism as a political project, nevertheless late in her life recommended if not utopianism than at least serious contemplation of "the inspiration for so imaginative and fascinating a form of literature [that] might revive to enlighten us again"—namely, utopian literature (Shklar, "What Use Is Utopia," in Hoffman, *Political Thought and Political Thinkers*, 190). Other essays in the volume *Liberalism and Illusions* that attempt to build a more "positive" liberal democratic politics from Shklar's negative "liberalism of fear" include "The Democracy of Everyday Life," by Nancy Rosenblum; "Judith Shklar's Dystopic Liberalism," by Seyla Benhabib; and "How Limited Is Limited Government?" by Amy Gutmann.

27. George Kateb, *The Inner Ocean: Individualism and Democratic Culture* (Ithaca, N.Y.: Cornell University Press, 1992), 32.

28. George Kateb, "On the 'Legitimation Crisis,'" *Social Research* 46 (1979): 705.

29. Alexis de Tocqueville, *Democracy in America*, trans. Harvey C. Mansfield and Delba Winthrop (Chicago: University of Chicago Press, 2000), Volume II, Book ii, chapter 15, 519.

30. Walt Whitman, "Democratic Vistas," *The Portable Walt Whitman*, ed. Mark Van Doren (New York: Penguin, 1973), 318, 325.

31. "The priest departs, the divine literatus comes" (Whitman, "Democratic Vistas," 321).

32. Ibid., 330.

33. Ibid., 367.

34. "Two cardinal principles of democratic faith are 'individual liberty' and 'universal community'" (J. Ronald Engel, "The Democratic Faith," *American Journal of Theology and Philosophy* 6 [1985]: 148–158). Cf. "Such a faith [i.e., democratic faith] is the only one that can unify society without imposing uniformity upon it" (Sidney Hook, "The Autonomy of the Democratic Faith," in idem, *Philosophy and Public Policy* [Carbondale: Southern Illinois University Press, 1980], 276).

35. Emerson's embrace of individualism was always conceived within a larger belief of human wholeness. See, especially, his essay, "The Oversoul," as well as descriptions of his belief in larger human "consciousness," in Robert D. Richardson Jr., *Emerson: The Mind on Fire* (Berkeley: University of California Press, 1995), 238, 255, 257–259, 317, 323, 333, 334–335, 353–354. For example, Emerson stated in his lecture, "Society," that "self-trust" was "not a faith in man's own whim or conceit as if he were quite severed from other beings and acted on his own private account, but a perception that the mind common to the universe is disclosed to the individual through his own nature" (Cited in Richardson, *Emerson*, 259).

36. C. Douglas Lummis, *Radical Democracy* (Ithaca, N.Y.: Cornell University Press, 1996).

37. Shortly thereafter, Lummis writes, "democratic faith is the decision to believe that a world of democratic trust is possible because we can see it in each person sometimes" (153).

38. Aristotle, *Politics*, trans. Peter L. Phillips Simpson, (Chapel Hill: University of North Carolina Press, 1997); citations given parenthetically in text. Here Aristotle is discussing the supposed "doglike" virtue of the guardians in Plato's *Republic*, and

thereby considerably complicating the easy assumption that one seeks to "help one's friends and harm one's enemies."

39. Aristotle's greater sympathy toward democracy is perceived by, among others, Josiah Ober in his analysis of several "antidemocrats" of antiquity, including Pseudo-Xenophon, Thucydides, and Plato, as well as Aristotle. See Ober, *Political Dissent in Democratic Athens: Intellectual Critics of Popular Rule* (Princeton, N.J.: Princeton University Press, 1998), chap. 6, esp. 319–324, 332–339. It is worth pointing out that Ober's book concludes with praise for the democratic pragmatism of John Dewey (373).

40. Among those who have regarded Aristotle's arguments on behalf of the "wisdom of the multitude" as problematic and dubious are Mary Nichols, *Citizens and Statesmen: A Study in Aristotle's Politics* (Lanham, Md.: Rowman and Littlefield, 1992), 66; and Richard Mulgan, *Aristotle's Political Theory: An Introduction for Students of Political Theory* (Oxford: Oxford University Press, 1977), 105. Those who interpret Aristotle's discussion in Book 3 as sympathetic toward democracy include, among others, Jeremy Waldron, "The Wisdom of the Multitude: Some Reflections on Book 3, Chapter 11, of Aristotle's *Politics*," *Political Theory* 23 (1995): 563–584; Thomas Lindsay, "Aristotle's Qualified Defense of Democracy through 'Political Mixing,'" *Journal of Politics* 56 (1992): 127–151; and Quentin P. Taylor, "Public Deliberation and Popular Government in Aristotle's *Politics*," *Interpretation* 29 (2002): 241–260.

41. Delba Winthrop writes, "no satisfactory proof is given that [the many] have either good taste or sound judgment about nutrition" ("Aristotle on Participatory Democracy," *Polity* 11 [1978]: 159).

42. Michael Davis argues that "Aristotle has not described a man here so much as an Aristophanic monster, which, lacking any hierarchical or ruling principle, is not a whole at all" (*The Politics of Philosophy: A Commentary on Aristotle's* Politics. [Lanham, Md.: Rowman and Littlefield, 1996], 54).

43. Aristotle subsequently offers a justification of rule by the many that stresses the superior discernment of those who "use" the products of the maker (*P* 1282a14–24). In this analogy Aristotle argues that a resident, pilot, and dinner guest can better judge the products of, respectively, a builder, carpenter, and dinner guest. Thus those who are affected by legislation are better able to perceive its virtues and drawbacks than are those who make it.

44. At this point, as if to damn democracy by faint praise, Aristotle advances a much more tepid justification of rule by the many on purely prudential grounds:

> For if they shared in the greatest offices, it would not be safe, since, on account of their injustice and unwisdom, they would do wrong in some things and go wrong in others. If, on the other hand, they were given no share and had no participation in office, it would be cause for alarm, since the city that has many in it who lack honor and are poor must of necessity be full of enemies. (1281b26–31)

45. Here I agree wholly with the assessment of Bernard Yack: "Aristotle, unlike Rousseau, did not believe that human beings need the denaturing exercise in 'self-transformation' that Rousseau and civic republicans celebrate. We certainly need law and moral education in order to live a fully human life, according to Aristotle. Without them we are unlikely to develop the virtues that are the foundation of a good life (*NE*, 1103a–b, 1179b–80a). But the training of the virtues is not for Aristotle a fight against nature, and certainly not a struggle to transform naturally self-regarding beings into other-regarding citizens. It is instead a process in which we draw out and

build on human beings' natural capacities and natural impulses for communal living" (*The Problems of a Political Animal: Community, Justice, and Conflict in Aristotelian Thought* [Berkeley: University of California Press, 1993], 14–15).

46. Winthrop, "Aristotle on Participatory Democracy," 155.

47. Richard Wollheim, "A Paradox in the Theory of Democracy," *Philosophy, Politics and Society*, ed. Peter Laslett and W. G. Runciman, 2nd series (New York: Barnes & Noble, 1962), 78.

48. Ibid., 84.

49. Recall J. Ronald Engel's profession of democratic faith: "Two cardinal principles of democratic faith are 'individual liberty' and 'universal community.'" ("The Democratic Faith," *American Journal of Theology and Philosophy* 6 [1985]: 148–158).

50. Winthrop, "Aristotle on Participatory Democracy," 156.

51. Hannah Arendt, "The Crisis in Culture," in idem, *Between Past and Future: Eight Exercises in Political Thought* (New York: Penguin, 1977), 220.

52. Ibid., 220–221.

53. I have discussed many of these "agonistic" thinkers in chapter 1. See, inter alia, Connolly, *Why I Am Not a Secularist*; Bonnie Honig, *Political Theory and the Displacement of Politics* (Ithaca, N.Y.: Cornell University Press, 1993); Chantal Mouffe, *The Return of the Political* (New York: Verso, 1993); Benjamin R. Barber, *Strong Democracy: Participatory Politics for a New Age* (Berkeley: University of California Press, 1984).

54. See, for example, Hadley Arkes, *First Things* (Princeton, N.J.: Princeton University Press, 1986).

55. Hannah Arendt, *On Revolution* (New York: Penguin, 1988), 129.

56. Ibid., 192–193.

57. Arendt, "Truth and Politics," in idem, *Between Past and Future*, 246.

58. Ibid.

59. "Four score and seven years ago our fathers brought forth on this continent, a new nation, conceived in Liberty, and dedicated to the proposition that all men are created equal" (Abraham Lincoln, "The Gettysburg Address," November 19, 1863). Lincoln's math was quite precise: he dated the origin of the American nation not in 1789, with the adoption of the Constitution, but in 1776, with the Declaration of Independence.

60. See, for example, Ronald Beiner, introduction to, and "Interpretive Essay" in, *Lectures on Kant's Political Philosophy* by Hannah Arendt, ed. Ronald Beiner (Chicago: University of Chicago Press, 1992), vii–viii, 89–156. Beiner suggests that the uncompleted third volume, "Judgment," would have been Arendt's "crowning achievement" (vii).

61. Hannah Arendt, *The Life of the Mind*, Vol. 2, *Willing* (New York: Harcourt Brace Jovanovich, 1978), 195–196.

62. Ibid., 200.

63. Ibid., 202. In this willingness to accept the fact of "We" as a given that cannot be philosophically comprehended, Arendt curiously anticipates Rorty's argument that liberalism must be embraced without seeking justification. See, for example, Richard Rorty, "The Priority of Democracy over Philosophy," in *Objectivity, Relativism, and Truth: Philosophical Papers* 3 vols. (New York: Cambridge University Press, 1991), 1:175–196.

64. Arendt, *Willing*, 202, 207.

65. Ibid., 216.

66. Ibid., 217.

67. Arendt, it should be recognized, sought to warn against excessive transformative energies in *On Revolution* by means of a favorable treatment of the American Revolution against a more critical assessment of the French and Russian Revolutions. Yet, for Arendt, what made all revolutions appealingly similar is the extent to which they "brought to light the new, secular, and worldly yearnings of the modern age ... [reflected by an] all-pervasive preoccupation with permanence, with a 'perpetual state.' . . . What lay behind them was the deeply felt desire for an Eternal City on earth" (*On Revolution*, 229).

68. Plato, *Republic*, trans. Allan Bloom (New York: Basic Books, 1968), 433a. Citations hereafter provided parenthetically in the text.

69. The most famous statement by Adam Smith in this regard is certainly his claim, "It is not from the benevolence of the butcher, the brewer, or the baker, that we expect our dinner, but from their regard to their own interest. We address ourselves, not to their humanity but to their self-love, and never talk to them of our own necessities but of their advantages" (*An Inquiry into the Nature and Causes of the Wealth of Nations*, 2 vols. (Indianapolis, Ind.: Liberty Press, 1981), 1:ii.

70. "Need" is a translation of *chreia*, which, in addition to its meaning as "lack" or "insufficiency," also contains connotations of "familiarity" or "intimacy." The exchange between Adeimantus and Socrates is permeated by the invocation of various words for "need," including the very outset of the decision to create a "city in speech": "Let's make a city in speech from the beginning. Our need [*chreia*], as it seems, will make it" (369c). Even political philosophy begins with an acknowledgment of its insufficiency.

71. John Locke, *Two Treatises of Government*, ed. Peter Laslett (New York: Cambridge University Press, 1988), Second Treatise, Section 95, 330. See also Michael P. Zuckert, *The Natural Rights Republic: Studies in the Foundation of the American Political Tradition* (South Bend, Ind.: Notre Dame University Press, 1996), chap. 1.

72. The relationship between the "two cities" is worthy of further exploration, but implicitly it certainly underlies the discussion between Socrates and Glaucon on why the philosopher-king, once having escaped and ascended above the cavern of opinion, would choose to re-descend where near-certain death awaited him. Socrates asserts that "it's not the concern of law that any one class in the city fare exceptionally well, but it contrives to bring this about for the whole city, harmonizing the citizens by persuasion and compulsion, making them share with one another the benefit that each class is able to bring to the commonwealth. And it produces such men in the city not in order that it may use them in binding one's city together, but in order that it may use them in binding the city together" (519e–520a). What once came as a natural and necessary course in the "city of utmost necessity" must now be forged by law, persuasion, and compulsion in the "feverish city" in which the connections between the work of citizens, and their mutual reliance, is no longer as easily perceived.

CHAPTER 4
PROTAGORAS UNBOUND: THE DEMOCRATIC MYTHOLOGY
OF PROTAGORAS'S "GREAT SPEECH"

1. Plato, *Theaetetus*, trans. M. J. Levett, rev. Myles Burnyeat, in *Plato: Complete Works*, ed. John Cooper (Indianapolis. Ind.: Hackett, 1997), 152a. Hereafter, page numbers to this work are given parenthetically in the text.

2. Henry Sidgewick, "The Sophists," *Journal of Philology* 4 (1872): 289.

3. G. B. Kerferd, *The Sophistic Movement* (Cambridge: Cambridge University Press, 1981); Mario Untersteiner, *The Sophists*, trans. Kathleen Freeman (New York: Philosophical Library, 1954); Jacqueline de Romilly, *The Great Sophists in Periclean Athens*, trans. Janet Lloyd (Oxford: Clarendon, 1992); Eric Havelock, *The Liberal Temper in Greek Politics* (London: J. Cape, 1957); Cynthia Farrar, *The Origins of Democratic Thinking: The Invention of Politics in Classical Athens,* (New York: Cambridge University Press, 1988); and Susan Jarrett, *Rereading the Sophists: Classical Rhetoric Refigured* (Carbondale: Southern Illinois University Press, 1991). These thinkers return to an even earlier tradition inaugurated by George Grote in which he criticized Plato and praised the Sophists in his classic *A History of Greece: From the Earliest Period to the Close of the Generation Contemporary with Alexander the Great* (London: J. Murray, 1872), vol. 8.

4. John Dewey, *The Quest for Certainty: A Study of the Relation of Knowledge and Action* (New York: Minton Balch, 1929).

5. Havelock, *The Liberal Temper in Greek Politics*, 18.

6. Richard Rorty, *Philosophy and the Mirror of Nature* (Princeton, N.J.: Princeton University Press, 1979), 147.

7. Farrar, *The Origins of Democratic Thinking*, 77. Many thinkers agree with Farrar. See Adolf Menzel, "Protagoras, die aelteste Theoretiker der Demokratie," *Zeitschrift fuer Politik* 3 (1910): 205–238; Kerferd, *The Sophistic Movement*, 144 ("Protagoras has produced for the first time in human history a theoretical basis for participatory democracy"); Jarratt, *Rereading the Sophists*; Donald Kagan, *The Great Dialogue: History of Greek Political Thought from Homer to Polybius* (New York: Free Press, 1965); Arlene W. Saxonhouse, *Athenian Democracy: Modern Mythmakers and Ancient Theorists* (South Bend, Ind.: University of Notre Dame Press, 1996); Capizzi, "Il 'Mito di Protagora' e la Polemica sulla Democrazia" *Cultura* 8 (1970): 552–571; A.W.H. Adkins, "Aretē, Technē, Democracy and Sophists," *Journal of Hellenic Studies* 93 (1973): 3–12. For dissenting views, see Peter P. Nicholson, "Protagoras and the Justification of Athenian Democracy," *Polis* 3 (1986): 14–24; and F. Rosen, "Did Protagoras Justify Democracy?" *Polis* 13 (1994): 12–30.

8. J. Peter Euben rehearses a number of these apparently democratic features in *Corrupting Youth: Political Education, Democratic Culture, and Political Theory* (Princeton, N.J.: Princeton University Press, 1997), 246–247, although he ultimately finds the full import of Protagoras's teaching to be deeply suspect from a democratic standpoint.

9. Some (e.g., G. B. Kerferd, "Plato's Account of the Relativism of Protagoras," *Durham University Journal* 9 [1949]: 20–26) argue that Protagoras's relativism only applied to individuals, but these passages in *Theaetetus* (167c, 172a–b) suggest that this relativism can be extended politically, which seems confirmed by arguments on behalf of "communal education" that he makes in the "Great Speech" of *Protagoras*. I discuss this latter point in greater detail below.

10. Farrar, *The Origins of Democratic Thinking*, 76.

11. Benjamin R. Barber, *Strong Democracy: Participatory Democracy for a New Age* (Berkeley: University of California Press, 1984), 152.

12. "Democratic faith," as has been argued to this point, is a phrase frequently used but rarely analyzed. See, for example, John Dewey, "The Democratic Faith and Education," *Antioch Review* 4 (1944): 274–283. More generally, see Ralph Henry Gabriel, *The Course of American Democratic Thought* (New York: Ronald Press, 1940), esp. chap. 2, "The Doctrines of the American Democratic Faith"; and chap. 31, "The Essence of the American Democratic Faith."

13. For example, Donald Kagan writes that "by far the fullest, perhaps the most beautiful, defense of the democratic practice of equality in public life is spoken by Protagoras of Abdera in the Platonic dialogue to which he gives his name" (*The Great Dialogue*, 81; cf. 92).

14. The dialogue is set in either the year 432 or 433 (J. S. Morrison, "The Place of Protagoras in Athenian Public Life," *Classical Quarterly* 35 [1941]: 2–16). In either event Plato was too young to be present, thus suggesting that the dialogue is a fictionalized account of what may or may not have been an actual meeting between Socrates and Protagoras.

15. I use the terms "shame" and "justice" for *aidos* and *dike*, rather than Lamb's "respect" and "right." Each term is complex and has multiple meanings. For a fuller explication of the word *aidos*, see Douglas L. Cairns, *Aid\mos: The Psychology and Ethics of Honour and Shame in Ancient Greek Literature* (Oxford: Clarendon, 1993); on *dik\me*, see E. A. Havelock, *The Greek Concept of Justice: From Its Shadow in Homer to Its Substance in Plato* (Cambridge, Mass.: Harvard University Press, 1978); and Hugh Lloyd-Jones, *The Justice of Zeus* (Berkeley: University of California Press, 1983).

16. Translations from both *Works and Days* and *Theogony* are drawn from Hesiod, *The Works and Days, Theogony, The Shield of Herakles*, trans. Richmond Lattimore (Ann Arbor: University of Michigan Press, 1987). Original Greek is drawn from Hesiod, *Homeric Hymns, Epic Cycle, Homerica*, trans. Hugh G. Evelyn-White (Cambridge, Mass.: Harvard University Press, Loeb Classical Library, 1936). Citations to *Works and Days* will appear as *WD* with a line number in the text. Citations to *Theogony* will appear as *T* with a line number in the text.

17. Jean-Pierre Vernant, "The Myth of Prometheus in Hesiod," *Myth and Society in Ancient Greece* (New York: Zone Books, 1988), 183.

18. On Prometheus as savior, see Carl Kerényi, *Prometheus: Archetypal Image of Human Existence*, trans. Ralph Manheim (Princeton, N.J.: Princeton University Press, 1991), 3–4.

19. The authorship of *Prometheus Bound* remains a contested issue. My assumption is that the authorship does not have any bearing on the main point of the analysis, which is to demonstrate the departures and resonances of Protagoras's Prometheus myth from that of *Prometheus Bound*. Most important for my argument is the relative dating of the two versions: *Prometheus Bound* is believed to have been performed in 457 or 456 BCE. The conversation between Socrates and Protagoras occurs later, most likely during Protagoras's second visit to Athens in 433 or 432 BCE. Thus it can be assumed that the Prometheus myth in *Prometheus Bound* would have been known to the interlocutors in Plato's *Protagoras* and, even more important, to Plato's audience.

20. I cite Aeschylus, *Prometheus Bound*, trans. David Grene, in *Aeschylus II* (Chicago: University of Chicago Press, 1956); hereafter citations given parenthically in text.

21. Timothy V. Kaufman-Osborn, *Creatures of Prometheus: Gender and the Politics of Technology* (Lanham, Md.: Rowman & Littlefield), 4.

22. Kerényi, *Prometheus*, 87–88.

23. W.K.C. Guthrie, *A History of Greek Philosophy* (Cambridge: Cambridge University Press, 1962), 255.

24. Ibid., 67–68; Danielle S. Allen, *The World of Prometheus: The Politics of Punishing in Democratic Athens* (Princeton, N.J.: Princeton University Press, 2000),

247–251. For a persuasive critique of Protagoras's views on punishment which shares many of my own suspicions of his "optimism," see Euben, *Corrupting Youth*, 229–249.

25. Joseph Cropsey has made a related compelling observation of the divine-mortal dynamic contained in the *muthos*:

We observe that without the contraband arts the human beings would have been not only unable to honor the mean and myopic Olympians with works of art but also unmoved to do so, since the possession of arts encourages introspective man to see a god within. As Plato fashions this skillful projection of Protagoras, the persistent tendency of the great sophist to link humanity to divinity through *technē* becomes clearer; and if we bear in mind that in the background of the discussion is the ever-present issue of teachability . . ., we can envision an important victory for Protagoras if he can produce the concurrence of divinity-qua-excellence and teachable art-qua-excellence. His pedagogy would then pass divinity from man to man, perfecting the philanthropy of Prometheus. (Joseph Cropsey, *Plato's World: Man's Place in the Cosmos* [Chicago: University of Chicago Press, 1995], 8)

26. Untersteiner, *The Sophists*, 60.
27. Havelock, *The Liberal Temper in Greek Politics*, 187.
28. Farrar, *The Origins of Democratic Thinking*, 78.
29. As Eric Havelock suggests, "The Greeks, so far as we know, were the first people to realize that the religious-metaphysical and the biological-historical furnished alternative explanations of the nature of man and man's culture" (*The Liberal Temper in Greek Politics*, 30).
30. Kagan, *The Great Dialogue*, 83–84.

CHAPTER 5
CIVIL RELIGION AND THE DEMOCRATIC FAITH OF ROUSSEAU

1. When citing Rousseau I use the following abbreviations for each work, placed within the text, followed by page numbers to that particular edition (in the case of *Oeuvres Complètes*, page numbers will be preceded by a roman numeral indicating the volume):

C: Confessions, trans. Christopher Kelly (Hanover: University Press of New England, 1995).

E: Emile, or on Education, trans. Allan Bloom (New York: Basic Books, 1979).

FD: First Discourse, in *The First and Second Discourses*, trans. Roger D. Masters and Judith R. Masters (New York: St. Martin's, 1964).

GM: Geneva Manuscript, in *On the Social Contract, with Geneva Manuscript and Political Economy*, trans. Judith R. Masters (New York: St. Martin's, 1978).

LV: "Letter to Voltaire" ("Letter on Providence"), in *The Discourses and Other Political Writings*, trans. Victor Gourevitch (New York: Cambridge University Press, 1997).

OC: Oeuvres Complètes, ed. Bernard Gagnebin and Marcel Raymond, 4 vols. (Paris: Gallimard, Bibliothèque de la Pléiade, 1959–69).

PE: Discourse on Political Economy, in *The Social Contract and other Later Political Writings*, trans. Victor Gourevitch (New York: Cambridge University Press, 1997).

SC: On the Social Contract, in *On the Social Contract, with Geneva Manuscript and Political Economy*, trans. Judith R. Masters (New York: St. Martin's, 1978).

SD: Second Discourse, in *The First and Second Discourses*, trans. Roger D. Masters and Judith R. Masters (New York: St. Martin's, 1964).

SW: Reveries of the Solitary Walker, trans. Peter French (New York: Penguin, 1979.

2. Rousseau adheres more closely to Plato's description of the Egyptian disapproval of the divine gift of writing, although Rousseau overlooks that the Egyptian king Thamus "said many things to Theuth [Thoth] in praise or blame of the various arts" and saved his strongest disapproval solely for writing, which threatened to weaken memory and give to the literate the appearance of wisdom without a thoughtful commitment to actual knowledge (*Phaedrus*, 274d–e; see, more generally, 274c–275b).

3. Plutarch, "How to Profit by One's Enemies," in *Plutarch's Moralia* (Cambridge: Loeb Classical Library, Harvard University Press, 1928), 9 (86f).

4. Ibid., 7 (86d).

5. From *Lettre à Lecat* (OC, III.102); translated and cited by Roger D. Masters, *The Political Philosophy of Rousseau* (Princeton, N.J.: Princeton University Press, 1968), 225–226.

6. Ibid., 226.

7. See, for example, Rousseau's *Letter to D'Alembert*, which warns against establishing a theater in Geneva.

8. *Animer*, as it does in English, includes the connotation of "bringing to life."

9. The Latin citation reads "Quem te Deus esse Jussit, et humana qua parte locatus in re, Disce" (*SD*, 97). The translation is provided by Masters (*SD*, 234 n. 17).

10. On "the pure state of nature," see Victor Gourevitch, "Rousseau's 'Pure' State of Nature," *Interpretation* 16 (1988): 23–59.

11. Leo Strauss, *Persecution and the Art of Writing* (Chicago: University of Chicago Press, 1952), 22–37.

12. Footnotes lettered b, c, d, e, f, g, j, m, and p all cite recent texts in the yet nascent social science literature of Rousseau's day. The frontispiece of the *Second Discourse* similarly undermines the claim that Rousseau will "set all the facts aside," inasmuch as it portrays a "Hottentot" fleeing civilization, a portrayal that follows the description drawn from *Histoire des voyages*. Rousseau's citation of the episode appears in note p (*SD*, 225–226). In this particular episode, the "facts" do little to assuage the aggressive defender of the Christian faith. Rousseau begins the note by observing (based on the "facts," of course) that humanity in the state of nature exhibits a studied avoidance of Christianity: "It is an extremely remarkable thing, for all the years that Europeans have been tormenting themselves [Rousseau avoids mentioning who else are possibly being tormented] to bring the savages of various countries in the world to their way of life, that they have not yet been able to win over a single one, not even with the aid of Christianity; for all our missionaries sometimes make Christians of them, but never civilized men. Nothing can overcome the invincible repugnance they have against adopting our morals and living in our way" (*SD*, 223). The "Hottentot" portrayed in the frontispiece leaves civilization with the following statement, also cited by Rousseau in this note: "Be so kind, sir, as to understand that I renounce this paraphernalia forever; I renounce also for my entire life the Christian religion; my resolution is to live and die in the religion, ways, and customs of my ancestors" (*SD*, 225–226).

13. John T. Scott also notes the implicit "theodicy" in Rousseau's portrayal of the fundamental "pure state of nature" of humanity in the *Second Discourse*. See John T. Scott, "The Theodicy of the *Second Discourse*: The 'Pure State of Nature' and

Rousseau's Political Thought," *American Political Science Review* 86 (September 1992): 696–711.

14. Compare to Rousseau's letter to Voltaire in which he denies that God devotes any attention to particular humans but, instead, concerns Himself solely with "the whole" (*LV*, 241).

15. Roger Masters glosses this passage similarly, though in my view he incorrectly suggests that it is the "goddess" that creates the laws, rather than a fiction that legitimates the laws: "Note . . . that a goddess is the source of laws whose purpose is the protection of property, and that these laws create a 'new kind of right'; it appears that gods are introduced by men to sanctify private property (which would otherwise be insecure)" (*SD*, 239 n. 39).

16. The passage is glossed again helpfully by Masters: "Note the implication that religion has served to protect illegitimate government from overthrow" (*SD*, 241 n. 53). See also Masters, *The Political Philosophy of Rousseau*, 190, esp. n. 142.

17. Christopher Kelly, *Rousseau's Exemplary Life: The* Confessions *as Political Philosophy* (Ithaca, N.Y.: Cornell University Press, 1987), 110–111. Kelly neglects to highlight Rousseau's explicit identification with the city's religion when he notes Rousseau's longing for this "self-contained sphere of family, friends, and city" (111). However, as I suggest below, this oversight may be entirely in keeping with the thrust of Rousseau's thought, inasmuch as one's religion is wholly subsumed by civic demands. Such a conclusion is complicated only by Rousseau's claim that he might have been "a good Christian" even while at the same time being "a good citizen" in light of his critique of Christianity in *On the Social Contract*, IV.8.

18. In addition to his reference in the *First Discourse*, Rousseau refers to the essay in *Reveries of a Solitary Walker* as he begins his famous (or infamous) reflection on lying (*SW*, 63). For a fruitful discussion of Rousseau's late use of Plutarch, see Michael Davis, *The Autobiography of Philosophy* (Lanham, Md.: Rowman & Littlefield, 1999), 148–151.

19. Plutarch, "How to Profit by One's Enemies," 9 (86f).

20. For Rousseau's most succinct discussions of civil religion and Christianity, see *On the Social Contract*, IV.8. On "natural religion," see "The Profession of Faith of the Savoyard Vicar," in Book IV of *Emile*, 266–313.

21. Of course, these broad features of "natural religion" accord point for point with Rousseau's description of the ideal dogmas of his civil religion described in *On the Social Contract*, IV.8, 131.

22. "The essential worship is that of the heart" (*E*, 308).

23. For a more sustained rejection of miracles, see *Lettres Ecrit de la Montagne*, Letter 3 (*OC*, III.727–754); and Ronald Grimsley's discussion in *Rousseau and the Religious Quest* (Oxford: Clarendon, 1968), 74–76.

24. For a fuller explication of the specific causes for Rousseau's hostility toward Christianity, see Arthur M. Melzer, "The Origin of the Counter-Enlightenment: Rousseau and the New Religion of Sincerity," *American Political Science Review* 90 (June 1996): 345–350. Melzer identifies seven features of Chrisitanty that pose a threat to political order: the tendency for Christian persecution; the destruction of republican virtue; the destruction of political unity; clerical tyranny and personal dependence; the weakening of morality; the weakening of the family; and the divided soul.

25. Cf. *Emile*, 273–277.

26. Cf. Ibid., 283.

27. On punishment and reward in the afterlife, cf. ibid., 284.

28. Cf. Ibid., 308.

29. Cf. Ibid., 309.

30. Melzer, "The Origin of the Counter-Enlightenment," 357.

31. With this passage Rousseau appears to clarify the ambiguities of his statement in the *Second Discourse* (discussed above) in which he said, "if religion had accomplished only this good for men, it would have been enough to oblige them all to cherish and adopt it, even with its abuses, since it spares even more blood than fanaticism causes to be shed" (*SD*, 170–171). His claim in the *Geneva Manuscript* of the inefficacy of religion to ensure domestic peace, even accepting its promotion of accompanying fanaticism, would appear to settle the question in the negative as to whether religion had accomplished even this one good for humanity.

32. Rousseau wrote that atheism, "this convenient philosophy of the happy and the rich, who make their paradise in this world, cannot long be that of the multitude, the victim of their passions, who, for want of happiness in this life, need to find here at least the hope and consolations of which that barbarous doctrine [atheism] deprives them" (*OC*, I.727; cited and translated by Melzer, "The Origin of the Counter-Enlightenment," 351).

33. Here Rousseau places a footnote citing Machiavelli, *Discourses on Titus Livy*, I.11:

> Nor in fact was there ever a legislator who, in introducing extraordinary laws to a people, did not have recourse to God, for otherwise they would not be accepted, since many benefits of which a prudent man is aware, are not so evident to reason that he can convince others of them. (*SC*, 142 n. 57)

For an informative discussion of Rousseau's reliance upon Machiavelli's new science of politics, see Masters, *The Political Philosophy of Rousseau*, 364–368.

34. As Daniel E. Cullen rightly rejects Benjamin R. Barber's understanding of the "general will" as a transformation that occurs *after* civic interaction in the public sphere:

> For Rousseau, the "artificial creation of civic communities" consists not in the public, political encounter with difference but in the suppression of particularity through a stance of moral asceticism toward one's self. The social tie is forged in the hearts of citizens rather than in their common space. (*Freedom in Rousseau's Political Philosophy* [DeKalb: Northern Illinois University Press, 1993], 155–156)

One needs only further observe that it is the legislator who initially "forges" this original willingness to engage in a kind of "moral asceticism." Rousseau's understanding of the initial "isolation" of all individuals, and the need to forge an "unnatural" communal bond between them, comports with Durkheim's later analysis of the constitutive social role of religion discussed in chapter 2, above.

35. Indeed, given the placement of Rousseau's discussion of "civil religion" at the very conclusion of *On the Social Contract*—at which point he has expressly stated that his concern is to recommend institutions that will slow the inevitable decline of the regime—perceptive commentators have noted that this latter appeal to "civil religion" represents a later addition to the state. See Masters, *The Political Philosophy of Rousseau*, 408 ("ultimately, Rousseau relies far more heavily on the institution of civil religion to restrain the inevitable tendency to moral corruption and despotism"). See also the seminal articles by Bertrand de Jouvenel: "Rousseau the Pessimistic Evolutionist," *Yale French Studies* 28 (1961): 83–96; and "Rousseau's Theory on the Forms of Government," in *Hobbes and Rousseau*, ed. Maurice Cranston and Richard

S. Peters (New York: Anchor, 1972), 484–497. Such a distinction between an *original* and founding form of religious belief at a regime's founding, and subsequent religious practices that arise in the course of the life of the regime, has precedence in Plato's *Republic*, which differentiates the founding "myth"—the "Noble Lie"—from specific practices that will arise in the regime.

36. An example, one among many, would be John Rawls, in *A Theory of Justice* (Cambridge, Mass.: Harvard University Press, 1971), who cites Rousseau's conception of the social contract as undergirding his own at several points (11, 264). Yet, Rawls neglects the collective aspect of Rousseau's depiction, as well as the necessary transformation of the human character *preceding* the entry into the contract. Thus Rawls's description of the necessary kind of contractual agreement that would accompany a just society lacks Rousseau's attentiveness to the practical means—means of "transformation"—by which a self-interested people would, *in the first instance*, sacrifice their own interests for the sake of the common good. Rawls never tells his readers *why* anyone would enter the "original position" in the first place. On this point, see Joseph Reisert's introduction to idem, *Jean-Jacques Rousseau: A Friend of Virtue* (Ithaca, N.Y.: Cornell University Press, 2003).

37. *Protagoras*, 322c.

38. Orpheus, as a musician and poet, has the ability required of the Legislator to "persuade without convincing." As Christopher Kelly has convincingly argued, this form of "persuasion" is less "rational" than poetic, and is highlighted as a kind of early and particularly musical communication in Rousseau's *Discourse on Languages*. See Christopher Kelly, "'To Persuade without Convincing': The Language of Rousseau's Legislator," *American Journal of Political Science* 31 (May 1987): 321–335.

39. Rousseau planned and commissioned the engravings for the illustration, and, Allan Bloom writes, he "considered them an integral part of the text" (*E*, 481 n. 6).

40. On the transformation of divine will to the general will, see Patrick Riley, *The General Will before Rousseau: The Transformation of the Divine into the Civic* (Princeton, N.J.: Princeton University Press, 1986).

41. "Optimism" is thus explicated by Roger Pearson in his introduction to Voltaire's *Candide*:

> In his Essais de Théodicée, written in French and published in 1710, Leibniz addressed the age-old question: what is the nature of divine Providence and how can we reconcile it with physical and moral evil and with the idea of free will? . . . One of the basic axioms in Leibniz's system is the so-called Principle of Sufficient Reason, which holds . . . that there must be some logical reason why anything is as it is. According to this axiom even God must have, or have had, a sufficient reason for His actions, and since He is by definition perfect, it must always be, or have been, the right reason. . . . Since God is perfection, and since God was creating something separate from Himself [when he created the material universe], it follows that what He created had necessarily to be imperfect. At the moment of Creation He had to decide between an infinite number of possible (i.e. imperfect) worlds. Following the Principle of Sufficient Reason He necessarily chose the best of all possible worlds (i.e. the least imperfect), namely that in which the greatest diversity might obtain and in which there would be the greatest excess of good over evil. By this token a world without evil, were it even logically possible, might be less good than a world with evil since some great goods are inevitably bound up with certain evils. . . . By this reasoning, then, the presence of evil is for a greater good. . . . Thus, all is for the best in the best of all possible worlds. (Roger Pearson, introduction to *Candide and Other Stories*, trans. idem [New York: Oxford University Press, 1998], xiv–xv).

42. Voltaire, "The Lisbon Earthquake: An Inquiry into the Maxim, 'Whatever Is, Is Right,'" trans. Tobias Smollet, in *The Portable Voltaire*, ed. Ben Ray Redman (New York: Viking, 1949), 556–569. Voltaire writes, "Leibnitz [*sic*] can't tell me from what secret cause / In a world governed by the wisest law, / Lasting disorders, woes that never end / With our vain pleasures real sufferings blend; / Why ill the virtuous with the vicious shares?" (567).

43. Pierre Burgelin has argued that Rousseau's philosophy is an effort to form a "second nature" for mankind, inasmuch as his "first nature" is no longer available. See Burgelin, *La Philosophie de l'existence de Jean-Jacques Rousseau* (Paris: Presses Universitaires de France, 1952); see also my discussion in *The Odyssey of Political Theory: The Politics of Departure and Return* (Lanham, Md.: Rowman & Littlefield, 2000), chap. 3.

CHAPTER 6
AMERICAN FAITH: THE TRANSLATION OF RELIGIOUS FAITH TO DEMOCRATIC FAITH

1. George Santayana, *The Life of Reason; or, The Phases of Human Progress*. 1-vol. ed. (London: Constable, 1954), 148 (chap. 5, "Reason in Society").

2. William James, "The Social Value of the College-Bred," in *William James: Writings, 1902–1912*, ed. Bruce Kuklick (New York: Library of America, 1987), 1245.

3. Edward Everett, "Oration Pronounced at Cambridge, before the Society of Phi Beta Kappa, August 26, 1824," in *The Transcendentalists: The Classic Anthology*, ed. Perry Miller (New York: MJF Books, 1978), 20, 21.

4. Henry Adams (Anonymous), *Democracy*, in *Henry Adams: Novels, Mont Saint Michel, The Education* (New York: Library of America, 1983), 40–41. Adams's disillusionment with democracy (one born of disappointed hopes) is captured in the title, given by his brother, Brooks Adams, in the introduction, of Adams's posthumously published collection, *The Degradation of the Democratic Dogma*, ed. Charles Hirschfield (New York: Macmillan, 1919).

5. See, for example, Richard J. Bernstein, "Creative Democracy: The Task Still Before Us," *American Journal of Theology and Philosophy* 21 (September 2000): 215–228.

6. Whitman uses the phrase "Religious Democracy" in *Democratic Vistas*, in *The Portable Walt Whitman*, ed. Mark Van Doren (New York: Penguin, 1973), 365. Richard Rorty approvingly notes that Dewey and Whitman regarded democracy as "something sacred" (*Philosophy and Social Hope* [New York: Penguin, 1999], 25).

7. It is tempting to treat many of these religiously derived invocations at greater length and to point to the ways that each is connected fundamentally to "democratic faith." A brief précis will have to suffice, however, since this takes us unnecessarily beyond the main line of the discussion.

Caritas is discussed sensitively in Romand Coles, *Rethinking Generosity: Critical Theory and the Politics of Caritas* (Ithaca, N.Y.: Cornell University Press, 1997). Coles, like many antifoundational thinkers, insists on the priority of agonism informed by "generous receptivity" as a necessary feature of democratic politics. Such generous "agonistic encounters" allow for "new possibilities for empowering transformations of perception, thought, and being. This sense is far more experiential than it is theological. Not that it is does not involve a certain faith. But such faith is akin to Merleau-Ponty's 'perceptual faith,' rooted in existence. . . . In a similar way, Adorno harbors a similar faith that, however obliquely, our greatest possibilities for enrichment of both the self and the surrounding world lie at the edge where identity opens onto the manifold forms of nonidentity" (136). Later Coles points out the similarity of Adorno's conception of self to that of Emerson, Whitman, and Dewey (212). Such faith is recommended in spite of an early rejection of the "malignancy" of traditional Christian forms of faith (3).

Paul Woodruff has recently sought to reclaim what he regards as the virtue of "reverence" for secular purposes in *Reverence: Renewing a Forgotten Virtue* (New York: Oxford University Press, 2001). While sometimes granting that reverence can be directed toward the divine, in the main Woodruff prefers recommending reverence as a necessary attitude in secular, and particularly political, settings in which it is to be expected that individuals become open to the views of others. "It is a natural mistake to think that reverence belongs to religion. It belongs, rather, to community. Wherever people try to act together, they hedge themselves around with some form of ceremony or good manners, and the observation of this can be an act of reverence. Reverence lies behind civility and all of the graces that make life in society bearable and pleasant" (5). For Woodruff, more often than not, religion is associated with strife and warfare, whereas "reverence" properly conceived in political settings can prevent all forms of unnecessary conflict. Above all, reverence reminds us of human limitations: "Reverence begins in a deep understanding of human limitations; from this grows the capacity to be in awe of whatever we believe lies outside our control— God, truth, justice, nature, even death. The capacity for awe, as it grows, brings with it the capacity for respecting human beings, flaws and all" (3). Woodruff does not dwell at any length on whether it is likely that humans often think that "truth, justice, nature or even death" lie outside human control, at least not without an accompanying belief in the irreducible distance that lies between God and humans (thereby suggesting that such humility may ultimately be equally inescapably theological as reverence is, notwithstanding Woodruff's arguments to the contrary).

Placing his argument firmly in an Emersonian frame, Jeffrey Stout argues in his book, *Democracy and Tradition* (Princeton, N.J.: Princeton University Press, 2004), that "democratic piety" is most needful for the full flourishing of democratic mutual respect and dialogic openness. Like Woodruff, Stout treats traditional religion as one of the key institutions against which modern democracy was rebelling in its initial formation. Nevertheless, Stout recommends three "religious" virtues of character for modern democratic citizens—"piety," "hope," and "love, or generosity [*caritas*]," although he insists that piety deserves more attention at least because it has been the most controversial of the three. Democratic piety, somewhat like reverence, "concerns the proper acknowledgment of the sources of our existence and our progress through life" (9). It is therefore more oriented as a respectful stance toward the past. Stout adopts Dewey's embrace of "warranted assertion" as a "realistic" standard of truth while sharing Dewey's distaste for most forms of religious faith as wishful thinking (246). Like Dewey, however, he assumes that human practice—shorn of the stultifying certainties advanced by religious belief—will result in the progress of knowledge, which he compares to the progression of individuals on a staircase without the prospect of an upper or top story. In spite of this image of infinite progress and perfectibility, Stout nevertheless, perhaps incongruously, recommends "humility" as a paramount democratic virtue (269).

By contrast, Richard Rorty explicitly rejects "humility" as needlessly negative (perhaps given its relationship to the word "humiliation"). He writes that "the big difference between an undesirable sense of humility and a desirable sense of finitude is that the former presupposes that there is, already in existence, something better and greater than the human. . . . A pragmatic sense of limits requires us only to think that there are some projects for which our tools are presently inadequate, and to hope that the future may be better than the past in this respect" (*Philosophy and Social Hope*, 51–52). Even while rejecting the formerly religious virtue of "humility," Rorty retains a secularized Christian, and more future-oriented, virtue of "hope" throughout his work, as this very passage, and the title of the book from which it is drawn, both attest. For a discussion of the religious virtue of "hope" in contrast to "optimism," see chapter 9, below.

8. Emile Durkheim, *The Elementary Forms of the Religious Life*, trans. Joseph Ward Swain (New York: Macmillan, 1915).

9. Robert Booth Fowler, *The Dance with Community: The Contemporary Debate in American Political Thought* (Lawrence: University Press of Kansas, 1991). See also Wilson Carey McWilliams, *The Idea of Fraternity in America* (Berkeley: University of California Press, 1973).

10. Of course, this reconciliation remains a goal of explicitly theological writing as well. See, for example, Miroslav Volf, *Exclusion and Embrace: A Theological Exploration of Identity, Otherness, and Reconciliation* (Nashville, Tenn.: Abingdon, 1986).

11. Rorty grasps the "utopianism" of his secularized religious vision, revealingly placing his own pragmatic devotions in a dubious (and not altogether internally compatible) tradition. He writes that,

> my candidate for the most distinctive and praiseworthy human capacity is our ability to trust and to cooperate with other people, and in particular to improve the future. Under favourable circumstances, our use of this capacity culminates in utopian political projects such as Plato's ideal state, Christian attempts to realize the kingdom of God here on earth, and Marx's vision of the victory of the proletariat. . . . In our century, the most plausible project of this sort has been the one to which Dewey devoted his political efforts." (*Philosophy and Social Hope*, xiii–xiv)

12. Generally, see Loyd D. Easton, *Hegels's First American Followers: The Ohio Hegelians* (Athens: Ohio University Press, 1966). Among others, Emerson encountered Hegel through the work of these thinkers as well as the subsequent school dubbed the "St. Louis Hegelians"; see Robert D. Richardson Jr., *Emerson: The Mind on Fire*, (Berkeley: University of California Press, 1995), 472–476. The influence of Hegel particularly on the early work of John Dewey has been well noted; see, for example, Alan Ryan, *John Dewey and the High Tide of American Liberalism* (New York: Norton 1995), 85–86, 95–97. Hegel especially influenced Dewey's thought on how to overcome the divide between the human reality and the ideal: "The gap between our own achievements and what we take to be perfection of character remained wide. . . . The separation of our imperfect selves from this image of what they might become reintroduced the lacerating separation of flesh and spirit, the actual and the ideal, that Dewey wanted to overcome" (97). See also Stephen C. Rockefeller, *John Dewey: Religious Faith and Democratic Humanism* (New York: Columbia University Press, 1991), chap. 2, esp. 78–83. Rockefeller stresses, in particular, Dewey's attraction to Hegel's "organicism," in which "there is no dualism of God and human nature. . . . The development of individual human consciousness is viewed as a process whereby the individual participates in and reproduces the universal and absolute mind of God, which 'consists in an eternal and ever-complete process of self-realization'" (83). Hegel's influence on "communitarian" thinking remains strong; see, esp., Charles Taylor, *Hegel* (New York: Cambridge University Press, 1975).

13. On the continuities between Augustinianism, Jansenism, and Calvinism, see Leszek Kolakowski, *God Owes Us Nothing: A Brief Remark on Pascal's Religion and on the Spirit of Jansenism* (Chicago: University of Chicago Press, 1995).

14. William Ellery Channing, "The Ideal of Humanity," in Miller, *The Transcendentalists*, 430.

15. Jonathan Edwards, "Dissertation II: The Nature of True Virtue," in *The Works of Jonathan Edwards: Ethical Writings*, Vol. 8, ed. Paul Ramsey (New Haven: Yale University Press, 1989), 540.

16. See also Edwards's many sermons in this Augustinian vein, if not his most famous, "Sinners in the Hands of an Angry God," more appropriately "God Glorified in Man's Dependence," as well as his treatise, "The Great Christian Doctrine of Original Sin Defended."

17. Edwards, "The Nature of True Virtue," 610.

18. Jonathan Edwards, "God Glorified in Man's Dependence," in *The Works of Jonathan Edwards* 2 vols. (Peabody, Mass.: Hendrickson, 2003), 2:7.

19. Christopher Lasch, *The True and Only Heaven: Progress and Its Critics* (New York: Norton, 1991), 248.

20. For a classic statement rejecting the hard and even degrading teachings of Calvinism, see William Ellery Channing, "The Argument against Calvinism," in *William Ellery Channing: Selected Writings*, ed. David Robinson (New York: Paulist, 1985), 103–121. Channing's rejection of Calvinism was required in order to arrive at, and yet also resulted from, his belief in fundamental human goodness that reflected humanity's inherent divinity. "I reverence human nature too much to do it violence. I see too much divinity in its ordinary operations to urge on it a forced and vehement virtue. To grow in the likeness of God we need not cease to be men" (William Ellery Channing, "Likeness to God," in Miller, *The Transcendentalists*, 25).

21. A leading statement of Emerson as "democratic individualist" is George Kateb, *Emerson and Self-Reliance*, (Thousand Oaks, Calif.: Sage, 1995), as well as idem, *The Inner Ocean* (Ithaca, N.Y.: Cornell University Press, 1992). See also Stanley Cavell's analysis of "Emersonian perfectionism," in Cavell, *Conditions Handsome and Unhandsome: The Constitution of Emersonian Perfectionism* (Chicago: University of Chicago Press, 1990). For a corrective to these interpretations, see Wilson Carey McWilliams, *The Idea of Fraternity in America* (Berkeley: University of California Press, 1973), 280–289.

22. Emerson, "The Over-Soul," in *Emerson: Essays & Poems* ed. Joel Porte (New York: Library of America, 1996), 386.

23. Ibid., 385.

24. Ibid., 386.

25. Emerson, "Worship," in *Essays & Poems*, 890–891.

26. Emerson, "The Over-Soul," 398. See also "Circles": "No facts are to me sacred; none are profane; I simply experiment, and endless seeker, with no Past at my back" (*Essays & Poems*, 412).

27. Emerson, "Fate," in *Essays & Poems*, 786.

28. Emerson, "New England Reformers," in *Essays & Poems*, 605, passim.

29. Ibid., 599, 602.

30. Ibid., 605, 607.

31. Ralph Waldo Emerson, "Fortune of the Republic," *Miscellanies*, in *The Complete Works of Ralph Waldo Emerson*, 12 vols. (New York: AMS Press, 1979), 11:517.

32. Ibid., 536–537.

33. Emerson, "The Young Americans," in *Emerson: Essays and Lectures*, ed. Joel Porte (New York: Library of America, 1983), 213.

34. Richard Falk, "The Making of Global Citizenship," in *Global Visions: Beyond the New World Order*, ed. Jeremy Brecher, John Brown Childs, and Jill Cutler (Cambridge, Mass.: South End Press, 1993), 51. See also the religious language throughout Jason D. Hill's *Becoming a Cosmopolitan: What It Means to Be a Human Being in the New Millennium* (Lanham, Md.: Rowman & Littlefield, 2000).

35. Emerson, "The Young Americans," 218.

36. Ibid., 217.

37. Christopher Lasch, "Against the 'Secularization Thesis,'" in idem, *The True and Only Heaven*, 47.

38. On the problems that even Hegel's conception entail, see Steven B. Smith, *Hegel's Critique of Liberalism* (Chicago: University of Chicago Press, 1989), 217–231. Even the seeming finality of Hegel's formulation gives way to a more "proceduralist" possibility. Writes Smith, "When applied to itself, Hegel's thesis about an end of history could not but become another stifling orthodoxy that would generate its own antithesis, namely, an end to the end of history" (230–231).

39. Lasch, "Against the 'Secularization Thesis,'" 48.

40. John Dewey, *The Early Works, 1882–1898*, 4:105. Citations to Dewey's works collected in the three editions of his *Complete Works* are so noted:

EW: Early Works: 1882–1898, ed. Jo Ann Boydston, 5 vols. (Carbondale: Southern Illinois University Press, 1967–72);

MW: Middle Works: 1899–1924, ed. Jo Ann Boydston, 15 vols. (Carbondale: Southern Illinois University Press, 1976–83);

LW: Later Works: 1925–53, ed. Jo Ann Boydston, 17 vols. (Carbondale: Southern Illinois University Press, 1981–90).

41. John Dewey, *Quest for Certainty* (New York: Minton, Balch, 1929), 23. For Dewey's general discussion of this topic, see, especially, chaps. 1, 2, 9, and 10; hereafter cited as *QC*.

42. Ibid., 23.

43. Ibid., 227.

44. Dewey, "Liberalism and Social Action," in *Excellence in Public Discourse: John Stuart Mill, John Dewey, and Social Intelligence*, ed. James Gouinlock (New York: Teacher's College Press, 1986 [1935]), 118.

45. John Dewey, *Reconstruction in Philosophy* (New York: New American Library, 1950), 147; hereafter cited as *RP*.

46. Ibid., 46. Dewey describes Bacon as the "real founder of modern thought" (10).

47. Ibid., 48; emphasis mine.

48. Dewey, "The Democratic Faith and Education," *Antioch Review* 4, no. 2 (1944): 274–283; quote at 277.

49. In this regard, Dewey criticizes existing educational practices as consisting of "the inculcation of fixed conclusions rather than the development of intelligence as a method of action" (*RP*, 252).

50. John Dewey, *Human Nature and Conduct* (New York: Henry Holt, 1944): 212–213; hereafter cited as *HNC*.

51. Ibid., 141; John Dewey, *Experience and Education* (New York: Macmillan, 1938), 28.

52. Dewey's trust evokes Max Weber's view that "the distinctive characteristic of a problem of social policy is indeed the fact that it cannot be resolved merely by technical considerations." To think otherwise, he argued, is simply "a matter of faith." See Max Weber, *Methodology of the Social Sciences* (New York: Free Press, 1949), 55–56.

53. Dewey, "Experience, Knowledge and Value: A Rejoinder," *EW*, 14:79.

54. Dewey's early struggles with his traditional religious upbringing suggest that even the seemingly "traditional" religious writings of the late-1800s were already pervaded with a different understanding of the role that faith and religion were to play in Dewey's philosophy. As Neil Coughlin relates (via a secondhand source),

> "One evening [in 1879] while [Dewey] sat reading," he had his one mystical experience. It came by way of "an answer to that question which still worried him: whether he really meant business when he prayed": "It was not a very dramatic mystic experience. There was no vision, not even a definable emotion—just a supremely blissful feeling that his worries were over. . . . 'I've never had any doubts since then, nor any beliefs.'" (Neil Coughlin, *Young John Dewey* [Chicago: University of Chicago Press, 1973], 8–9)

55. Dewey, "Obligation to Knowledge of God," *EW*, 1:63. In a remarkable passage, Dewey wrote, "The scriptures are uniform in their treatment of skepticism. There is an obligation to know God, and to fail to meet this obligation is not to err intellectually, but to sin morally. Belief is not a privilege but a duty—'whatsoever is not faith is sin'" (ibid., 1:61).

56. Dewey, "Christianity and Democracy," *EW*, 4:4.

57. Ibid., 4:8.

58. Ibid., 4:9.

59. Dewey, "What I Believe," *Forum* 83 (March 1930): 180.

60. Dewey, "Christianity and Democracy," *EW*, 4:6.

61. Ibid., 4:10.

62. 4:9.

63. John Dewey, *A Common Faith* (New Haven: Yale University Press, 1934), 9–10; hereafter cited as *CF*. "[The religious] denotes attitudes that may be taken toward every object and every proposed end or ideal" (10).

64. While Dewey is careful to avoid associating Christianity too closely with more "primitive" religions, he does reflect, "have not some religions, including the most influential forms of Christianity, taught that the heart of man is totally corrupt? How could the course of religion in its entire sweep not be marked by practices that are shameful in their cruelty and lustfulness, and by beliefs that are degraded and intellectually incredible? What else than what we find could be expected, in the case of people having little knowledge and no secure method of knowing; with primitive institutions, and with so little control that they lived in a constant state of fear?" (*CF*, 5–6).

65. Dewey, "Intelligence and Power," *New Republic*, April 25, 1934, 306.

66. Dewey, "Creative Democracy—The Task Before Us," in *LW*, 2:287–288. Dewey's appreciative reception of Walter Lippmann is found in his review of Lippman's *Public Opinion*, entitled "Public Opinion," in *MW* 13:337. Dewey regarded *Public Opinion* as "perhaps the most effective indictment of democracy as currently ever penned" (337). See Robert Westbrook's invaluable discussion in his *John Dewey and American Democracy* (Ithaca, N.Y.: Cornell University Press, 1991), chap. 9.

67. Dewey, *Democracy and Education*, (New York: Macmillan, 1916), 59; *MW*, 12:181.

68. Dewey, "John Dewey Responds," in *John Dewey at Ninety*, ed. Harry W. Laidler (New York: League for Industrial Democracy, 1950), 34.

69. These struggles are extensively discussed by John Patrick Diggins in his *Promise of Pragmatism* (Chicago: University of Chicago Press, 1994), chap. 6. Diggins quite ably reveals one of the great deficiencies of Dewey's reliance on "experience" as revealed by his changing stance during the two wars. Believing in Wilson's claim that democracy could best be served by American intervention in World War I, Dewey supported U.S. participation, much to the chagrin of his colleagues at the *New Republic* (as Randolph Bourne remarked at one point, "if war is too strong for you to prevent, how is it going to be weak enough for you to control and mould to your liberal purposes?"). However, based on his disillusionment with the war's outcome, he concluded that American intervention in World War II would be a mistake. Reflecting an almost unpragmatist assumption, Dewey concluded that "no matter what happens, stay out" (*The Promise of Pragmatism*, 274). Diggins points out that "America's encounter with so unprecedented a phenomenon as Nazism raises a question as old as the study of history itself: can a novel event be dealt with by experience?" (274–275). Dewey's response to both wars—the certainty that in each case he had derived the right position based on experience—suggests a significant flaw in applying Dewey's philosophy to the world of politics. As Diggins concludes, "In Dewey's thoughts one finds no whisper of scepticism about the mind's ability to understand what is happening. Nor is there any suggestion of the 'fallibalism' or 'temporalism' that intellectual historians regard as the genius of pragmatism" (275).

70. Dewey, "The Democratic Faith and Education," 274.

71. Ibid., 277.

72. Ibid., 282–283.

73. Ibid., 283.

74. Cited in Rockefeller, *John Dewey*, 170.

75. Dewey's infatuation with Bellamy is recorded in Ryan, *John Dewey and the High Tide of American Liberalism*, 43–44.

76. John Patrick Diggins is among the few I have encountered. Another scholar attuned to this paradox in Dewey's thought is David Fott, who observes that "when [Dewey] says that he is willing to put his faith in scientific method to the test, he mentions an experimental test. If science is to test science, he is obviously begging the question" (*John Dewey: America's Philosopher of Democracy* [Lanham, MD: Rowman & Littlefield, 1998], 148).

77. The best expression of this aspect of Dewey's thought is in Dewey, *The Public and Its Problems* (Athens, Ohio: Swallow, 1927) esp. chaps. 4–6. Current theorists who view their work in a Deweyan mode include Richard Rorty, *Achieving Our Country* (Cambridge, Mass.: Harvard University Press, 1998), chap. 1; Benjamin R. Barber, "Foundationalism and Democracy," in *Democracy and Difference: Contesting the Boundaries of the Political*, ed. Seyla Benhabib (Princeton, N.J.: Princeton University Press, 1996), 348–359; and Amy Gutmann, "Democracy, Philosophy, and Justification," in Benhabib, *Democracy and Difference*, 340–347.

78. Lasch, *The True and Only Heaven*, 390–393.

79. Reinhold Niebuhr, *Moral Man and Immoral Society* (New York: Scribner's, 1932), 81.

80. On the long-standing debate between Niebuhr and Dewey on these and other

themes, see Daniel F. Rice, *Reinhold Niebuhr and John Dewey: An American Odyssey* (Albany: State University of New York Press, 1993), esp. chaps. 5 and 12; see also my discussion of Niebuhr in chapter 9, below.

81. *CF*, 80.

82. Richard Rorty, *Achieving Our Country: Leftist Thought in Twentieth-Century America* (Cambridge, Mass.: Harvard University Press, 1998). Rorty writes that "for both Whitman and Dewey, the terms 'America' and 'democracy' are shorthand for a new conception of what it is to be human—a conception which has no room for obedience to a nonhuman authority, and in which nothing save freely achieved consensus among human beings has any authority at all" (18).

83. Rorty, *Philosophy and Social Hope*, 160.

84. Ibid., 162.

85. Richard Rorty, *Contingency, Irony, and Solidarity* (New York: Cambridge University Press, 1989), 86.

86. Richard Rorty, *Essays on Heidegger and Others, Philosophical Papers*, Vol. 2 (Cambridge: Cambridge University Press, 1991), 33.

87. Rorty, *Achieving Our Country*, 143 n. 12.

88. Rorty, *Philosophy and Social Hope*, 161.

89. Ibid., 27.

90. Ibid., 163.

91. Ibid., 51–52.

CHAPTER 7
"A PATTERN LAID UP IN HEAVEN": PLATO'S DEMOCRATIC IDEAL

1. Karl R. Popper, *The Open Society and Its Enemies*, Vol. 1, *The Spell of Plato*, (Princeton, N.J.: Princeton University Press, 1962); Sheldon S. Wolin, *Politics and Vision: Continuity and Innovation in Western Political Thought* (Boston: Little, Brown, 1960), chap. 2; R.H.S. Crossman, *Plato Today* (London: Unwin, 1959), 285; Jean Bethke Elshtain, *Public Man, Private Woman* (Princeton, N.J.: Princeton University Press, 1981), 20–41; Benjamin R. Barber, "Misreading Democracy: Peter Euben and the *Gorgias*," in *Demokratia: A Conversation on Democracies, Ancient and Modern*, ed. Josiah Ober and Charles Hedrick. (Princeton, N.J.: Princeton University Press, 1996), 361–375; Cynthia Farrar, *The Origins of Democratic Thinking: The Invention of Politics in Classical Athens* (New York: Cambridge University Press 1988), 1.

2. Leo Strauss, *The City and Man* (Chicago: University of Chicago Press, 1964), 127.

3. Ibid., 131. See also the similar argument by Strauss's student, Allan Bloom, in his "Interpretive Essay," in *The Republic of Plato*, trans. Allan Bloom (New York: Basic Books, 1968), 421–422.

4. Other notable contributions to this subtle reading of Plato as a democratic thinker include Arlene Saxonhouse, *Athenian Democracy: Modern Mythmakers and Ancient Theorists* (Notre Dame: University of Notre Dame Press, 1996), 87–114; S. Sara Monoson, *Plato's Democratic Entanglements* (Princeton, N.J.: Princeton University Press, 2000); John Wallach, *The Platonic Political Art: A Study of Critical Reason and Democracy* (University Park: University of Pennsylvania Press, 2001); Christopher Rocco, *Tragedy and Enlightenment: Athenian Political Thought and the Dilemmas of Modernity* (Berkeley: University of California Press, 1997); Gerald M.

Mara, *Socrates' Discursive Democracy: Logos and Ergon in Platonic Political Philosophy* (Albany: State University of New York Press, 1997). See also my review essay, "Chasing Plato," *Political Theory* 28 (2000): 421–439.

5. See J. Peter Euben, *The Tragedy of Political Theory: The Road Not Taken* (Princeton, N.J.: Princeton University Press, 1990); idem, *Corrupting Youth: Political Education, Democratic Culture, and Political Theory* (Princeton, N.J.: Princeton University Press, 1997); and idem, *Platonic Noise* (Princeton, N.J.: Princeton University Press, 2003).

6. Euben, *The Tragedy of Political Theory*, 270.

7. Euben, *Corrupting Youth*, 208.

8. As Euben points out in a commentary on the *Gorgias,* "Socrates dismisses majority rule as an absurd way of deciding on the best way of life or even the best polity. . . . Even democracy's friends have often worried about what majority rule can mean in the face of elite manipulation" (Euben, "Reading Democracy: 'Socratic' Dialogues and the Political Education of Democratic Citizens," in Ober and Hedrick, *Demokratia*, 333).

9. Plato, *Republic*, trans. Allan Bloom (New York: Basic Books, 1968, 368c–369a; hereafter Stephanus numbers are provided parenthetically within the text.

10. Bernard Williams, "The Analogy of the City and the Soul in Plato's *Republic*," in *Exegesis and Argument*, ed. E. N. Lee (New York: Humanities, 1973): 196–206.

11. Ibid., 199.

12. Ibid. At this point Williams attempts to apply this proper interpretation of the rational element's "weakening" of the "desiring" portion of the soul *back* to the city, resulting in a picture of domination rather than cooperation, thereby leading to Williams's conclusion that it is "a less attractive picture" (199).

13. Despite his perceptive argument about the incongruities of the analogy, Williams allows those incongruities to lead him to conclusions about Plato's aims in establishing a hierarchical city, rather than guiding him toward a conclusion about the priority of the soul (ibid., 199ff.).

14. Here I use the translation of Tom Griffith, which, perhaps peculiarly, although less literal in its translation of *"aporia oikeion"* than Bloom's "shortage at home," nevertheless more clearly conveys the statement (Plato *Republic*, trans. Tom Griffith (New York: Cambridge University Press, 2000).

15. Jacob Klein rightly notes that even the "abruptness" of *Meno*'s first line would nevertheless convey an extensive set of prior understandings to the immediate Greek audience, including aspects of the character of Meno. As described by Xenophon in *Anabasis*, he is well known to be "a totally unscrupulous man, eager above all to accumulate wealth and subordinating everything else to that end, consciously putting aside all accepted norms and rules of conduct, perfidious and treacherous, and perfectly confident in his own cunning and ability to manage things to his own profit" (Jacob Klein, *A Commentary on Plato's* Meno [Chicago: University of Chicago Press, 1989 (1965)], 36). For the portrayal of Meno in Xenophon, see *Anabasis* II.6: 21–29.

16. *Meno*, trans. G.M.A. Grube, in *Plato: Complete Works*, ed. John M. Cooper (Indianapolis: Hackett, 1997).

17. Although some commentators dismiss the "paradox" as a ploy by Meno to divert the conversation and consider Socrates' willingness to engage it as wholly ironic, Alexander Nehamas rightly views the "paradox" to be central to the Socratic

project. See Alexander Nehamas, "Meno's Paradox and Socrates as a Teacher," in *Plato's* Meno *in Focus*, ed. Jane M. Day (New York: Routledge, 1994), 221–229.

18. Many philosophic investigations have attempted to explicate, clarify, verify, or reject the apparent teaching of this doctrine of recollection, although often, indeed almost always, without regard to the explicit content of the "framing" story or myth by which Socrates (or, more often, a theory attributed to Plato) presents the doctrine. Consider, for example, the essays in Day, *Plato's* Meno *in Focus*, especially Gregory Vlastos's "*Anamnesis* in the *Meno*," Julius Moravcsik's "Learning as Recollection" and Kathleen V. Wilkes, "Conclusions in the *Meno*," in which she writes that "for the purposes of this paper, the doctrine of reincarnation [*sic*] is best ignored" (219 n. 4). These essays are representative of the avoidance of considerations of dramatic and dialogic developments in the dialogue that one finds throughout the philosophical profession.

19. See, for example, Vlastos, "*Anamnesis* in the *Meno*," 88–111.

20. Commentators who have noted this difficulty in the doctrine include Jerome Eckstein, *The Platonic Method: An Interpretation of the Dramatic-Philosophic Aspects of the* Meno (New York: Greenwood, 1968); Klein, *A Commentary on Plato's* Meno, 96–97; Vlastos, "*Anamnesis* in the *Meno*," 102–103.

21. For a helpful diagram of the divided line, see Bloom's annotation in his introduction to *The Republic of Plato*, 464 n. 39.

22. See Klein, *A Commentary on Plato's Meno*, 96, on the inculcation of courage that results from a belief in *anamnēsis*.

23. Jerome Eckstein similarly notes that "pragmatically, there is no cognitive difference between the alternates' consequence [i.e., "learning" vs. "recollection"]. It is all the same whether man has no prenatal knowledge, or whether he has eternal knowledge of everything but forgets it at birth; in both cases he must encounter in this life questions and experiences that will elicit from him 'learning' and 'remembrance'" (*The Platonic Method*, 47).

24. Klein more accurately calls it a "story" rather than a "theory" (*A Commentary on Plato's Meno*, 96).

25. Socrates compares *orthē doxa* to the "statues of Daedelus" who, "like acquiring a runaway slave," is only worth much "if tied down." This "tying down" of "true opinion," thereby making it "knowledge," is accomplished through "recollection" (97e–100b). For further elaboration on these passages, see Nehamas, "Meno's Paradox and Socrates as a Teacher," 229–245.

26. *Apology*, trans. G.M.A. Grube, in *Plato: Complete Works*.

CHAPTER 8
THE ONLY PERMANENT STATE: TOCQUEVILLE ON RELIGION AND DEMOCRACY

1. Examples of proponents on each side of this debate are too numerous to cite, but the looming authority defending the idea of "public reason," and arguing for limits on religious ideas (or "comprehensive doctrines") in the public sphere, is John Rawls, *Political Liberalism* (New York: Columbia University Press, 1993), esp. 212–254. In these pages Rawls admits the "limits of public reason" by acknowledging that his own theory, strenuously applied, might have limited claims made by abolitionists and civil rights leaders. However, he concludes that, given historical circumstances applicable at that time, "it was not unreasonable for them to act as they did [i.e., not employing "public reason" but rather a "comprehensive doctrine" of reli-

gion] for the sake of the ideal of public reason itself" (251). It is not entirely clear whether Rawls believes it was on this basis that these people acted (i.e., anticipating Rawls) or whether it is Rawls's judgment that now gives their otherwise untoward evocation of religion a retrospective legitimacy. This begs the question, however, of how we are to act in the future, unless we assume, as Rawls apparently does, that we have reached the end of philosophy, if not the end of history. Here Rawls presents himself as the modern Hegel. For a forceful defense of the role of religion in the public sphere, see Richard John Neuhaus, *The Naked Public Square: Religion and Democracy in America* (Grand Rapids, Mich.: Eerdmans, 1986).

2. On the dangers posed by various kinds of fundamentalism, see S. Scott Appleby, *The Ambivalence of the Sacred: Religion, Violence, and Reconciliation* (Lanham, Md.: Rowman & Littlefield, 2000), esp. chaps. 2 and 3; on the call for a firming of moral and communal underpinnings in modern democracy, see Amitai Etzioni, *The Spirit of Community: The Reinvention of American Society* (New York: Touchstone, 1993); and idem, ed., *New Communitarian Thinking: Persons, Virtues, Institutions, and Communities* (Charlottsville: University Press of Virginia, 1995).

3. See Alexis de Tocqueville, *Democracy in America*, trans. George Lawrence, ed. J. P. Mayer (New York: Harper and Row, 1969), 297–301. All subsequent citations from *Democracy in America* are from this edition, and, hereafter, parenthetically are given within the text. Citations from the French are drawn from Tocqueville, *Oeuvres*, Vol. 2, ed. André Jardin (Paris: Éditions Gallimard, 1992). William Galston describes how *Democracy in America* has come increasingly to apply to the contemporary "partial Europeanization of America" in "Tocqueville on Liberalism and Religion," *Social Research* 54 (1987), 501. Stephen Macedo's recent work, *Diversity and Distrust: Civic Education in a Multicultural Democracy* (Cambridge: Harvard University Press, 2000) suggests that the suspicion and even hostility toward religion in the "public sphere" remains, at base, motivated by a deep suspicion of Catholicism's commitments to democratic values. For a critique of this hostility toward Catholicism in particular, see Richard Boyd, "Including Us Out," *Commonweal* 127 (September 22, 2000), 25–6.

4. Tocqueville, *Oeuvres*, 2:7. I have changed Lawrence's translation here from "dread" to the more accurate "terror."

5. As described by Harvey C. Mansfield and Delba Winthrop, "The democrat considers others to be like himself and if they are truly different, he *sees* them to be like himself regardless. He ignores or flattens out any differences that might call equality into question" (introduction to *Democracy in America* by Alexis de Tocqueville [Chicago: The University of Chicago Press, 2000], xlvii). Cynthia J. Hinckley similarly recognizes this "psychological predisposition," although, in my view, excessively stresses the sense of "equality of opportunity" that informs the American view ("Tocqueville on Religious Truth and Political Necessity," *Polity* 23 [1990]: 39–52). While this is clearly one aspect of the American sense of equality recognized by Tocqueville, even at the stage when one "gets ahead" there is rarely a claim made by either those who succeed—or those who do not—that one has achieved a form of moral excellence deserving special praise (44–45).

6. See Tocqueville's letter to Gobineau, dated September 5, 1843, in which he noted one of the primary inheritances of Christianity was to put "in grand evidence the equality, the unity, the fraternity of all men." See Tocqueville, *The European Revolution and Correspondence with Gobineau*, ed. and trans. John Luckacs (Westport,

Conn.: Greenwood, 1959), 191. See also his letter to Gobineau dated January 14, 1857, in which he forcefully rejects Gobineau's racialist theories:

> How can this [Christian] spirit be reconciled with a doctrine that tries to make the races distinct and unequal, with differing capacities of understanding, of judgment, of action, due to some original and immutable disposition which invisibly denies the possibility of improvement for certain peoples? Evidently Christianity wishes to make all men brothers and equals. Your doctrine makes them cousins at best whose common father is very far away in the heavens; to you down here are only victors and vanquished, masters and slaves, due to our different birthright. (305)

For a more extensive discussion of the Tocqueville-Gobineau correspondence, with particular emphasis on their radical differences regarding fundamental human equality (or inequality), see James W. Ceaser, *Reconstructing America: The Symbol of America in Modern Thought* (New Haven: Yale University Press, 1997), chaps. 4–6.

7. The vast literature examining the role of judicial review as a forum of counter-majoritarian redress speaks to Tocqueville's concern. Theorists who are suspect of democratic majorities tend to be supportive of a strong role for judicial review, for example, John Hart Ely, *Democracy and Distrust: A Theory of Judicial Review* (Cambridge, Mass.: Harvard University Press, 1980); and Ronald Dworkin, *Law's Empire* (Cambridge, Mass.: Harvard University Press, 1986). Recently some theorists have suggested that courts need to be more deferential toward democratic majorities; see Jeremy Waldron, *The Dignity of Legislation* (Cambridge: Cambridge University Press, 1999); and Mark Tushnet, *Taking the Constitution Away from the Courts* (Princeton, N.J.: Princeton University Press, 1999). What this literature often overlooks is Tocqueville's understanding that the American system is based, in the words of James Madison, on "the majority principle." While courts can postpone or delay the fruition of the majority's views, a sustained majority opinion will be successful either through the amendment process (in the event that a majority is also a supermajority) or through the electoral process, by which presidents are able to appoint justices whose views are more in line with their own.

8. I follow Henry Reeve's and George Lawrence's traditional translation of Tocqueville's word "inquiet" to be "restlessness." However, in their recent translation, Mansfield and Winthrop employ the word "restive" instead, which, in their view, more fully captures Tocqueville's sense of "rebelliousness and intent" rather than the more random sense of "restless" (introduction to *Democracy in America* by Tocqueville, xciii). Perhaps even better would be the word "inquietude," although it is somewhat archaic even as it captures the same Latin root of the French term. These connotations should be kept in mind as informing the imperfectly translatable sense of Tocqueville's term.

9. Tocqueville would almost certainly have found the popular bumper sticker, "Whoever dies with the most toys wins," to be revealing of this American tendency, and not entirely in jest.

10. Tocqueville shies away from exploring what might be regarded as the dangers of a belief in human perfectibility in the chapter in which he discusses its particularly democratic manifestation. He notes that Americans are wont to view all contemporary conditions as imminently outmoded, and hence to construct objects with a view to their almost immediate obsolescence (453). While Tocqueville speaks of a sailor's view of shipbuilding in this context, one must wonder if this principle might be extended more generally to other "objects" of human endeavor whose permanence Tocqueville views as essential to the health of the democratic project, including fam-

ilies, associations, and communities—all of which might be viewed as equally subject to obsolescence on the grounds of human perfectibility. He does not investigate some of the more malevolent implications of the belief in perfectibility as they are manifested in politics. Wilfred M. McClay in *The Masterless: Self and Society in Modern America* (Chapel Hill: University of North Carolina Press, 1994), has pointed to some contemporary aspects of Tocqueville's observations that point to these more alarming consequences of "perfectibility":

> The emergence of this temper can easily be correlated with the rise of Jackson, including the decline of deferential politics and the status of older governing elites, the intensifying disdain for all forms of privilege and ascriptive status, the veneration of "the common man," the general weakness of institutional authority, the seeming fluidity of social boundaries, the sense of immense economic opportunity presented by a vast and unexploited American continent, the swell of enthusiasm for a plethora of social reforms, each driven by its own impassioned dream of the perfectibility of man. All these elements seem to merge and coalesce into a heroic fantasy of boundless individual potential, a vision of personal infinitude that impatiently brushed aside the severe and impassible limits imposed by custom, by history, by accidents of birth, or even by the venerable doctrine of original sin. The spread-eagle rhetoric of Manifest Destiny and continental expansion seemed to find its counterpart in a spread-eagle, expansive understanding of the self. (42)

11. Joshua Mitchell describes this condition as arising from humanity's "Augustianian self," by which humans are simultaneously drawn "inward" toward an excessive concern with self and "outward" toward an excessive devotion to things of the world. Although this condition is endemic to the human situation, according to Augustine and described by Mitchell, democracy exacerbates each tendency and makes democratic man manifest extreme versions of both at the same time. See Joshua Mitchell, *The Fragility of Freedom: Tocqueville on Religion, Democracy and the American Future* (Chicago: University of Chicago Press, 1995), 3–39.

12. In a letter to Gobineau, dated December 20, 1853, Tocqueville suggested that these extremes were being manifested in postrevolutionary France:

> The last century had an exaggerated and somewhat childish trust in the control which men and peoples were supposed to have of their own destinies. It was the error of those times; a noble error, after all; it may have led to many follies, but it also produced great things, compared to which we shall seem quite small in the eyes of posterity. The weary aftermath of revolutions, the weakening of the passions, the miscarriage of so many generous ideas and of so many great hopes have led us to the opposite extreme. After having felt ourselves capable of transforming ourselves, we now feel incapable of reforming ourselves; after having had excessive pride, we have now fallen into excessive self-pity; we thought we could do everything, and now we think we can do nothing; we like to think that the struggle and effort are henceforth useless and that our blood, muscles, and nerves will always be stronger than our will power and courage. This is really the sickness of our age. (Tocqueville, *The European Revolution*, 231–232)

If Tocqueville appears uncharacteristically forgiving of the extreme optimism of the revolutionaries in this letter, it is part because he is trying foremost to combat what he regards as the self-defeating resignation and passivity underlying Gobineau's theories on the inequality of the races.

13. Aristotle, *Nicomachean Ethics*, trans. Martin Ostwald (New York: Macmil-

lan, 1962), 1108b11–1109b15, esp. 1108b27–28 ("the extremes are more opposed to one another than each is to the median").

14. Ibid., 1109b4–5.

15. "There is therefore no question of reconstructing an aristocratic society, but the need is to make freedom spring from that democratic society in which God has placed us" (695).

16. Tocqueville precedes this discussion of religious "enthusiasm" by reiterating what he had said earlier regarding faith being the "only permanent state of mankind" (297): "It was not man who implanted in himself the taste for the infinite and love of what is immortal. These sublime instincts are not the offspring of some caprice of the will; their foundations are embedded in nature; they exist despite a man's efforts. Man may hinder and distort them, but he cannot destroy them" (534–535).

17. Tocqueville saw these two "propensities" as inescapably part of the human predicament. In a letter to his friend Kergolay he wrote,

> Do what you will, you cannot change the fact that men have bodies as well as souls—that the angel is enclosed in the beast. . . . Any philosophy, any religion which tries to leave entirely out of account one of these two things may produce a few extraordinary examples, but it will never influence humanity as a whole. This is what I believe, and it troubles me, for you know that, no more detached from the beast than anyone else, I adore the angel and want at all costs to see him predominate. (Cited in Tocqueville, *The European Revolution*, trans. Lukacs, 27–28).

18. Pierre Manent, *Tocqueville and the Nature of Democracy*, trans. John Waggoner (Lanham, Md.: Rowman & Littlefield, 1996), 132.

19. On the avoidance of "impiety" even by the most ardent revolutionaries, see Wilson Carey McWilliams, "Civil Religion in the Age of Reason: Thomas Paine on Liberalism, Redemption, and Revolution," *Social Research* 54 (1987): 447–490. McWilliams maintains that even Paine, whose subtle interpretation of Scripture suggests an underlying atheism, nevertheless must seek to recommend a form of liberal "civil religion" only by indirection in the face of colonial mistrust toward atheists. Tocqueville was aware that the religious underpinnings of the United States had a particularly Puritan basis, one that understood freedom as distinct from license. He favorably quotes from Cotton Mather's *Magnalia Christi Americana* on precisely this point:

> "Nor would I have you to mistake in the point of your own *liberty*. There is a *liberty* of corrupt nature, which is affected by *men* and *beasts* to do what they list; and this *liberty* is inconsistent with *authority*, impatient of all restraint; but this *liberty*, *Sumus Omnes Deteriores*, 'tis the grand enemy of *truth* and *peace*, and all the *ordinances* of God are bent against it. But there is a civil, a moral, a federal *liberty*, which is the proper end and object of *authority*; it is a *liberty* for that only which is *just* and *good*. . . . This *liberty* is maintained in a way of *subjection* to *authority*; and the *authority* set over you will in administrations for your good be quietly submitted to, by all but such as have a disposition to *shake off the yoke*, and lose their true *liberty*, by their murmuring at the honour and power of *authority*." (cited on 46)

20. John C. Koritansky maintains that Rousseau was Tocqueville's model for the development of his civil religion, whereas Sanford Kessler argues that Montesquieu was the source of Tocqueville's inspiration. Tocqueville noted the particular influence of three scholars in his thought: "There are three men with whom I live a bit every day, Pascal, Montesquieu, and Rousseau" (letter to Kergolay, November 10, 1836;

cited in James T. Schleifer, *The Making of Tocqueville's Democracy in America*, 2nd ed. [Indianapolis: Liberty Fund, 2000], 32). See John C. Koritansky, "Civil Religion in Tocqueville's *Democracy in America*," *Interpretation* 17 (1990): 389–400; and Sanford Kessler, *Tocqueville's Civil Religion: American Christianity and the Prospects for Freedom* (Albany: State University of New York, 1994), chap. 3, esp. 59.

21. Jack Lively, *The Social and Political Thought of Alexis de Tocqueville* (Oxford: Clarendon, 1965), 197.

22. Marvin Zetterbaum, *Tocqueville and the Problem of Democracy* (Stanford: Stanford University Press, 1967), 122.

23. Among those scholars critical of Lively and Zetterbaum are Mitchell, *The Fragility of Freedom*; Catherine Zuckert, "Not by Preaching Alone: Tocqueville on the Role of Religion in American Democracy," *Review of Politics* 43 (1981): 259–280, esp. 275–280; and Hinckley, "Tocqueville on Religious Truth and Political Necessity"; in addition, without explicit mention, Pierre Manent is also critical of the view that Tocqueville can be understood to be speaking of religion in wholly utilitarian terms (*Tocqueville and the Nature of Democracy*, chap. 8).

24. Manent, *Tocqueville and the Nature of Democracy*, 88.

25. Ibid., 91.

26. He variously states that he considers religions "from a purely human point of view" (297, 445) or that he makes a judgment about religion's utility in a democracy by considering "the interests of this world" (442). The phrase and perspective was likely drawn from the method of François Guizot, who claimed also to look at religion "always under a human point of view" in lectures that appear in *The History of Civilization in Europe* (ed. Larry Siedentop [New York: Penguin, 1997], 39), lectures which Tocqueville attended in 1828. On the influence of these lectures, and the thought of Guizot generally, on Tocqueville's thought, see Andre Jardin, *Tocqueville: A Biography*, trans. Lydia Davis (New York: Farrar, Straus and Giroux, 1988), 81–82; Larry Siedentop, *Tocqueville* (Oxford: Oxford University Press, 1994) chap. 2; and Aurelian Craiutu, "Tocqueville and the Political Thought of the French Doctrinaires," *History of Political Thought* 30 (autumn 1999): 456–494.

27. "Plato's *Apology of Socrates*," in *Four Texts on Socrates*, trans. Thomas G. West, rev. ed. (Ithaca, N.Y.: Cornell University Press, 1998), 23b.

28. Tocqueville here refers to a passage from, but does not explicitly cite, Pascale's *Pensées*, Fragment 72. See Tocqueville's reference to Pascale's influence in note 17, above.

CHAPTER 9
HOPE IN AMERICA: THE CHASTENED FAITH OF REINHOLD NIEBUHR AND CHRISTOPHER LASCH

1. Richard Rorty, The End of Leninism, Havel, and Social Hope," in *Truth and Progress: Philosophical Papers*, Vol. 3 (Cambridge: Cambridge University Press, 1998), 228. The essay appeared originally under the title "The End of Leninism and History as Comic Frame," in *History and the Idea of Progress*, ed. Arthur M. Melzer, Jerry Weinberger, and M. Richard Zinman (Ithaca, N.Y.: Cornell University Press, 1995), 211–226.

2. Richard Rorty, *Achieving Our Country: Leftist Thought in Twentieth-century America* (Cambridge, Mass.: Harvard University Press. 1998), 14. Rorty's self-iden-

tification with the "party of hope" drawn from Emerson's description of a "party of hope" and a "party of memory" in the latter's 1841 essay "The Conservative."

3. Rorty, "The End of Leninism," 236.

4. Ibid., 243.

5. Václav Havel, *Disturbing the Peace* (New York: Vintage, 1991), 181.

6. Ibid.

7. Ibid.

8. Ibid.

9. Václav Havel, *The Art of the Impossible: Politics as Morality in Practice* (New York: Fromm International, 1997), 238–239. Of course, this speech had not been delivered when Rorty delivered the remarks on which his original essay was based in 1991 (*Philosophical Papers*, 3:14 n. 12). However, the republication and retitling of Rorty's essay in his *Philosophical Papers,* Vol. 3, in 1998 postdates the publication of Havel's speech on hope in 1997.

10. Augustine, *Enchiridion on Faith, Hope, and Love* (Washington, D.C.: Regnery, 1961), 7.

11. Ibid., 132. Of the respective sections addressing faith, hope, and love, respectively, in Augustine's *Enchiridion*, a full ninety-four sections deal with faith; merely three with hope; and five with love. In keeping with what we have seen in the essays by Rorty and Havel, although hope "occupies" a central place in the thought of Augustine's work, it is in fact little discussed, perhaps reflecting its ultimate mystery.

12. Thomas Aquinas, *Theological Texts*, ed. and trans. Thomas Gilby (Oxford: Oxford University Press, 1955), 203.

13. Ibid.

14. Thomas Aquinas, *Treatise on the Virtues*, trans. John A. Oesterle (Englewood Cliffs, N.J.: Prentice Hall, 1966), 122.

15. Aquinas, *Theological Texts*, 203–204.

16. Ibid., 204.

17. Joseph Pieper, *Faith, Hope, Love* (San Francisco: Ignatius, 1986), 101.

18. Ibid., 102.

19. Christopher Lasch, *The True and Only Heaven: Progress and Its Critics* (New York: Norton, 1991), 389. On the distinction that both Niebuhr and King draw between hope and optimism, see ibid., chap. 9 ("The Spiritual Discipline against Resentment"), especially the section entitled "Hope without Optimism" (390–393). See also my treatment of Lasch in this chapter, below.

20. Martin Luther King Jr., *A Testament of Hope*, ed. James Melvin Washington (New York: Harper, 1991).

21. Cornel West, "The Moral Obligations of Living in a Democratic Society," in *The Good Citizen*, ed. David Batstone and Eduardo Mendieta (New York: Routledge, 1999), 5, 9, 12.

22. Ibid., 10.

23. Václav Havel, "Forgetting We Are Not God," *First Things* (March 1995): 50.

24. This view of science as a corrective to narrow local prejudice is, of course, one of the great assumptions of the Enlightenment, animating, for example, Diderot's introduction to the *Encyclopedie*. While such optimistic expressions would appear to be largely discredited in the late twentieth century, they survive less in academia (with the exception of departments in the natural sciences) and more in the arena of popular nonfiction, such as in the recent book by Virginia Postrel, *The Future and Its Enemies* (New York: Free Press, 1998). For an exploration of some contemporary expressions

of this confidence in the natural sciences, for example, in the areas of artificial intelligence and genetic engineering, see David F. Noble, *The Religion of Technology: The Divinity of Man and the Spirit of Invention* (New York: Knopf, 1998), chaps. 8–11.

25. As Havel writes elsewhere,

> Thirty years after [collectivization] swept the traditional family farm off the face of the earth, scientists are amazed to discover what even a semi-literate farmer previously knew—that human beings must pay a heavy price for every attempt to abolish, radically, once for all and without a trace, that humbly respected boundary of the natural world, with its tradition of scrupulous personal acknowledgment. They must pay for the attempt to seize nature, to leave not a remnant of it in human hands, to ridicule its mystery; they must pay for the attempt to abolish God and to play at being God. (*Living in Truth*, ed. Jan Valdislav [Boston: Faber and Faber, 1986], 141).

26. Reinhold Niebuhr, *Man's Nature and His Communities* (New York: Scribner's, 1965), 24.

27. Reinhold Niebuhr, *The Irony of American History* (New York: Scribner's, 1952), 63; hereafter *IAH*.

28. For a superb exploration of the long dispute (and many agreements) between Niebuhr and Dewey, see Daniel F. Rice, *Reinhold Niebuhr and John Dewey: An American Odyssey* (Albany: State University of New York Press, 1993).

29. Reinhold Niebuhr, *Moral Man and Immoral Society: A Study in Ethics and Politics* (New York: Scribner's, 1960 [1932]); hereafter *MMIS*. On the shift in Niebuhr's thought, marked by the publication of this book and its extraordinary reception, see Richard Wightman Fox, *Reinhold Niebuhr: A Biography* (Ithaca, N.Y.: Cornell University Press, 1996), esp. chap. 6. As Fox points out regarding Niebuhr's early thought, "despite his fulminations against sentimental liberalism, against complacent faith in the redemptive character of human goodwill, Reinhold remained a thoroughgoing liberal. . . . His faith was built not upon abandoning himself to God's will but upon the old liberal dream of transforming human society" (134). See also Ernest F. Dibble, *Young Prophet Niebuhr: Reinhold Niebuhr's Early Search for Social Justice* (Washington, D.C.: University Press of America, 1977), 26–95.

30. *MMIS*, 35, xxii.

31. Ibid., xiii.

32. Reinhold Niebuhr, "Intellectual Biography," in *Reinhold Niebuhr: His Religious, Social, and Political Thought*, ed. Charles W. Kegley and Robert W. Bretall (New York: Macmillan, 1961), 15.

33. Reinhold Niebuhr and Paul S. Sigmund, *The Democratic Experience* (New York: Praeger, 1969), 11.

34. "Educators who emphasise the pliability of human nature, social and psychological scientists who dream of 'socialising' man and religious idealists who strive to increase the sense of moral responsibility, can serve a very useful function in society in humanizing individuals within an established social system and in purging the relations of individuals of as much egoism as possible. In dealing with the problems and necessities of radical social change they are almost invariably confusing in their counsels because they are not conscious of the limitations in human nature which finally frustrate their efforts" (*MMIS*, xxiv).

35. Reinhold Niebuhr, *The Nature and Destiny of Man*, 2 vols. (New York: Scribner's, 1941–43), 1:121; hereafter, *NDM*.

36. Ibid., 1:96.

37. Ibid., 1:178–79.

38. "The religious presuppositions which form the framework for most modern scientific examinations of the human scene contain two very dubious articles, which must be held responsible for most of the errors and illusion in these examinations: A) The idea of the perfectibility of man and B) the idea of progress" (Reinhold Niebuhr, *Christian Realism and Political Problems* [New York: Scribner's, 1953), 3; hereafter, *CRPP*.

39. *NDM*, 1:201. Elsewhere Niebuhr wrote that "faith proves its absoluteness precisely where its insights make it possible to detect the relativity of the interpretations and to question the validity of any claim, including our own, that we have been redeemed. At those points it is proved that faith has discerned and is in contact with the 'true' God and not with some idol of our imagination." See "A Reply," in Kegley and Bretall, *Reinhold Niebuhr*, 443. On this self-critical aspect of Niebuhr's theology, see Langdon Gilkey, *On Niebuhr: A Theological Study* (Chicago: University of Chicago Press, 2001), esp. chap. 6 ("Sin: Anxiety, Pride, and Self-Deception), 102–123.

40. In response to *Moral Man and Immoral Society* Dewey wrote:

> The situation is such that it is calculated to make one look around, even if from sheer desperation, for some other method, however desperate. And under such circumstances, it also seems as if the effort to stimulate resort to the method of intelligence might present itself as at least one desperate recourse, if not the only one that remains untried. In view of the influence of the collective illusion of the past, some case might be made out for the contention that even if it be an illusion, exaltation of intelligence and experimental method is worth a trial. Illusion for illusion, this particular one may be better than those upon which humanity has usually depended. ("Intelligence and Power," *New Republic*, April 25, 1934, 306).

41. For a theological treatment of Niebuhr on hope, see Keith Ward, "Reinhold Niebuhr and the Christian Hope," in *Reinhold Niebuhr and the Issues of Our Times*, ed. Richard Harries (London: Mowbray, 1986), 61–87.

42. Robin W. Lovin, *Reinhold Niebuhr and Christian Realism* (New York: Cambridge University Press, 1995), 198; see also 9–11 ("The Limits of Political Realism").

43. Reinhold Niebuhr, "The Relevance of an Impossible Ethical Ideal," in *An Interpretation of Christian Ethics* (Harper and Brothers, 1935), 113; hereafter *CE*.

44. Ibid., 111.

45. Ibid., 118.

46. Ibid., 120–121.

47. For Niebuhr, justice is a species, albeit a lower species, of love; nevertheless, it is a necessary goal as an approximation of love given the intractability of human selfishness: "The effort to substitute the law of love as the fulfillment and the highest form of the spirit of justice is derived from the failure to measure the power and persistence of self-interest" (Reinhold Niebuhr, *Love and Justice: Selections from the Shorter Writings of Reinhold Niebuhr*, ed. D. B. Robertson [New York: Meridian, 1957], 25). See also *NDM*, 2:246–247: "Love is both the fulfillment and the negation of all achievements of justice in history" (246).

48. The recognition of the unachievability of the "law of love" is critically important in resisting tyrannical efforts to force its promulgation: "The tragic character of our moral choices, the contradiction between various equal values of our devotion, and the incompleteness of all our moral striving, prove that 'if in this life only

we had hoped in Christ, we are of all men most miserable.' No possible historic justice is sufferable without the Christian hope. But any illusion of a world of perfect love without these imperfect harmonies of justice must ultimately turn the dream of love into a nightmare of tyranny and injustice" (Niebuhr, *Love and Justice*, 29).

49. Reinhold Niebuhr, "Optimism, Pessimism, and Religious Faith," in *The Essential Reinhold Niebuhr: Selected Essays and Addresses*, ed. Robert McAfee Brown (New Haven: Yale University Press, 1986), 7; hereafter *ERN*.

50. *CE*, 121. The term "ultimate optimism" appears in *ERN*, 6.

51. Reinhold Niebuhr, *The Children of Light and the Children of Darkness: A Vindication of Democracy and a Critique of Its Traditional Defense* (New York: Scribner's, 1960 [1944]), xiv; hereafter *CLCD*.

52. See Langdon Gilkey's personal recollection of the impact of Niebuhr's darker prophetic words in the early part of the twentieth century in his *On Niebuhr*, 3–15.

53. For example, Niebuhr criticized democratic faith based upon the perfection of political institutions, upon the possibility of a thoroughly just economic system, or (here indicating his long-standing critique of Dewey) upon "a more perfect educational process to redeem man from his partial and particular loyalties" (*CLCD*, 17).

54. *CLCD*, 135. Charles T. Mathewes writes that "Niebuhr's famous skepticism about claims to innocence or purity is not a disabling, paralyzing hermeneutics of suspicion, but rather an 'enabling humility'" (*Evil and the Augustinian Tradition* [New York: Cambridge University Press, 2001], 133).

55. *CLCD*, 29.

56. Niebuhr bases the book's title on Luke 16:8: "The children of this world are in their generation wiser than the children of light."

57. Of Madison, Niebuhr admiringly wrote:

> James Madison was the only one of the founding fathers who made a realistic analysis of both power and interest from a political and democratic perspective. He was governed by a basic insight of political realism, namely the "intimate relation" between reason and self-love. Unlike the idealists, he knew the need for strong government. Unlike Thomas Hobbes, he feared the dangers of strong government and thought that the "separation of powers" itself would prevent tyranny. Madison shared the fear of "factions" with all the Founding Fathers, but gave us the best pre-Marxist analysis of the basis of collective and class interests of varying classes. (*MNHC*, 66–67)

By contrast, Thomas Jefferson was the preferred Founding Father for Dewey, who regarded Jefferson's "deep-seated faith in the people and their responsiveness to enlightenment properly presented . . . [as] the cardinal element bequeathed by Jefferson to the American tradition" (John Dewey, "Presenting Thomas Jefferson," in *The Later Works: 1925–1953*, ed. Jo Ann Boydston, 17 vols. (Carbondale: Southern Illinois University Press, 1981–1990), 14: 204, 205. For further discussion of the contrast between Niebuhr and Dewey on the American founders, see Rice, *Reinhold Niebuhr and John Dewey*, 255–259.

58. *CLCD*, 119.

59. Hobbes, *Leviathan*, chap. 30.

60. *NDM*, 2:275.

61. Alexander Hamilton, James Madison, and John Jay, *Federalist Papers*, ed. Clinton Rossiter (New York: Mentor Books, 1999), no. 55, 310.

62. *MMIS*, xi–xii. Recognizing that his distinction may be drawn "too unqualifiedly" (xi), Niebuhr later wrote that the more appropriate title would have been

"The Not So Moral Man and His Less Moral Communities" (*MNHC*, 22), but even these qualifiers indicate that he held the distinction throughout his career to be descriptively true and politically significant.

63. *CLCD*, 41.

64. *IAH*, 142–143. While expressing skepticism about the likelihood of world government, Niebuhr notes that "human communities are subject to 'organic' growth" (142).

65. Reinhold Niebuhr, "The Illusion of World Government," in *CRPP*, 29.

66. *MMIS*, 277. Note that both Niebuhr and Dewey conclude that humankind is in need of salutary illusion in order to pursue the perfection of society (see Dewey on illusion, cited above in note 39). The difference lies in Niebuhr's sense that we must first be disillusioned to allow ourselves to embrace that illusion more clearly; for Dewey, we must be "re-illusioned" away from the disillusionment to which traditional religion inclines us. As Daniel Rice has noted, Niebuhr and Dewey share far more in common philosophically than either was likely to acknowledge (Rice, *Reinhold Niebuhr and John Dewey*, xvii, 238: "Niebuhr perhaps should have articulated more fully than he did his basic agreement with the nexus in Dewey's writings between liberal idealism and democracy"). See also Cornel West, *The American Evasion of Philosophy* (Madison: University of Wisconsin Press, 1989), 150–164, who places Niebuhr firmly within the pragmatist tradition: "Even after Niebuhr turned to the Pauline and Augustinian traditions he remained a liberal Christian. I suggest this is so because Niebuhr's roots in American pragmatism do not permit him to decenter human creative powers" (155). For a fascinating argument on behalf of the "illusion" of religion, see Reinhold Niebuhr, "As Deceivers, Yet True," in idem, *Beyond Tragedy: Essays on the Christian Interpretation of History* (New York: Scribner's, 1937), 1–24.

67. Reinhold Niebuhr, "Augustine's Political Realism," in *ERN*, 128. See Niebuhr's discussion of Augustine's rejection of world government in ibid., 127.

68. *NDM*, 2:85.

69. *CLCD*, 153.

70. Ibid., 158, 160, 162–163.

71. Ibid., 168.

72. Ibid., 186.

73. For a sustained and penetrating analysis of Niebuhr's consistent endorsement of perfectionist liberalism, see Wilson Carey McWilliams, "Reinhold Niebuhr: New Orthodoxy for Old Liberalism," *American Political Science Review* 56 (December 1962): 874–885. For a related critique in a more theological register, see Stanley Hauerwas, *With the Grain of the Universe: The Church's Witness and Natural Theology* (Grand Rapids, Mich.: Brazos, 2001), chaps. 4 and 5.

74. James Madison, "Is Universal Peace Possible?" in *The Complete Madison: His Basic Writings*, ed. Saul K. Padover (New York: Harper and Brothers, 1953), 260.

75. Madison's argument presages that of Kant, who states in "Perpetual Peace" that,

as hard as it may sound, the problem of organizing a nation is solvable even for a people comprised of devils (if only they possess understanding). The problem can be stated this way: "So order and organize a group of rational beings who require universal laws for their preservation—though each is secretly inclined to exempt himself from such laws—that, while their private attitudes conflict, these nonetheless so cancel one another that these beings behave publicly just as if they had no evil attitudes." (Immanuel Kant, "Perpetual Peace," in *Perpetual Peace and Other Essays*, trans. Ted Humphrey [Indianapolis, Ind.: Hackett, 1983], 124).

76. Madison, "Is Universal Peace Possible?" 261.

77. Ibid., 262.

78. Arthur Schlesinger Jr., "Reinhold Niebuhr's Role in American Political Thought and Life," in *Reinhold Niebuhr: His Religious, Social, and Political Thought*, ed. Charles W. Kegley and Robert W. Bretall (New York: Macmillan, 1961), 214.

79. Reinhold Niebuhr, *Faith and Politics: A Commentary on Religious, Social and Political Thought in a Technological Age*, ed. Ronald H. Stone (New York: George Braziller, 1968), 42.

80. Many of Niebuhr's theological critics offer a healthy corrective to Niebuhr's submerged optimism, particularly his brother H. Richard Niebuhr, Karl Barth, and, more recently, Stanley Hauerwas. On H. Richard's reservations to Niebuhr's "humanistic religion," see Fox, *Reinhold Niebuhr*, 132–134; Hauerwas expresses his own reservations about Niebuhr, and contrasts him to Barth, in *With the Grain of the Universe*, chaps. 4–7. Nevertheless, arguably it is the very *theological* emphasis of these critics that leads them to overlook the role and influence of "democratic faith" in the backdrop of Niebuhr's optimism, and why a "secular" thinker is best positioned to see that relationship more clearly.

81. Lasch, *The True and Only Heaven*; and idem, *The Revolt of the Elites and the Betrayal of Democracy* (New York: Norton, 1995).

82. Ralph Waldo Emerson, "The Conservative," in *Emerson: Essays and Lectures*, ed. Joel Porte (New York: Library of America, 1996), 173. For Lasch, "hope" relied equally upon memory and the rejection of "nostalgia" (*The True and Only Heaven*, 82–119); see also idem, "The Politics of Nostalgia: Losing History in the Mists of Ideology," *Harper's*, November 1984, 66–70.

83. Lasch was unsurprised that his book *The True and Only Heaven*, was strongly attacked by critics on both the Left and the Right. See Lasch, "A Reply to Jeffrey Isaac," *Salmagundi* 93 (winter 1992): 98–109.

84. Among helpful and sympathetic recent treatments of Lasch's thought, especially recommended are Jean Bethke Elshtain, "The Life and Work of Christopher Lasch: An American Story," *Salmagundi* 106–107 (spring 1995): 146–161; and idem, "Limits and Hope: Christopher Lasch and Political Theory," *Social Research* 66 (summer 1999): 531–543; and Peter A. Lawler, *Postmodernism Rightly Understood* (Lanham, Md.: Rowman & Littlefield, 1999), chap. 5 ("Moral Realism versus Therapeutic Elitism: Christopher Lasch's Populist Defense of American Character"). Sometimes insightful, but finally less helpful, is Louis Menand, "Christopher Lasch's Quarrel with Liberalism," in idem, *American Studies* (New York: Farrar, Straus and Giroux, 2002), 198–220.

85. Lasch, *The Revolt of the Elites*, 82–83.

86. Lasch, *The True and Only Heaven*, introduction; idem, *The Revolt of the Elites*, chap. 2. The phrase "secession of the successful" is drawn from a similar argument posed by Robert Reich. See Robert B. Reich, "The Secession of the Successful," *New York Times Magazine*, January 20, 1991, 16.

87. Lasch, *The Revolt of the Elites*, 5–6, 29, 34–35, 79. See also David Brooks, *Bobos in Paradise: The New Upper Class and How They Got There* (New York: Simon and Schuster, 2000).

88. Lasch, *The Revolt of the Elites*, 39–47. On these competing conceptions of equality, see John Schaar, "Some Ways of Thinking about Equality," *Journal of Politics* 26 (November 1964): 867–895. See also Wilson Carey McWilliams, "On Equality as the Moral Foundation for Community," in *The Moral Foundations of the American Republic*, ed. Robert H. Horwitz (Charlottesville: University Press of Virginia, 1986), 183–213.

89. Christopher Lasch, *The Culture of Narcissism: American Life in an Age of Diminishing Expectations* (New York: Norton, 1979); idem, *Haven in a Heartless World: The Family Besieged* (New York: Basic Books, 1977); and idem, *The Revolt of the Elites*, 105–107.

90. Unsurprisingly Lasch expressed admiration for Foucault's early analysis of the rise of the modern disciplines. See his review of Foucault's *The Birth of the Clinic*, *New York Times Book Review*, February 24, 1974, 6.

91. Lawler, *Postmodernism Rightly Understood*, 159.

92. Lasch, *The True and Only Heaven*, 530; idem, *The Revolt of the Elites*, 85–86.

93. Lasch, *The Revolt of the Elites*, 82–83. On this point, see also Wilson Carey McWilliams, "The Discipline of Freedom," in *To Secure the Blessings of Liberty: First Principles of the Constitution*, ed. Sarah Baumgartner Thurow (Lanham, Md.: University Press of America, 1988), 31–63.

94. This aspect of Lasch's argument bears extensive resemblance to that advanced generally by Wendell Berry, *The Art of the Common Place: The Agrarian Essays of Wendell Berry*, ed. Norman Wirzba (Washington, D.C.: Counterpoint, 2002); see also Kimberly K. Smith, *Wendell Berry and the Agrarian Tradition: A Common Grace* (Lawrence: University Press of Kansas, 2003).

95. Here Lasch echoes Hannah Arendt, who wrote that "men, not Man, live on earth and inhabit the world" (*The Human Condition*, 2nd ed. [Chicago: University of Chicago Press, 1998], 7).

96. Ray Oldenburg, *The Great Good Place: Cafés, Coffee Shops, Community Centers, Beauty Parlors, General Stores, Bars, Hangouts, and How They Get You through the Day* (New York: Paragon, 1989).

97. Lasch, *The Revolt of the Elites*, chap. 5 ("Communitarianism or Populism? The Ethic of Compassion and the Ethic of Respect").

98. Ibid., chaps. 6 and 9, esp. 117, 119, 124.

99. Ibid., 171.

100. In an interesting reversal of expectations, Lasch also appealed to "late" Emerson—particularly as the author of the essay "Fate"—as one resource for understanding the limits on the human attempt to control all external phenomena. If Emerson is partly responsible for disassociating the language of "hope" from the language of limits—as he does in the essay "The Conservative"—then perhaps Lasch believed that turnabout was fair play, and therefore drafted Emerson in the project of recoupling hope and humility (*The True and Only Heaven*, 261–279).

101. See Christopher Lasch, "The Infantile Illusion of Omnipotence and the Modern Ideology of Science," *New Oxford Review* (October 1986): 14–18. This article was the first in a series appearing in the *New Oxford Review* maintaining that modern belief in human mastery, scientific control, and the possibility of overcoming alienation was a fundamental restatement of the second-century heresy of Gnosticism. To Elaine Pagel's question, "Why would a God who is 'almighty'—all powerful—create a world that includes suffering, pain, disease," Lasch gently if chidingly

responded (in a tone reminiscent of one a parent might take with an indignant child), "One answer, of course, is that human happiness may not be the purpose of creation" (15).

102. I draw again upon William F. May's distinction between "accepting love" and "transforming love," which was discussed in the introduction and is available at: http://bioethicsprint.bioethics.gov/transcripts/jan02/jansession2intro.html. Lasch's most extensive discussion of the nonliberal aspect of the family is found in *Haven in a Heartless World*; see also *Women and the Common Life: Love, Marriage, and Feminism*, ed. Elisabeth Lasch-Quinn (New York: Norton, 1997).

103. Lasch, *The True and Only Heaven*, 491. To this extent, the "pro-life" movement has erred beyond measure in itself adopting the language of "rights" to defend the fetus, inasmuch as this language is derived precisely from the liberal voluntarist model. For further Lasch-influenced discussion of abortion as a belief in "the power over life," see Christopher Shannon, *Conspicuous Criticism: Tradition, the Individual, and Culture in American Social Thought, from Veblen to Mills* (Baltimore, Md.: The Johns Hopkins University Press, 1996), 186–187. Lasch was well aware that the same ethic which defended abortion on demand would lead inevitably to the call for libertarian genetic engineering (*The True and Only Heaven*, 188–189).

104. Lasch, *The Revolt of the Elites*, 25–79.

105. Lasch, *The True and Only Heaven*, 527.

106. In his assessment of Lasch's "argument with liberalism," Louis Menand rightly points out that the populist tradition to which Lasch appealed had its fair share of bigots, isolationists, racists, and demagogues. In response, Menand can only seek to restate the grounds of the disagreement: liberalism offers "rights" as a corrective to, and limitation upon, democracy and, in doing so, ultimately defines democracy as co-extensive with the progressive extension of rights. Menand suggests that Lasch was insufficiently aware of liberalism's reliance upon rights as a constitutive component of progress. This is implausible: if anything, Lasch believed that the liberal emphasis upon rights insufficiently attended to duties and obligations that accompanied rights (e.g., with the right to "free speech," there must be an accompanying duty to speak civilly and listen attentively). Moreover, Menand gives insufficient attention to the extent to which the extension of rights has relied upon, and indeed in many cases been driven by, economic nationalization and globalization, the destruction of local forms of life, and the decline of democratic engagement by citizenries in "advanced" nations. Lasch sought to refute the all-too-easy liberal assumption that such forms of local life were the endemic and unavoidable sources of narrowness, and that democracy so conceived was not sufficiently informed by forms of toleration which eschewed judgments that led to such claims of superiority of "one's own" way of life or one's own kind of people. Finally, it should also be observed that liberalism has been insufficiently attentive to conceiving of ways to abridge objectionable forms of exclusion and bigotry without seeking to uproot all forms of "parochialism," partiality, or community. See Menand, "Christopher Lasch's Quarrel with Liberalism," 217–220. See also Lasch's discussion of the substantial civic virtues that the invocation of rights presupposes in his "Age of Limits," in *History and the Idea of Progress*, ed. Arthur M. Melzer, Jerry Weinberger, and M. Richard Zinman (Ithaca, N.Y.: Cornell University Press, 1995), 233.

107. This dynamic has been dissected with unparalleled perceptiveness by Wilson

Carey McWilliams in *The Idea of Fraternity in America* (Berkeley: University of California Press, 1973).

108. Lasch, *The Revolt of the Elites*, 244.

109. Lasch's analysis has been extended in rich historical detail by Christian Smith in his introduction to *The Secular Revolution: Power, Interests, and Conflict in the Secularization of American Public Life*, ed. Christian Smith (Berkeley: University of California Press, 2003), 1–96.

110. Lasch was concerned far more with rebutting liberal criticisms of religion than with theological complacency among religious believers, but the implications of his analysis concerning the former apply equally to the latter. In this regard, Lasch would likely be equally if not more critical of contemporary forms of "personalized and individualistic" religion that Alan Wolfe analyzes in his recent book *The Transformation of American Religion: How We Actually Live Our Faith* (New York: Free Press, 2003), as well as his earlier book *Moral Freedom: The Search for Virtue in a World of Choice* (New York: Norton, 2002). For an articulation of such a critique, see Wilson Carey McWilliams, "American Democracy and the Politics of Faith," in *Religion Returns to the Public Square: Faith and Policy in America*, ed. Hugh Heclo and Wilfred M. McClay (Washington, D.C.: Woodrow Wilson Center Press, 2003), 143–162.

111. Lasch, *The Revolt of the Elites*, 15–16; also 90 and 244–246.

112. For Lasch's discussion of Edwards, see *The True and Only Heaven*, 246–256.

113. Leszek Kolakowski, *God Owes Us Nothing: A Brief Remark on Pascal's Religion and on the Spirit of Jansenism* (Chicago: University of Chicago Press, 1995). Kolakowski's interest in both thinkers centers on their fundamental Augustinianism; see ibid., 30–61.

114. Lasch, *The True and Only Heaven*, 248. For a characteristic statement of this belief, see Jonathan Edwards, "God Glorified in Man's Dependence," in *The Works of Jonathan Edwards* 2 vols. (Peabody, Mass.: Hendrickson, 2003), 2:3–7.

115. Lasch, *The Revolt of the Elites*, 243. Prideful men, caught up in rebellion against their dependence, find it "impossible (unless their hearts [are] softened by grace) to reconcile their expectations of worldly success and happiness, so often undone by events, with the idea of a just, loving, and all-powerful creator" (Lasch, *The True and Only Heaven*, 248). For a characteristic expression of this incomprehension, see William Ellery Channing's 1820 essay "The Moral Argument against Calvinism," in *William Ellery Channing: Selected Writings*, ed. David Robinson (New York: Paulist, 1985), 103–121; as well as Lasch's discussion in *The True and Only Heaven*, 260–261.

116. Lasch, *The True and Only Heaven*, 248; idem, *The Revolt of the Elites*, 246.

117. For Lasch's discussion of "hope without optimism," see *The True and Only Heaven*, 14, 39, 78–81, 390–393, 536. His discussion of "the spiritual discipline against resentment" is found in ibid., 329–411, and features largely admiring portraits of Reinhold Niebuhr and Martin Luther King.

118. Cited by Elshtain, "The Life and Work of Christopher Lasch," 161.

119. Christopher Lasch, *The Minimal Self: Psychic Survival in Troubled Times* (New York: Norton, 1984), 259.

CONCLUSION
A MODEL OF DEMOCRATIC CHARITY

1. President George W. Bush, "Inaugural Address," *New York Times*, January 21, 2001, 14.

2. Wilfred M. McClay has seen this relationship perhaps more clearly than anyone, writing that George W. Bush's faith is well within the tradition of American civil religion: "Despite much public worrying about President Bush's easy resort to "God-talk," his oratory lies well within the established historical pattern of American civil-religious discourse." McClay goes on to suggest that Bush's faith is in accordance with John Dewey's call for a "common faith" ("The Soul of a Nation," *Public Interest* 155 [spring 2004], 18, 19). Another acute observer of the president's optimism is David Brooks, who has chronicled George W. Bush's (as well as his own) overly optimistic belief in the ease of democratizing Iraq, and has argued further that modern conservatism following Ronald Reagan is notable for its eschewal of the dour views once associated with Russell Kirk and Richard Weaver. See, in particular, his column, "Reagan's Promised Land," *New York Times*, June 8, 2004, A25, in which Brooks writes that Reagan "was an optimist," evinced in particular by his "boyish faith in science" and overarching belief in progress. Reagan, much like Bush, articulated a view of America that unquestioningly assumed God's favor, saying at one point, "I, in my own mind, have always thought of America as a place in the divine scheme of things that was set aside as a promised land" (A25). For one among many theologically based critiques of George W. Bush's Christianity, see, for example, Sidney Callahan, "A Pro-life Case against Bush," *Commonweal*, June 4, 2004, 15–18.

3. Sidney Hook, *Pragmatism and the Tragic Sense of Life* (New York: Basic Books, 1974), ix.

4. Ibid., xiii–xiv.

5. Richard Rorty, "Truth without Correspondence to Reality," in idem, *Philosophy and Social Hope* (New York: Penguin, 1999), 29.

6. Richard Rorty, "Religious Faith, Intellectual Responsibility and Romance," in idem, *Philosophy and Social Hope*, 163. See also idem, "Justice as Larger Loyalty," in *Cosmopolitics: Thinking and Feeling beyond the Nation*, ed. Pheng Cheah and Bruce Robbins (Minneapolis: University of Minnesota Press, 1998), esp. 56–57.

7. Ralph Waldo Emerson, "The Fortune of the Republic," *Miscellanies*, in *The Complete Works of Ralph Waldo Emerson* (New York: AMS Press, 1979), 515.

8. H. W. Brands has persuasively shown that America's self-confidence of its special place in the world—what Lincoln described as "the last, best hope—has taken different forms. The first, more passive and benign, form is the American self-understanding as an "exemplary" nation; the other, more interventionist type, involves the American self-conception as "vindicationist" or "redeemer" nation. See H. W. Brands, *What America Owes the World: The Struggle for the Soul of Foreign Policy* (New York: Cambridge University Press, 1998). See also Walter McDougall, *Promised Land, Crusader Nation: America's Encounter with the World since 1776* (New York: Houghton Mifflin, 1997); and Ernest Lee Tuveson, *Redeemer Nation: The Idea of America's Millennial Role* (Chicago: University of Chicago Press, 1968).

9. Emerson, "The Fortune of the Republic," 537.

10. Christopher Lasch, *The Revolt of the Elites and the Betrayal of Democracy* (New York: Norton, 1995), 244.

11. Cornel West, "Pragmatism and the Sense of the Tragic," in *The Cornel West*

Reader (New York: Basic Books, 1999), 174–182. There West writes, "Dewey failed to seriously meet the challenge posed by Lincoln—namely, defining the relation of democratic ways of thought and life to a profound sense of evil" (175). Further, "the culture of democratic societies requires not only the civic virtues of participation, tolerance, openness, mutual respect and mobility, but also dramatic struggles with the two major culprits—disease and death—that defeat and cut off the joys of democratic citizenship. Such citizenship must not be so preoccupied—or obsessed—with possibility that it conceals or represses the ultimate facts of the human predicament" (179). West rightly stresses Lincoln's sense of the ineradicablity of "evil" but dangerously reduces evil to physical phenomena that might lead a pragmatist to conclude that science and medicine can aim to cure what ails us. Lincoln's belief that human "illness" was lodged in our will to power and aim at mastery (including the denial of our fundamental equality) stands as a necessary corrective to even West's insufficient but still bracing view.

12. Abraham Lincoln, *Speeches and Writings*, ed. Donald E. Fehrenbacher, 2 vols. (New York: Library of America, 1989), 1:28–36, 81–90; hereafter, citations to Lincoln will be indicated by volume and page number parenthetically within the text. Harry V. Jaffa and students have particularly advanced an understanding of Lincoln's thought that stresses the central importance of these two early speeches. See Harry V. Jaffa, *Crisis of the House Divided: An Interpretation of the Issues in the Lincoln-Douglas Debates* (Chicago: University of Chicago Press, 1982), 183–272; see also Lucas E. Morel, *Lincoln's Sacred Effort: Defining Religion's Role in American Self-Government* (Lanham, Md.: Lexington Books, 2000). For a corrective, see Glen E. Thurow, *Abraham Lincoln and American Political Religion* (Albany: State University of New York Press, 1976); and Stewart Winger, *Lincoln, Religion and Romantic Cultural Politics* (DeKalb: Northern Illinois University Press, 2003).

13. In his magisterial biography of Lincoln, Allen C. Guelzo has stressed Lincoln's attraction to rationalist and Enlightenment thinkers as well as his religious skepticism during his young adult years. See Guelzo's *Abraham Lincoln: Redeemer President* (Grand Rapids, Mich.: Eerdmans, 1999), chaps. 1 and 4. Harry V. Jaffa has stressed Lincoln's contractarianism initially in *Crisis of the House Divided* (313–315, and chaps. 14–15 generally) and has forcefully reiterated these views in *A New Birth of Freedom: Abraham Lincoln and the Coming of the Civil War* (Lanham, Md.: Rowman & Littlefield, 2000), chap. 2. There Jaffa writes that "disinterested human intelligence" and "unassisted human reason" determine that "a free society is in harmony with the nature of man because it recognizes that the human good arises from human freedom" (105). See also Daniel Farber, *Lincoln's Constitution* (Chicago: University of Chicago Press, 2004).

14. A brief account of Lincoln's correspondence with Eliza Gurney is provided by Ronald C. White Jr., *Lincoln's Greatest Speech: The Second Inaugural* (New York: Simon and Schuster, 2002), 141–143. For a sensitive treatment of the role of divine providence that governed Lincoln's late thought especially, see Guelzo, *Abraham Lincoln*, epilogue.

15. On Witherspoon's influence, see Garrett Ward Sheldon, *The Political Philosophy of James Madison* (Baltimore, Md.: The Johns Hopkins University Press, 2001); and Jeffry Morrison, "John Witherspoon and 'The Public Interest of Religion,'" *Journal of Church and State* 41 (summer 1999): 551–573.

16. In contrast to Locke, Calvin held that politics was natural, even if particular regimes were not. See Sheldon S. Wolin, *Politics and Vision* (Boston: Little, Brown,

1960), 155–165. Calvin wrote that government was "equally as necessary to mankind as bread and water, light and air, and far more excellent" (cited in ibid., 162).

17. Calvinists and liberals were able to make common cause in the years leading up to the American Revolution. The "Declaration of Independence"—often understood by such thinkers as Jaffa as the ur-text of Enlightenment liberalism—was, in fact, written with craft and political acumen in such a manner to hold together that fragile coalition. See Garrett Ward Sheldon, "Eclectic Synthesis: Jesus, Aristotle, and Locke," in *Thomas Jefferson and the Politics of Nature*, ed. Thomas S. Engeman (Notre Dame, Ind.: University of Notre Dame Press, 2000), 81–98.

18. See Guelzo, *Abraham Lincoln*, 151–152; White, *Lincoln's Greatest Speech*, esp. chap. 6. See also Winger, *Lincoln, Religion and Romantic Cultural Politics*, chaps. 6–7.

19. In Book XII of the *Confessions*, Augustine writes that,

> all these valid points of view are available to people who entertain no doubts about their truth because you have granted them the grace to discern these matters. . . . I will have no truck with any . . . who think that Moses could have said what is untrue. But as for those who feed on your truth in wide pastures of charity . . ., let us approach the words of your book together, and there seek your will as expressed through the will of your subject. . . . A great variety of interpretations, many of them legitimate, confronts our exploring minds as we search among these words to discover your will. (Augustine, *The Confessions of Saint Augustine*, trans. Maria Boulding [Hyde Park, N.Y.: New City Press, 1997], 262, 265).

In effect, Augustine argues that it is only those who begin with a ground assumption of the truth of Scripture that can engage in charitable interpretation, precisely because they at once recognize the truth of the Bible and, through that acknowledgment, recognize the necessary imperfection of humanity in comprehending with utter certainty the will of God expressed therein. See also Peter Brown, *Augustine of Hippo: A Biography* (Berkeley: University of California Press, 1967), 260–269.

20. Jaffa, *The Crisis of the House Divided*, 305–306.

21. John Calvin, *Commentaries on the Book of Genesis*, trans. John King (Grand Rapids, Mich.: Baker Books, 2003), 176. Calvin notes that Adam's sin—eating from the Tree of the Knowledge of Good and Evil—indicated the human propensity to "desire to be wise above measure" (126).

22. Lincoln's insight into the source of human equality was restated with particular acuity and brevity by C. S. Lewis in a short essay entitled "Equality." Lewis states, "I am a democrat because I believe in the Fall of Man." Unlike those "democratic enthusiasts," influenced, in his view, by Rousseau, who believe that humans are "wise and good," Lewis counters that "the real reason for democracy is just the reverse. Mankind is so fallen that no man can be trusted with unchecked power over his fellows." Lewis accords some tentative agreement with Aristotle's argument for the existence of natural slaves but then sharply differs when considering whether any natural leaders even exist: "I reject slavery because I see no men fit to be masters." Democracy is justified in the end not because humans are capable of ultimate perfection but because we are equally burdened with imperfection, partiality, and, above all, original sin. See C. S. Lewis, "Equality," in *Present Concerns*, ed. Walter Hooper (New York: Harcourt Brace Jovanovich, 1986), 17.

23. This phrase is drawn from Lincoln's 1842 "Address to the Washington Temperance Society of Springfield." While Stewart Winger identifies this speech as among

Lincoln's most "optimistic productions," nevertheless he rightly concludes that its overarching message reflected Lincoln's "habitual belief that one was not entirely in control of one's own choices. One therefore needed to adopt a posture of humility, forgiveness, and thankfulness. . . . It was a profoundly Christian counter to any self-congratulatory pharisaism that might have crept in among the faithful" (Winger, *Lincoln, Religion and Romantic Cultural Politics*, 188, 189).

24. Daniel Elazar has compared Lincoln's invocation of an American covenant to that of John Winthrop in the *Arabella* speech in *The Covenant Tradition in American Politics*, available at: http://www.jcpa.org/dje/books/ct-vol3-ch1.htm. See also John H. Schaar's argument that Lincoln advanced a form of "covenanted patriotism" in "The Case for Patriotism," *American Review: The Magazine of New Writing* 17 (May 1973): 59–99. Matthew Holland has helped me see the similarities between these two speeches, although he differs with me on how closely their respective theologies are related.

25. John Winthrop, "A Model of Christian Charity," in *The American Puritans: Their Prose and Poetry*, ed. Perry Miller (New York: Columbia University Press, 1956), 79.

26. Ibid., 79–80.

27. Ibid., 80.

28. Ibid., 82.

29. Winthrop's—and Lincoln's—understanding that the virtue of charity arises foremost from a recognition of our individual insufficiency accords fully with Calvin's statement to the same end:

> No member [of the human body] has its power for itself, nor applies it to its private use, but transfuses it among its fellow members, receiving no advantage from it but what proceeds from the common convenience of the whole body. So, whatever ability a pious man possesses, he ought to possess it for his brethren, consulting his own private interest in no way inconsistent with a cordial attention to the common edification of the church. . . . Whatever God has conferred upon us, which enables us to assist our neighbor, we are stewards of it, and must one day render an account of our stewardship. (cited in Wolin, *Politics and Vision*, 183).

30. Timothy P. Jackson, *The Priority of Love: Christian Charity and Social Justice* (Princeton, N.J.: Princeton University Press, 2003), 172. Jackson is speaking here specifically in respect to abortion policies, although its sentiments certainly extend throughout the human and political life span.

31. Calvin, *Commentary on Genesis*, 178.

32. Mark Noll, *America's God: From Jonathan Edwards to Abraham Lincoln* (New York: Oxford University Press, 2002), 434, 435. On the triumphalism of most major Northern theologians, see 422–445.

33. Cited in ibid., 423.

34. Ibid., 432.

35. "We shall nobly save, or meanly lose, the last best, hope of earth" ("1862 Annual Message to Congress," 2:415); "I am exceedingly anxious that this Union, the Constitution, and the liberties of the people shall be perpetuated in accordance with the original idea for which that struggle was made, and I shall be most happy indeed if I shall be an humble instrument in the hands of the Almighty, and of this, his almost chosen people, for perpetuating the object of that great struggle" ("Address to the New Jersey Senate," 2:209).

36. Lincoln rightly understood that the existence of slavery deprived American

democracy of its claim to exemplary equality in a world hostile to democratic equality: "I hate [slavery] because it deprives our republican example of its just influence in the world—enables the enemies of free institutions, with plausibility, to taunt us as hypocrites" ("Speech on the Kansas-Nebraska Act," October 16, 1854, 1:315). As he further argued—against the exclusion of any people from the Declaration's defense of human equality—"when it comes to this I should prefer emigrating to some country where they make no pretense of loving liberty—to Russia, for instance, where despotism can be taken pure, and without the base alloy of hypocrisy" ("Letter to Joshua Speed," August 24, 1855, 1:363).

NEW FORUM BOOKS

New Forum Books makes available to general readers outstanding original interdisciplinary scholarship with a special focus on the juncture of culture, law, and politics. New Forum Books is guided by the conviction that law and politics not only reflect culture but help to shape it. Authors include leading political scientists, sociologists, legal scholars, philosophers, theologians, historians, and economists writing for nonspecialist readers and scholars across a range of fields. Looking at questions such as political equality, the concept of rights, the problem of virtue in liberal politics, crime and punishment, population, poverty, economic development, and the international legal and political order, New Forum Books seeks to explain—not explain away—the difficult issues we face today.

PAUL EDWARD GOTTFRIED
After Liberalism: Mass Democracy in the Managerial State

PETER BERKOWITZ
Virtue and the Making of Modern Liberalism

JOHN E. COONS AND PATRICK M. BRENNAN
By Nature Equal: The Anatomy of a Western Insight

DAVID NOVAK
Conventional Rights: A Study in Jewish Political Theory

CHARLES L. GLENN
*The Ambiguous Embrace: Government and Faith-Based Schools
and Social Agencies*

PETER BAUER
From Subsistence to Exchange and Other Essays

ROBERT P. GEORGE, ed.
Great Cases in Constitutional Law

AMITAI ETZIONI
The Monochrome Society

DANIEL N. ROBINSON
Praise and Blame: Moral Realism and Its Applications

TIMOTHY P. JACKSON
The Priority of Love: Christian Charity and Social Justice

SOTIRIOS A. BARBER
Welfare and the Constitution

JEFFREY STOUT
Democracy and Tradition

JAMES HITCHCOCK
*The Supreme Court and Religion in American Life:
Volume 1, The Odyssey of the Religion Clauses;
Volume 2, From "Higher Law" to "Sectarian Scruples"*

CHRISTOPHER WOLFE, ed.
That Eminent Tribunal: Judicial Supremacy and the Constitution

PATRICK J. DENEEN
Democratic Faith